A History of Graphic Design
Second Edition

Philip B. Meggs

A History of Graphic Design

Second Edition

VNR Van Nostrand Reinhold
New York

Library of Congress Catalog Number 91-9281

ISBN 0-442-31895-2

Printed and bound in the United States of America by Arcata/Halliday.

Van Nostrand Reinhold
115 Fifth Avenue
New York, New York 10003

Chapman and Hall
2-6 Boundary Row
London, SE1 8HN, England

Thomas Nelson Australia
102 Dodds Street
South Melbourne 3205
Victoria, Australia

Nelson Canada
1120 Birchmount Road
Scarborough, Ontario MIK 5G4, Canada

16 15 14 13 12 11 10 9 8 7 6 5 4 3 2 1

Library of Congress Cataloging-in-Publication Data
Meggs, Philip B.
   A history of graphic design/Philip B. Meggs.—2nd ed.
     p. cm.
   Includes bibliographical references and index.
   ISBN 0-442-31895-2
    1. Printing, Practical—Layout—History. 2. Graphic arts—
History. 3. Book design—History. I. Title.
Z244.5.M42 1991
686.2′09—dc20   91-9281
                                     CIP

For my parents,
Wallace N. Meggs and
Elizabeth Pruitt Meggs

1. the creative process is not performed by the skilled hand alone, but must be a unified process in which "head, heart, and hand play a simultaneous role."

2. I quote the Japanese saying, "first acquire an infallible technique and then open yourself to inspiration."

3. the human being as a manifestation of the supreme spirit or the source of life "performs what he is given to do." in the consciousness of I of myself can do nothing the artist becomes a transparency through which the creative principle operates.

herbert bayer
16 march 1979

Preface

The first edition of *A History of Graphic Design* attempted to chronicle the evolution of graphic design. It might also be seen as the author's personal diary of discovery, compiled over a decade of research. Its wide distribution placed a heavy responsibility upon the second edition, demanding an improved research methodology and extensive efforts to corroborate sources.

There are numerous possible approaches to an investigation of the evolution of graphic design. These include: an exploration of the relationship between design and its audience; analysis of the evolution of formal or stylistic attributes; and study of the social and economic impact of design activities. The intent of this book is to identify and document innovation in semantic and syntactic aspects of visual communications. The graphic designs of each period discussed have been investigated and assessed in an attempt to distinguish works and their creators that influenced the ongoing evolution of the discipline. This information can provide a conceptual overview useful for further study and practice.

The traditional research methods of art historians do not fully take into account the complexities of graphic design. A focus upon individual artists, organized into schools or movements, with their masterpieces and unique contributions identified, cannot adequately address graphic design history. Often new developments are shaped by technology, such as the invention of lithography or phototypesetting, or evolve over time as a public dialog by graphic designers eclectically influenced by one another's work. In some periods, a collective vision and imagery evolve which cannot be easily attributable to specific individuals. However, those who seek to deny the role of pivotal individuals—and call for a collective view of design history—produce an equally biased vision. There are pivotal individuals who shaped the direction of graphic design in their times by inventing new typographic and symbolic forms, innovative ways to structure information in graphic space, pioneering imagery, and original methodologies for signifying messages. It would be foolhardy to deny the unique contributions to our graphic heritage by such individuals as John Baskerville or El Lissitzky. Careful analysis of dates of similar works often proves that seemingly collective directions do in fact have an identifiable point of origin; however, when a collective evolution such as Victorian graphics does occur, many works typify the essence of the direction and time period.

Concurrent analysis from two historical points of view—synchrony and diachrony—can help steer an exploration of graphic design around many pitfalls. Synchrony is simultaneous occurrence; while diachrony is a study of phenomena as they occur and change over time. One pondering the significance of, for example, E. McKnight Kauffer's 1918 poster for *The Daily Herald* (Pl. 46) can examine its synchronic relationship to other graphic designs of its time, then examine it in relationship to the graphic designs preceding and following it. This poster appears to be unlike other graphic designs of its immediate time and its antecedents; but it significantly influenced work by Kauffer and others in the months and years following its publication. Because the concepts embodied in this poster drew inspiration from advanced art, an understanding of Cubism and Futurism is needed to fully comprehend this poster. Due to the rampart plagiarism and eclecticism in mass communication, synchrony and diachrony are critical to the design historian's efforts to identify an innovator from his or her army of imitators. Sometimes short time spans exist between the creative act and the imitation, making this separation very difficult and prone to error. Influence must not be read as plagiarism, for the evolution of graphic design has often been a continuum, evolving over time. The evolution of 17th-century typography and design, discussed in Chapter 9, is but one example of a dialog transcending decades and national boundaries. A building process enabled designers to achieve a gradual transition from Renaissance design to the modern epoch.

Criteria for selection of illustrations are often influenced by issues other than the author's preference or aesthetic judgments. Often final selections of illustrations for this book were based on the clarity with which they demonstrated a concept, spatial arrangement, or graphic form, even though other examples might arguably possess superior attributes. In other instances, difficulties in securing reproduction permissions and/or suitable photography determined the selection.

Many of the works in this book *stand for* a school, a movement, a style, or an approach. The problem of the "masterpiece," traditionally viewed as a work made with exceptional skill or brilliance, or as an artist's most accomplished or climactic work representing the pinnacle of his or her creativity, also plagues the study of graphic design. A 20th-century designer working over a thirty-year career as art director of monthly periodicals will be responsible for 360 magazine covers and thousands of editorial pages. His or her publications will likely be in an ongoing competitive interaction with other periodicals addressing the same audience and subject matter, and he or she will be assisted by a changing staff of assistants and apprentices. When a cover and editorial spread are selected for a historical anthology, it is often appropriate to view them as an example from a series rather than as a singular masterwork. The concept of the elevated masterpiece yields to work that becomes a paradigm of an era, style, or the spirit of its times. Further, the work selected might even have been conceived and executed by an assistant while the art director was on vacation. In some—but certainly not all—cases the art director or studio head becomes, not a singular designer, but a figurehead for a collective enterprise. Graphic design is often a collaborative process involving designers or art directors and their assistants, photographers, illustrators, typesetters, printers, and clients. Credits for all participants were frequently not available. I am deeply appreciative to those who have shared their knowledge and advised me on problems of attribution, interpretation, and dating of material in the first edition. Information amplifying or correcting attributions, dates, etc., and permitting amendment should a revised edition be possible in the future will be greatly appreciated.

Establishing the parameters for this book posed major difficulties. The evolution of graphic design is closely bound to the evolution of illustration, photography, and printing technology; yet, it was not possible to imbed a comprehensive discussion of these closely related disciplines within the scope of one book. While important interchanges among these disciplines are included, these areas only appear in the context of their impact upon the evolution of graphic design.

In recent years, graphic design has expanded beyond its traditional boundaries and now encompasses kinetic and environmental graphic design. Limitations of space prevented exploration of these extraordinary new areas, although they are represented by two examples of animated graphics by Saul Bass and important environmental graphic designs for Olympic games in three countries.

This book should not be perceived as an all-encompassing encyclopedia of graphic-design history, for such a complete evolution would require at least three volumes this size. This book attempts to provide a conceptual and pictorial overview of significant stages in graphic design's development. Many significant graphic-design accomplishments, such as Persian manuscript illustration, the early Japanese print, and Dutch graphic design since World War II, could not be included due to production limitations. In making painful decisions about which material to include, a line of descendancy toward contemporary graphic design in post-industrial culture was a primary determinant. For example, visual communications and printing in early Chinese culture have an important lineal impact, while synchronous work from the Indus Valley does not have a similar direct influence. Cubism altered the course of graphic design, but Fauvism did not. This approach

places significance upon western civilization, in contrast to the current vogue for minimizing western civilization and emphasizing other cultures. Some historians have suggested that if Muslim forces had prevailed at the Battle of Poitiers (also called the Battle of Tours) in 732 A.D., they might have conquered Europe and established Muslim culture there, including Arabic writing. Under the methodology used for this book, such a shift in the cultural evolution would have resulted in the Greek and Latin alphabets receiving minor treatment as visual-language systems, rather than as the wellsprings for postindustrial typography.

For the first edition, Van Nostrand Reinhold set a limitation of 300 pages and 600 illustrations, but I delivered a manuscript accompanied by 1,000 illustrations and requiring a 500-page book. Much to my amazement, they consented to publish the entire work. For the second edition, illustrations have been eliminated to make room for additional work. Difficult decisions about material to be included have been necessary, and many graphic designers who can make equal claim to documentation in this book could not be included due to space limitations. The author expresses profound apologies to designers whose accomplishments merit inclusion in a design history survey, but who could not be included due to limitations of space.

Anyone who sees this book as a mere chronicle of style misunderstands graphic design. Today the word *style* is often used to define superficial surface characteristics, which are sometimes dictated by marketing considerations. Its original meaning—distinctive excellence of artistic expression achieved by appropriate forms and their relationships to one another in space—has been corrupted. While the visual attributes of graphic design are critical to the discipline and receive appropriate emphasis in this book, I am equally concerned about designers' underlying philosophic viewpoints, the meaning graphic design holds for its culture and audience, and the signification of forms and their syntactic relationships. In some eras, such as late 19th- and early 20th-century Art Nouveau, a pervasive style made it appropriate to label a chapter by the style. In other instances, naming a chapter after a style would have artificially limited the content. Thus several general titles, such as "Popular Graphics of the Victorian Era," "Pictorial Modernism," and "The Conceptual Image" are used to encompass works having underlying conceptual similarities but very different visual manifestations. Had the "Pictorial Modernism" chapter been dubbed "Art Deco," for example, it would have forced the elimination of important works falling outside the parameters of that term.

Authors and curators structuring visual arts books and exhibitions often confront the dilemma of chronological versus thematic organization. Alternative structures were considered before deciding to organize this book into five general chronological sections, which are then divided thematically into chapters. The difficulties of a purely chronological structure can be quickly grasped by considering the design practices of Paul Rand and Bradbury Thompson, both of whom have been involved in graphic design from the 1930s until the 1990s, a span of over a half-century. A chronological organization by decades might require placing them in as many as six chapters, with confusing results. A time line has been designed for each section to facilitate chronological comparisons.

It has been gratifying to learn that many designers and students, along with many other communications professionals and general readers, have found the first edition of *A History of Graphic Design* to be a useful resource in spite of its many flaws. I hope that this new edition, with its expanded content, revised format and typography, timelines for each section, expanded bibliography organized by chapters, and color section, will prove to be even more useful.

Preface to the first edition

There is a German word, *Zeitgeist,* that does not have an English equivalent. It means the spirit of the time, and refers to the cultural trends and tastes that are characteristic of a given era. The immediacy and ephemeral nature of graphic design, combined with its link with the social, political, and economic life of its culture, enable it to more closely express the Zeitgeist of an epoch than many other forms of human expression. Ivan Chermayeff, a noted designer, has said: the design of history is the history of design.

Since prehistoric times, people have searched for ways to give visual form to ideas and concepts, to store knowledge in graphic form, and to bring order and clarity to information. Over the course of history, these needs have been filled by various people, including scribes, printers, and artists. It was not until 1922, when the outstanding book designer William Addison Dwiggins coined the term "graphic design" to describe his activities as an individual who brought structural order and visual form to printed communications, that an emerging profession received an appropriate name. However, the contemporary graphic designer is heir to a distinguished ancestry. Sumerian scribes who invented writing, Egyptian artisans who combined words and images on papyrus manuscripts, Chinese block printers, medieval illuminators, and fifteenth-century printers and compositors who designed early European printed books all become part of the rich heritage and history of graphic design. By and large, this is an anonymous tradition, for the social value and aesthetic accomplishments of graphic designers, many of whom have been creative artists of extraordinary intelligence and vision, have not been sufficiently recognized.

History is in large measure a myth, because the historian looks back over the great sprawling network of human struggle and attempts to construct a web of meaning. Oversimplification, ignorance of causes and their effects, and the lack of an objective vantage point are grave risks for the historian. When we attempt to record the accomplishments of the past, we do so from the vantage point of our own time. History becomes a reflection of the needs, sensibilities, and attitudes of the chronicler's time as surely as it represents the accomplishments of bygone eras. As much as one might strive for objectivity, the limitations of individual knowledge and insights ultimately intrude.

The concept of art for art's sake, a beautiful object that exists solely for its aesthetic value, did not develop until the nineteenth century. Before the Industrial Revolution, the beauty of the forms and images that people made were linked to their function in human society. The aesthetic qualities of Greek pottery, Egyptian hieroglyphics, and medieval manuscripts were totally integrated with useful values; art and life were unified into a cohesive whole. The din and thunder of the Industrial Revolution turned the world upside down in a process of upheaval and technological progress that continues to accelerate at an ever-quickening pace. By jolting the arts and crafts from their social and economic roles, the machine age created a gulf between people's material life and their sensory and spiritual needs. Just as voices call for a restoration of humanity's unity with the natural environment, there is a growing awareness of the need to restore human and aesthetic values to the man-made environment and mass communications. The design arts—architecture, product, fashion, interior, and graphic design—offer one means for this restoration. Once more a society's shelter, artifacts, and communications might bind a people together. The endangered aesthetic and spiritual values might be restored. A wholeness of need and spirit, reunited through the process of design, can contribute in great measure to the quality and raison d'etre of life in urban societies.

This chronicle of graphic design is written in the belief that if we understand the past, we will be better able to continue a culture legacy of beautiful form and effective communication. If we ignore this legacy, we run the risk of becoming buried in a mindless morass of a commercialism whose molelike vision ignores human values and needs as it burrows forward into darkness.

Acknowledgments

Several hundred people generously provided information, assistance, pictorial material, and reproduction permissions. Unfortunately, it is not possible to thank each one of them here. The contribution of many people has been so critical to this effort that I wish to express deep and sincere gratitude.

At the Library of Congress, Elaina Millie of the Poster Collection and Katheleen Hunt of the Rare Book and Special Collections Division provided invaluable information and courteous assistance beyond normal expectations. Robert Coates of the Museum of Modern Art Design Study Center and Susan Reinhold of the Reinhold-Brown Galleries generously shared research materials. At the Virginia Commonwealth University Libraries, Sue Bass, Janet Dalberto, Suzanne Freeman, and Arts Librarian Joan Muller made important contributions to my research. Dr. Robert Godwin-Jones and Marion Betta assisted in numerous translations. Continuing support has been provided by Murry N. DePillars and John DeMao.

George Nan, Allen Jones, and Catheleen Crone provided invaluable advice and assistance on photographic matters, and Jerry Bates assisted in the reconstruction of graphic materials which would not have been otherwise available.

Aaron Burns, Arthur A. Cohen, Elaine Lustig Cohen, Marty Fox, Edward Gottschall, Steven Heller, Janet Conradi, Ellen Lupton of Cooper Union's Herb Lubalin Study Center, John Malinoski, Jacqui Morgan, and Roger Remington generously shared information and materials. Victor Margolin and Nic Chaparos furnished valuable insights.

Charlene Crosby and Harriet Turner have provided secretarial assistance. Margaret Hill Bates and Diana Lively supplied invaluable logistic and editorial support. Keith Jones contributed research assistance in preparing material for the second edition.

My understanding of the modern movements of twentieth-century art has been greatly informed by Richard Carlyon. John T. Hilton contributed immeasurably to my comprehension of the humanist and social role of design activities. Robert C. Carter generously shared research materials and his understanding of the Bauhaus era, and the late Mallory Callan's insights into the genesis of the modern design movement have proven invaluable. Professor Han Schroeder was most helpful in providing information about the de Stijl movement, particularly the Schroeder house.

With but rare exception, the contemporary designers whose work is in this book provided their work and reproduction permission. It is not possible to list them all here, but they are identified in the picture captions. The estates and families of many deceased twentieth-century designers provided information, materials, and reproduction permissions. I am particularly indebted to Joella Bayer, Dorothy Beall, Carla Binder, Elaine Lustig Cohen, Tom Golden, Hattula Moholy-Nagy, Siegfried Poppe, Cornelia Tschichold, and Joanne Beall Westerman.

Research leading to publication of this book was made possible by the generous support of two Design Fellowships from the Design Arts Program of the National Endowment for the Arts. Likewise, two research grants from the Faculty Grants-in-Aid program from Virginia Commonwealth University was critical to my pictorial and bibliographic research. These grants enabled me to travel to major archives, museums, and study centers to research original artifacts and primary resource materials.

At Van Nostrand Reinhold, Lilly Kaufman shared my view that the second edition should be completely redone due to inappropriate typography and layout, and she successfully pursued this goal. Amanda Miller, Paul Lukas, and Joy Aquilino made invaluable editorial contributions. Monika Keano made superb recommendations about the format design and designed almost all of the chapter pages. Kurt Andrews was the production manager.

My wife, Libby Phillips Meggs, and children, Andrew and Elizabeth, provided unwavering support and indispensable sangfroid.

Contents

The Prologue to Graphic Design:
The visual message
from prehistory
through the medieval era

World Events	1 The Invention of Writing	2 Graphic Communications in Ancient Egypt	3 The Asian Contribution	4 The Alphabet	5 The Medieval Manuscript
Note: Many dates on these timelines are approximate, because exact dates are difficult to establish in early history, and some dates are in dispute.					
c. 15,000-10,000 B.C. Cave paintings at Lascaux					
c. 3500 B.C. Sumerians settle in Mesopotamia					
c. 3200 B.C. Menes, first Pharaoh, unites Egypt					
c. 3000 B.C. Copper tools and weapons	c. 3600 B.C. Blau Monument combines images and early writing				
	c. 3100 B.C. Early Sumerian pictographic scripts on clay tablets	c. 3100 B.C. King *Zet's* ivory tablet, earliest Egyptian pictographic writing			
	c. 2900 B.C. Early cylinder seals				
	c. 2800 B.C. Sumerian scribes turn pictographic writing on its side				
c. 2750 B.C. Formal land-sale contracts written in cuneiform					
		c. 2600 B.C. Early surviving papyrus manuscripts			
c. 2500 B.C. Great Pyramids at Giza	c. 2500 B.C. Early cuneiform writing				
		c. 2345 B.C. Pyramid Texts in tomb of Unas			
		c. 2100 B.C. Coffin Texts in noblemen's tombs			
				c. 2000 B.C. Early Cretan pictographs	
				c. 2000 B.C. Phaistos Disk	
c. 1792-1750 B.C. Hammurabi, Babylonian king, rules Mesopotamia	c. 1750 B.C. Law Code of Hammurabi		c. 1800 B.C. Legendary Ts-ang Chieh invents writing		
c. 1600 B.C. Bronze in general use					
		c. 1500 B.C. *Hieratic* scripts	c. 1500 B.C. Oracle bone writing	c. 1500 B.C. Ras Shamra script	
		c. 1420 B.C. Papyrus of Ani			
c. 1300 B.C. Temple of Ramses III at Thebes		c. 1300 B.C. Many *Book of the Dead* papyrus scrolls			
c. 1100 B.C. Iron is widely used for weapons and tools					
			c. 1000 B.C. Bronze script writing	c. 1000 B.C. Early Greek alphabet	

World Events

753 B.C. Romulus establishes Rome
c. 750-700 B.C. Homer's *Odyssey*
683 B.C. Democracy in Athens
c. 600 B.C. Nebuchadrezzar II builds the "Tower of Babel"
551 B.C. Confucius is born
c. 528 B.C. Gautama, supreme Buddha
447-432 B.C. Parthenon built in Athens
332-330 B.C. Alexander conquers Egypt
c. 300 B.C. Euclid's geometry
221 B.C. Shih Huang-ti unites China; The Great Wall of China is underway
44 B.C. Julius Caesar assassinated
c. 1 A.D. Birth of Christ
79 A.D. Roman Colosseum
325 A.D. Rome adopts Christianity
330 A.D. Constantine moves Roman capital to Constantinople
410 A.D. Visigoths sack Rome
476 A.D. Fall of western Roman Empire
570 A.D. Birth of Mohammad
660 A.D. Organ used in church services
700 A.D. *Beowulf* epic
771 A.D. Moors defeat Spanish army
800 A.D. Charlemagne crowned Emperor
c. 1000 A.D. Gunpowder in use in China
1150 A.D. Compass is invented
1095-1099 A.D. First Crusade
1215 A.D. King John signs Magna Carta
1265 A.D. Marco Polo to China
1348-1350 A.D. The Black Plague
1415 Florence humanists study classical manuscripts

1 The Invention of Writing / 2 Graphic Communications in Ancient Egypt

c. 400 B.C. *Demotic* script
c. 197 B.C. Rosetta Stone
c. 394 A.D. Lost hieroglyphic inscription

3 The Asian Contribution

c. 250 B.C. "Small-seal" calligraphy
105 A.D. Ts'ai Lun invents paper
c. 165 A.D. Stone-carved Confucian classics
c. 200 A.D. "Regular-style" calligraphy
c. 300 A.D. Chops are used as identifying seals
c. 770 A.D. Early datable Chinese relief printing
868 A.D. *Diamond Sutra:* Earliest extant printed manuscript
c. 1040 A.D. Pi Sheng invents movable type

4 The Alphabet

c. 190 B.C. Parchment is used for manuscripts
c. 100 A.D. Pompeian wall writing
c. 114 A.D. Trajan's Column
c. 200 A.D. Codex form of the book
c. 250 A.D. Greek uncials
c. 200-500 A.D. Roman square capitals and rustic capitals

5 The Medieval Manuscript

c. 425 A.D. Vatican Vergil
c. 500 A.D. Uncial lettering flourishes
c. 600 A.D. Insular script
c. 680 A.D. Book of Durrow
c. 698 A.D. Lindisfarne Gospels
751 A.D. Arabs learn papermaking from Chinese prisoners
c. 781 A.D. Alcuin establishes school at Aachen; Caroline minuscules
c. 800 A.D. *Book of Kells; Coronation Gospels*
1047 A.D. *Beatus of Fernando and Sancha*
c. 1265 A.D. *Douce Apocalypse*
c. 1300 A.D. *Ormesby Psalter*
c. 1415 A.D. *Les Tres Riches Heures*
c. 1450 A.D. Movable type in Germany

The Invention of Writing

It is not known precisely when or where the biological species of conscious, thinking people, *Homo sapiens,* emerged. The search for our prehistoric origins continues to push back into time the early innovations of our ancestors. It is believed that we evolved from a species that lived in the southern part of Africa. These early humanoids ventured out onto the grassy plains and into caves as the forests slowly disappeared in that part of the world. In the tall grass, they began to stand erect. Perhaps this adaptation was a result of the need to watch for predators in the tall grass, to help discourage enemies by increasing the humanoids' apparent size, or to hold branches as weapons. In any event, the hand developed a magnificent ability to carry food and hold objects. Found near Lake Turkana in Kenya, a nearly three-million-year-old stone that had been sharpened into an implement proves the thoughtful and deliberate development of a technology—a tool. Early shaped stones may have been used to dig for roots or to cut away flesh from dead animals for food. While we can only speculate about the use of early tools, we know that they mark a major step in the human species's immense journey from primitive origins toward a civilized state. A number of quantum leaps provided the capacity to organize a community and gain some measure of control over human destiny. Speech—the ability to make sounds in order to communicate with one another—was an early skill developed by the species in the long evolutionary trail from its archaic beginnings. Writing is the visual counterpart of speech. Marks, symbols, pictures, or letters drawn or written upon a surface, or *substrate,* became a graphic counterpart of the spoken word or unspoken thought. The limitations of speech are the fallibility of human memory and an immediacy of expression that cannot transcend time and place. Until the present electronic age, spoken words vanished without a trace, while written words remained. The invention of writing brought people the luster of civilization and made it possible to preserve hard-won knowledge, experiences, and thoughts.

The development of writing and visible language had its earliest origins in simple pictures, for a close connection exists between the drawing of pictures and the marking of writing. Both are natural ways of communicating ideas, and primitive man used pictures as an elementary way to record and transmit information.

Prehistoric visual communications
The earliest human markings found in Africa are over 200,000 years old. From the early Paleolithic to the Neolithic periods (35,000 B.C. to 4000 B.C.), early Africans and Europeans left paintings in caves, including the famous Lascaux caves in southern France (Pl. 1 and Fig. 1-1). A black was made from charcoal, and a range of warm tones, from light yellows through red-browns, were made from red and yellow iron oxides. This palette of pigments was mixed with fat as a medium. Images of animals were drawn and painted upon the walls of these former subterranean water channels occupied as a refuge by prehistoric men and women. Perhaps the pigment was smeared onto the walls with a finger, or a brush was fabricated from bristles or reeds. This was not the beginning of *art* as we know it. Rather, it was the dawning of visual communications, because these early pictures were made for survival and were created for utilitarian and ritualistic purposes. The

1-1. Cave painting from Lascaux, c. 15,000–
10,000 B.C. Random placement and shifting
scale signify prehistoric people's lack of
structure and sequence in recording their
experiences.

presence of what appears to be spear marks in the sides of some of these animal
images indicates that they might have been used in magical rites designed to gain
power over animals and success in the hunt. Or perhaps they were teaching aids to
instruct the young on the process of hunting as a cooperative group effort. Abstract
geometric signs, including dots, squares, and other configurations, are intermingled
with the animals in many cave paintings. Whether they represent man-made objects or are protowriting is not known, and will never be known with any certainty,
because they were made before the beginning of recorded history (the 5,000-year
period during which people have recorded in writing a chronicle of their knowledge
of facts and events). The animals painted on the caves are *pictographs*—elementary pictures or sketches to represent the things depicted.

1-2. Found carved and sometimes painted on
rocks throughout the western portion of the
United States, these petroglyphic figures,
animals, and signs are similar to those found
all over the world.

Throughout the world, from Africa to North America to the islands of New Zea-
land, prehistoric man left numerous *petroglyphs* (Fig. 1-2), which are carved or
scratched signs or simple figures on rock. Many of the petroglyphs are pictographs,
and some may be *ideographs,* or symbols to represent ideas or concepts.

1-3. Engraved drawing on a deer antler,
c. 15,000 B.C. This prehistoric image is shown
in a cast made by rolling the antler onto clay.

A high level of observation and memory is evidenced in many prehistoric drawings. In an engraved reindeer antler found in the cave of Lorthet in southern
France (Fig. 1-3), the scratched drawings of deer and salmon are remarkably accurate. Even more fascinating, however, are two diamond-shaped forms with interior

1-2

1-3

marks, which imply an early symbol-making ability. The early pictographs evolved in two ways: First, they were the beginning of pictorial art—the objects and events of the world were recorded with increasing fidelity and exactitude as the centuries passed; second, pictographs also evolved into writing. The images, whether the original pictorial form was retained or not, ultimately became symbols for spoken-language sounds.

The Paleolithic artist developed a tendency toward simplification and stylization. Figures became increasingly abbreviated and were expressed with a minimum number of lines. By the late Paleolithic period, some petroglyphs and pictographs had been reduced to the point of almost resembling letters.

The cradle of civilization

Until recent discoveries indicated that early peoples in Thailand may have practiced agriculture and manufactured pottery at an even earlier date, archaeologists had long believed that the ancient land of Mesopotamia, "the land between rivers," was the cradle of civilization. Between the Tigris and Euphrates rivers, which flow from the mountains of eastern Turkey across the land that is now Iraq and into the Persian Gulf, there lies a flat, once-fertile plain whose wet winters and hot, dry summers proved very attractive to early humankind. It was here that early humans ceased their restless nomadic wanderings and established a village culture. Around 8000 B.C., wild grain was planted, animals were domesticated, and agriculture began. By the year 6000 B.C., objects were being hammered from copper; the Bronze Age was ushered in about 3000 B.C., when copper was alloyed with tin to make durable tools and weapons, followed by the invention of the wheel.

The leap from village culture to high civilization occurred after the Sumerian people arrived in Mesopotamia near the end of the fourth millennium B.C. The origin of the Sumerians remains a great mystery. Before 3000 B.C., they had settled in the lower part of the fertile crescent. As vital as the technologies developed in Mesopotamia were for the future of the human race, the Sumerians' contribution to social and intellectual progress had even more impact upon the future. The Sumerians invented a system of gods, headed by a supreme deity named Anu, who was the god of the heavens. An intricate system of god–man relationships was developed. The city emerged, with the necessary social order for large numbers of people to live together. But of the numerous inventions in Sumer that launched man onto the path of civilization, the invention of writing brought about an intellectual revolution that had a vast impact upon social order, economic progress, and technological and cultural developments.

The history of Mesopotamia records waves of invaders who flooded onto the fertile plain and conquered the peoples living there. The culture established by the Sumerians conquered the invaders in turn, and the sequence of ruling peoples adopted and developed civilization. The peoples who dominated Mesopotamia during its long history include Akkadians, Assyrians, Babylonians, and Chaldeans. Persians from the west and Hittites from the north also conquered the area and spread Mesopotamian civilization beyond the fertile crescent.

The invention of writing

Religion dominated life in the Mesopotamian city-state, just as the massive ziggurat, a stepped temple compound, dominated the city. These vast, multistory brick temples were constructed as a series of recessed levels becoming smaller toward the top of the shrine. Inside, priests and scribes (Fig. 1-4) wielded enormous power as they controlled the inventories of the gods and the king and ministered to the magical and religious needs of the people. Writing may have evolved because this temple economy had a desperate need for record keeping. The temple chiefs must have consciously sought a system for setting down information.

In human memory, time can become a blur, and important facts are sometimes forgotten. In Mesopotamian terms, such important facts might include the answers to questions like who delivered their taxes in the form of crops? How much food

1-4. Alabaster relief from the palace of King Tiglath-Pileser III at Nimrud, c. 500 B.C. In this bas-relief, two Assyrian scribes compile lists of the spoils of war upon clay tablets with their styli, as dictated by the official on the left.

1-5. Early Sumerian pictographic tablet, c. 3100 B.C. This archaic pictographic script contained the seeds for the development of writing. Information is structured by horizontal and vertical division into zones.

was stored, and was it adequate to meet community needs before the next harvest? How much seed must be held until planting time to ensure that the next crop will be an abundant one, and how much can be used for human and animal food? As even these relatively simple questions show, an accurate continuum of knowledge became imperative if the temple priests were to be able to maintain the order and stability necessary in the city-state. One theory holds that the origin of visible language evolved from the need to identify the contents of sacks and pottery containers used to store food. Small clay tags were made that identified the contents with a pictograph and the amount in an elementary decimal numbering system, inspired by the ten human fingers.

The earliest written records are tablets from the city of Uruk (Fig. 1-5). They apparently list commodities by pictographic drawings of objects, accompanied by numerals and personal names inscribed in orderly columns. An abundance of clay in Sumer made it the logical material for record keeping, and a reed stylus sharpened to a point was used to draw the fine, curved lines of the early pictographs. The clayey mud tablet was held in the left hand, and pictographs were scratched in the surface with the wooden stylus. Beginning in the top right corner of the tablet, the lines were written in careful vertical columns. The inscribed tablet was dried in the hot sun or baked rock-hard in a kiln.

This writing system underwent an evolution over several centuries. A *grid system* was developed to contain writing in horizontal and vertical spatial divisions. Sometimes the scribe would smear the writing as his hand moved across the tablet. Around 2800 B.C., the scribes turned the pictographs on their sides and began to write in horizontal rows, from left to right and top to bottom (Fig. 1-6). This made writing easier, and it made the pictographs less literal. About three hundred years later, writing speed was increased by replacing the sharp-pointed stylus with a triangular-tipped one. This stylus was *pushed into* the clay, instead of being dragged through it. The characters were now composed of a series of wedge-shaped strokes, rather than of a continuous line drawing (Fig. 1-7). This innovation radically altered the nature of the writing; pictographs evolved into an abstract sign writing called *cuneiform* (from the Latin for "wedge-shaped").

The early Sumerian Blau monument (Pl. 2) is an etched and carved shale artifact from the third quarter of the fourth millennium B.C. It is the oldest extant artifact combining images and writing.

While the graphic form of Sumerian writing was evolving, its ability to record information was expanding. From the first stage, when picture-symbols represented animate and inanimate objects, signs became ideographs and began to rep-

1-6. This clay tablet demonstrates how the Sumerian symbols for star (which also meant heaven or god), head, and water evolved from early pictographs (3100 B.C.). The latter were turned on their side by 2800 B.C. and evolved into the early cuneiform writing by 2500 B.C.

resent abstract ideas. The symbol for sun, for example, began to represent ideas such as "day" and "light." As early scribes developed their written language so that it would function in the same way as their speech, the need to represent in easily depicted spoken sounds arose. Adverbs, prepositions, and personal names often could not be adapted to pictographic representation. Picture symbols began to represent the sounds of the objects depicted instead of the objects themselves. Cuneiform became *rebus writing,* which is pictures and/or pictographs representing words and syllables with the same or similar sound as the object depicted. Pictures were used as *phonograms,* or graphic symbols for sounds. The highest development of cuneiform was its use of abstract signs to represent syllables, which are sounds made by combining more elementary sounds.

Cuneiform was a difficult writing system to master, even after the Assyrians simplified it into only 560 signs. Youngsters selected to become scribes began their schooling at the *edubba,* the writing school or "tablet house," before the age of ten and worked from sunrise to sunset every day, with only six days off per month (Fig. 1-8). Professional opportunities in the priesthood, estate management, accounting, medicine, and government were reserved for these select few. Writing took on important magical and ceremonial qualities. The general public held those who could write in awe, and it was believed that death occurred when a divine scribe etched one's name in a mythical Book of Fate.

The knowledge explosion made possible by writing was astounding. Libraries were organized and contained thousands of tablets about religion, mathematics, history, law, medicine, and astronomy. Literature sprang up, as poetry, myths, hymns, epics, and legends were recorded on the clay tablets. Writing fostered a deep sense of history, and tablets chronicled with meticulous exactitude the events that occurred during the reign of each monarch. Thousands of commercial contracts and records still remain.

Writing enabled society to stabilize itself under rule and law. Measurements and weights were standardized and guaranteed by written inscription (Fig. 1-9). Law codes, such as the Code of Hammurabi, dating from the period 1792–1750 B.C., spelled out crimes and their punishments, thus establishing social order and justice. The Code of Hammurabi is written in careful cuneiform on a 2.44-meter (8-foot) tall *stele,* an inscribed or carved stone or slab, used for commemorative purposes (Figs. 1-10 and 1-11). The stele contains 282 laws gridded in twenty-one columns. Steles with Hammurabi's reformed law code were erected in the main temple of Marduk at Babylon and in other cities. Written in a precise style, harsh penalties were expressed with clarity and brevity. Some of these commandments include: "a thief stealing from a child is to be put to death"; "a physician operating on a slightly wounded man with a bronze scalpel shall have his hands cut off"; and "a builder who builds a house that falls and kills the owner shall be put to death."

1-7. Cuneiform tablet, c. 2100 B.C. This clay tablet lists expenditures of grain and animals.

1-8. Sumero-Akkadian exercise tablet, third millennium B.C. On this rare surviving tablet, a student in the *edubba* practiced writing the words *God Urash* three times.

1-9. Black stone duck weight, c. 3000 B.C. The cuneiform inscription states that this weight is dedicated to the god Nanna by the King of Ur, and confirms a weight of five *minas.* Each Mesopotamian *mina* weighed about 0.559 kilograms, or 18 ounces.

1-11. Detail of the Code of Hammurabi, c. 1800 B.C. Whether pressed into clay or carved into stone as shown here, Mesopotamian scribes achieved a masterful control in their writing and arrangement of the strokes in the partitioned space.

1-10. *Stele* bearing the Code of Hammurabi, which was initially written between 1792–1750 B.C. Above the densely textured law code, King Hammurabi is shown on a mountaintop with the seated sun god Shamash, who orders the king to write down the laws for the people of Babylon. A graphic image of divine authority as the source for the code becomes powerful visual persuasion.

Visual identification

Two natural by-products of the rise of village culture were the ownership of property and the specialization of trades or crafts. Both made visual identification necessary. Cattle brands and proprietary marks were developed so that ownership could be established, and the maker of pottery or other objects could be identified if problems developed or if superior quality inspired repeat purchases. A means of identifying the author of a clay cuneiform tablet, certifying commercial documents and contracts and proving the authority of religious and royal proclamations, was needed. The fascinating Mesopotamian cylinder seals, which provided a forgery-proof method of sealing documents and proving their authenticity, were developed (Figs. 1-12 and 1-13). In use for over three thousand years, these small cylinders had images and writing etched into their surfaces. When they were rolled across the damp clay tablet, a raised impression of the depressed design, which became a "trademark" for the owner, was formed. Because the image carved into the round stone appeared on the tablet as a raised flat design, it was virtually impossible to duplicate or counterfeit. Many such stones had a hollow perforation running through them so that they could be worn on a string around the neck or wrist.

The widely traveled Greek historian Herodotus (c. 500 B.C.) wrote that the Babylonians each wore a cylinder seal on a cord around their wrists like a bracelet. Prized as ornaments, status symbols, and unique personal signatures, cylinder seals were even used to mark a damp clay seal on the house door when the occupants were away, to indicate whether burglars had entered the premises. Cutters of cylinder and stamp seals developed great skill and a refined sense of design. The earliest seals were engraved with simple pictures of kings, a line of cattle, or mythic creatures. Later, more narrative images developed; for instance, one god would present a man (probably the seal's owner) to another god, or a man would figure prominently in fighting a battle or killing a wild animal. In the later Assyr-

1-12

1-13

1-12. Hittite cylinder seal, undated. Thought to portray a ritual, possibly with a sacrificial offering on the right, this seal combines decorative ornamentation with figurative images. It has both a rolled image on the side and a stamped image on the bottom.

1-13. Mesopotamian cylinder seals, c. 1880–1550 B.C. The diversity of cylinder-seal design ranged from the highly structured and figurative to the random and abstract.

1-14 and 1-15. Persian stamp seal, c. 500 B.C. Incised into a precious pale blue quartz called chalcedony in a gold mount, this seal, with its symmetrical design of a pair of heraldic beasts locked in combat, probably belonged to a member of the royal family or the high priesthood.

ian period, north of Mesopotamia, a more stylized and heraldic design approach developed. Stories of the gods were illustrated and animals were shown engaged in battle (Figs. 1-14 and 1-15).

The last glory of Mesopotamian civilization occurred during the long reign of King Nebuchadnezzar (d. 562 B.C.) in the city-state of Babylon. But in 538 B.C., after less than a century of great power, during which Babylon became the richest city in the world, with a population reaching perhaps a million people, Babylon and Mesopotamia fell to the Persians. The Mesopotamian culture began to perish as Mesopotamia became a province of Persia, then of Greece and Rome. By the time of the birth of Christ, great cities such as Babylon were abandoned, and the ziggurats had fallen into ruins. The dawning of visible language, the magnificent gift to the future of mankind that was writing, passed forward to the Phoenicians, who reduced the formidable complexity of cuneiform to simple phonetic signs.

1-14

1-15

Graphic Communications in Ancient Egypt

2-1. Ivory tablet of King Zet, First Dynasty. This five-thousand-year-old tablet is perhaps the earliest known example of the Egyptian pictographic writing that evolved into hieroglyphics.

The Nile River courses 6,689 kilometers (4,157 miles) through the northwest corner of Africa toward the Mediterranean Sea. The basin of this ancient river—the planet's longest—has yielded stone implements that are one hundred thousand years old. The early flint-implement inhabitants lived in a warm, moist climate, but thousands of years ago the region began to grow more arid. Deserts slowly crept toward the narrower Nile River, and twenty thousand years ago the area that became Egypt had become a vast sandy desert, devoid of life except for the lush flood plain clinging to each side of the river. Perhaps it was five or six thousand years ago that agriculture began in the Nile Valley. The early tillers of the soil deified this great river, whose cycle of floods nourished their crops and animals.

By the time King Menes unified the land of Egypt and formed the First Dynasty around the year 3100 B.C., a number of inventions from the Sumerians in Mesopotamia had reached the Egyptians, including the cylinder seal, architectural designs of brick, a number of decorative design motifs, and the fundamentals of writing. Unlike the Sumerians, who evolved their pictographic writing into the abstract cuneiform, the Egyptians retained their picture-writing system, called *hieroglyphics* (Greek for "sacred carving" after the Egyptian for "the god's words"), for almost three and a half millennia. The earliest known hieroglyphs (Fig. 2-1) date from about 3100 B.C., and the last known written hieroglyphic inscription was carved in 394 A.D., many decades after Egypt had become a Roman colony.

Egyptian hieroglyphs

For nearly fifteen centuries, people looked with fascination upon Egyptian hieroglyphs without understanding their meaning. The last people to use this language system were fourth-century A.D. Egyptian temple priests, and they were so secretive that Greek and Roman scholars of the era believed that this amazing writing was nothing more than magical symbols for sacred rites. In August of 1799, Napoleon's troops were digging a foundation for an addition to the fortification in the Egyptian town of Rosetta, which they were occupying. A black slab was unearthed, bearing an inscription in two languages and three scripts: Egyptian hieroglyphics, Egyptian demotic script, and Greek (Fig. 2-2). This decree had been written in 197 or 196 B.C., after a great council of Egyptian priests met to commemorate the ascension of Pharaoh Ptolemy V (born c. 210 B.C.) to the throne of Egypt nine years earlier. It was realized that the inscription was probably the same in the three languages, and efforts to translate it began. In 1819, Dr. Thomas Young (1773–1829) proved that the direction in which the glyphs of animals and people faced was the direction from which hieroglyphics should be read and that the cartouche for Ptolemy occurred several times (Fig. 2-3).

The major deciphering of the Rosetta Stone hieroglyphs was done by Jean François Champollion (1790–1832). He realized that some of the signs were alphabetic, some were syllabic, and some were determinatives (signs that determined how the preceding glyphs should be interpreted). Realizing that the hieroglyphs often functioned as phonograms and not simply pictographs, Champollion was able to sound out the names Ptolemy and Cleopatra. This breakthrough happened in 1822, after Champollion had been given a photograph of an obelisk, a tall, totemlike Egyptian

11

Graphic Communications in Ancient Egypt

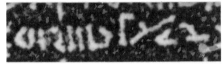

2-3

2-4

2-2

2-2. The Rosetta Stone, c. 197–196 B.C. From top to bottom, the concurrent hieroglyphic, demotic, and Greek inscriptions provided the key to the secrets of ancient Egypt.

2-3. Details of the Rosetta Stone, showing the name *Ptolemy* in hieroglyphics (top) and as the Greek word *Ptolemaios* (bottom).

2-4. Cartouche of Sesostris I, c. 1950 B.C. The cartouche—as shown in this example etched on iridescent mother of pearl—is a bracketlike plaque containing the glyphs for an important name.

monument bearing an inscription. As Champollion studied the photograph, he was stunned to see the cartouches—bracketlike plaques containing the glyphs of important names (Fig. 2-4)—of both Ptolemy and Cleopatra, which he had recognized earlier. Champollion assigned sounds to the three glyphs found in both words: *p, o,* and *l*. Then he patiently sounded out the others until he had a dozen hieroglyphic translations (Fig. 2-5). Armed with this new knowledge, he proceeded to decipher the cartouche for Alexander.

Champollion gathered all the cartouches he could find from the Greco-Roman era and quickly translated eighty, building a large vocabulary of glyphs in the process. After his death at the age of forty-two, Champollion's *Egyptian Dictionary* and *Egyptian Grammar* were both published. He had made such progress toward translating hieroglyphics that the Egyptologists who followed during the nineteenth century were able to unlock the mysteries of Egyptian history and culture that had been silently preserved in this beautiful graphic-language system.

When the early Egyptian scribes were confronted with words difficult to express in visual form, they probably devised a rebus, using pictures for sounds, to write the desired word (Fig. 2-6). At the same time, they designated a pictorial symbol for every consonant sound and combination of consonants in their speech. Even

2-5. Alphabet characters have been applied beside each hieroglyph in the cartouches of Ptolemy and Cleopatra to demonstrate the approximate phonetic sounds deciphered by Champollion.

2-6. These Egyptian hieroglyphs illustrate the rebus principle. Words and syllables are represented by pictures of objects and by symbols whose names are similar to the word or syllable to be communicated. These hieroglyphs mean *bee, leaf, sea,* and *sun.* As rebuses (using the English language), they could also mean belief and season.

2-7. Offering Niche of the Lady Sat-tety-lyn, Sixth Dynasty. In contrast to the raised images in the lower registers, these hieroglyphs are carved into the surface and are contained in a mathematical grid of carved lines.

though they never developed signs for the connecting sounds, combining the various glyphs formed a skeletonized form of every word. By the time of the New Kingdom (1570–1085 B.C.), this remarkably efficient writing system had over seven hundred hieroglyphs, over one hundred of which remained strictly visual pictographs or word-pictures. The remainder had become phonograms. Because the Egyptian language contained so many homonyms (such as, for example, a *pool* of water and the game of *pool*), determinatives were used after these words to ensure that the reader correctly interpreted them. *Hinew,* for example, could refer to a liquid measure or neighbors. In the former case, it was followed by the glyph for beer pot; in the latter, by glyphs for a man and a woman.

The ancient Egyptians had an extraordinary sense of design, and they were sensitive to the remarkable decorative and textural qualities of their hieroglyphs. This monumental visible language system was everywhere. Hieroglyphs were carved into stone as raised images or incised relief (Figs. 2-7 and 2-8), and color was often applied. These covered the interior and exterior of temples and tombs. Furniture, coffins, clothing, utensils, buildings, and jewelry all bore hieroglyphs with both decorative and inscriptional purposes. Frequently, magical and religious values were ascribed to certain hieroglyphs. The hieroglyph *ankh* was a cross surmounted by a loop, and had modest origins as the symbol for a sandal strap. Due to the phonetic similarity, it gained meaning as a symbol for life and immortality, and was widely used as a sacred emblem throughout the land.

The design flexibility of hieroglyphics was greatly increased by the choice of writing direction. One started from the direction in which the living creatures were facing. The lines could be written horizontally or vertically, so the designer of an artifact or manuscript had four choices: left to right horizontally; left to right in vertical columns; right to left horizontally; and right to left in vertical columns. Sometimes, as demonstrated in the schematic of the sarcophagus of Aspalta (Fig. 2-9), these design possibilities were combined in one work.

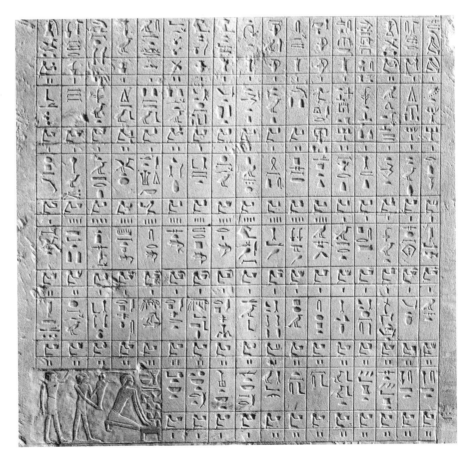

2-9

2-8. Hieroglyphic praise to Sesostris I, c. 1971–1928 B.C. In this beautiful carved relief, some of the pictographs become detailed pictorial sculpture. Sesostris I's cartouche is seen at the bottom, left of center.

2-9. Sarcophagus of Aspalta, King of Ethiopia, c. 593–568 B.C. This detail of the designs scribed into this granite sarcophagus demonstrates the flexibility of hieroglyphics.

Papyrus and writing

A major forward step in Egyptian visual communications was the development of *papyrus,* a paperlike substrate for writing manuscripts. In ancient times the *Cyperus papyrus* plant grew along the Nile in shallow marshes and pools, and the Egyptians made extensive use of this plant. A 5-meter (about 15-foot) root about as thick as a man's wrist grew along the bottom of the shallows. Smaller feeder roots were sunk into the mud, and 4.6-meter (about 15-foot) stems grew up above the water. Papyrus flowers were used for garlands at the temples, and the root was used for fuel and utensils. From the stem the Egyptians made sails, mats, cloth, rope, sandals, and, most importantly, papyrus.

In his *Natural History,* Roman historian Pliny the Elder (23–79 A.D.) tells how papyrus was made. After the rind was peeled away, the inner pith of the stems was cut into longitudinal strips, laid side by side. A second layer of strips was then laid on top of the first layer, at right angles to it. These two layers were soaked in the Nile River and then pressed or hammered until they were a single sheet—apparently, the glutinous sap of the papyrus stem acted as an adhesive. After the sheets dried in the sun, an ivory or stone polisher was used to smooth them. If such flaws as spots, stains, or spongy areas appeared, a sheet would be peeled apart and remade. Eight different papyrus grades were made, for uses ranging from royal proclamations to daily accounting. The finished sheet had an upper surface of horizontal fibers called the *recto* and a bottom surface of vertical fibers called the *verso.* The tallest papyrus sheets measured 49 centimeters (19½ inches), and up to

twenty sheets would be pasted together and rolled into a scroll, with the recto side facing inward.

As in Sumer, knowledge was power, and the scribes gained significant authority in Egyptian society. Learning to read and write the complex language took many years, and the profession of scribe was highly respected and brought many privileges, not the least of which was exemption from taxation.

The wooden palette used by the scribe was a trademark, identifying the carrier as being able to read and write (Fig. 2-10). The example shown is 32.5 centimeters (12¾ inches) long. One end has at least two depressions, to hold black, red, and sometimes other ink cakes. With a gum solution as a binder, carbon was used to make black ink and ground red ocher to make red ink. These were dried into cakes not unlike contemporary watercolors, and a wet brush would then be rubbed onto the cake to return the ink to a liquid state for writing. A slot in the middle of the palette held the brushes, which were made from rush stems. The stem tips were cut on an angle and chewed by the scribe to separate the fibers into a brush.

Holding the scroll with his left hand, the scribe would begin at the outer-right edge and write a column of hieroglyphs from top to bottom, writing column after column as shown in the detail of the *Book of the Dead* of Tuthmosis III (Fig. 2-11). This hieroglyphic book handwriting evolved from the monumental form—the scribes simplified the inscriptional hieroglyphs from a carefully constructed picture to a quickly drawn gesture.

By 1500 B.C., a cursory *hieratic* (from the Greek for "priestly") script, a kind of penstroke simplification of the hieroglyphic book hand, was developed by the priests for religious writings. The earliest hieratic script differed from the hieroglyphs only in that the use of a rush pen, instead of a pointed brush, produced more abstract characters with a terse, angular quality. An even more abstract script called *demotic* (from the Greek word for "popular") came into secular use for commercial and legal writing by the year 400 B.C. The hieroglyph for scribe was a pictorial image of the very early brush-holder, palette, and sack of ink. The characters accompanying the photograph of these artifacts show this evolution (Fig. 2-12). Hieratic and demotic scripts supplemented rather than supplanted hieroglyphs, which continued in use for religious and inscriptional purposes.

2-10. Egyptian scribe's palette with an inscription in hieratic script.

2-11. Detail from the *Book of the Dead* of Tuthmosis III, c. 1450 B.C. Written hieroglyphics were simplified, but they maintained their pictographic origin.

2-11

Graphic Communications in Ancient Egypt

2-12. The hieroglyph for scribe depicted the Old Kingdom palette, the drawstring sack for dried ink cakes, and a reed brush holder. The changes in this glyph demonstrate the evolutionary process (from left to right): hieroglyphic, 2700 B.C.; hieroglyphic manuscript hand, c. 1500 B.C.; hieratic script, c. 1300 B.C.; and demotic script, c. 400 B.C.

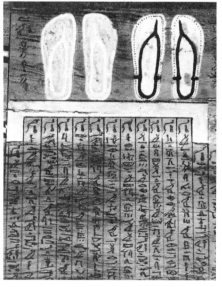

2-13. Detail, the coffin of Diehurty-Matcht's wife, Twelfth Dynasty. Portions of the Coffin Text are shown on the inside of this wooden coffin. The registers of pictorial images, including these two pairs of sandals, could become real food, objects, and clothing in the afterlife.

The first illustrated manuscripts

The Egyptians were the first people to produce illustrated manuscripts in which words and pictures combined to communicate information. This was particularly evident in Egyptian mythology. A preoccupation with death and a strong belief in the afterlife compelled the Egyptians to evolve a complex mythology about the journey into the afterlife. Mythology was early man's way to deal with natural phenomena and other unknown aspects of life and the world. By inventive myth and legend, the inexplicable could be explained and faced. A final judgment would ultimately allow the deceased either to be admitted into the company of the gods or to suffer eternal damnation. The prayer of every Egyptian was to be cleansed of sin and found worthy at the final judgment. Scribes and artists were commissioned to prepare funerary papyri, called *The Chapters of Coming Forth by Day.* A nineteenth-century scholar named them *The Book of the Dead,* and this name is generally used today.

The Book of the Dead was a logical evolution of the need for funerary texts. Beginning with the pyramid of Unas (c. 2345 B.C.), the walls and passages of the pyramids were covered with the *Pyramid Texts* of hieroglyphic writings, including myths, hymns, and prayers relating to the godlike Pharaoh's life in the afterworld. This practice was followed by the *Coffin Texts* (Fig. 2-13). All surfaces of the wooden coffin and/or stone sarcophagus were covered with writings carved into the surface, and often illustrated with pictures of possessions for the afterlife. Thus, high officials and noblemen could now enjoy the benefits of the funerary texts even though the cost of a pyramid was beyond their means.

The dawning of the New Kingdom around 1580 B.C. saw papyrus manuscripts come into use for funerary texts. Even citizens of fairly limited means could afford to have at least simple papyri to accompany them on the journey into the afterlife. From pyramid to coffin to papyri: This evolution toward cheaper and more widespread use of funerary texts paralleled the increasingly democratic and secular aspects of Egyptian life (Fig. 2-14).

The Book of the Dead was written in a first-person narrative by the deceased and placed in the tomb to help triumph over the dangers of the Underworld. The artists who illustrated *The Book of the Dead* papyrus were called upon to foretell what would occur after the subject died and entered the afterlife (Fig. 2-15). Magical spells could enable the deceased to turn into powerful creatures; passwords to enter various states of the Underworld were provided; and the protection of the gods was sought. Wonderful futures are illustrated in various *Books of the Dead*. One might dwell in the Fields of Peace, ascend into the heavens to live as a star, travel the sky with the sun god, Ra, in his solar boat, or help Osiris rule the Underworld.

The journey into the Underworld is depicted as a chronological narrative. The final judgment is shown in the c. 1420 B.C. *Papyrus of Ani* (Pl. 3). Ani, a royal scribe, temple accountant, and grainery manager from Thebes, and his wife, Thuthu, approach the scales where the jackal-headed god Anubis, keeper of the dead, prepares to weigh Ani's heart against a feather symbolizing truth to see if he is "true of voice" and free from sin. Thoth, the ibis-headed scribe of the gods and keeper of the magical arts, is poised with a scribe's palette to write the verdict. To the right, the monster Ammit, the devourer of the dead, stands poised for action should Ani fail to pass the moment of judgment. An imaginative visual symbol, Ammit has the head of a crocodile, the torso of a lion, and the hindquarters of a hippopotamus. A register across the top shows twelve of the forty-two gods who sit in judgment. Addressing each god in turn, a "negative confession" denies a host of sins: "I have not done evil; I have not stolen; I have not killed people; I have not stolen food. . . ." After making this negative confession, Ani spoke to his heart: "Set now thyself to bear witness against me. Speak not against me in the presence of the judges, cast not your weight against me before the Lord of the Scales." Upon being found virtuous, Ani is presented to Osiris, Lord of the Underworld, then his

2-14. Vignette from the Papyrus of Nekht, c. 1250 B.C. Standing between their house and ornamental pool, this military scribe and his wife worship Osiris and the goddess Maat. The pool is shown as a flat projection, and "wind-catchers" are on the roof of the house.

2-15. Detail from the Papyrus of Hunefer, c. 1370 B.C. Hunefer and his wife are worshiping the gods of Amenta. The sun-god Ra bears an *ankh* symbol on his knee, and Thoth holds the *udjat,* the magical protective "sound eye" of the god Horus.

soul spends the night after death traveling into the Underworld. On the following morning, he arrives at his "coming forth by day."

A consistent design format evolved for the illustrated Egyptian papyri. One or two horizontal bands, usually colored, ran across the top and bottom of the manuscript. Vertical columns of writing separated by ruled lines were written from right to left. Images were inserted adjacent to the text illustrated. Often, images stood on the lower horizontal band, and the columns of text hung down from the top horizontal band. Frequently, a horizontal friezelike register ran along the top of a sheet. Sometimes, a sheet was divided into rectangular zones to separate text and images. The functional integration of text and image was aesthetically pleasing, for the dense texture of the brush-drawn hieroglyphs contrasted handsomely with the illustration's open spaces and flat planes of color. In the earlier *Books of the Dead,* the scribe designed the manuscript. If it was to be illustrated, blank areas were left which the artist would fill in as best he could. The vignettes gradually became more important and dominated the design. The artist would draw these illustrations first. Then the scribe would write the manuscript, trying to avoid awkward blank spaces and sometimes writing in the margins if the illustrator did not leave adequate room for the text. Excellent artists were retained to create the images, but the scribes who did this work were not scholars. Often, passages were omitted for purposes of layout or through poor workmanship. The manuscript illustrations were drawn in simplified contour lines using black or brown ink, then flat color was applied using white, black, brown, blue, green, and sometimes yellow pigments. Perhaps the extensive use of luminous blue and green together in the papyri was a response to the intense blue of the Nile and the rich green of the foliage along its banks, a cool streak of life winding through vast reaches of desert.

Wall paintings and papyri shared the same vocabulary of design conventions. These are shown clearly in the dry fresco wall painting of a fowling scene from the Tomb of Nakht at Thebes (Fig. 2-16). Men had darker skin color than women, and important persons were shown in larger scale than less important persons. The human body was drawn as a two-dimensional schematic. The frontal body had arms, legs, and head in profile. The stylized eye reads simultaneously as both profile and frontal image. The concern for design regularity and geometry is seen in the repetition of papyrus plants, which were reduced to simplified symbols. Action was frozen. Even though the flatness was maintained, the Egyptian artists were capable of sensitive observation and recording of details, as shown in the birds flying up from the papyrus swamp.

2-16. *Fowling in the Marshes,* fresco painting from the Tomb of Nakht, c. 1450 B.C. Armed with throw-sticks, Egyptians ventured into the Nile delta area on light boats to hunt birds.

One could commission a funerary papyrus, or purchase a stock copy and have one's name filled in in the appropriate places. The buyer could select the number and choice of chapters, the number and quality of illustrations, and the length. Excepting the 57-meter (185-foot) great Turin Papyrus, *The Book of the Dead* scrolls ranged from 4.6 meters (15 feet) to 27.7 meters (90 feet) long and were from 30 centimeters (about 12 inches) to 45 centimeters (about 18 inches) tall. Toward the final collapse of the Egyptian culture, *The Book of the Dead* often consisted merely of sheets of papyrus, some of which were only a few inches square.

2-17

Visual identification

The Egyptians used cylinder seals and proprietary marks on such items as pottery very early in their history. The seals certainly were inherited from the Sumerians, and the proprietary marks may have been also. A uniquely Egyptian contribution that expressed love of natural form and decoration was the scarab seal (Figs. 2-17 and 2-18). From prehistoric times, the scarab beetle was venerated in ancient Egypt as being sacred or magical. In the Twelfth Dynasty, carved scarab emblems were commonly used as identification seals. These oval stones, usually of a glazed steatite, were sculpted likenesses of the scarab beetle. Because steatite was soft enough for carving but also held up well under the heat needed to apply a glaze, it became the stone of choice for the scarabs. The flat underside, engraved with a hieroglyphic inscription, was used as a seal. Sometimes, the scarab was mounted as a signet ring. Every Egyptian of any standing had a personal seal. Interestingly, very little evidence of scarabs actually being used for sealing has survived. Possibly the communicative function was secondary to the scarab's value as talisman, ornament, and symbol of resurrection. The scarab beetle was connected with the creator sun god, Kheper, and the scarab was sometimes depicted rolling the sun across the sky just as the living scarab or dung beetle was seen forming a ball of dung and rolling it across the sand to its burrow to be eaten over the following days. The ancient Egyptians mistakenly believed that the scarab beetle laid its eggs in this ball, and felt that the life cycle of the scarab represented the daily rebirth of the sun. A scarab called a "heart-scarab" was placed over the heart of a mummy with its wrappings. Its engraved undersurface had a brief plea to the heart not to act as a hostile witness in the Hall of Justice of Osiris.

The majestic Egyptian culture survived for over three thousand years. Hieroglyphics, papyrus, and illustrated manuscripts are its visual communications legacy. Along with the accomplishments of Mesopotamia, these innovations triggered the development of the alphabet and graphic communications in Phoenicia and the Greco-Roman world.

2-18

2-17 and 2-18. Scarab of Ikhnaton and Nefertiti, c. 1370 B.C. This 6-centimeter (2.4-inch) scarab bears the cartouche of Ikhnaton on the side shown. The engraved hieroglyphs of the flat bottom were etched with a bronze needle.

3　The Asian Contribution

3-1. The top row of pictographs are *chia-ku-wen* or "bone-and-shell" script, attributed to the legendary Ts-ang Chieh. The lower row shows the same words from Li Ssu's unified *hsiao chuan* or "small-seal" style. From left: sun, moon, water, rain, wood, and dog.

3-2. Oracle bone inscribed with *chia-ku-wen* or "bone-and-shell" script, c. 1300 B.C. The 128 characters inscribed on this scapula concern a diviner's predictions of calamities during the next ten-day period.

Civilization sprang seemingly from nowhere along the banks of the Tigris and Euphrates rivers in Mesopotamia and along the course of the Nile River in Egypt. The origins of the splendid civilization that developed in the vast ancient land of China are shrouded in similar mystery. Legend suggests that by the year 2000 B.C., a culture was evolving in virtual isolation from the western pockets of civilization. Among the many innovations of the ancient Chinese, some proved to change the course of human events. The compass made exploration and seafaring possible. Gunpowder, which fueled that warlike aspect of human nature and changed the nature of war, was used by the Chinese for fireworks instead of for weapons. Chinese calligraphy, an ancient writing system, is used today by more people than any other visual language system. Paper, a magnificent and economical substrate for transmitting information, and printing, the duplication of words and images, made possible the wide communication of thought and deed. The adoption of these Chinese inventions became the means that allowed Europeans to set forth and conquer the world: The compass (which may have been developed independently in Europe) directed early explorers across the seas and around the globe; firearms enabled them to subjugate the native populations of Africa, Asia, and the Americas; printing on paper became the method for spreading European language, culture, religion, and law throughout the world.

Chinese calligraphy

Chinese calligraphy is a purely visual language. It is not alphabetical, and every symbol is composed of a number of differently shaped lines within an imaginary square. Legend holds that calligraphy was invented about 1800 B.C. by Ts-ang Chieh, who was inspired to invent writing by contemplating the clawmarks of birds and footprints of animals. Ts-ang Chieh proceeded to develop elementary pictographs of things in nature. These images were highly stylized and composed of a minimum number of lines, but they are easily deciphered. The Chinese sacrificed the realism found in hieroglyphs for more abstract designs. Aesthetic considerations seem to have interested the Chinese from the early beginnings of their writing. Simple nouns were developed first, and the language slowly matured and became enriched as characters were invented to express feelings, actions, colors, sizes, and types. Chinese calligraphic characters are *logograms,* graphic characters or signs that represent an entire word. (The sign $, for instance, is a logogram to represent the word "dollar.") Ideographs and phonetic loans—borrowing the sign of a similar-sounding word—were developed, but calligraphy was never broken down into syllable signs, like cuneiform, or alphabetic signs for elementary sounds. Therefore, there is no direct relationship between the spoken and written Chinese languages. Both are independent systems for conveying thought; a sound from the mouth to the ear, and a sign from the hand to the eye. Learning the total vocabulary of forty-four thousand characters was the sign of wisdom and scholarship.

The earliest known Chinese calligraphy is a writing called *chia-ku-wen,* or "bone-and-shell" script (Figs. 3-1 and 3-2), used from 1800–1200 B.C. It was closely bound to the art of divination, an effort to foretell future events through communication with the gods or long-dead ancestors. This ancient writing—as in hieroglyphics and cuneiform—was pictographic. Dating from the eighteenth century before Christ, Chinese pictographs are found incised on tortoise shells and large animals' flat shoulder bones, called "oracle bones," which contain communications between the living and the dead. When one wished to consult an exalted ancestor or a god, the royal diviner was asked to inscribe the message on a polished animal bone. The diviner pushed a red-hot metal bar into a hole in the inscribed bone, and the heat produced an intricate web of cracks. The diviner could read these cracks, which were believed to be messages from the dead.

The next phase of Chinese calligraphy, called *chin-wen* or "bronze" script, consisted of inscriptions on cast-bronze objects, including food and water vessels, musical instruments, weapons, mirrors, coins, and seals. Inscriptions were scribed in the casting molds to preserve answers received from gods and ancestors during divination. The permanence of bronze also made it suitable for important treaties, penal codes, and legal contracts. Ceremonial vessels used to hold food offerings in ancestor worship and inscribed vessels with dedications (Fig. 3-3) contain well-formed characters in orderly alignment. Most inscriptions were made inside the vessels, and these characters were more studied and regular than the bone-and-shell inscriptions.

Artists in different places developed different writing styles until Chinese calligraphy was unified under the powerful Emperor Shih Huang Ti (259–210 B.C.). During his reign, Confucian scholars were buried alive and their books burned. Thousands of lives were sacrificed building the Great Wall of China to protect the emperor and his empire. But he also unified the Chinese people into one nation and issued royal decrees standardizing weights, measures, the axle length on carts, laws, and writing. Prime minister Li Ssu (c. 280–208 B.C.) was charged with designing the new writing style. This third phase in the design evolution of calligra-

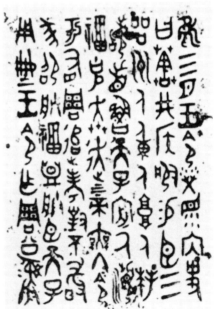

3-3. Four-handled vessel with *chin-wen* or "bronze" script inscription, eleventh century B.C. Bold regular strokes are used to form the sixty-four characters of an eight-line dedication, forming a rectangle in the vessel's bottom.

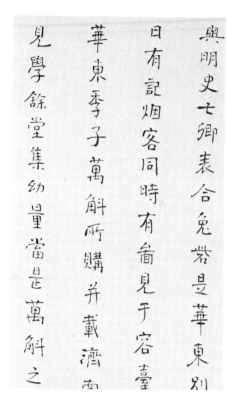

3-4. Wo-yun-sheng (formerly attributed to Tung Yuan, 907–980), detail of the colophon from "A Clear Day in the Valley." This handscroll detail is an excellent example of *chen-shu* or "regular-style" calligraphy.

3-5. *Li* (three-legged pottery vessel), late neolithic period. The evolution of the calligraphic character *Li* stemmed from this pot: oracle bone pictograph, bronze script, 1000 B.C., and *chen-shu* or regular style, 200 B.C.

phy is called *hsiao chuan* or "small-seal" style (Fig. 3-1). The lines are drawn in thicker, more even strokes. More curves and circles are used in this graceful, flowing style, which is much more abstract than the earlier two styles. Each character is neatly balanced and fills its imaginary square primly.

The final step in the evolution of Chinese calligraphy is called *chen-shu* (also, *k'ai-shu* or "regular" style) (Fig. 3-4) and has been in continuous use for nearly two thousand years. In regular style, every line, dot, and nuance of the brush can be controlled by the sensitivity and skill of the calligrapher. An infinite range of design possibilities exists within every word. Structure, composition, shape, stroke thickness, and the relationship of strokes to each other and to the white spaces surrounding them are design factors determined by the writer. Regular-style calligraphy has an abstract beauty that rivals humanity's highest attainments in art and design. Indeed, it is considered to be the highest art form in China, more important, even, than painting. Oriental painting and calligraphy have close bonds. Both are executed with ink on paper or silk using gestured strokes of the brush.

The evolution of Chinese calligraphy can be traced from its pictographic origins through one of the early characters; for example, the prehistoric character for the three-legged pot called a *li,* which is now the word for "tripod" (Fig. 3-5). The *li* was an innovative product design, for the black discolorations on some surviving examples indicate that it stood in the fire to heat its contents rapidly. In the oracle-bone script, it was an easily recognized pictograph. In the 1000 B.C. bronze script, this character had evolved into a simpler form. The chen-shu script character echoes the three-part bottom and flat top of the earlier forms.

The painting of bamboo from the *Album of Eight Leaves* (Fig. 3-6) by Li Fang-Yin (1695–1754) shows how the vividly descriptive brushstrokes with a bamboo brush join calligraphy and painting, poem and illustration, into a unified communication. Nature is the inspiration for both, and every stroke and dot is given the energy of a living thing. Children begin their early training by drawing bamboo leaves and stems with the brush to learn the basic strokes.

Spiritual states and deep feelings can be expressed in calligraphy. Thick, languid strokes become mournful, and poems written in celebration of spring have a light exuberance. A master calligrapher was once asked why he dug his ink-stained fingers so deeply into the hairs of his brush. He replied that only then could he feel the *tao* (cosmic spirit that operates throughout the universe in animate and inanimate things) flow from his arm, into the brush, and onto the paper.

Calligraphy was said to have bones (authority and size), meat (the proportion of the characters), blood (the texture of the fluid ink), and muscle (spirit and vital force). The exuberance of master calligrapher Chu-Yun-Ming's *Eight Immortals of the Wine Cup* (Fig. 3-7) shows just how dynamic and inventive calligraphy could be, with broad strokes thrusting down the page in contrast to lively, delicate strokes of smaller characters.

Mountain and River Landscape (Fig. 3-8) by Tao Chi (1630–c. 1707 A.D.) demonstrates calligraphy's ability to evoke natural objects, forming movement and energy into an organic whole.

The invention of paper

Dynastic records attribute the invention of paper to the eunuch and high governmental official Ts'ai Lun, who reported his invention to Emperor Ho in 105 A.D. Whether Ts'ai Lun truly invented paper, perfected an earlier invention, or patronized its invention is not known. He was, however, deified as the god of the papermakers.

In earlier times, the Chinese wrote on bamboo slats or wooden strips, using a bamboo pen with a dense and durable ink, the origins of which are obscure. Lampblack or soot was deposited on a dome-shaped cover over a vessel of oil with several burning wicks. The lampblack was collected, mixed thoroughly with a gum solution using a mortar and pestle, and then molded into sticks or cubes. For writing, these were returned to the liquid state by rubbing it in water on an inking stone. The

3-6. Li Fang-Yin, from the *Album of Eight Leaves,* number six, 1744. The design of the total space, with the bamboo bending out into the open space in contrast to the erect column of writing, is exquisite.

3-7

3-8

strips of wood were used for short messages; 23-centimeter (about 9-inch) pieces of bamboo tied together with leather strips or silk string were used for longer communications. Although these substrates were abundant and easy to prepare, they were heavy. After the invention of woven silk cloth, it too was used as a writing surface. However, it was very costly.

Ts'ai Lun's process for making paper continued almost unchanged until papermaking was mechanized in nineteenth-century England. Natural fibers, including mulberry bark, hemp fishnets, and rags, were soaked in a vat of water and beaten into a pulp with pounding mortars. A vatman dipped a screen-bottomed framelike mold into the pulp solution, taking just enough of the solution onto the mold for the sheet of paper. With skill and split-second judgment, the vatman raised the mold from the vat while oscillating and shaking the mold to cross and mesh the fibers as the water drained through the bottom. Then the paper was couched, or pressed onto a woolen cloth, to which it adhered while it dried. The mold was free for immediate reuse. The couched sheets were stacked, pressed, and then hung to dry. The first major improvement in the process was the use of starch sizing or gelatin to stiffen and strengthen the paper and increase its ability to absorb the ink.

In paper's early decades, some ancient Chinese often considered it to be a cheap substitute for silk or bamboo, but as time went on, its light weight, economical manufacture, and versatility overcame all reservations. The coarse, long-fibered quality of this early paper caused no problems because the hair brush, invented

3-7. Chu-Yun-Ming, handscroll with poem, *Eight Immortals of the Wine Cup,* eighth century A.D. The imaginative powers for inventive design were unleashed in the writing of this poem.

3-8. Tao Chi, *Mountain and River Landscape,* detail of scroll. The visual design qualities of calligraphy—from delicate and lacy to thunderous and bold—are contrasted in this scroll.

The Asian Contribution

3-9. Chinese chop, c. 1500 A.D. As this example, carved in yellow field stone, shows, the chop is beautiful at both ends. The identification stamp was inscribed into the bottom of a small decorative sculpture.

3-10. Buddhist dedicatory stela, c. 562 A.D. This votive limestone tablet illustrates the early Chinese practice of permanently and accurately rendering inscriptions by carving them on stone.

many centuries earlier, was the primary writing instrument. Scrolls for writing were made by gluing together sheets of paper, sometimes delicately stained slate blue, lemon yellow, or a pale, warm yellow. These sheets were rolled onto dowels of sandalwood or ivory, which were sometimes tipped with jade or amber. In addition to writing, the Chinese used their new material as wrapping paper, wallpaper, toilet paper, and napkins.

The discovery of printing

Printing, a most important invention in human history, was invented by the Chinese. This was *relief printing:* the spaces around an image on a flat surface are cut away; the remaining raised surface is inked; and a sheet of paper is placed over the surface and rubbed to transfer the inked image to the paper. Two hypotheses have been advanced about the invention of printing. One is that the use of engraved seals to make identification imprints evolved into printing. As early as the third century B.C., seals or stamps were used to make impressions in soft clay. Often, bamboo or wood strips bearing writing were wrapped in silk, which was then sealed with clay that bore an impression.

During the Han Dynasty (third century A.D.), seals called chops (Fig. 3-9) were made by carving calligraphic characters into a flat surface of jade, silver, gold, or ivory. The flat surface was inked by pressing it into a pastelike red ink made from cinnabar, then the chop was pressed onto a substrate to form an impression, similar in method to present-day rubber stamps. The impression was a red shape with white characters. Around 500 A.D., chops came into use upon which the artisan had cut away the negative area surrounding the characters, so that the characters could be printed in red surrounded by white paper. The fundamental technique for block printing was now available. Yuan Chao Meng-fu's fourteenth century A.D. painting of a goat and sheep (Pl. 4) has both types of chops imprinted upon its surface: white characters reversed from a solid ground, and solid characters surrounded by a white ground.

The second theory about the origins of printing focuses on the early Chinese practice of making inked rubbings from inscriptions carved in stone (Fig. 3-10). Beginning in 165 A.D., Confucian classics were carved into stone to ensure an accurate, permanent record. The disadvantages of these stone "books" were their weight and the space required. One historical work required thirteen acres for storage of the tablets, which were arranged like rows of tombstones. Soon, copies of these inscriptions were pulled by making ink rubbings: A damp sheet of thin paper was laid on the stone. The paper was pressed into the depressions of the inscription with a stiff brush. Then, an inked cloth pad was lightly rubbed over the surface to produce an ink image from the incised inscription. Although the ink is applied to the top of the paper rather than to the relief image in this method, the process is related to relief printing.

As early as the second century A.D., rubbings were also made from stone relief sculptures carved as offering shrines and tombs (Fig. 3-11). In a sense, these reliefs were closer to painting than to sculpture, for the figures crowding the complex designs were handled as flat silhouettes with linear detail and little effort to create spatial depth. In retrospect, these votive and tomb carvings resemble neither sculpture nor painting as much as they do a relief woodblock printing plate.

Whether relief printing evolved from chops, rubbings from stone inscriptions, or a synthesis of both is not known. Just who invented relief printing and when and where it began remain a mystery. The route is marked by undated relics: printed fabrics, stencil pictures, and thousands of stamped impressions of the Buddha figure. By the time the earliest existing datable relief printing was produced, around 770 A.D., the technique had been well developed: Using a brush and ink, the material to be printed was prepared on a sheet of thin paper. Calligraphy was written, images were drawn. The blockcutter applied this thin page to the smooth wooden block, image side down, after wetting the surface with a paste or sizing. When the paste or sizing was thoroughly dry, the paper was carefully rubbed off. A faint

3-11. Chinese relief tomb sculpture and rubbing, Tang Dynasty (c. 618–907 A.D.). Illustrative images from the life of the deceased are captured in stone and with ink on paper.

inked imprint of the image, which was now reversed, remained on the surface of the block.

Working with amazing speed and accuracy, the blockcutter carved away the surface around the inked image, leaving it in high relief. The printer inked the raised surface, applied a sheet of paper over it, then rubbed the back of the paper with a rubber or stiff brush to transfer the ink to the page, which was then lifted from the block. So efficient is this method that a skilled printer could pull over two hundred impressions per hour.

During the eighth century, Chinese culture and the Buddhist religion were exported to Japan, where the earliest surviving datable printing was produced. Mindful of the terrible smallpox epidemic three decades earlier, the Japanese Empress Shōtoku decreed that one million copies of Buddhist *dhāranī* ("charms") be printed and placed inside one million miniature pagodas about 11.5 centimeters (4½ inches) tall (Fig. 3-12). The Empress was attempting to follow the teachings of Buddha, who had advised his followers to write seventy-seven copies of a *dhāranī* and place them in a pagoda, or place each one in its own small clay pagoda. This would lengthen one's life and eventually lead to paradise. Empress Shōtoku's efforts failed, for she died about the time the charms were being distributed, rolled up in their little three-story wooden pagodas. But the sheer number produced, combined with their sacred value, enabled numerous copies to survive to this day.

The oldest surviving printed manuscript is the *Diamond Sutra* (Fig. 3-13). It consists of seven sheets of paper pasted together to form a scroll 4.9 meters (16 feet) long and 30.5 centimeters (12 inches) high. Six sheets of text convey Buddha's revelations to his elderly follower Subhuti; the seventh is a complex linear woodcut

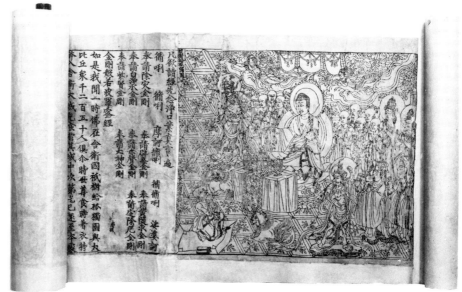

3-13

illustration of the Buddha and his disciples. Buddha decreed that whosoever repeats this text shall be edified. Apparently one Wang Chieh responded to the Buddha's charge, for the final lines of text declare that he made the *Diamond Sutra* for wide, free distribution to honor his parents on the date equivalent to 11 May 868 A.D. The excellence of the printing indicates that the craft had advanced to a high level by the time it was produced.

During the early ninth century A.D., the Chinese government began to issue paper certificates of deposit to merchants who deposited metal currency with the state. When a critical provincial shortage of iron money developed shortly before the year 1000, paper money was designed, printed, and used in lieu of metal coins. The government took control of the currency's production, and millions of notes per year were printed. Inflation and devaluation soon followed, as did efforts to restore confidence: Money was printed on perfumed paper of high silk content; some money was printed on colored paper; and the penalty for counterfeiting was death. China thus became the first society in which ordinary people had daily contact with printed images. In addition to paper money, religious block prints bearing religious images and texts received wide distribution (Fig. 3-14).

During the tenth century, errors in the Confucian classics came to light. Chinese prime minister Fêng Tao became deeply concerned and felt that new master texts should be made. Lacking the resources needed for extensive cutting of stone inscriptions, Fêng Tao turned to the rapidly developing block printing method for this monumental task. With the great scholars as editors and a famous calligrapher overseeing the writing of the master copies, producing the 130 volumes of the nine Confucian classics with their commentaries took twenty-one years, from 932–953 A.D. The goal was not spreading knowledge to the masses, but authenticating the texts. Fêng Tao took a fairly obscure craft and thrust it into the mainstream of Chinese civilization.

The scroll was replaced with paged formats in the ninth or tenth century. First, folded books that opened accordion-style were developed. These resembled scrolls that were folded, like a railroad timetable, instead of rolled. In the tenth or eleventh century, stitched books were developed. Two pages of text were printed from one block. Then the sheet was folded down the middle with the unprinted side of the sheet facing inward and the two printed pages facing out. Sequences of these folded and printed sheets were gathered and sewn to make a codex-style book. The pages from the *Pen ts'ao* medical herbal (Fig. 3-16) were assembled in this fashion. Illustrations and calligraphy were used for headings. A graphic design used to separate the text into sections was shown in the center of the right-hand page.

3-12. *Dhāranī* Buddhist charms, c. 770 A.D. Rolled up and inserted in little pagodas, these earliest surviving specimens of relief printing had the text printed in Chinese calligraphy on one side and in Sanskrit on the other.

3-13. The *Diamond Sūtra*, 868 A.D. Wang Chieh sought spiritual improvement by commissioning the duplication of the *Diamond Sūtra* by printing; the wide spread of knowledge was almost incidental.

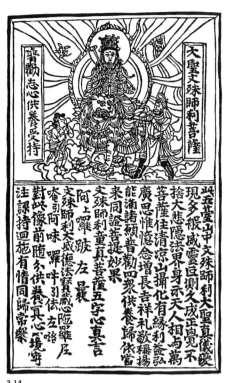

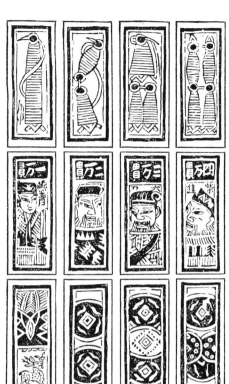

3-14

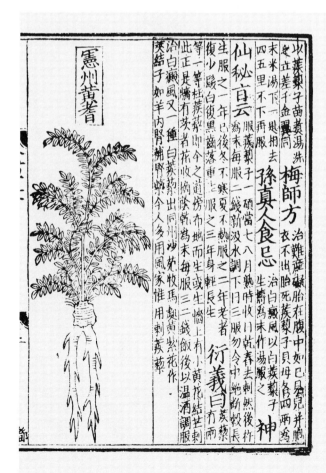

3-15

3-14. Chinese woodblock print, c. 950 A.D. An illustration of Mañjuśrī, the Buddhist personification of supreme wisdom, riding a lion is placed above a prayer text.

3-15. Chinese playing cards, undated. Many of the design conventions used here—numerical sequences of images signifying the suits and the depiction of royalty—survive in playing cards to this day.

3-16. Pages from the *Pen ts'ao,* 1249 A.D. In this illustrated woodblock book on Chinese herbal medicine, a generous top margin and ruled lines bring order to the page.

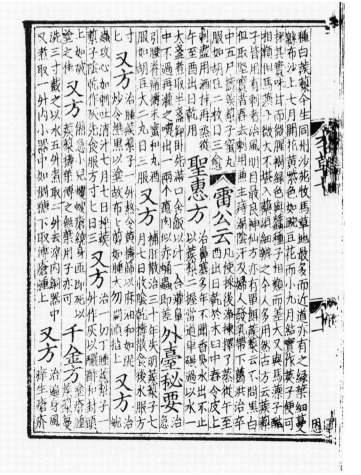

3-16

3-17. Chinese movable types, c. 1300 B.C. This group of carved wood types ranges in size from about 1.25 to 2.5 centimeters (½ to 1 inch) in height.

Another early form of Chinese graphic design and printing was playing cards (Fig. 3-15). These "sheet dice" were first printed on heavy paper cards about the time that paged books replaced manuscript scrolls.

A benchmark in block printing—reproducing beautiful calligraphy with perfection—was established in China by 1000 A.D. and has never been surpassed. The calligrapher was listed with the author and printer in the colophon. State printers were joined by private printers as histories and herbals, science and political science, poetry and prose were carved onto blocks of wood and printed. The quiet revolution that printing wrought upon Chinese intellectual life brought about a renaissance of learning and culture just as surely as Johann Gutenberg's invention of movable type in the West did over five hundred years later.

The invention of movable type

In a woodblock print, such as Figure 3-14, the wood around each calligraphic character is painstakingly cut away. Around 1040 A.D., the Chinese alchemist Pi Sheng (1023–1063 A.D.) extended this process by developing the concept of movable type. If each character were an individual raised form, he reasoned, then any number of characters could be placed in sequence on a surface, inked, and printed. He made his types from a mixture of clay and glue. These three-dimensional calligraphic characters were baked over a straw fire until they hardened. To compose a text, Pi Sheng placed them side by side upon an iron plate coated with a waxy substance to hold the characters in place. The plate was gently heated to soften the wax, and a flat board was pressed upon the types to push them firmly in place and equalize their height from the surface of the form. After the wax cooled, the page of calligraphic types was printed exactly like a woodblock. After the printing was complete, the form was heated again to loosen the wax, so that the characters could be filed in wooden cases.

Since calligraphy is not alphabetical, types were organized according to rhymes. The large number of characters in oriental languages made filing and retrieving the characters difficult. Later, the Chinese cast letters in tin and cut them from wood (Fig. 3-17), but movable type never replaced the handcut woodblock in the Orient.

A notable effort to print from bronze movable type began in Korea under government sponsorship in 1403 A.D. Characters cut from beechwood were pressed into a trough filled with fine sand, making a negative impression. A cover with holes was placed over the impression, and molten bronze was poured into it. After the bronze cooled, a type character was formed. These metal characters were, of course, less fragile than Pi Sheng's earthenware types.

It is curious that movable type was first invented in cultures whose language systems numbered not in the hundreds but in the thousands of characters. With a total of over forty-four thousand characters, it is not surprising that movable type never came into widespread Far Eastern use. One interesting effort to simplify sorting and setting types was the invention of a revolving "lazy susan" table with a spinning tabletop 2.13 meters (7 feet) in diameter (Fig. 3-18). The compositor could sit at this table and rotate it to bring the section with the character within reach.

The Chinese contribution to the evolution of visual communications was formidable. During the Western world's thousand-year medieval period, China's invention of paper and printing spread slowly westward, arriving in Europe just as it was rising from its long night to awaken into a renaissance of learning and culture.

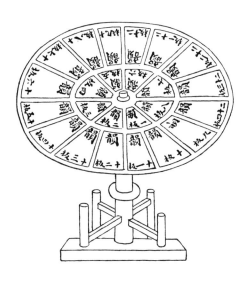

3-18. Woodblock image of a revolving typecase, c. 1313 A.D. This quaintly stylized illustration shows the revolving case designed to make typesetting more efficient.

The Alphabet

Early visual language systems, including cuneiform, hieroglyphs, and Chinese calligraphy, contained a built-in complexity. In each, pictographs had become rebus writing, ideographs, logograms, or even a syllabary. But these early writing systems remained unwieldy and required long, hard study to master. The number of individuals who gained literacy was small. Their access to knowledge enabled them to acquire great power in the early cultures. The subsequent invention of the *alphabet* (from the first two letters of the Greek alphabet, *alpha* and *beta*) represents a major step forward in human communications.

An alphabet is a series of simple visual symbols that stand for elementary sounds. They can be connected and combined to make a visual configuration for any and every sound, syllable, and word uttered by the human mouth. The hundreds of signs and symbols required by cuneiform and hieroglyphs were replaced by twenty or thirty easily learned elementary signs. Figure 4-1 shows major steps in the evolution of the alphabet.

Various theories have been advanced about the origins of the alphabet, but the inventor of this magnificent idea remains unknown. Theories naming cuneiform, hieroglyphs, prehistoric geometric signs, and early Cretan pictographs as the source of the alphabet have been advanced. Some scholars even wonder if the alphabet was invented by an isolated genius, independent of the existing writing systems.

Cretan pictographs

The Minoan civilization that existed on the Mediterranean island of Crete ranks behind only Egypt and Mesopotamia in its early level of advancement in the ancient Western world. Minoan picture symbols were in use as early as 2800 B.C. Short pictographic inscriptions have been found that were written as early as 2000 B.C. About 135 surviving pictographs include figures, arms, and other parts of the body, animals, plants, and some geometric symbols. By 1700 B.C., these pictographs seem to have yielded to linear script writing, a precursor to the spoken Greek language.

One of the most extraordinary relics of the Minoan civilization is the Phaistos Disk (Pl. 4), which was unearthed on Crete in 1908. Lacking precedent or parallel, this modest, flat, *terra cotta disk,* 16.5 centimeters (6½ inches) in diameter, has pictographic and seemingly alphabetic forms imprinted on both sides in spiral bands. These 241 signs include a man in a plumed headdress, a hatchet, an eagle, a carpenter's square, an animal skin, and a vase. Typelike stamps were used to impress each character carefully into the wet clay; thus the principle of movable type was used in a western culture as early as 2000 B.C. Just what the inscriptions say, who made them, and whether the stamps or types were used to make messages upon papyrus or other perishable substrates may never be known. The Phaistos Disk remains one of the great mysteries in the history of graphic design and communications—some scholars have speculated that it may have originated from some location other than Crete, but there is no evidence to support or reject this theory.

Early Name	Probable Meaning	Greek Name	Cretan pictographs	Phoenician	Early Greek	Classical Greek	Latin	Modern English
Āleph	Ox	Alpha				A	A	A
Bēth	House	Bēta				B	B	B
Gimel	Camel	Gamma				Γ	C	C
Dāleth	Folding door	Delta				Δ	D	D
Hē	Lattice window	Epsilon				E	E	E
Wāw	Hook, nail						F	F
							G	G
Zayin	Weapon	Zēta				Z		
Hēth	Fence, barrier	Ēta				H	H	H
Tēth	A winding (?)	Thēta				θ		
Yōd	Hand	Iōta				I	I	I
								J
Kaph	Bent hand	Kappa				K	K	K
Lāmed	Ox-goad	Lambda				Λ	L	L
Mēm	Water	Mu				M	M	M
Nūn	Fish	Nu				N	N	N
Sāmek	Prop (?)	Xei				Ξ		
'Ayin	Eye	Ou				O	O	O
Pē	Mouth	Pei				Π	P	P
Sādē	Fish-hook (?)							
Kōph	Eye of needle (?)	Koppa					Q	Q
Rēsh	Head	Rho				P	R	R
Shin, sin	Tooth	Sigma, san				Σ	S	S
Taw	Mark	Tau				T	T	T
						Y	V	U
								V
								W
						X	X	X
							Y	Y
							Z	Z

4-1. This diagram displays the heritage of the contemporary alphabet. The controversial theory speculating that early Cretan pictographs are the source of our alphabet is based on similarities between their forms and the Phoenician alphabet.

The Phoenician alphabet

The earliest known alphabetical writings come from the ruins of ancient Phoenicia, a culture that developed in what is now Lebanon and parts of Syria and Israel. Situated on the Mediterranean Sea between the Egyptian and Mesopotamian civilizations, the Phoenicians absorbed influences and ideas from both. During the second millennium B.C., the Phoenicians developed as a seafaring and merchant society, with settlements throughout the Mediterranean world. The Phoenician city-states exported pine and cedar woods from Lebanon, fine linens woven in their city-states of Byblos and Tyre, metal and glass work, wine, salt, and dried fish; in exchange, they received precious metals and gems, papyrus, ostrich eggs, ivory, silk, spices, and horses. Their sailing ships were the fastest and best engineered in the ancient world. They invented a beautiful deep crimson dye, which was so costly that wearing purple robes became a mark of royalty. But the Phoenician contributions of commerce, ships, and dye fade in comparison to their major contribution to human civilization: the phonetic alphabet.

Geography has wielded great influence upon the affairs of man. Even the development of the alphabet may have been an act of geography, for the Phoenician city-states where the alphabet apparently developed had become the hub of the ancient world. Their location on the western shores of the Mediterranean Sea enabled Phoenicia to become the crossroads of international trade. Before 1000 B.C., the Phoenicians received cuneiform from Mesopotamia in the west, and Egyptian hieroglyphics and scripts from the south. It is probable that the Phoenicians, sailors that they were, had knowledge of the Cretan pictographs and scripts and may have been influenced by them. Faced with this range of visible languages, it is not surprising that they started experimenting with alternative possibilities. They seemed to have preferred cuneiform written on clay tablets to the hieroglyphics written on papyrus, leather, or stone. Cylinder seals were used to sign their clay tablets. Apparently Phoenicians' ethnic pride and practical nature made them want a writing system for their own northern Semitic speech, and evidence of a number of localized experiments has been unearthed.

Around the year 1500 B.C., Semitic workers in Egyptian turquoise mines in the Sinai desert area designed an achrophonic adaptation of hieroglyphs. Achrophonic means using a pictograph to stand for the initial sound of the depicted object. In this mostly undeciphered *Sinaitic script,* a pictorial symbol or hieroglyph for an object was used for the initial sound of the name of the object.

Clay tablets written in a true Semitic alphabetical script, using thirty characters to represent elementary consonant sounds, have been unearthed in the ruins of the ancient city of Ugarit. At first glance, this writing looks like cuneiform. The signs are written with wedge-shaped marks resembling cuneiform because a similar stylus is used. This *Ras Shamra script* (Fig. 4-2) has no vowels, and its "alphabetical order"—the sequence in which the letters are memorized—is the same as those used in the later Phoenician and Greek alphabets.

It is believed that the alphabet was born in the oldest Phoenician city-state, Byblos. The Greeks named papyrus *byblos,* because it was exported through the port of Byblos. The English word "Bible" derives from Byblos, from the Greek phrase meaning "the [papyrus] book." A writing script developed there, called *sui generis,* used pictographic signs devoid of any remaining pictorial meaning. The stone and bronze documents, written about 2000 B.C. and having a syllabary of over a hundred characters, were a major step on the road to an alphabet.

The writing system exported by the Phoenicians that conquered the world is a totally abstract and alphabetical system of twenty-two characters (see Fig. 4-1) that was in use by 1500 B.C. One of the oldest datable inscriptions in the Phoenician alphabet is found on the limestone sarcophagus of the Byblos King Ahiram (c. 11th century B.C.). This sarcophagus is supported by four carved lions and has relief figures carved on the sides, ends, and lid top. A lengthy inscription is carved along the side of the lid. It is believed that the Phoenicians' right-to-left writing style developed because stonemasons carved inscriptions by holding a chisel in the

4-2. *Ras Shamra* script, c. 1500 B.C. Used for bureaucratic and commercial documents, myths and legends, the *Ras Shamra* script, reducing cuneiform to a mere thirty-two characters, has—oddly enough—only been found in Ugarit.

left hand and a hammer in the right. The Phoenitic or northern Semitic script was also written on papyrus with a brush or pen. Unfortunately, Phoenician literature written on papyrus in this early alphabet, including, for instance, one Byblos author's nine-book work on mythology, has perished.

The alphabet that has survived from Phoenicia is the historical beginning of the alphabet, but it probably descended from an earlier, lost prototype design. It is likely that the same protoalphabet that produced the Phoenician alphabet evolved into Hebrew and Arabic alphabets elsewhere in the region. The graphic forms of the Hebrew alphabet are squared, bold letters with the horizontal strokes thicker than the vertical ones. Basically, the Hebrew alphabet is the twenty-two consonant letters of the ancient northern Semitic alphabet. The Arabic visible language of curving calligraphic gestures contains the twenty-two original sounds of the Semitic alphabet, plus six additional characters at the end. Both of these functional and beautifully designed letter systems are still written from right to left in the manner of their early origins.

Just as the invention of printing launched a quiet revolution in Chinese culture, the alphabet written on papyrus slowly turned western society upside down. Easy to write and learn, this system of simple signs for elementary sounds made literacy available to large numbers of people. The alphabet is a democratic or people's writing, in contrast to the theocratic writing of the temple priests of Mesopotamia and Egypt. Scribes and priests thus lost their monopolies on written knowledge, and their political power and influence were shattered. Secular and military leaders came to the fore as the leaders of the classical world of Greece and Rome.

The Greek alphabet

Greek civilization laid the foundation for most of the accomplishments of the Western world—science, philosophy, and democratic government all developed in this ancient land. Art, architecture, and literature are a priceless part of the Greek heritage. It is therefore fitting that the Greeks adopted the alphabet and vastly developed its beauty and utility.

The date when the Phoenician alphabet was adopted by the ancient Greeks and spread through their city-states was probably about 1000 B.C. The oldest inscriptions date from the eighth century B.C., but the Greek alphabet (Fig. 4-3), occupying a supreme position in the evolution of graphic communication, may have developed earlier. The Greeks took the Phoenician or northern Semitic alphabet and

4-3. Archaic Greek votive wheel, c. 525 B.C. A dedication to Apollo is clearly legible through the medium green patina of this metal wheel, 16 centimeters (6¼ inches) in diameter, used for worship purposes.

changed five consonants to vowels, which are connecting sounds that join consonants to make words. These have evolved into the present letters *a, e, i, o,* and *u.* When vowel sounds are spoken, the human breath channel is not constricted or blocked enough to create an audible friction. It is not known for certain who transported the alphabet from Phoenicia to Greece, but both mythology and tradition, which, in the ancient world, frequently became scrambled with oral history, point toward Cadmus of Miletus (dates unknown). According to various ancient accounts, Cadmus invented history or created prose or designed some of the letters of the Greek alphabet. These alleged accomplishments raise the possibility that Cadmus may have brought the alphabet to Greece.

In an enigmatic parallel, early Greek mythology reports that Cadmus, King of Phoenicia, set forth to find his sister Europa after she was abducted by Zeus. During his journey, King Cadmus killed a dragon that had slain his traveling companions. On the advice of Athena, he planted the dragon's teeth like seeds, and an army of fierce men sprang forth from them. Tradition holds that King Cadmus brought the alphabet to Greece. Perhaps myth and oral history hint at a blinding truth: The power of Cadmus to raise armies from nowhere could be due to his command of the alphabet. Troop movements, scouting reports, and orders to the field could be delivered by writing. Power came not from Cadmus's ability to plant dragon's teeth but from his ability to raise and direct armies using the alphabet as an information and communication tool that was as advanced in the ancient world as instantaneous electronic communications are today.

Perhaps Cadmus's story is a myth, and Phoenician traders brought the alphabet to Greece and other Mediterranean areas. Local Greek regions adapted the alphabet to their own needs until about 400 B.C., when Athens officially adopted a version that became standard throughout Greece.

The period around 700 B.C. is significant in the development of Greek culture. Homer's epic poems, the *Odyssey* and *Iliad,* had been composed, and architects had begun to build in stone. On pottery the human figure was starting to appear as a major subject, and large freestanding sculpture was only decades away. The city-state of Athens, cradle of representative government, had organized the towns of the Attica region into a unified political unit and was moving toward the establishment of an aristocratic republic with elected archons—the nine chief magistrates first voted into one-year terms in 683 B.C. During this cultural renaissance, the alphabet came into increasing use in Greek city-states.

4-5. Votive stela with four figures, fifth century B.C. The design excellence of Greek inscriptions is clearly shown in this fragment. By using a three-sided square with a central dot for the *E* and a V-shaped horizontal in the *A,* the designer engaged in a personal inventiveness with form.

4-4. Timotheus, *The Persians,* papyrus manuscript, fourth century B.C. This excellent example of the Greek alphabet shows the symmetrical form and even visual rhythm that evolved. These qualities made the Greek alphabet the prototype for subsequent developments.

From a graphic design standpoint, the Greeks took the cockeyed Phoenician characters and converted them into art forms of great harmony and beauty. The written form, as shown in *The Persians* by Timotheus (Fig. 4-4), has a visual order and balance as the letters march along a baseline in an even repetition of form and space. The letters and their component strokes are somewhat standardized because a system of horizontal, vertical, curved, and diagonal strokes is used. In the inscriptional form, such as the fifth-century B.C. votive stela with four figures (Fig. 4-5), the letters became symmetrical geometric constructions of timeless beauty. Stonecarvers took imaginative liberties with letterform design while still maintaining the basic structure of the twenty-four-character alphabet that had stabilized by the classical period and is still in use in Greece today. In this inscription, letterforms including the *E* and *M* are based on a square, *A* is constructed from an equilateral triangle, and the design of the *O* is a near perfect circle.

Initially, the Greeks adopted the Phoenician style of writing from right to left. Later, they developed a writing method called *boustrophedon,* which has been compared to plowing a field with an ox, for every other line reads in the opposite direction. Line one will read from right to left, then the characters do an about-face, and line two reads from left to right. The lines alternate direction in this manner, and the reader can scan the text with a continuous back and forth eye movement, unhindered by the need to return to the opposite edge of the column to read each line. Finally, the Greeks adopted the left-to-right reading movement that has continued to this day in Western civilization.

As early as the second century A.D., the Greeks developed a more rounded writing style called *uncials* (Fig. 4-6). These could be written more quickly because their rounded letters were formed with fewer strokes. In addition to use on manuscripts, uncials were written on wood and soft materials, such as wax tablets and clay. Uncials also demonstrated how writing tools and substrates influence written forms. Greek scribes made their pens from hard reeds, cut into a nib and split at the tip to aid ink flow. These pens gave their writing a totally different character from writing by Egyptian scribes, who used soft reeds to brush ink onto the substrate.

The Golden Age of Athens (c. 500 B.C.) was the high point of Greek culture. Democracy or "people rule" was practiced. Aristotle called democracy "a state where freemen and the poor, being in a majority, are invested with the power of the State." The vote of the majority became law. Visual communications played a secondary role in the oral culture of the Greek city-state. All citizens could attend the popular assembly and vote, and all elected officials were responsible to it. The orator who could speak persuasively to the assembly, the actor, and the lecturer were paramount in these city-states, where the total population, including the surrounding countryside, seldom exceeded ten thousand people. The historian or poet who wrote rather than spoke was less seriously regarded.

Nonetheless, the alphabet played a role in democracy; it enabled the use of allotment tokens when selecting citizens by lot for public service (Fig. 4-7). Secret voting by jurors was possible through the use of metal ballots with alphabet inscriptions (Fig. 4-8). The freedom and equality of Greek citizens did not extend to a concept of equality for all people. The system was, in fact, based on slavery, because slave labor freed citizens to devote their time and energy to public affairs.

4-6. Greek wooden tablet with uncials, 326 A.D. The rounded uncials allowed an *A* to be made with two strokes instead of three, and an *E* to be made with three strokes instead of four.

4-7. Greek allotment tokens, c. 450–430 B.C. In the Greek city-state, some public officials were elected, and others were selected by lot. These tokens were used in the selection process.

4-8

To authorize and endorse documents, wealthy Greek citizens used signature seals, which could be stamped into wax or clay (Fig. 4-9). Exquisite designs were engraved into the flat, oval bottom of a translucent precious stone called chalcedony, which is a pale blue or gray variety of quartz. Animals were a favorite motif. The refined forms, harmonious balance, and wholeness that we associate with Greek sculpture were achieved in these small (about 2-centimeter, or ¾-inch) signature seals used to impress a personal identification.

From the Macedonian city-state of Pella at the top of the Greek peninsula, Alexander the Great (356–323 B.C.) smashed the power of the Persian Empire and carried Hellenistic culture throughout the ancient world, including Egypt, Mesopotamia, and India. Reading and writing had become more important by the time of Alexander, because the expansion of information and knowledge exceeded the ability of an oral culture to contain and document it. Alexander therefore formed libraries. A major one, in the colonial outpost of Alexandria in Egypt, housed several hundred thousand scrolls.

The format design of the papyrus scroll was usually 10.5 meters (about 35 feet) long, 24 centimeters (9 or 10 inches) high, and, when rolled, 4 to 6 centimeters (about 1½ to 2¼ inches) in diameter. The text layout was in flush-left/random-right columns about 8 centimeters (3 inches) wide, with generous 2.5-centimeter (about 1-inch) ditches between them.

Unfortunately, most of the great storehouse of knowledge and culture compiled by the Greek civilization has been lost due to the fragile nature of papyrus scrolls and the dampness of the Greek climate. Only thirty thousand scrolls remain. Of the 330 plays by the great Greek playwrights, for instance, only forty-three have survived.

After Alexander's death in Babylon at the age of thirty-two, his generals split his empire into separate Hellenistic kingdoms. Greek civilization and its alphabet now became an influence throughout the world. The Greek alphabet fathered the Etruscan, Latin, and Cyrillic alphabets, and, through these ancestors, became the grandfather of alphabet systems used throughout the world today.

The Latin alphabet

The rise of Rome from a small village to the great imperial city that ruled the known world, and the eventual awesome collapse of this mighty empire, constitutes one of the great sagas of history. Perhaps as early as 750 B.C., Rome existed as a humble village on the Tiber River in central Italy. By the first century A.D., the Roman Empire stretched from England in the north to Egypt in the south, and from Spain in the west to the Persian Gulf at the base of the ancient land of Mesopotamia in the east.

From a farm near Rome, the great poet Horace (65–8 B.C.) wrote that "Captive Greece took Rome captive." After the Roman conquest of Greece, scholars and whole libraries were packed and moved to Rome. The Romans captured Greek literature, art, and religion, adapted them to the conditions of Roman power and confidence, and spread them throughout the vast Roman Empire.

The Latin alphabet (see Fig. 4-1) came to the Romans from Greece by way of the ancient Etruscans (Fig. 4-10), an early people who dominated the Italian peninsula

4-9

4-8. Greek juror's ballots, fourth century B.C. A juror voted "not guilty" with a ballot having a solid hub, and a hollow-hubbed ballot was used to cast a "guilty" vote.

4-9. Greek signature seals, fifth century B.C. The leaping dolphin was photographed from a plaster impression made from the seal. A heron standing on one leg, a ewe rising from the ground, and a racehorse with broken reins are reproduced from the actual small carvings.

4-10. Etruscan Bucchero vase, seventh or sixth century B.C. A prototype of the educational toy, this toy jug in the shape of a rooster bears an inscription of the Etruscan alphabet.

during the early first millennium B.C. After the letter *G* was designed by one Spurius Carvilius (c. 250 B.C.) to replace the Greek letter *Z* (zēta), which was of little value to the Romans, the Latin alphabet contained twenty-one letters: *A, B, C, D, E, F, G, H, I, K, L, M, N, O, P, Q, R* (which evolved as a variation of *P*), *S, T, V,* and *X*. Following the Roman conquest of Greece during the first century B.C., the Greek letters *Y* and *Z* were added to the end of the Latin alphabet to accommodate Greek words containing these sounds that were being borrowed by the Romans. Three additional letters were added to the alphabet during the Middle Ages to arrive at the twenty-six letters of the contemporary English alphabet. The *J* is an outgrowth of *I*, which was lengthened in fourteenth-century manuscripts to indicate use with consonant force, particularly as the first letter of some words. Both *U* and *W* are variants of *V*, which was being used for two sounds in medieval England. At the beginning of the tenth century, *U* was designed to represent the soft vowel sound in contrast to the harder consonant sound of *V*. The *W* began as a ligature, which is a joining of two letters. In twelfth-century England two *V* letterforms were joined into *VV* to represent "double U."

Rome took great pride in its imperial accomplishments and conquests, and created monumental letterforms for architectural inscriptions celebrating the generals and victories. Roman inscriptions were designed to have great beauty and permanence. The simple geometric lines of the *capitalis monumentalis* ("monumental capitals") were drawn in thick and thin strokes, with organically unified straight and curved lines (Figs. 4-11 and 4-12). Each letterform was designed to become one form rather than merely the sum of its parts. Careful attention was given to the shapes of spaces inside the letters and between the letters. A Roman inscription became a sequence of linear geometric forms adapted from the square, triangle, and circle. Combined into an inscription, these letterforms molded the negative shapes around and between them into a measured graphic melody of spatial forms, achieving an eternal wholeness.

Much debate has centered on the elegant Roman serifs, which are small lines extending from the ends of the major strokes of a letterform. One theory holds that the serifs were originally chisel marks made by the "cleanup" strokes as the stonemason finished carving a letter. Others argue that the inscriptions were first drawn on the stone with a flat signwriter's brush, and that the signwriter gave a short gesture before lifting the brush to sharpen the termination of the stroke. Regardless of which tool initiated the serif as a design element, we do know that the original letters were drawn on the stone with a brush. The shapes and forms defy mathematical analysis or construction with a T-square and compass. A letter found several times on an inscription will have subtle differences in width and proportion. In some inscriptions, lines with more letters will have both the letterforms and the negative spaces between them slightly condensed to accommodate the information. This represents an artistic judgment by the brushwriter rather than a measured calculation. Some Roman inscriptions even contain minute particles of red paint that have adhered to the stone through the centuries, leaving little doubt that the letters were painted. Monumental capitals were carved as wedge-shaped troughs. The edges of the letterforms were not sharp 90-degree angles with the flat surface of the stone; rather, a more gentle, angled taper created a shallower edge that resisted chipping and wearing.

The Roman written hand took several design styles. The most important are the *capitalis quadrata* ("square capitals"), which were widely used from the second century A.D. until the fifth century A.D. Written carefully and slowly with a flat pen, square capitals (Fig. 4-13) had stately proportions and outstanding legibility. The space between lines and letters was generous, but there was no space left between words. The letters were written between two horizontal baselines, and the *F* and *L* extended slightly above this line. The letter designs are amazingly similar to the letters we call *capitals* today. Serifs were added with the pen and strengthened the ends of the strokes.

The *capitalis rustica* ("rustic capitals") were used during the same period

(Fig. 4-14). These extremely condensed letterforms saved space. Parchment and papyrus were expensive, and rustic capitals enabled the writer to squeeze half again as many rustic capitals on the page in comparison to square capitals. One interesting design element was the lack of a horizontal stroke on the letter *A*. Rustic capitals were written quickly and are hard to read.

From the ruins of Pompeii and Herculaneum, we have learned that Roman brushwriters wrote notices (Fig. 4-15), political campaign material, and advertising announcements on exterior walls, using both square capitals and rustic capitals. In addition to wall writing, poster messages were painted on reusable panels, which were set up in the streets. Placards and picture signboards were executed by professional letterers. Trademarks were widely used to identify the firm or place of origination of handcrafted products. Commercial records, documents of state, and literature were written on a variety of substrates. Papyrus from Egypt was supple-

4-11. Carved inscription from the base of Trajan's column, c. 114 A.D. Located in Trajan's forum in Rome, this masterful example of *capitalis monumentalis* gives silent testimony to the ancient Roman dictum, "The written word remains."

4-12. Detail, inscription on a tomb along the Appian Way, Rome. The controlled brush drawing of the forms onto the stone combines with the precision of the stonemason's craft to create letterforms of majestic proportion and harmonious form.

mented by wood, clay, flat pieces of metal, and wax tablets held in wooden frames. Writing was scratched into the wax with a stylus, the flat end of which was used to erase the writing in the soft wax so that the tablet could be used again.

Around 190 B.C., the use of *parchment* as a substrate for writing came into common use. Tradition holds that Ptolemy V (ruled c. 205–181 B.C.) of Alexandria and King Eumenes II (ruled 197–160 B.C.) of Pergamum were engaged in a fierce library-building rivalry, and that Ptolemy placed an embargo on papyrus shipments to prevent Eumenes from continuing his rapid production of scrolls. Parchment, a writing surface made from the skins of domestic animals—particularly calves, sheep, and goats—was invented to overcome the embargo. These refined leather sheets are made by first washing the skin and removing all hair or wool. Then, the skin is stretched tightly on a frame and scraped to remove all traces of hair and flesh. After being whitened with chalk, it is smoothed with pumice. Larger, smoother, and more durable and flexible than papyrus sheets, parchment became very popular as a writing surface. The highest quality of parchment is called *vellum* and is made from the smooth skins of newborn calves.

A revolutionary format design called the *codex* began to supplant the scroll (called a *rotulus*) in Rome and Greece, beginning about the time of Christ. Parchment was gathered in signatures of two, four, or eight sheets. These were folded, stitched, and combined into codices with pages like a modern book. The parchment codex had several advantages over the papyrus scroll. The clumsy process of unrolling and rolling scrolls to look up information yielded to the quick process of opening a codex to the desired page. Papyrus was too fragile to be folded into pages, and the vertical strips on the back of a papyrus scroll made writing on both sides impractical. Since both sides of the parchment pages in a codex could be used for writing, storage space and material costs both dropped.

During the rise of Christianity, from after 1 A.D. until around 400 A.D., scrolls and codices were used side by side. The durability and permanence of the codex appealed to Christians because their writings were viewed as sacred words from God. With a whole pantheon of gods and little clear distinction between god and man, pagan scholars were less inclined to revere their religious writings. Traditionally, pagan writings were on scrolls. Christians were involved in comparative study of different texts, particularly the Gospels. It is easy to have several codices open on a table, but virtually impossible to have several scrolls unrolled for comparative reference. Christians sought the codex format to alienate themselves from the pagan scroll; pagans clung to their scrolls in resistance to Christianity. Graphic format thereby became a symbol of religious belief during the late decades of the Roman Empire. The world outlook of Christianity, which sought universality and

4-13. *Capitalis quadrata* ("square capitals") from a manuscript, *Virgil,* c. 400 A.D. The flat pen held at an angle produced thick-and-thin strokes and serifs.

NIMARTISQ·DOLOSETD
CHAODENSOSDIVVMN
NEQVOCAPTAEDVMFV

4-14. *Capitalis rustica* ("rustic capitals") from a manuscript, *Virgil,* c. 400 A.D. The flat-nibbed pen was held in an almost vertical position, creating a staccato rhythm of thin verticals contrasting with elliptical round and arched diagonal strokes.

IOCEANISPRETOSPEDEREPPVL
DEMSIDVSFVGIENSVBIPISCIS
ORTTIBERNASCAELODESCEN

4-15. Wall writing from Pompeii, first century A.D. This inscription is one of over sixteen hundred messages ranging from passages from Virgil to crude obscenities that were preserved under more than 3.6 meters (12 feet) of volcanic ash.

the conversion of all peoples, elevated books and writing to far greater importance than their previous roles in the ancient world.

Christianity was adopted as the state religion of Rome in 325 A.D. by the Emperor Constantine (d. 337 A.D.). The Roman legions, which had once persecuted Christians, now began to carry a monogram of Christ into battle as a symbol of salvation.

The Roman Empire's collapse was as dramatic as its rise from humble origins. In the first century A.D., Rome began to experience hostile actions from tribal peoples (called "Barbarians" by the Greeks) living beyond the Danube and Rhine Rivers. In 325 A.D., Emperor Constantine moved the capital from Rome to the Greek town of Byzantium (later renamed Constantinople), located astride the mouth of the Black Sea. Quite naturally, this weakened the strength of the western provinces, and the warlike Huns began to put great pressure against Rome's border neighbors. In 376 A.D., the Visigoths were allowed to settle west of the Danube inside the Roman Empire after their defeat by the Huns; two years later, the Visigoths killed the Emperor Valens (c. 328–378 A.D.) and two-thirds of his army in a pivotal battle. The Empire was permanently divided in half in 395 A.D., and Rome itself was sacked by the Visigoths in 410 A.D. The Emperor moved his court to Ravenna, which became the capital of the western Roman Empire. Then, in 476 A.D., Ravenna fell to the Barbarians and became the capital of an Ostrogothic Kingdom. This marked the final dissolution of the Roman Empire. But Rome left a legacy that includes its architecture, engineering, law, language, and literature. The grandeur of Roman society informed many aspects of later human culture, and its alphabet became the design form for visible languages in the western world.

5 The Medieval Manuscript

The collapse of the Roman Empire was followed by an era of dislocation and uncertainty in the West. After the Empire was divided in 395 A.D., the eastern half, with Byzantium (Constantinople) as its capital, thrived as the sophisticated Byzantine civilization. The western portion saw the light of civilization flicker and almost vanish. The thousand-year medieval era lasted from the fall of Rome in the fifth century A.D. until the fifteenth-century Renaissance. Cities in the western half of the Roman Empire degenerated and became small villages; officials left their duties and moved to their country estates; government and law ceased to exist. Trade and commerce slumped and almost became nonexistent, for travel became extremely dangerous. The regional languages, customs, and geographic divisions of Europe started to form in isolated areas during this period. The general population languished in illiteracy, poverty, and superstition. A feudal society was established, in which land-owning noblemen had dictatorial power over the peasants who toiled in the fields.

But the centuries following the fall of Rome saw Barbarian and Roman influences combine to produce a rich and colorful design vocabulary in the arts and crafts. Although the medieval era has been called "The Dark Ages," there was nothing dark about the crafts of the period, which included the making of books.

The knowledge and learning of the classical world were almost entirely lost. The Christian belief in sacred religious writings became the primary impetus for the preservation of books. Christian monasteries became the centers of cultural, educational, and intellectual activities. The preservation of knowledge within the monastery included the making of *illuminated manuscripts,* which in the strictest sense are handwritten books embellished with gold or silver. However, the term has come to mean any handwritten book that was decorated, illustrated, and produced during the medieval period. For the medieval Christian, the sacred writings had great meaning. The use of graphic and illustrative embellishment to expand the word visually became very important, and the illuminated manuscripts were produced with extraordinary care and design sensitivity.

Illuminated manuscript production was costly and time consuming. Parchment or vellum took hours to prepare, and a large book might require the skins of three hundred sheep. Black ink for lettering was prepared from fine soot or lampblack. Gum and water were mixed with sanguine or red chalk to make a red ink used for headings and paragraph marks, and irongall (a mixture of iron sulfate and oak apples, which are oak galls caused by wasp larvae) was used to make a brown ink. Mineral, animal, and vegetable substances were used to make colors for the illustrations. A vibrant, deep blue was made from lapis lazuli, a precious mineral mined only in Afghanistan that found its way to monasteries as far away as Ireland. Gold (and less frequently silver) was applied in two ways: Sometimes it was ground into a powder and mixed into a gold paint, but this left a slightly grainy surface, so the preferred application method was hammering the gold into a fine sheet of gold leaf, which was applied over an adhesive ground. Burnishing for texture, punching, and tooling with metalworking tools were sometimes used for design effects. The dazzling luminosity of the gold leaf when it caught and reflected light spawned the term *illuminated manuscript.* The book covers were wooden boards usually covered with leather. Decorative patterns were applied by tooling the leather, and important liturgical manuscripts often had precious jewels, gold and silverwork, enameled designs, or ivory carving on their covers.

During the early medieval era, nearly all books were created in the monastic *scriptorium,* or writing room. Christian scriptures were the most important works produced. The head of the scriptorium was the *scrittori,* a well-educated scholar who understood Greek and Latin and functioned as an editor and art director with overall responsibility for the design and production of the manuscripts. A *copisti* was a production letterer, who spent his days bent over a writing table penning page after page in a trained lettering style. The *colophon* of a manuscript or book is an inscription, usually at the end, containing facts about the production. Often the scribe, designer, or, later, printer, is identified. A number of colophons inform us that the work of the copisti was difficult and tiring. In the colophon of one illuminated manuscript, a scribe named George declared that "As the sailor longs for a safe haven at the end of his voyage, so does the writer for the last word." Another scribe, Prior Petris, described writing as a terrible ordeal that "dims your eyes, makes your back ache, and knits one's chest and stomach together. . . ." The reader was then advised to turn the pages carefully and to keep his finger far from the text. The *illuminator* or illustrator was an artist responsible for the execution of ornament and image in visual support of the text. The word was supreme, and the scrittori controlled the scriptorium. He would lay out the pages to indicate where illustrations were to be added after the text was written. Sometimes this was done

5-1. The *Vatican Virgil*. The death of Laocoön, early fifth century A.D. The vibrant red of Laocoön's cape creates a focal point and echoes the bright red border framing the illustration.

with a light sketch, but often a note jotted in the margin told the illustrator what to draw in the space.

The illustration and ornamentation were not mere decoration. The monastic leaders were mindful of the educational value of pictures and ability of ornament to create mystical and spiritual overtones. Most illuminated manuscripts were small enough to fit into a saddlebag. This portability enabled manuscripts to transmit knowledge and ideas from one region to another and one time period to another. Manuscript production over the thousand-year course of the medieval era created a vast vocabulary of graphic forms, page layouts, illustration and lettering styles, and techniques. Regional isolation and difficult travel caused innovation and influences to spread very slowly, so identifiable regional design styles emerged. Some of the more distinctive schools of manuscript production can be ranked as major innovations in graphic design.

The classical style

In classical antiquity, the Greeks and Romans designed and illustrated manuscripts, but none have survived. The Egyptian *Book of the Dead* was probably an influence, and the fabulous Greek library at Alexandria, where late Egyptian culture met early classical culture, probably contained many wonderful, illustrated manuscripts that are now lost. This great library reportedly housed seven hundred thousand scrolls when it was destroyed by fire at the time of Julius Caesar (100–44 B.C.). In the few fragments of illustrated scrolls that survive, the layout approach uses numerous small illustrations drawn in a crisp, simple style and inserted throughout the text. The frequency with which these appear creates a cinematic graphic sequence not unlike the contemporary comic book.

The invention of parchment, which was so much more durable than papyrus, and the codex format, which could take thicker paint because it did not have to be rolled, opened new possibilities for design and illustration. Literary references refer to manuscripts on vellum, with a portrait of the author as a *frontispiece*.

The earliest extant illuminated manuscript from the late antique and early Christian era is the *Vatican Virgil* (Fig. 5-1). Created in the late fourth century or early fifth century A.D., this volume contains two of the three great poems of Publius Vergilius Maro (70–19 B.C.). Virgil was the greatest Roman poet. The *Vatican Virgil* contains his *Georgics,* a poem on farming and country life, and the *Aeneid,* an epic narrative about Aeneas, who left the flaming ruins of Troy and set out to found a new city in the west. A consistent graphic design approach is used: The text is lettered in crisp rustic capitals, with one wide column on each page; illustrations, framed in bright bands of color (frequently red) and the same width as the text column, are placed at the top, middle, or bottom of the page to be adjacent to the passage illustrated; there are six full-page illustrations, the illustrator neatly lettered the name of the major figures upon the illustration in the manner of present-day political cartoonists.

The *Vatican Virgil* is completely Roman and pagan in its conception and execution. The lettering is Roman, and the illustrations echo the rich colors and illusionistic space of the wall frescoes preserved at Pompeii. The demise of Laocoön, a priest who was punished by death for profaning the temple of Apollo, is shown in a sequence within one image. On the left, Laocoön calmly prepares to sacrifice a bull at the temple of Poseidon, oblivious to the approach of two serpents in the lake at the upper-left corner. On the right, Laocoön and his two young sons are attacked and killed by the serpents.

This pictorial and historical style of book illustration, so similar to late Roman painting and combined with rustic capitals, represents the *classical style*. It was used in many of the earliest Christian manuscripts and surely was the book-design style of the late Roman Empire.

As early as the third century A.D., a dazzling design effect was achieved in early Christian manuscripts by dyeing parchment a deep and costly purple color. Lettering was executed in silver or gold to produce some of the most elegant pages in the

INTERUOS CONQU
OENSUNUSOETU
AÇISTERAOTULIFI

derllodixicibr quemmrœ
uœoq·minoneſtquraeœpat
muſetfiliurcumdicit·ſiaut

history of graphic design. These monastic graphic artists were severely reprimanded by St. Jerome (c. 347–420 A.D.) who, in his preface to a manuscript Book of Job, blasted the practice as a useless and wasteful extravagance.

The evolution of writing styles was a continuing search for simpler and faster letterform construction and writing ease. Two important new writing styles came into prominence during the course of the late antique and early Christian period. Both were primarily used within the Christian church from the fourth until the ninth century A.D. and have retained this association. As mentioned earlier, the *uncials* (Fig. 5-2) (so named because they were written between two guidelines that are one *uncia* [the Roman inch] apart) were actually invented by the Greeks as early as the third century B.C. In the Greek wooden tablet from 326 A.D. (see Fig. 4-6), the primary characteristics of uncials are seen. Uncials are rounded, freely drawn majuscule letters more suited to rapid writing than either square capitals or rustic capitals. The curves reduced the number of strokes required to make many letterforms, and the number of angular joints—which have a tendency to clog or close up with ink—was significantly reduced. Certain letters in the uncial style threaten to develop ascenders (strokes ascending above the top guideline) or descenders (strokes descending below the baseline), but the design remains that of a majuscule or capital letter. A step toward the development of minuscules (small or "lowercase" letterforms) was the *semi-uncial* or *half-uncial* (Fig. 5-3). Four guidelines instead of two were used, and strokes were allowed to soar above and sink below the two principal lines, creating true ascenders and descenders. The pen was held flatly horizontal to the baseline, which gave the forms a strong vertical axis. Half-uncials were easy to write and had increased legibility because the visual differentiation between letters was improved. Although some half-uncials appeared in the third century A.D., it was not until the late sixth century A.D. that the style began to flourish.

Celtic book design

The period from the collapse of Rome until the eighth century was a time of migration and upheaval throughout Europe as different ethnic tribes fought for territory. These unsettled times were the blackest decades of the medieval era. Wandering hordes of Germanic Barbarians did not invade the island of Ireland, tucked in the far corner of Europe, and the Celts living there enjoyed relative isolation and peace. In the early fifth century A.D., the legendary St. Patrick and other mission-

5-5

5-4. *The Book of Durrow,* the lion, symbol for Mark, c. 680 A.D. Reflecting a pagan and barbarian ancestry, this symbolic lion has a head of red dots; body stripes, tail, and feet in intense yellow contour lines; and a body of red and green diamond shapes.

5-5. *The Book of Durrow,* the man, symbol of Matthew, c. 680 A.D. As flat as a Cubist painting and constructed from simple geometric forms, this figure, facing the opening of the Gospel of St. Matthew, wears a checkered pattern of red, yellow, and green squares and tile-like patterned textures.

aries began to rapidly convert the Celts to Christianity. In a bizarre melding of culture and religion, pagan temples were converted to churches and Celtic ornaments were applied to chalices and bells brought to Ireland by the missionaries.

Celtic design is abstract and extremely complex: Geometric linear patterns weave, twist, and fill a space with thick visual textures; bright, pure colors are used in close juxtaposition. This Celtic craft tradition of intricate, highly abstract decorative patterns was applied to book design in the monastic scriptoria, and a new concept and image of the book emerged. A series of gospel books containing the four narratives of the life of Christ, which are the first four books of the New Testament of the Christian Bible, represent the height of the Celtic style. Written and designed around 680 A.D., *The Book of Durrow* (Figs. 5-4 and 5-5) is the earliest fully designed and ornamented Celtic book. *The Lindisfarne Gospels,* written by Eadfrith, Bishop of Lindisfarne, before 698 A.D., represents the full flowering of the Celtic style. The masterwork of the epoch is *The Book of Kells,* created in the scriptorium at the island monastery of Iona around 800 A.D. Countless hours of work were lavished upon individual pages, whose vibrant color and form are in stunning contrast to the stark reclusive environment and rule of silence found in the monastic scriptorium.

Ornament was used in three ways: Ornament frames or borders were created to enclose portraits of the apostles and other full-page illustrations; opening pages of each gospel and other important passages were singled out for illumination, particularly by the design of ornate initials; full pages of decorative design called *carpet pages* were bound into the manuscript. This name developed because the densely packed design has the intricate patterning associated with oriental carpets. As a carpet page from the *Lindisfarne Gospels* shows (Fig. 5-6), a cross or other geometric motif becomes an organizing form that brings structure to the interlaces and lacertines filling the space. The *interlace* is a two-dimensional decoration formed by a number of ribbons or straps woven into a complex, usually symmetrical design. It is evident that drafting instruments were used to construct many of the designs in Celtic manuscripts. Interlaces created by animal forms were called *lacertines*. Most of the forms were either invented from imagination or based on earlier models. Careful observation of nature was not required of the Celtic designer or illustrator.

Large initials on the opening pages grew bigger in newer books as the decades passed. The need to integrate these initials with the rest of the text was a challenging design problem that was beautifully resolved in the scriptoria. In the opening page of the Gospel of Saint Mark in *The Book of Durrow* (Fig. 5-7), the first letters

5-6. *The Lindisfarne Gospels,* carpet page facing the opening of St. Matthew, c. 698 A.D. A mathematical grid buried under swirling lacertine birds and quadrupeds brings structure to the textured areas, and a red, contoured cross with white circular "buttons" brings timeless stability to one of the most animated pages in the history of design.

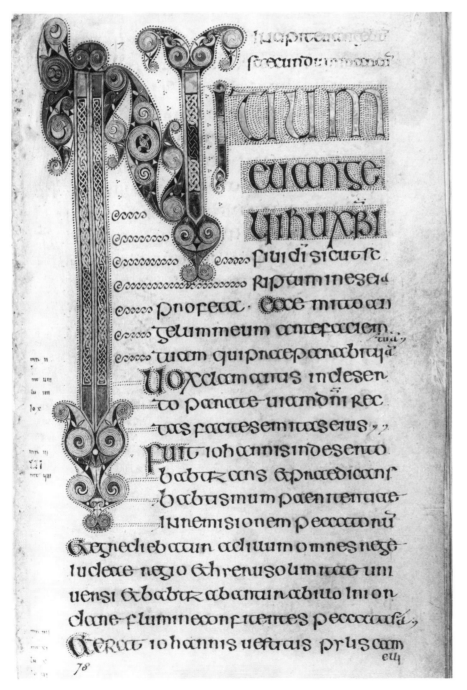

5-7. *The Book of Durrow,* opening page, the Gospel of Saint Mark, c. 680 A.D. Linked into a ligature, an *I* and an *N* become an artform of interlaced threads and coiling spiral motifs in a black, yellow, red, and white color scheme.

The Medieval Manuscript

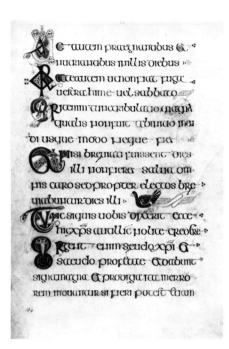

5-8. *The Book of Kells,* text page with ornamental initials, c. 795–806 A.D. The incredible originality of the hundreds of illustrated initials is suggested by the variety of imaginative forms in the six initials on this one page.

of the word "Initium" create a large monogram thrusting down the page. A graphic principle called *diminuendo,* which is the decreasing scale of graphic information, is operative in this page design. The large double initial is followed in decreasing size by a smaller initial, the last four letters of the first word, the next two words, and the text. This descending scale unites the large initial to the text. Red S-shaped lines or dots align each line of text to the initial and further unify the elements. The red-dot pattern transforms the first three words into rectangles and contours the first letters of each verse. Ultimately, a thoughtful and harmonious design system is created. These red dots were used profusely, and watercolor washes were often used to fill in the negative areas inside and between letters. Sometimes pigments were handled thickly and opaquely; at other times they were as thin and translucent as enamel.

One of the most important moments in the Gospels occurs when the name of Christ is first mentioned in the eighteenth verse of the first chapter of Matthew. The writer announces that "Now the birth of Christ was on this wise. . . ." Upon arriving at the word "Christ," the illuminator created a graphic explosion using the monogram *XPI.* This monogram—used to write Christ in manuscripts—is called the *Chi-Rho,* after the first two letters of the Greek word for Christ, Chi (*X*) and Rho (*P*). The Chi-Rho in *The Book of Kells* (Pl. 6) is composed of shimmering color and intricate convoluted form, blossoming over a whole page. Amidst the intricate patterns of spirals and lacertines, the artist has drawn thirteen human heads. At the base of the plunging descender of the *X,* two cats and two mice calmly watch as two other mice tug at a wafer. An otter holds a salmon in another niche at the base of the monogram.

In the Celtic manuscript, a radical design innovation is the practice of leaving a space between words to enable the reader to separate the string of letters into words more quickly. The half-uncial script of late antique codices journeyed to Ireland with the early missionaries and was transformed into the *scriptura scottica,* or insular script (Figs. 5-7 and 5-8), as it is now called. These half-uncials became the national letterform style in Ireland and are still used for special writings and as a type style. Starting with the half-uncial, the Celts subtly redesigned the alphabet to suit their visual traditions. Written with a slightly angled pen, the full, rounded characters have a strong bow with ascenders bending to the right. A heavy triangle perches at the top of ascenders, and the horizontal stroke of the last letter of the word, particularly an *e* or *t,* zips out into the space between words. The text page from *The Book of Kells* (Fig. 5-8) shows how carefully the insular script was lettered. Characters are frequently joined at the waistline or the baseline.

Ironically, beautiful, carefully lettered half-uncials convey a text that is careless and incorrect, containing numerous misspellings and misreadings. Even so, *The Book of Kells* is the zenith of Celtic illumination. Its noble design has generous margins and huge initial letters. Far more full-page illustrations than in any other Celtic manuscript are executed with a remarkable density and complexity of form (Fig. 5-9). Over twenty-one hundred ornate capitals make every page a visual delight. Here and there through the course of its 339 leaves, a sentence blooms into a full page of illumination.

The magnificent Celtic school of manuscript design ended abruptly before *The Book of Kells* was completed. In 795 A.D. northern raiders made their first appearance on the Irish coast, and a period of intense struggle between the Celts and the Vikings followed. Both Lindisfarne and Iona, seats of two of the greatest scriptoria in medieval history, were destroyed. When the invading Northmen swarmed over the island of Iona, where *The Book of Kells* was being completed in the monastery scriptorium, escaping monks took it to Kells and continued to work on it there. It can only be guessed whether or not majestic illuminated manuscripts were lost, or what magnificent volumes might have been designed had peace and stability continued for the Celts of Ireland.

5-9. *The Book of Kells,* symbols of the Gospel authors, c. 795–806 A.D. Winged and stylized almost to abstraction, Matthew's man, Mark's lion, Luke's ox, and John's eagle float in four rectangles wrapped in a densely ornamented frame.

The Caroline graphic renewal

When Charlemagne (742–814), King of the Franks since 768 and the leading ruler of central Europe, rose from prayer in St. Peter's Cathedral in Rome on Christmas Day, 800 A.D., Pope Leo III (d. 816) placed a crown on his head, and declared him emperor of what became known as the Holy Roman Empire. The whole of central Europe was united under Charlemagne in an empire that was neither Roman nor particularly holy. Nevertheless, it attempted to recapture the grandeur and unity of the Roman Empire in a Germanic and Christian federation. In addition to restoring the concept of empire to the West, Charlemagne introduced the feudal system in an effort to bring order to chaotic medieval society.

Although by some reports he was illiterate except to sign his name, Charlemagne fostered a revival of learning and the arts. England of the 700s had seen much intellectual activity, and Charlemagne recruited the English scholar Alcuin of York (c. 732–804) to come to his palace at Aachen and establish a palace school. Except for the Celtic pattern-making tradition, book design and illumination had sunk to an inept low in most of Europe. Illustrations were poorly drawn and composed, and writing had become localized and undisciplined in the hands of poorly trained scribes. Many manuscripts were difficult, if not impossible, to read. Charlemagne mandated reform by royal edict in 789. At the court in Aachen, a *turba scriptorium* ("crowd of scribes," as Alcuin called them) was assembled to prepare master copies of the important religious texts. Then books and scribes were dispatched throughout Europe to disseminate the reforms.

Standardization of page layout, writing style, and decoration was attempted. The alphabet was successfully reformed. For a model, the ordinary writing script of the late antique period was selected and molded into an ordered uniform script called *Caroline minuscules* (Fig. 5-10). Ideas from this late Roman cursive script were combined with some of the Celtic innovations in their insular script, including the use of four guidelines, ascenders, and descenders. The Caroline minuscule is the forerunner of our contemporary lowercase or small-letter alphabet. This clear set of letterforms was practical and easy to write. Characters were set apart instead of joined, and the number of ligatures was reduced. Much writing had become a slurred scrawl; the new alphabet restored legibility. The Caroline minuscule became the standard throughout Europe for a time, but as the decades passed, various areas veered toward a regional style. Roman capitals were studied and adopted for headings and initials of great beauty. These were not calligraphic, but carefully drawn and built up with more than one stroke. The use of a dual alphabet was not fully developed in the sense that we use capital and small letters today, but a process in that direction had begun. In addition to graphic reforms, the court at Aachen reformed sentence and paragraph structure and punctuation. The Caroline revival of scholarship and learning stayed a serious loss of human knowledge and writings that had been occurring through the early medieval period.

When early manuscripts from the late antique period and the Byzantine culture were imported for study, illuminators were shocked and stunned when they saw the naturalism and illusion of deep space of the illustrations. The two-dimensional, decorative style suddenly seemed passé in the face of this "picture-window" style, where space moved back into the page from a decorative frame, and clothes seemed to wrap the forms of a living human figure. Lacking the skill or basic knowledge of the antique artists, Caroline illuminators began to copy these images with sometimes uneven results. The classical heritage was revived as accurate drawing and illusionistic techniques were mastered by some illuminators. Figurative imagery and ornament, which had been scrambled together in earlier medieval illumination, became separate and distinct design elements.

In a manuscript book such as the *Coronation Gospels,* designed and produced at the court of Charlemagne in the late eighth century, a dignified classical elegance emerges. In the beginning of each gospel as shown in Plate 7, the opening pages of Saint Mark's Gospel, the figure of the author sits in a natural landscape on a page of deep crimson stained parchment. The facing page is stained a deep purple and has gold lettering. These two facing pages are unified by their exactly equal margins. The initial letters echo Roman monumental capitals, and the text appears to be closely based on the insular script of Ireland. Furthermore, supplementary ma-

5-10. Caroline minuscules from the *Alcuin Bible,* ninth century A.D. An economy of execution and good legibility characterized this new writing style.

terials, including chapter lists, introductory words, and prefaces, are lettered in rustic capitals. Whether this book was designed, lettered, and illuminated by scribes brought in from Italy, Greece, or Constantinople is not known. The creators of this book had a precocious understanding of both the lettering styles and painting techniques of classical culture. (Legend claims that in the year 1000, Emperor Otto III [980–1002] of the Holy Roman Empire journeyed to Aachen, where he opened the tomb of Charlemagne and found the Emperor seated on a throne with the *Coronation Gospels* on his lap.)

Spanish pictorial expressionism

On the Spanish peninsula, surrounded by oceans and isolated from the rest of Europe by mountains, the scriptoria did not experience the initial impact of the Caroline renewal. In 711 A.D., a Moorish army under the Arab governor of Tangier crossed the Straits of Gibraltar and smashed the Spanish army. Even the Spanish King was among the missing-in-action. Moorish settlers brought an Islamic presence that mingled with Christian traditions to create unique manuscript designs during the medieval period.

A number of Islamic design ideas filtered into Spanish Christian manuscripts. Flat shapes of intense color were used. Sometimes they were sprinkled with stars, rosettes, polygons, or garlands in optically active contrasting colors. Flat, schematic drawing had prominent outlines. The two-dimensional aggressive color created a frontal intensity that obliterated any hint of atmosphere or illusion. A pagan tradition of totemlike animals dates back through Islamic northern Africa to Persia to ancient Mesopotamia, and these ghastly creatures reared their frightful heads in Spanish illumination. Decorative frames enclosed most illustrations with intricate patterns evoking the richly colored geometric designs applied to Moorish architecture in tilework, and molded and chiseled decorations.

Great delight was taken in designs of intricate geometry and intense, pure color. In the commemorative labyrinth from Pope Gregory's *Moralia in Iob* (*Commentary on Job*) of 945 A.D., the scribe Florentius designed a *labyrinth page* (Fig. 5-11), bearing the words "Florentius indignum memorare," which modestly ask the reader to "remember the unworthy Florentius." The humility of Florentius' message is incongruous with the dazzling graphic treatment and his decision to put his full-page labyrinth opposite the monogram of Christ. The labyrinth arrangement of commemorative messages dates to ancient Greece and Rome and was quite popular in medieval manuscripts.

For the medieval faithful, life on earth was but a prelude to eternal salvation, if the individual could triumph in the battle between good and evil being raged on earth. Supernatural explanations were still assigned to natural phenomena that were not understood; eclipses, earthquakes, plague, and famine were seen as dire warnings and punishments. It was believed that a terrible destruction awaited the earth, and this tragic end was encouraged by the Biblical Book of Revelation, which foretold a horrible doomsday. Revelation suggested a date, "When the thousand years had expired . . . ," as a likely time for the last judgment. This led many individuals to consider the year 1000 A.D. as the probable end of the world, and concern mounted as the year drew nigh. A number of interpretations of Revelation were written. Most potent and widely read was *The Commentary of Beatus on the Apocalypse of Saint John the Divine*. The monk Beatus (730–798 A.D.) of Liebana in northern Spain wrote this harrowing interpretation in 776 A.D. In numerous copies penned and illustrated throughout Spain, graphic artists were called upon to give visual form to the fearful events of the end of the world. The monastic dictum, *Pictura est laicorum literatura* ("The picture is the layman's literature"), evidences the concern for conveying information to the illiterate citizenry that prompted the creation of illustrations. Combining Christian prophecy with Moorish design influences, they succeeded admirably. Revelation is laced with rich, imaginative imagery, and in designing copies of Beatus's commentary, scrittori gave pictures an importance that rivaled the text's. Full-page illustrations appeared frequently.

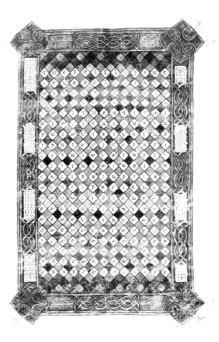

5-11. Commemorative labyrinth from *Moralia in Iob,* 945 A.D. Starting in the center of the top line, the inscription reads down, left, and right, establishing a labyrinth of letterforms. The checkered diamonds are bright yellow, red, orange, and purple.

5-12. The Four Horsemen of the Apocalypse from *Beatus of Fernando and Sancha,* 1047 A.D. Unlike the usual interpretations, Beatus's commentary saw the first horseman —being crowned by an angel—as an envoy of God whose arrows pierce the heart of nonbelievers. The demon at lower right is bright blue against an orange background.

The twenty-three surviving copies of Beatus's commentary represent a high-water mark of graphic expressionism. Over sixty different passages have been illustrated in the surviving copies. Stark, symbolic imagery challenged the artist's mind as Beatus's interpretation of this prophecy was visualized. This is the most forceful interpretation of the Apocalypse in graphic art before Albrecht Dürer's intricate woodcut illustrations in the early 1500s (see Fig. 7-12).

On New Year's Eve, 999 A.D., people all over Europe gathered to await the final judgment. It is reported that many spent the night naked on their cold rooftops waiting for the end. When nothing happened, new interpretations of the "thousand years" phrase were made, and manuscript copies of Beatus's *Commentary* continued to be produced. In the masterful *Beatus of Fernando and Sancha* of 1047 A.D., the scribe and illuminator Facundus drew schematic figures acting out the final tragedy in a hot and airless space created by flat horizontal bands of pure hue. The thick color is bright and clear. Chrome yellow, cobalt blue, red ocher, and intense green are slammed together in jarring contrasts. The Four Horsemen of the Apocalypse (Fig. 5-12), which are traditionally war, famine, pestilence, and death, ride forth in front of blue, yellow, orange, and tan stripes to unleash their terror upon the world.

A passage in Revelation tells that "the fourth angel sounded, and the third part of the sun was smitten, and the third part of the moon, and the third part of the stars, so as the third part of them was darkened, and the day shown not for a third part of it, and the night likewise" (Rev. 8:12). The illuminator pushed the angel to the left in a space structured with bands of intense blue, yellow, and red (Fig. 5-13). The sun (labeled "sol") and the moon (labeled "luna") are pie charts that are one-third white and two-thirds red, to illustrate that one-third had fallen away. Finally, a sinister eagle flies into the space screaming "Woe, woe, woe to those who dwell on the earth. . . ." Angel and eagle bear wings, with feathers as sharp and menacing as daggers. As an iconic symbol, the angels in the *Beatus* illustrations are worlds away from the pure white angel of hope found in later Christian imagery. Inspired by the words from the Apocalypse, "I am the alpha and the omega, the beginning and the end," Facundus designed the first page of the *Beatus of Fernando and Sancha* as a huge illuminated *A* (alpha, the first letter of the Greek alphabet), and the last page as a huge illuminated *O* (omega, the last letter of the Greek alphabet).

During the early eleventh century A.D., the balance of power in Spain swung away from the Moors and toward the Christians. Communications with other European countries improved, and Spanish graphic design tilted toward the continental mainstream that developed from the Caroline style. The expressionistic style that filled Bibles, commentaries, and most especially the *Commentary of Beatus* faded from fashion.

Late medieval illuminated manuscripts

The Romanesque period, c. 1000–1150, was a period of renewed religious fervor and even stronger feudalism. Christendom was united in a vigorous effort to conquer the Holy Land through the Crusades. Monasticism reached its peak, and large liturgical books, including Bibles, Gospels, and Psalters, were produced in the booming scriptoria. For the first time, a universal design style seemed possible, as visual ideas traveled back and forth on the pilgrimage routes. The illusionistic revival of the Caroline era was replaced by a new emphasis on linear drawing and a willingness to distort figures to meld with the overall design of the page. The representation of deep space became even less important, and figures were placed against backgrounds of gold leaf or textured patterns.

During the middle of the twelfth century, the Romanesque period developed into the Gothic period, which lasted from 1150 until the Renaissance of European culture that began in fourteenth-century Italy. This transitional period saw the power of the feudal lords constrained by reasonable laws. The towns and villages began to grow into cities. Agriculture yielded to international trade as the foundation of

5-13. The fourth angel from *Beatus of Fernando and Sancha*, 1047 A.D. Wings, tail, and trumpet bring a lively counterpoint of angles to the static bands of color.

political power, and money replaced land as the primary measure of wealth. Europe was slowly rousing from its long centuries of slumber and was preparing to move into a glorious renaissance. Particularly in France and England, monarchy was established by powerful noblemen, enabling more stable central governments to emerge. Uncertainty and fear, which had been the daily companions of medieval peoples for centuries, diminished as the social and economic environment became more predictable, replacing the wildly inconsistent conditions that still prevailed in Romanesque times.

During the 1200s, the rise of the universities created a demand for books that expanded the market. Of the hundred thousand residents of Paris, for example, twenty thousand were students who had flocked to the city to attend the university. Literacy was on the rise, and professional lay illuminators were active to help meet the growing demand for books.

The Book of Revelation had a surge of unexplained popularity in England and France during the 1200s. A scriptorium at St. Albans with high artistic standards seems to have figured prominently in this development. At least ninety-three copies of the *Apocalypse* survive from this period. The horror and anxiety of the earlier

Spanish editions is replaced with a straightforward naturalism anchored in this world rather than a future one.

The *Douce Apocalypse* (Fig. 5-14), written and illustrated around 1265, is one of the many masterpieces of the Gothic style. Each of a hundred illustrated pages (three are now missing) has an illustration at the top with two columns of beautifully lettered text below. The scribe used the *textura* style of lettering, which looks like a picket fence with its rigid repetition of verticals capped with pointed serifs. Textura, from the Latin *texturum,* which means woven fabric or texture, appears to have been the favored name for the dominant lettering style of the Gothic period. Other terms, such as the French *lettre de forme* and the English *blackletter* and *Old English,* are vague and misleading. During its time, textura was called *littera moderna,* which is Latin for "modern lettering." This style was quite functional, for all the vertical strokes in a word were drawn first, then the scribe would add the serifs and other strokes needed to transform the group of verticals into a word.

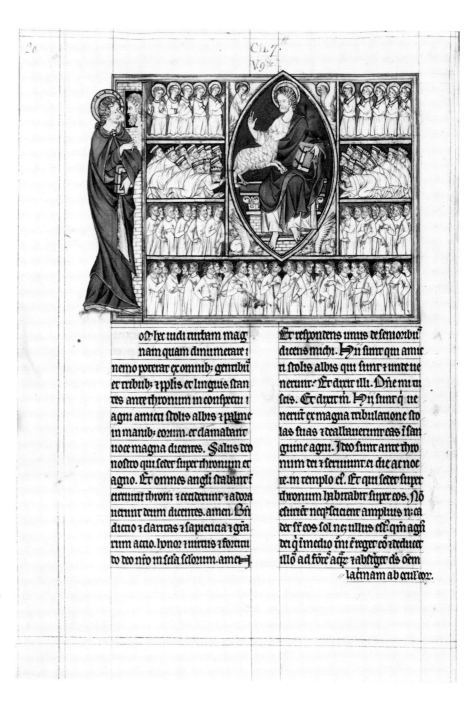

5-14. The multitude worshiping God from the *Douce Apocalypse,* c. 1265. In many of the images, St. John, the roving reporter of the final doom, is shown at the left of the scene peering curiously into the rectangular image.

Rounded strokes are almost eliminated, and the letters and the spaces between them are condensed in an effort to save space on the precious parchment. The overall effect is one of a dense black texture. On every page, an open square is left in the upper-left corner for an initial, but these were never added. Illustrations that were drawn but never painted show an even line of great sensitivity and decisiveness. The illustrations are divided into segments by elaborate framing. In the illustration for the last passage of the seventh chapter of Revelation, the triumphant white-robed multitude who survived the great tribulation are shown surrounding a very human-looking God with his Lamb. St. John's soft-blue robe and rust-brown cloak set the tone for a mellow palette of blues, greens, reds, browns, grays, and yellows.

The *Douce Apocalypse* is one of a new breed of picture books that established the graphic design approach of the fifteenth-century woodblock books after printing came to Europe. The scribe and illuminator are not known; in fact, scholars have argued over whether the *Douce Apocalypse* was created in England or France. This blurring of national origin evidences the trend toward an *international Gothic style,* which pervaded the late Gothic period. It is characterized by elongated figures that rise upward in a vertical movement, often wearing elegant fashionable costumes or flowing robes. It is a style of increasing naturalism. Even though the figures are pulled upward, there is a conviction of solid, almost monumental weight and an expression of human dignity. Elements from the national styles of various countries were combined, and increased commissions for private books, particularly from royal patrons, enabled scribes and illuminators to travel and disseminate artistic conventions and techniques.

Liturgical books of the late medieval era contained incredible designs. The *Ormesby Psalter* (Fig. 5-15), designed and produced during the early 1300s in England, is a stunning example. Its generous 33.6-centimeter (about 13½-inch) height allows for illustrated capital initials containing biblical scenes with gold-leaf backgrounds. The large text is written in the textura writing style. The text area is surrounded by an intricate frame filled with decorative pattern capital initials, and rich marginalia, which are thought to be visual clues suggesting appropriate parables and stories to the priest after he completes the scriptural reading to the congregation. The page illustrated in Figure 5-15 has an owl/horse conferring with a man/snail at the top. At the bottom, a demon smugly watches a betrothal. The young maiden eagerly reaches for the falconer's engagement ring; the symbolic cat and mouse below the couple hint that someone is being victimized. The everyday life of the people had found its way into the margins of religious books. Some historians have seen this as an indication of the first promise of the coming humanism of the Renaissance, with its concern for the quality of human life on earth.

The Christian faith did not have a monopoly on illuminated manuscripts, for parallel graphic traditions evolved among followers of the Hebrew and Islamic religions. Hebrew illuminated manuscripts are rare, but the ones that have survived are jewels of graphic design. In the *Darmstadt Haggādāh* (Fig. 5-16), a dense black calligraphy and dominance of browns and other earth tones give a weighty elegance to the volume. The large, decorated initials become focal points for the pages. Drawings of figures, animals, and birds are executed with great sensitivity.

Perhaps even more than Christians and Jews, people of the Muslim faith are devoted to their sacred books. The relationship of calligraphy to the Prophet Mohammed's Koran made calligraphy the Islamic world's major artform. The finest Muslim manuscripts were designed during the sixteenth century. In the Persian Empire (centered in what is now Iran), the ruling Shahs patronized the creation of shimmering pages of great beauty and intricacy (Fig. 5-17).

The production of illuminated manuscripts for private use became increasingly important, and in the early 1400s the *Book of Hours* became the most popular book. This private devotional book contained religious texts for each hour of the day, prayers, and calendars listing the days of important saints. The pinnacle of the illuminated book was reached in the early fifteenth century, when a passionate

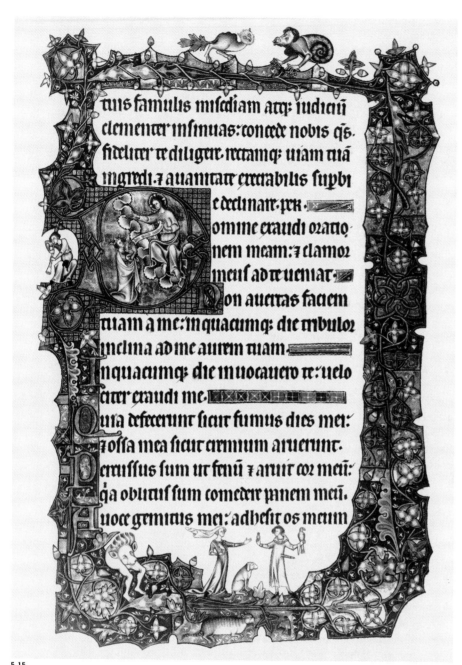

5-15

5-16

5-15. Page from the *Ormesby Psalter,* c. early fourteenth century. A bright red and blue color scheme dominates the ornaments and illustrations of this and other late-Gothic English manuscripts.

5-16. Page from the *Darmstadt Haggādāh,* c. 1420. This masterpiece of Hebrew illumination has exquisitely drawn birds and animals, well-formed calligraphy in the Hebrew alphabet, and superb initials contained in earth-toned plaques.

lover of beautiful books, the French nobleman and brother of King Charles V, Jean, Duc de Berry (1340–1416), who owned a vast portion of central France, installed the Limbourg brothers of Dutch origin in his castle to establish a private scriptorium. Little is known about the brief lives of Paul, Herman, and Jean Limbourg. It is believed that all three were born after 1385. Sons of a Dutch wood sculptor, all three apprenticed as goldsmiths, then probably trained at an important Paris scriptorium after 1400. The Duc de Berry employed Paul Limbourg in 1408 to head his workshop. Paul was probably the designer responsible for layout and design.

The Duc de Berry, whose library of 155 books included fourteen Bibles and fifteen *Books of Hours,* owned one of the largest private libraries in the world at that time. He followed the design and execution of each page with keen interest. Apparently a close rapport developed between patron and designer/illustrators, for on New Year's Day of 1411 the Limbourg brothers gave the Duc a bogus book consisting of a wooden block bound in white velvet and locked with an enameled clasp decorated with the Duc's coat of arms.

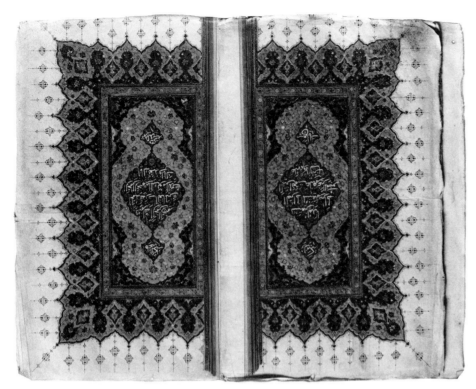

5-17. Pages from a Persian manuscript Koran, c. sixteenth century. This Islamic manuscript has the intricate floral and geometric patterns with interlocked positive and negative areas associated with architectural decorations and carpets designed in Muslim countries.

In the early fifteenth century, the Limbourgs were the avant-garde of the evolution toward the interpretation of visual experience. The Gothic tendency toward abstraction and stylized presentation was reversed. The Limbourgs sought a convincing realism. Atmospheric perspective was used to push planes and volumes back in deep space, and a consistent effort toward linear perspective was made. The Limbourgs' exceptional gifts of observation combined with remarkable painting skill enabled them to propel book design and illustration to its zenith. There is a strong sense of mass and volume, and in some illustrations highlights and cast shadows are created by a single light source.

The Limbourg brothers' masterpiece is *Les Tres Riches Heures du Duc de Berry* (Pl. 8 and Figs. 5-18 and 5-19), which was produced between 1413 and 1416. The first twenty-four pages are an illustrated calendar. Each month has a double-page spread with a genre illustration relating to seasonal activities of the month on the left page and a calendar of the saints' days on the right page. Each month's miniature painting is crowned with a graphic astronomical chart depicting constellations and the phases of the moon. The winter farm scene for February includes a cutaway building with people warming themselves by the fire. The calendar page lists the saints' days and uses vibrant red and blue inks for the lettering. A pencil grid structure establishes the format containing the information.

Plate 8 shows The Annunciation, with the angel Gabriel bearing a white lily and scroll containing his message as he visits the Virgin Mary. In the pages with prayers and scriptures, layouts are built around illustrations contained in gold outlines. Circular extensions to the rectangular illustrations were a favorite design device. On many pages, a mere four lines of text are lettered in two columns aligned under the illustrations. Decorated initials spin off whirling acanthus foliage, which is sometimes accompanied by angels, animals, or flowers in the generous margins. Apprentices were kept busy grinding colors on a marble slab with a muller. The medium was water mixed with arabic or tragacanth gum as a binder to adhere the pigment to the vellum and preserve the image. The Limbourg brothers used a palette of ten colors plus black and white. These included cobalt and ultramarine blue and two greens, one made from a carbonate of copper, the other from

5-18 and 5-19. The Limbourg brothers, February pages from *Les Tres Riches Heures du Duc de Berry,* 1413–1416. Both pictorial and written information are presented with clarity indicating a high level of observation and visual organization.

iris leaves. Gold-leaf and gold-powder paint were used in profusion. The minute detail achieved implies that a magnifying lens might have been used.

The Limbourg brothers did not live to complete this masterpiece, for all three died before February of 1416, and the Duc de Berry died on 15 July 1416, perhaps the victims of a terrible epidemic or plague that is believed to have swept through France that year. The inventory of the Duc de Berry's library, taken after his death, indicates that half his books were religious works, and a third were history books, with geography, astronomy, and astrology volumes rounding out the collection. During the same years that the Limbourgs were working on their great graphic designs, a new means of visual communication—woodblock printing—was appearing in Europe. The invention of movable type in the West was but three decades away. The production of illuminated manuscripts continued through the fifteenth century and even into the early decades of the sixteenth century, but this thousand-year-old craft dating back to antiquity was doomed to eventual extinction with the coming of the typographic book.

A Graphic Renaissance:
The origins of European typography and design for printing

World Events	6 Printing Comes to Europe	7 The German Illustrated Book	8 Renaissance Graphic Design	9 An Epoch of Typographic Genius
1415 Florence humanists study classical manuscripts				
1431 Joan of Arc burned at Rouen	1423 St. Christopher, early dated woodblock print			
c. 1445 Fra Angelico paints *The Annunciation*	c. 1440s Gutenberg perfects typographic printing c. 1450 Copperplate engraving begins			
1462 Mainz, Germany, sacked by Adolf of Nassau	c. 1455 *42-line Bible* completed 1457 Fust and Schoeffer, *Psalter in Latin* 1468 Gutenberg dies			
1480 da Vinci invents the parachute		c.1460 Pfister, illustrated typographic book 1465 Sweynheym and Pannartz, 1st Italian printing press 1470 1st printing press in France 1475 Caxton, 1st English language typographic book 1486 Reuwich illustrates trip to Holy Land	1469 de Spira, 1st Venice printing press 1470 Jenson's roman typeface 1476 Ratdolt: *Calendarium* title page	
1492 Columbus discovers America 1494 France invades Italy 1503 da Vinci, *Mona Lisa*		1493 Koberger, *The Nuremberg Chronicle* 1498 Durer, *The Apocalypse*	1494 Manutius, The Aldine Press 1495 Griffo designs and cuts Bembo type 1501 Griffo designs and cuts italic type 1505 Tory returns to France from Italy 1506 Tory, *Les Heures de Jean Lallement*	
1509 Henry VIII, King of England 1512 Michelangelo completes Sistine Chapel ceiling 1517 Luther launches the Reformation 1522 Circumnavigation of the globe 1527 French army sacks Rome		1514-17 de Brocar, *Polyglot Bible* 1517 Schoensperger, *Teuerdank*	1522 Arrighi's writing manual 1525 Tory, his 1st Book of *Hours* 1529 Tory, *Champ Fleury* c. 1530 Garamond establishes an independent type foundry	
1534 Luther, German language Bible		1538 1st printing press in Mexico		
1553 Lucas Cranach dies			1555 Plantin establishes his Antwerp press c. 1557 Granjon, *Civilite* type 1561 Kerver, French version of *Poliphili* 1569-72 Plantin, *Polyglot Bible*	
1569 Mercator, modern cartography				
1573 Drake sees Pacific from Panama				
1584 Raleigh lands in Virginia				
1594 Shakespeare, *Romeo and Juliette*				
1597 Spain's naval war on England fails				

6 Printing Comes to Europe

c. 1400 Woodblock playing cards are used in Europe

7 The German Illustrated Book

8 Renaissance Graphic Design

9 An Epoch of Typographic Genius

1692 French king Louis XIV commissions the Romain du Roi
1702 1st book using Romain du Roi

1722 Caslon, 1st Caslon Old Style font

1737 Fournier le Jeune, standardized type sizes; John Pine, *Opera* of Horatii
1742 Fournier le Jeune, *Modeles des characteres de l'Imprimere*

1757 Baskerville, *Virgil*

1764 Fournier le Jeune publishes 1st volume of *Manuel Typographique*
1771 Luce, *Essai d'une Nouvelle Typographie*
1784 Didot, true modern style type

1789 Blake, *Songs of Innocence*
c. 1790 Neoclassical Style dominant; Bodoni, typefaces bearing his name; Bewick, *General History of Quadrupeds*
1796 Bewick and Bulmer, *The Chase*

1609 Regularly published German newspapers

1621 *Weekly Newes*, 1st English newspaper

1640 Daye, *Whole Book of Psalmes*
1642 Bosse, *Printing Shop—The Plate Printer*

1667 Schipper, Calvin's *Commentary*

1608 Lippersheim invents the telescope

1629 English settlements in Massachusetts

1639 Descartes, analytical geometry

1652 Dutch found Capetown
1653 Walton, *The Compleat Angler*

1667 Milton, *Paradise Lost*

1689 Peter the Great, Czar of Russia

1700 Sewall, *Story of Joseph*, 1st American protest against slavery

1719 Daniel Defoe, *Robinson Crusoe*
c. 1720 Rococo designs appear in Paris
1721 Bach, *Brandenburg concertos*

1726 Swift, *Gulliver's Travels*

1760 George III becomes King of England

1769 Watt patents steam engine
1770 Boston Massacre

1774 Louis XVI becomes King of France
1776 Declaration of Independence
1784 David, *Oath of the Horatii*
1788 Washington, 1st U.S. President
1789 French Revolution begins

1793 Louis XVI beheaded
1799 Napoleon rules France

6 Printing Comes to Europe

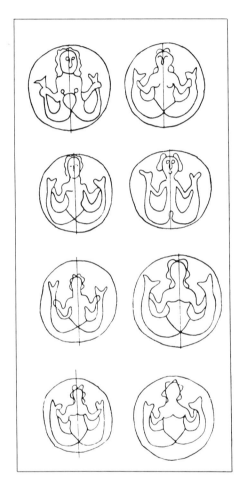

6-1. French watermark designs, fifteenth century. These mermaid designs were produced by bent wire attached to the mold used in making paper.

Xylography is the technical term for the relief printing from a raised surface that originated in the Orient. *Typography* is the term for printing through the use of independent, movable, and reusable bits of metal, each of which has a raised letterform on its top. This dry definition belies the immense potential for human dialogue and the new horizons for graphic design that were unleashed by this extraordinary invention in the mid-1400s by a restless German inventor whose portrait and signature are lost to the relentless passage of time. The invention of typography is one of the most important advances in civilization after the creation of writing. Writing gave the human family a means of storing, retrieving, and documenting knowledge and information that transcended time and place; typographic printing allowed the economical and multiple production of alphabet communication. Knowledge spread rapidly, and literacy increased as a result of this remarkable invention.

Several factors created a climate in Europe that made typography feasible. The demand for books had become insatiable as Europe was slowly aroused from the medieval era into the Renaissance. The emerging literate middle class and students in the rapidly expanding universities had snatched the monopoly on literacy from the clergy, creating a vast new market for reading material. The slow and expensive process of bookmaking had changed little in one thousand years. A simple two-hundred-page book required four or five months' labor by a scribe, and the twenty-five sheepskins needed for the parchment were even more expensive than his labor.

In 1424 the university at Cambridge had only 122 manuscript books in its library, and the library of a wealthy nobleman whose books were his most prized and sought-after possessions would probably number less than two dozen volumes. The value of a book was equal to the value of a farm or vineyard. The steady growth of demand had led independent merchants to develop an assembly-line division of labor with specialists trained in lettering, decorative initialing, gold ornamentation, proofreading, and binding. Even this exploding production of manuscript books was unable to meet the demand.

Without paper, the speed and efficiency of printing would have been useless. Papermaking had completed a long, slow journey from China to Europe, so a plentiful substrate was available. Over six hundred years passed before papermaking, which spread westward following caravan routes from the Pacific Ocean to the Mediterranean Sea, reached the Arab world. After repelling a Chinese attack on the city of Samarkand in 751 A.D., the Arab occupation forces captured some Chinese papermakers. Abundant water and bountiful crops of flax and hemp enabled Samarkand to become a papermaking center, and the craft spread to Baghdad, Damascus, and reached Egypt by the tenth century. From there, it spread across North Africa and was introduced into Sicily in 1102 and into Spain by the Moors during the middle of the twelfth century. By 1276 a paper mill was established in Fabriano, Italy. Troyes, France, had a paper mill in 1348.

The watermark (Fig. 6-1), a translucent emblem produced by pressure from a raised design on the mold and visible when the sheet of paper is held to the light, was used in Italy by 1282. The origin of this design device is unknown. Trademarks

6-2. Jack of Diamonds, woodblock playing card, c. 1400. The flat, stylized design conventions of playing cards have changed little in over five hundred years. Visual signs to designate the suits began as the four classes of medieval society. Hearts signified the clergy; spades (derived from *spada,* "sword," in Italy) stood for the nobility; the leaflike club represented the peasantry; and diamonds denoted the burghers.

for paper mills, individual craftsmen, and perhaps religious symbolism were early uses. As successful marks were imitated, they began to be used as a designation for sheet and mold sizes and paper grade. Mermaids, unicorns, animals, flowers, and heraldic shields were frequent design motifs.

Early European block printing

The origins of woodblock printing in Europe are shrouded in mystery. After the Crusades opened Europe to an eastern influence, relief printing arrived on the heels of paper. Playing cards and religious-image prints were early manifestations. Circumstantial evidence implies that, like paper, relief printing from woodblocks had also spread westward from China. By the early 1300s pictorial designs were being printed on textiles in Europe. Card playing was popular, and in spite of being outlawed and denounced by zealous churchmen, this pastime stimulated a thriving underground block-printing industry, possibly before 1400.

In 1415 the Duke of Milan played cards with ivory slats bearing images painted by famous artists, and Flemish nobles used engraved silver plates. Throughout Europe, the working class gathered in taverns and by the roadside to play with grimy cards that were block-printed and stenciled on coarse paper (Fig. 6-2). The first graphic designs to move into an illiterate culture, these cards are the earliest manifestation of printing's democratizing ability in Europe, for the games of kings could now become the games of peasants and craftsmen. As these cards introduced the masses to symbol recognition, sequencing, and logical deduction, their intrinsic value transcended idle entertainment.

The first known European block printing with a communications function were devotional prints of saints (Figs. 6-3 and 6-4), ranging from small images fitting in a person's hand to larger images of 25 by 35 centimeters (about 10 by 14 inches). Image and lettering were cut from the same block of wood. These early graphic designs evolved into the *block books* (Figs. 6-5 and 6-6), which were woodcut picture books with religious subject matter and brief text. Each page was cut from a block of wood and printed as a complete word and picture unit. Since most of the few surviving copies were printed in the Netherlands after 1460, it is not known whether the block book preceded the typographic book. Drawn in a simplified illustration style, with the visual elements dominant as in contemporary comic books, the block book was used for religious instruction of illiterates. This form gradually declined during the fifteenth century as literacy increased. Common subjects included the Apocalypse, a forewarning of the final doom and destruction of the world. *Ars Moriendi* (art of dying) advised one on the preparation and meeting of the final hour. In a Europe that had been decimated by the great cycles of plague, called the black death, which claimed one-fourth of the population during the fourteenth century and caused a thousand villages either to vanish totally or to be critically depopulated, death was an ever present preoccupation.

In the *Ars Moriendi* shown (Fig. 6-7), eleven illustrations depict the temptation of the devil and the comfort of the angel on subjects such as faith, impatience, vainglory, and the final hour of death. Thirteen pages are block-print text. While the apparent raison d'être of the *Ars Moriendi* was to help people meet death, it also must be considered as one of the first examples of printed propaganda, for it urges the dying to put aside the desire to provide for one's family and to will the estate to the church. *Biblia Pauperum* (bible of the poor) was a compendium of events in the life of Christ, including testimony about how Old Testament prophecy was fulfilled (Fig. 6-8). The pages from *Ars Memorandi per figuras Evangelistarum,* c. 1470 (Pl. 9), demonstrate the graphic power of the block book with fluid washes of watercolor applied to enliven its symbolic imagery.

Most block books contained from thirty to fifty leaves. In addition to hand coloring and the use of stencils to apply flat areas of color to textile, playing card, and later block-book woodcuts, some fifteenth-century prints exist where woodblocks were used to print paste or gum, sprinkled with tinsel (minute sparkling fragments of metal), incrustation (minute quartz crystals with color), or flocking (powdered

Printing Comes to Europe

6-3

6-4

6-3. Woodblock print of St. Christopher, 1423. The unknown illustrator depicted the legendary saint, a giant who carried travelers safely across a river, bearing the infant Christ. The inscription below reads: "In whatsoever day thou seest the likeness of St. Christopher/In that same day thou wilt at least from death no evil blow incur/1423." One of the earliest dated European block prints, this image has an effective use of changing contour-line width to show form.

6-4. Blockprint of The Annunciation, undated. The black area between the angel and Virgin becomes an effective focal point and serves to unify the two figures. The scroll, with a Latin inscription, serves the same communicative function as a "talk balloon." (The upper-left corner of this print is missing.)

6-5. Block-book page from *The Story of the Blessed Virgin,* 1400s. This page attempts to justify the Immaculate Conception by a series of "logical" parallels: If the light of Venus's temple cannot be extinguished, if the moon is reflected in water, if a person can be changed into stone, and if man can be painted on stone, why should not the Blessed Virgin be able to generate?

6-6. Letter *K* from a Grotesque Alphabet, c. 1464. This page from a twenty-four–page, abecedarium block-book presented each letter of the alphabet by composing figures into the shape of the letter.

6-7. Pages from *Ars Moriendi*, 1466. In the illustration, a tight montage effect is achieved by juxtaposing the deathbed scene with a view of the subject's estate. One demon urges, "Provide for your friends," while the other advises, "Attend to your treasures." The densely textured text page suggests that one's earthly goods should be given to the church.

6-8. Page from a *Biblia Pauperum,* 1465. In this typical layout, a crosslike architectural structure brings order to a complex page. Bible verses appear in the upper corners; David and three other prophets are above and below with a quotation from each on a scroll. Across the center, the creation of Eve, the Crucifixion of Christ, and Moses striking the rock for water are shown.

6-8

wool). These were used as design elements to bring a vibrant tactile quality and luminosity to the image. The earliest block books were printed with a hand rubber in brown or gray ink; later versions were printed in black ink on a printing press. Because the hand rubber created too much indention to allow double-sided printing, the earliest block books are only printed on one side of the paper. Each double-page spread was followed by two blank pages, which were usually pasted together to preserve the visual flow of images and text. While the monastic designer might also cut his own woodblock, in the secular world the distinction between *designer* and *cutter (formschneider)* was vigorously upheld by trade guilds. The cutters who worked from the designer's ink layout on either paper or woodblock were often members of carpentry guilds.

Movable typography in Europe

With the availability of paper, relief printing from woodblocks, and the growing demand for books, the mechanization of book production by such means as movable type was sought by printers in Germany, the Netherlands, France, and Italy. In Avignon, France, goldsmith Procopius Waldfoghel was involved in the production of "alphabets of steel" around 1444, but with no known results. The Dutchman Laurens Janszoon Coster of Haarlem allegedly explored the concept of movable type by cutting out letters or words from his woodblocks for reuse. The judgment of history, however, is that Johann Gensfleisch zum Gutenberg (c. 1387–1468) of Mainz, Ger-

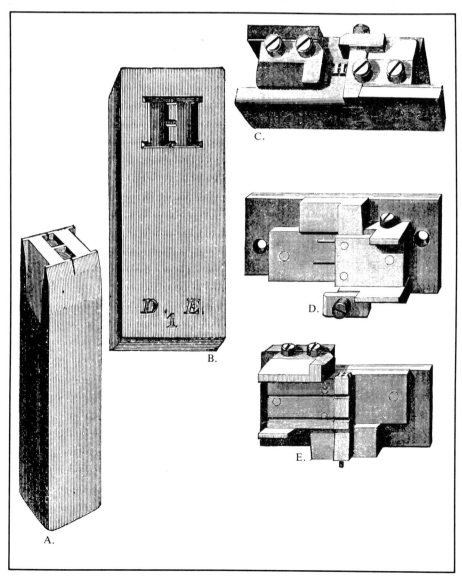

6-9. These early nineteenth-century engravings illustrate Gutenberg's system for casting type. A steel punch is used to stamp an impression of the letterform into a softer brass matrix. After the matrix is slipped into the bottom of the two-part type mold, the mold is filled with the molten lead alloy to cast a piece of type. After the lead alloy cools, the type mold is opened and the type is removed.

A. Punch

B. Matrix

C. Type Mold (with matrix removed to show a newly cast *H*)

D. & E. Type Mold (opened so that the newly cast *H* can be removed) many, brought together the complex systems and subsystems necessary to print a typographic book around the year 1450. The third son of the wealthy Mainz patrician Friele Gensfleisch, Johann Gutenberg apprenticed as a goldsmith, developing the metalworking and engraving skills necessary for making type. In September 1428, he was exiled from Mainz for his leadership role in a power struggle between the landed noblemen and the burghers of the trade guilds who sought a greater political voice. He relocated in Strasbourg, one hundred miles to the southwest, and became a successful and prosperous gem cutter and metalworker.

Early in 1438, Gutenberg formed a contractual partnership with Strasbourg citizens Andreas Dritzehen (who had received gem-cutting training from Gutenberg) and Andreas Heilmann (who owned a paper mill). He agreed to teach them a secret process for making mirrors to sell at an Aachen pilgrimage fair the following year. Mirrors were rare and difficult to manufacture: Molten lead was poured over glass and formed a reflective surface when it cooled; the difficulty was preventing the glass from cracking from the heat. When the fair was postponed until 1440, Gutenberg entered a new five-year contract to teach his partners another secret process.

When Dritzehen died in late 1438, his brothers Georg and Claus sued Gutenberg for either admission to the partnership or a refund. On 12 December 1439, the court ruled in Gutenberg's favor because his original contract specified that only one hundred florins would be paid to any partner's heirs. The record of this trial shows conclusively that Gutenberg was involved in printing. Several witnesses mention that the partners owned a press; woodturner Conrad Saspach testified that he had constructed the press. Testimony mentions type, a stock of lead and other metals, and a mysterious four-piece instrument secured by double handscrews (probably a type mold). Goldsmith Hans Dünne testified that as early as 1436 he had sold Gutenberg one hundred guilders' worth of material "solely for that which belonged to printing." In the mid-1440s, Gutenberg moved back to Mainz, where he resolved the technical, organizational, and production problems that had plagued earlier typographic printing efforts. He had labored for ten years before his first printing and twenty years before printing the first typographic book, called the forty-two-line Bible. Typographic printing did not grow directly out of block printing because wood was too fragile. Block printing was advantageous for the Chinese because alignment between characters was not critical and sorting over five thousand basic characters was untenable. By contrast, the need for exact alignment and the modest alphabet system of about two dozen letters made the printing of text material from independent, movable and reusable type highly desirable in the West.

A number of steps were necessary in the creation of typographic printing. A style of letter had to be selected. Gutenberg made the obvious choice of the square, compact textura lettering style commonly used by German scribes of his day. Early printers sought to compete with calligraphers by imitating their work as closely as possible. This "picket fence" style of block letter with no subtle curves was so well developed by Gutenberg that the characters in the forty-two-line Bible are hardly distinguishable from good calligraphy. Next, each character in the font—small and capital letters, numbers, punctuation, ligatures—had to be engraved into the top of a steel bar to make a punch. This punch was then driven into a matrix of softer copper or brass to make a negative impression of the letterform.

The key to Gutenberg's invention was the type mold (Fig. 6-9), used for casting the individual letters. Each character had to be plane parallel in every direction and the exact same height. Gutenberg's two-part type mold, which adjusted to accept matrixes for narrow characters (i) as well as wide ones (m), solved the need to cast large volumes of type made to critical tolerances. Type required a metal soft enough to cast but hard enough to hold up for thousands of impressions. It must not expand and contract when melted, poured into the type mold, then returned to a solid state as it cooled. As a metalsmith, Gutenberg had learned that the silvery white metal antimony would expand when it cooled from a liquid to a solid state, in contrast to most metals, which contract when cooled. He developed a unique alloy

A.

B.

C.

D.

E.

F.

G.

H.

6-10. Jost Amman, woodcut illustrations for *Ständebuch* ("Book of Trades"), 1568. This little book presented over a hundred occupations, from the Pope to the scissors sharpener. Amman's crisp illustrations were accompanied by prolific poet Hans Sachs's descriptive rhymes. The occupations of the graphic arts are shown here.

A. The parchment maker is shown scraping animal skins to produce a smooth surface after they have been washed, stretched, and dried.

B. The papermaker lifts his mold out of the vat as he forms each sheet by hand.

C. The typefounder is depicted pouring the melted lead into the type mold to cast a character. The foreground basket is filled with newly cast type.

D. One printer is shown removing a newly printed sheet from the press while the other one inks the type. In the background, compositors are shown setting type at typecases.

E. The designer is illustrated as he draws an image in preparation for a woodcut or copper engraving. (This is probably Amman's self-portrait.)

F. The woodblock cutter carefully cuts the drawing or design into a block of wood.

G. The illuminator, who applied gold leaf and color—originally to manuscripts—continued his craft on the typographically printed page.

H. Bookbinders are presented as one collates the pages of a volume by hand. The other prepares a book for the application of the covers.

of 80 percent lead, 5 percent tin, and 15 percent antimony to maintain a constant mass throughout the process of manufacturing type. Gutenberg needed as many as fifty thousand single pieces of type in use at a time, so the speed, accuracy, and economy achieved by this type mold and its casting process were critical. The type was stored in compartmented cases and pulled out letter by letter to set the lines. After a page was printed, the type was returned to the compartments letter by letter.

The medieval block printer used a thin, watery ink made from oak gall. Since the woodblock could absorb excess moisture, this ink worked fine, but it would run off or puddle on metal type. Gutenberg used boiled linseed oil colored with lampblack, which produced a thick, tacky ink that could be smoothly applied. To ink type, a dollop of ink was placed on a flat surface and smeared with a soft leather ball, coating the ball's bottom. The ball was then daubed onto the type to apply an even coating of ink.

A strong, sturdy press capable of sufficient force to pressure the ink from the type onto the paper surface was needed. Ample prototypes existed in presses used in making wine, cheese, and baling paper, and Gutenberg adapted their designs, which were based on a large screw lowering and raising a plate, to printing. Gutenberg's press and system were used for four hundred years with moderate improvements. This precision machine, sometimes underrated, allowed tremendous printing speed and consistent quality in comparison to the hand-rubbing method of the Orient and early European block printers. Later improvements included a frisket to protect margins and other unprinted areas, modification of the screw to lessen the energy needed to print, and a quick release feature so that less energy was needed to lift the plate than to lower it. Eventually, a mechanical linkage replaced the screw. The graphic arts craftsmen involved in book production are illustrated in Figure 6-10.

Among the assorted surviving examples of early typographic design and printing —a German poem on the Last Judgment, four calendars, and a number of editions of a *Latin Grammar* by Donatus—the earliest *dated* specimens are the 1454 "Letters of Indulgence" issued in Mainz (Fig. 6-11). Pope Nicholas V issued this pardon

6-11. Johann Gutenberg, thirty-one-line *Letters of Indulgence*, c. 1454. The written additions in this copy indicate that on the last day of December 1454, one Judocus Ott von Apspach was pardoned of his sins.

Incipit liber bresith quē nos genesim dr̄ Jn principio creauit deus celū dicimus2j. et terram. Terra autem erat inanis et vacua:et tenebre erāt sup facie abissi. et sps dūi ferebat sup aquas. Dixitꝙ deus. Fiat lux. Et facta ē lux. Et vidit deus lucem ꝙ esset bona:ꞇ diuisit lucē a tenebris.appellauitꝙ lucem diem ꞇ tenebras noctem. Factūꝙ est vespe et mane dies vnius. Dixit ꝙ deus. Fiat firmamentū in medio aquaꝛ:ꞇ diui dat aquas ab aquis. Et fecit deus fir mamentū:diuisitꝙ aquas que erāt sub firmamento ab hijs ꝗ erant sup firmamentū:et factū ē ita. Vocauitꝙ deus firmamentū celū:ꞇ factū ē vespe et mane dies secūd9. Dixit vero deus. Congregentꝛ aque que sub celo sūt in locū vnū ꞇ appareat arida. Et factū ē ita. Et vocauit deus aridam terram: congregationesꝙ aquaꝛ appellauit maria. Et vidit deus ꝙ esset bonū.et ait. Germinet terra herbā virentem et facientē semen:ꞇ lignū pomiferꝛ faciēs fructū iuxta genus suū.cui9 semen in semetipso sit sup terrā. Et factū ē ita. Et protulit terra herbā virentē ꞇ facientē semē iuxta genus suū:lignūꝙ faciēs fructū ꞇ habēs vnūqdꝗ sementē scdm speciē suā. Et vidit deus ꝙ esset bonū: et factū est vespe et mane dies tercius. Dixitꝙ autē deus. Fiant luminaria in firmamēto celi:ꞇ diuidāt diem ac noctem:ꞇ sint in signa ꞇ tpa et dies ꞇ annos.ut luceāt in firmamēto celi et illuminēt terrā. Et factū ē ita. Fecitꝙ deus duo luminaria magna:luminare maius ut pesset diei et luminare min9 ut pesset nocti ꞇ stellas.ꞇ posuit eas in firmamēto celi ut lucerent sup terrā:et

pessent diei ac nocti.ꞇ diuiderent lucē ac tenebras. Et vidit de9 ꝙ esset bonū: et factū ē vespe ꞇ mane dies quartus. Dixit eciā de9. Producāt aque reptile aīme viuentis ꞇ volatile super terrā sub firmamēto celi. Creauitꝙ deus cete grandia.et omnem aīam viuentē atꝗ motabilē quā pduxerāt aque ī species suas.ꞇ omne volatile scdm gen9 suū. Et vidit deus ꝙ esset bonū.benedixitꝙ eis dicens. Crescite ꞇ mltiplicamini.ꞇ replete aquas maris.auesꝗ mltipli centꝛ sup terrā. Et factū ē vespe ꞇ mane dies quitus. Dixit quoꝗ deus. Pro ducat terra aīam viuentē in gene suo. iumenta ꞇ reptilia.ꞇ bestias terre scdm species suas. Factūꝙ ē ita. Et fecit de9 bestias terre iuxta species suas.iumen ta ꞇ omne reptile terre ī genere suo. Et vidit deus ꝙ esset bonū.et ait. Facia mus hoīem ad ymaginē ꞇ silitudinē nostrā.ꞇ presit piscibꝯ maris.et vola tilibꝯ celi ꞇ bestijs vniūseꝗ terre.omniꝗ repti qd mouetur ī terra. Et creauit deus hoīem ad ymaginē ꞇ silitudinē suā.ad ymaginē dī creauit illū.ma sculū ꞇ feminā creauit eos. Benedixit ꝗ illis deus.ꞇ ait. Crescite ꞇ mltiplica mini ꞇ replete terrā.et sbicite eā.et dīa mini piscibꝯ maris.et volatilibꝯ celi. et vniuersis animātibꝯ que mouentꝛ sup terrā. Dixitꝙ de9. Ecce dedi vobꝯ omne herbā afferentē semen sup terrā. et vnīusa ligna que hūt in semetipis sementē genis sui.ut sint vobis ī escā ꞇ cunctis aīantibꝯ terre.omniꝗ volucri celi ꞇ vniuersis ꝗ mouētur in terra.ꞇ ī quibꝯ est anima viuēs.ut habeāt ad vescendū. Et factū est ita. Viditꝙ deus cuncta que fecerat.ꞇ erāt valde bona.

of sins to all Christians who had given money to support the war against the Turks. Apparently the agents selling manuscript copies early in 1454 learned of Gutenberg's work and realized the value of printing this letter in quantity. Seven editions in two styles were ordered during 1454 and 1455.

Because the relentless expenses of research and development were a constant drain on Gutenberg's financial resources, in 1450 he found it necessary to borrow eight hundred guilders from Johann Fust (c. 1400–1460), a wealthy Mainz burgher and merchant, to continue his work. The printing equipment was offered as collateral. At some point, Gutenberg conceived the idea of printing a Bible. Around 1452 he had to borrow another eight hundred guilders from Fust "for their common profit," establishing a partnership "in the production of books."

A heroic effort was required to produce this first typographic book, which is also one of the finest examples of the printer's art (Fig. 6-12). The large 30-by-40.5-centimeter (11¾-by-16-inch) pages have two columns of type with a generous 2.9-centimeter (¾-inch) margin between them. The first nine pages have forty lines per column, the tenth page has forty-one lines per column, and the rest have forty-two lines per column. It is not known whether Gutenberg followed a manuscript like this or whether he began a forty-line Bible and then increased the number of lines per column for economy. With 1,282 pages in a two-volume work, the increase of two lines per column saved an additional sixty pages. This fantastic project began with two presses, which were increased to six presses. With lines of about thirty-three characters, each page had over 2,500 characters set from a font of 290 different characters. The generous number of alternate characters and ligatures enabled Gutenberg to achieve the richness and variety of the manuscript page. For further enrichment, blank spaces were left for decorative initials to be drawn in later by a scribe. A rigorous justification of the columns was possible because Latin words could be abbreviated freely by up to six letters by the use of abbreviation symbols above the words. The edition of 210 copies consisted of 180 on paper and thirty on fine vellum, requiring five thousand carefully prepared calfskins.

In 1455, as work neared completion, Fust suddenly sued Gutenberg for 2,026 guilders in payment of loans and interest. On 6 November 1455, the courts ruled in favor of Fust with the requirement that he appear at the local monastery and swear before God that he was paying interest on some of the money he had loaned Gutenberg. Fust appeared and fulfilled the edict of court by taking the oath. Gutenberg did not attend. Instead, he sent two friends to beg Fust to give him more time. Fust found himself in possession of Gutenberg's printing equipment and all work in progress; on the eve of completion of the immensely valuable forty-two-line Bible, which would have enabled him to pay all debts, Gutenberg was locked out of his printing shop.

Fust immediately entered into an agreement with Peter Schoeffer (d. 1502), who was Gutenberg's skilled assistant and foreman. An artist/designer experienced as an illuminator and manuscript dealer and a scribe at the University of Paris in 1449, Schoeffer quite possibly played a key role in the format development and type design for the forty-two-line Bible. If so, he may have been the first typeface designer. With Fust as business manager and Schoeffer in charge of printing, the firm of Fust and Schoeffer became the most important printing firm in the world and established a hundred-year family dynasty of printers, publishers, and booksellers, for Schoeffer married Fust's daughter, Christina, around 1467. The new partnership's first venture was the completion of the forty-two–line Bible. Since one of the forty-seven surviving copies bears a marginal notation that the hand rubrication, which is the application of red-ink initials and titling by a scribe, was completed on 24 August 1456, we can presume that Fust acquired a nearly complete production when he foreclosed.

Sales of the forty-two-line Bible were brisk as Fust traveled widely to distribute them. An early author relates that Fust carried a parcel of Bibles to Paris and attempted to sell them as manuscripts. The forty-two-line Bible had no title page, no page numbers, or other innovations to distinguish it from handmade manu-

6-12. Johann Gutenberg, first page of Genesis from the Gutenberg Bible, 1450–1455. The superb typographic legibility and texture, generous margins, and excellent presswork make this first printed book a canon of quality that has seldom been surpassed. The header and initial were added in color by an illuminator.

scripts. Both Gutenberg and his customers probably wanted it this way. After the French observed the number and conformity of the volumes, they decided that witchcraft was involved. To avoid indictment and conviction, Fust was forced to reveal his secret. It has been claimed that this event is the basis for the popular story, related by several authors, of the German magician Dr. Faustus (Johann Faust in an early version), who grew dissatisfied with the limits of human knowledge and sold his soul to the devil in exchange for knowledge and power.

On 14 August 1457, Fust and Schoeffer published a magnificent *Psalter in Latin* with a monumental 30.5-by-43.2-centimeter (12-by-17-inch) page size (Pl. 10). The large red and blue initials were printed from two-part metal blocks which were either inked separately, reassembled, and printed with the text in one press impression or stamped after the text was printed. These famous decorated two-color initials were a major innovation, whose typographic vitality and elegance rival the most beautiful manuscript pages. The *Psalter in Latin* was also the first book to bear a printer's trademark and imprint, printed date of publication, and colophon (Fig. 6-13). A translation of the colophon reads: "This book of the Psalms, decorated with beautiful capitals, and with an abundance of rubrics, has been fashioned thus by an ingenious invention of printing and stamping without use of a pen. And to the worship of God it has been diligently brought to Completion by Johann Fust, a citizen of Mainz, and Peter Schoeffer of Gernsheim, in the year of Our Lord 1457, on the eve of the Feast of the Assumption."

Another important innovation appeared in Fust and Schoeffer's 1459 edition of *Rationale divinorum officiorum* (Fig. 6-14). This long volume explaining religious ceremonies was the first typographic book that used a small-sized type style to conserve space and increase the amount of text on each page. This achieved significant economy in the amount of presswork, ink, and parchment needed to print the edition.

Other major works included a beautiful Latin Bible, 1462, and an edition of Cicero's *De officiis,* 1465, which was the first printing of a classic from antiquity. Typography spurred the interest in ancient Greek and Roman culture. As knowledge of the ancient world began to exist alongside knowledge of the medieval era, the fusion became a catalyst for the creation of the modern world.

During a 1466 Paris trip to sell books, Johann Fust died, probably of plague. Peter Schoeffer and his associate, Conrad Henkis, who married Fust's widow the

6-13. Fust and Schoeffer, colophon and trademark from *Psalter in Latin,* 1457. The double crests are thought to symbolize the two printers.

6-14. Jan Fust and Peter Schoeffer, page from *Rationale divinorum officiorum*, 1459. The innovative small type is combined with wonderfully intricate printed red and blue initials that evidence the early printer's efforts to mimic the design of the manuscript book.

year after Fust died, continued this highly successful printing business producing broadsheets, books, and pamphlets.

While Fust and Schoeffer were selling Bibles and printing Psalters, Johann Gutenberg, who, like many innovators, was running a heartbeat ahead of his time, drifted into bankruptcy and in 1458 defaulted on interest payments for a 1442 loan. Although he was sixty years of age and down and out, he had perfected his craft and completed his research. It is believed that with financial support from Mainz citizen Dr. Conrad Homery, Gutenberg was able to establish a new printing shop. Some scholars view him as the printer of the thirty-six-line Bible, a late-1450s reprint of the forty-two-line Bible with similar but less refined type. His *Catholicon,* an encyclopedic dictionary, was published in 1460 with a colophon—perhaps in Gutenberg's own words—stating that the work was published "with the protection of the Almighty, at whose will the tongues of infants become eloquent and who often reveals to the lowly what he hides from the wise." On 17 January

Printing Comes to Europe

6-15. The Master of the Playing Cards, *The Three of Birds,* c. 1450. Masterful design and placement of the images in the space enhanced the sureness of drawing and use of line for tonal effects.

6-16. The Master of the Playing Cards or his follower, *Vine Ornament with Two Birds,* c. 1440–1450. This design is one of the earliest copperplate engravings. Its designer has achieved a remarkable overall pattern and convincing form using linear shading.

1465, Archbishop Adolf of Mainz appointed Gutenberg courtier with the rank of nobleman, entitling him to clothing, keep, and "twenty matter of corn and two fudder of wine each year." The flyleaf of a book owned by a Mainz priest bears an inscription that "the honorable Master Johann Gutenberg died 3 February 1468." Based on prior agreements, Dr. Homery petitioned the courts for ownership of the "forms, letters, instruments, tools, and other things pertaining to the work of printing" that belonged to the late Gutenberg. On 26 February 1468, the archbishop transferred possession to Dr. Homery, who promised to keep this equipment in Mainz and give first preference to Mainz citizens in the event of future sale.

For a brief few years, printing was centered in Mainz as Fust and Schoeffer, Gutenberg, and former apprentices who had established their own firms were located there. Ironically, the swift spread of printing was created by a bloody conflict. German princes and lords were involved in power struggles, which erupted into full-scale war. Leading an army of eight hundred horsemen and several thousand foot soldiers, Adolf of Nassau descended upon Mainz in 1462 and sacked the town. Plundering and looting brought trade and commerce to a halt. Warnings from other towns in Adolf's path enabled many Mainz merchants and craftsmen to load everything possible on wagons and carts and scatter like seeds in the wind. Many younger printers and apprentices did not return. Rather, presses were soon established as far away as France and Italy.

Copperplate engraving

During the same time and in the same section of Europe that Johann Gutenberg invented movable type, an unidentified artist called the Master of the Playing Cards created the earliest known copperplate engravings (Figs. 6-15 and 6-16). *Engraving* is printing from an image that is incised or cut into the printing surface. To produce a copperplate engraving, a drawing is scratched into a smooth metal plate. Ink is applied into the depressions, the flat surface is wiped clean, and paper is pressed against the plate to receive the ink image. The Master of the Playing Cards's finest work is a set of playing cards using birds, animals, and wild men as images. The quality of his drawing suggests that he probably trained as an artist rather than as a goldsmith. The masterful execution implies that these playing cards were designed and engraved by someone who had already mastered engraving, not someone struggling to perfect a new graphic technique.

Scholars have speculated that Johann Gutenberg, in addition to inventing typographic printing, may have been involved in the research and development of copperplate engraving. Images by the Master of the Playing Cards have now been associated with Mainz illuminators, including artists associated with Gutenberg's printing works during the 1450s. The links that bind these early researchers into printing together are illustrations of birds, animals, flowers, and figures that are duplicated in the engraved playing cards, an illuminated Bible produced in Mainz during the early 1450s, and the illumination added to a surviving copy of the forty-two-line Bible.

This circumstantial evidence has raised an exciting possibility: was Johann Gutenberg striving to perfect the printing not just of scribe's lettering but of the magnificent ornamentation and illustration of the medieval manuscript as well? Was engraving pioneered as a means to print illustrations onto the typographic pages, which could then be handcolored? Did Gutenberg explore using engraving plates as molds to cast relief versions, so that illustrations could be printed with type? These provocative questions, still without definite answers, indicate that Gutenberg's research might have carried the printed book in a different direction from its subsequent development. But when Johann Gutenberg's world came crashing down and he was locked out of his printing shop in 1455, research into these possibilities ended.

7

The German Illustrated Book

The Latin word *Incunabula* means "cradle" or "baby linen." Its connotations of birth or beginning caused seventeenth-century writers to adopt it as a name for books printed from Gutenberg's invention of typography until the end of the century. (This date is completely arbitrary; this chapter traces the logical continuation of design and typography into the early 1500s.) Printing's rapid spread is evidenced by the fact that by 1480, twenty-three northern European towns, thirty-one Italian towns, seven French towns, six Spanish and Portuguese towns, and one English town had presses. By 1500, printing was practiced in over 140 towns. It is estimated that over thirty-five thousand editions for a total of nine million books were produced. In 1450, Europe's monasteries and libraries housed a mere fifty thousand volumes. In addition, a vast array of ephemera—including religious tracts, pamphlets, and broadsides—was produced for free distribution or sale. Broadsides —single-leaf pages printed on one side—eventually evolved into printed posters, advertisements, and newspapers. Four years after printing came to Venice, a dismayed scribe complained that the city was "stuffed with books." The boom in this new craft led to overproduction and proliferation of firms. From the ranks of over one hundred printing firms established in Venice before 1490, only ten survived until the end of the century.

Printing was resisted in some quarters. The scribes in Genoa, Italy, banded together and demanded that the town council forbid printing in that town. They argued that greedy printers were threatening their livelihood. The council did not support the petition, and within two years Genoa joined the mushrooming list of towns with printers. Parisian illuminators filed suits in the courts in a vain attempt to win damages from printers who were engaged in unfair competition that caused the demand for manuscript books to decline. Some bibliophiles maintained that type was inferior to calligraphy and unworthy of their libraries. In 1492, a cardinal, who later became Pope Julius II, ordered scribes to handletter a copy of a typographic book for his library. But typographic printing reduced the cost of books to a fraction of their earlier cost and turned the serious shortage of books (and the knowledge they contained) into an abundance. The tide of progress could not be stayed, and manuscript production slowly declined. The philosopher Alfred N. Whitehead once observed that a major technical advance is a process that wrecks the society in which it occurs. Typography, the major communications advance between the invention of writing to that of electronic mass communications in the twentieth century, played a pivotal role in the social, economic, and religious upheavals that occurred during the fifteenth and sixteenth centuries. The modern nation developed as a result of the vigorous spirit of nationalism that swept over Europe and led to the American and French revolutions of the late eighteenth century. In addition to being a powerful vehicle to spread ideas about the rights of man and the sovereignty of the people, printing stabilized and unified languages. People all across France, for example, were reading the same material in the French language, which formerly had many provincial idiosyncrasies of spelling and grammar. The French, English, and German tongues became typographic mass media that communicated to audiences of unprecedented size with one voice. Illiteracy, the inability to read and write, began a long, steady decline. Literacy

73

was of limited value to a medieval peasant who had no hope of gaining access to books. But tumbling book prices, the beginnings of such popular writing as romantic novels, and the proliferation of the ever-present broadsheet made reading desirable and increasingly necessary for the Renaissance townspeople. The medieval classroom had been a scriptorium of sorts, where each student penned his own book. Typography radically altered education. Learning became an increasingly private, rather than communal, process. Human dialogue, extended by type, began to take place on a global scale that bridged time and space. Gutenberg's invention was the first mechanization of a skilled handicraft. As such, it set into motion, over the next three hundred years, the machinations that would lead to the industrial revolution.

The Renaissance innovators altered our perception of information by creating two visual systems. Painting evoked illusions of the natural world on flat surfaces through such means as the single light source and light and shadow modeling, the fixed viewpoint and linear perspective, and atmospheric perspective. Typography created a sequential and repeatable ordering of information and space. It led man toward linear thought and logic, and a categorization and compartmentalization of information that formed the basis for empirical scientific inquiry. It developed the individualism that has been a dominant aspect of Western society since the Renaissance.

As edition after edition of the Bible was published, increased study led men throughout Europe to formulate their own interpretations instead of relying on religious leaders as the locus of truth. This led directly to the Reformation, which shattered Christianity into hundreds of sects. After Martin Luther (c. 1483–1546) posted his ninety-five theses for debate on the door of Castle Church in Wittenberg, Germany, on 31 October 1517, his friends passed copies to printers. By December, his proclamation had spread throughout central Europe. Within a few months, thousands of people all over Europe knew his views. Without typography, it is doubtful that the Protestant movement of the Reformation era could have happened. Both Luther and Pope Leo X used printed broadsides and tracts in a theological dispute before a mass audience of the entire continent.

By the end of the Incunabula, presses had been established throughout Europe, but very few of these printers contributed to the development of graphic design. Most were content to print copies of manuscripts or earlier printed editions. Although the press replaced the copisti in producing the running text, the same division of labor found in the scriptorium continued. Multicolor printing was used in Fust and Schoeffer's *Psalter in Latin,* but rubrication, decoration, and illumination in early Incunabula books were almost always by hand. Perhaps the difficulties of multicolor printing made it more expensive, or maybe enough political pressure was generated by the rubricators and illuminators to allow them to continue their crafts on typographic books.

Design innovation took place in Germany, where woodcut artists and typographic printers collaborated to develop the illustrated book and broadsheet. In Italy, the letterstyles and format design inherited from illuminated manuscripts gave way to a design approach unique to the typographic book. Early printers followed the manuscript custom of putting the title and author at the top of the first page, in the same size and style of lettering as the text. A short space was skipped, then *Incipit* ("Here Begins") launched the book. Early in the Incunabula, a printed *ex libris,* or bookplate (Fig. 7-1), was pasted into the front of a book to identify the owner. As printing spread from Mainz, so did the use of the printer's trademark as a visual identifier.

Scribes and woodcut artists were often called upon to make *exemplars,* or layouts, for illustrated books and broadsides. Manuscript books have been discovered with editorial notes, marginal notes to indicate where typeset pages ended, inky fingerprints, and sketches for woodblocks. These indicate their use as a layout and manuscript for printed books. In one such manuscript, the scribe's colophon is scratched out, in the printed book it is replaced by a typeset version.

7-1. Ex libris design for Johannes Knabensberg, c. 1450s. One of the earliest extant bookplates, it bears an inscription, "Hans Igler that the hedgehog may kiss you." *Igler,* his nickname, is similar to the German word for *hedgehog,* making an early graphic pun.

7-2. Albrecht Pfister (printer), illustration from the second edition of *Der Ackerman aus Böhmen (The Farmer from Bohmen),* c. 1463. Death sits as a king on his throne, flanked by a widower and his child on the left, and the deceased wife on the right.

7-3. Günther Zainer (printer), illustration from *Spiegel des menschlichen Lebens*, 1475. In this illustration of a voice instructor, the triangular pattern on the tile floor introduces a lively tonal contrast.

.xiij.

De Marsepia & Lampedone reginis amazonū. C. xi

Arsepia seu marthesia & lampedo soro res fuere Amazonum inuicem regine/ & ob il lustrem bellox gloriam sese martis vocaué silias Quax qm pegrina sit historia paulo altr̃ assumēda est/ e scithia eigo ea rēpestate siluestri & fere in accessa exteris regione/ & sub artheo se in ocea num vsq ab eusino sinu ptendente / Siliscus & scolo picus(vt aiunt)regij iuuenes factione maiox pulsi cū parte pplox iuxta thermodohonté cappadocie amnem deuenē/& tirps occuparis aruis raptu viué & incolas latrocinijs infestare cepé, A quibus tractu temporis p insidias fere omnes trucidati sunt homines. Qō cum egrederent viduate coniuges/ & in ardoré vindicte de: ueniffent feruide/ cum paucis qui supuixerint viris in arma prorupere. Et primo impetu facto hostes a suis demouere fimbus/inde vltro circumstantibus intulere bellum/demum arbitrantes suiruté potius q̃ oiugiū/ si exteris adhererent hoinibus / & feminas solas posse

7-4. Johann Zainer, page from *De mulieribus claris* by Boccaccio, 1473. In this book about famous women, the woodcuts are all designed in rectangles the width of the type column and dropped in flush to it.

Origins of the illustrated typographic book

Block printers and woodcarvers feared typographic printing as a serious threat to their livelihood. But early in the evolution of the typographic book, Bamberg printer Albrecht Pfister began to illustrate his books with woodblock prints. About 1460, he used five woodblocks (Fig. 7-2) and the types from Gutenberg's thirty-six-line Bible to print his first edition of *Der Ackerman aus Böhmen (The Farmer from Böhmen)*. Pfister's nine editions of five books were popular literature, in contrast to the theological and scholarly works published by most other early printers. As the decades passed, typographic printers dramatically increased their use of woodblock illustrations. This created a booming demand for blocks, and the stature of graphic illustrators increased. Augsburg and Ulm, centers for woodblock playing card and religious print production, became centers for illustrated books. In the 1470s, Günther Zainer (d. 1478) established a press in Augsburg, and his relative Johann Zainer established one about 70 kilometers (43 miles) to the east at Ulm. Both were scribes and illuminators who had learned printing at Strasbourg.

Günther Zainer met resistance from the Augsburg woodcutter's guild when he wanted to illustrate his books with woodblocks. A 1471 agreement allowed Zainer to use woodblock illustrations as long as he commissioned them from members of the guild. His first illustrated books used a rounded Gothic type and woodblocks set into a type column of the same width. By 1475, his illustrated books, including *Spiegel des menschlichen Lebens (The Mirror of Life),* which analyzes the positive and negative aspects of various careers, used woodcuts with textured areas and some solid blacks (Fig. 7-3). This introduced a greater tonal range to the page design. Fortune smiled upon Günther Zainer, for the sale of over thirty-six thousand books printed in over a hundred editions enabled him to become one of Augsburg's most prominent and affluent citizens.

In Ulm, Johann Zainer used eighty woodcuts in his 1473 edition of *De mulieribus claris (Of Famous Women)* by Boccaccio (Fig. 7-4). These illustrations have a very even line weight, and the capital initials are printed rather than added later by hand. These are wonderful little woodblock letters formed by birds, snakes, and plants. Woodcuts were used over and over in different books. For example, the two hundred woodcuts in Johann Zainer's 1476 Aesop's *Vita et fabulae* appear again in the edition by Ulm printer Anton Sorg four years later (Fig. 7-5). Many of these illustrations are not completely enclosed with rectangular borders, which allows

The German Illustrated Book

Das viero puch   Das · xxxix.blat .

Die erst fabel von dem fuchs vmd dem trauben·

In fuchs lieff für ein hohe weinreben vmd
sabe daran hangen zeitig trauben·der begeret
er zeessen/vmd süchet manigerley wege
wie jm die traube werden möchten mit klimen
vmd springen·Aber sy stünden so hoch das sy jm
nit werden mochten·do er daz mercket lief er hinweg
vmd verkeret sein anfechtung vmd lust zü den traube
in freüde vmd sprache· Nun seind doch die trauben
noch sawer·Ich wölt sy auch nit essen/ob ich sy wol
möcht erlangen · Dise fabel bedeutet das ein weiser
man sol sich lassen beduncken/er wöl vn müg des nit.
das er nit gehaben mag.

Die ander fabel von der wisel vmd der müß.

7-6

7-5. Anton Sorg, page from Aesop's *Vita et fabulae,* c. 1479. Sorg used a wider column width than Zainer's earlier version of Aesop's *Fables* and tried to compensate for the lack of alignment between the woodcut and the type column by a margin of white space above and below the illustration.

7-6. Erhard Reuwich (illustrator), page from *Peregrinationes in montem Syon,* 1486. With his accurate observations and brilliant illustrations, Reuwich launched pictorial journalism.

7-7. George Alt, title page for the index to the *Nuremberg Chronicle,* 1493. This dazzling calligraphy reads, "Registry [index] for this Book of Chronicles with illustrations and portraits from the initiation of the world." The design for this woodblock is attributed to Alt (c. 1450–1510), a scribe who assisted Hartmann Schedel in lettering the Latin exemplar and translated the Latin manuscript into German for that version.

7-8. Anton Koberger, pages from the *Nuremberg Chronicle,* 1493. The raised hand of God in the initial illustration becomes a visual theme appearing over the next several pages that chronicle the biblical story of creation.

white space to flow from the wide margins into the pictures. Simple outline initials extend this light design effect. Typographic paragraph marks leave nothing for the rubricator in this volume; the printed book was becoming independent of the manuscript.

The first illustrator to be identified as such in a book was Erhard Reuwich, for his work in *Peregrinationes in montem Syon (Travels in Mount Syon),* printed with Schoeffer's types in 1486 (Fig. 7-6). Reuwich was a careful observer of nature who introduced cross-hatch illustration in this volume, which had fold-out illustrations, including a view of Venice that stretches out almost 1.5 meters (4 feet, 9 inches). The author of this interesting narrative, Bernardus de Breidenbach, traveled to the Holy Land and took Reuwich along to illustrate his writing.

Nuremberg becomes a printing center

Because printing required a huge capital investment and large trained labor force, it is not surprising that Nuremberg, which had become central Europe's prosperous center of commerce and distribution, housed Germany's most esteemed printer by the end of the century. Anton Koberger (c. 1440–1513) printed over two hundred editions, including fifteen Bibles, at his printing firm, which was staffed by a hundred craftsmen operating twenty-four presses. As a bookseller, he owned sixteen shops and had agents throughout Europe. By the 1490s, most printers had trouble selling large books and abandoned the huge format of the liturgical Bibles. They adopted smaller page sizes that were more convenient and economical for the private customer. Koberger, however, continued to publish and sell large books. As a printer working in concert with master illustrators, he produced three masterpieces. The 1491 *Schatzbehalter,* a religious treatise, contains ninety-two full-page woodcuts by the painter and woodcut illustrator Michael Wolgemuth (1434–1519).

Published in German and Latin versions in 1493, the six-hundred-page *Liber Chronicarum (Nuremberg Chronicle)* by Dr. Hartmann Schedel is an ambitious history of the world from the dawn of creation until 1493. One of the masterpieces of Incunabula graphic design, the *Nuremberg Chronicle* (Pl. 11 and Figs. 7-7 through 7-11) has 1,809 woodcut illustrations in its complex, carefully designed 47.5-by-32.7-centimeter (18¾-by-12⅞-inch) pages. The exemplars (a handmade model layout and manuscript text used as a guide for the woodcut illustrations, typesetting, page design, and makeup) for both editions survive and provide rare insight into the design and production process. The publishers contracted Michael Wolgemuth and his stepson, Wilhelm Pleydenwurff (d. 1494), to create the exemplars, draw the illustrations, and cut, correct, and prepare the woodblocks for printing. Also, one or the other had to be present at the printshop during typesetting and printing. For this work the artists were paid a one-thousand-guilder advance and guaranteed one-half of the net profits.

Because many woodcuts were used several times, only 645 different woodcuts were required. For example, 598 portraits of popes, kings, and other historical personages were printed from ninety-six blocks.

Koberger's contract required him to order and pay for paper, which had to be as good as or better than the sample he had supplied; print the book according to the exemplars in an acceptable type style; maintain the security of a locked room for the project; and provide a workroom for Wolgemuth and Pleydenwurff. Koberger was paid four guilders for every ream (five hundred sheets) of four-page sheets printed. During the months of production, Koberger could bill the publishers periodically for portions of the book that had been printed and gathered into twelve-page, three-sheet signatures.

The exemplars or layouts for the *Nuremberg Chronicle* are the work of several "sketch artists" and numerous scribes, whose lettering in the exemplar has the same character count as the typefont to ensure an accurate conversion. The variety and diversity of page layouts range from a full double-page illustration of the city

7-7

7-10. Anton Koberger, pages from the *Nuremberg Chronicle,* 1493. This complex layout is ordered by the use of rules around the illustrations. These convert the silhouette images into rectangles, which can be tightly fitted with the rectangles of type.

7-9. Anton Koberger, pages from the *Nuremberg Chronicle,* 1493. As the story of the creation unfolds, it is illustrated by symbolic circular designs contained in a square ruled line.

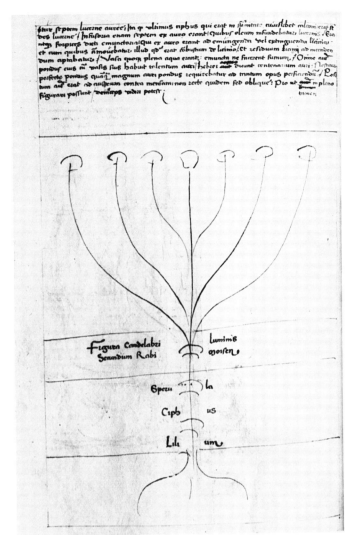

7-11. Studio of Michael Wolgemuth and Wilhelm Pleydenwurff, pages from the *Nuremberg Chronicle*, Latin exemplar, pre-1493. This layout and manuscript provided guidance for the compositors, although liberties were taken in the final layout.

of Nuremberg to unillustrated type pages. On some pages, woodcuts are inserted into the text; on others, woodcuts are lined into horizontal columns. Rectangular illustrations are placed under or above type areas. When the layout threatens to become repetitious, the reader is jolted by an unexpected page design. The dense texture and rounded strokes of Koberger's sturdy Gothic types contrast handsomely with the tones of the woodcuts. The illustrators' imaginations enabled them to create unseen monstrosities, unvisited cities, awful tortures, and to express the story of creation in graphic symbols.

Koberger was godfather to Albrecht Dürer (1471–1528), whose goldsmith father apprenticed him to Michael Wolgemuth for almost four years beginning in 1486. Perhaps the young Dürer, who grew up three houses down the street in Nuremburg from Wolgemuth's home and studio, assisted in the layout and illustration for the *Nuremberg Chronicle*.

In 1498, publication of Latin and German editions of *The Apocalypse* (Fig. 7-12), which contain Dürer's monumental sequence of fifteen woodcuts illustrating St. John's Revelation, brought the twenty-seven-year-old graphic artist and painter fame throughout Europe. This thirty-two-page book with 44.5-by-30.5-centimeter (17½-by-12-inch) pages has fifteen layouts with two columns of Koberger's gothic type on the left, facing one of Dürer's illustrations on the right. Dürer's *Apocalypse* has an unprecedented emotional power and graphic expressiveness. Volume and depth, light and shadow, texture and surface are created by black ink on white paper, which becomes a metaphor for light in a turbulent world of awesome powers.

7-13. Albrecht Dürer, title page for *The Life of the Virgin,* 1511. Dürer's mature work achieved a mastery in the use of line as tone. A linear sunburst effect surrounds "The Virgin in Glory" with a dazzling luminosity seldom achieved with black ink on white paper. The triangular shape of the title above the illustration echoes the angular lines radiating from the figures, and the text below repeats the horizontal sky tone below the figures.

The colophon reads, "Printed by Albrecht Dürer." Given his prodigious volume of prints, we may assume that he had a press in his workshop. Since the types used are Koberger's, we don't know if Dürer acquired set type from his godfather and printed the *Apocalypse,* printed the blocks and sent the sheets to Koberger's shop for typographic imprinting, or commissioned Koberger to print the edition under Dürer's supervision.

In 1511, Dürer issued a new edition of the *Apocalypse* and published two other large-format volumes, the *Large Passion* and *The Life of the Virgin* (Fig. 7-13). Dürer's broadsides were very popular, and at least eight editions of his rhinoceros (Fig. 7-14) went out of print.

Trips to Venice for six months at age twenty-three and for one and a half years when he was thirty-four enabled Dürer to absorb the painting theory and technique, as well as the humanist philosophy, of the Italian Renaissance. Dürer became a major influence in the cultural exchange that saw the Renaissance spirit filter into Germany. His feeling that German artists and craftsmen produced inferior work to the Italians because they lacked the theoretical knowledge of their

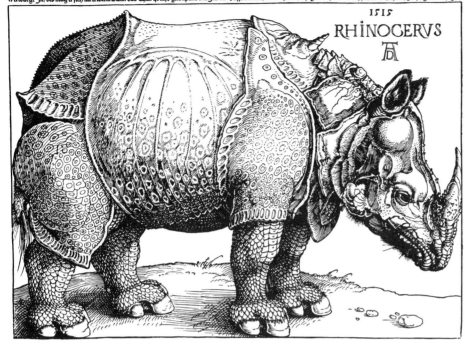

1515
RHINOCERVS

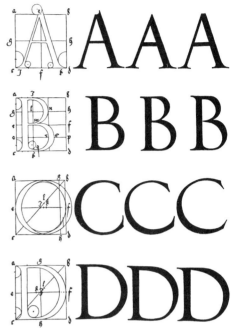

7-14. Albrecht Dürer, broadside, 1515. Dürer developed his woodcut illustration from a sketch and description sent from Spain, after the first rhinoceros in over a thousand years arrived in Europe. The text was undoubtedly carefully edited so that the five lines of metal type form a perfect rectangle of tone that aligns with the woodcut border.

7-15. Albrecht Dürer, from *Underweisung der Messung,* 1525. Dürer presented variations for each character in the alphabet. Recognizing the value of art and perception over geometry, Dürer advised his readers that certain construction faults could only be corrected by a sensitive eye and trained hand.

fellow professionals to the south inspired Dürer to author the first of his three books, *Underweisung der Messung mit dem Zirckel und Richtscheyt* (*A course in the Art of Measurement with Compass and Ruler*) in 1525. The first two chapters are theoretical discussions of linear geometry and two-dimensional geometric construction. The third chapter explains the application of geometry to architecture, decoration, engineering, and letterforms. Dürer's beautifully proportioned Roman capitals with clear instructions for their construction made a significant contribution to the evolution of alphabet design (Fig. 7-15). Relating each letter to the square, Dürer worked out a construction method using a one-to-ten ratio of the heavy stroke to the height. This is the approximate proportion of the Trajan alphabet, but Dürer did not base his designs on any single source. This book also presents his modular system for textura, the German manuscript hand. It begins with a lowercase *i*, which is composed of six stacked squares with the top and bottom units tilted to form the serifs. From this construction, Dürer proceeds to build an entire alphabet (Fig. 7-16). The fourth chapter covers the construction of geometric solids, linear perspective, and mechanical aids to drawing (Fig. 7-17).

The illustrated book *De Symmetria Partium Humanorum Corporum (Treatise on Human Proportions)* (Fig. 7-18), which first appeared in Nuremberg shortly after Dürer's death in 1528, shared Dürer's tremendous knowledge of drawing, the human figure, and the advances of Italian Renaissance artists with German painters and graphic artists.

7-16. Albrecht Dürer, page from *Underweisung der Messung,* 1525. This diagram illustrates Dürer's modular system for constructing a gothic alphabet.

The German Illustrated Book

7-17. Albrecht Dürer, page from *Underweisung der Messung,* 1525. This mechanical aid in drawing, explained by Dürer, consists of a frame device for drawing foreshortened perspective views of objects.

7-18. Albrecht Dürer, woodcut from *De Symmetria Partium Humanorum Corporum,* 1532. To assist his fellow artists, Dürer offers a "through-the-looking-grid" device as an aid to drawing.

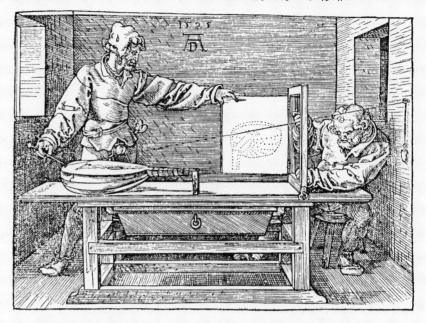

7-17

7-18

The further development of the German illustrated book

While graphic artists and printers in Italy and France evolved toward Renaissance book design (discussed in the next chapter), German graphic design continued its tradition of textura typography and vigorous woodcut illustrations. One of Dürer's former students, Hans Schäufelien, was commissioned to design the illustrations for Pfintzing's *Teuerdank* (Fig. 7-19), an adventure of chivalry and knighthood that was printed by Johann Schoensperger the Elder at Nuremberg in 1517. Commissioned by Emperor Maximilian to commemorate his marriage to Mary of Bur-

7-19. Johann Schoensperger (printer), pages from *Teuerdank,* 1517. The flamboyant calligraphic gestures are appropriate for this romantic novel about chivalry. The swashes are carefully placed to animate the pages in the layout of the book.

gundy, this lavish book required five years in production time. The types for *Teuerdank,* designed by court calligrapher Vincenz Rockner, were one of the earliest examples of the Gothic style known as *fraktur.* Some of the rigid, angular straight lines found in textura letterforms were replaced with flowing curved strokes. In comparing the design qualities of Rockner's fraktur with Gutenberg's textura (see Fig. 6-12), one might almost say that flowers and vines are now growing on the picket fence to soften the overall effect.

Rockner carried this design quality even further in a heroic effort to duplicate the gestural freedom of the pen. As many as eight alternate characters were designed and cast for each letterform. These had sweeping calligraphic flourishes, some of which flowed deep into the surrounding space. Other printers insisted that these ornamental letterforms had to be printed from woodblocks, for they refused to believe that it was possible to achieve these effects with cast metal types. (An inverted *i* in the 1517 edition, however, conclusively proves that metal types were used to print *Teuerdank.*)

Technically speaking, a *broadside* is a single leaf of paper printed on one side only. When both sides are printed, the usual designation is a *broadsheet.* When the printed sheet is folded, a pamphlet, tract—and later, a newspaper—is the result. This ubiquitous and ephemeral form of graphic communications became a major means for information dissemination from the invention of printing until the middle of the nineteenth century. Content ranged from announcements of deformed births and natural phenomena to portraits of famous secular and religious leaders

7-20

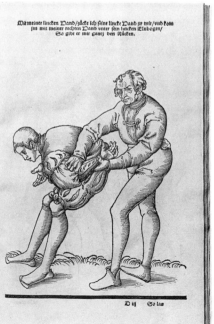

7-20. Grunenberg (printer) and Lucas Cranach the Elder (illustrator), pages from *Passional Christi und Antichristi*, 1521. In a biting visual contrast of travel, Christ labors under the weight of his cross while the Pope travels in style in a sedan chair.

7-21. Hans Lufft (printer) and Lucas Cranach the Younger (illustrator), pages from Auerswald's *Ringer-Kunst*, 1539. In this how-to-do-it book on the art of wrestling, Lufft printed Cranach's eighty-seven woodcuts without the usual border. This enables them to move dynamically on the page. The centered captions above and thick rule below restore balance in this predominantly pictorial book.

7-21

(see Fig. 7-22). Festivals and fairs were advertised, and the sale of lottery tickets and indulgences were announced. Political causes and religious beliefs were expounded, and invasions and disasters were proclaimed. The design of a broadside was often the task of the compositor, who organized the space and made typographic decisions while setting the type. Woodblock illustrations were commissioned from artists. Once available, a given woodblock might appear in a number of broadsides, or be sold or loaned to another printer.

As Martin Luther pressed his breach with the Catholic Church that began in 1517, his presence at the university in Wittenberg brought importance to the graphics produced there. Luther found a fast friend and follower in the artist Lucas Cranach the Elder (1472–1553), who had been called to Wittenberg by the electors of Saxony. In addition to his studio with a number of well-trained assistants, Cranach operated a printing office, a bookshop, and a paper mill, and even found time to serve as mayor of Wittenberg twice. He turned his considerable energy to the Reformation by portraying the Reformers and their cause in books and broadsides. When Luther traveled to Worms for his celebrated trial in 1521, his portraits by Cranach filled the town on printed matter proclaiming his beliefs. And yet, Cranach regularly accepted commissions for Madonnas and Crucifixions from Catholic clients, and many of the woodcuts he produced for the Luther Bible were also used in a subsequent Catholic edition. A most effective example of propaganda is Cranach's work for the *Passional Christi und Antichristi* (Fig. 7-20), printed by Grunenberg in 1521. Inspired by Luther, graphic contrast is achieved on facing pages as scenes from the life of Christ and biting depictions of the papacy are juxtaposed. Both of Cranach's sons, Hans Cranach (d. 1537) and Lucas Cranach the Younger (1515–1586), joined their father's studio; few examples of Hans's work remain, but the younger son continued to work in the family style for many years after his father's death (Figs. 7-21 and 7-22). The epitaph on Lucas Cranach the Elder's tomb honors him as *pictor celerrimus*—the swiftest of painters!

Typography spreads from Germany

Italy, which was at the forefront of Europe's slow transition from the medieval world into a cultural and commercial revival, sponsored the first printing press to be set up outside of Germany. Although fifteenth-century Italy was a political patchwork of city-states, monarchies, republics, and papal domains, it was at the zenith of its wealth and splendid patronage of the arts and architecture in the Renaissance. In 1465, Cardinal Turrecremata of the Benedictine monastery at Subiaco invited two printers, Conrad Sweynheym (d. 1477) of Mainz, who had been employed by Peter Schoeffer, and Arnold Pannartz (d. 1476) of Cologne, to Subiaco to establish a press. The Cardinal wished to publish Latin classics and his own writings.

The types designed by Sweynheym and Pannartz (Fig. 7-23) marked the first step toward roman-style typography based on the humanistic writing that had been developed by Italian scribes. These scholars had discovered copies of lost Roman classics written in ninth-century Caroline minuscules. They mistakenly thought that authentic Roman writing had been discovered in contrast to the black, medieval writing that they erroneously believed to be the writing style of the barbarians who had destroyed Rome. Sweynheym and Pannartz created a typographic "double alphabet" by combining the capital letters of ancient Roman inscriptions with the rounded minuscules that had evolved in Italy from the Caroline minuscule. They tried to unify these contradictory alphabets by adding serifs to some of the minuscule letters and redesigning others. After three years in Subiaco, Sweynheym and Pannartz moved to Rome, where they designed a more fully roman alphabet that became the prototype for the roman alphabets still in use today. By 1473, the partnership had printed over fifty editions, usually in press runs of 275 copies. Ten Italian cities also had printers publishing Latin classics, and the market could not absorb the sudden supply of books. The partnership of Sweynheym and Pannartz suffered a financial collapse and was dissolved.

7-22. Lucas Cranach the Younger, broadside, 1551. This commemorative portrait of Martin Luther bears the identification of the illustrator (Cranach's flying snake device) and the block cutter, a craftsman named Jörg, who is identified typographically above the date.

The German Illustrated Book

bat ille ihefus:q quom p̄mū aufes uocaret moifes figurā
ihefum uocari: ut dux miliṭiẹ delectus effet aduerfus am
nabant filios ifrabel: et aduerfariū debellaret p noīs figu

effe fenfum femitaf quẹ̄tur. tanq̄ illi ad cogita
quadrigif opuf eēt. Democrituf quafi in puteo q
ut funduffit nulluf: ueritatem iacere demerfam

7-23. Conrad Sweynheym and Arnold Pannartz, specimens of the first (top, 1465) and second (bottom, 1467) typefaces in the evolution toward roman-style typefaces are shown near original size.

Early volumes printed in Italy continued the pattern of the early German printed books. Initials, folios, headings, and paragraph marks were not printed. Space was left for these to be rubricated by a scribe with red ink. Often, a small letter would be printed in the space left for an illuminated initial to tell the scribe what initial to draw. In many volumes from the Incunabula, the paragraph marks were not drawn in red in the spaces provided. Eventually, the blank space alone indicated a paragraph.

After apprenticing in the English textile trade, William Caxton (c. 1421–1491) left his native land for the textile center of Bruges in the low countries, where he prospered. In the early 1470s, he spent a year and a half in Cologne, where he translated the *Recuyell of the Histories of Troy* from French into English, and learned printing. On returning to Bruges, he enlisted the help of the illuminator and calligrapher Colard Mansion, and in 1475 Caxton's translation became the first typographic English language book. In the epilogue to the third part, Caxton tells the reader that "my pen is worn, my hand is weary and shaky, my eyes are dimmed from too much looking at white paper"; thus he "practiced and learned at great expense how to print it."

After printing an English translation of *The Game and Playe of the Chesse* (1476) and two or three French language books, the partners separated (Fig. 7-24). Mansion remained in Bruges and printed twenty-seven editions before 1484, when he was forced to flee the city to escape his creditors. Caxton moved his types and press across the English Channel and established the first press on English soil. He had printed the first book in English; now he printed the first book in England, at the Sign of the Red Pail in Westminster.

The roughly ninety books that he published in Westminster encompassed nearly all the major English literature up to the fifteenth century, including Chaucer's *Canterbury Tales* and Sir Thomas Malory's *Morte d'Arthur*. He is a pivotal figure in the development of a national English language, for his typographic work stabilized and unified the constantly changing, diverse dialects in use throughout the islands. Primarily a scholar and translator, Caxton contributed little to the evolution of graphic design and printing, as his work had a crude vigor devoid of graphic elegance or refinement. Woodcut illustrations from his volumes have a brash forcefulness and awkward drawing, and the workmanship of his printing is inferior to continental printing of the same period. Caxton's printer's mark (Fig. 7-25) evokes the carpets woven at Bruges, and a broadside advertising one of his books is the earliest extant English poster (Fig. 7-26).

After Caxton's death, his foreman, Wynkyn de Worde, continued his work and published nearly four hundred titles over the following four decades.

Printing came to France in 1470 when three German printers—Michael Freiburger, Ulrich Gering, and Martin Kranz—were sponsored by the Prior and the Librarian of the Sorbonne to establish a press there. At first they used a roman letter (Fig. 7-27), inspired by Italian types, and reprinted classics, but after they lost their Sorbonne sponsorship in 1473, they began to print with Gothic types that were more familiar to their French audience. The inevitable competition appeared

7-24. William Caxton and Colard Mansion, page from *The Game and Playe of the Chesse*, c. 1476. The kinky, jerky type used by Caxton ushered the era of the typographic book into the British nation.

7-25. William Caxton, printer's trademark, after 1477.

7-26. William Caxton, advertising poster/ handbill, 1477. A copy of this announcement for "Pyes of Salisbury Use" in a Manchester, England, library bears a handwritten request, "Pray, do not pull down the advertisement."

7-27. Michael Freiburger, Ulrich Gering, and Martin Kranz, first page of *Letters* by Gaspari, 1470. In this first book printed in Paris, the ornamental woodcuts and rude roman typography are harbingers of the golden era of French typography that bloomed after the turn of the century.

This first chapiter of the first tractate sheweth vnder
what kynge the play of the chesse was founden and
maad .:.

Monge all the euyll condicions and signes
that may be in a man the first and þ grettest
is whan he feereth not/ne dredeth to displese
and make wroth god by synne / and the
peple by lyuyng disordynatly/whan he rec-
cheth not / ner taketh hede vnto them that repreue hym
and his vices/But sleeth them/In suche wyse as dide the
emperour Nero/whiche dide do slee his maister seneque.
For as moche as he might not suffre to be repreuid and
taught of hym In lyke wyse was somtyme a kynge in
Babiloine that was named Emsmerodach a Jolye man
with oute Justice and so cruell that he dyde do hewe his
faders body in thre honderd pieces / And gaf hit to ete
and deuour to thre honderd birdes that men calle wultres
And was of suche condicion as was Nero/And right
well resembled and was lyke vnto his fader Nabogo-
donosor / whiche on a tyme wold do slee alle the sage
and wyse men of Babylonye / For as moche as they
coude not telle hym his dreme that he had dremed on a
nyght and had forgoten hit lyke as it is wreton in the
bible in the book of danyell / Vnder this kynge than
Emsmerodach was this game and playe of the chesse
founden/Trewe it is that some men wene/that this playe
was founden in the tyme of the bataylles & siege of troye
But that is not soo For this playe cam to the playes of
the caldees as dyomedes the greek sayth and rehercceth .
That amonge the philosophrs was the most renomed
playe amonge all other playes/ And after that/cam this

7-24

7-25

Galparini pergamensis clarissimi orato'
ris/epistolaru̅ liber foeliciter incipit.

Audeo plurimum ac lætor in
ea te sentêtia esse:ut nihil a
me fieri sine causa putef.Ego
eni̅ etsi multos uerebar suspi
tionef,q̃ a me semproniu̅ antiquu̅ fami
liare meu̅ reiieieba̅:tame̅ cu̅ ad incredibi
le animi tui sapiêtia̅ iudiciu̅ meu̅ refere̅
ba̅:nihil erat q̃re id a te improbari pu
tarem·Nam cum & meos nossef mores:&
illius natura̅ n̅ ignorares:n̅ dubitaba̅ qd
de hoc facto meo iudicaturus esses. Non
igit̅ hac ad te scribo lrãs/quo nouam tibi
de rebus a me gestis opinionem facia̅:sed
ut si quando aliter homies nostros de me
sentire intelliges:tu q probe causam mea̅
nosti,defensione mea̅ suscipias·Hæc si fe
ceris:nihil est quo ulterius officium tu'
um requitam·Vale ;

7-27

If it plese ony man spirituel or temporel to bye ony
pyes of two and thre comemoracio̅s of salisburi vse
enpryntid after the forme of this preset lettre whiche
ben wel and truly correct,late hym come to westmo-
nester in to the almonesrye at the reed pale and he shal
haue them good chepe .·.

Supplico stet cedula

7-26

before long. Nowhere else in Europe did block printers and typographic printers join forces in an attempt to duplicate the design of illuminated manuscripts as in France. Late Gothic illumination was the zenith of French art at that time, and early French printing surrounded its Gothic type and woodcut illustrations with modular blocks that filled the space with flowers and leaves, birds and animals, patterns, and portraits. Jean Dupré printed France's first outstanding typographic book, St. Augustine's *La Cité de Dieu*, in 1486. Philippe Pigouchet's *Horae* (*Book of Hours*) (1485–1515) established the graphic excellence of this popular form (Fig. 7-28). He appears to have introduced the *criblé* technique, in which the black areas of a woodblock are punched with white dots, giving the page a lively tonality.

Spain also received three German printers, who arrived in Valencia in 1473 under the auspices of a major, German import–export firm. The Spanish design sense, which favored dark masses balancing decorative detail, influenced their graphic design, particularly their large woodblock title pages (Fig. 7-29). A particular masterpiece of Spanish typographic design is Arñao Guillen de Brocar's *Polyglot Bible* (Fig. 7-30) of 1514–1517. Composed of correlated texts in multiple languages, this massive research project drew scholars from all over Europe to the

7-29. Diego de Gumiel, title page for *Aureum Opus*, 1515. The title almost becomes an afterthought in this title page. The use of white on black woodblocks and heraldic imagery is typical of early Spanish graphic design.

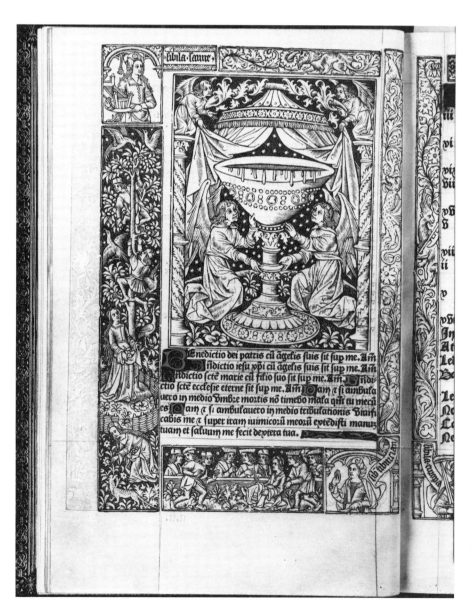

7-28. Philippe Pigouchet, page from *Horae Beatus Virginis Mariae*, 1498. The dense complexity of illustration, typography, and ornaments compressed into the space is typical of Pigouchet's design style.

7-30

7-31

University of Alcalá de Henares. The printer had to design a page format to accommodate five simultaneous typographic presentations.

Christopher Columbus discovered the New World in 1492, and a spice-laden but badly leaking vessel, *Victoria,* limped back to Portugal with the seventeen survivors of Ferdinand Magellan's expedition to circumnavigate the globe in 1522. An energetic competition by European nations to colonize new territory began. A missionary zeal for converting the natives in the colonies to Christianity characterized this expansion. On Columbus' second voyage, a Roman Catholic priest was on board. In 1539, the Franciscan archbishop in Mexico, Juan de Zumarraga, made arrangements to establish the first printing press in the New World for the instruction and conversion of the Indians. An Italian printer, Giovanni Paoli (Juan Pablos in Spanish), contracted to sail to Mexico, establish a press, and remain for a decade. His first works are lost to history; the earliest known survivor is the 1540 *Manual de Adultos* (Fig. 7-31), which was published a century before the first printing press was established in British North America.

During the remarkable first decades of typography, German printers and graphic artists established a national tradition of the illustrated book and spread the new medium of communication throughout Europe and even to the New World. Simultaneously, a cultural renaissance emerged in Italy and swept graphic design in unprecedented new directions.

7-30. Arñao Guillen de Brocar, page from the *Polyglot Bible,* 1514–1517. The grid system developed for this volume used uneven columns to compensate for the different running lengths of the different languages.

7-31. Giovanni Paoli, page from *Manual de Adultos* by Juan de Zumarraga, 1540. In this earliest extant book printed in America, Paoli established a handsome rhythm by indenting every other line.

Renaissance Graphic Design

8-1. Johannes de Spira, typography from Pliny the Elder's *Historia Naturalis,* 1469. The vertical stress and sharp angles of textura that remained in Sweynheym and Pannartz's fonts yielded to an organic unity of horizontal, vertical, diagonal, and circular forms.

8-2. Nicolas Jenson, typography from Eusebius's *De Praeparatione Evangelica,* 1470. A new standard of excellence was established with wider letterforms, lighter tone, and a more even texture of black strokes on the white ground.

The word *Renaissance* means "revival" or "rebirth." Originally, this term was used to denote the period that began in the fourteenth and fifteenth centuries in Italy, when the classical literature of ancient Greece and Rome was revived and read anew. Frequently, however, the word is used to encompass the period marking the transition from the medieval world to the modern world. In the history of graphic design, the renaissance of classical literature and the work of the Italian humanists are closely bound to an innovative approach to book design. Type design, page layout, ornaments, illustration, and even the total design of the book were all rethought by Italian printers and scholars. The prototype roman alphabet designs of Sweynheym and Pannartz (see Fig. 7-23) and the coarse decorative borders of early French books (see Fig. 7-27) were the first tentative steps toward a unique, Renaissance design style. The flowering of a new approach to the design of the book that was independent of the German illustrated book started in Venice and continued there during the last three decades of the fifteenth century.

Graphic design of the Italian Renaissance

It was not Florence, where the wealthy Medicis scorned printing as inferior to manuscript books, but Venice—the center of commerce and Europe's gateway to trade with the eastern Mediterranean nations, India, and the Orient—that led the way in Italian typographic book design. A Mainz goldsmith, Johannes de Spira (d. 1470), was given a five-year monopoly on printing in Venice, publishing his first book, *Epistolae ad Familiares* by Cicero, in 1469. His innovative and handsome roman type (Fig. 8-1) cast off some of the gothic qualities found in the fonts of Sweynheym and Pannartz, and he claimed that it was an original invention. In partnership with his brother, Vindelinus, de Spira's 1470 edition of *De Civitate Dei* was the first typographic book with printed page numbers. Vindelinus de Spira inherited his brother's press—but not the exclusive right to printing in Venice—upon Johannes de Spira's untimely death.

Nicolas Jenson (c. 1420–1480), from France, who had been Master of the Royal Mint of Tours, was a highly skilled cutter of dies used for striking coin. He established Venice's second press shortly after de Spira's death. In 1458, King Charles VII of France had sent Jenson to Mainz to learn printing. It has been said that

Nam ut reiectio facta est clamoribus maximis: primis postul ectione ille effugare non poterat: qui mesti inter sui dissimiles sed iudicium si queris quale fuerit: incredibili exitu: sicundatur.

8-1

Hæc igitur ispiciés diuinus ille uir mœnibus ferreis & iuiolabili a cæteris gétibus separe nos uoluit: quo pacto facilius corpore a imaculatos lógeqȝ ab huiuscemodi falsis opinioibus remotos for

8-2

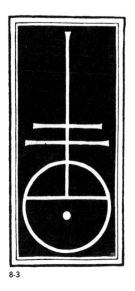

8-3   8-4   8-5

8-3. Attributed to Nicolas Jenson, mark for
The Society of Venetian Printers, 1481. One
of man's oldest symbols, the orb-and-cross
motif is found in a chamber of Cheop's
pyramid at Giza, where it was hewn into
stone as a quarry mark. In Jenson's time it
symbolized that "God shall reign over earth."

8-4. Laurentius de Rubeis, printer's mark,
1482. This orb and cross was designed in the
town of Ferrara located about 90 kilometers
(55 miles) southwest of Venice.

8-5. Pere Miguel, printer's mark, 1494.
Dozens of Incunabula printers adopted an
orb-and-cross mark. Miguel worked in
Barcelona, Spain.

Jenson chose not to return to France after Louis XI ascended to the French throne
in 1461. Jenson's fame as one of history's greatest typeface designers and punch
cutters rests on the types first used in Eusebius's *De Praeparatione Evangelica*,
which was the full flowering of roman type design (Fig. 8-2).

Part of the lasting influence of Jenson's fonts is their extreme legibility, but it
was his ability to design the spaces between the letters and within each form to
create an even tone throughout the page that places the mark of genius on his
work. During the last decade of his life, Jenson designed outstanding Greek and
Gothic fonts and printed approximately 150 books that brought him financial success and artistic renown. The characters in Jenson's fonts aligned more perfectly
than those of any other printer of his time.

The Renaissance had a love for floral decoration. Wildflowers and vines were
applied to furniture, architecture, and the manuscript. The book continued to be a
collaboration between a typographic printer—in the Incunabula period typography
was sometimes called "artificial writing"—and the illuminator who added initials
and ornaments. The logical evolution was to print everything on a printing press.
Many early printers designed trademarks to identify their books (Figs. 8-3 through
8-5). Erhard Ratdolt (1442–1528) achieved significant design innovations toward a
totally printed book. A master printer from Augsburg, Germany, Ratdolt worked in
Venice from 1476 until 1486. Working closely with his partners, Bernhard Maler
and Peter Loeslein, Ratdolt's 1476 *Calendarium* by Regiomontanus had the first
complete title page used to identify the book (Fig. 8-6). In addition to the innovative title page, *Calendarium* contained sixty diagrams of solar and lunar eclipses
printed in yellow and black. These used a grid system of metal rules to bring order
and legibility to this record of past and future eclipses (Pl. 12). Fear and superstition were being swept away, as scientists began to understand natural phenomena,
and printers disseminated this knowledge. Eclipses moved from black magic to
predictable fact. In the rear of the book, there is a three-part mathematical wheel
for calculating the solar cycles (Fig. 8-7).

Yet another innovation by Ratdolt is the way woodcut borders and initials were
used as design elements. These decorative designs include naturalistic forms inspired by western antiquity and more patterned forms derived from the eastern
Islamic cultures. Partner Bernhard Maler (also called Pictor) was probably the
designer of these borders. Both fine-line ornaments and reversed designs (white
forms on a solid background) were used; sometimes, these were printed in red ink.
A three-sided woodcut border used on the title page for a number of Ratdolt's editions became a kind of trademark. It is used in the title page of Euclid's *Geometriae
elementa* of 1482 (Fig. 8-8). This geometry book's format design uses a large outer
margin about half as wide as the text column width (Fig. 8-9). Small geometric

8-6. Erhard Ratdolt, Peter Loeslein, and
Bernhard Maler, title page for *Calendarium*
by Regiomontanus, 1476. The title and
author are identified in verse describing the
book. The date and printers' names in Latin
appear below.

Renaissance Graphic Design

8-7. Erhard Ratdolt, Peter Loeslein, and Bernhard Maler, pages from *Calendarium* by Regiomontanus, 1476. The three-part diagram on the left is similar in structure to a contemporary proportion wheel. The two top circles are printed on heavy paper, cut out, and mounted over the larger woodcut with tape and a string. This may be the first "die-cut" and hand tip-in graphic material in a printed book.

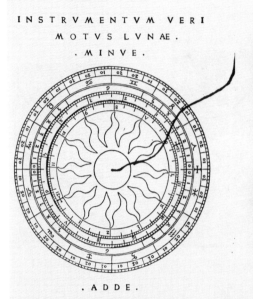

8-8. Erhard Ratdolt, Peter Loeslein, and Bernhard Maler, title page for Euclid's *Geometriae elementa,* 1482. A dazzling "white-on-black" design brackets the text, and incredibly fine line diagrams in the wide margin visually define Euclid's terms.

LIBER

Propofitio .36.

[Euclid diagram and Latin text in Gothic type]

Propofitio· .1.

8-9. Erhard Ratdolt, Peter Loeslein, and
Bernhard Maler, page from Euclid's
Geometriae elementa, 1482. The wide outer
margin is maintained throughout the book
for explanatory diagrams. Two sizes of initial
letters denote sections and subsections.

8-10. Giovanni and Alberto Alvise, title page
from *Ars Moriendi*, 1478. The vocabulary of
graphic design possibilities was expanded by
the design and casting of metal decorative
ornaments which could be composed as part
of the page along with type.

figures, whose sheer delicacy of line represents a technical breakthrough, are
placed in these margins adjacent to the supporting text.

When Ratdolt decided to leave Venice and return to his native Augsburg, he
publicized his return by issuing the first printer's type specimen sheet. This
showed his range of typographic sizes and styles. Ratdolt remained an active
printer until his death at age eighty-one. The innovations of Ratdolt and his partners during his decade in Venice were not immediately adopted by other Venetian
printers. The full flowering of graphic decoration in the printed book did not begin
until the turn of the century.

The *Ars Moriendi* was a best seller during the fifteenth century. At least sixty-
five editions including manuscripts, blockbooks, and typographic books were produced before 1501. An edition published on 28 April 1478 by the Italian printers
Giovanni and Alberto Alvise in Verona is believed to be the first design that used
printers' flowers (fleurons), which are decorative elements cast like type. The Verona *Ars Moriendi* used these as graphic elements in the title-page design and as
fillers in short lines that left blank areas in the text blocks (Fig. 8-10).

Quite possibly, a printer identified as Johannes Nicolai de Verona, who printed a
manual on warfare entitled *De re militari* by Roberto Valturio in 1472, was Giovanni Alvise. If so, he scored an earlier design innovation; the light contour style of

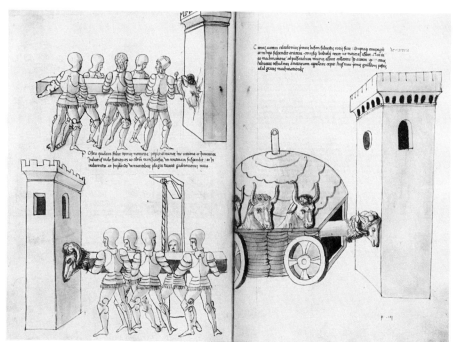

8-11. Manuscript book of Roberto Valturio's *De re militari*, undated. Freely drawn in brown pen and ink, the illustrations have brown and ochre washes applied.

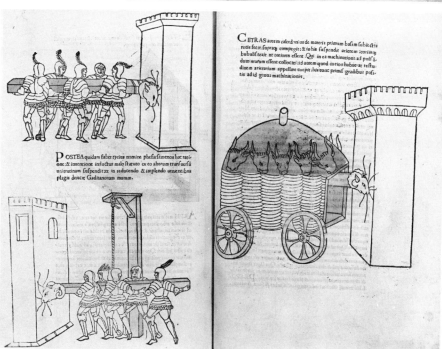

8-12. Johannes Nicolai de Verona (printer), pages from Roberto Valturio's *De re militari*, 1472. Detail and gestural line quality are lost in the translation from manuscript original to printed volume, but the basic layout remains the same.

woodblock illustration used in *De re militari* initiated the fine-line style that became popular in Italian graphic design during the later decades of the fifteenth century.

A fascinating manuscript copy of *De re militari* (Figs. 8-11 and 8-12) shows the relationship between the typographic book and the manuscript books which were used as exemplars or layouts. This manuscript book is written in semi-Gothic script, but has marginal corrections in a roman hand. Because these corrections are incorporated by the printer, it is believed that this manuscript version was corrected by the author. Then, it was used as corrected copy by the compositors, as a layout by the blockcutters, and as a guide for page design and makeup by the pressman.

This extraordinary book, a manual on warfare, is a compendium of the latest techniques and devices (many imaginary) for scaling walls, catapulting missiles, ramming fortifications, and torturing enemies. The page designs are unique. The text is set in a tight column with wide outer margins, and the freely shaped images sprawl across the pages in dynamic asymmetrical layouts. In the spread showing battering rams, the repetition of the towers and rams' heads gives the pages a lively visual rhythm.

Medieval Christianity fostered a belief that the value of human life was primarily its effect on God's judgment after death. A turning away from medieval beliefs toward a new concern for human potential and value characterized Renaissance *humanism,* a philosophy of human dignity and worth that defined man as capable of using reason and scientific inquiry to achieve both an understanding of the world and self-meaning. This new spirit was accompanied by a renewed study of classical writings from Greek and Roman cultures. An important humanist and scholar of the Italian Renaissance, Aldus Manutius (1450–1515), established a printing press in Venice at age forty-five to realize his vision: He would publish the major works of the great thinkers of the Greek and Roman world. Important scholars and skilled technical personnel were recruited to staff his Aldine Press, which rapidly became known for its editorial authority and scholarship. From 1494 until 1498, a five-volume edition of Aristotle was published.

A most important member of the Aldine staff was Francesco da Bologna, surnamed Griffo (1450–1518). Manutius called this brilliant typeface designer and punch cutter to Venice, where Griffo cut Roman, Greek, Hebrew and the first italic types for Aldine editions. His initial project in Venice was a roman face for *De Aetna* (Fig. 8-13) by Pietro Bembo in 1495. Griffo researched pre-Caroline scripts to produce a roman type that was more authentic than Jenson's designs. This style survives today as the book text face Bembo.

While the German 15th century closed with Koberger and Dürer creating a technical and artistic masterpiece in *The Apocalypse,* in Italy Aldus Manutius ended the epoch with his 1499 edition of Fra Francesco Colonna's *Hypnerotomachia Poliphili* (*The Strife of Love in a Dream* or *The Dream of Poliphilus*) (Figs. 8-14 through 8-16). This romantic fantasy tells of young Poliphilus's wandering quest for his lover, who had taken a vow to preserve her chastity, which takes him through classical landscapes and architectural environments. A celebration of paganism, with erotic overtones and a few explicit illustrations, it probably escaped scandal only because of its high cost and limited Venetian audience.

This masterpiece of graphic design achieved an elegant harmony of typography and illustration that has seldom been equaled. The communicative coordination of the illustrations with the text and the exceptional design integration of images and typography indicate that the printer, type designer, author, and artist worked in close collaboration. The name of the artist who designed the 168 delicate linear illustrations is lost to history. Griffo designed new capitals for use with the Bembo lowercase. These capitals were based on the most precise research and study of Roman inscriptions available and used the one-to-ten (stroke weight-to-height) proportion advanced by leading mathematicians of the era whose search for mathematical laws of proportion included a study of Roman inscription lettering. Griffo made his lowercase ascenders taller than the capitals to correct an optical color problem—the tendency of capitals to appear too large and heavy in a page of text—that had plagued earlier Roman fonts. Griffo's typefaces became the model for the talented French type designers who perfected these letterforms during the following century. Exquisite chapter headings in capitals that are the same size as those used in the text, large outline initials surrounded by stylized floral ornamentation, and an overall lightness to the page—combined with generous margins, beautiful paper, and meticulous presswork—excited printers and designers throughout Europe. *Poliphili* was Manutius's only illustrated book. After it was published, the Aldine staff turned their attention to scholarly editions.

In 1501, Manutius addressed the need for smaller, more economical books by publishing the prototype of the "pocket book." This edition of Virgil's *Opera* had a 7.7-by-15.4-centimeter (3¾-by-6-inch) page size and was set in the first italic type

8-13. Aldus Manutius, from Pietro Bembo's *De Aetna,* 1495–1496. As the model for Garamond in the sixteenth century, this typeface became the prototype for two centuries of European typographic design.

8-14. Aldus Manutius, typographic page from *Hypnerotomachia Poliphili,* 1499. The texture of the headings (set in all capitals), the text typography, and the outline initial have a subtle yet beautiful contrast. The one-line intervals of space separating the information into three areas introduces light and order into the page.

Renaissance Graphic Design

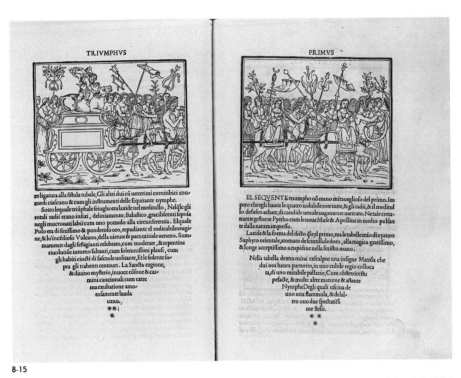

8-15. Aldus Manutius, illustrated spread from *Hypnerotomachia Poliphili,* 1499. The exquisite symmetry of each page is emphasized by the shaped type that tapers down to Griffo's light ornaments. The illustrations of the triumphant pagan procession form a continuous image, unifying the spread.

8-16. Aldus Manutius, illustrated spread from *Hypnerotomachia Poliphili,* 1499. The asymmetrical balance is unusual for its time. The arched borders of the two illustrations on the right echo the arch form in the illustration on the left. This repetition of shape increases the unity of the layout.

font. Between the smaller size type and the narrower width of italic characters, a 50-percent gain in the number of characters in a line of a given measure was achieved over Jenson's fonts and Griffo's type for *De Aetna.* Italic (Fig. 8-17) was closely modeled on the *cancelleresca* script, a slanted handwriting style which was finding favor among scholars who liked its writing speed and informality. On 14 November 1502, Manutius was granted a monopoly on Greek publishing and italic printing by the Venetian government, and shortly thereafter Griffo and Manutius quarreled and separated. Manutius wished to protect his huge investment in type design and production; Griffo found that he could not sell his original and popular typeface designs to other printers. With the parting of ways of this printer–publisher and his brilliant staff designer, graphic-design innovation in Venice ended.

Until his death in 1515, Manutius published numerous classical editions in the small format and italics of Virgil's *Opera*. These made the Aldine Press logo—a dolphin and anchor inspired by one of the illustrations in *The Dream of Poliphilus*—famous throughout Europe (Fig. 8-18). Griffo returned to Bologna, where he vanished from the historical record after being charged for the murder of his son-in-law, who was bludgeoned with an iron bar in 1516.

The typographic book came to Italy from Germany as a manuscript book printed with types. A series of design innovations including the title page, roman and italic type, printed page numbers, woodblock and cast metal ornaments, and innovative approaches to the layout of illustrations with type, enabled the Italian printers of the Renaissance to pass on to posterity the basic format of the typographic book as we know it today.

Italian writing masters

Ironically, the inevitable decline in manuscript writing that followed on the heels of typographic printing occurred while new opportunities opened for master calligraphers almost as a side effect of printing. The rapid growth of literacy created a huge demand for writing masters to teach this fundamental skill, and the attendant expansion of government and commerce created a demand for expert calligraphers to draft important state and business documents. The first of many sixteenth-century writing manuals was created by Italian master calligrapher, printer, and type designer Lodovico Arrighi (d. c. 1527). His small volume of 1522, entitled *La Operina da imparare di scrivere littera cancellaresca* (Fig. 8-19), was a

8-17. Aldus Manutius, page from Juvenal and Persius, *Opera*, 1501. This was one of the first books using Griffo's new italic type. Note the unfilled space for a rubricated initial, the letterspaced, all-capital heading, and the capital roman letter at the beginning of each line.

8-18. Aldus Manutius, printer's trademark, c. 1500. The swiftest of sea creatures combines with an anchor to signify the epigram, "Make haste slowly."

8-19. Lodovico Arrighi, page from *La Operina da imparare di scrivere littera cancellaresca,* 1522. The ample spaces between lines in Arrighi's brilliant writing leave room for the plumelike ascenders waving to the right in elegant counterpoint to the descenders sweeping gracefully to the left.

8-19

brief course using magnificent examples to teach the cancelleresca script. Arrighi's masterful writing was meticulously cut onto woodblocks by engraver Ugo da Carpi. Arrighi's directions were so clear and simple that the reader could learn this hand in a few days. *La Operina . . . cancellaresca* sounded the deathknell for the scriptorium as an exclusive domain for the few who could write; it rang in the era of the writing master and public writing skill. A follow-up 1523 volume, entitled *Il Modo de temperare le penne,* presented a dozen handwriting styles. Among those influenced by Arrighi, Giovanni Battista Palatino (c. 1515–c. 1575) produced the most complete and widely used writing manuals of the sixteenth century.

The Renaissance in Italy began to fade with the sack of Rome in 1527 by the combined forces of the Holy Roman Emperor Charles V and his Spanish allies. One of the victims of this outrage appears to be Lodovico Arrighi. He was working in Rome at the time, after which his name vanishes from the historical record without a trace.

Innovation passes to France

Filled with glorious dreams of romantic conquest and empire, the French king Charles VIII (1470–1498) crossed into Italy with a vast army in 1494 and attempted to gain control of the Kingdom of Naples. This began an absurd fifty-year effort by French kings to conquer Italy. Although vast outlays of money and men gained little except fleeting glory, the cultural vitality of the Italian Renaissance was imported to France. Francis I (1494–1547) ascended to the French throne on 1 January 1515 and began his spectacular reign. Under his patronage, the French Renaissance flowered as he gave generous support to humanists, authors, and visual artists.

This cultural epoch was a fertile one for graphic design and printing, and the sixteenth century has become known as "the golden age of French typography." The initial design impetus was imported from Venice. Henri Estienne (d. 1520) was one of the early French scholar-printers (Fig. 8-20) who became enthusiastic about Aldus's *Poliphilus.* Soon books printed in roman types, with title pages and initials inspired by the Venetians, were sprouting all over Paris. Estienne's untimely death left his wife with three young sons. The widowed mother quickly married Estienne's foreman, Simon de Colines (d. 1546), who ran the family business until his stepson, Robert Estienne (1503–1559), was able to take over in 1526. At this time, Simon de Colines opened his own firm. Robert Estienne became a brilliant printer of scholarly works in Greek, Latin, and Hebrew (Fig. 8-21). His growing reputation as a publisher of great books, including a major Latin dictionary, enabled young Estienne to join his stepfather as one of the leading figures in this grand period of book design and printing.

Censorship became an increasingly difficult problem during the 1500s as church and state sought to maintain their authority and control. Propagating ideas, not pressing inked type onto paper, was the main purpose of the scholar-printers, who often found their quest for knowledge and critical study in conflict with religious leaders and the royalty. In spite of war and censorship, however, the humanist spirit took hold in France and produced both excellent scholarship and a graceful school of graphic design. The leading printers produced books of fine proportions, outstanding legibility, beautiful typography, and elegant ornamentation. Two brilliant graphic artists, Geoffroy Tory (1480–1533), and a typeface designer and punch cutter, Claude Garamond (c. 1480–1561), created visual forms that were embraced for two hundred years.

The term "renaissance man" is often used to identify a unique individual of genius whose wide-ranging activities in various philosophic, literary, artistic, or scientific disciplines result in important contributions to more than one field. Such a person was Geoffroy Tory. His range of accomplishments is staggering: professor, scholar, and translator; poet and author; publisher, printer, and bookseller; calligrapher, designer, illustrator, and engraver. He translated, edited, and often published Latin and Greek texts. As a reformer of the French language, he introduced

8-20. Henri Estienne, title page for Aristotle's *Metaphysics,* 1515. By setting the type in geometric shapes, Estienne achieved a distinctive graphic design with minimal means.

8-21. Robert Estienne, title page for a Bible, 1540. As with many printers' marks of the era, Estienne's olive tree with a branch falling off became a pictorial illustration.

the apostrophe, the accent, and the cedilla. In the graphic arts, he played a major role in importing the italianate influence. Then, he proceeded to develop a uniquely French Renaissance style of book design and illustration.

Born of humble means in Bourges, Tory's brilliance captured the attention of the city's leading citizens, who made it possible for him to journey to Italy for study at the universities in Rome and Bologna. Returning to France in 1505, Tory became a lecturer in philosophy at the University of Paris, sometimes worked as a reader at

Henri Estienne's printing office, and was active as a scribe and illuminator. His boundless enthusiasm for the visual forms of the Italian Renaissance included a deep love for roman letterforms. Tory's lettering, developed in Italy and used in the 1506 manuscript book, *Les Heures de Jean Lallemant* (Pl. 13), is a light roman with long ascenders and descenders. The background of the armorial frontispiece and forty vignettes are decorated with orderly rows of the twenty-three letterforms of the Latin alphabet in front of a striking blue field with red and white stripes. Some scholars believe that Tory designed early roman types used by Henri Estienne and Simon de Colines.

After a period of publishing with Simon de Colines, Tory made a second extended trip to Italy from 1516 until 1518 to improve his abilities as an artist and designer. Upon returning to Paris, Tory seems to have turned first to manuscript illumination for his livelihood, which quickly yielded to the design and engraving of woodblocks commissioned by printers. After Simon de Colines's 1520 marriage to Henri Estienne's widow, he began to commission borders, floriated letters, trademarks, and an italic typeface from Tory. It was this collaboration between the master printer and graphic artist that established the new open, lighter style.

In sixteenth-century France, engravers were usually booksellers. In keeping with this tradition, Tory opened a Parisian bookselling firm on the Petit Pont at the sign of the *Pot Cassé* ("broken urn"), where he illustrated, published, bound, and—for several years—printed books. Tory sought out excellent craftsmen and trained them in his approach to book design, which chased the dense, claustrophobic page layout and heavy, Gothic typography from French printing.

The symbolic origin of the *Pot Cassé* trademark (Fig. 8-22), which quickly became a symbol for the fresh winds of the French Renaissance, is poignant. On 25 August 1522 Tory's ten-year-old daughter Agnes died suddenly. The devastated father wrote and published a poem in her memory. At the end of the text, the first engraving of the Pot Cassé appears. This shattered antique urn, chained to a closed, locked book and bearing the inscription "non plus" (no longer, or nothing more), seems to symbolize the tragic death of his daughter. This interpretation is strengthened by the small winged figure in the upper-right corner, a detail that had been cut away from the woodblock by the time this same cut was used in a book published by Tory a year later.

Nothing captured the imagination of French printers as did several series of initials designed by Tory. Roman capital initials (Fig. 8-23) are set into black squares that come alive with meticulous floral designs and *criblé*. Along with matching printer's ornaments and headpieces, these initials were the perfect accompaniment for the lighter new roman types by Garamond. Tory's influence gained momentum in 1525, when he initiated a series of *Horae* (Book of Hours) (Figs. 8-24 and 8-25), printed for him by Simon de Colines, that set the style for the era. It was a new clarity of thought, an innovative attitude toward form, and a precise harmony of the various elements—text, capital initials, borders, and illustrations—that mark the 1525 *Horae* as a milestone in graphic design. The patchwork quilt of woodblocks filling the space of early Books of Hours became passé. A light, delicate effect is achieved in the complex illustrations and ornamental borders because Tory used a fine contour line with air flowing around and within his graceful curves. The texture and tone of these visual elements echo the typographic lightness. Tory selected a size and weight of initial that added just the right darker accent, and he used outline initials with his headings. He cut the woodblocks for these borders and illustrations himself. The creative momentum in publishing and graphic design had now passed to France, and King Francis I honored Tory's contribution by naming him *imprimeur du roi* ("printer to the king") in 1530.

Tory's *Champ Fleury* (subtitled *The art and science of the proper and true proportions of the attic letters, which are otherwise called antique letters, and in common speech roman letters*), first published in 1529 (Fig. 8-26), was his most important and influential work. It consists of three books. In the first, he attempted to establish and order the French tongue by fixed rules of pronunciation and speech. The

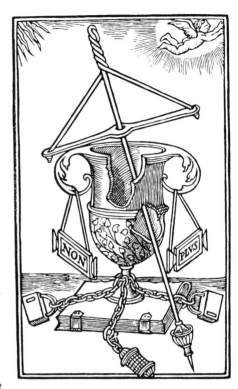

8-22. Geoffroy Tory, Pot Cassé emblem, 1524. Later, Tory explained that the broken jar symbolized one's body, the toret or auger symbolized fate, and the book held shut by three padlocked chains signified the book of a life after it is shut by death.

8-23. Geoffroy Tory, capital from a series of criblé initials, c. 1526. Engraved for Robert Estienne, this alphabet of roman capitals brought elegance and "color" to the pages of books printed at Estienne's press.

8-24. Geoffroy Tory, pages from *Horae ad usum Romanum,* 1531. This layout from Tory's book of hours demonstrates the delicate lightness of his woodcut borders and illustrations. The bird becomes a powerful accent of black.

8-25. Geoffroy Tory, pages from *Horae in laudem Virgin Marie,* 1541. A set of border components, filled with plant and animal motifs, are combined and recombined throughout the book. The open line quality facilitates the application of color by hand. The crowned *F* in the bottom center of the left-hand page is an homage to King Francis I.

second discusses the history of roman letters and compares their proportions with the ideal proportions of the human figure and face. Errors in Albrecht Dürer's letterform designs in the recently published *Underweisung der Messung* are carefully analyzed, then Dürer is forgiven his errors because he is a painter. Painters—according to Tory—rarely understand the proportions of well-formed letters. The third and final book offers instructions in the geometric construction of the twenty-three letters of the Latin alphabet on background grids of one hundred squares

LE SEGOND LIVRE.

LE SEGOND LIVRE. FEVIL.XXX.

LE TRIVM PHE DA, POLLO ET DE SES MVSES.

b
BACCHVS
CERES ET
VENVS
SONT ICY
MENEZCA
PTIFZ

Trium phe Da pollo,& fens mo ral dicel luy. Frances fco Pe traccha.

OR voyez doncques le beau triumphe Dapollo, auec fes Mufes & autres dames compaignes qui nous monftrent a loeul commant au moyen des bonnes lettres & Sciences tout homme en bien vfant peut paruenir a confom= me hôneur & immortalite de fon nom. Si a ce propos on defiroit en veoir plus a plain, quon fen aille efbatre a lire aux Triûphes de meffer Erancefco Petrar cha,& on trouuera au Triûphe de Renômee coimât les Poetes, les Philofo= phes, & les Orateurs par leur ftudieufe vertus, côbien quilz foiêt pieça morts corporellement, viuent fpirituellement, & viuront plufque nulz autres tant vertueulx ayent ilz peu eftre.

La gou te dor. Iupiter, Acrifius, Danae, Moly. Homere.

IE porrois cy adiouxter dauâtage, & approprier, pareillement moralifer La goute dor en la quelle, felon les Poetes & Philofophies anciens Iupiter fe tranfmua pour defcendre du Ciel en Terre en la tour de Acrifius Roy de Gre= ce, & pere de la belle Danae. Semblablement ie porrois auffi efcrire de lherbe & verge mercurialle nômee en Grec Moly. De la quelle Homere faict menfion en fon Odiffee, au dixiefme liure, mais laiffant ces chofes a rumyner aux bons efperits, Ie pafferay oultre, & viendray a proportiôner & defcrire toutes noz lettres Attiques & Abecedaires lune apres lautre felon leur ordre vulgaire. Et pour y commancer, auec laide de Dieu, Il me fouuient que iay pieça dit cy

Lifflabe. Diofcori de, Mar= cel Vir= gile, Hyacin= thiol.

deffus, que toutes nofdites lettres Attiques font faictes & participantes de le I. & de le O. & que I. & A. auoient efte fantafiez en la fleur dun lis ayant cou= leur de pourpre, quon dit en Paris Lifflamble, & que Diofconde, femblable= ment fon tranflateur Florentin nôme Marcel virgile, appellent Hyacinthus, que le langage vulgaire Italien nôme & dit Hyacintiol, ien fays cy prefvng de= feing au quel le A.eft affis fus vng dit Lifflambe en quadrature & rotondite pareillement eft faict de le I.multiplie en triangle, ou fi voules autrement dire, dittez que le A, eft faict de trois I, affis & logez lun fus lautre, en prenât de cha= cun ce quil conuient a former vng A parfaict, comme pouuez veoir au dit de= feing enfuyuant, au quel iay faict le A, noir, & le refte des trois I, Ie lay laiffe en blanc comme chofe fuperabundante du dit A. Le defeing eft tel quil fen= fuyt.

VEla donques comme iay dit, commant le I, eft le modele & proportion aux lettres At e tiques, Ceft a fcauoir, a celles qui ont iambes dro ittes. Nous verrons de le O.ou nous ferons le B. qui eft de le I. & de le O. entendu quil a iambe & panfe qui denote brifeure.

EN ceft endroit louuant noftre feigneur Dieu, Ie feray fin a noftre Segond liure, au quel auons felon noftre petit entendement demon= ftre lorigie des lettres Attiques & auôs voulu fua= der & prier, la quelle chofe encores prions, que quelques bons efperits feuertuaffent a mettre no= ftre langue francoife par reigle, afin quen peuf= fions vfer honneftement & feurement a coucher par efcript les bonnes Sciences, quil nous fault mendier des Hebreux, des Grecs, & des Latins, & que ne pouuons auoir fans grans coufts / fraiz/ & defpens de temps & dargent.

LA FIN DV SEGOND LIVRE.

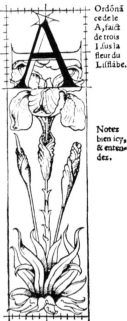

Ordõnã ce de le A, faict de trois I. fus la fleur du Lifflabe.

Notez bien icy, & enten= dez.

(Fig. 8-27). Finally, it closes with Tory's designs for thirteen other alphabets, including Greek, Hebrew, Chaldean, and his extraordinary fantasy style made of handtools (Fig. 8-28).

Champ Fleury is a personal book written in a rambling conversational style with frequent digressions into Roman history and mythology. And yet its message about the Latin alphabet came through loud and clear to a generation of French printers and punch cutters, and Tory became the most influential graphic designer of his century.

During the 1530s and 1540s, Robert Estienne achieved a wide reputation as a great printer (Figs. 8-29 and 8-30) renowned for the scholarship and intellectual acumen that he brought to the editorial process. During the same time, Colines earned a similar reputation based on the elegance and clarity of his book designs (Figs. 8-31 and 8-32). Illustrated title pages, typographic arrangements, ornaments and borders, and fine presswork contributed to this reputation.

Claude Garamond was the first punch cutter to work independently of printing firms. His roman typefaces (Fig. 8-33) were designed with such perfection that French printers in the sixteenth century were able to print books of extraordinary legibility and beauty. Garamond is credited, by the sheer quality of his fonts, with a major role in eliminating Gothic styles from compositors's cases all over Europe, except in Germany. Around 1510, Garamond apprenticed as a punch cutter under Antoine Augereau. Just how much credit for the evolution of roman type should go to Augereau, whose religious beliefs led him to the gallows in 1534, Geoffroy Tory, with whom Garamond worked about 1520, and Garamond himself is somewhat

8-26. Geoffroy Tory, pages from *Champ Fleury*, 1529. This double-page spread discusses how the Roman philosophers, poets, and orators live in spirit through the power of the Roman letters, illustrated by woodcuts of mythological subjects about which we have knowledge through the alphabet. The final paragraph of this "second book" introduces the "third book," the construction of roman letters, with an illustration showing the construction of an *A* from three *I*s.

8-27. Geoffroy Tory, construction of the letter *Q* from *Champ Fleury*, 1529. Tory used five compass centers in his effort to construct geometrically an ideal roman *O*, and he used an additional two compass centers to add a tail for the *Q*.

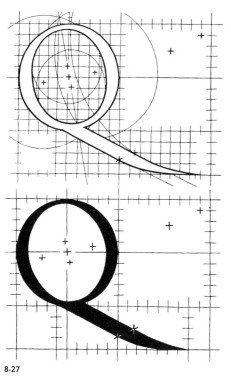

8-27

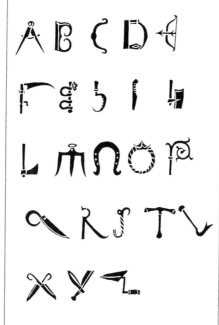

8-28

8-28. Geoffroy Tory, fantastic alphabet from *Champ Fleury*, 1529. The thirteen alphabets concluding this book (Hebrew, Greek, Persian, and so on) included this whimsical sequence of pictorial letterforms composed of tools. *A* is a compass, *B* is a fusy (steel used to strike a flint to start a fire), and *C* is a handle.

8-29. Robert Estienne, page from Paolo Giovio's *Vitae duodecim Vicecomitum Mediolani Principum,* 1549. Estienne used Garamond's roman fonts and Geoffroy Tory's initials in this book. Headings are set in one line of letterspaced capitals and two lines of lowercase.

8-30. Robert Estienne, page from a Greek New Testament, 1550. The great scholar-printer designed the pages of his Greek volumes using, once again, graphic material created by punch cutter Claude Garamond and engraver Geoffroy Tory.

5

PAVLI IOVII NOVOCOMEN-
fis in Vitas duodecim Vicecomitum Mediolani
Principum Præfatio.

ETVSTATEM nobi-
liſſimæ Vicecomitum fami-
liæ qui ambitioſius à præalta
Romanorú Cæſarum origi-
ne, Longobardíſq; regibus
deducto ſtemmate, repete-
re contédunt, fabuloſis pe-
nè initiis inuoluere viden-
tur. Nos autem recentiora
illuſtrioráque, vti ab omnibus recepta, ſequemur:có-
tentíque erimus inſigni memoria Heriprandi & Gal-
uanii nepotis, qui eximia cum laude rei militaris, ci-
uilíſque prudentiæ, Mediolani principem locum te-
nuerunt. Incidit Galuanius in id tempus quo Medio-
lanum à Federico AEnobarbo deletú eſt, vir ſumma
rerum geſtarum gloria, & quod in fatis fuit, inſigni
calamitate memorabilis. Captus enim, & ad trium-
phum in Germaniam ductus fuiſſe traditur: ſed non
multo póſt carceris catenas fregit, ingentíque animi
virtute non ſemel cæſis Barbaris, vltus iniurias, patriã
reſtituit. Fuit hic(vt Annales ferunt)Othonis nepos,
eius qui ab inſigni pietate magnitudinéque animi, ca
nente illo pernobili claſſico excitus, ad ſacrú bellum
in Syriam contendit, communicatis ſcilicet conſiliis
atque opibus cú Guliermo Montiſferrati regulo, qui
à procuritate corporis, Longa ſpatha vocabatur. Vo-
luntariorum enim equitum ac peditum delectæ no-
A.iii.

8-29

125

Η ΠΡΟΣ ΕΒΡΑΙΟΥΣ ΕΠΙΣΤΟΛΗ
ΠΑΥΛΟΥ.

8-30

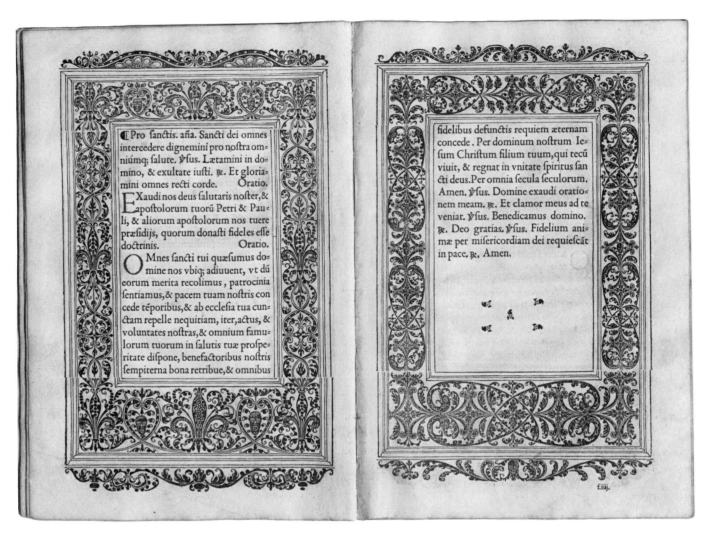

muddled. Perhaps these three Frenchmen, all of whom developed a passionate love
for roman letterforms designed by Griffo, each had a hand in the struggle to perfect
roman fonts.

Around 1530, Garamond established his independent type foundry to sell to
printers cast type ready to distribute into the compositor's case. This was a first
step away from the "scholar-publisher-typefounder-printer-bookseller," all in one,
that began in Mainz some eighty years earlier. The fonts Garamond cut during the
1540s achieved a mastery of visual form, a snugness of fit, that allowed closer
wordspacing, and a harmony of design between capitals, lowercase, and italic.
These types permit books such as the French language *Poliphili,* printed by
Jacques Kerver in 1546, to maintain their status as benchmarks of typographic
beauty and readability to this day. The influence of writing as a model diminished
in Garamond's work, for typography was evolving a language of form rooted in the
processes of making steel punches, casting metal type, and printing instead of imitating forms created by hand gestures with an inked quill on paper. Old age did not
treat Garamond kindly, and he was desperately poor when he died at age eighty-
one. His widow sold his punches and matrixes. No doubt this contributed to the
wide use of his fonts, which remained a major influence until the late 1700s.

Oronce Finé (1494–1555) was a mathematics professor and author whose abilities as a graphic artist complemented his scientific publications. In addition to
illustrating his mathematics, geography, and astronomy books, Finé became interested in book ornament and design. His contemporaries had equal admiration for
his contributions to science and graphic arts. He worked closely with printers, notably Simon de Colines, in the design and production of his books (Fig. 8-34). Also,

8-31. Simon de Colines (printer) and Geoffroy
Tory (designer), pages from a Book of Hours,
1543. This dense border design is no longer
a schematic for the application of color
by hand.

8-32. Simon de Colines, title page for *De natura stirpium libri tres,* 1536. The typography is surrounded by an illustration that takes great liberties with natural scale and perspective to create a joyous interpretation of the natural bounty of the earth's flora.

8-33. Robert Estienne, opening page from *Illustrissimae Galliaru reginae Helianorae,* 1531. It is believed that the types used in this book are made from Claude Garamond's early type punches and matrices.

he made an excellent contribution as an editor and designer involved in numerous other titles. While Tory's inspiration is evident, Finé's mathematical construction of his ornaments and the robust clarity of his graphic illustration are the work of an innovative graphic designer.

During the 1540s, Robert Estienne was caught up in the turmoil of the Reformation. The protection King Francis I (1494–1547) provided for his "dear printer" ended with the king's death, and Estienne's work as a scholar and printer of "pagan language" Latin, Greek, and Hebrew Bibles incurred the wrath of Catholic theologians at the Sorbonne, who suspected that he was a heretic. After a 1549 visit to Geneva, Switzerland, to meet Protestant Reformation leader John Calvin (1509–1564), Estienne began careful preparations to move his printing firm to that city the following year. In choosing to relocate in Switzerland, Estienne was mindful of the fate of Étienne Dolet (1509–1546), whose two-volume *Commentarii lin-*

Renaissance Graphic Design

guage Latinae had made a major contribution to classical scholarship. On three occasions, officials' displeasure with the books Dolet published had caused him to be imprisoned. Finally, he was accused of atheism, tried, and condemned by the Sorbonne Theological Faculty. On 3 August 1546, thirty-seven-year-old Dolet was burned at the stake, and his books were used to fuel the flames. Ironically, his first work, *Cato christianus,* had been a profession of his Christian creed.

Comparison of the editions of *Poliphili* printed by Jacques Kerver (Figs. 8-35 and 8-36) during the middle of the sixteenth century with Manutius's 1499 edition (see Figs. 8-14 through 8-16) shows just how rapidly the French Renaissance printers expanded the range of graphic design. Manutius produced his *Poliphili* with one size of roman type and used capitals as his only means of emphasis; Kerver called upon a large range of roman and italic type sizes in designing his pages. Manutius used a set of ornamental initials and little starlike ornaments; Kerver selected from an elegant stock of headpieces, tailpieces, and printers' flowers to embellish the printed page. The illustrations in Manutius's *Poliphili* use a monotone contour line; Kerver's illustrator achieved a broad range of tonal effects. And a fully developed title page in the Kerver editions set the tone for his volume.

Early typographic books in each European country had an identifiable national style. The unified structure and tone of the French book produced during the golden age of French typography was admired throughout the continent.

8-34

8-35

8-36

8-34. Simon de Colines (printer) and Oronce Finé (designer), title page for Oronce Finé's *Arithmetica,* 1535. In this title-page border, Finé used carefully measured strapwork, symbolic figures representing areas of knowledge, and a criblé background. De Colines's exquisite typography combines with this border to create a masterpiece of Renaissance graphic design.

8-35. Jacques Kerver, title page from *Poliphili,* 1561. A satyr and a nymph eyeing each other amidst an abundant harvest clue the reader to the pagan adventures within the book.

8-36. Jacques Kerver, typographic page from *Poliphili,* 1561. Bracketed by white space, Kerver's heading uses three sizes of type with capitals and lowercase, all capitals, and italic to bring variety to the design.

Comment ilz fignifioient Dieu.

Pour fignifier dieu ilz paignoient vng oeil pource que ainfi que loeil veoit & regarde ce qui eft audeuant de luy dieu veoit confidere & congnoit toutes chofes.

8-37. Jacques Kerver (printer), page from *Hora pollo,* 1543. An unsettling Surrealism springs from the woodblock illustrations in this small volume, where eyes and disembodied feet float in the sky.

As Garamond-derived type fonts and Tory-inspired initials and ornaments became available throughout Europe, printers began to emulate the light elegance and ordered clarity of Parisian books. As a result, the first international style of typographic design flourished as the dominant graphic theme of the sixteenth century.

Basel and Lyons become design centers

Scholarship and book production flourished in many cities, but only a few—notably Nuremberg, Venice, and Paris—emerged as centers for design innovation. During the 1500s Basel, which became a part of Switzerland in 1501, and Lyons, a French city located 300 kilometers (180 miles) southwest of Basel, developed into major centers for graphic design. Printers in the two towns enjoyed a lively exchange. Types, woodcut borders, and illustrations from Basel were on many Lyons presses, and Lyons printers often produced editions for their busy Basel counterparts. Johann Froben (1460–1527) came to the sophisticated college town of Basel to attend the university, then began to print there in 1491. He became Basel's leading printer and attracted the outstanding humanist scholar of the Northern Renaissance, Desiderius Erasmus (1466–1543), to Basel. For eight years beginning in 1521, Erasmus worked with Froben as author, editor, and advisor on matters of scholarship. Unlike most of his German contemporaries, Froben favored hearty, solid roman types instead of gothics.

A twenty-three-year-old painter, Hans Holbein the Younger (1497–1543), arrived in Basel from Augsburg in the autumn of 1519, was received as a master in the *Zum Himmel* guild, and was engaged by Froben to illustrate books. His border designs were sculptural and complex and often included a scene from the Bible or classical literature. His prolific designs for title pages (Fig. 8-38), headpieces, tailpieces, and several sets of illustrated initials ranged from the humorous (peasants chasing a fox), to the genre (dancing peasants and playing children), to a morbid series of initials depicting the Dance of Death. Before leaving for England in 1526, Holbein was probably already working on his greatest graphic work, the forty-one woodcuts illustrating *Imagines Mortis (The Dance of Death)* (Fig. 8-39). The Dance of Death, a procession in which skeletons or corpses escort the living to their graves, was a major theme in the visual arts, as well as in music, drama, and poetry. This use of art as an ominous reminder to the unfaithful of the inevitability of death originated in the fourteenth century, when the great waves of the plague swept over Europe. By separating the procession into individual scenes, Holbein was able to intensify the suddenness and personal tragedy of death. Numerous editions were printed from the blocks engraved by Hans Lutzelburger after Holbein's drawings.

After Froben's death, Johann Oporinus became Basel's leading printer. His masterpiece is the enormous 667-page folio, *De humani corporis fabrica* (Fig. 8-40), by the brilliant founder of modern anatomy from Brussels, Andreas Vesalius (1514–1564). This important book was illustrated by full-page woodcuts of remarkable clarity and accuracy by artists working from dissected corpses under Vesalius's supervision. Many of the anatomical figures are gracefully posed in landscapes. Oporinus set Vesalius's turgid, wordy text in tight pages of roman type with precise page numbers, running heads, marginal notes in delicate italic type, and no paragraph indications. A curious note of humor is introduced by illustrated, square initials that break up the text. In them, *cherubs* curiously examine bones, circumcise one of their little friends, and perform a dissection on a wild boar. If imitation is the sincerest form of flattery, *De humani corporis fabrica* ranks as a great book, for it was pirated, translated, reprinted, copied, and abridged by printers all across Europe. In fact, King Henry VIII of England ordered the production of an English pirated edition in 1545. Its carefully executed, copperplate-engraved illustrations—copied from the original woodcut title page and illustrations—mark this copy as the first successful book with engraved illustrations.

In Lyons, most of the forty printers churned out such routinely designed material as popular romances for the commercial market using Gothic type. In 1542, Jean de Tournes (1504–1564) opened his firm in Lyons and began to use Garamond types with initials and ornaments designed by Tory. But de Tournes was not content to imitate Parisian graphic design; he retained his fellow Lyonese, Bernard Salomon, to design headpieces, arabesques, *fleurons* (printers' flowers), and woodblock illustrations. The excellent book design of these collaborators was further enhanced (Figs. 8-41 and 8-42) when they were joined by a Parisian type designer working in Lyons, Robert Granjon (d. 1579), who married Salomon's daughter Antoinette.

The most original of the designers inspired by Garamond's roman faces, Granjon created delicate italic fonts, which had beautiful italic capitals with swashes. Books set in italic lowercase had been using regular capitals. Granjon attempted to add a fourth major style—in addition to Gothic, roman, and italic—when he designed and promoted the *caractères de civilité* (Fig. 8-43), a typographic version of the French secretarial writing style then in vogue. The distinctive appearance of these typefaces with flamboyant cursive ascenders was insufficient compensation for their poor legibility. Therefore, *civilité* was just a passing fancy. The fleurons designed by Granjon were modular and could be put together in endless combinations to make headpieces, tailpieces, ornaments, and borders. Garamond's type designs were so beautiful and legible that for two hundred years, from about 1550 until the mid-1700s, most typeface designers followed Granjon by merely refining and altering Garamond's forms.

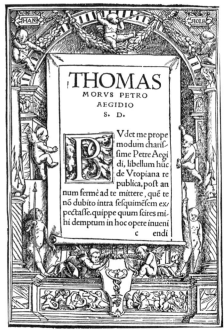

8-38

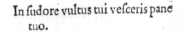

8-38. Johann Froben (printer) and Hans Holbein (illustrator), title page for Sir Thomas More's *Utopia*, 1518. Complex of image and tone, this title-page design unifies the typography to the illustration by placing it on a hanging scroll.

8-39. Joannes Frellonius (printer) and Hans Holbein the Younger (illustrator), pages from *Imagines Mortis* ("The Dance of Death"), 1547. The terror of a child suddenly taken from his home by death is in striking contrast to the modest size (6.65 centimeters or 2⅝ inches) of the illustrations and the understated elegance of Frellonius's typography.

8-40. Johann Oporinus (printer), page from *De humani corporis fabrica*, 1543. Anatomical illustrations of skeletons and muscles in natural poses appear in pages of italic captions set in three columns to the page.

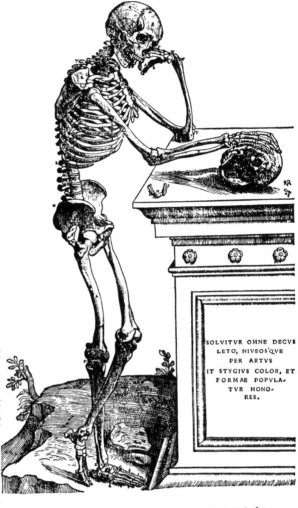

8-40

On 1 March 1562, a conflict between French troops and a Reformed church congregation ended in a massacre. This began four decades of religious wars that effectively ended the innovation of the golden age of French typography. Many Huguenot (French Protestant) printers fled to Switzerland, England, and the Low Countries to escape religious strife, censorship, and rigid trade laws. Just as the momentum for innovative graphic design had moved from Italy to France, it now passed from France into the Low Countries, especially the cities of Antwerp and Amsterdam.

A serious arm injury in the early 1550s ended the outstanding bookbinding career of Christophe Plantin (1514–1589). Thus he changed his career to printing in mid-life, and the Netherlands found its greatest printer. Plantin was born in a rural French village near Tours, apprenticed as a bookbinder and bookseller in Caen, then set up shop in Antwerp at age thirty-five. While de Tournes's dedication to quality and unsurpassed design standards have led many authorities to proclaim him the sixteenth century's "best printer," Plantin's remarkable management sense and publishing acumen could earn him the same accolade for different reasons. Classics and Bibles, herbals and medicine books, music and maps—a full

Renaissance Graphic Design

range of printed matter—poured from what became the world's largest and strongest publishing house. Even Plantin got into trouble during this dangerous time for printers. While he was in Paris in 1562, his staff printed a heretical tract, and his assets were seized and sold. He recovered much of the money, however, and within two years was reorganized and going strong. Plantin's design style (Fig. 8-44) was a more ornamented, weightier adaptation of French typographic design.

Granjon was called to Antwerp for a period as type designer in residence. Plantin loved Granjon's fleurons and used them in profusion, particularly in his ever-popular emblem books. Plantin published fifty emblem books, which contained illustrated verses or mottos for moral instruction or meditation. At the estate sales of Colines and Garamond, Plantin secured numerous punches and types. Under the patronage of King Phillip II of Spain, Plantin published the second of the great Polyglot Bibles (Fig. 8-45) from 1569–1572. This eight-volume work almost bankrupted him when the promised patronage was slow to materialize.

The use of copperplate engravings, instead of woodcuts, to illustrate his books was Plantin's main design contribution. He commissioned masters of this flourishing printmaking medium to design title pages and to illustrate books. Soon engraving was replacing the woodcut as the major technique for graphic images throughout Europe. After Plantin's death, his son-in-law, John Moretus, continued the firm, which remained in the family until 1876, when the town of Antwerp purchased it and turned this amazing house and printing firm into a unique museum of typography and printing, containing two presses dating from Plantin's time.

The seventeenth century

After the remarkable progress in graphic design that took place during the brief decades of the Incunabula, and the exquisite typography and book design of the Renaissance, the seventeenth century was a relatively quiet time for graphic design innovation. An abundant stock of ornaments, punches, matrices, and woodblocks from the 1500s was widely available, so there was little incentive for printers to commission new graphic materials. Graphic design and printing were characterized by a business-as-usual attitude. An awakening of literary genius occurred during the seventeenth century, however. Immortal works by gifted authors, including the British playwright and poet William Shakespeare (1564–1616)

8-42. Jean de Tournes, title page for a Bible, 1558. This delicate, open arabesque border is typical of the innovative design style developed by de Tournes and his associates in Lyons.

8-43. Robert Granjon, title page for *Le Premier Livre des Narrations Fabuleuses,* 1558. The script letterforms are Granjon's *caractères de civilité* (characters of civility), which were used for the entire text of this 128-page book. The serpent device, elegantly bracketed by the motto in roman capitals, is Granjon's trademark.

8-44. Christophe Plantin, title page for *Centvm fabvlae ex antiqvis* by Gabriello Faerno, 1567. Dignified and architectural, this title page is typical of the Plantin house style.

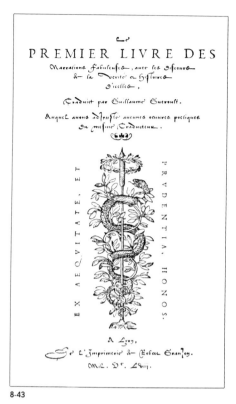

8-43

8-44

8-45. Christophe Plantin, page from the *Polyglot Bible*, 1569–1572. A double-page format, with two vertical columns over a wide horizontal column, contained the Hebrew, Latin, Aramaic, Greek, and Syriac translations of the Bible.

and the Spanish novelist, playwright, and poet Miguel de Cervantes Saavedra (1547–1616), were widely published. Unfortunately, similar innovation was lacking in the graphic arts. There were no important new layout approaches or typefaces to provide a distinctive format for outstanding new literature. Louis XIII of France, under the influence of his prime minister, Cardinal Richelieu, established the *Imprimerie Royale* ("royal printing office") at the Louvre in 1640 in an effort to restore the earlier quality.

The oldest surviving newspaper dates from early in the century. This was the *Avisa Relation oder Zeitung,* printed in the German town of Augsburg on a regular basis in 1609. Others appeared in many German cities and other European countries. England, for example, had its first two-page "running news" publications, called *corantos,* in 1621.

Printing came to the North American colonies when a British locksmith named Stephen Daye (c. 1594–1668) contracted with a wealthy dissenting clergyman, Reverend Jesse Glover, to sail with him to the New World and establish a printing press. Glover died during the sea voyage in the autumn of 1638 and was buried at sea. Upon arrival in Cambridge, Massachusetts, Glover's widow assisted Daye in setting up the printing office. The first printing was done in early 1639, and the first book to be designed and printed in the English American colonies was *The Whole Book of Psalmes* (now called *The Bay Psalm Book*) of 1640 (Fig. 8-46). As the title page, with its dominant word "whole" and border of cast metal printers' flowers, demonstrates, the design and production of this volume was diligent but understandably lacking in refinement. Stephen's son Matthew, who was second in charge and had apprenticed in a Cambridge, England, printing shop before sailing to America, probably did the typesetting and took responsibility for the design of the broadsides, books, and other matter produced at this press. In spite of strong censorship and a stamp tax on both newspapers and advertising, printing grew steadily in the colonies. By 1775, there were about fifty printers in the thirteen colonies, and they fueled the revolutionary fever that was brewing. Just as printing had hurled Europe toward the Protestant Reformation during its early decades, it now pushed the American colonies toward revolution.

The copperplate engraving continued to grow in popularity as technical refinements greatly increased its range of tone, textures, and detail. Independent engraving studios were established, as shown in the combined etching and engraving by Abraham Bosse (1602–1676) illustrating the plate printers in his printing shop (Fig. 8-47). In addition to commissions for copperplate engravings to be bound into books as illustrations, these studios produced engravings for hanging on the wall. This enabled persons who were unable to afford oil paintings to have images in

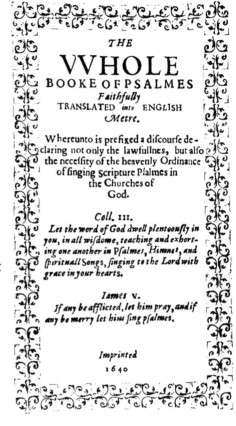

8-46. Stephen and Matthew Daye, title page for *The Whole Book of Psalmes*, 1640. In the title typography, a rich variety is achieved by combining three type sizes and using all capitals, all lower case, and italics to express the importance and meaning of the words.

8-47. Abraham Bosse, *Printing Shop—The Plate Printer*, 1642. A convincing range of lights and darks is built from scratched lines.

Habit de Rôtisseur

COMMENTARIORUM
JOANNIS CALVINI
IN
EUANGELIUM
SECUNDUM JOANNEM
PRÆFATIO
Magnificis Dominis, Syndicis, Senatuique
Genevenſi, Dominis ſuis vere obſervandis Joan. Calvinus *Spi-*
ritum prudentiæ & fortitudinis, proſperumque guber-
nationis ſucceſſum à Domino precatur.

Quoties in mentem venit illa Chriſti ſententia, qua tanti
æſtimat quod hoſpitibus colligendis impenditur huma-
nitatis officium, ut in ſuas rationes acceptum ferat, ſimul
occurrit quam ſingulari vos honore dignatus fit, qui urbem veſtram non unius vel paucorum, ſed commune Eccleſiæ ſuæ ho-
ſpitium eſſe voluit. Semper apud homines profanos non modo
laudata, ſed una ex præcipuis virtutibus habita fuit hoſpitalitas :
ac proinde in quibus extremam barbariem ac mores prorſus effe-
ratos damnare vellent, eos ... vel (quod idem valet) inhoſpitales
vocabant. Laudis autem veſtræ longe potior eſt ratio, quod tur-
bulentis hiſce miſeriſque temporibus Dominus vos conſtituit quo-
rum in fidem præſidiumque ſe conferent pii & innoxii homines,
quos non ſæva minus quam ſacrilega Antichriſti tyrannis è patriis
ſedibus fugat ac diſpellit. Neque id modo, ſed ſacrum etiam apud
vos domicilium nomini ſuo dicavit, ubi pure colatur. Ex his duo-
bus quiſquis minimam partem vel palam reſcindere, vel furtim
auferre conatur, non hoc agit modo ut nudatam præcipuis ſuis
ornamentis urbem veſtram deformet, ſed ejus quoque ſaluti ma-
ligne invidet. Quamvis enim quæ Chriſto & diſperſis ejus mem-
bris præſtantur hic pietatis officia, caninos impiorum latratus pro-
vocent, merito tamen hæc vobis una compenſatio ſatis eſſe debet
quod è cælo Angeli & ex omnibus mundi plagis filii Dei benedi-

8-49

8-48. After N. de Larmessin, *"Habit de Rotisseur,"* from *The Trades*, 1690. A stately symmetry and somber demureness intensify the outrageous humor of this image.

8-49. Jan Jacob Schipper, page from Calvin's *Commentary*, 1667. Using types designed by Christoffel van Dyck, Schipper's mixture of sizes, letterspacing, and leading in the heading material is an exemplary representation of the Baroque sensibility.

their homes. Broadsheets, advertising cards, and other printed ephemera were produced by the engraving studios. The wonderful imagination that was sometimes displayed is seen in the set of engravings called *The Trades* (Fig. 8-48), originally created by N. de Larmessin in 1690. The tools or products of each trade were turned into lavish costumes on the figures. The nature of engraving—scratching fine lines into metal—encouraged the development of script letterforms of extreme fineness and delicacy.

During the seventeenth century, the Netherlands prospered as a mercantile and seafaring nation whose cultural attainment included the master artists Rembrandt and Vermeer. During this century, books became an important export commodity as a result of the accomplishments of yet another family dynasty of printers, founded by Louis Elzevir (1540–1617). Their handy and practical little volumes had solid, legible Dutch types surrounded by economically narrow margins, and featured engraved title pages. Competent editing, economical prices, and convenient size enabled the Elzevirs to pioneer an expansion of the book-buying market. The format design of their volumes was amazingly consistent, leading one prominent printing historian to declare that if you have seen one, you have seen them all! Editors were hired for Dutch, English, French, German, and Latin books that were exported throughout Europe. Many of their types were designed by the great Dutch designer and punchcutter Christoffel van Dyck. Designed to resist the wear and tear of printing, his types had stubby serifs with heavy bracketing (the connecting curve that unifies the serif to the main stroke of the letter) and the hairline elements were fairly stout (Fig. 8-49). Van Dyck's matrices and types were used continuously until 1810, when the fashion for the extreme thicks and thins of modern style types led the Haarlem foundry, which owned these, to thoughtlessly melt them down to reuse the metal.

9

An Epoch of Typographic Genius

After the drought of graphic-design creativity during the seventeenth century, the 1700s were an epoch of spectacular typographic originality. In 1692, Louis XIV, who had a strong interest in printing, ordered the establishment of a committee of scholars to develop a new type, whose letters were to be designed by "scientific" principles. Headed by mathematician Nicolas Jaugeon, the academicians studied all previous alphabets and writers on type design.

To construct the new roman capital letters, a square was divided into a grid of sixty-four units, then each of these squares was divided into thirty-six smaller units, for a total of 2,304 tiny squares. Italics were constructed on a similar parallelogram. The refined designs that were developed had less of the calligraphic properties inspired by the chisel and flat pen; a mathematical harmony was achieved by measurement and drafting instruments. However, these designs were not merely mechanical constructions, for ultimately the final decisions were made by the eye.

This *Romain du Roi,* as the new typeface was called, had increased contrast between thick and thin strokes, sharp horizontal serifs, and an even balance to each letterform. The master alphabets were engraved as large copperplate prints (Figs. 9-1 and 9-2) by Louis Simonneau (1654–1727). Philippe Grandjean (1666–1714) cut the punches for the reduction in size from the master alphabets to text type. The minute refinement on a 2,304-square grid proved absolutely worthless when reduced to text-size types; the delicacy of Grandjean's meticulous punch cutting and his aesthetic judgments became as important as the committee's lengthy deliberations and Simonneau's engravings as a source for the new typestyle.

Types designed for the Imprimerie Royale were for use only by that office for royal printing; other use constituted a capital offense. Other typefounders quickly cut types with similar characteristics, but they made sure the designs were sufficiently distinct to avoid confusion with Imprimerie Royale fonts.

In 1702, the *Médailles* folio was the first book to use the new types. As the first important shift from the Venetian tradition of Old Style roman type design, the Romain du Roi (Fig. 9-3) initiated a category of types called *transitional roman.* These break with a tradition of calligraphic qualities, bracketed serifs, and relatively even stroke weights of Old Style fonts. The *Romain du Roi* (as William Morris observed in the late nineteenth century) saw the calligrapher replaced by "the engineer" as the dominant typographic influence.

Graphic design of the Rococo era

The fanciful French art and architecture that flourished from about 1720 until around 1770 is called *Rococo.* Florid and intricate, Rococo ornament was composed of *S*- and *C*-curves with scrollwork, tracery, and plant forms derived from nature, classical art, oriental, and even medieval sources. Light pastel colors were often used with ivory white and gold in asymmetrically balanced designs. This lavish expression of the era of French King Louis XV (1710–1774) found its strongest graphic design impetus in the work of Pierre Simon Fournier le Jeune (1712–1768), the youngest son of a prominent family of printers and typefounders. At age twenty-four, Fournier le Jeune established an independent type design and foundry operation after studying art and apprenticing at the Le Bé foundry oper-

9-1 and 9-2. Louis Simonneau, master alphabets for the *Romain du Roi,* 1695. These copperplate engravings were intended to establish graphic standards for the new alphabet.

9-3. Philippe Grandjean, specimen of *Romain du Roi,* 1702. Compared to Old Style roman fonts, the crisp geometric quality and increased contrast of this first transitional typeface are clearly evident. The small spur on the center of the left side of the lowercase *l* is a device used to identify types of the Imprimerie Royale.

114

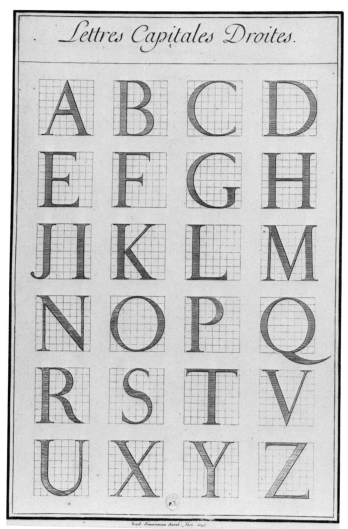

9-1

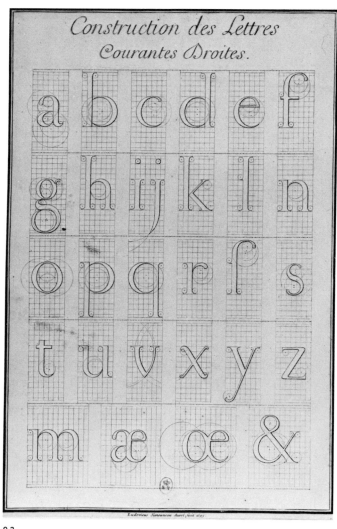

9-2

PREMIERE PARTIE
LES ÉPOQUES.

PREMIERE ÉPOQUE
ADAM OU LA CREATION.

Premier age du Monde.

*L'intention principale de Bossuet est de faire obser-
ver dans la suite des temps celle de la religion et
celle des grands Empires. Après avoir fait aller
ensemble selon le cours des années les faits qui
regardent ces deux choses, il reprend en particulier
avec les réflexions nécessaires premièrement ceux
qui nous font entendre* la durée perpétuelle de
la religion, *et enfin ceux qui nous découvrent les*
causes des grands changements arrivés dans les
empires.

La première époque vous présente d'abord un
grand spectacle : Dieu qui crée le ciel et la terre
par sa parole, et qui fait l'homme à son image.
C'est par où commence Moïse, le plus ancien

9-3

ated by his older brother, where he had cut decorative woodblocks and learned
punchcutting.

Eighteenth-century type measurement was chaotic, for each foundry had its own
type sizes, and nomenclature varied. In 1737, Fournier le Jeune pioneered standardization when he published his first Table of Proportions. The *pouce* (a now-
obsolete French unit of measure slightly longer than an inch) was divided into
twelve lines, each of which was divided into six points. Thus, his Petit–Romain size
was one line, four points, or about equal to contemporary ten-point type; his Cicero
size was two lines, or similar to contemporary twelve-point type.

Fournier le Jeune published his first specimen book, *Modèles des Caractères de
l'Imprimerie,* shortly before his thirtieth birthday in 1742. It presented 4,600 characters. Over a six-year period, he had both designed and cut punches for all of
these by himself. His roman styles were transitional forms inspired by the Romain
du Roi of 1702. However, his variety of weights and widths innovated the idea of a
"type family" of fonts that are visually compatible and can be mixed. He personally
designed and set the more complex pages, which were richly garlanded with his
exquisite typographic flowers that could be used singly or multiplied for unlimited
decorative effect. His explorations into casting enabled him to cast single, double,
and triple ruled lines up to 35.5 centimeters (about 14 inches) and to offer the
largest metal type (equivalent to contemporary 84- and 108-point sizes) yet made.
His decorative types (Fig. 9-4)—outline, shaded, flowered, and exotic—worked remarkably well with his roman fonts, ornaments, and rules.

Printing has been called "the artillery of the intellect." It might be said that

9-4

9-5

9-4. Pierre Simon Fournier le Jeune, specimen page of decorative types, 1768. Within each of Fournier's ornamental display letterforms, there is the structure of a well-proportioned roman letter.

9-5. Pierre Simon Fournier le Jeune, title page for *Ariette, Mise en Musique,* 1756. Vast numbers of floral, curvilinear, and geometric ornaments were needed to construct designs like this, which set the standard of excellence of the Rococo period.

9-6. Joseph Gerard Barbou, pages from *Contes et nouvelles en vers* by Jean La Fontaine, 1762. To adorn a poem about a painter's romantic interlude with his subject, Barbou used Eisen's etching of the event, a topical tailpiece by Choffard, and Fournier le Jeune's ornamented type.

Fournier le Jeune stocked the arsenals of Rococo printers with a complete design system (roman, italic, script, and decorative type styles, rules, and ornaments) of standardized measurement whose parts integrated both visually and physically (Fig. 9-5). Since French law now prevented a type founder from printing, Fournier le Jeune delivered made-up pages to Jean Joseph Barbou, the printer of his *Modèles des Caractères.* His nephew, Jean Gerard Barbou, was closely associated with Fournier le Jeune. In addition to publishing all of Fournier le Jeune's other books, the younger Barbou produced volumes of exceptional Rococo design, combining Fournier le Jeune's decorative types and copperplate engravings by Charles Eisen (1720–1778), who specialized in illustrations of graceful intricacy and sensual intimacy in vogue with royalty and the wealthy. Add the talents of the engraver Pierre Philippe Choffard (1730–1809), who specialized in ornate tailpieces and spot illustrations, and the results are book designs such as Jean La Fontaine's *Contes et nouvelles en vers* of 1762 (Fig. 9-6). In a small number of copies for a special audience, the coy romantic escapades in Eisen's engravings were replaced with other versions depicting explicit sexual conduct. In the *éditions de luxe,* the typefounder, printer, and illustrator combined their talents to project the psychology of the Rococo era: extravagant, sensuous, and pastoral; a joyous fantasyland oblivious to the misery and growing militancy of the poverty-stricken masses. These wildly popular books remained in vogue until the French Revolution of 1789 brought the monarchy and Rococo era tumbling down.

Fournier le Jeune planned a four-volume *Manuel Typographique* (Fig. 9-7) for many years, but only produced two volumes: *Type,* its cutting and founding, 1764; and *Type Specimens* (originally planned as volume four), 1768. An improved measurement system, based on the *point* (instead of the line and point), was introduced. He did not live to complete the other two volumes, one on printing and one on the great typographers' lives and work. Although his crowning achievement, the *Manuel Typographique,* was only half completed, Fournier le Jeune made more typographic innovations and had a greater impact on graphic design than any other person of his era.

9-7. Pierre Simon Fournier le Jeune, pages from *Manuel Typographique,* 1764 and 1768. In addition to showing the design accomplishments of a lifetime, Fournier's type manual is a masterwork of Rococo design.

9-6

LE BÂT.

Un peintre étoit, qui jaloux de sa femme,
Allant aux champs, lui peignit un baudet
Sur le nombril, en guise de cachet.
Un sien confrere amoureux de la Dame,
La va trouver, & l'âne efface net,
Dieu sçait comment ; puis un autre en remet,
Au même endroit, ainsi que l'on peut croire.
A celui-ci, par faute de mémoire,
Il mit un Bât ; l'autre n'en avoit point.
L'époux revient, veut s'éclaircir du point.
Voyez, mon fils, dit la bonne commere ;
L'âne est témoin de ma fidélité.
Diantre soit fait, dit l'époux en colere,
Et du témoin, & de qui l'a bâté.

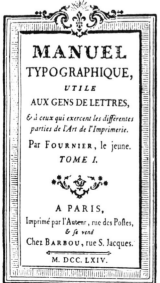

**MANUEL
TYPOGRAPHIQUE,**
UTILE
AUX GENS DE LETTRES,
*& à ceux qui exercent les differentes
parties de l'Art de l'Imprimerie.*
Par FOURNIER, le jeune.
TOME I.

A PARIS,
Imprimé par l'Auteur, rue des Postes,
& se vend
Chez BARBOU, rue S. Jacques.
M. DCC. LXIV.

9-7

**MANUEL
TYPOGRAPHIQUE.**

PREMIÈRE PARTIE.

LA GRAVURE,
OU TAILLE DES POINÇONS.

Pour être un bon Graveur de Caractères,
il faut être Typographe, c'est-à-dire, savoir
tous les détails du méchanisme de la Fonderie
& de l'Imprimerie, afin d'y assujétir son travail.
Maître de l'art, le Graveur doit tout prévoir
dans la fonte & dans l'impression. C'est par-là
que les Simon de Colines, les Garamond, les

A

N°. XXXVI. 34

CICÉRO, PETIT ŒIL.

Le Directeur à la mode, sem-
blable au Médecin, flatte, con-
sole, encourage, entretient la
délicatesse & la sensibilité sur
soi-même ; il n'ordonne que de
petits remèdes benins, & qui se
tournent en habitude. On ne
fait que tournoyer dans un petit cercle de vertus communes,
au-delà desquelles on ne passe
jamais généreusement.

Certains Dévots n'aiment jamais tant Dieu que lorsqu'ils
ont obtenu leurs satisfactions
temporelles ; ils ne prient jamais mieux que quand l'esprit
& la chair sont contens & qu'ils
prient ensemble.

Des faits éloignés de nos yeux
Ces Caractères nous instruisent,
Et par cet Art ingénieux,
Tous les talens s'immortalisent.

While even the most extravagant designs of Fournier le Jeune and his followers maintained the vertical and horizontal alignment that is part of the physical nature of metal typography, engravers were free to take tremendous liberties with form. Basically, an engraving is a drawing made with a graver instead of a pencil as the drawing tool and a copperplate instead of a sheet of paper as the substrate. Because this free line was an ideal medium for expressing the florid curves of the Rococo sensibility, engraving flourished throughout the 1700s. Delicate detail and fine lines made this medium (Fig. 9-8) much prized for labels, business cards, and announcements. Writing masters of the period developed flamboyant pen-and-ink flourishes, which translated well into engraving. Typical of this collaboration is the title page for George Shelley's *The Second Part of Natural Writing* (Fig. 9-9). Shelley's compendium of virtuoso writing styles was faithfully translated into the printed medium by George Bickham.

As engravers became increasingly skillful, they even began to produce books independent of the typographic printers by hand-engraving both illustrations and text. Englishman John Pine (1690–1756) was one of the best. His books, including the 1737 *Opera* of Horatii (Fig. 9-10), were sold by subscription before publication, and a list naming each subscriber was engraved in script in the front of the volume. Because serifs and thin strokes of letterforms were reduced to the delicate scratch of the engraver's finest tool, the contrast in the text material was dazzling and inspired imitation by typographic designers. As each letter was inscribed by hand, the text has a slight vibration giving it a handmade quality instead of a mechanical uniformity.

9-8. Robert Clee, trade card for a liquor dealer, eighteenth century. The design of copperplate engraved trade cards used extravagantly ornate border configurations and florid scripts.

9-9. George Shelley (designer) and George Bickham (engraver), title page for *The Second Part of Natural Writing*, c. 1709. Writing master Shelley designed the title page for his book as an opulent demonstration of his writing styles, ornaments, and "delightful fancies."

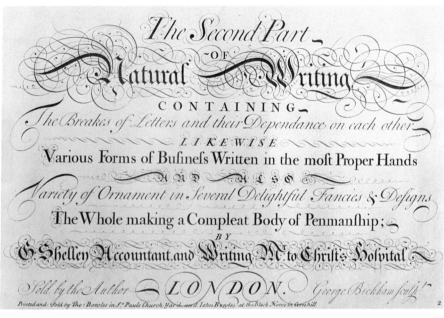

9-10. John Pine, page from Horatii's *Opera*, Volume II, 1737. The illustration and text were hand-engraved upon a copper printing plate and printed in one pass through the press.

Pine's book design and production shared his time with his position as chief engraver of seals for the king of England and production of large portfolios of etchings. One extraordinary set printed in 1753 depicts the 1588 defeat of the Spanish Armada in jumbo 52-by-36-centimeter (20½-by-14¼-inch) prints. These naval clashes were printed from two copperplates using black and blue-green ink. The effect is not unlike a subtle duotone.

Caslon and Baskerville

For over two and a half centuries after the invention of movable type, England had looked to the continent for typography and design leadership. Civil war, religious persecution, harsh censorship, and government control of printing had created a climate that was not conducive to graphic innovation. Upon ascending to the throne in 1660, Charles II had demanded that the number of printers be reduced to twenty "by death or otherwise."

Type and design ideas were imported across the English channel from Holland until a native genius emerged in the person of William Caslon (1692–1766). After apprenticing to a London engraver of gunlocks and barrels, young Caslon opened his own shop and added silver chasing and the cutting of gilding tools and letter stamps for bookbinders to his repertoire of engraving skills. The printer William Bowyer encouraged Caslon to take up type design and founding, which he did in 1720 with almost immediate success. His first commission was an Arabic font for the Society for Promoting Christian Knowledge. This was followed closely by the first size of Caslon Old Style with italic (Fig. 9-11) in 1722, and his reputation was made. For the next sixty years, virtually all English printing used Caslon fonts, and these types followed English colonialism around the globe. Printer Benjamin Franklin (1706–1790) introduced Caslon into the American colonies, where it was used extensively, including for the official printing of the Declaration of Independence by a Baltimore printer.

Caslon's type designs were not particularly fashionable or innovative. They owed their tremendous popularity and appeal to an outstanding legibility and sturdy texture that make them "comfortable" and "friendly to the eye." Beginning with the Dutch types of his day, Caslon increased the contrast between thick and thin strokes by making the thick elements slightly thicker. This was in direct opposition to fashion on the continent, which was embracing the lighter texture of the *Romain du Roi*. Caslon's fonts have a variety of design, giving them an uneven, rhythmic texture that adds to their visual interest and appeal. The Caslon foundry continued under his heirs and operated until the 1960s.

DOUBLE PICA ROMAN.
Quousque tandem abutere, Catilina, patientia noftra ? quamdiu
nos etiam furor ifte tuus eludet ?
quem ad finem fefe effrenata jac-
ABCDEFGHJIKLMNOP

GREAT PRIMER ROMAN.
Quousque tandem abutêre, Catilina, patientia noftra ? quamdiu nos etiam furor ifte tuus eludet ? quem ad finem fefe effrenata jactabit audacia ? nihilne te nocturnum præfidium palatii, nihil urbis vigiliæ, nihil timor populi, nihil con-
ABCDEFGHIJKLMNOPQRS

Double Pica Italick.
Quousque tandem abutere, Catilina, patientia noftra ? quamdiu nos etiam furor ifte tuus-eludet ? quem ad finem fefe effrenata jac-
ABCDEFGHJIKLMNO

Great Primer Italick.
Quousque tandem abutêre, Catilina, patientia noftra ? quamdiu nos etiam furor ifte tuus eludet ? quem ad finem fefe effrenata jactabit audacia ? nihilne te nocturnum præfidium palatii, nihil urbis vigiliæ, nihil timor populi, nihil con-
ABCDEFGHIJKLMNOPQR

9-11. William Caslon, specimens of Caslon roman and italic, 1734. The straightforward practicality of Caslon's designs made them the dominant roman style throughout the British empire far into the nineteenth century.

William Caslon worked in a tradition of Old Style roman typographic design that had begun over two hundred years earlier during the Italian Renaissance. This tradition was bolstered by John Baskerville (1706–1775), an innovator who broke the prevailing rules of design and printing in fifty-six editions produced at his Birmingham, England, press. Baskerville was involved in all facets of the bookmaking process. He designed, cast, and set type, improved the printing press, conceived and commissioned new papers, and designed and published the books he printed. This native of rural Worcestershire, who had "admired the beauty of letters" as a boy, moved to Birmingham as a young man and became established as a master writing teacher and stonecutter (Fig. 9-12). While still in his thirties, Baskerville became a manufacturer of japanned ware. These frames, boxes, clock cases, candlesticks, and trays were made from thin sheet metal, often decorated with hand-painted fruit and flowers, and finished with a hard, brilliant varnish. Manufacturing earned Baskerville a fortune, and he built an estate, Easy Hill, near Birmingham. Around 1751, he returned to his first love, the art of letters, and began to experiment with printing. As an artist who wanted to control all aspects of book design and production, he sought graphic perfection and was able to invest the time and resources necessary to achieve his goals. He was assisted by John Handy, a punch cutter, and Robert Martin, an apprentice who later became his foreman. Baskerville's type designs, which bear his name to this day, represent the zenith of the transitional style bridging the gap between Old Style and modern type design. His letters possessed a new elegance and lightness. In comparison with earlier designs, his types are wider, and the weight contrast between thick and thin strokes is increased. Placement of the thickest part of the letter is different. The treatment of serifs is new. The serifs flow smoothly out of the major strokes and terminate as refined points. His italic fonts most clearly show the influence of master handwriting.

As a book designer in a period of intricate, engraved title pages and illustrations, and generous use of printers' flowers, ornaments, and decorated initials, Baskerville opted for the pure typographic book (Figs. 9-13 and 9-14). Generous margins and a liberal use of space between letters and lines were used around his magnificent alphabets. To maintain an elegant purity of typographic design, an unusually large percentage of each press run was rejected, and he melted down and recast his type after each printing.

Baskerville's improvements for his four presses, built in his own workshops, focused on perfect alignment between the inch-thick brass platen and the smooth, stone press bed. The packing behind the sheet of paper being printed was unusually hard and smooth. As a consequence, he achieved even, overall impressions.

Trial and error led to the development of an ink composed of boiled linseed oil which was aged for several months after black or amber resin had been added. Then, a fine lampblack—acquired from "glass pinchers' and solderers' lamps"—

9-12

9-12. John Baskerville, *The gravestone slate,* undated. This demonstration stone showed potential customers young Baskerville's carving skill and range of lettering styles.

9-13. John Baskerville, title page for the *Virgil,* 1757. Baskerville reduced the design to letterforms symmetrically arranged and letterspaced; he reduced content to author, title, publisher, date, and city of publication. Economy, simplicity, and elegance resulted.

9-14. John Baskerville, sectional heading page from the *Virgil,* 1757. The stately order of Baskerville's page design results from the harmony of elements and the spatial intervals that separate them.

PUBLII VIRGILII

MARONIS

BUCOLICA,

GEORGICA,

ET

AENEIS.

BIRMINGHAMIAE:

Typis JOHANNIS BASKERVILLE.

MDCCLVII.

9-13

P. VIRGILII MARONIS

GEORGICON.

LIBER SECUNDUS.

HACTENUS arvorum cultus, et fidera cœli:
Nunc te, Bacche, canam, nec non filveftria tecum
Virgulta, et prolem tarde crefcentis olivæ.
Huc, pater o Lenæe; (tuis hic omnia plena
5 Muneribus: tibi pampineo gravidus autumno
Floret ager; fpumat plenis vindemia labris)
Huc, pater o Lenæe, veni; nudataque mufto
Tinge novo mecum direptis crura cothurnis.
  Principio arboribus varia eft natura creandis:
10 Namque aliæ, nullis hominum cogentibus, ipfæ
Sponte fua veniunt, campofque et flumina late
Curva tenent: ut molle filer, lentæque geniftæ,
Populus, et glauca canentia fronde falicta.
Pars autem pofito furgunt de femine: ut altæ
15 Caftaneæ, nemorumque Jovi quæ maxima frondet
Aefculus, atque habitæ Graiis oracula quercus.
Pullulat ab radice aliis denfiffima filva:
Ut cerafis, ulmifque: etiam Parnaffia laurus
Parva fub ingenti matris fe fubjicit umbra.
20 Hos natura modos primum dedit: his genus omne
Silvarum, fruticumque viret, nemorumque facrorum.
Sunt alii, quos ipfe via fibi repperit ufus.
Hic plantas tenero abfcindens de corpore matrum
                                        Depofuit

9-14

was ground into it. The resin added a sheen to this unusually dense black ink whose luster bordered on purple.

The smooth, glossy surface of the paper in Baskerville's books had not been seen before. This quality was achieved by using hot-pressed wove paper. Before Baskerville's *Virgil,* books were printed on laid paper, which has a textural pattern of horizontal lines. This pattern is created in manufacture by wires that form the screen in the papermaker's mold. This wire screen had close parallel wires supported by larger wires running at right angles to the thinner wires. The wove paper manufactured for Baskerville was formed by a mold having a much finer screen made of wires woven in and out like cloth. The texture from wire marks was virtually eliminated from this paper.

All handmade papers have a coarse surface. When paper was moistened before printing on a hand press, it became even coarser. Baskerville's desire for elegant printing led him to hot-press the paper after it was printed to produce a smooth, refined surface. How he hot-pressed or calendered his paper is controversial, because early sources give conflicting reports. One version reports that Baskerville designed and constructed a smoothing press with two copper rollers 21.6 centimeters (8½ inches) in diameter and almost a meter (39 inches) long. A second version explains that Baskerville employed a woman and a little girl to operate a pressing or glazing machine that worked in a manner not unlike ironing clothes. Yet another version declares that as each page was removed from the press, it was sandwiched between two highly polished heated copperplates which expelled moisture, set the ink, and created the smooth, glossy surface. Since Baskerville closely guarded his innovations, we can only guess which of these methods were employed. Realizing the potential market for mirror-smooth writing paper, he used his process to develop a steady stationery business through booksellers.

The net result of this effort was books of dazzling contrast, simplicity, and refinement. Professional jealousy caused Baskerville's critics to dismiss him as an "amateur," although his work set a high standard of quality. Some of his critics argued that reading Baskerville type hurt their eyes because it was so sharp and contrasty. Benjamin Franklin, who admired Baskerville, wrote him a letter relating that he, Franklin, had torn the foundry name from a Caslon specimen sheet, told an acquaintance who was complaining about Baskerville's type that it was Baskerville's specimen sheet, and asked the man to point out the problems. The victim of Franklin's whimsy proceeded to pontificate on the problems, complaining that just looking at it was giving him a headache.

While Baskerville met with indifference and even hostility in the British Isles, the design of his type and books became important influences on the continent, as the Italian Giambattista Bodoni (1740–1813) and the Didot family in Paris became enthusiastic about his work.

The imperial designs of Louis René Luce

An imperial and stately graphic design style was achieved by another type designer and punch cutter at the Imprimerie Royale, Louis René Luce (d. 1773). During the three decades from 1740 until 1770, Luce designed a series of types that were narrow and condensed, with serifs as sharp as spurs. Engraved borders were being widely used in graphic designs, and these required a second printing. Luce created a large series of letterpress borders, ornaments, trophies, and other devices of impressive variety and excellent printing quality. These were designed with a mechanistic perfection that projects an air of imperial authority. Cast in modular sections, these ornaments were then assembled into the desired configuration by the compositor. The density of line in Luce's ornaments was carefully planned to be visually compatible with his typefaces and often had an identical weight so that they would look as if they belonged together in a design. In 1771, Luce published his *Essai d'une Nouvelle Typographie (Essay on the New Typography)* with ninety-three plates presenting the range of his design accomplishments (Figs. 9-15 and 9-16). Mindful of the power of his patron, King Louis XV, Luce made his layout for

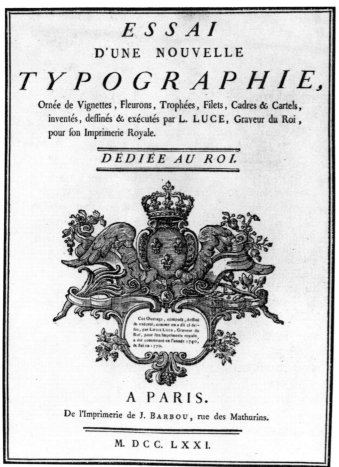

9-15

9-16

the first of eleven foldout, hypothetical graphic designs showing his ornaments and types in use a "Frontispiece for a history of the King." Both Fournier le Jeune and Luce died before the French Revolution tore apart the world in which they lived and served, the *ancien régime* of the French monarchy. The majestic design styles in architecture, interiors, and graphics patronized by royalty lost all social relevance in the world of democracy and equality that emerged from the chaos of revolution. Perhaps the ultimate irony occurred in 1790, when *Romain du Roi* typefaces commissioned by Louis XIV were used to print radical political tracts in support of the French Revolution.

The modern style

The son of a poor printer, Giambattista Bodoni was born in Saluzzo in northern Italy. As a young man, he traveled to Rome and apprenticed at the Propaganda Fide, the Catholic press that printed missionary materials in native tongues for use around the globe. Bodoni learned punch cutting, but his interest in living in Rome declined after his mentor, Ruggeri—who was the director—committed suicide. Shortly thereafter, Bodoni left the Propaganda Fide with the idea of journeying to England and perhaps working with Baskerville. While visiting his parents before leaving Italy, twenty-eight-year-old Bodoni was asked to take charge of the Stamperia Reale, the official press of Ferdinand, Duke of Parma. Bodoni accepted the charge and became the private printer to the court. He printed official documents and publications desired by the Duke, in addition to projects conceived and initiated by Bodoni. His initial design influence was Fournier le Jeune, whose foundry supplied type and ornaments to the Stamperia Reale after Bodoni took charge. The quality of Bodoni's design and printing, even though scholarship and proofreading were sometimes lacking, created a growing international reputation. In 1790, the

9-15. Louis René Luce (designer) and Jean Joseph Barbou (printer), title page from *Essai d'une Nouvelle Typographie,* 1771. By replacing the floral lushness of Rococo design with a more rigorous design feeling, Luce pointed toward the Modern style of Bodoni and the Didots.

9-16. Louis René Luce (designer) and Jean Joseph Barbou (printer), ornaments page from *Essai d'une Nouvelle Typographie,* 1771. These meticulously constructed cornices and borders express the authority and absolutism of the French monarchy.

An Epoch of Typographic Genius

9-17. Giambattista Bodoni, title page from *Saggio tipografico,* 1771. The tremendous influence of Fournier le Jeune upon Bodoni's earlier work is evident in this page design.

9-18. Giambattista Bodoni, page from *Pel battesimo d.S.A.R. Ludovico,* 1774. Moving away from Fournier le Jeune's influence, Bodoni began to favor more geometric ornaments and white space.

9-19. Giambattista Bodoni, section-heading page for Virgil's *Opera,* Volume II, 1793. In graphic designs so pure and simple, every adjustment of letterspace and line space becomes critical to the overall design harmony.

Vatican invited Bodoni to Rome to establish a press for printing the classics there, but the Duke countered with an offer of expanded facilities, greater independence, and the privilege of printing for other clients. Bodoni elected to remain in Parma.

At about the same time, the cultural and political climate was changing. Politically, the revolt against the French monarchy led to a total rejection of the lush styles so popular during the reigns of Louis XV and XVI. To fill the formal void, architects, painters, and sculptors enthusiastically embraced the classical forms of Greek and Roman antique art, which were captivating the public by the 1790s. Excavations, mostly at Herculaneum, Pompeii, and around Rome, fueled the mania. Graphic design required another language of form to replace the seemingly outmoded Rococo style. It was Bodoni who took a leadership role in evolving new typefaces and page layout. Figures 9-17, 9-18, and 9-19 show Bodoni's evolution from Fournier le Jeune–inspired Rococo to the modern style.

The term *modern,* which defines a new category of roman type, was first used by Fournier le Jeune in his *Manuel Typographique* to describe the design trends that culminated in Bodoni's mature work. The initial impetus was the thin, straight serifs of Grandjean's *Romain du Roi* commissioned by Louis XIV, followed by engraved graphic designs by artists including Pine. Next came the letterforms and page layouts of Baskerville, particularly his practice of making the light strokes of his characters thinner to increase the contrast between thicks and thins. Also, Baskerville's rejection of ornament and his generous use of space were factors. Another trend, the design of narrower, more condensed letterforms, gave type a taller and more geometric appearance. Finally, all of these evolutionary trends were encouraged by a growing sensibility for a lighter typographic tone and texture, and this new fashion reinforced the other trends.

Around 1790, Bodoni redesigned the roman letterforms with a more mathematical, geometric, and mechanical appearance. He reinvented the serifs by making them hairlines that formed sharp right angles with the upright strokes. There is no tapered flow of the serif into the upright stroke as in Old Style roman. The thin strokes of his letterforms were trimmed to the same weight as the hairline serifs,

9-17

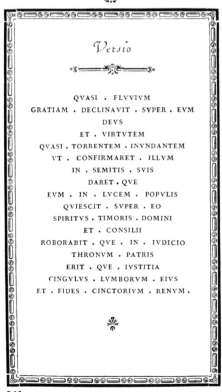

9-18

9-19

creating a brilliant sharpness and a dazzling contrast that had not been seen before. Bodoni defined his design ideal as cleanness, good taste, charm, and regularity. This regularity—the standardization of units—was a concept of the emerging industrial era of the machine. Bodoni decided that the letters in a type font should be created through combinations of a very limited number of identical units. This standardization of forms that could be measured and constructed marked the death of calligraphy and writing as the wellspring for type design and the end of the imprecise cutting and casting of earlier type design. Bodoni's precise, measurable, and repeatable forms expressed the vision and spirit of the machine age. It is noteworthy that as Bodoni was constructing alphabets of interchangeable parts, American inventor Eli Whitney was assembling firearms of interchangeable parts in his New Haven, Connecticut, factory, foreshadowing the mass-production techniques soon to revolutionize western society.

In Bodoni's page layouts, the borders and ornaments of the earlier decorative style that had brought international fame to the Stampera Reale were cast aside for a severe economy of form and efficiency of function. The severe purity of Bodoni's late graphic design style has affinities with twentieth-century functional typography. Open, simple page design with generous margins, wide letter- and line spacing, and large areas of white space became his hallmark. Lightness was increased by using a smaller x-height and longer ascenders and descenders. In some fonts, letters were cast on oversized metal so the type could not be set solid. As a result, these fonts always had the appearance of generous leading.

Like a majority of books of his time, most of the 345 books that Bodoni published were new editions of Greek and Roman classics. Critics hailed Bodoni's volumes, like the great Roman poet Virgil's *Opera,* as the typographic expression of Neoclassicism and a return to "antique virtue." This is surprising, for Bodoni was breaking new ground. Bodoni designed about three hundred type fonts and planned a monumental specimen book presenting this work. After his death, his widow, Signora Bodoni, and foreman, Luigi Orsi, persisted with the project and published the two-volume *Manuale Tipografico* (Fig. 9-20) in 1818. This monumental celebration of the aesthetics of letterforms and homage to Bodoni's genius is a milestone in the history of graphic design.

In 1872, the citizens of Saluzzo honored their native son by erecting a statue of Bodoni. Ironically, they carved his name in the base in Old Style roman letters!

A family dynasty of printers, publishers, papermakers, and typefounders began in 1713 when Françoise Didot (1689–1757) established his printing and bookselling firm in Paris. In 1780, his son, François Ambroise Didot (1730–1804), introduced a highly finished, smooth paper of wove design modeled after the paper commissioned by Baskerville in England. The Didot typefoundry's constant experimentation led to *maigre* (thin) and *gras* (fat) type styles similar to the condensed and expanded fonts of our time. Around 1785, François Ambroise revised Fournier's typographic measurement system and created the point system used in France today. François Ambroise realized that the Fournier scale was subject to shrinkage after being printed on moistened paper, and even Fournier's metal master had no standard for comparison. Therefore, François Ambroise adopted the official *pied de roi,* divided into twelve French inches, as his standard. Then each inch was divided into seventy-two points. Didot discarded the traditional nomenclature for various type sizes (Cicero, Petit-Romain, Gros-Text, and so on) and identified them with the measure of the metal type body in points (ten-point, twelve-point, and so on). The Didot system was adopted in Germany, where it was revised by Hermann Berthold in 1879 to work with the metric system. In 1886, the Didot system—revised to suit the English inch—was adopted as a standard point measure by American typefounders, and England adopted the point system in 1898. The fonts brought out beginning in 1775 by François Ambroise are the first to possess the Didot touch (Fig. 9-21), a lighter, more geometric quality similar in feeling to the evolution occurring in Bodoni's designs under Baskerville's influence.

François Ambroise had two sons: Pierre l'aîné Didot (1761–1853), who took

9-20. Giambattista Bodoni, page from *Manuale Tipografico,* 1818. The crisp clarity of Bodoni's letterforms are echoed by the *scotch rules.* Composed of double and triple thick-and-thin elements, these rules and borders echo the weight contrasts of Bodoni's modern types.

AVIS

AUX SOUSCRIPTEURS

DE

LA GERUSALEMME

LIBERATA

IMPRIMÉE PAR DIDOT L'AÎNÉ

SOUS LA PROTECTION ET PAR LES ORDRES

DE MONSIEUR.

LES ARTISTES choisis par MONSIEUR pour exécuter son édition de LA GERUSALEMME LIBERATA demandent avec confiance aux souscripteurs de cet ouvrage un délai de quelques mois pour en mettre au jour la première livraison. Il est rarement arrivé qu'un ouvrage où sont entrés les ornements de la gravure ait pu être donné au temps préfix pour lequel il avoit été promis : cet art entraîne beaucoup de difficultés qui causent des retards forcés ; et certainement on peut regarder comme un empêchement insurmontable les jours courts et obscurs d'un hiver long et rigoureux. D'ailleurs la quantité d'ouvrages de gravure proposés actuellement par

9-21. François Ambroise Didot, typography from a prospectus for Tasso's *La Gerusalemme Liberata,* 1784. Designed at the Didot foundry, the typeface used in this announcement for a forthcoming romantic novel is a very early presentation of a true Modern style letterform. Straight hairline serifs, extreme contrast between thick and thin strokes, and construction on a vertical axis are characteristics that mark this break with transitional letterforms.

charge of his father's printing office, and Firmin Didot (1764–1836), who succeeded his father as head of the Didot type foundry. Firmin's notable achievements included the invention of *stereotyping.* This process is casting a duplicate of a relief printing surface by pressing a molding material (damp paper pulp, plaster, or clay) against it to make a matrix. Molten metal is poured into the matrix to form the duplicate printing plate. Stereotyping made longer press runs possible.

After the Revolution, the French government honored Pierre l'aîné by granting him the printing office formerly used by the Imprimerie Royale at the Louvre. There he gave the neoclassical revival of the Napoleonic era its graphic design expression in a series of *éditions du Louvre* (Fig. 9-22). These magnificent classics included Virgil (1798), Horace (1799), Racine (1801–1805), and Aesop (1802). The lavish margins set off Firmin Didot's modern typography, which is even more mechanical and precise than Bodoni's. The engravings of flawless technique and sharp value contrast were designed by various artists working in the Neoclassical manner of the painter Jacques Louis David (1748–1825). In seeking to imitate nature in her most perfect form, these artists created figures as ideally modeled as Greek statues, who are frozen in shallow picture boxes. A seldom equaled, though brittle, perfection is achieved.

Bodoni and the Didots were rivals and kindred spirits. Comparisons and speculation about who innovated and who followed become inevitable. They shared common influences and the same cultural milieu. In the opinion of this writer, their influence upon each other was reciprocal, for Bodoni and the Didots each attempted to push the modern style farther than the other. In so doing, each pushed the aesthetics of contrast, mathematical construction, and neoclassical refinement to the ultimate possible level. Bodoni is credited with greater skill as a designer and printer, but the Didots possessed greater scholarship. Bodoni proclaimed that he sought only the magnificent and did not work for common readers. In addition to their extravagant folio editions, the Didots used their new stereotyping process to produce much larger editions of economical books for a broader audience. A year after the *Manuale Tipografico* appeared, the 1819 *Spécimen des Nouveaux Caractères . . . de P. Didot l'aîné* was published in Paris.

The illuminated printing of William Blake

During the waning years of the eighteenth century, an unexpected counterpoint to the severe typography of Bodoni and Didot appeared in the illuminated printing of the visionary English poet and artist, William Blake (1757–1827). As a child, Blake reported seeing angels in a tree and the prophet Ezekiel in a field. After completing an engraving apprenticeship and studying at the Royal Academy, Blake opened a printing shop at age twenty-seven, where he was assisted by his younger brother Robert. Upon Robert's death three years later, Blake reported that he saw Robert's soul joyfully rising through the ceiling. Blake informed friends that Robert appeared to him in a dream and told about a way to print Blake's poems and illustrations as relief etchings without typography.

Blake began to publish books of his poetry, and each page was printed as a monochrome etching combining word and image. Blake and his wife then either hand-colored each page with watercolor or printed colors, handbound each copy in paper covers, and sold them at modest prices. The lyrical fantasy, glowing swirls of color, and imaginative vision that Blake achieved in his poetry and accompanying designs represent an effort to transcend the material of graphic design and printing to achieve a spiritual expression. The 1789 title page from *Songs of Innocence* (Pl. 14) shows how Blake integrated letterforms into illustrations. The swirls of foliage that spin from the serifs of the letters become leaves for the tree; small figures frolic among these letters that are set against a vibrant sky.

Blake's single-minded unworldliness and spiritual beliefs led some people to dismiss him as being mad, and he died in poverty and neglect. His reaction against the Neoclassical emphasis on reason and the intellect, combined with his focus upon the imagination, introspection, and emotions as a wellspring for his work,

AENEIDOS

LIBER QUINTUS.

Interea medium Aeneas jam classe tenebat
Certus iter, fluctusque atros Aquilone secabat,
Moenia respiciens, quae jam infelicis Elissae
Collucent flammis. Quae tantum accenderit ignem
Causa latet; duri magno sed amore dolores
Polluto, notumque furens quid femina possit,
Triste per augurium Teucrorum pectora ducunt.
    Ut pelagus tenuere rates, nec jam amplius ulla
Occurrit tellus, maria undique et undique coelum;
Olli caeruleus supra caput adstitit imber,
Noctem hiememque ferens; et inhorruit unda tenebris.
Ipse gubernator puppi Palinurus ab alta:
Heu! quianam tanti cinxerunt aethera nimbi?
Quidve, pater Neptune, paras? Sic deinde locutus,
Colligere arma jubet, validisque incumbere remis;
Obliquatque sinus in ventum, ac talia fatur:
Magnanime Aenea, non, si mihi Juppiter auctor

make Blake a harbinger of nineteenth-century romanticism. His bright colors and swirling organic forms are forerunners to expressionism, Art Nouveau, and abstract art.

The epoch closes

British national pride led to the establishment of the Shakespeare Press in 1786 to produce editions of splendor to rival the folio volumes of Paris and Parma. The state of English printing was such that a printing house, typefoundry, and ink manufactory had to be established to produce work of the desired quality. Punch cutter William Martin (d. 1815), former apprentice to Baskerville and brother of Baskerville's foreman Robert Martin, was called to London to design and cut types "in imitation of the sharp and fine letter used by the French and Italian printers." His types combined the majestic proportions of Baskerville with the sharp contrasts of modern fonts. William Bulmer (1757–1830) was chosen by publishers John and Josiah Boydell and George and W. Nicol to print, in nine volumes, *The Dramatic Works of Shakespeare,* 1792–1802. These were followed by a three-volume edition of Milton.

As a boy in Newcastle, Bulmer had a close friend in Thomas Bewick (1753–1828), who is called the father of wood engraving (Figs. 9-23 and 9-24). After apprenticing to engraver Ralph Beilby and learning to engrave sword blades and door plates, Bewick turned his attention to the wood engraving of illustrations. His "white-line" technique employed a fine graver to achieve delicate tonal effects by cutting across the grain on woodblocks of Turkish boxwood instead of with the grain on the blocks of softer wood used in creating woodcuts. Publication of his *General History of Quadrupeds* in 1790 brought renown to Bewick and his techniques, which became a major illustration method in letterpress printing until the

9-22. Pierre l'âiné Didot (printer), pages from Virgil's *Bucolica, Georgica, et Aeneis,* 1798. This double-page spread shows the splendid perfection, lavish margins, and cool understatement of Neoclassical graphic design.

9-23. Thomas Bewick, "Old English Hound" from the *General History of Quadrupeds,* 1790. Bewick achieved his dazzling tonal range by combining "white-line-on-black" techniques—much like drawing in chalk on a blackboard—with a more usual "black-line-on-white" treatment in the lighter tonal areas.

9-24. Thomas Bewick, "The Yellow Bunting" from *British Birds,* 1797. "Sticking to nature as closely as he could," Bewick achieved a tonal range and accuracy of drawing which set the standard of excellence for wood-engraved illustrations.

9-25. Thomas Bewick (engraver) and William Bulmer (printer), page from William Somerville's *The Chase,* 1796. Simplicity becomes exquisite, for the paper, type, printing, and engravings all reflect a perfection of craft.

advent of photomechanical halftones nearly a century later.

Bulmer used Martin's types and Bewick's wood engravings together in a series of volumes, including *Poems by Goldsmith and Parnell* in 1795 and William Somerville's *The Chase* of 1796 (Fig. 9-25), in which the clean, spacious design of Bodoni and Didot was tempered by a traditional English legibility and warmth. These gentle volumes might be called a lyrical envoi of a three-and-a-half-century period of graphic design and printing that began with Gutenberg in Mainz. Printing had been a handicraft, and graphic design had involved the layout of metal type and related material with illustrations printed from handmade blocks. The eighteenth century closed with stormy political revolutions in France and the American colonies. England was the nucleus for the gathering forces of the vast upheavals of the Industrial Revolution. The sweeping changes ushered in by the conversion of an agrarian, rural society with handicraft manufacture to the industrial society of machine manufacture shook Western civilization to its very foundations. All aspects of the human experience, including visual communications, were transformed by profound and irrevocable changes.

In Albion's isle, when glorious Edgar reign'd,
He, wisely provident, from her white cliffs
Launch'd half her forests, and, with numerous fleets,
Cover'd his wide domain: there proudly rode,
Lord of the deep, the great prerogative
Of British monarchs. Each invader bold,
Dane and Norwegian, at a distance gazed,
And, disappointed, gnash'd his teeth in vain.
He scour'd the seas, and to remotest shores
With swelling sails the trembling corsair fled.
Rich commerce flourish'd; and with busy oars
Dash'd the resounding surge. Nor less, at land,
His royal cares; wise, potent, gracious prince!
His subjects from their cruel foes he saved,

9-25

1. Cave painting from Lascaux, France, c. 15,000–10,000 B.C.

2. The Blau Monument, c. 3750 B.C.

3. *The Final Judgment* from the Papyrus of Ani, c. 1420 B.C.

4. Painting by Yuan Chao Meng-fu, c. 1400 A.D.

5. Phaistos Disk, c. 2000 B.C.

6. *Chi-Rho* from the Book of Kells, c. 795–806 A.D.

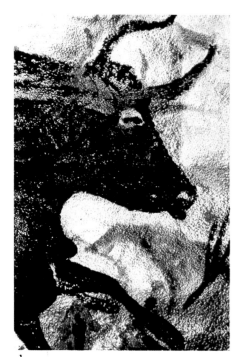

1

2

3

4

5

6

7. Pages from the Coronation Gospels, c. 800 A.D.

8. Limbourg Brothers, page from *Les Tres Riches Heures du Duc de Berry*, 1413–1416.

9. Pages from *Ars memorandi per figuras Evangelistarum*, c. 1470.

10. Fust and Schoeffer, detail from *Psalter in Latin*, 1459.

11. Anton Koberger, pages from *The Nuremberg Chronicle*, 1493.

12. Erhard Ratdolt, Peter Loeslein, and Bernhard Maler, pages from *Calendarium*, 1476.

7

8

11

9

10

12

13. Geoffroy Tory, page from *Les Heures de Jean Lallement,* 1506.

14. William Blake, *Songs of Innocence* title page, 1789.

15. J. H. Bufford's Sons, *The Swedish Song Quartett* poster, c. 1867.

16. Riverside Print Company, *Carry-Us-All* poster, undated.

17. Morris Père and Fils, and Emile Levy, *Cirque D'Hiver* poster, 1871.

18. William Morris, *Rose* fabric design, 1883.

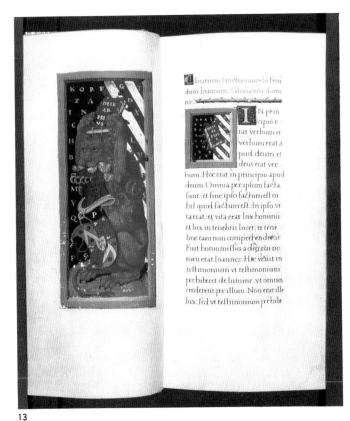

13

15

16

14

17

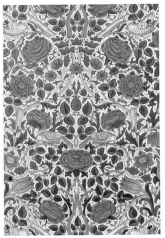

18

19. Lucien Pissarro, pages from *Ishtar's Descent to the Nether World*, 1903.

20. Frederic Goudy, Caxton Company booklet cover, 1911.

21. Jules Chéret, Élysée Montmartre *Bal Masqué* poster, 1896.

22. Eugène Grasset, exhibition poster, c. 1894.

23. The Beggarstaffs, Harper's poster, 1895.

24. Henri de Toulouse-Lautrec, Moulin Rouge poster, 1891.

25. Théophile-Alexandre Steinlen, Guillot poster, 1897.

19

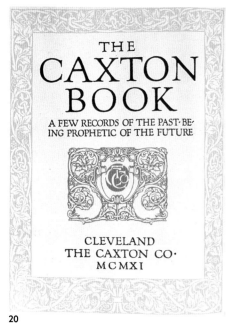

20

22

21

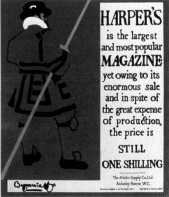

23

24

25

26. Alphonse Mucha, *Gismonda* poster, 1894.

27. Emmanuel Orazi, La Maison Moderne poster, 1905.

28. Will Bradley, *The Inland Printer* poster, 1895.

29. Edward Penfield, *Harper's* poster, 1897.

30. Henri van de Velde, Tropon poster, 1899.

31. Gisbert Combaz, *La Libre Esthetique* poster, 1898.

26

27

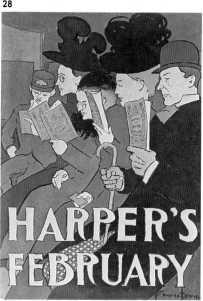

28

29

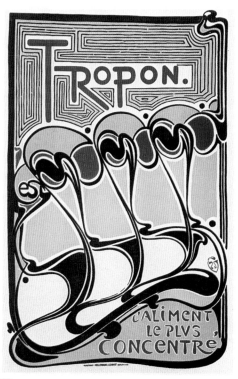

30

31

32. Hans Christiansen, *Jugend* cover, 1899.

33. J. Herbert McNair with Margaret and Frances Macdonald, Glasgow Institute of Fine Arts poster, 1895.

34. Koloman Moser, Thirteenth Vienna Secession exhibition poster, 1902.

35. Alfred Roller, Fourteenth Vienna Secession exhibition poster, 1902.

36. Peter Behrens, AEG poster, 1910.

37. Fernand Léger, page from *La fin du Monde . . .* , 1919.

38. Fortunato Depero, New Futurist Theater poster, 1924.

39. Fortunato Depero, cover for *Dinamo-Azari*, 1927.

32

34

35

37

38

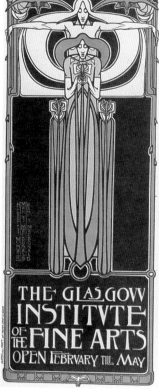

33

36

39

40. Lucien Bernhard, Priester poster, c. 1905.

41. Hans Rudi Erdt, Opel poster, 1911.

42. Julius Klinger, eighth bond drive poster, 1917.

43. James Montgomery Flagg, military recruiting poster, 1917.

44. Jesse Wilcox Smith, American Red Cross poster, 1917.

45. Ludwig Hohlwein, Marque PKZ poster, 1908.

40

42

43

44

41

45

46. E. McKnight Kauffer, *Daily Herald* poster, 1918.

47. A. M. Cassandre, *L'Intransigeant* poster, 1925.

48. A. M. Cassandre, "L'Atlantique" poster, 1931.

49. Austin Cooper, London Electric Railway poster, 1924.

50. Austin Cooper, London Electric Railway poster, 1924.

51. Kasmir Malevich, Suprematist Composition, 1915.

52. El Lissitzky, *Beat the Whites with the Red Wedge* poster, 1919.

53. El Lissitzky, pages from *For the Voice*, 1923.

46

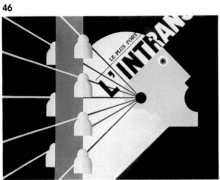

47

48

49

50

51

53

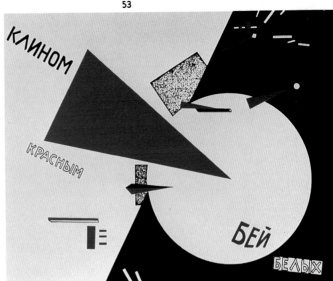

52

54. Georgy and Vladimir Stenberg, film poster, undated.

55. Bart van der Leck, Batavier-Line poster, 1916.

56. Theo van Doesburg, cover for *Grundbegriffe der Neuen Gestaltenden Kunst,* 1925.

57. Joost Schmidt, Bauhaus exhibition poster, 1923.

58. Herbert Bayer, Kandinsky exhibition poster, 1926.

59. Jan Tschichold, *Die Hose* film poster, 1927.

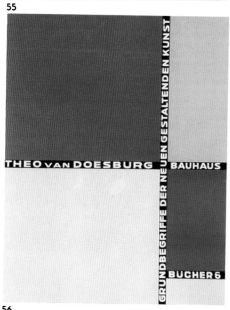

54

55

58

57

59

56

60. Piet Zwart, brochure page for N. V. Druckerei Trio, 1930.

61. Willem Sandberg, cover for a museum journal, 1963.

62. Herbert Matter, Pontresina tourist poster, 1935.

63. Lester Beall, Rural Electrification Administration poster, 1937.

64. Lester Beall, Rural Electrification Administration poster, c. 1937.

65. Joseph Binder, New York World's Fair poster, 1939.

60

63

61

62

64

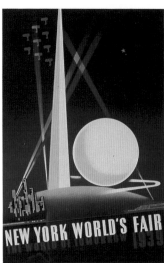

65

66. Will Burtin, cover image for *The Architectural Forum*, 1940.

67. Jean Carlu, "America's Answer! Production" poster, 1941.

68. E. McKnight Kauffer, poster supporting the Greek resistance, 1940.

69. Ben Shahn, U.S. Office of War Information poster, 1943.

70. Theo Ballmer, exhibition poster, 1928.

71. Max Bill, poster for an exhibition of U.S. architecture, 1945.

67

66

68

69

70

71

72. Max Huber, Monza automobile race poster, 1948.

73. Josef Müller-Brockmann, poster for an exhibition of lamps, 1975.

74. Rudy de Harak, *Personality and Psychotherapy* book cover, 1964.

75. Paul Rand, cover design for American Institute of Graphic Arts, 1968.

76. Bradbury Thompson, pages from *Westvaco Inspirations*, 216, 1961.

77. Saul Bass, *Exodus* film poster, 1960.

72

73

77

74

75

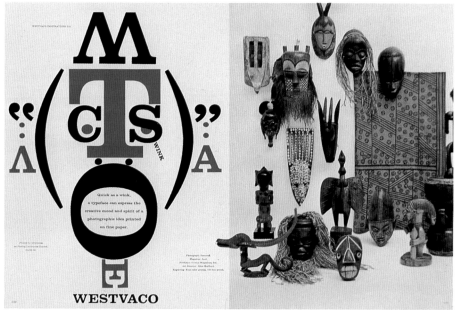

76

66. Will Burtin, cover image for *The Architectural Forum*, 1940.

67. Jean Carlu, "America's Answer! Production" poster, 1941.

68. E. McKnight Kauffer, poster supporting the Greek resistance, 1940.

69. Ben Shahn, U.S. Office of War Information poster, 1943.

70. Theo Ballmer, exhibition poster, 1928.

71. Max Bill, poster for an exhibition of U.S. architecture, 1945.

66

67

68

69

70

71

72. Max Huber, Monza automobile race poster, 1948.

73. Josef Müller-Brockmann, poster for an exhibition of lamps, 1975.

74. Rudy de Harak, *Personality and Psychotherapy* book cover, 1964.

75. Paul Rand, cover design for American Institute of Graphic Arts, 1968.

76. Bradbury Thompson, pages from *Westvaco Inspirations*, 216, 1961.

77. Saul Bass, *Exodus* film poster, 1960.

72

73

77

74

75

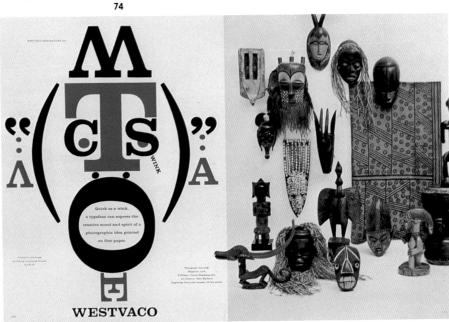

76

78. Herb Lubalin, poster announcing Davida Bold typeface, 1965.

79. George Lois, *Esquire* magazine cover, 1968.

80. Giovanni Pintori, Olivetti Elettrosumma 22 poster, 1956.

81. Lance Wyman and Beatrice Cole, Mexico City Olympics tickets, 1968.

82. Otl Aicher, Munich Olympics poster, 1972.

83. Deborah Sussman, *Design Quarterly* cover, 1985.

78

79

80

81

82

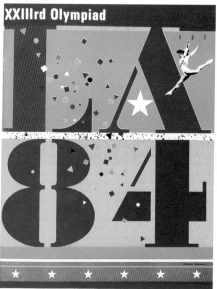

83

84. Tadeusz Trepkowski, "No!" antiwar poster, 1953.

85. Milton Glaser, poster for Bob Dylan, 1967.

86. Seymour Chwast, *The Three Penny Opera* record album cover, undated.

87. Paul Davis, theater poster, 1977.

88. Gunter Rambow, *South African Roulette* theater poster, 1988.

89. Grapus, exhibition poster, 1982.

84

85

87

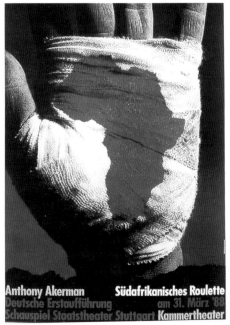

88

89

86

90. Kazumasa Nagai, "Tradition et Nouvelles Techniques" poster, 1984.

91. Ikko Tanaka, "Nihon Buyo" poster, 1981.

92. Takenobu Igarashi, Igarashi Poster Calendar, 1990.

93. Kochi Sato, Ellipse Music '84 poster, 1984.

94. Rosmarie Tissi, Anton Schob folder, 1981.

90

92

91

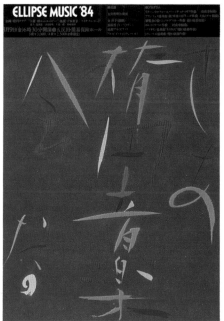

93

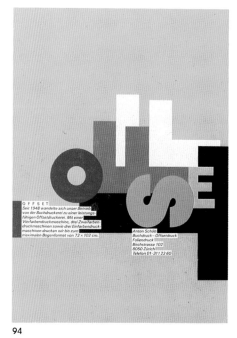

94

95. Wolfgang Weingart, Kunstkredit poster, 1982.

96. Michael Vanderbyl, California Public Radio poster, 1979.

97. Michael Cronin and Shannon Terry, Beethoven Festival poster, 1983.

98. Paula Scher, CBS Records jazz poster, 1979.

99. Lance Hidy, Sioux City Public Library poster, 1990.

100. Woody Pirtle, photomontage for Mead Paper Company, 1985.

101. April Greiman, health care symposium poster, 1987.

95

96

98

99

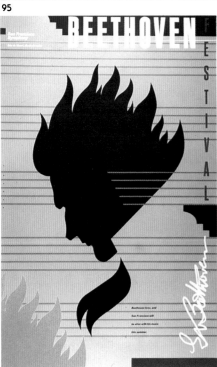

97

100

101

The Industrial Revolution:
The impact of industrial
technology upon
visual communications

World Events	10 Typography for an Industrial Age	11 Photography: The New Communications Tool	12 Popular Graphics of the Victorian Era	13 The Arts and Crafts Movement	14 Art Nouveau
	c. 1765 Cotterell, 12-line pica type		1796 Senefelder invents lithography		
1800 Library of Congress formed	1800 Lord Stanhope, cast-iron press				
	1803 Thorne, 1st Fat Face type; 1st production paper machine				
1804 Napoleon crowned Emperor					
1806 Webster, Dictionary					
1808 Beethoven, Fifth Symphony					
1810 Goya, "Disasters of War"					
1812 War of 1812 begins					
	1814 Koenig, steam-powered press				
1815 Napoleon defeated at Waterloo	1815 Figgins, Egyptian and Tuscan type				
	1816 Caslon, 1st sans-serif type				
1819 Florida ceded to U. S.					
				1820s Pickering begins publishing, emphasizing the design of his books	
1821 Champollion deciphers hieroglyphics		c. 1822 Niepce, photolithographic print			
1823 Monroe Doctrine					
1825 Bolshoi Ballet starts in Moscow		1826 Niepce, 1st photograph from nature			
	1827 Wells, wood display type				
1828 Democratic Party formed					
1831 Henry, 1st electric motor					
	1833 Figgins, 2-line Pearl, Outline				
1834 Braille, writing system for blind	1834 Leavenworth, pantograph driven router		1834 Pugin begins medieval-inspired ornamental designs for British Houses of Parliament		
1835 Barry & Pugin, British Houses of Parliament		1835 Talbot, 1st photographic negative			
1837 Victoria becomes Queen of the United Kingdom					
1839 Goodyear vulcanizes rubber		1839 Daguerre announces the daguerreotype process; Talbot announces his photographic process			
			1840 Sharp introduces lithography to America		
1841 British seize Hong Kong					
		c. 1843 Hill & Adamson, early portraits	1843 Bufford, Boston lithography firm		
1844 Morse, telegraph		1844 Talbot, The Pencil of Nature	1844 Adams, Harper's Bible		
1845 Annexation of Texas	1845 Besley, 1st Clarendon; Caslon, Ionic type		c. 1845 Rouchon, stencil posters in France		
			1846 Hoe, rotary lithographic press		
1848 Marx, Communist Manifesto					
		1850 Archer, wet-plate collodion process			

World Events	10 Typography for an Industrial Age	11 Photography: The New Communications Tool	12 Popular Graphics of the Victorian Era	13 The Arts and Crafts Movement	14 Art Nouveau
1851 Melville, *Moby Dick*					
1853 Perry, treaty with Japan					
1854 Republican Party formed	1850s & 1860s Woodtype posters dominate the hoardings	1850s Ambrotypes and tintypes are widely used			
1857 *Atlantic Monthly* founded			1856 Jones, *Grammar of Ornament*; Prang opens Boston lithography firm; Morse, woodcut circus poster		
1859 Darwin, *Origin of Species*		1858 Nadar, 1st aerial photography			
1861 U. S. Civil War begins		1861–65 Brady & staff photograph the U. S. Civil War		1861 Morris opens art-decorating firm	
1863 Emancipation Proclamation		1864–74 Cameron, portrait photography	1862 Nast joins *Harper's Weekly*		
1865 Lincoln assassinated			1865 Crane, his 1st children's book		1866 Cheret, *La Biche au Bois* poster
1867 Strauss, *Blue Danube Waltz*		1867–69 O'Sullivan, geological expedition	1866 Ihlenburg joins Philadelphia foundry as type designer		
1869 Suez Canal opens					
1871 Boss Tweed indicted	1870s Woodtype posters begin to decline as lithography becomes dominant	1871 Moss, commercially feasible photoengraving	1871 Walker, *Woman in White* poster; French *Cirque D'Hiver* poster		
1872 Yellowstone National Park					
1874 Tiffany opens his glassworks		1875 Gillot, 1st French photographic printing plates		1877 Morris makes his 1st public lectures on design	
1876 Bell, telephone		c. 1877 Muybridge, sequence photography			
1879 Edison, electric lamp		1880 Horgan, experimental halftone screen	1879 Greenaway, *Under the Window*	1881 Mackmurdo, chair with curvilinear pattern	
1881 Barnum & Bailey, circus		1880s Dry plates replace wet plates		1883 Mackmurdo, *Wren's City Churches*	1883 Grasset, *Historie des Quartre Fils Aymon*
1883 Stevenson, *Treasure Island*		1885 Ives, halftone screen		1884 Art Worker's Guild is formed; *Hobby Horse* published	
1884 Twain, *Huckleberry Finn*					1886 Grasset, 1st poster
1886 Statue of Liberty	1886 Mergenthaler, Linotype machine	1888 Eastman, Kodak camera makes photography "every person's art form"		1888 Morris plans Kelmscott Press and designs Golden type; Arts and Crafts Exhibition Society, 1st exhibit	
1888 National Geographic Society	1887 Lanston, Monotype machine				1890 Cheret, Legion of Honor
1889 Van Gogh, *Starry Night*				1891 & 1894 Morris & Crane, *The Story of the Glittering Plain*	1891 Toulouse-Lautrec, Moulin Rouge poster; Grasset, *Harper's* cover
1891 Edison, kinetoscopic camera	1892 American Typefounders is formed			1893 Morris, Chaucer type	1893 Beardsley, *Mort D'Arthur*
1893 Ford, his 1st gasoline motor					1894 Mucha, *Gismonda*; Bradley, covers
1894 Nicholas II becomes Russian Czar				1895 Goudy's Camelot, his 1st typeface	1895 Bing, l'Art Nouveau gallery opens
1895 Lumiere Bros., Cinematographie				1896 Morris, Kelmscott *Chaucer*; Pissarro founds Eragny Press; Rogers joins Riverside Press; Hornby starts Ashendene Press; Morris dies	1896 *Jugend*; Steinlen, *La Rue* poster
1896 Sousa, *Stars and Stripes Forever*					1897 Vienna Secession formed
1897 Thompson discovers the electron	1898 Berthold, Akzidenz Grotesk				1898 Combaz, *La Libre Esthetique* poster
1898 Curie discovers radium					1899 van de Velde, *Tropon* poster
1899 Freud, *The Interpretation of Dreams*					
1900 Boxer Rebellion					
1901 Queen Victoria dies				1902 Ashbee, Essex House *Psalter*	

Typography for an Industrial Age

Although it might be said that the Industrial Revolution first occurred in England during the period from 1760 until 1840, it was a radical process of social and economic change rather than a mere historical period of time. A major impetus for this conversion from an agricultural society into an industrial one was energy. Until James Watt (1736–1819) perfected the steam engine, which was deployed rapidly starting in the 1780s, animal- and humanpower were the primary sources of energy. During the course of the nineteenth century, the amount of energy generated by steam power increased a hundredfold. During the last three decades of the century, electricity and gasoline-fueled engines further expanded productivity. A factory system with machine manufacturing and divisions of labor was developed. New materials, particularly iron and steel, became available.

Masses of people left a subsistence existence living on the land and sought employment in the factories. Cities grew rapidly, and there was a wider distribution of wealth. Political power shifted away from the aristocracy and toward capitalist manufacturers, merchants, and even the working class. The growing scientific knowledge was applied to manufacturing processes and materials, and man's sense of dominion over nature and faith in the ability to exploit the earth's resources to satisfy material wants and needs created a heady confidence.

The capitalist replaced the landowner as the most powerful force in western countries, and capital investment in machines for mass manufacture became the basis for change in industry after industry. A spiraling production cycle was created. Demand from a rapidly growing urban population with increased buying power stimulated technological improvements. In turn, this enabled mass production, which increased availability and lowered costs. The cheaper, more abundant merchandise now available stimulated a mass market and even greater demand. Graphics played role in marketing factory output, as this cycle of industrial supply and demand became the force behind the relentless industrial developments.

The giddy developments of the Industrial Revolution were not without their social costs. Workers who traded overpopulated rural areas for urban factories worked thirteen-hour days for miserable wages and lived in filthy, unsanitary tenements. This huge work force of men, women, and children often suffered from shutdowns caused by earlier overproduction, depressions, economic panics, business and bank failures, and the loss of jobs to newer technological improvements. On measure, however, the overall standard of living of people in Europe and America improved dramatically over the course of the nineteenth century. Critics of the new industrial age cried that civilization was shifting from an interest in humanist values toward a preoccupation with material goods, and that people were losing their communion with nature, aesthetic experience, and spiritual values.

The greater degree of equality that sprang from the French and American Revolutions led to increased public education and literacy. The audience for reading matter expanded accordingly, and this unsettled period of fluid change was characterized by greater importance and availability of graphic communications. As with other commodities, technology lowered unit costs and increased the production of printed materials. In turn, the greater availability created an insatiable demand, and the era of mass communications dawned.

Handicrafts almost completely vanished. The unity of design and production ended. Earlier, a craftsman designed and fabricated a chair or pair of shoes, and a printer was involved in all aspects of his craft from typeface design and page layout to the actual printing of books and broadsheets. Over the course of the nineteenth century, however, the specialization of the factory system fractured graphic communications into separate design and production components. The nature of visual information was profoundly changed. The range of typographic sizes and letterform styles exploded. The invention of photography—and later, the means to print photographic images—expanded the meaning of visual documentation and pictorial information. Color lithography put sensual and colorful printing into every home in a democratic revolution that enabled the aesthetic experience of colorful images to pass from the privileged few to the whole society. This dynamic, exuberant, and often chaotic century witnessed a staggering parade of new technologies, imaginative forms, and expanded applications of graphic design. The nineteenth century was the most inventive and prolific period for new typeface designs, ranging from the totally new categories of Egyptian and sans serif to fanciful and outrageous novelty styles.

Innovations in typography

Many authorities of typography and printing history have deplored the Pandora's box of typographic design unleashed by the Industrial Revolution. In doing so, they fail to recognize the shifting social and economic role of typographic communication. Before the nineteenth century, dissemination of information, primarily through the medium of the book, had been the dominant function. The faster pace and mass-communications needs of an increasingly urban and industrialized society produced a rapid expansion of jobbing printers, advertising, and posters. Larger scale, greater visual impact, and new tactile and expressive characters were demanded, and the book typography that had slowly evolved from handwriting did not fulfill these needs.

It was no longer enough for the twenty-six letters of the alphabet to function only as phonetic symbols. The industrial age required that these signs be transformed into abstract visual forms projecting powerful concrete shapes of strong contrast and large size from the billboards. At the same time, letterpress printers were under increasing competitive pressure from lithographic printers, whose skilled craftsmen rendered plates directly from an artist's sketch and produced images and letterforms limited only by the artist's imagination. The letterpress printers turned to the typefounders to expand their design possibilities, and the founders were only too happy to comply. The early decades of the nineteenth century saw an outpouring of new type designs without precedence.

As in many other aspects of the Industrial Revolution, England played a pivotal role and major design innovations were achieved by London typefounders. In a

10-1. Thomas Cotterell, twelve-line pica, letterforms, c. 1765. These display letters, shown actual size, seemed gigantic to eighteenth-century compositors who had been used to setting handbills and broadsides using types that were rarely even half this size.

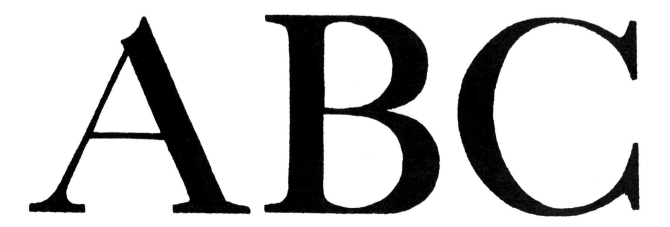

Typography for an Industrial Age

MINT main.

Quousque tandem abutere, Catilina, patientia nostra? quamdiu nos etiam furor is te tuus eludet? quem after CONSTANTINOPLE £1234567890

10-2. Robert Thorne, fat face types, 1821. Although the dated record of these designs is William Thorowgood's 1 January 1821 publication of *New Specimen of Printing Types, late R. Thorne's,* it is generally thought that Thorne designed the first fat faces in 1803.

sense, it might almost be said that the first William Caslon was grandfather of this revolution. In addition to his heirs, two of his former apprentices who were dismissed for leading a workers' revolt, Joseph Jackson (1733–1792) and Thomas Cotterell (d. 1785), became successful type designers and founders in their own right. Apparently Cotterell began the trend of sand casting large, bold display letters as early as 1765, when his specimen book displayed, in the words of one of his amazed contemporaries, a "proscription, or posting letter [Fig. 10-1], of great bulk and dimension, as high as the measure of twelve *lines of pica!*" (about 5 centimeters or 2 inches).

The idea of larger and fatter letters was embraced by other founders, and type grew steadily bolder by the decade. This led to the invention of *fat faces* (Fig. 10-2), a major category of type design innovated by Cotterell's pupil and successor, Robert Thorne (d. 1820), possibly around 1803. A fat-face typestyle is a roman face whose contrast and weight have been increased by expanding the thickness of the heavy strokes. The stroke width has a ratio of 1:2.5 or even 1:2 to the capital height. These bulldozer bold fonts were only the beginning, as Thorne's Fann Street Foundry began a lively competition with William Caslon IV (1781–1869) and Vincent Figgins (1766–1844). The full range of Thorne's accomplishment as a type designer was documented after his death, when William Thorowgood—who was not a type designer, punch cutter, or printer, but used lottery winnings to offer the top bid when Thorne's Fann Street Foundry was auctioned after Thorne's death—published the 132-page book of specimens that had been typeset and was ready to go onto the press when Thorne died.

One of Joseph Jackson's apprentices, Vincent Figgins, stayed with him and took full charge of his operation during the three years preceding Jackson's death from scarlet fever in 1792. Figgins failed in his efforts to purchase his master's foundry because William Caslon III offered the highest bid. Undeterred, Figgins established his own typefoundry and quickly built a reputation for quality type design and mathematical, astronomical, and other symbolic material numbering in the hundreds of sorts. By the turn of the century, Figgins had designed and cast a complete range of romans and had begun to produce scholarly and foreign faces. The rapid tilt in typographic design taste toward modern-style romans and new jobbing styles after the turn of the century seriously affected him. But he rapidly responded, and his 1815 printing specimens showed a full range of modern styles, *antiques* (Egyptians)—the second major innovation of nineteenth-century type design (Fig. 10-3)—and numerous jobbing faces, including "three-dimensional" fonts.

Having a bold, machinelike feeling, these antiques were characterized by slab-like rectangular serifs, an evenness of weight throughout the form, and short ascenders and descenders. In Thorowgood's 1821 specimen book of Thorne's type, the name *Egyptian*—which continues to be used for this style—was used for the slab-serif fonts shown (Fig. 10-4). Perhaps the fascination for all aspects of ancient Egyptian culture, which was intensified by Napoleon's 1798–1799 invasion and

10-3. Vincent Figgins, Two Lines Pica, Antique, 1815. The inspiration for this highly original design, first shown by Figgins, is not known. Whether Figgins, Thorne, or an anonymous sign painter first invented this style is another mystery surrounding the sudden appearance of slab-serif letterforms.

ABCDEFGHIJ KLMNOPQR STUVWXYZ&,:;.- £1234567890

Quosque tandem abutere Catilina patientia FURNITURE 1820

Quosque tandem abutere Catilina patientia nostra? quamdiu nos W. THOROWGOOD.

10-4. Robert Thorne, Egyptian type designs, 1821. Comparison with Figgins's design reveals subtle differences. Thorne based this lower case on the structure of Modern-style letters, but he radically modified the weight and serifs.

Quousque tandem abutere, Catilina, patientia nostra? quamdiu nos e-tiam furor iste tuus eludet? quem ad finem sese effrenata jactabit audacia? nihilne te nocturnum præsidium palatii, nihil urbis vigiliæ, nihil ABCDEFGHIJKLMN ABCDEFGHIJKLMNOPQR £ 1234567890

10-5. Henry Caslon, Ionic type specimen, mid-1840s. Bracketing refers to the curved transition from the main strokes of a letterform to its serif. Egyptian type replaced the bracket with an abrupt angle; Ionic type restored a slight bracket.

10-6. Robert Besley (designer, with Thorowgood), specimen of an early Clarendon, 1845. An even more subtle adaptation of Ionic than Ionic was of Egyptian, Clarendon styles were wildly popular after their introduction. When the three-year patent expired, numerous imitations and piracies were issued by other founders.

occupation, inspired this name. It may be that design similarities were seen between the chunky geometric alphabets and the visual qualities of some Egyptian artifacts. As early as the 1830s, a variation of Egyptian, having slightly bracketed serifs and increased contrast between thicks and thins, was called Ionic (Fig. 10-5). In 1845, William Thorowgood and Company copyrighted a modified Egyptian called Clarendon (Fig. 10-6). Similar to the Ionics, these letterforms were condensed Egyptians with stronger contrasts between thick and thin strokes and somewhat lighter serifs.

Figgins's 1815 specimen book also presented the first nineteenth-century version of Tuscan-style letters (Fig. 10-7). This style, characterized by serifs that are extended and curved, was put through an astounding range of variations during the nineteenth century, often with bulges, cavities, and ornaments.

It seemed that the English typefounders were trying to invent every possible design permutation by modifying forms or proportions and applying all manner of decoration to their alphabets. In 1815, Vincent Figgins showed styles that projected the illusion of three dimensions (Fig. 10-8) and appeared as bulky objects rather than two-dimensional signs. This device proved to be very popular, and specimen books began to show perspective clones for every imaginable style. An additional variation was the depth of shading, which ranged from pencil-thin shadows to deep perspectives. Realizing that every device—perspective, outline (Fig. 10-9), reversing (Fig. 10-10), expanding, contracting—could multiply each style into a kaleidoscope of design possibilities, the designers proliferated styles with boundless enthusiasm. The mechanization of manufacturing processes during the industrial revolution made the application of decoration more economical and efficient. Designers of furniture, household objects, and even typefaces delighted in design intricacy. During the first half of the century, pictures, plant motifs, and decorative designs were applied to display letterforms (Fig. 10-11).

The third major typographic innovation of the early 1800s, *sans-serif* type, whose most obvious characteristic is the absence of serifs, made its modest debut in an 1816 specimen book issued by William Caslon IV (Fig. 10-12). Buried among the decorative display fonts of capitals in the back of the book, one line of medium-weight monoline serifless capitals proclaimed "W CASLON JUNR LETTER FOUNDER." It looked a lot like an Egyptian face with the serifs removed, which is probably how Caslon IV designed it. The name—Two Lines English Egyptian—Caslon adopted for this style tends to support the theory that it had its origins in an Egyptian style. (English denoted a type size roughly equivalent to today's fourteen-point; thus, Two Lines English indicated a display type of about twenty-eight points.) Sans serif, which became so important to twentieth-century graphic design, had a tentative beginning. The inelegant early sans serifs were primarily used for subtitles and descriptive material under sledgehammer bold fat faces and Egyptians.

Sans serifs were little noticed until the early 1830s, when several typefounders introduced new sans-serif styles. Each designer and foundry seems to have invented a name: Caslon used Doric, Thorowgood called his fonts grotesques, Blake and Stephenson named their version sans-surryphs, and in the United States the Boston Type and Stereotype Foundry asserted independence from the British origins by naming its first American sans-serif faces Gothics. Perhaps the rich

Quousque tandem abutere Catilina, patientia nostra? quamdiu nos etiam furor iste tuus eludet? quem ad finem sese effrenata jactabit audacia? nihilne te nocturnum præsidium palatii, nihilne urbis vigiliæ, nihil timor populi, nihil consensus bonorum omnium, nihil hic munitissimus habendi senatus locus, nihil horum £1234567890

10-7. The top two specimens are typical Tuscan styles with ornamental serifs, and demonstrate the diversity of expanded and condensed widths produced by nineteenth-century designers. The bottom specimen is an Antique Tuscan with slab-serifs that have been curved and slightly pointed. Note the care given to the design of the negative shapes that surround the letters.

10-9. Vincent Figgins, Two-Line Pearl, Outline, 1833. In outline and open fonts, a contour line of even weight encloses the alphabet shape that usually appears black.

10-10. William Thorowgood, Six-line Reversed Egyptian Italic, 1828. Types that appeared white against a printed black background enjoyed a brief popularity during the middle decades of the nineteenth century, then went out of fashion.

10-8. Vincent Figgins, Five Lines Pica, In Shade, 1815. The first three-dimensional or perspective fonts were fat faces. Perhaps designers were seeking to compensate for the lightness of the thin strokes, which tended to reduce the legibility of fat faces at a distance.

10-11. Woods and Sharwoods, letters from ornamented fonts, 1838–1842. The wide fat-face letterforms provided a background for pictorial and decorative elements.

10-12. William Caslon IV, Two-line English Egyptian, 1816. This specimen quietly introduced what was to become a major resource for graphic design.

black color of these display types seemed similar to the density of Gothic types. But it was Vincent Figgins who dubbed his 1832 specimen sans serif (Fig. 10-13), in recognition of the font's most apparent feature, and the name stuck. German printers had a strong interest in sans serifs, and by 1830 the Schelter and Giesecke foundry had issued the first sans-serif fonts with a lowercase alphabet. By midcentury, serifless alphabets were seeing increased use.

The wood-type poster

As the size of display types crept upward, problems magnified for both printer and founder. In casting, it was difficult to keep the metal in a liquid state while pouring, and uneven cooling often created slightly concave printing surfaces. Many printers found large metal types to be prohibitively expensive, brittle, and heavy. For example, a wide twelve-line capital might weigh as much as five hundred grams (about 1.1 pounds). It is easy to imagine the problems in setting, handling, storing, and shipping that resulted. An American printer named Darius Wells (1800–1875) began to experiment with handcarved wooden types while recovering from a serious illness, and in 1827 he invented a lateral router that enabled the economical mass manufacture of wood types for display printing. Durable, lighter, and costing less than half as much as large metal types, wood type rapidly overcame printers' initial objections and had a significant impact on poster and broadsheet design. Beginning in March of 1828, when Wells launched the wood-type industry with his first specimen sheets, American wood-type manufacturers imported type design ideas from Europe and exported wood type. Soon, however, European countries began to develop their own wood-type manufactories, and American firms began to create innovative decorative alphabets by midcentury.

After William Leavenworth (1799–1860) combined the pantograph with the router in 1834, new styles could be introduced so easily that customers were invited to send a drawing of one letter of a desired new style; the manufactory offered to design and produce the entire font based on the sketch without an additional charge for design and pattern drafting.

The impetus of this new display typography and the increasing demand for public posters by clients (Fig. 10-14), ranging from traveling circuses and vaudeville troupes to clothing stores and the new railroads, led to poster houses specializing in letterpress display material. In the eighteenth century, job printing had been a sideline of the newspaper and book printers. The design of handbills, wood-type posters, and broadsheets at the poster houses did not involve a graphic designer in the twentieth-century sense. The compositor, often in consultation with the client, selected and composed the type, rules, ornaments, and wood-engraved or metal-stereotyped stock illustrations that filled the typecases. Armed with this infinite typographic range of sizes, styles, weights, and novel ornamental effects, the design philosophy was to use it! The need to lock all the elements tightly on the press enforced a horizontal and vertical stress onto the design; this became the basic organizing principle (Fig. 10-15).

Design decisions were pragmatic. Long words or copy dictated condensed type, and short words or copy were set in expanded fonts. Important words were given emphasis through the use of the largest available type sizes. There was a practical side to the extensive mixing of styles in job printing, because many fonts, each having a limited number of characters, were available at the typical print shop. Wood and metal types were used together freely. In the avalanche of nineteenth-century ephemera (Figs. 10-16 and 10-17) printed by letterpress, a surprising number of well-designed posters and handbills were produced among the more typical workaday compositions. The typographic poster houses that developed with the advent of wood type began to decline after 1870, as improvements in lithographic printing resulted in more pictorial and colorful posters by that process. Also, the importance of traveling entertainment shows—a mainstay among their clients—declined. The growth of magazines and newspapers with space advertising, and the legislative restrictions on posting, began to shift commercial communications away

TWO-LINE GREAT PRIMER SANS-SERIF.

TO BE SOLD BY AUCTION, WITHOUT RESERVE; HOUSEHOLD FURNITURE, PLATE, GLASS, AND OTHER EFFECTS. VINCENT FIGGINS.

10-13. Vincent Figgins, Two-line Great Primer Sans-serif, 1832. Both the name and wide use of sans-serif typography were launched by the awkward black display fonts in Figgins's 1832 *Specimens of Printing Types.*

10-14. Paul Gavarni (1804–1866), *An afficheur at work,* 1845. The famous French illustrator and cartoonist lampooned the proliferation of posters by showing an *afficheur* ("poster hanger") pasting his posters over competitive messages.

10-15. Brown's Steam-power Job Printing Establishment, wood-type poster, 1854. By letterspacing lines to be flush left and right, centering the type, and creating a rhythm of horizontals moving down the space, the compositor managed to bring order to a combination of novelty, sans-serif, slab-serif, fat face, and Modern styles.

10-16. Printer's proof, 1888. Proofed on tissue-thin, translucent paper, with pale blue stripes for checking alignments, this poster for a Leap Year Ball is typical of the job printing produced by letterpress printers in small towns and provincial centers all across Europe and America.

10-16

from posted notices. The unique graphic design form of the letterpress poster houses, alive with typographic variety and textural richness, had almost vanished by the end of the century.

A revolution in printing

The printing presses used by Baskerville and Bodoni were remarkably similar to the first one used by Gutenberg over three centuries earlier. Inevitably, the relentless progress of the Industrial Revolution radically altered printing. Inventors

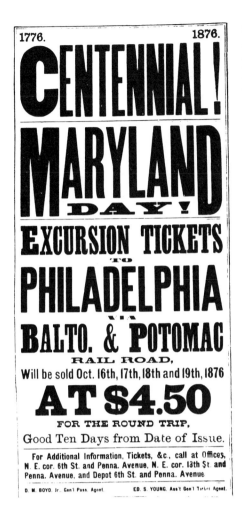

10-17. Handbill for an excursion train, 1876. To be bolder than bold, the compositor used heavier letterforms for the initial letter of important words. Oversized terminal letterforms are used effectively with condensed and extended styles in the phrase, "Maryland Day!"

sought to apply mechanical theory and metal parts to the hand press to increase its efficiency and the size of its impression. Several improvements to make the hand press stronger and more efficient culminated in Lord Stanhope's printing press (Fig. 10-18) constructed completely of cast iron parts in 1800. The metal screw mechanism required approximately one-tenth the manual force needed to print on a wooden press, and Stanhope's press enabled a doubling of the printed sheet's size. William Bulmer's printing office installed and experimented with Lord Stanhope's first successful prototype. These innovations served to improve a partially mechanized handicraft. The next step was to convert printing into a high-speed factory operation.

Far more crucial, however, were the accomplishments of Friedrich Koenig, a German printer who arrived in London around 1804 and presented his plans for a steam-powered printing press to major London printers. Finally receiving financial support from Thomas Bensley in 1807, Koenig obtained a patent in March, 1810, for his press, which produced its first production trial—three thousand sheets for the *Annual Register*—during April, 1811. This press printed four hundred sheets per hour in comparison to the hourly output of 250 sheets on the Stanhope hand press. Koenig's first powered press was designed much like a hand press connected to a steam engine. Other innovations included a method of inking the type by rollers instead of the hand inking balls. The horizontal movement of the type forms in the bed of the machine and the movement of the *tympan* and *frisket* were automated. This press was a prelude to Koenig's development of the stop-cylinder steam-powered press, which enabled much faster operation. In this design, the type form was on a flat bed, which moved back and forth beneath a cylinder. During the printing phase, the cylinder rotated over the type, carrying the sheet to be printed. It stopped while the form moved from under the cylinder to be inked by rollers. While the cylinder was still, the pressman fed a fresh sheet of paper onto the cylinder.

John Walter II of *The Times* in London commissioned Koenig to build two double-cylinder steam-powered presses (Fig. 10-19). These were capable of printing 1,100 impressions an hour on sheets of paper that were 90 centimeters (35½ inches) long and 56 centimeters (22 inches) wide. Fearing the sabotage that often destroyed new machinery when workers felt their jobs were endangered, Walter had the new presses moved to Printing House Square in absolute secrecy. Employees who had threatened Koenig and his invention were directed to wait for news from the continent on the fateful morning of 29 November 1814. At six o'clock, Walter entered the press room to announce that "*The Times* is already printed—by steam." That day's edition informed its readers that "Our Journal of this day presents to the public the practical result of the greatest improvement connected with printing since the discovery of the art itself. The reader of this paragraph now holds in his hand one of the many thousand impressions of *The Times* newspaper, which were taken off last night by a mechanical apparatus." An immediate savings resulted in the composing room, for *The Times* had been typesetting a duplicate of each edition so the two hand presses could print each page. Also, the news could be printed to reach subscribers several hours earlier.

In 1815, William Cowper obtained a patent for a printing press using curved stereotyped plates wrapped around a cylinder. This press achieved 2,400 impressions per hour, and it could be used to print 1,200 sheets on both sides. In 1827, *The Times* commissioned Cowper and his partner, Ambrose Applegath, to develop a four-cylinder steam-powered press using curved stereotyped plates made rapidly from *papier-mâché* molds. This press printed four thousand sheets per hour—on both sides.

All across Europe and North America, book and newspaper printers began to retire their hand presses and replace them with steam-powered ones. The Industrial Revolution had caught up with the printer; the Applegath and Cowper steam-powered multiple-cylinder press produced thirty-two impressions for every one

Typography for an Industrial Age

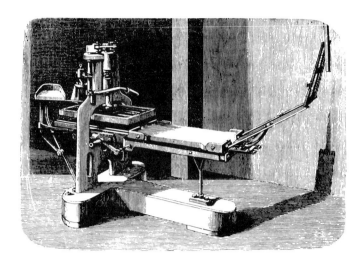

10-19

10-18. This engraved illustration depicts the printing press of all-iron parts invented in England by Charles, third Earl of Stanhope.

10-19. The first steam-powered cylinder press, 1814. Koenig's invention caused the speed of printing to skyrocket while the price dropped considerably.

printed on the Stanhope hand press. The cost of printing began to plunge downward as the size of editions soared upward. By the 1830s, printing began its incredible expansion, as newspaper, book, and jobbing printers proliferated. While early printers served the relatively limited needs of the church and scholars, this conveyor of literacy now served all facets of society.

The value of high-speed, steam-powered printing would have been limited without an economical and abundant source of paper. A young clerk in the Didot paper mill in France, Nicolas-Louis Robert, developed a prototype for a paper-making machine in 1798, but political turmoil in France prevented him from perfecting it. In 1801, English patent number 2487 was granted to John Gamble for "an invention for making paper in single sheets without seam or joining from one to twelve feet and upwards wide, and from one to forty-five feet and upwards in length." In 1803, the first production paper machine was operative at Frogmore, England. This machine, which was similar to Robert's prototype, poured a suspension of fiber and water in a thin stream upon a vibrating wire-mesh conveyor belt. As long as the supply of pulp was maintained and the conveyor belt continued to move and shake, an unending sheet of paper could be manufactured. The rights were acquired by Henry and Sealy Fourdrinier, who invested their fortune financing and promoting what is called the Fourdrinier machine to this day. Ironically, although the Fourdrinier brothers perfected the paper-making machine and gave the world economical and abundant paper, they ruined themselves financially in the process.

The mechanization of typography

Setting type by hand and then redistributing it into the job case remained a slow and costly process. By the middle of the nineteenth century, presses could produce twenty-five thousand copies per hour, but each letter in every word in every book, newspaper, and magazine had to be set by hand. While scores of experimenters attempted to invent the motor car and flying machine, dozens more worked to perfect a machine to compose type. The first patent for a composing machine was registered in 1825. By the time Ottmar Mergenthaler (1854–1899) perfected his *Linotype machine* in 1886, about three hundred machines had been patented in Europe and America, and several thousand patent claims were on file. Millions of dollars were invested in the search for automatic typesetting. Before the Linotype was invented, the high cost and slow pace of composition limited even the largest daily newspapers to eight pages, and books remained fairly precious.

Mergenthaler was a German immigrant working in a Baltimore machine shop who struggled for a decade to perfect his typesetter. On 3 July 1886, the thirty-two-year-old inventor demonstrated his keyboard-operated machine (Fig. 10-20) in the office of the *New York Tribune*. Whitelaw Reid, the editor of the *Tribune*, reportedly exclaimed "Ottmar, you've done it! A line o' type." The new machine received its name from this enthusiastic reaction.

10-20. Ottmar Mergenthaler demonstrates the Blower Linotype, the first line-casting keyboard typesetter, to editor Whitelaw Reid on 3 July 1886.

10-21. The Model 5 Linotype became the workhorse of printing, with keyboards and matrices in over a thousand languages.

Many earlier inventors had tried to make a machine that would compose metal type mechanically by automating the traditional typecase. Others had tried a typewriter affair that pressed letters into a papier-mâché mold or attempted to transfer a lithographic image into a metal relief. Mergenthaler's brilliant breakthrough involved the use of small brass matrices with female impressions of the letterforms, numbers, and symbols. Ninety typewriterlike keys controlled vertical tubes that were filled with these matrices. Each time the operator pressed a key, a matrix for that character was released. It slid down a chute and was automatically lined up with the other characters in that line. Melted lead was poured into the line of matrices to cast a slug bearing the raised line of type.

In 1880, the New York newspapers offered over half a million dollars in prizes to any inventor who could create a machine that would reduce the compositor's time by 25 to 30 percent; Mergenthaler's Linotype machine could do the work of seven or eight hand compositors! The rapid deployment of the Linotype replaced thousands of highly skilled hand typesetters, and strikes and violence threatened many installations. But the new technology caused an unprecedented explosion of graphic material, creating thousands of new jobs. The three-cent price of an 1880s newspaper, which was too steep for the average citizen, plunged to one or two pennies, while the number of pages multiplied and circulation soared. Book publishing expanded rapidly, with fiction, biographies, technical books, and histories joining the educational texts and literary classics that were being published. The Linotype aided in a revolution in periodicals (Fig. 10-21), and illustrated weeklies, including *The Saturday Evening Post* and *Collier's,* reached audiences of millions by the turn of the century. Another American, Tolbert Lanston (1844–1913), invented the *Monotype machine,* which cast single characters from hot metal, in 1887. It was a decade before the Monotype was efficient enough to be put into production.

Handset metal type faced a dwindling market. Most text type was machine set, and display type was hand set. Devastating price wars and cutthroat competition featured discounts of 50 percent plus another 10 percent for cash payment. Consortiums, such as the 1892 merger of fourteen foundries into the American Type Founders Company, were formed in an effort to stabilize the industry. Design piracy was rampant. Foundries would commission new typeface designs, but competitors would immediately electroplate the new designs, then cast and sell types from the counterfeit matrices.

Technological advances permitted machine-set typography to be printed on machine-manufactured paper on high-speed steam-powered printing presses. This opened a new era of knowledge, education, and expanding literacy. There was a global spread of words and pictures, and the age of mass communications arrived.

Photography, the New Communications Tool

11

The making of pictorial images and the preparation of printing plates for reproducing pictorial images remained a handwork process until the invention of photography and its application to graphic production. A series of inventions through the course of the nineteenth century swept the production and reproduction of images forward into the machine age.

The concept behind the device used for making images by photochemical processes, the *camera obscura* (Latin for "dark chamber"), was known in the ancient world as early as the time of Aristotle in the fourth century B.C. A camera obscura is a darkened room or box with a small opening or lens in one side. Light rays passing through this aperture are projected onto the opposite side and form a picture of the bright objects outside. Artists have used the camera obscura as an aid to drawing for centuries. Around 1665, small, portable boxlike camera obscuras were developed (Fig. 11-1). As the only additional element necessary to "fix" or make permanent the image projected into a camera obscura was a light-sensitive material capable of capturing this image, it is not surprising that the early inventors of photography used their camera obscuras as the basis for their experiments.

The inventors of photography

Photography and graphic communications have been closely linked, beginning with the first experiments to capture an image of nature with a camera. Joseph Niepce (1765–1833), the Frenchman who first produced a photographic image, began his experiments by seeking an automatic means for transferring drawings onto printing plates. As a lithographic printer of popular religious images, Niepce depended

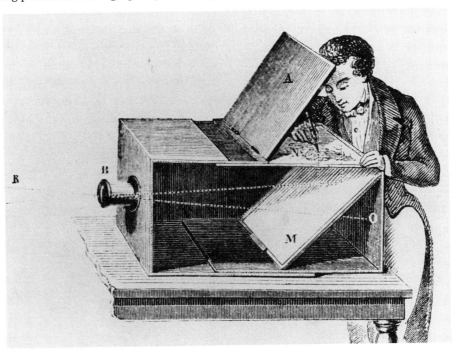

11-1. As this early nineteenth-century portable camera obscura demonstrates, the optical principles for photography were well understood and used by artists as a drawing aid.

on his son, Isadore, to make transfer drawings onto lithographic stones. Isadore was drafted into the army, and the father did not have the drawing skills necessary to continue this work. Niepce searched for a way to make plates other than by drawing. In 1822, he coated a pewter sheet with a light-sensitive asphalt, called bitumen of Judae, which hardens when exposed to light. Then a drawing, which had been oiled to make it transparent, was contact-printed to the pewter with sunlight. Niepce washed the pewter plate with lavender oil to remove the parts not hardened by light, then he etched it with acid to make an incised copy of the original. Niepce called his invention *heliogravure* ("sun engraving"). A photographically etched printing plate made from an engraving of Cardinal d'Ambroise and subsequently used for printing (Fig. 11-2) marked the dawning of photogravure.

In 1826, Niepce had an exciting idea. By putting one of his pewter plates in the back of his camera obscura and pointing it out the window, could he not make a picture directly from nature? The earliest extant photograph is a pewter sheet that Niepce exposed all day (Fig. 11-3). After removing it from the camera obscura that night and washing it with lavender oil, a hazy image of the sunlit buildings outside his workroom window was captured. Niepce continued his research with light-sensitive materials, including silver-coated copper. He became very guarded when a theatrical performer and painter who had participated in the invention of the diorama, Louis Jacques Daguerre (1799–1851), contacted him. Daguerre had been conducting similar research, and after Niepce warmed to him, the two men became friends and began to share ideas until Niepce died of a stroke in 1833.

Daguerre persevered, and on 7 January 1839 his perfected process was presented to the French Academy of Sciences. The members marveled at the clarity and minute detail of his *daguerreotype* prints (Fig. 11-4) and the incredible accuracy of the images. In his perfected process, a highly polished silver-plated copper sheet was sensitized by placing it, silver side down, over a container of iodine crystals. After the rising iodine vapor combined with the silver to produce light-sensitive silver iodide, the plate was placed in the camera and exposed to light coming through the lens, to produce a latent image. The visible image was formed by placing the exposed plate over a dish of heated mercury. After the mercury vapors formed an alloy with the exposed areas of silver, the unexposed silver iodide was removed and the image was fixed with a salt bath. The bare metal appeared black in areas where no light had struck it. The luminous, vibrant image was a bas-relief of mercury and silver compounds that varied in density in direct propor-

11-2. Joseph Niepce, photolithographic print of Cardinal d'Ambroise, c. 1822. This routine portrait print is the first image printed from a plate that was created by the photochemical action of light, rather than by the human hand.

11-3. Joseph Niepce, the first photograph from nature, 1826. Looking out over the rear courtyard of the Niepce home, the light and shadow patterns formed by (from left to right) a wing of the house, a pear tree, the barn roof in front of the low bakehouse with its chimney, and another wing of the house are seen.

11-4. Louis Jacques Daguerre, *Paris Boulevard,* 1839. In this early daguerreotype, the wagons, carriages, and pedestrians were not recorded because the slow exposure could only record stationary objects. On the lower-left street corner, a man stopped to have his boots polished and became the first person ever to be photographed.

tion to the amount of light that had struck the plate during exposure. In one giant leap, the technology of the Industrial Revolution had caught up with creating pictorial images. Cries of fraud were stilled after the French government acquired Daguerre's process and the Academy of Sciences made it available to the public. In one early year, a half million daguerreotypes were made in Paris.

Daguerreotypes had limitations, for each plate was a one-of-a-kind image of predetermined size, and the process required meticulous polishing, sensitizing, and development. The polished surface had a tendency to produce glare, and unless it was viewed at just the right angle, the image had a curious habit of reversing itself and appearing as a negative.

In parallel research, an Englishman, William Henry Fox Talbot (1800–1877), pioneered the process that became the basis for both photography and the use of photomechanical platemaking in printing. While sketching in the Lake Como region of Italy in 1833, Talbot became frustrated with his lack of drawing ability and the difficulties of recording the beautiful fleeting image of the landscape (Fig. 11-5). He thought "how charming it would be if it were possible to cause these natural images to imprint themselves durably, and remain fixed upon the paper." Talbot knew that silver nitrate was a light-sensitive chemical, and after returning that fall to his estate, Lacock Abbey, he began a series of experiments with paper treated with silver compounds. In his early explorations, he floated paper in a weak brine solution, let it dry, and then treated it with a strong solution of silver nitrate to form an insoluble light-sensitive silver-chloride compound in the paper. When he held a piece of lace or a leaf tight against the paper with a pane of glass and exposed it in sunlight, the paper around the object slowly darkened. Washing this image with a salt solution or potassium iodide would fix it somewhat by making the unexposed silver compounds fairly insensitive to light.

Talbot called these images, made without a camera, *photogenic drawings* (Fig. 11-6); today we call images made by manipulating the light striking photographic paper with objects *photograms.* This technique has been valuable to twentieth-century graphic designers in their quest for form. During the course of his 1835 experiments, Talbot combined his new techniques with a microscope to produce the first microphotographs. Plant cross-sections so small that they could not be studied with the naked eye were photographed. Talbot began to use his treated paper in the camera obscura to create minute photographic images, which had

11-5. William Henry Fox Talbot, *View toward Lecco, 6 October 1833*. Able only to capture the basic lines of the landscape in his camera obscura drawings, Talbot was inspired to begin research toward the invention of photography.

light areas rendered dark and dark areas appearing light. Also, these images were mirror images of nature. About one of his early pictures of a building, he once wrote, "I believe this to be the first instance on record of a house having painted its own portrait."

Having satisfied his initial scientific curiosity, Talbot let his research drop and turned to other interests for almost three years until the sudden international hullabaloo over Daguerre spurred him to action. Talbot rushed his work to London, and on 31 January 1839, three weeks after Daguerre stunned the world with his announcement, Talbot presented a hastily prepared report, "Some Account of the Art of Photogenic Drawing," to the Royal Society.

Upon learning about the research of Daguerre and Talbot, the eminent astronomer and chemist Sir John Herschel (1792–1871) tackled the problem. In addition to duplicating Talbot's results, he innovated the use of sodium thiosulfate to fix or make permanent the image by halting the action of light. On 1 February 1839, he shared this knowledge with Talbot. Both Daguerre and Talbot adopted this means of fixing the image in their processes. During February, Talbot solved the problem of the reversed image by contact printing his reverse image to another sheet of his sensitized paper in sunlight. Herschel named the reversed image a *negative* (Fig. 11-7) and called the contact print restoring the values of nature a *positive* (Fig. 11-8). These terms and Herschel's later name for Talbot's invention, *photography* (from the Greek *photos graphos,* meaning "light drawing") have been adopted throughout the world.

Late in 1840, Talbot achieved a further breakthrough and was able to increase the light sensitivity of his paper, expose a latent image, then develop it after it was removed from the camera. He called his new process *calotype* (from the Greek *kalos typos,* meaning "beautiful impression"). Later he adopted the name *talbotype* at the suggestion of his friends. In 1844, Talbot began publishing his book, *The Pencil of Nature,* in installments for subscribers (Fig. 11-9; see also Fig. 12-1). There were twenty-four photographs mounted into each copy by hand. In the foreword, he expressed a desire to present "some of the beginnings of the new art." Each photograph was presented opposite a text explaining the picture and forecasting future uses of the new medium. As the first volume completely illustrated with photographs, *The Pencil of Nature* was a milestone in the history of the book.

The crystal clarity of daguerreotypes was superior to the softness of calotype

11-6. William Henry Fox Talbot, cameraless shadow picture of flowers, 1839. By sandwiching the flowers between his photographic paper and a sheet of glass and exposing the light-sensitive emulsion to sunlight, Talbot invented the *photogram.*

11-7. William Henry Fox Talbot, the first photographic negative, 1835. This image was made on Talbot's light-sensitive paper in the camera obscura, which pointed toward the leaded glass windows in a large room of his mansion, Lacock Abbey.

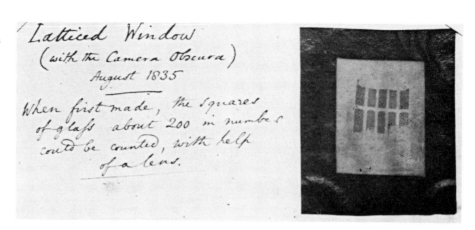

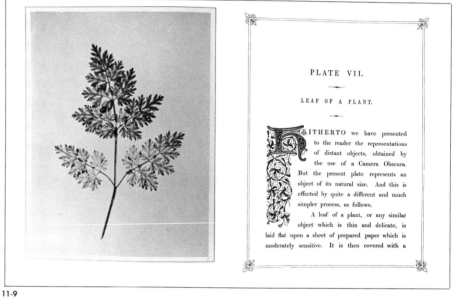

11-9

11-8. William Henry Fox Talbot, print from the first photographic negative. The sun provided the light source to contact print the negative to another sheet of sensitized paper, producing this positive image of the sky and land outside the windows.

11-9. Pages from Talbot's *The Pencil of Nature,* 1844. This first book to be illustrated entirely with photographs had original prints mounted onto the printed page. Plate VII is a photogram. (The use of Modern-style type with ornate initials is typical of early Victorian book design.)

images. To make a positive calotype print, a sheet of the light-sensitive paper was tightly sandwiched underneath the calotype negative and placed in bright sunlight. Because the sun's rays were diffused by the fibers of the paper negative, the positive print was slightly blurred. But because a negative could be exposed to other light-sensitive materials to make an unlimited number of prints and could later be enlarged, reduced, and used to make photoprocess printing plates, Talbot's invention radically altered the course of both photography and graphic design. In photography's earliest decades, however, Daguerre's process was dominant, because Talbot's potpourri of exclusive patents slowed the spread of his methods for a time.

While the softness of calotypes was not without character, having a textural quality similar to charcoal drawing, a search for a suitable vehicle to adhere light-sensitive material to glass for negatives of extreme detail and for positive lantern slides was underway. Many substances, including the slime left by snails, were explored before Abel Niepce de Saint Victor (1805–1870), nephew of Joseph Niepce, invented the albumen process, in which a glass plate is coated with beaten egg white containing potassium/iodine compounds, which could then be sensitized with silver nitrate.

This slow process was replaced by the wet collodion process announced by the English sculptor Frederick Archer (1813–1857) in the March 1850 *Chemist*. By candlelight in a darkroom, a clear viscous liquid collodion—made of pyroxyline (guncotton) dissolved in alcohol and ether and sensitized with iodine compounds—is poured over a glass plate, immersed in a bath of silver nitrate, and exposed and developed in the camera while still wet. Archer's wet-plate collodion process was adopted by photographers throughout the world. Archer did not patent his process, and because it enabled much shorter exposure times than daguerreotypes and calotypes, it almost completely replaced them by the mid-1850s.

For economical portraiture, Archer and his friend P. W. Fry devised an interesting modification. Sir John Herschel had observed that when a negative was viewed by reflection against a black background, it appeared to be a positive; by backing an underexposed negative with black velvet or paper, this phenomenon was used to produce the very popular *ambrotype* portraits (Fig. 11-10). When the collodion material was coated on black lacquered metal, the portrait was called a *tintype*. Ambrotypes and tintypes were produced by the tens of thousands, and citizens of modest means could have their image fixed for immortality for the first time in history.

The scope of photography was seriously limited by the need to prepare a wet plate immediately before making the exposure and develop it immediately afterwards. Innovations by many experimenters finally led to the commercial manufacture of gelatin emulsion dry plates by several firms in 1877. The three-decade heyday of the collodion wet plate rapidly yielded to the dry-plate method after 1880 (Fig. 11-11).

An American dry-plate manufacturer, George Eastman (1854–1932), put the power of photography into the hands of the lay public when he introduced his Kodak camera (Fig. 11-12) in 1888. It was an invention without precedent, for ordinary citizens now had an ability to create images and preserve a graphic record of their lives and experiences.

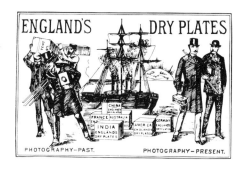

11-11. Advertisement for dry plates, c. 1884. The dry plate's important advantage—an end to the need to haul a clumsy portable darkroom and lab for preparing and processing plates—is graphically illustrated in this ad.

11-12. Advertisement for the Kodak camera, c. 1889. George Eastman's camera, so simple that "anyone can use it who can wind a watch," played a major role in making photography "every man's art form."

11-10. An ambrotype was a photographic negative whose positive–negative character was reversed by placing black cloth or paper behind it to make the clear areas of the negative black, while the emulsion's opaque surface reflected light to take on the quality of a dull, positive print.

The application of photography to printing

Beginning in the 1840s, the rising level of wood engraving that started with Thomas Bewick fostered more frequent and effective use of images in editorial and advertising communications. Because wood-engraving blocks were type high and could be locked into a letterpress and printed with type, while copperplate and steel engraving or lithographs had to be printed as a separate press run, wood engraving dominated book, magazine, and newspaper illustration. However, the preparation of wood-engraved printing blocks was very costly, and numerous inventors and tinkerers continued the search begun by Niepce to find an economical and reliable photoengraving process for preparing printing plates. Inventors tended to keep their innovations top-secret instead of patenting them. Once a patent became a matter of record, competitors would start looking for a loophole that would allow them to get around the inventor's legal rights. This has made identification of the true inventor of the many techniques difficult.

In 1871, John Calvin Moss of New York pioneered a commercially feasible photoengraving method for translating line artwork into metal letterpress plates. A negative of the original illustration was made on a copy camera suspended from the ceiling by a rope to prevent vibration (Fig. 11-13). In a highly secret process, a negative of the original art was contact printed to a metal plate coated with a light-sensitive gelatin emulsion, then etched with acid. To preserve his secret method, only Mrs. Moss and two other trusted employees were taught the process. After hand tooling for refinement, the metal plate was mounted on a type-high block of wood. The gradual implementation of photoengraving cut the cost and time required to produce printing blocks, and achieved greater fidelity to the original.

Close on the heels of Moss, the Frenchman Firmin Gillot perfected his *gillotage* method for the photographic transfer of planographic images into letterpress plates. In 1875, his son Charles opened Paris's first photorelief printing firm.

Before it was possible to print photographs, photography was used as a research tool in developing wood-engraved illustrations. The documentary reality of photography aided the illustrator in his studio in capturing current events. During the 1860s and 1870s, wood engravings drawn from photographs became prevalent in mass communications (Figs. 11-14 and 11-15). An example is found in the photo-

11-13. Illustration of Moss's photographic department from *Scientific American,* 1877. When this major science journal reported on the rise of photoengraving, it revealed that, unknown to its readers, thousands of photoengravings had been used side by side with hand engravings during the 1870s with no recognizable differences.

11-14

11-15

graph, "Freedmen on the Canal Bank in Richmond," attributed to Mathew Brady. Arriving in Richmond, Virginia, shortly after the evacuation and destruction by fire of most of the business district on 2 April 1865, when the Union forces broke through the Confederate defenses of the city, Brady turned his camera upon a group of former slaves who suddenly found themselves to be freedmen. A moment in time was preserved; a historical document to aid man in his understanding of his history was formed with the timeless immediacy of photography.

Since the means to reproduce this image was not yet available, *Scribner's* magazine turned to an illustrator to reinvent the image in the language of the wood engraving so that it could be reproduced. It was reprinted in *Scribner's Popular History of the United States.* This book was issued on the Centennial of the founding of the United States and drew heavily from the magazine's editorial and illustrative material.

The passionate search for a way to print photographs on printing presses continued. Experimenters, beginning with Talbot, realized that if a photographic printing plate that could print the subtle nuances of tone found in a photograph was to be invented, a method to separate continuous tones into dots of varying sizes was necessary. Then, tones could be achieved in spite of the even ink application of the relief press. During the 1850s, Talbot experimented with gauze as a way to break up tones.

Many individuals worked on the problem and contributed to the evolution of this process. An 1857 French patent protected a single-direction line screen produced by scratching a series of horizontal lines in an opaque background. The solution came with a major breakthrough on 4 March 1880, when the *New York Daily Graphic* printed the first reproduction of a photograph with a full tonal range in a newspaper (Figs. 11-16 and 11-17). Entitled *A Scene in Shantytown,* it was printed from a crude *halftone screen* invented by Stephen H. Horgan. The screen broke the image into a series of minute dots, whose varying sizes created tones. Values from pure white paper to solid black ink were simulated by the amount of ink printed in each area of an image.

A mechanically ruled pattern of horizontal and vertical lines on film was used by Frederick E. Ives to print halftones in 1885. The amount of light that could pass through each little square formed by the lines determined how big that dot would be. The sum of all these dots made an image that gave the illusion of continuous tones. In 1893, brothers Max and Louis Levy produced consistent commercial halftones using etched glass screens. A ruling machine was used to scribe parallel lines in an acid-resistant coating on optically clear glass. After acid was used to etch the ruled lines into the glass, the indented lines were filled with an opaque material,

11-14. Attributed to Mathew Brady, photograph, *Freedmen on the Canal Bank at Richmond,* 1865. The photographer supplied the visual evidence needed by the illustrator to document an event.

11-15. John Macdonald, wood engraving, *Freedmen on the Canal Bank at Richmond.* The tonality of the photographer's image was reinvented in the visual syntax of wood-engraved line.

11-16

11-17

and two sheets of this ruled glass were sandwiched, face to face, with one set of lines running horizontally and the other set running vertically. Superb halftone images could be made from the Levys' screens, and the era of photographic reproduction had arrived.

Printing full-color images was an important goal. The first photomechanical color illustrations were printed by the Paris magazine *L'Illustration* in the 1881 Christmas issue. Complicated and time-consuming, photomechanical color separation remained experimental until the end of the century. During the 1880s and '90s, photomechanical reproduction was in the air, and technology began to rapidly eliminate the "middle man." The highly skilled craftsmen who transferred artists' designs into handmade printing plates witnessed the death of their craft, forcing early retirements and occupational changes. Years of apprenticeship and professional practice were suddenly rendered obsolete by the click of a camera. Up to a week had been required to prepare a complex wood engraving; the photographic processes reduced the time from art to printing plate to one or two hours with greatly reduced costs.

Defining the medium

During the same decades that eager inventors were expanding the technical boundaries of the new photographic medium, the image-making potential was being explored by artists and adventurers. In photography's first years, just pointing the camera to capture an image was sufficiently magical to satisfy most needs. An early effort to introduce design concerns into photography began in May of 1843, when the Scottish painter David Octavius Hill (1802–1870) decided to immortalize the 474 ministers who withdrew their congregations from the Presbyterian Church and formed the Free Church of Scotland. Hill badly needed portraits as reference materials for this giant group portrait, so he teamed up with Edinburgh photographer Robert Adamson (1821–1848), who had been making calotypes for about a year. Using forty-second exposures, Hill posed their subjects in sunlight using all the compositional skill and figurative knowledge gained in two decades of portraiture (Fig. 11-18). The resulting calotypes were lauded as superior to Rembrandt's paintings. Hill and Adamson created landscape photographs that echoed the visual order found in landscape paintings of the period. When a Newhaven minister began a campaign for improved fishing-boat design to lessen job dangers for his parishioners, Hill and Adamson made photographs to document the problems. This was probably the first use of photography as visual communications to inform an audience.

When Julia Margaret Cameron (1815–1879) received a camera and the equipment for processing collodion plates as a forty-ninth-birthday present from her daughter and son-in-law, the note said, "It may amuse you, Mother, to photograph." From 1864 until 1874, this homely wife of a high British Civil Servant extended the artistic potential of photography through portraiture that recorded

11-16 and 11-17. Stephen H. Horgan, experimental photoengraving, 1880. This first halftone printing plate to reproduce a photograph in a newspaper heralded the potential of photography in visual communications.

11-18. David O. Hill and Robert Adamson, *Reverend Thomas H. Jones,* c. 1845. The painter's attention to lighting, characterization, placement of hands and head, and composition within the rectangle replaced the "mug-shot" sensibility of earlier photographers.

11-19. Julia Margaret Cameron, *Sir John Herschel*, 1867. Moving beyond descriptive imagery, Cameron's compelling psychological portraits revealed her subjects' inner being.

11-20. F. T. Nadar, *Sarah Bernhardt*, 1859. The famous actress took Paris by storm and became a major subject for the emerging French poster.

11-21. Honoré Daumier (1808–1879), "Nadar elevates photography above the art of Lithography," c. 1870. The famous French cartoonist and social commentator lampooned Nadar's gas-balloon aerial photography. Note the number of photography signs in the Parisian streets.

"faithfully the greatness of the inner man as well as the features of the outer man." Converting a chicken coop into a studio and her coal bin into a darkroom, Cameron produced portraits that have been hailed by scientists, writers, and artists as a major contribution to images expressing the human condition (Fig. 11-19).

A lively contribution to photography was made by the Frenchman F. T. Nadar (1820–1910). In the early 1850s, this freelance writer looked for a more lucrative livelihood after marrying. He hesitated when a friend told him about a photography setup that was for sale, because he did not want to betray his artist friends. Portraits and other visual documentary matter provided artists with their principal income, and photography was already eroding it. Nonetheless, he did pursue photography, and his portraits of writers, actors (Fig. 11-20), and artists have a direct and dignified simplicity and provide an invaluable historical record.

In 1858, Nadar made the first aerial photographs from a captive balloon (Fig. 11-21). The two-story car of his 1863 gas balloon could hold forty-nine people and contained both a darkroom and a printing press for printing leaflets to be distributed from the air. On its third descent, the anchors failed to hold, and the balloon dragged Nadar, tangled in the ropes, over French farmland for several hours. He broke both legs, and renounced ballooning.

Nadar pioneered artificial light photography by using gas illumination to photograph the ancient catacombs and extensive sewers under Paris. In 1886, the first photographic interview was published in *Le Journal Illustré* (Fig. 11-22). A series of twenty-one photographs was made by Nadar's son Paul as Nadar interviewed the eminent hundred-year-old scientist Marie Eugene Chevreul. The elderly man's expressive gestures accompanied his answers to Nadar's questions.

The ability of photography to provide a historical record and define human history for forthcoming generations was dramatically proven by the prosperous New York studio photographer Mathew Brady (c. 1823–1896). When the American Civil War began, Brady set out in a white duster and straw hat carrying a handwritten card from Abraham Lincoln reading, "Pass Brady—A. Lincoln." During the war, Brady invested a $100,000 fortune to send a score of his photographic assistants, including Alexander Gardner (1821–1882) and Timothy O'Sullivan (c. 1840–1882), to document every phase of the American Civil War. From Brady's photography

11-22. Paul Nadar, *Nadar Interviewing Chevreul*, 1886. The words spoken by the one-hundred-year-old chemist were recorded below each photograph to produce a visual–verbal record of the interview.

Photography, the New Communications Tool

11-23. Mathew Brady, *Dunker Church and the Dead*, 1862. Made in the aftermath of the Battle of Antietam, the bloodiest battle of the Civil War, this photograph shows how visual documentation took on a new level of authenticity with the arrival of photography. So fearsome was the fighting that in one nearby cornfield, "the green corn that grew upon it looked as if it had been struck by a storm of bloody hail."

11-24. Timothy H. O'Sullivan, *Sand Dunes near Sand Springs, Nevada,* 1867. The virgin territory of the American West was documented by expedition photographers. O'Sullivan's photography wagon—isolated by the almost Oriental space of the sand dunes —becomes a symbol of these lonely journeys over vast distances.

11-23

11-24

wagons, called "Whatsit" by the Union troops, a great national trauma was etched forever in the collective memory by the thin unblinking photographic emulsion. Brady's photographic documentation had a profound impact upon the public's romantic ideal of war (Fig. 11-23). Battlefield photographs joined artist's sketches as reference materials for wood-engraved magazine and newspaper illustrations.

After the Civil War, photography became an important documentary and communications tool in the exploration of new territory and the opening of the American West. Photographers including Tim O'Sullivan were hired by the Federal government to accompany expeditions into the wild, unexplored western territories (Fig. 11-24). From 1867 until 1869, O'Sullivan accompanied the Geological Explo-

11-25. Eadweard Muybridge, *The Horse in Motion,* 1878. Sequence photography indicated that graphic images could record time and space relationships, and the notion of moving images became a possibility.

ration of the Fourth Parallel, beginning in western Nevada. Returned to the East and translated into illustrations for reproduction, images of the West inspired the great migratory wanderlust that eventually conquered all of North America.

One of the expedition photographers, Eadweard Muybridge (1830–1904), settled in San Francisco after photographing Yosemite and Alaska. An entrepreneur of the Central Pacific Railway, Leland Stanford, commissioned Muybridge to document whether or not a trotting horse lifted all four feet off the ground simultaneously; a twenty-five-thousand-dollar wager rested on the outcome. While working on the problem, Muybridge became interested in photographing a horse's stride at regular intervals. Success came in 1877 and 1878, when a battery of twenty-four cameras —facing an intense white background in the dazzling California sunlight—was equipped with rapid drop shutters that were slammed down by springs and rubber bands as a trotting horse broke threads attached to the shutters. The simultaneity of time and space was arrested on a graphic surface (Fig. 11-25). The development of motion-picture photography, the kinetic medium of changing light passing through a series of still photographs joined by the human eye through the persistence of vision, was the logical extension of Muybridge's innovation.

Nineteenth-century inventors like Talbot, documentarists like Brady, and visual poets like Cameron had a significant collective impact upon graphic design. By the arrival of the twentieth century, photography was becoming an increasingly important tool in the reproduction of graphic design. New technologies radically alter existing ones, and both graphic techniques and illustration changed dramatically. Photography—the visual truth at ¹⁄₁₂₅th of a second—asserts an authority as undeniable document, unmatched by other image-making processes. As photomechanical reproduction replaced handmade plates, illustrators gained a new freedom of expression. Photography gradually monopolized factual document and pushed the illustrator away toward fantasy and fiction. The textural and tonal properties of the halftone image changed the visual appearance of the printed page.

Popular Graphics of the Victorian Era

12-1. Title page, 1844. This title page demonstrates the eclectic confusion of the Victorian Era. Medieval letterforms, Baroque plant forms, and geometric interlaces are combined into a dense symmetrical design.

The long reign of Victoria (1819–1901), who became Queen of the United Kingdom of Great Britain and Ireland in 1837, spanned two-thirds of the nineteenth century and is called the Victorian Era. This was a time of strong moral and religious beliefs, proper social conventions, and optimism. "God's in his heaven, all's right with the world" was a popular motto. The Victorian period was an era in search of a style. Aesthetic confusion led to a number of often contradictory design styles and philosophies mixed together in a helter-skelter fashion (Fig. 12-1). A taste for the Gothic, which suited the pious Victorians, was fostered by the English architect A. W. N. Pugin (1812–1852), who designed the ornamental details of the British House of Parliament. The first nineteenth-century designer to articulate a philosophy, Pugin defined design as a moral act that achieved the status of art through the designer's ideals and attitudes. Although he said that he looked to earlier periods—particularly Gothic—not for *style,* but for a *principle,* the net result of Pugin's influence was a wide mimicking of Gothic architecture, ornament, and letterforms.

Popular narrative and romantic painting of the Victorian Era was closely linked with the graphic pictorialism of chromolithographers, including Louis Prang (1824–1909). Prang often commissioned art and held competitions to acquire subjects for use in his printed images. The English designer, author, and authority on color, Owen Jones (1809–1874), became a major design influence at midcentury. During his midtwenties, Jones traveled to Spain and the Near East and made a systematic study of Islamic design. Jones introduced Moorish ornament to western design in his 1842–1845 book, *Plans, Elevations, Sections, and Details of the Alhambra.* His main influence was through his widely studied 1856 book of large color plates, *The Grammar of Ornament.* This catalog of design possibilities from eastern and western cultures, "savage" tribes, and natural forms became the nineteenth-century designer's bible of ornament. The Victorian love of complexity and fussiness was expressed by "gingerbread" woodwork applied to domestic architecture, ornate extravagant embellishments on manufactured products from silverware to large furniture, and elaborate borders and lettering in graphic design.

In the 1850s, the word *Victorian* began to be used to express a new consciousness of the industrial era's spirit, culture, and moral standards. In 1849, Prince Albert, husband of Queen Victoria, conceived the idea of a grand exhibition with hundreds of exhibitors from all industrial nations. This became the Great Exhibition of 1851, an important summation of the progress of the Industrial Revolution and a catalyst for future developments. Six million visitors reviewed the products of thirteen thousand exhibitors.

This exhibition is commonly called the Crystal Palace Exhibition, after the 800,000-square-foot steel and glass prefabricated exhibition hall that remains a landmark in architectural design. The competition to design the exhibition hall was won by a landscape and greenhouse designer, Sir Joseph Paxton (1801–1865).

Sweetness and piety embraced traditional values of home, religion, and patriotism in graphic images and designs that captured and conveyed the values of an era (Fig. 12-2). Sentimentality, nostalgia, and a canon of idealized beauty were expressed by images of children, maidens, puppies, and flowers. The production

12-2. Diecut and embossed Valentine, c. 1890. The intricacy of the design and its production demonstrates the high craftsmanship of the designer, diemaker, and pressman.

medium for this outpouring of Victorian popular graphics was *chromolithography,* an innovation of the Industrial Revolution that enabled thousands of copies of colorful naturalistic images to be printed.

The development of lithography

Lithography (from the Greek, literally "stone printing") was invented by Aloys Senefelder (1771–1834) of Bavaria in 1796. Senefelder, an author, was seeking a cheap way to print his own dramatic works and was experimenting with etched stones and metal reliefs. One day his mother called out a laundry list for him before he went out. Lacking a handy sheet of paper in his workroom, Senefelder wrote the list with a grease pencil on a flat printing stone. Suddenly, it dawned upon him that the stone could be etched away around the grease pencil writing and made into a printing plate. Senefelder began a series of experiments that culminated in the invention of lithographic printing, in which the image to be printed is neither raised, as in relief printing, nor incised, as in intaglio printing. Rather, it is formed on the flat plane of the printing surface.

Lithography is based on the simple, chemical principle that oil and water do not mix. An image is drawn on a flat stone surface with an oil-based crayon, pen, or pencil. Water is spread over the stone to moisten all areas except the oil-based image, which repels the water. Then an oil-based ink is rolled over the stone, adhering to the image but not to the wet areas of the stone. A sheet of paper is placed over the image and a printing press is used to transfer the inked image onto the paper. In the early 1800s, Senefelder began experimenting with multicolor lithography, and in his 1819 book he predicted that one day this process would be perfected to allow reproduction of paintings. German printers spearheaded the development of color lithography, and the French printer Godefroy Engelmann named the process *chromolithographie* in 1837. One plate, usually printed in black, established the image, and other plates put flat color or tints behind it.

Popular Graphics of the Victorian Era

12-3. William Sharp, *Reverend F. W. P. Greenwood,* chromolithograph, 1840. Printed from two or perhaps three lithographic stones, the image is constructed much like a duotone. Apparently tan, flesh, and gray tones come together and combine to produce this image, which launched chromolithography in America.

The Boston school of chromolithography

American chromolithography began in Boston, and several outstanding practitioners there innovated a school of lithographic realism that achieved technical perfection and naturalistic convincing imagery of compelling realism. By 1840, English lithographers were producing color book illustrations. One of them, William Sharp (b. 1803), introduced chromolithography to America. Sharp was a London painter and drawing teacher who opened a lithography shop in 1829. He emigrated to Boston in the late 1830s, intent upon establishing steady commissions as a portrait painter. In 1840, Sharp was retained by the Congregation of Kings Chapel to create the first chromolithograph in America (Fig. 12-3). This was a portrait of the Congregation's minister, the Reverend F. W. P. Greenwood. Dark gray, tan, and flesh-tone inks were printed from two or three stones. When these separate colors were overprinted, a muted naturalistic color range emerged. From these humble beginnings, American chromolithography was born. During the next quarter century, Sharp applied his subtle crayon drawing style to sheet music cover designs, portraits, floral plates, and book illustrations. Sharp's intent was to reproduce the painted image as closely as possible.

In 1846, the American inventor and mechanical genius Richard M. Hoe (1812–1886) perfected the rotary lithographic press (see Fig. 12-6), which was nicknamed the "lightning press" because it increased lithographic production sixfold relative to the flat-bed presses then in use. This innovation proved to be an important boost in lithography's competition with letterpress and released the floodgates of lithography. Economical color printing, ranging from art reproductions for middle-class parlors to advertising graphics of every description, poured from the presses in millions of impressions each year.

The next major innovator of chromolithography in Boston was John H. Bufford (d. 1870), a masterful draftsman whose crayon-style images achieved a stunning realism. After training in Boston and working in New York, Bufford returned to Boston in 1840. He became the first American lithographer not associated with Sharp to experiment with chromolithography beginning in 1843. Specializing in art prints, posters, covers, and book and magazine illustrations, Bufford often used five or more colors. The meticulous tonal drawing of his black stone always became the master plate. Working from an original master drawing for an edition such as the c. 1867 Swedish Song Quartett poster (Pl. 15), for example, the precise tonal drawing was duplicated on a lithographic stone. Then, separate stones were prepared to print the flesh tones, reds, yellows, blues, and slate-gray background color. Browns, grays, and oranges were created when these five stones were overprinted in perfect registration. The color range of the original was separated in component parts, then reassembled in printing. The near-photographic lithographic crayon drawing glowed with the bright underprinted yellows and reds of the folk costumes.

In 1864, Bufford's sons entered his firm as partners. The senior Bufford maintained artistic direction responsibilities until his death in 1870. The hallmark of Bufford designs was meticulous and convincing tonal drawing. A major graphic-design concern of this firm was the integration of image and lettering into a unified design. In the Swedish Song Quartett poster, the arcs of the words move gracefully in the space above the seven carefully composed members of this musical group. The large capital letters in the name are placed adjacent to the heads of the three standing women to establish a visual relationship between word and image.

In their political campaign graphics, such as the poster for Grover Cleveland and Thomas A. Hendricks in the 1884 presidential campaign (Fig. 12-4), a rich vocabulary of patriotic motifs, including eagles, flags, banners, columned frames, and Liberty clothed in the flag, were used to establish a patriotic tone.

The Bufford firm folded in 1890. The two decades after the founder's death were a period of declining quality, cut-rate pricing, and emphasis on cheap novelties. The Cleveland and Hendricks poster is atypical of the later period; it recaptures both the style and the quality of John Bufford's finer work.

American lithography maintained a German heritage. Both the highly skilled

12-4. S. S. Frizzall (artist) and J. H. Bufford's Sons (printers), poster for the Cleveland and Hendricks presidential campaign, 1884. The loose style of the flags and other symbolic imagery framing the candidates emphasizes the extreme realism of the portraits.

craftsmen who prepared the stones for printing and the excellent Bavarian lithographic stones themselves were exported from Germany to nations all around the world. The four decades from 1860 until 1900 were the heyday of chromolithography; it became the predominant printing medium. Popular graphics of the Victorian Era found its most prolific innovator in a German immigrant to America, Louis Prang, whose work and influence were international.

After mastering the complexities of his father's fabric-printing business, twenty-six-year-old Prang arrived in America in 1850 and settled in Boston. His knowledge of printing chemistry, color, business management, designing, engraving, and printing was of great value when he formed a chromolithography firm with Julius Mayer in 1856. Initially, Prang designed and prepared the stones, and Mayer did the printing on a single hand press. The popularity of Prang's colorful work provided the impetus for growth, and there were seven presses when Prang bought Mayer's share of the firm and named it L. Prang and Co. in 1860.

In addition to art reproductions and Civil War maps and scenes, Prang put vivid color into the lives of every citizen through the production of literally millions of album cards called *scrap*. Collecting these "beautiful art bits" was a major Victorian pastime, and Prang's wildflowers, butterflies, children, animals, and birds became the ultimate expression of the period's love for sweetness, nostalgia, and traditional values.

Prang followed closely in the tradition of Sharp and Bufford, for his meticulously drawn, naturalistic images were duplicated as precisely as possible. Prang has been called "The Father of the American Christmas Card" for his pioneering work in graphics for holiday celebrations. He had begun to produce Christmas images suitable for framing in the late 1860s, then he published a Christmas card for mailing in England in 1873. His first American Christmas card was designed the following year. Typical images of these first Christmas cards were Santa Claus, reindeer, and Christmas trees. A full line of designs followed, and Easter, birthday, Valentine, and New Year's Day cards were produced annually by L. Prang and Company during the early 1880s. Prang sometimes used as many as forty stones for one design. Part of the exceptional quality of his firm's work was the fact that Bufford's master black plate was dropped in favor of a slow building and heightening of the image through the use of many plates bearing subtle colors.

The album chromolithographs evolved into the advertising trade card in the 1870s. Prang's claim that he invented this graphic form does not hold up, for cop-

Popular Graphics of the Victorian Era

perplate engravers of the eighteenth century produced large numbers of illustrated advertising cards. Certainly, however, Prang's distribution of twenty to thirty thousand business cards with floral designs at the 1873 Vienna International Exhibition helped to popularize the use of chromolithographic trade cards for advertising. Unlike many of his competitors who jumped into the field, Prang seldom identified his firm on advertising materials, making verification of L. Prang & Company designs difficult. Competition was fierce, and Prang was constantly developing new ideas to stay ahead of imitators who were undercutting his prices by using fewer stones for similar designs.

Prang made a lifelong contribution to art education after he started to give his daughter art lessons in 1856. Unable to find quality, nontoxic art materials for children, Prang began to manufacture and distribute watercolor sets and crayons. Finding a complete lack of competent educational materials for teaching industrial artists, fine artists, and children, Prang devoted tremendous energy to developing and publishing art-instruction books. On two occasions, Prang ventured into magazine publishing: *Prang's Chromo* was a popular art journal first published in 1868, and *Modern Art Quarterly,* published from 1893 until 1897, showed Prang's ability to continue to grow and explore new artistic possibilities in his old age.

The design language of chromolithography

From Boston, chromolithography quickly spread to other major cities, and by 1860 about sixty chromolithography firms employed eight hundred people. A phenomenal growth put chromolithographers in every American city, and by 1890 over eight thousand people were employed by seven hundred lithographic printing firms. Fig-

12-5. L. Prang and Company and others, c. 1880–1900. This album page shows the range of graphic ephemera collected by Victorian children.

ure 12-5 shows the diversity of chromolithographs produced by Prang and his competitors. Pasted around a nursery catalogue cover, clockwise from the top left, are: a thread company card with nine babies clustered behind the label; a diecut friendship card; an album card from one of Prang's bird series; a trade card for Hunt's remedy, which is advertised on the back as a cure to restore proper healthy action to the kidney, liver, and bowels when all else fails; an early Christmas card; lions from a pack of jungle animal album cards; two clowns performing acrobatics with a spool of the advertiser's thread; a diecut figure from a sheet of stickers; two patriotic little girls appearing on behalf of a cod liver oil tonic; and a beautifully printed image of a loving mother, daughter, and cat drenched in Victorian sweetness. Sold in bulk, this last card enabled the merchant or manufacturer to imprint an advertising message on the back.

Letterpress printers and admirers of fine typography and printing were appalled by the design language that emerged with the growth of lithography. Design was done on the artist's drawing board instead of the compositor's metal press bed. Without traditions and lacking the constraints of letterpress, chromolithograph designers could invent any letterform that suited their fancy and allow lettering to run in angles and arcs or flow right over images. In addition, the lithographer had an unlimited palette of bright vibrant color, the likes of which had never been seen in printed communications. It is little wonder that chromolithography began to drive letterpress posters from the market (Fig. 12-6).

The vitality of this revolution in graphics grew from the talented artists who created original designs, frequently working in watercolor, and the highly skilled craftsmen who traced the original art onto the stones. These disciplined workers interpreted the design by making five, ten, twenty, or even more separate stones, whose colors would come together in perfect registration, magically to create hundreds or even thousands of glowing duplicates of the original. The name of the lithography firm that produced the design, rather than the graphic artists or craftsmen who created it, appeared on the work. Therefore, the names of many designers who defined the medium by bringing an original vision to chromolithography are lost to history. Among the firms around the nation which attained a high level of Victorian design, Schumacher & Ettlinger Lithography of New York, The Strobridge Litho. Company and the Krebs Lithographing Company in Cincinnati, Riv-

12-7. Schumacher & Ettlinger, Lithographers, stock advertising trade card, undated. By printing these in great quantity, with a blank area for the client to imprint an advertising message, the lithographer was speculating that business firms would like the designs offered.

12-9. The Strobridge Litho. Company, *The Original Black Crook,* theatrical poster, c. 1881. The idealized young woman, floral motif, and curvilinear scroll suggest the Victorian roots from which Art Nouveau sprang a decade later.

12-8. Schumacher & Ettlinger, Lithographers, cover and pages from *Our Navy* premium booklet, 1888. Contrasting sizes and perspectives combine with ornaments that move forward and backward in space to create complex illusions.

erside Print Company in Milwaukee, and A. Hoen and Company of Baltimore and Richmond created engaging graphic designs.

Schumacher & Ettlinger's art staff was particularly skilled at combining imagery with Victorian ornament. The "peacock" trade card (Fig. 12-7) demonstrates the integration of illustration with decorative patterns not unlike material found in the *Grammar of Ornament.* The upper-left corner of this design is being peeled away to reveal a geometric pattern underneath. Trompe-l'oeil devices such as this delighted nineteenth-century graphic artists. In the 1888 premium booklet, *Our Navy* (Fig. 12-8), commissioned by the Allen & Ginter Company, a montage effect is achieved through the use of complex ornaments and ribbons that become compositional devices and unify the layouts by tying disparate elements together.

Cincinnati emerged as a design center, led by the Strobridge Litho. Company (Fig. 12-9), which became internationally famous for the quality of its chromos, particularly the large posters created for circuses and other theatrical traveling entertainments. The graphic clarity of designs by the Strobridge art department— which combined convincing pictorial images with simple and legible lettering, often placed on brightly colored shapes or bands across the top of the image—found great favor with producers of entertainment spectaculars. The Strobridge firm continued to produce chromolithographs, particularly for circuses, well into the twentieth century.

Plate 16 is an undated poster for the C. W. Parker Company's *Carry-Us-All* portable carousels. Parker's carousels, manufactured in Kansas, were very popular in midwestern nomadic carnivals. This poster was designed and printed by the River-

12-10. Krebs Lithographing Company, poster for the Cincinnati Industrial Exposition, 1883. Glowing with a rich palette of yellow and golden tones, this poster expresses a buoyant optimism in industrial progress.

12-11. W. J. Morgan and Co., Cleveland, lithographic theater poster, 1884. Graphic designers developed a complex montage effect by combining many images with shifting scale, perspective planes, and depth.

12-10

12-11

Popular Graphics of the Victorian Era

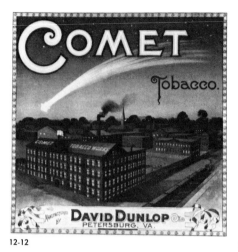

12-12

12-13

12-12. A. Hoen and Company, label for *Comet* Tobacco, 1880s. Nineteenth-century manufacturers loved to display their buildings, and the designer accommodated with a giant comet flaming above the client's facilities.

12-13. A. Hoen and Company, label for *Tiger Brand* tobacco, 1880s. A yellow circle in a red and yellow square border is dissolved by the illustration, which overlaps these borders.

side Print Company of Milwaukee, using the bright primary colors favored in graphics for entertainment shows and fairs. The bright yellow band at the top was left blank to provide a place for local printers to imprint the dates and location of the carnival's visit.

A high design standard was also maintained by the firm of Adolph Krebs (b. 1833). One of the finest designs by this firm is the poster for the 1883 Cincinnati Industrial Exposition (Fig. 12-10). The Victorian passion for allegory inspired a mythic scene in front of the exhibition hall. An allegorical figure representing the "Queen City," as Cincinnati loved to call itself, accepts machinery, agricultural products, and manufactured goods from symbolic figures representing the various states participating in the exhibition. W. J. Morgan and Company's design staff also produced superb work, excelling in complex montage posters for theatrical performances (Fig. 12-11).

Label design, for the numerous and newly coined brand names identifying products, was an important use of chromolithography. A. Hoen of Baltimore and Richmond counted labels as one of its specialties. The rapidly growing tobacco industry provided A. Hoen's art staff with dozens of names like Indian Queen, Cora, Comet (Fig. 12-12), Crusader, Black Swan, Golden Eagle, and Tiger Brand (Fig. 12-13), all of which needed graphic interpretation. Fantasy and the exotic were used to bring drama to ordinary products.

By the mid-1890s, the golden era of chromolithography was coming to a close. Changing public tastes and the development of photoengraving were making the use of chromolithography from hand-prepared stones obsolete. Perhaps the end of the chromolithographic era can be marked by the year 1897, when Louis Prang—mindful of the revolution that was occurring in tastes and technology—merged his firm with Clark Taber & Company, a printing firm specializing in the new photographic-process reproduction of artwork. By contrast, the famous art reproduction firm of Currier & Ives continued to print graphic expressions of outmoded Victorian sentiment by stone lithography and went bankrupt shortly after the turn of the century.

The battle on the signboards

The ascendency of the letterpress poster and broadsheet was challenged in the middle of the nineteenth century by a more visual and pictorial poster. Lithography was the graphic medium allowing a more illustrative approach to public communication. During the late 1840s, posters from the French printing firm of Rouchon, which acted as an art director and adviser to book publishers, theatrical producers, and fashion houses, pioneered the graphic impact that could be achieved by simplification. Rouchon commissioned design from leading artists of the day, including Paul Baudry (1828–1886). A stencil process was used to print flat planes of color that combined to construct a stylized representational image (Fig. 12-14).

12-14. Poster for *L'Algerie*, c. 1845. In this poster for a book describing life in Algeria, the use of a large central figure dominating the space is typical of posters produced by Rouchon.

12-15

12-16

An unusual design quality of Rouchon posters was the unprecedented use of bright, often violently contrasting colors that caused these images seemingly to leap from the billboards in striking contrast to the more typical graphic designs of the period.

The letterpress printers responded to competition from the fluid and colorful lithographs beginning to be pasted on the signboards by midcentury with heroic and ingenious efforts to extend their medium. Witness, for example, the 344-centimeter (11-foot) multicolored woodcut poster designed by Joseph Morse of New York for the Sands, Nathan and Company Circus in 1856 (Fig. 12-15). The enormous wooden blocks were printed in sections to be assembled by the poster hangers.

In his work from the 1860s, James Reilley of New York would design ingenious ways to increase the pictorial impact of the letterpress poster. The 1866 poster for John O'Brien's Consolidated Six Shows is an excellent example of Reilley's imaginative design solutions (Fig. 12-16).

Another approach was the "if you can't beat 'em, join 'em" philosophy. In France, letterpress poster houses and lithographers collaborated. In these graphic "piggyback" designs, each medium did what it could do best, for colorful lithographic illustrations were pasted onto large woodtype posters. A masterpiece of the genre is the 1871 *Cirque D'Hiver* ("Winter Circus") poster, of which only one copy survives (Pl. 17). The Morris Pere et Fils printing firm commissioned a lithographer, Emile Levy, to illustrate an acrobatic dance act called *Les Papillons* (The Butterflies). The spectacular finale of this crowd-thrilling act featured two young female performers —one black and one white—being hurled through the air. Levy illustrated them as surreal butterfly women.

Another important designer in the development of lithographic posters in France was Jules Chéret (1836–1932), who carried the poster from his complex Victorian early style all the way into the twentieth century and became one of the major innovators of the Art Nouveau style (see Figs. 14-2 through 14-4).

In England, the 1871 poster for a play, *The Woman in White,* at the Olympic Theatre, is considered to be one of the first British visual posters (Fig. 12-17).

Images for children

Before the Victorian era, western countries had a tendency to treat children as "little adults." The Victorians developed a more doting and tender attitude toward their offspring, and this was expressed through the development of *toy books,* colorful picture books for preschool children. Three English illustrators achieved good page design, excellent pictorial composition, and a restrained use of color in their

12-15. Joseph Morse, colored woodcut poster, 1856. The heroic scale—262 by 344 centimeters (11 by 8½ feet)—allowed the presentation of life-sized figures. The pictorial images in this circus poster dominate the headline, *Five Celebrated Clowns Attached to Sands, Nathan Co.'s Circus,* which is pushed into the background.

12-16. James Reilley (printer and engraver), poster for John O'Brien's Circus, 1866. Several wood engravings are pieced together to create an endless circus parade.

Popular Graphics of the Victorian Era

12-17. Frederick Walker, theater poster, 1871. This oversized wood engraving has a fluid, calligraphic quality in the drawing of the clothing in contrast to the rectangular forms of the door frame and lettering.

work. Standards and an approach to children's graphics were established, and their influence still lingers.

Many of the earliest toy books were not dated, so just who pioneered this graphic form is not clear. It is generally acknowledged, however, that Walter Crane (1845– 1915) was one of the earliest and the most influential designers of children's picture books (Fig. 12-18). Apprenticed as a wood engraver as a teenager, Crane was twenty years old in 1865 when his *Railroad Alphabet* was published. A long series of his toy books broke with the traditions of printed material for children. Earlier graphics for children insisted on a didactic or moral purpose, and always taught or preached to the young; Crane sought only to entertain. He was the first to be influenced by the Japanese woodblock, and introduced it into western art. He had acquired some Japanese prints from a British sailor in the late 1860s and was inspired by the use of flat color and flowing contours. This unprecedented design quality in his work produced a tremendous volume of commissions to design tapestries, stained-glass windows, wallpaper, and fabrics. Crane remained active into the twentieth century. He played an important role in the Arts and Crafts Movement and had a significant impact upon art and design education.

T stands for Tom, the son of the piper,
May his principles change as his years grow riper.

U for the Unicorn, keeping his eye on
The coveted crown, and its counsel the Lion.

V for the Victuals, including the drink.
The old woman lived on surprising to think!

12-18. Walter Crane, page from *Walter Crane's Absurd A.B.C.*, 1874. Animated figures are placed against a black background, and large letterforms are integrated with the imagery.

While Crane entertained children, Randolph Caldecott (1846–1886) set forth to amuse them (Fig. 12-19). As a bank clerk in his twenties, Caldecott developed a passion for drawing and took evening lessons in painting, sketching, and modeling. He learned anatomy by dissecting birds and animals. A steady stream of freelance assignments encouraged him to move to London and turn professional at the age of twenty-six. He possessed a devastating sense of the absurd, and his ability to exaggerate movement and facial expressions of both people and animals brings his work to life. Caldecott created a world where dishes and plates are personified, cats make music, children are at the center of society, and adults become servants. His humorous drawing style became a prototype for children's books and animated films.

Kate Greenaway's (1846–1901) expressions of the childhood experience captured the imagination of the Victorian era, although her work was static and humorless compared to Caldecott's. As a poet and illustrator, Greenaway created a modest small world of childhood happiness; as a book designer, she sometimes pushed her graceful sense of page layout to innovative levels (Fig. 12-20). White space, silhouetting of images, and asymmetrical balance combined with a soft color sense to create pages of great charm.

The clothes Greenaway designed for her models had a major influence on children's fashion design. Walter Crane, however, complained that Greenaway "overdid the big bonnet, and her little people are almost lost in their clothes." In the thousands of little pictures created by Greenaway, childhood became an idealized fantasy world. This led one child psychologist to denounce her for creating "a false and degenerate race of children in art," but the Victorian love of sentiment and idealization made Greenaway an internationally famous graphic artist whose books are still in print.

12-19. Randolph Caldecott, illustration from *Hey Diddle Diddle,* c. 1880. Oblivious to the outlandish elopement, Caldecott's dancing dinnerware moves to a driving musical rhythm.

12-20. Kate Greenaway, page from *Under the Window,* 1879. Often Greenaway would leave out the background as a means of simplifying the page design and focusing on the figures. Her use of white space was without immediate precedent.

12-19

Up you go, shuttlecocks, ever so high!
Why come you down again, shuttlecocks—why?
When you have got so far, why do you fall?
Where all are high, which is highest of all?

12-20

Popular Graphics of the Victorian Era

The rise of American editorial and advertising design

The Harper brothers, James (1795–1869) and John (1797–1875), using modest savings and their father's offer to mortgage the family farm if necessary, established a New York printing firm in 1817. Their younger brothers Wesley (1801–1870) and Fletcher (1807–1877) joined the firm in 1823 and 1825, respectively. Eighteen-year-old Fletcher Harper was made the firm's editor when he became a partner, and the firm's own publishing ventures grew dramatically over the decades. By midcentury, Harper and Brothers had become the largest printing and publishing firm in the world. In the role of senior editor and manager of publishing activities, Fletcher Harper shaped graphic communications in America for half a century.

Inventive book design was not a concern for most publishing firms in America and Europe, including Harper and Brothers, during most of the nineteenth century. With the rapid expansion of the reading public, and the economies resulting from new technologies, publishers focused on large press runs and modest prices.

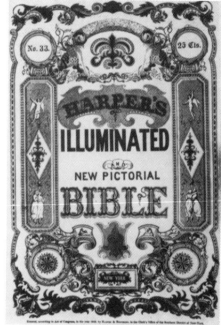

12-22

12-21. Joseph A. Adams, page from *Harper's Illuminated and New Pictorial Bible,* 1846. In the first page of the Old and the New Testaments, the two-column format with a central margin for annotation was disrupted by centering the first few verses.

12-22. Joseph A. Adams, cover design, installment thirty-three of *Harper's Illuminated and New Pictorial Bible,* 1844. This two-color engraving achieves the pomp and grandeur of Victorian design. Extravagant floral elements soften the architectonic symmetrical structure.

Modern-style fonts, often second-rate derivatives of Bodoni and Didot designs, were composed in workaday page layouts.

During the 1840s, Harper and Brothers launched a monumental project that was destined to become the finest achievement of graphic design and book production to date in the young country's history. *Harper's Illuminated and New Pictorial Bible,* printed on presses specially designed and built for its production, contained 1,600 wood engravings from illustrations by Joseph A. Adams (Fig. 12-21). Its publication in fifty-four installments of twenty-eight pages each was heralded by a carefully orchestrated advertising campaign. Each segment was handsewn and bound in heavy paper covers printed in two colors (Fig. 12-22). During the preliminary preparations for this work, Adams invented an electrotyping process. This involved pressing the wood engraving into wax to make a mold, which was dusted with graphite to make it electroconductive. Then an electrodeposit of metal (usually copper) was made in the mold. The resulting thin shell was backed with lead, and this harder printing surface enabled Harper to publish fifty thousand copies in installments. A hardbound edition of twenty-five thousand copies with handtooled gold gilding on morocco leather binding was bound and sold after the series of installments was completed. The format consisted of two columns of text with a central margin bearing annotations. Illustrations included large images the width of two columns contained in ornate Victorian frames and hundreds of spot illustrations dropped into the text. Every chapter opened with an illuminated initial.

The firm opened its era of the pictorial magazine in 1850 when the 144-page *Harper's New Monthly Magazine* began publication with serialized English fiction

12-23. Richard G. Tietze, poster for *Harper's Magazine,* 1883. An impressionist quality is achieved in an illustration divided into three zones, with the middle holly area providing a background for the message while separating the images.

12-24. After A. H. Wald, cover for *Harper's Weekly,* 1864. Engraved after a sketch from a "visual journalist" in the field, this cover is a forerunner of the newsmagazine coverage of current events.

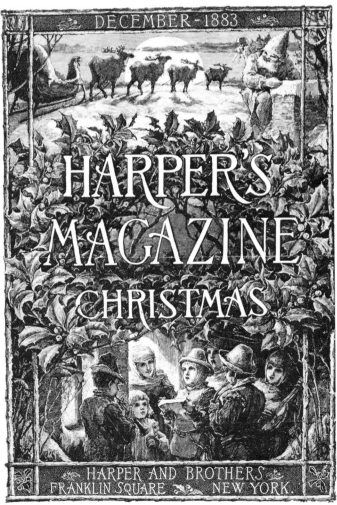

12-23

12-24

Popular Graphics of the Victorian Era

and numerous woodcut illustrations created for each issue by the art staff
(Fig. 12-23). The monthly magazine was joined by a weekly periodical that functioned as a newsmagazine, *Harper's Weekly,* in 1857. *Harper's Bazar* (*sic*) for
women was founded in 1867, and the youth audience was addressed with *Harper's
Young People* in 1879. *Harper's Weekly* billed itself as "a journal of civilization" and
developed an elaborate division of shop labor for the rapid production of woodblocks for printing cartoons and graphic reportage (Fig. 12-24) based on drawings
from artist/correspondents, including Thomas Nast (1840–1902).

Nast, a precociously talented artist, had switched from public school to art school
after the sixth grade and began his career as a four-dollar-per-week staff illustrator for *Leslie's Weekly* when he was fifteen years old. Fletcher Harper hired him
when he was twenty-two to make battlefield sketches during the Civil War. The
power of his work was such that President Abraham Lincoln called Nast "the best
recruiting sergeant" and General Ulysses S. Grant declared that Nast had done as
much as anyone to bring the conflict to a close. Public response to Nast's work was
a major factor in propelling *Harper's Weekly*'s circulation from one hundred thousand to three hundred thousand copies per issue.

After the war, Nast remained with *Harper's Weekly,* where he would draw his
images directly on the woodblock in reverse for the craftsmen to cut. His deep
social and political concerns led him to strip away detail and introduce symbols and
labels for increased communicative effectiveness in his work. He has been called
the "Father of American Political Cartooning." The graphic symbols Nast popularized and focused include a number of important images: Santa Claus, John Bull (as
a symbol for England), the Democratic donkey, the Republican elephant, Uncle
Sam, and Columbia (a symbolic female signifying democracy that became the prototype for the Statue of Liberty).

The potential of visual communications was demonstrated when Nast took on
the governmental corruption of the political boss William Marcy Tweed, who controlled New York politics from infamous Tammany Hall. Tweed exclaimed that he
did not care what the papers wrote, because voters couldn't read, but "they could
sure see them damn pictures." Nast's relentless graphic attack culminated on Election Day, in a double-page cartoon of the "Tammany tiger" loose in the Roman
Coliseum, devouring liberty, while Tweed as the Roman emperor surrounded by his
elected officials, presided over the slaughter (Fig. 12-25). The opposition won the
election.

After Fletcher Harper died in 1877, a more conservative editorial staff took over
the magazine, leading Nast to declare that "policy always strangles individuals."

12-26. Charles Dana Gibson, poster for
Scribner's, 1895. Although the exquisite
beauty of the "Gibson Girls" was captured
with facility and control, Gibson was
unconcerned with the design of type and
image as a cohesive whole. In this poster, the
printer added type in incompatible typefaces.

So effective were Nast's graphics for the Republican Party that President Theodore Roosevelt appointed him Consul General to Ecuador. Nast died of yellow fever six months after his arrival in that tropical country.

Charles Parsons became the art editor of Harper and Brothers in 1863, and his efforts contributed to a higher standard of pictorial images in the publications. Parsons had a superb eye for young talent, and the illustrators he brought along included a master of pen-and-ink drawing, Edwin Austin Abbey (1852–1911); Charles Dana Gibson (1867–1944), the creator of beautiful young women (Fig. 12-26) and square-jawed men who established a canon of perfection in the mass media that endured for decades; and Arthur B. Frost (1851–1928), a teen-aged wood engraver who joined Harper's staff in 1876 and became loved for his pen-and-ink drawings of animals and rural American folk.

Among the many illustrators encouraged by Parsons, Howard Pyle (1853–1911) had the broadest influence. Pyle's own work and his remarkable gifts as a teacher made him the major force that launched the period called the "Golden Age of American Illustration." Spanning the decades from the 1890s until the 1940s, this period saw visual communications in America dominated by the illustrator. Magazine art editors selected the illustrators, whose work dominated rather routine typographic formats. Advertising layouts were often guides for the illustrator, indicating how much room to leave for the type, which was often *pub-set* (composed by the publication and locked into the letterpress chase to be printed with the plates for the illustration).

Pyle published over 3,300 illustrations and two hundred texts, ranging from simple children's fables to his monumental four-volume legend of King Arthur. The meticulous research, elaborate staging, and historical accuracy of Pyle's work (Fig. 12-27) inspired a younger generation of graphic artists, who carried forward the tradition of realism in America. The impact of photography, the new communications tool, upon graphic illustration can be traced in Howard Pyle's career, which evolved with the new reproduction technologies. He was twenty-three years old when he received his first illustration commission from *Scribner's Monthly* in 1876. Like nearly all magazine and newspaper illustration of the time, it was an ink line drawing, which was turned over to a wood engraver to be cut into a relief block that could be locked in place with type and printed by letterpress.

A decade later, in 1887, Pyle was thirty-four years old when he received his first commission for a tonal illustration. The new photomechanical halftone process (discussed in the preceding chapter) made possible the conversion of the blacks, whites, and grays in Pyle's oil and gouache painting into minute black dots that were blended by the human eye to produce the illusion of continuous tone. In addition to this process's impact upon engravers, illustrators were faced with the need either to shift to tonal, painted illustrations instead of pen-and-ink art or to face a dwindling market for their work.

Another advance occurred for Pyle in 1893, when the forty-year-old illustrator created his first two-color illustration. Pink flesh tones and browns were mixed from the limited palette of black, white, and red paint. The image was printed from two halftone plates. One impression was in black ink, and the other—shot with a filter—separated the red tones from the blacks and grays. This plate was inked with a red ink closely matched to Pyle's red paint. Four years later, in 1897, Pyle had passed his forty-fourth birthday when he had a first opportunity to apply his spectacular sense of color to a full-color illustration assignment. This image was printed by the developing four-color process system. All of Pyle's full-color illustrations were painted during the fourteen years from 1897 until his death at age fifty-eight in 1911.

Harper's Weekly's leading competitors in the magazine field were the *Century* magazine (1881–1930) and *Scribner's Monthly* (1887–1939). All three of these major periodicals were printed at the printing firm of Theodore Low De Vinne (1824–1914). De Vinne and his staff gave a quiet, dignified, but rather dry layout to all three. In the *Century,* for example, text was set in two columns of ten-point

12-27. Howard Pyle, illustration from *The Merry Adventures of Robin Hood,* 1883. Pyle sought authenticity in every detail of setting, props, costume, and characterization.

type, and the wood engravings were dropped in adjacent to the copy discussed. Article titles were merely set in twelve-point, all capitals, and centered above the beginning page of the article. De Vinne was dissatisfied with the thin modern typefaces used in this magazine, so he commissioned type designer Linn Boyd Benton to cut a blacker, more readable face that is slightly extended with thicker thin strokes and short slab serifs. Now called Century, this unusually legible style is still widely used today. Its large x-height and slightly expanded characters have made it very popular for children's reading matter.

The rising tide of literacy, plunging production costs, and the growth of advertising revenues pushed the number of newspapers and magazines published in the United States from eight hundred to five thousand between 1830 and 1860. During the 1870s, magazines were being used extensively for general advertising. This additional revenue lowered prices for the readers, which caused even greater circulation increases.

Closely bound to the growth of magazines was the development of advertising agencies. In 1841, Volney Palmer of Philadelphia opened what is considered to be the first advertising agency. He sold space for publishers much as a travel agent sells tickets for airlines today, and received a 25 percent commission on his sales. The advertising agency as a consulting firm with an array of specialized skills was pioneered by another Philadelphia advertising agent, N. W. Ayer and Son. In 1875, Ayer gave his clients an open contract, which allowed them access to the real rates publications were charging the agencies. Then, Ayer received an additional per-

12-28. Advertisements, 1880–1890. This potpourri of advertisements demonstrates the range of Victorian advertising, from small typographic to full-page ads with a dominant pictorial image.

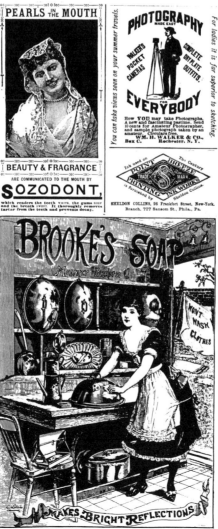

centage for placing the advertisements. In the 1880s, Ayer provided services clients were not equipped to perform and publishers did not offer, such as copywriting. By the end of the century, Ayer was well on the way toward offering a complete spectrum of services: copywriting, art direction, production, and media selection.

Many of the conventions of persuasive selling were developed during the last two decades of the nineteenth century. Advertisements from the English and American magazines of the period demonstrate some of these techniques (Fig. 12-28): An aura of glamour and adventure is projected by the exotic hunters in the International Fur Store advertisement; an appeal to self-improvement and idealized beauty is conveyed by the ad for Sozodont, which will turn one's teeth into "pearls in the mouth"; a demonstration of product excellence in the Brook's Soap ad shows how this product turns pots and pans into bright reflecting mirrors; for Cadbury's Cocoa, the celebrity testimonial is pioneered by none other than Queen Victoria herself, enjoying the product in her royal train coach. The design of this page demonstrates the makeup of Victorian advertising pages—printing plates for the various ads are locked together with little concern for a total design. By the end of the century, magazines, including *Cosmopolitan* and *McClure's,* were carrying over a hundred pages of advertisements in every monthly issue. Frequently an engraved illustration would have type set above or below it, and often the prevalent practice of chromolithography, superimposing lettering on top of a pictorial image, was adopted by engravers.

12-29. Cover for Frank Tousey's *Wide Awake Library,* 1888. Speculating visually about the form of the new, nineteenth-century graphic artists often wrapped the future in the forms of the past.

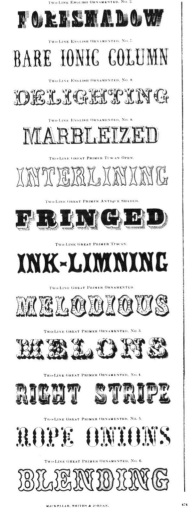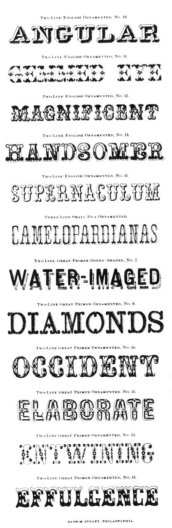

12-30. MacKellar, Smiths, & Jordan, page from *Book of Specimens,* 1881. The two dozen styles of type on this page suggest the bewildering range of possibilities available to the nineteenth-century designer of printing.

12-31. Herman Ihlenburg, typeface designs.

12-32. John F. Cumming, typeface designs.
The bottom two typefaces show a marked
shift in Cumming's design approach under
the influence of the Kelmscott Press, which is
discussed in Chapter 13.

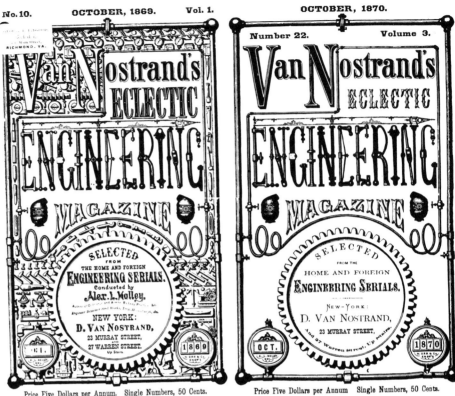

12-33

On 20 June 1877 a new graphic format was launched by the Pictorial Printing Company of Chicago, when the first issue of *The Nickel Library* hit newsstands throughout America. Called nickel novels or story papers, these weekly publications hired graphic artists to design and illustrate action-filled covers interpreting tales of Civil War, Indians, and the western frontier. The typical format was sixteen to thirty-two pages, set with two to four type columns per page. The 20.3-by-30.5-centimeter (8-by-12-inch) page size allowed the artists to create strong visual impact on the news dealer's shelf.

Typical of the many imitators was publisher Frank Tousey's (1876–1902) *Wide Awake Library* (Fig. 12-29), which was eagerly purchased by thousands of young people who followed the weekly adventures written by such authors as Luis P. Senarens (1865–1939). Writing under the pseudonym "Noname," Senarens drew upon his considerable scientific knowledge to make believable the astounding inventions of young inventor Frank Reade, Jr., whose electric horses, helicopters, airships, and other inventions accurately forecast future technologies.

Victorian typography

As the Victorian Era progressed, the taste for ornate elaboration became a major influence upon typeface and lettering design. As discussed in Chapter 10, early nineteenth-century elaborated types were based on letterforms with traditional structure. Shadows, outlines, and embellishments were applied while retaining the classical proportions (see Fig. 10-11). In the second half of the century, advances in industrial technology permitted metal-type foundries to push elaboration, including the fanciful distortion of basic letterform structure, to an extreme degree. To produce more intricate types, punch cutters cut their designs in soft metal, then electroplated them to make a harder punch able to stamp the design into a brass matrix. Chromolithography, with its uninhibited lettering, was a major source of inspiration for foundries and letterpress printers desperately seeking to maintain their share of a fiercely competitive graphic-arts industry.

A major Victorian typeface designer was Berlin-born Hern Ihlenburg (b. 1843), who spent most of his career from 1866 until after the turn of the century with the

12-33. Covers for *Van Nostrand's Eclectic Engineering,* 1869–1870. Apparently, a design decision to simplify the cover format radically was made between October of 1869 and October of 1870.

12-34. Trademark for Moss Engraving Company, 1872. Graphic complexity and slogans often embellished Victorian trademarks.

12-34

MacKellar, Smiths & Jordan foundry in Philadelphia, which became a major component of the American Type Founders Company when the monopoly was formed in 1892. MacKellar, Smiths & Jordan played a significant role in the design and production of Victorian display typefaces (Fig. 12-30), and Ihlenburg was a leading member of their design staff. Before the end of the century, Ihlenburg had designed over eighty display typefaces and cut punches for over thirty-two thousand typographic characters. This becomes even more remarkable in light of the extreme complexity of many of his designs (Fig. 12-31).

John F. Cumming (b. 1852) designed numerous elaborated typefaces for the Dickinson Type Foundry in Boston (Fig. 12-32), but the passion for ornate Victorian typefaces began to decline in the 1890s, yielding to the revival of classical typography, inspired by the English Arts and Crafts Movement (see Chapter 13). Cumming rode the tides of change, and designed faces derivative of Arts and Crafts designs.

Outlandish and fantasy lettering, as evidenced by the *Eclectic Engineering* magazine covers (Fig. 12-33) enjoyed great popularity, and many trademarks of the era reflect the Victorian love of ornamental complexity (Fig. 12-34). Typographic purists view the typeface designs of Ihlenburg, Cumming, and their contemporaries as aberrations in the evolution of typography, a commercial venture intended to give advertisers novel visual expressions to garner attention to their messages while providing foundries with a constant stream of original new typefaces to sell to printers, but it has also been argued that these ornate expressions connote the spirit of an era characterized by unbridled optimism, technological development, and economic expansion.

The popular graphics of the Victorian Era stemmed not from a design philosophy or artistic convictions but from the prevalent attitudes and sensibilities of the period. Undaunted by the revolutionary design ideas that developed during the 1890s or by the decline of chromolithography, many conventions of Victorian design could still be found during the early years of the twentieth century, particularly in commercial promotion.

The Arts and Crafts Movement

13-1. William Pickering, title page for *The Book of Common Prayer,* 1844. The intricacy of Gothic architecture and heraldic devices are convincingly depicted in this red and black title page.

As the nineteenth century wore on, the quality of book design and production became a casualty of the Industrial Revolution, with a few notable exceptions, such as the books by the English publisher William Pickering (1796–1854). At age fourteen, Pickering apprenticed to a London bookseller and publisher; at age twenty-four, he established his own bookshop, specializing in old and rare volumes. Shortly thereafter, this young man with a deep love of books and outstanding scholarship began his publishing program. Pickering played an important role in the separation of graphic design from printing production, for he maintained control over the format design, type selection, illustrations, and all other visual considerations. The actual production of his books was commissioned from printers, who worked under Pickering's close supervision. A cordial working relationship between publisher/designer and printer was established by Pickering and Charles Whittingham (1795–1876) of the Chiswick Press. Whittingham's excellent craftsmanship complemented Pickering's demands for quality very nicely. In books of prose and poetry, such as Pickering's fifty-three-volume series of "Aldine Poets," his design sense moved toward classic simplicity. In collaboration with Whittingham, Pickering revived Caslon types, which he loved for their straightforward legibility. Pickering's liturgical books, including the 1844 *The Book of Common Prayer* (Fig. 13-1), are some of the finest examples of the revival of Gothic forms that infested the nineteenth century.

In spite of the efforts of Pickering and others, the decline in book design was not checked until late in the century, when a book-design renaissance began. This revival—which treated the book as a limited-edition art object, then influenced commercial production—was largely a byproduct of the Arts and Crafts Movement, which flourished in England during the last decades of the nineteenth century as a reaction against the social, moral, and artistic confusion of the Industrial Revolution. Design and a return to handicraft were advocated, and the "cheap and nasty" mass-produced goods of the Victorian Era were abhorred. The leader of the English Arts and Crafts Movement, William Morris (1834–1896), called for a fitness of purpose, truth to the nature of materials and methods of production, and individual expression by both designer and worker.

The writer and artist John Ruskin (1819–1900) inspired the philosophy of this movement. Asking how society could "consciously order the lives of its members so as to maintain the largest number of noble and happy human beings," Ruskin rejected the mercantile economy and pointed toward the union of art and labor in service to society, as exemplified in the design and construction of the medieval Gothic cathedral. Ruskin called this the social order that Europe must "regain for her children." According to Ruskin, a process of separating art and society had begun after the Renaissance. Industrialization and technology caused the severing of art from society to reach a critical stage, isolating the artist. The consequences were eclecticism of historical models, a decline in creativity, and design by engineers without aesthetic concern. Inherent in all of this was Ruskin's notion that beautiful things were valuable and useful precisely because they were beautiful. From the philosophy of art, Ruskin became concerned for social justice, advocating improved housing for industrial workers, a national education system, and retirement benefits for the elderly.

Among the artists, architects, and designers who embraced a synthesis of Ruskin's aesthetic philosophies and social consciousness, William Morris is a pivotal figure in the history of design. The eldest son of a wealthy wine importer, Morris grew up in a Georgian mansion on the edge of Epping Forest, where the near-feudal way of life, ancient churches and mansions, and beautiful English countryside made a profound impression. In 1853, he entered Exeter College, Oxford, where he began his lifelong friendship with Edward Burne-Jones (1833–1898). Both planned to enter the ministry, and their wide reading included medieval history, chronicles, and poetry. Writing became a daily activity for Morris, who published his first volume of poems at age twenty-four. Throughout his career, he produced a steady flow of poetry, fiction, and philosophical writings, which filled twenty-four volumes when his daughter May (1862–1938) published his collected works after his death.

While traveling in France on a holiday in 1855, Morris and Burne-Jones decided to become artists instead of clergymen, and after graduation Morris entered the Oxford architectural office of G. E. Street. There, Morris formed a close friendship with young architect Philip Webb (1831–1915), who was his supervisor. Morris found the routine of an architectural office stifling and dull, so in the fall of 1856 he left architecture and joined Burne-Jones in the pursuit of painting. Since Morris's family estate provided an income of nine hundred pounds a month, he could follow his ideas and interests wherever they led. The two artists fell under the influence of the Pre-Raphaelite painter Dante Gabriel Rossetti (1828–1882). Morris struggled with his romantic paintings of medieval pageantry but was never fully satisfied with his work. He married his hauntingly beautiful model, Jane Burden, daughter of an Oxford stableman, and, during the process of establishing their home, began to find his design vocation.

Red House, designed for them by Philip Webb, is a landmark in domestic architecture. Instead of featuring rooms in a rectangular box behind a symmetrical façade, the L-shaped plan grew out of functional interior space planning. Here and there the exterior façade darts in or out, in response to interior needs. When it came time to furnish the interior, Morris suddenly discovered the appalling state of Victorian product and furniture design. Over the next several years, he designed and supervised the execution of furniture, stained glass, and tapestries for Red House.

As a result of this experience, Morris joined with six friends in 1861 to establish the art-decorating firm of Morris, Marshall, Faulkner and Company. Growing rapidly, the firm established London showrooms and began to assemble teams of craftsmen that eventually included furniture and cabinet makers, weavers and dyers, stained glass fabricators, and ceramic and tile makers (Fig. 13-2). Morris

13-2. J. P. Seddon, cabinet designed for Morris and Company, 1861. Paintings illustrating the honeymoon of the fifteenth-century Italian King René of Anjou by Ford Madox Brown, Edward Burne-Jones, and D. G. Rossetti grace this cabinet. The structure and ornamental carving allude to design from the late medieval era.

proved to be a brilliant two-dimensional pattern designer. He created over five hundred pattern designs for wallpapers, textiles, carpets, and tapestries. His 1883 fabric design, "Rose" (Pl. 18), demonstrates his close study of botany and drawing fluency in creating willowy patterns weaving decorative arabesques of natural forms. A similarly large number of stained glass windows were created under his supervision. Medieval arts and botanical forms were his main inspirations. The firm reorganized in 1875 as Morris and Company, with Morris as the sole owner.

Deeply concerned about the problems of industrialization and the factory system, Morris tried to implement Ruskin's ideas: The tastelessness of mass-produced goods and the lack of honest craftsmanship could be addressed by a reunion of art with craft; art and craft could combine to create beautiful objects, from buildings to bedding; workers could find joy in their work once again, and the man-made environment—which had declined into industrial cities of squalid, dismal tenements filled with tacky, manufactured goods—could be revitalized.

A moral concern over the exploitation of the poor led Morris to embrace socialism. Dismay over the wanton destruction of the architectural heritage motivated him to found the Society for the Protection of Ancient Buildings, called "Anti-Scrape." Disgust at the false and misleading claims of advertising caused him to become involved in the Society for Checking the Abuses of Public Advertising, which confronted offenders directly.

During the 1880s and 1890s, the Arts and Crafts Movement was underpinned by a number of societies and guilds, which sought to establish democratic artistic communities united for the common good. These ranged from exhibition cooperatives to communes based on socialist and religious ideals.

The Century Guild

A twenty-six-year-old architect, Arthur H. Mackmurdo (1851–1942), met William Morris and was inspired by Morris's ideas and accomplishments in applied design. In trips to Italy in 1878 and 1880, Mackmurdo filled his sketchbooks with studies of Renaissance architectural structure and ornament, in addition to extensive drawings of botanical and other natural forms. Back in London, Mackmurdo led a youthful group of artists and designers who banded together in 1882 to establish the Century Guild. The group included designer/illustrator Selwyn Image (1849–1930) and designer/writer Herbert P. Horne (1864–1916). The goal of the Century Guild was "to render all branches of art the sphere, no longer of the tradesman, but of the artist. . . ." The design arts were to be elevated to "their rightful place beside painting and sculpture." The group evolved a new design aesthetic as Mackmurdo and his friends, who were about two decades younger than Morris and his associates, incorporated Renaissance and Japanese design ideas into their work. Their graphic designs provide a link from the Arts and Crafts Movement to the floral stylization of Art Nouveau.

Featuring the work of guild members, *The Century Guild Hobby Horse* began publication in 1884 as the first finely printed magazine devoted exclusively to the visual arts. The medieval passions of the Arts and Crafts Movement were reflected in the graphic designs of Image and Horne. However, several designs by Mackmurdo have swirling organic forms that are pure Art Nouveau in their conception and execution. He first explored abstract intertwining floral patterns in an 1881 carved chair back (Fig. 13-3). The 1883 title page for his book, *Wren's City Churches* (Fig. 13-4), was followed by fabric designs (Fig. 13-5), the Century Guild trademark (Fig. 13-6), and *Hobby Horse* graphics (Fig. 13-7). In retrospect, these were seminal innovations that could have launched a movement; but these designs were born before their time. Mackmurdo did not explore this direction further, and Art Nouveau did not explode into a movement until the following decade.

The *Hobby Horse* (Figs. 13-8 and 13-9), which sought to proclaim the philosophy and goals of the Century Guild, was produced with painstaking care under the tutelage of the master printer and typographer at the Chiswick Press, Sir Emery Walker (1851–1883). Its careful layout and typesetting, handmade paper, and in-

13-3. Arthur H. Mackmurdo, chair, 1881. In developing this decorative pattern, Mackmurdo carefully considered visual design qualities and structural strength. Unifying construction and ornament became an important characteristic of Art Nouveau.

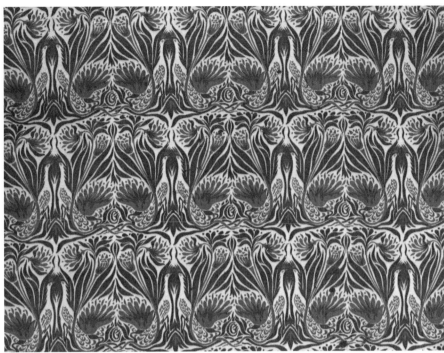

13-4

13-5

tricate woodblock illustrations made it the harbinger of the growing Arts and Crafts interest in typography, graphic design, and printing. Mackmurdo, in addition to anticipating Art Nouveau, was a forerunner of the private press movement and the renaissance of book design. This private press movement should not be confused with amateur or hobby presses. Rather, it was a design and printing movement advocating an aesthetic concern for the design and production of beautiful books. It sought to regain the design standards, quality materials, and careful workmanship of printing that existed before the Industrial Revolution. The *Hobby Horse* was the first 1880s periodical to introduce the British Arts and Crafts viewpoint to a European audience and to treat printing as a serious design form. Mackmurdo later related that he showed William Morris a copy of *Hobby Horse* and discussed the difficulties of typographic design, including the problems of proportions and margins, letterspacing and leading between lines, choosing paper, and typefaces. Reportedly, Morris was filled with enthusiasm about the possibilities of book design as he admired the well-crafted typographic pages, generous margins, wide linespacing, and meticulous printing alive with handcut woodblock illustrations, head-and-tail pieces, and ornamented capitals. Original etchings and lithographs were printed as fine plates and bound into the quarterly issues.

In an article entitled "On the Unity of Art" in the January 1887 issue of *Hobby Horse,* Selwyn Image passionately argued that all forms of visual expression deserved the status of art. He suggested that "the unknown inventor of patterns to decorate a wall or a water-pot" who "employs himself in representing abstract lines and masses" deserves equal claim to being called an artist as the painter, Raphael, who represented "the human form and the highest human interests." He chided the Royal Academy of Art by recommending that its name be changed to the Royal Academy of Oil Painting because it was so limited relative to the total range of art and design forms. In perhaps the most prophetic observation of the decade, Image concluded that "For when you begin to realize, that all kinds of invented Form, and Tone, and Colour, are alike true and honorable aspects of Art, *you see something very much like a revolution looming ahead of you*" [emphasis added].

Although it received ample commissions, the Century Guild disbanded in 1888. Emphasis had been upon collaborative projects, but now the members were becom-

13-4. Arthur H. Mackmurdo, title page for *Wren's City Churches,* 1883. Mackmurdo's plant forms are stylized into flamelike, undulating rhythms that compress the negative space between them. This establishes a positive and negative interplay between black ink and white paper.

13-5. Arthur H. Mackmurdo, "Peacock" design, 1883. Mackmurdo applied forms and images similar to those on his famous title page to this printed cotton fabric.

13-6. Arthur H. Mackmurdo, trademark for the Century Guild, 1884. Flame, flower, and initials are compressed and tapered into proto-Art Nouveau forms.

13-7. Arthur H. Mackmurdo, design element from the *Hobby Horse,* 1884. The design is a reversal of the title-page design (see Fig. 13-4), for the stylized plant forms, undulating rhythms, animation of the space, and visual tension between positive and negative spaces are created by white forms on a black field instead of black forms on a white field.

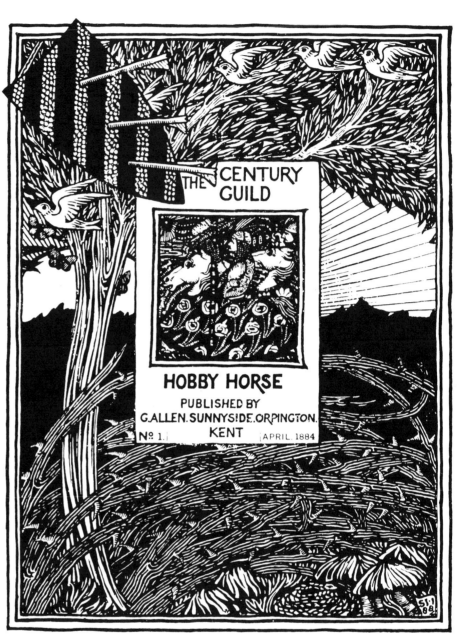

13-8. Selwyn Image, title page to *The Century Guild Hobby Horse,* 1884. Packing it with detail, Image designed a "page within a page" that reflects the medieval preoccupation of the Arts and Crafts Movement.

13-9. Selwyn Image, woodcut from the *Hobby Horse,* 1886. The potential of shape and pattern as visual means to express thought and feeling is realized in this graphic elegy for illustrator/engraver Arthur Burgess. A black bird flies toward the sun over mournful downturned tulips that hover above flamelike leaves.

ing more preoccupied with their individual work. Selwyn Image designed typefaces, innumerable illustrations, mosaics, stained glass, and embroidery. Mackmurdo focused on social politics and the development of theories to reform the monetary system. Almost in defiance of the mainstream concern for ornament, Herbert Horne designed books with classic simplicity and restraint (Fig. 13-10). His educational background had included typesetting, and his layouts have a concise sense of alignment, proportion, and balance.

The Kelmscott Press

A number of groups and individuals concerned with the craft revival combined to form the Art Worker's Guild in 1884. The guild's activities were expanded in 1888, when a splinter group formed the Combined Arts Society, elected Walter Crane as its first president, and planned to sponsor exhibitions. By the October, 1888, open-

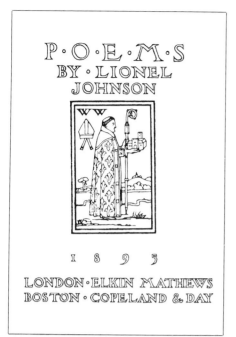

P·O·E·M·S
BY · LIONEL
JOHNSON

1 8 9 5

LONDON · ELKIN MATHEWS
BOSTON · COPELAND & DAY

13-10. Herbert Horne, title page for *Poems by Lionel Johnson,* 1895. Symmetry, outline type, letterspacing, and alignment are the design qualities of Horne's work. The outline quality of the letterforms is a perfect companion for the illustration.

ing of the first exhibition, the name had been changed to the Arts and Crafts Exhibition Society.

Early exhibitions featured demonstrations and lectures. In 1888, these included William Morris on tapestry weaving, Walter Crane on design, and Emery Walker on book design and printing. In his November 15th lecture, Walker showed lantern slides of medieval manuscripts and Incunabula type design. Advocating a unity of design, Walker told his audience that "the ornament, whatever it is, picture or pattern-work, should form part of the page, should be part of the whole scheme of the book." Walker considered book design similar to architecture, for only careful planning of every aspect—paper, ink, type, spacing, margins, illustration, and ornament—could result in a design unity. As Morris and Walker, who were friends and neighbors, walked home together after the lecture that autumn evening, Morris resolved to plunge into typeface design and printing. This was a possibility he had considered for some time, and he began work on his first typeface design that December. Morris had incunabula typefaces photographically enlarged to five times their original size so that he could study their forms and counterforms.

It is not surprising that Morris decided to tackle graphic design and printing, for he had long been interested in books. His library included some magnificent medieval manuscripts and Incunabula volumes. Earlier, Morris had made a number of manuscript books, writing the text in beautifully controlled scripts and embellishing them with delicate borders and initials with flowing forms and soft, clear colors. An 1866 attempt to publish a folio edition of *The Earthly Paradise* failed. Morris had hand-cut woodblocks for thirty-five of Burne-Jones's one hundred illustrations, with the rest cut by other engravers, and the Chiswick Press had proofed specimen pages in Caslon type. But when both the woodblocks and typography evidenced technical defects as press trials began, the project was dropped.

Morris named his first typeface Golden (Fig. 13-13), because his original plan was to print *The Golden Legend* by Voragine as his first book, working from William Caxton's translation. Golden was based on the Venetian roman faces designed by Nicolas Jenson between 1470 and 1476 (see Fig. 8-2). Morris studied large photographic prints of Jenson's letterforms, then drew them over and over. Punches were made and revised for the final designs, which captured the essence of Jenson's work but did not slavishly copy it. Typefounding of Golden began in December of 1890. Workmen were hired, and an old handpress rescued from a printer's storeroom was set up in a rented cottage near Kelmscott manor in Hammersmith, which Morris had purchased as a country home. Morris named his new enterprise Kelmscott Press (Fig. 13-14), and its first production was *The Story of the Glittering Plain* by William Morris with illustrations by Walter Crane (Figs. 13-15 and 13-16). Initially, twenty copies were planned, but as word of the enterprise spread, Morris

13-11. Herbert Horne, trademark for the Chiswick Press, c. 1895. Whether the Chiswick Lion is paying homage to the Aldine dolphin or moving it out of the way is an amusing ambiguity.

13-12. Walter Crane, trademark for the Chiswick Press, c. 1898. The literal and medieval overtones of Crane's version of the Chiswick mark, in contrast to the simplified version by Horne, demonstrate the divergent viewpoints of the period.

13-11

13-12

13-14

THE ARTS AND CRAFTS OF TODAY.
BEING AN ADDRESS DELIVERED IN
EDINBURGH IN OCTOBER, 1889. BY
WILLIAM MORRIS.
'Applied Art' is the title which the Society has
chosen for that portion of the arts which I have to
speak to you about. What are we to understand by
that title? I should answer that what the Society

13-13

13-13. William Morris, Golden typeface, 1888–1890. This alphabet design was the inspiration for a renewed interest in Venetian and Old Style typography. Designers, type founders, and printers began to study and use these forms.

13-14. William Morris, trademark for the Kelmscott Press, 1892.

was persuaded to increase the press run to two hundred paper copies and six on vellum. From 1891 until the Kelmscott Press disbanded in 1898, two years after Morris's death, over eighteen thousand volumes of fifty-three different titles were produced.

Careful study of the Incunabula gothic types of Peter Schoeffer (see Pl. 10), Anton Koberger (see Figs. 7-8 through 7-10), and Günther Zainer informed Morris's design of Troy, the remarkably legible blackletter typeface designed for *The Story of the Glittering Plain*. Morris made the characters wider than most gothic types, increased the differences between similar characters, and made the curved characters rounder. A smaller version of Troy, called Chaucer, was the last of Morris's three typeface designs. These stirred a renewed interest in Jenson and gothic styles and inspired a number of other versions in Europe and America.

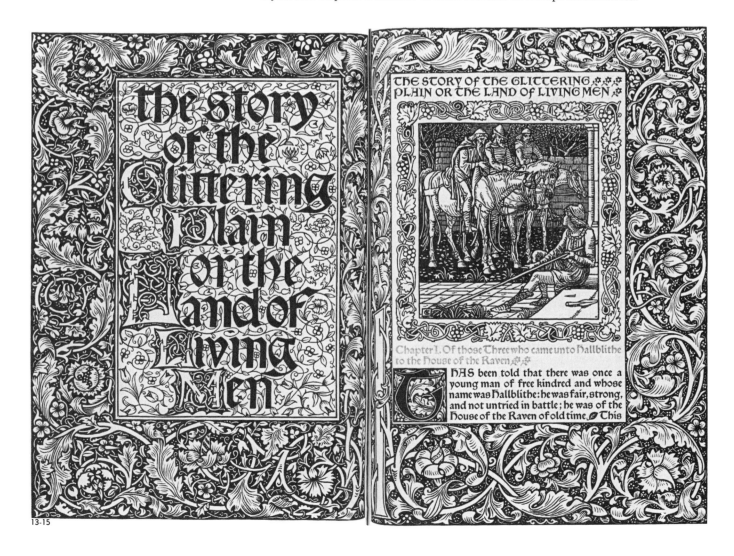

13-15

Sea-eagle said to him: "Here am I well honoured and measurelessly happy; and I have a message for thee from the King". ✪ "What is it?" said Hallblithe; but he deemed that he knew what it would be, and he reddened for the joy of his assured hope.✪Said the Sea-eagle: "Joy to thee, O shipmate! I am to take thee to the place where thy beloved abideth, & there shalt thou see her, but not so as she can see thee; & thereafter shalt thou go to the King, that thou mayst tell him if she shall accomplish thy desire".✪Then was Hallblithe glad beyond measure, & his heart danced within him, & he deemed it but meet that the others should be so joyous and blithe with him, for they led him along without any delay, and were glad at his rejoicing; and words failed him to tell of his gladness.

BUT as he went, the thoughts of his coming converse with his beloved curled sweetly round his heart, so that scarce anything had seemed so sweet to him before; & he fell a-pondering what they twain, he and the Hostage, should do when they came together again; whether they should abide on the Glittering Plain, or go back again to Cleveland by the Sea and dwell in the House of the Kindred; and for his part he yearned to behold the roof of his fathers and to tread the meadow which his scythe had swept, and the acres where his hook had smitten the wheat. But he said to himself: "I will wait till I hear her desire hereon".✪Now they went into the wood at the back of the King's pavilion and through it, and so over the hill, and beyond it came into a land of hills and dales exceeding fair and lovely; and a river wound about the dales, lap-

g 3   85

13-16

13-15. William Morris (designer) and Walter Crane (illustrator), title-page spread for *The Story of the Glittering Plain,* 1894. Operating on his compulsion to ornament the total space, Morris created a luminous range of contrasting values.

13-16. William Morris (designer) and Walter Crane (illustrator), pages from *The Story of the Glittering Plain,* 1894. Legibility was as important to Morris as decoration. The border around Crane's illustration was carefully selected to frame the darker illustration in a lighter tone, and generous margins set off the Troy type.

The Kelmscott Press was committed to recapturing the beauty of Incunabula books. Meticulous hand-printing, handmade paper, handcut woodblocks, and initials and borders similar to those used by Ratdolt turned the picturesque cottage into a time machine swinging back four centuries into the past. The book became an art form.

The design style of the Kelmscott Press was established in its early books. Decorative borders and initials designed by Morris were engraved on wood by William H. Hooper (1834–1912), a master craftsman lured from his retirement to work at the press. These have a wonderful visual compatibility with Morris's types and woodblock illustrations cut from drawings by Burne-Jones, Crane, and C. M. Gere. Morris designed 644 blocks for the press, including initials, borders, frames, and title pages. First, he lightly sketched the main lines in pencil; then, armed with white paint and black ink, he worked back and forth, painting the background in black and, over it, the pattern in white. The entire final design would be developed through this fluid process, for Morris believed that meticulous copying of a preliminary drawing squeezed the life from a work.

The outstanding volume from the Kelmscott Press is the ambitious 556-page *The Works of Geoffrey Chaucer* (Figs. 13-17 and 13-18). Four years in the making, the Kelmscott *Chaucer* has eighty-seven woodcut illustrations from drawings by Burne-Jones and fourteen large borders and eighteen smaller frames around the illustrations cut from designs by Morris. In addition, Morris designed over two hundred initial letters and words for use in the Kelmscott *Chaucer,* which was printed in black and red in large folio size. An exhaustive effort was required by everyone involved in the project. This edition, 425 copies on paper and thirteen on

13-18

13-17. William Morris, illustrated page from *The Works of Geoffrey Chaucer,* 1896. A system of types, initials, borders, and illustrations were combined to create the dazzling Kelmscott style.

13-18. William Morris, text page from *The Works of Geoffrey Chaucer,* 1896. Beautiful pages of texture and tone contain an order and clarity that make the author's words legible and accessible.

vellum, was the final achievement of Morris's career. On 2 June 1896, the bindery delivered the first two copies to the ailing designer. One was for Burne-Jones, the other for Morris. Four months later, on 3 October, William Morris died at age sixty-two.

The paradox of William Morris is that as he sought refuge in the handicraft of the past, he developed design attitudes that charted the future. His call for workmanship, truth to materials, making the utilitarian beautiful, and fitness of design to function are attitudes adopted by succeeding generations who sought to unify not art and craft but art and industry. Morris taught that design could bring art to the working class, but the exquisite furnishings of Morris and Company and the magnificent Kelmscott books were available only to the wealthy.

The extraordinary influence of William Morris and the Kelmscott Press upon graphic design, particularly book design, was evidenced not just in the direct stylistic imitation of the Kelmscott borders, initials, and typestyles; Morris's concept of the well-made book, his beautiful typeface designs based on earlier models, and his sense of design unity with the smallest detail relating to the total concept inspired a whole new generation of book designers (Fig. 13-19). Ironically, this crusader for handicraft became the inspiration for a revival of fine book design that lasted well into the twentieth century and filtered into commercial printing.

The incredible complexity of Morris's decorations tends to draw attention away from other accomplishments. His books achieved a harmonious whole, and his typographic pages—which formed the overwhelming majority of the pages in his books—were conceived and executed with readability in mind. Morris's searching

13-19. Walter Crane, layout sketches from *The Bases of Design*, 1898. Crane used these sketches to demonstrate the relationship of two pages that form a double-page unit, and how the margins can be used for decorative effect.

13-20. Charles R. Ashbee, emblem for the Essex House Press, c. 1902. This full-page woodcut, which seems to compare the quality work of the Guild of Handicrafts with the bee seeking a flower, sometimes appeared on the colophon page of Ashbee's books.

reexamination of earlier typestyles and graphic design history touched off an energetic redesign process that resulted in a major improvement in the quality and variety of fonts available for design and printing.

One final irony is that while Morris was returning to printing methods of the Incunabula, he used initials, borders, and ornaments that were modular, interchangeable, and repeatable. A basic aspect of industrial production was applied to the printed page.

The private press movement

Architect, graphic designer, silversmith, and jeweler, the indefatigable Charles R. Ashbee (1863–1942) founded the Guild of Handicraft on 23 June 1888, with three members and only fifty pounds, British sterling, as working capital. Although William Morris was dubious and threw "a great deal of cold water" upon Ashbee's plan, the guild met with unexpected success in its endeavors. Ashbee also founded the School of Handicraft, which attempted to unify the teaching of design and theory with workshop experience. Ashbee sought to restore the holistic experience of apprenticeship, which had been destroyed by the subdivision of labor and machine production. During a decade, about seven hundred students received a dualistic education with practical skill development, supplemented by readings from Ruskin and study of the application of art principles to materials. Able neither to secure state support nor to compete with the state-aided technical schools, the School of Handicraft finally closed. The Guild of Handicraft, on the other hand, flourished as a cooperative where workers shared in governance and profits. It was inspired by both socialism and the Arts and Crafts Movement. In 1890, the guild leased Essex House, an old Georgian mansion in what had declined into a grimy and desolate section of industrial London.

After the death of William Morris, Ashbee opened negotiations with the executors of the estate to transfer the Kelmscott Press to Essex House. When it became known that the Kelmscott woodblocks and types were to be deposited in the British Museum with the stipulation that they not be used for printing for a hundred years, Ashbee resolved to hire key personnel from the Kelmscott Press, to purchase the equipment that was available for sale, and to form the Essex House Press (Fig. 13-20). The *Psalter* of 1902 was the design masterpiece of the Essex House Press (Fig. 13-21). The text is in vernacular sixteenth-century English from the c. 1540 translation of Archbishop Thomas Cranmer of Canterbury. Ashbee developed a graphic program for each psalm, consisting of a roman numeral, the Latin title in red capitals, an English descriptive title printed in black capitals, an illustrated woodcut initial, and the body of the psalm. Verses are separated by woodcut leaf ornaments printed in red. Ashbee's design for the Essex House type was a curious cross between an Egyptian and a roman type imbued with a medieval feeling. Calligraphic touches, such as the swash on the lowercase *h, n,* and *m,* gave it a curious but engaging quality. Its even stroke weight and unusually large x-height provided an interesting texture, handsome in the mass of text and contrasting effectively with the tone of Ashbee's ever-present woodcut initials.

In 1902, the guild moved to the rural village of Chipping Campden and began the ambitious task of turning the village into a communal society for guild workers and their families. The large costs involved, combined with the expenses of maintaining the guild's retail store on Brook Street in London, forced the guild into deficit finances, which led to voluntary bankruptcy in 1907. Many of the craftsmen continued to work independently, and the undaunted Ashbee returned to his architectural practice, which had lain fallow during his noble experiments over two decades. Although he was a leading design theorist and follower of the ideals of Ruskin and Morris at the turn of the century, after World War I, Ashbee began to question the belief that industrial manufacturing was inherently evil, and he began to formulate a design policy relevant to the industrial age. Thus, Ruskin's follower who went farthest in establishing an idyllic workshop paradise became a major English voice calling for integration of art and industry in a later era.

13-21. Charles R. Ashbee, page from the Essex House *Psalter,* 1902. Hand-cut woodblock initials, calligraphic type, handmade paper, and hand-press printing combine to re-create the quality of the Incunabula.

13-22. T. J. Cobden-Sanderson and Emery Walker, page from the Doves Press *Bible,* 1903. This book's purity of design and flawless perfection of craft have seldom been equaled.

In 1900, the bookbinder T. J. Cobden-Sanderson (1840–1922) joined Emery Walker in establishing the Doves Press at Hammersmith. They set out to "attack the problem of pure Typography" with the view that "the whole duty of Typography is to communicate to the imagination, without loss by the way, the thought or image intended to be conveyed by the Author." Books from the Doves Press, including their monumental masterpiece, the 1903 Doves Press *Bible* (Fig. 13-22), are remarkably beautiful typographic books. Illustration and ornaments were rejected in the approximately fifty volumes produced there. Fine paper, perfect presswork, and exquisite type and spacing were relied upon to produce inspired graphic design. Their five-volume Bible used a few stunning initials designed by Edward Johnston (1872–1944). This master calligrapher of the Arts and Crafts Movement had been inspired by William Morris and abandoned his medical studies for the life of a scribe. Johnston's study of pen techniques and early manuscripts, as well as his teaching activities, made him a major influence upon the art of letters.

Established in 1895, the Ashendene Press, directed by C. H. St. John Hornby of London, proved to be an exceptional private press (Fig. 13-23). The type designed for Ashendene was inspired by the semi-Gothic types used by Sweynheym and Pannartz in Subiaco. It possessed a ringing elegance and straightforward legibility with modest weight differences between the thick and thin strokes and a slightly compressed letter.

A curious twist in the unfolding of the Arts and Crafts Movement is the case of the American Elbert Hubbard (1856–1915), who met William Morris in 1894. Hubbard established an arts-and-crafts center called the Roycrofters in East Aurora, New York. Books, inspirational booklets, and his two magazines were wrapped in the look of Kelmscott volumes, and the Roycrofters became a tourist mecca where four hundred employees produced artistic home furnishings, copperware, leather

13-23. C. H. St. John Hornby, pages from St. Francis of Assisi's *Legend,* 1922. A liberal use of all-capital type and initial words printed in color brought distinction to Ashendene Press page layout.

13-24. Lucien Pissarro, excerpt from *Of Typography and the Harmony of the Printed Page,* c. 1900. Using his legible Brook type, which combined roman structure with slab serifs and a few decorative Art Nouveau details, Pissarro's page design typifies the structural unity and workmanship of the private press movement.

goods, and printing. When May Morris visited America, she declined an invitation to visit "that obnoxious imitator of my dear father."

Even after Hubbard's death in 1915 aboard the ill-fated *Lusitania,* the Roycrofters continued until 1938. Hubbard's detractors claim that he tarnished the whole movement, while his defenders counter that the Roycrofters brought beauty into the lives of ordinary people who otherwise would not have had an opportunity to enjoy the fruits of the reaction against industrialism's mediocre products.

Lucien Pissarro (1863–1944) learned drawing from his father, the impressionist painter Camille Pissarro, then apprenticed as a wood engraver and illustrator under the renowned book illustrator Auguste Lepère. Disillusioned with the response to his work in France, and learning of a revival of interest in wood-engraved illustrations in England, Pissarro crossed the English Channel to join the movement. Captivated by the Kelmscott books, Pissarro established the Eragny Press (named after the Normandy village where he was born and studied with his father). The design of three- and four-color woodblock illustrations at Hammersmith in 1894 is a unique design feature of Eragny Press books. Pages from the 1903 *Ishtar's Descent to the Nether World* (Pl. 19) show the influence of expressionism and Art Nouveau upon Pissarro's volumes.

Pissarro and his wife collaborated on designing, wood engraving, and printing the books produced at the Eragny Press. His Brook type (Fig. 13-24) was also a Jenson-inspired design. Younger than most members of the Arts and Crafts Movement, Pissarro combined the traditional medieval sensibilities of the private press movement with an interest in the blossoming Art Nouveau movement. This proved to be even more true of Charles Ricketts (1866–1931), who founded the Vale Press in 1896 and spent more time as a consulting graphic designer working in the Art Nouveau style than as a private press operator.

A book-design renaissance

The long-range effect of William Morris was a significant upgrading of book design and typography throughout the world. In Germany, this influence inspired a renaissance of arts-and-crafts activities, wonderful new typefaces, and a significant improvement in book design.

The most important of the German men of letters was Rudolf Koch (1876–1934), a powerful figure who was deeply mystical and medieval in his viewpoints. A de-

13-25. Rudolf Koch, title page demonstrating *Eine deutsche Schrift,* 1910. Koch's gothic revivals achieved unusual legibility, striking typographic color and spatial intervals, and many original forms and ligatures.

13-26. Rudolf Koch, specimen of *Neuland,* 1922–1923. A dense texture is achieved in this intuitively designed typeface with unprecedented capital *C* and *S* forms. The woodcut-inspired ornaments are used to justify this setting into a crisp rectangle.

vout Christian, Koch taught at the Arts and Crafts School in Offenbach am Main, where he led a community of writers, printers, stonemasons, and metal and tapestry workers in a creative community. He regarded the alphabet as a supreme spiritual achievement of humanity. Basing his pre–World War I work on pen-drawn calligraphy, Koch sought the medieval experience through the design and lettering of handmade manuscript books. But he did not merely seek to imitate the medieval scribe; he tried to build upon the calligraphic tradition by creating an original, simple expression from his gestures and materials. After the war, Koch turned to hand-lettered broadsides and handicrafts, then became closely associated with the Klingspor Type Foundry. His type designs ranged from original interpretations of medieval letterforms (13-25) to unexpected new designs, such as the rough-hewn chunky letterforms of his Neuland face (13-26).

In America, the influence of the Arts and Crafts Movement upon the revitalization of typography and book design moved forward in the hands of two young men from the Midwest who fell under the spell of the Kelmscott Press during the 1890s. Book designer Bruce Rogers (1870–1956) and typeface designer Frederic W. Goudy (1865–1947) each inspired for a lifetime of creative work, had long careers filled with a love of books and diligent work that enabled them to carry their exceptional sense of book design and production well into the twentieth century.

Even as a boy in Bloomington, Illinois, Frederic Goudy had a passionate love of letterforms. He later related that he cut over three thousand letters from colored paper and turned the church he attended into a multicolored environment of Biblical passages on the walls. Goudy was working in Chicago as a bookkeeper in the early 1890s when he became involved in printing and publicity. Books from the Kelmscott Press, including their *Chaucer,* and from other private presses at the rare book department of the A. C. McClurg Bookstore, fired Goudy's imagination. He became interested in art, literature, and typography on "a higher plane than mere commercialism."

In 1894, Goudy started the Camelot Press with a friend, then left it and returned to bookkeeping the following year when disagreements developed. In 1895, he set up the short-lived Booklet Press, then designed his first typeface during the period of unemployment that followed. Named Camelot, his pencil drawing of capitals was mailed to the Dickinson Type Foundry of Boston with an offer to sell the design for five dollars. After a week or two, a check for ten dollars in payment for the design arrived. In 1899, Goudy became a freelance designer in Chicago specializing in lettering and typographic design. Another venture in printing, the Village Press, was modeled on the private press ideal of handicraft.

The Village Press was moved first to Boston, then to New York, where a terrible fire completely destroyed it in 1908. That same year marked the end of Goudy's efforts as a printer; he turned his energy to the design, cutting, and casting of typefaces. It was also the year when Goudy began a long association with the Lanston Monotype Company, which commissioned some of his finest fonts. Goudy designed a total of 122 typefaces by his own count, including a few faces that were never produced and counting roman and italic variations as two faces. A staunch traditionalist, Goudy based many of his designs, including variations developed by other designers, upon Renaissance and Medieval models (Fig. 13-27).

With an amiable and witty personality and wonderful writing ability, Goudy became a link between William Morris and his ideals and the everyday printers. His readable books include *The Alphabet* (1908), *Elements of Lettering* (1921), and *Typologia* (1940). The two journals he edited, *Ars Typographica* and *Typographica,* impacted the course of book design. In 1923 Goudy established the Village Letter Foundry in an old mill on the Hudson River. There he designed types, cut matrices, and cast and sold type. In 1939 a second disastrous fire burned the mill to the ground, destroying about seventy-five of the seventy-four-year-old designer's original type designs and thousands of matrices. Undaunted, Goudy continued to work until his death at age eighty-two.

A student of Goudy's at the turn of the century named William Addison Dwig-

Goudy Old Style
Goudy Old Style Italic
Goudy Catalogue
Goudy Bold
Goudy Extra Bold
Goudy Heavyface
Goudy Handtooled
Goudy Mediaeval

13-27. Frederic Goudy and others. The Goudy series of Old Style fonts captures the feeling of Venetian and French Renaissance typography.

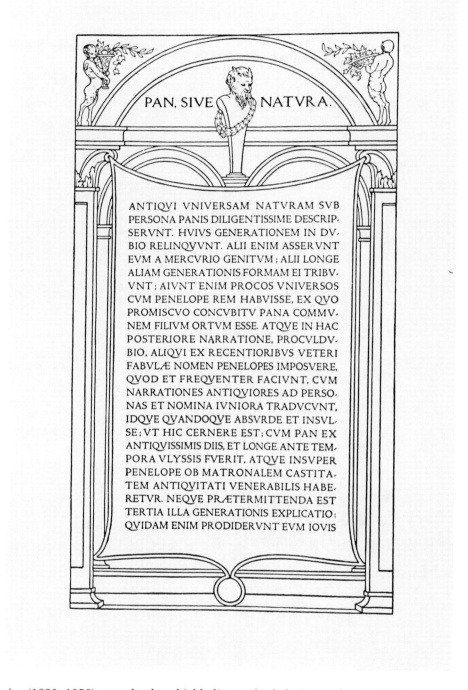

13-28. Bruce Rogers, typographic page of classical typography. Venetian in concept, this design uses a similar weight in the type strokes and frame lines. The light coming through the all-capitals type makes a value close to the tone of the architectural motif, which further unifies the two elements.

gins (1880–1956) proved to be a highly literate book designer who established a house style for the Alfred A. Knopf publishing company and designed hundreds of volumes for this firm. During the early 1920s, Dwiggins first coined the term *graphic designer* to describe his professional activities. In 1938, he designed one of the most widely used book faces in America, Caledonia.

Albert Bruce Rogers of Lafayette, Indiana, evolved from his Kelmscott roots in the 1890s and became the most important American book designer of the early twentieth century. After graduating from college, where he was active as a campus artist, Rogers became a newspaper illustrator in Indianapolis. Dismayed by the ambulance-chasing school of pictorial reportage that included frequent trips to the local morgue, Rogers tried landscape painting, worked for a Kansas railroad, and did book illustrations for an Indianapolis studio in the typical saga of the young man in search of himself. When he was shown Kelmscott books by a close friend,

13-29. Bruce Rogers, page from *The Centaur* by Maurice de Guerin, 1915. The headpiece, initial, and page layout echo the wonderful graphic designs of the French Renaissance.

THE CENTAUR. WRITTEN BY MAURICE DE GUÉRIN AND NOW TRANSLATED FROM THE FRENCH BY GEORGE B. IVES.

Was born in a cavern of these mountains. Like the river in yonder valley, whose first drops flow from some cliff that weeps in a deep grotto, the first moments of my life sped amidst the shadows of a secluded retreat, nor vexed its silence. As our mothers draw near their term, they retire to the caverns, and in the innermost recesses of the wildest of them all, where the darkness is most dense, they bring forth, uncomplaining, offspring as silent as themselves. Their strength giving milk enables us to endure without weakness or dubious struggles the first difficulties of life; yet we leave our caverns later than you your cradles. The reason is that there is a tradition amongst us that the early days of life must be secluded and guarded, as days engrossed by the gods.

My growth ran almost its entire course in the darkness where I was born. The innermost depths of my home were so far within the bowels of the mountain, that I should not have known in which direction the opening lay, had it not been that the winds at times blew in and caused a sudden coolness and confusion. Sometimes, too, my mother returned, bringing with her the perfume of the valleys, or dripping wet from the streams to which she resorted. Now, these her homecomings, although they told me naught of the valleys or the streams, yet, being attended by emanations therefrom, disturbed my thoughts, and I wandered about, all agitated, amidst my darkness. 'What,' I would say to myself, 'are these places to which my mother goes and what power reigns there which summons her so frequently? To what influences is one there exposed,

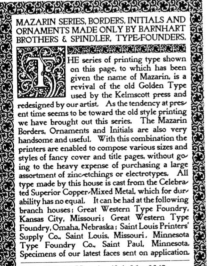

13-30. Mazarin typeface, Barnhart Brothers & Spindler, 1895. This face is but one of numerous imitations of Morris typefaces offered with Kelmscott-inspired borders and initials.

J. M. Bowles, his interest immediately shifted toward the total design of books. Bowles was running an art supply store and editing a small magazine called *Modern Art*. Louis Prang became interested in this periodical and invited Bowles to move to Boston and edit what then became an L. Prang and Company periodical. A typographic designer was needed, so Rogers was hired at fifty cents an hour with a twenty-hour-per-week guarantee.

Rogers joined the Riverside Press of the Houghton Mifflin Company in 1896, and designed a number of books with a strong Arts and Crafts influence. In 1900, the Riverside Press established a special department for producing quality limited editions, and Rogers became the designer for the series. Sixty limited editions produced at Riverside over the next twelve years enabled Rogers to emerge as an

Alternate Gothic

Century Schoolbook

Clearface

Cloister Bold

Franklin Gothic

News Gothic

Souvenir

Stymie Medium

13-31. Morris F. Benton, typeface designs: Alternate Gothic, 1906; Century Schoolbook, 1920; Clearface, 1907; Cloister Bold, 1913; Franklin Gothic, 1905; News Gothic, 1908; Souvenir, 1914; Stymie Medium, 1931.

influential book designer, and his work set the standard for the well-designed twentieth-century book. Beatrice Warde wrote that Rogers "managed to steal the Divine Fire which glowed in the Kelmscott Press books, and somehow be the first to bring it down to earth." Rogers applied the ideal of the beautifully designed book to commercial production. He has been called an allusive designer, for his work recalls earlier years and styles. For inspiration, he shifted from Incunabula volumes of Jenson and Ratdolt, with their sturdy types and strong woodblock ornaments, to the lighter, graceful books of the French Renaissance (Fig. 13-28).

In 1912, Rogers left the Riverside Press to become a freelance book designer. In spite of some difficult years, Rogers needed freedom to be able to realize his full potential as a graphic artist. His 1915 typeface design, Centaur, is one of the finest of the numerous styles based on the 1470 style by Jenson. It was first used in Rogers's design for *The Centaur* by Maurice de Guerin, one of Rogers's most elegant book designs (Fig. 13-29). In 1916, he journeyed to England for an unsuccessful effort to collaborate with Emery Walker and stayed on as a consultant to the Cambridge University Press until 1919. Again from 1928 through 1932, when his commissions included the design of the monumental Oxford Lectern Bible, Rogers worked in England.

Very much an intuitive designer, Rogers possessed an outstanding sense of visual proportion and of "rightness." Design is a decision-making process; the culmination of subtle choices about paper, type, margins, leading between lines, and so on can combine to create either a unity or a disaster. Rogers wrote that "the ultimate test, in considering the employment or the rejection of an element of design or decoration, would seem to be: does it look as if it were *inevitable,* or would the page look as well or better for its omission?" So rigorous were Rogers's design standards that when he compiled a list of successful books from among the seven hundred he designed, he only selected thirty! The first book on his list was predated by over a hundred earlier ones. While Rogers was a classicist who revived the forms of the past, he did so with a sense of appropriate form for outstanding book design. Rogers, like Frederic Goudy, lived a long life and was honored for his accomplishments as a graphic designer during his twilight years.

William Morris, the Arts and Crafts Movement, and the private presses inspired a vigorous revitalization of typography. The passion for Victorian typefaces started to decline in the 1890s, as imitations of Kelmscott typefaces (Fig. 13-30; see also Fig. 12-32) were followed by revivals of other classical typeface designs. Garamond, Plantin, Caslon, Baskerville, and Bodoni—these typeface designs of past masters were studied, recut, and offered for hand and keyboard composition during the first three decades of the twentieth century. In the United States, the prolific designer Morris F. Benton (1872–1948), head of typeface development for the American Type Founders Company, designed important revivals of Bodoni and Garamond. His revival of Nicolas Jenson's type was issued as the Cloister family. From 1901 to 1935, Benton designed approximately 225 typefaces, including nine additional members of the Goudy family and over two dozen members of the Cheltenham family, which began as one typeface by architect Bertram Goodhue. Benton carefully studied human perception and reading comprehension to develop Century Schoolbook, designed for and widely used in textbooks. Figure 13-31 shows examples from seven of Benton's type families.

The legacy of the Arts and Crafts Movement extends beyond style. Its attitudes about materials, function, and social value became an important inspiration for twentieth-century designers. Its positive impact upon graphic design continues a century after William Morris's death, through the revivals of earlier typeface designs, the continued efforts toward excellence in book design and typography, and the private press movement that continues to this day.

Art Nouveau

14

Art Nouveau is an international decorative style that thrived during the two decades (c. 1890–1910) that girded the turn of the century. It encompassed all the design arts—architecture, furniture and product design, fashion, and graphics— and consequently touched all aspects of the man-made environment: posters, packages, and advertisements; teapots, dishes, and spoons; chairs, door frames, and staircases; factories, subway entrances, and houses. Art Nouveau's identifying visual quality is an organic, plantlike line. Freed from roots or gravity, it can either undulate with whiplash energy or flow with elegant grace as it defines, modulates, and decorates a given space. Vine tendrils, flowers (such as the rose and lily), birds (particularly peacocks), and the human female form were frequent motifs from which this fluid line was adapted.

To dismiss Art Nouveau as surface decoration is to ignore its pivotal role in the evolution of all aspects of design. Art Nouveau is the transitional style that evolved from the *historicism* that dominated design for most of the nineteenth century. By replacing historicism—the almost servile use of past forms and styles instead of the invention of new forms to express the present—with innovation, Art Nouveau became the initial phase of the modern movement, preparing the way for the twentieth century by sweeping this historicizing spirit from design.

Ideas, processes, and forms in twentieth-century art bear witness to this catalytic importance. Modern architecture, graphic and industrial design, surrealism, and abstract art have roots in Art Nouveau's underlying theory and concepts. In Art Nouveau graphics, the organic linear movements frequently dominate the spatial area and other visual properties, such as color and texture. In earlier three-dimensional design, ornaments often were mere decorative elements applied to the surface of a building or object; but in Art Nouveau objects, the basic forms and shapes were formed by, and evolved with, the design of the ornament. This was a new design principle, unifying decoration, structure, and intended function. Because Art Nouveau forms and lines were often invented rather than copied from nature or the past, there was a revitalization of the design process that pointed toward abstract art. Perhaps the seminal genius of the movement was Belgian architect Baron Victor Horta (1861–1947). His 1892 townhouse for Emile Tassel was unified by tendrilous curvilinear networks unlike anything yet seen in England or on the continent at that time.

During this period, there was a close collaboration between visual artists and writers. The French Symbolist movement in literature of the 1880s and 1890s, with its rejection of realism in favor of the metaphysical and sensuous, was an important influence, and led artists to symbolic and philosophic attitudes. In a skeptical era with scientific rationalism on the rise and traditional religious beliefs and social norms under assault, art was seen as a potential vehicle to a much-needed spiritual rejuvenation. Birth, life, and death; growth and decay—these became symbolic subject matter. The complexity of this era and movement has allowed contradictory interpretations: Because of its decorativeness, some observers see Art Nouveau as an expression of late-nineteenth-century decadence; others, however, noting Art Nouveau's quest for spiritual and aesthetic values, see it as a reaction *against* the decadence and materialism of this epoch.

14-1. Hishikawa Ryuoku, *Woman Standing before a Large Pot of Chrysanthemums*, woodblock print, nineteenth century. Characteristics that excited nineteenth-century artists and designers are flowing curved contours, flat shapes of color, and decorative patterns.

Art Nouveau graphic designers and illustrators attempted to make art a part of everyday life. Their fine-arts training had educated them about art forms and methods developed primarily for aesthetic considerations. At the same time, they enthusiastically embraced applied-art techniques that had evolved with the development of commercial printing processes. As a result, they were able to upgrade significantly the visual quality of mass communications. The international character of Art Nouveau was expedited by advances in transportation and communications technology. Contact between artists in various nations through print media and international exhibitions allowed cross-fertilization to take place. The many art periodicals of the 1890s served this purpose while simultaneously introducing the new art and design to the larger public.

The numerous sources often cited for Art Nouveau are diffuse and wide ranging. They include William Blake's book illustration, Celtic ornament, the Rococo style, the Arts and Crafts Movement, Pre-Raphaelite painting, and Japanese decorative design and woodblock prints. The treaties that resulted from American Commodore Matthew C. Perry's naval expeditions to Japan, beginning in 1853, led to the collapse of Japan's traditional isolationist policy and the opening of trade with the West. Japanese art and artifacts began to pour into Europe, and several books on Japanese art and ornament were published during the 1880s. The influence of the Japanese print included calligraphic line drawing, the simplification of natural appearances, flat silhouette shapes and color, and decorative areas of pattern (Fig. 14-1). Important inspiration also came from the painting of the late 1880s, which had fallen under the oriental spell. The swirling forms of Vincent Van Gogh (1853–1890), the flat color and stylized organic contour of Paul Gauguin (1848–1903), and the work of the Nabis group of young artists all played a role. The Nabis explored symbolic color and decorative patterns, and concluded that a painting was, first of all, an arrangement of color in two-dimensional patterns.

Chéret and Grasset

The transition from Victorian graphics to the Art Nouveau style was a gradual one. Two graphic artists working in Paris, Jules Chéret (1836–1933) and Eugène Grasset (1841–1917), played important roles in the transition.

In 1881, a new French law concerning freedom of the press lifted many censorship restrictions and allowed posters anywhere except on churches, polls, and areas designated for official notices. This new law led to a booming poster industry of designers, printers, and *afficheurs*. The streets became an art gallery for the nation, as even the poorest worker saw the environment transformed by images and color. Respected painters felt no shame at creating advertising posters. The Arts and Crafts Movement was creating a new respect for the applied arts, and Jules Chéret had shown the way. Now acclaimed as the father of the modern poster, Chéret was the son of a poor typesetter, who paid four hundred francs to secure a three-year lithographic apprenticeship for his son at age thirteen. The teenager spent his weekdays lettering backwards on lithographic stones and his Sundays absorbing art at the Louvre. After completing his apprenticeship, he worked as a lithographic craftsman and renderer for several firms and took drawing classes. At the age of eighteen, he headed for London but could only find work making catalogue drawings of furniture, so he returned to Paris after six months. He moved into the small attic room of his brother, Joseph, also a lithographer, where they took turns sleeping on the bed and the floor.

These were difficult years for Chéret. He was convinced that pictorial lithographic posters would replace the typographic letterpress posters, which filled the urban environment and only occasionally had small woodcut illustrations, but he could not convince advertisers of this. At the age of twenty-two, he produced a blue-and-brown poster for Offenbach's operetta, *Orphée aux Enfers* (*Orpheus in Hades*). When further commissions were not forthcoming, he returned to London. English color lithography was more advanced, and Chéret soon mastered it. A poster commission for a family of clowns he had befriended was the turning point, leading to

14-2

14-3

label commissions from the philanthropist and perfume manufacturer Eugene Rimmel. Several years of close association and friendship with Rimmel were marked by extensive design and production experience, culminating in Rimmel financing Chéret to establish a printing firm in Paris in 1866. The latest English technology and custom-crafted, oversized lithographic stones were purchased, and Chéret was poised to begin the process of running letterpress typography from the signboards. The first poster from his shop (Fig. 14-2) was a monochromatic design for the theatrical production *La Biche au Bois* (*The Doe in the Wood*), starring the twenty-two-year-old Sarah Bernhardt. Artist and actress took Paris by storm, as Bernhardt became the leading actress of her day and Chéret pioneered the visual poster. During the 1870s, Chéret evolved away from Victorian complexity, simplifying his designs and increasing the scale of his major figures and lettering (Fig. 14-3).

In 1881 Chéret sold his printing company to the larger printing firm Imprimerie Chaix and became its artistic director, a move that allowed more time for art and design. In the mornings he drew from the model, then spent the afternoons painting at his easel, drawing pastels, and working on his huge lithographic stones. By 1884, some Chéret posters were produced in sizes of up to two meters (seven feet) tall by printing the images in sections, which were joined on the wall by the afficheurs. The total annual press runs of his designs were almost 200,000 copies. At least eight French printers specialized in posters, and Chéret was joined by a score of other poster designers.

Chéret's artistic influences included the idealized beauty and carefree lifestyle painted by Watteau and Fragonard, the color luminosity of Turner, and the churning movement of Tiepolo, whose figures expressed energy and movement through twisting torsos and extended limbs. Chéret worked directly on the stone, in contrast to the standard practice of commissioning an artist's design for execution on the stones by craftsmen. During the 1880s, he used a black line with the primary colors (red, yellow, and blue). He achieved a graphic vitality with these bright colors, and subtle overprinting allowed an astonishing range of colors and effects: stipple and crosshatch; soft watercolor-like washes and bold calligraphic chunks of color; scratching, scraping, and splattering—all were used in his work. His typical composition is a central figure or figures in animated gesture, surrounded by swirls of color, secondary figures or props, and bold lettering that often echoes the shapes and gestures of the figure. His unending production for music halls and the the-

14-2. Jules Chéret, poster for *La Biche au Bois*, 1866. Printed in green and black, Chéret's early poster used the multiple-image format so popular in the 1860s. The lettering is a harbinger of the swirling forms of Chéret's mature style.

14-3. Jules Chéret, poster for *Valentino's Ball*, 1872. The lively dynamic figures and efforts to unify words and images visually—hallmarks of Chéret's mature style—are developing.

14-5. Eugène Grasset, title page for *Histoire des Quatre Fils Aymon*, 1883. Dividing the space into zones, Grasset unified lettering, illustration, and decorative patterns into a total page design.

14-6. Eugène Grasset, pages from *Histoire des Quatre Fils Aymon*, 1883. Typography is set in shapes designed to fit around illustrations that fade out behind the type.

14-4. Jules Chéret, *Palais de Glace* ("Ice Palace") poster, 1896. Parisian elegance, a carefree grace, and astounding technical mastery are present. The figures create a lively play of angles, linking the lettering at bottom left and top right.

ater, beverages and medicines, entertainers, and publications transformed the walls of Paris (Pl. 21 and Fig. 14-4).

The beautiful young women he created, dubbed "the Chérette" by an admiring public, were archetypes—not only for the idealized presentation of women in mass media, but for a generation of French women who used their dress and apparent life-style as inspiration. One pundit has dubbed Chéret "the father of women's liberation," because his women introduced a new role model as the Victorian Era gave way to the Gay Nineties. Options for women had been limited, and the proper lady in the drawing room and the tramp in the bordello were stereotyped roles, when into this dichotomy swept the Chérette. Neither prudes nor prostitutes, these self-assured, happy women enjoyed life to the fullest, wearing low-cut dresses, dancing, drinking wine, and even smoking in public. While Chéret preferred the large format, saying that since "a well-made woman is about 150 centimeters [five feet], a poster 240 centimeters [7½ feet] in length affords ample space for drawing a figure full length," his output ranged from life-size images to the diminutive.

Chéret's contribution was recognized in 1889, when he received a gold medal at the International Exhibition and enjoyed the acclaim of leading critics reporting on his major one-man show. A petition was circulated, which led in 1890 to Chéret being named to the Legion of Honor by the French government. He was cited for creating a new branch of art that advanced printing and served the needs of commerce and industry. By the turn of the century, when Chéret's poster production nearly ceased as he spent more time on pastels and paintings, he had produced over a thousand posters. He retired to Nice, where the Jules Chéret Museum opened, preserving his work, shortly before his death at the age of ninety-seven.

Swiss-born Eugène Grasset was the first illustrator/designer to rival Chéret in public popularity. Grasset had studied medieval art intensely, and this influence, mingled with a love of exotic oriental art, was reflected strongly in his designs for furniture, stained glass, textiles, and books. A bellwether achievement, both in graphic design and printing technology, was the 1883 publication of *Histoire des Quatre Fils Aymon* (Figs. 14-5 and 14-6), which was designed and illustrated by Grasset. It was printed in an aquatint grain/color photo-relief process from plates made by Charles Gillot, who transformed Grasset's line and watercolor designs into subtle, full-color printed book illustrations. Grasset and Gillot collaborated closely on this two-year project, with Grasset working extensively on the plates. The design is important for its total integration of illustrations, format, and typography. Some of Grasset's design ideas that were rapidly assimilated after publication include the decorative borders framing the contents, the integration of

14-5

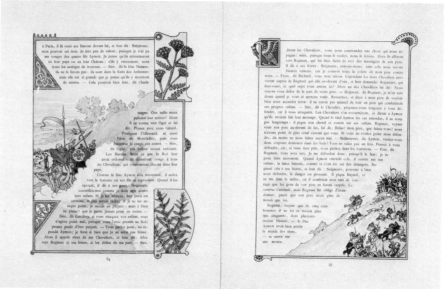

14-6

illustration and text into a unity, and the design of illustrations so that typography is printed over skies and other areas. Spatial segmentation is used as an expressive component in the page layouts.

In 1886, Grasset received his first poster commission. His willowy maidens—who wore long, flowing robes and static poses to advertise inks, chocolates, and beer—soon began to grace French streets. Quietly demure instead of exuberant, Grasset's figures project a resonance very different from that of the Chérette. The c. 1894 exhibition poster (Pl. 22) illustrates what has been called his "coloring-book style" of thick black contour drawing that locks forms into flat areas of color in a manner similar to medieval stained glass windows. His figures echo Botticelli and medieval clothing; his stylized, flat cloud patterns reflect his study of Japanese woodblocks. Grasset's formal composition and muted color contrasted strongly to Chéret's informally composed, brightly colored work. In spite of Grasset's tradition-bound attitude, his flowing line, subjective color, and ever-present floral motifs pointed toward French Art Nouveau. His oeuvre included wallpaper and fabric design, stained-glass windows, typefaces, and printer's ornaments (Fig. 14-7).

English Art Nouveau

In England, the Art Nouveau movement was primarily concerned with graphic design and illustration rather than architectural and product design. Its sources, in addition to those listed earlier, included Gothic art and Victorian painting. A strong momentum toward an international style was created by the inaugural issue of *The Studio* in April of 1893. The first of nearly a dozen upstart European art periodicals of the 1890s, the April issue reproduced the work of Aubrey Beardsley (1872–1898) (Fig. 14-8); *The Three Brides,* by the Dutch artist Jan Toorop (1858–1928), was included in the September issue (Fig. 14-9). The collective influence of these two artists was enormous. Early issues of *The Studio* also included work by Walter Crane (an early innovator in the application of Japanese ornamental pattern and Eastern interpretations of nature to the design of surface pattern) and furniture and textiles produced for the Liberty and Company store.

Aubrey Beardsley was the *enfant terrible* of Art Nouveau with his stunning pen line, vibrant black-and-white work, and shockingly exotic imagery. A strange cult figure, he was furiously prolific for only five years and died of tuberculosis at age twenty-six. He became famous at age twenty, when his illustrations for a new edition of Malory's *Mort D'Arthur* (Figs. 14-10 and 14-11) began to appear in monthly installments, augmenting a strong Kelmscott influence with strange and imaginative distortions of the human figure and powerful black shapes. Japanese blockprints and William Morris were synthesized into a new style. Beardsley's unique line was reproduced by the photoengraving process, which, unlike the hand-cut woodblock, retained complete fidelity to the original art.

William Morris was so angry when he saw Beardsley's *Mort D'Arthur* that he considered legal action. Beardsley had, to Morris's mind, vulgarized the design ideas of the Kelmscott style by replacing the formal, naturalistic borders with more stylized, flat patterns (Fig. 14-12). Burne-Jones's classical woodcut illustrations yielded to dramatic contrasts of black-and-white shapes. Walter Crane, always ready with an unequivocal viewpoint, declared that Beardsley's *Mort D'Arthur* had mixed the medieval spirit of Morris with a weird "Japanese-like spirit of deviltry and the grotesque," which Crane thought fit only for the opium den.

In spite of Morris's anger, the enthusiastic response to Beardsley's work resulted in numerous commissions. Beardsley was named art editor for *The Yellow Book,* a magazine whose bright yellow cover on London newsstands became a symbol for the new and outrageous. In 1894, Oscar Wilde's *Salomé* received widespread notoriety for the obvious erotic sensuality of Beardsley's illustrations of women (Fig. 14-13). Late-Victorian English society was shocked by this celebration of evil, which reached its peak in Beardsley's work for an edition of Aristophanes's *Lysistrata*. Banned by English censors, it was widely circulated on the continent.

During the last two years of his life, Beardsley was an invalid. When he could

14-7. Eugène Grasset, from *Ornaments Typographiques,* c. 1894. During the 1880s, Grasset designed three dozen sets of headpieces, tailpieces, and ornamental initials, which were gathered together in this 1894 printer's specimen book.

14-8. Aubrey Beardsley, first cover for *The Studio,* 1893. Beardsley's career was launched when editor C. Lewis Hine featured him on this cover and reproduced eleven of his illustrations in the inaugural issue.

14-9. Jan Toorop, *The Three Brides,* 1893. In this pencil and colored-crayon drawing on brown paper, the undulating flow of stylized ribbons of hair symbolizes sound pouring forth from the bells. Toorop's curvilinear drawing inspired his contemporaries.

14-10. Aubrey Beardsley, *Mort D'Arthur,* full-page illustration, 1893. This image shows Beardsley's emerging ability to compose contour line, textured areas, and black-and-white shapes into powerful compositions. The contrast between geometric and organic shapes reflects the influence of the Japanese print.

14-11. Aubrey Beardsley, *Mort D'Arthur,* chapter opening, 1893. William Morris's lyrical bouquets were replaced by rollicking mythological nymphs in a briar border design.

14-9

HOW LA BEALE
ISOVD NVRSED
SIR TRISTRAM

14-10

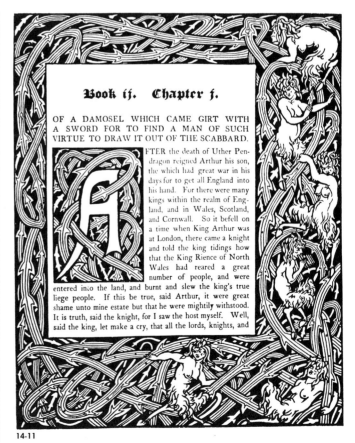

Book ij. Chapter j.

OF A DAMOSEL WHICH CAME GIRT WITH A SWORD FOR TO FIND A MAN OF SUCH VIRTUE TO DRAW IT OUT OF THE SCABBARD.

AFTER the death of Uther Pendragon reigned Arthur his son, the which had great war in his days for to get all England into his hand. For there were many kings within the realm of England, and in Wales, Scotland, and Cornwall. So it befell on a time when King Arthur was at London, there came a knight and told the king tidings how that the King Rience of North Wales had reared a great number of people, and were entered into the land, and burnt and slew the king's true liege people. If this be true, said Arthur, it were great shame unto mine estate but that he were mightily withstood. It is truth, said the knight, for I saw the host myself. Well, said the king, let make a cry, that all the lords, knights, and

14-11

14-12

14-13

14-12. William Morris, page from *The Recuyell of the Historyes of Troye,* 1892. Comparison of page designs by Morris and Beardsley reveals that the differences reflect a dichotomy of philosophy, life-style, and social values.

14-13. Aubrey Beardsley, illustration for Oscar Wilde's *Salomé,* 1894. John the Baptist and Salomé, who was given his head on a platter by Herod after her dance, are remarkable symbolic figures. The dynamic interplay between positive and negative shapes has seldom been equaled.

work, he employed a more naturalistic and romantic style (Fig. 14-14), inspired by such eighteenth-century French painters as Antoine Watteau. Even as he lingered toward a tragically early death, Beardsley's lightning influence penetrated the design and illustration of every European country and America.

Beardsley's leading rival among English graphic designers working in the wake of the Arts and Crafts Movement and on the crest of Art Nouveau was Charles Ricketts, who maintained a lifelong collaboration with his close friend Charles Shannon (1863–1931). Ricketts began as a wood engraver and received training as a compositor; therefore, his work was based on a thorough understanding of printed production. While Beardsley tended to approach his works as illustrations to be inserted between pages of typography, Ricketts approached the book as a total entity to be designed inside and out, focusing upon a harmony of the parts: binding, end sheets, title page, typography, ornaments, and illustrations (which were frequently commissioned from Shannon). After working as an engraver and designer for several printing firms, Ricketts established his own studio and publishing firm.

In 1893, Ricketts's first total book design appeared, and the following year he produced his masterful design for Oscar Wilde's exotic and perplexing poem, "The Sphinx" (Figs. 14-15 through 14-17). Although Ricketts owed a debt to Morris, he usually rejected the density of Kelmscott design. Ricketts's page layouts are lighter, his ornaments and bindings more open and geometric (Fig. 14-18), and his designs have a vivid luminosity. The complex, intertwining ornament of Celtic design and the flat, stylized figures painted on Greek vases, which he studied in the British Museum, were major inspirations. Like Beardsley, who also studied Greek vase painting, Ricketts learned how to indicate figures and clothing with minimal lines and flat shapes with no tonal modulation.

In 1896, Ricketts launched the Vale Press. This was not a private press in the sense of the Kelmscott Press, for Ricketts did not own a press or do his own printing. Rather, he placed his typesetting and presswork with printing firms who labored under his exacting requirements. When William Morris was shown Vale Press books during his final illness, he cried in admiration of the great beauty and design of Ricketts's volumes.

The well-known author Laurence Housman (1865–1959) was active as a book designer at the turn of the century. Arguing that it was as unreasonable to ask

14-14. Aubrey Beardsley, illustration for *The Pierrot of the Minute,* 1897. In his later work, Beardsley turned from the celebration of evil to a more lyrical and romantic style. The flat patterns and dynamic curves of Art Nouveau yielded to a more naturalistic tonal quality, and dotted contours softened the decisive line of his earlier work.

14-15. Charles Ricketts, binding design for *The Sphinx*, 1894. A linear structure, stamped in gold upon white vellum, evokes Japanese interiors and frames the stunning apparition placed in dynamic balance with the narrator.

14-16. Charles Ricketts, title page for *The Sphinx*, 1894. Ricketts's unconventional title page, dominated by an illustration, is placed on the left rather than the right. The text is set in all capitals.

14-17. Charles Ricketts, pages from *The Sphinx*, 1894. The white space and typography printed in rust and olive green ink are without precedent.

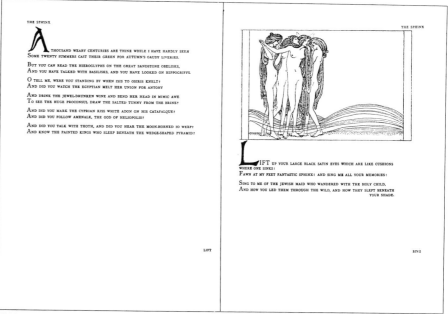

14-16

14-17

book designers to work always with the standard format sizes as it would be to require painters to work only on stretchers of a fixed size and proportion, Housman designed tall, narrow books and square books. His title pages were often unique and unconventional (Fig. 14-19), and his decorative designs were executed with meticulous detail. After the turn of the century, Housman's soaring reputation as a writer and his failing eyesight closed his graphic design career.

One of the most remarkable moments in the history of graphic design is the brief career of The Beggarstaffs. James Pryde (1866–1941) and William Nicholson (1872–1949) were brothers-in-law who had been close friends since art school. Respected academic painters, they decided to open an advertising design studio in 1894 and felt it necessary to adopt pseudonyms to protect their fine-arts reputations. One of them found a sack of corn in a stable with a hearty old English name, "The Beggarstaff Brothers," on it. They adopted the name, dropping "Brothers" from it, and plunged into business. During their brief collaboration they developed

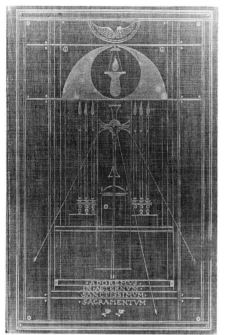

14-18

T HE WERE-WOLF
BY CLEMENCE HOUSMAN
WITH SIX ILLUSTRATIONS
BY LAURENCE HOUSMAN

LONDON: JOHN LANE
AT THE BODLEY HEAD
CHICAGO: WAY AND
WILLIAMS 1896

14-19

14-18. Charles Ricketts, binding design for *Poems of Adoration* by Michael Fields, c. 1900. Christian symbolism is abstracted into elemental forms with rigorous rectangles punctuated with a few well-placed circles and arches.

14-19. Laurence Housman, title page design for *The Were-Wolf,* 1896. An ornamental Art Nouveau initial and typographic information are compressed into three rectangles.

a new technique, later named *collage.* Cut pieces of paper were moved around, changed, and pasted into position on board. The resulting style of absolutely flat planes of color had sensitive edges "drawn" with scissors. Often they presented an incomplete image, challenging the viewer to participate in the design by deciphering the subject (Pl. 23). They were immune to the prevalent floral Art Nouveau as they forged this new working method into posters of powerful colored shapes and silhouettes.

Unfortunately, their work was an artistic success but a financial disaster. They attracted few clients, and only a dozen of their designs were printed. Their most famous poster, for Sir Henry Irving's production of *Don Quixote* at the Lyceum Theater (Fig. 14-20), was never printed, because Irving decided it was a bad likeness. They billed him for only fifty pounds; he paid them twice that. Later, the poster was published in a limited edition, reduced size for collectors.

When it became economically advisable for Nicholson and Pryde to terminate the partnership, each returned to painting and received some measure of recognition. Nicholson also developed a woodcut style of illustration that maintained some of the graphic economy of Beggarstaff posters (Fig. 14-21). Ironically, their brief months as The Beggarstaffs overshadow their individual accomplishments.

Like Nicholson and Pryde, British painter and illustrator Dudley Hardy (1866–1922) also turned to poster and advertising design. He was instrumental in introducing the graphic pictorial qualities of the French poster to London billboards during the 1890s. In much of Hardy's strongest work (Fig. 14-22), lettering and figures appear against simple flat backgrounds.

The further development of French Art Nouveau

During the 1880s, Grasset was a regular at Rodolphe Salis's La Chat Noir nightclub, a gathering place for artists and writers that opened in 1881. It was there that he met and shared his enthusiasm for color printing with younger artists in their twenties: Henri de Toulouse-Lautrec (1864–1901), Georges Auriol (1863–1939), and fellow Swiss artist Théophile-Alexandre Steinlen (1859–1923).

Even Jules Chéret had to concede that Lautrec's 1891 poster, *La Goulue au Moulin Rouge,* broke new ground in poster design (Pl. 24). A dynamic pattern of flat planes—black spectator's silhouettes, yellow ovals for lamps, and the stark white undergarments of the notorious cancan dancer, who performed with trans-

14-20. The Beggarstaffs, poster for *Don Quixote,* 1896. Cut-paper shapes—a black windmill, a brown torso and horse contour, and a light-brown head—produce a graphic image whose simplicity and technique were ahead of their time.

14-21. William Nicholson, illustration from *An Alphabet,* 1897. The reductive simplicity of Beggarstaff posters is maintained.

14-22. Dudley Hardy, theatrical poster, 1898. The actor and play title stand out dramatically against the stark black background.

14-21

14-22

parent or slit underwear—move horizontally across the center of the poster. In front of this is the profile of the dancer Valentine, known as "the boneless one" because of his amazing flexibility. In this milestone of graphic design, simplified symbolic shapes and dynamic patterns are the material forming expressive and communicative images.

The son of the Count of Toulouse, Henri de Toulouse-Lautrec had turned obsessively to drawing and painting after breaking both hips in an accident at age thirteen. Further growth of his legs was stunted, leaving him crippled. He became a master draftsman in the academic tradition after moving to Paris two years later. Japanese art, Impressionism, and Degas's design and contour excited him, and he haunted Paris cabarets and bordellos, watching, drawing, and developing a journalistic, illustrative style that captured the night life of *la belle epoque* ("the beautiful era," a term used to describe glittering late-nineteenth-century Paris). Primarily a printmaker, draftsman, and painter, Toulouse-Lautrec produced only thirty-two posters (Figs. 14-23 and 14-24)—the commissions for which were negotiated in the cabarets in the evenings—and a modest number of music- and book-jacket designs. His command of direct drawing on the lithographic stone was exuberant. He often worked from memory with no sketches and used an old toothbrush that he always carried to achieve tonal effects with a careful splatter technique.

There is an affinity, in the fluid reportorial line and flat color, between the posters and prints of Steinlen and those of his friend and sometime rival for commissions, Toulouse-Lautrec. The debate over which one influenced the other is probably irrelevant, because Steinlen and Lautrec drew inspiration from similar sources and each other. Steinlen, whose work maintained a naturalistic quality, joined the urban migration that was swelling Europe's cities. He arrived in Paris at age twenty-two with his young wife, a great love of drawing, and a mania for cats. His first Paris commissions were cat drawings for La Chat Noir. Steinlen was a prolific illustrator during the 1880s and 1890s, and his radical political views, socialist affiliations, and anticleric stance led him toward a social realism depicting poverty, exploitation, and the working class. His black-and-white lithographs often had color printed by a stencil process. He experimented with subtle colors overprinted to create additional colors. His vast oeuvre included over two thousand magazine-cover and interior illustrations, nearly two hundred sheet-music covers, over a hundred book-illustration assignments, and three dozen large posters.

14-23. Henri de Toulouse-Lautrec, poster for Aristide Bruant, 1893. The influence of the Japanese print is clearly evident in the flat silhouette, unmodulated color, and stylized curvilinear drawing.

14-24. Henri de Toulouse-Lautrec, poster for Jane Avril, 1893. The gestural expressiveness of Toulouse-Lautrec's direct drawing on the lithographic stone captures the vitality of the dancer. This poster was created from sketches made during a performance.

14-23

14-24

14-25. Théophile-Alexandre Steinlen, *La Rue* ("The Street"), 1896. A cross section of Parisian society—a mother and baby, a washerwoman, two workers, Steinlen's daughter Colette with her nanny, a businessman, and sophisticated shoppers—promenades in a nearly life-sized echo of the adjacent sidewalks.

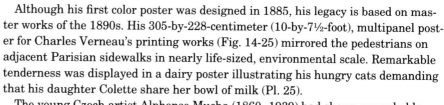

14-26. Eugène Grasset, poster for Sarah Bernhardt as Joan of Arc, 1894. The visual relationships of the figure, lettering, and background cacophony of clouds and spears are somewhat awkward, but the drama and historical period are expressed well.

Although his first color poster was designed in 1885, his legacy is based on master works of the 1890s. His 305-by-228-centimeter (10-by-7½-foot), multipanel poster for Charles Verneau's printing works (Fig. 14-25) mirrored the pedestrians on adjacent Parisian sidewalks in nearly life-sized, environmental scale. Remarkable tenderness was displayed in a dairy poster illustrating his hungry cats demanding that his daughter Colette share her bowl of milk (Pl. 25).

The young Czech artist Alphonse Mucha (1860–1939) had shown remarkable drawing ability when he was growing up in the small Moravian village of Ivancice. After journeying to Paris at age twenty-seven, Mucha spent two years of study supported by a benefactor. This financial support ended suddenly, and a period of deep poverty ensued. But Mucha gained steady acceptance as a dependable illustrator with strong drawing skills.

On Christmas Eve, 1894, Mucha was at the Lemercier's printing company, dutifully correcting proofs for a friend who had taken a holiday. Suddenly, the printing firm's manager burst into the room, upset because the famous actress Sarah Bernhardt was demanding a new poster for the play *Gismonda* by New Year's Day. Since Mucha was the only artist available, he received the commission. Using the basic pose from Grasset's earlier poster for Bernhardt in *Joan of Arc* (Fig. 14-26) and sketches of Bernhardt made at the theater, Mucha elongated Grasset's format, used Byzantine-inspired mosaics as background motifs, and produced a poster totally distinct from any of his prior work. Even though the bottom portion of this poster was unfinished because only a week was available for design, printing, and posting, it created an overnight sensation with its life-sized figure, mosaic pattern, and elongated shape (Pl. 26). Because of its complexity and muted colors, Mucha's work lacked Chéret's impact from afar. But once they stepped closer, Parisians were astounded.

On New Year's Day, 1895, as Mucha began his meteoric rise, a number of influences throughout Europe were converging into what would be labeled l'Art Nouveau. Although Mucha resisted this label, maintaining that art was eternal and could never be new, the further development of his work and of the visual poster are inseparably linked to this diffuse international movement and must be considered as part of its development. Just as the English Arts and Crafts Movement was a special influence of that country's Art Nouveau, the light and fanciful flowing

14-27. Alphonse Mucha, poster for Job cigarette papers, 1898. The warm pinks and brown hair of the figure glow against a deep-purple background and icy, green letterforms in this vintage example of *le style Mucha*. Mucha delighted in filling the total space with animated form and ornament.

14-28. Alphonse Mucha, illustration from *Ilsée, Princesse de Tripoli*, 1901. This masterful example of Mucha's page design has contour lines printed in dark blue-gray. Five other lithographic stones printed light blue-gray, metallic gold, pink, yellow, and brown.

curves of eighteenth-century French Rococo were a special resource in France. The new art was hailed as *le style moderne* until December 1895, when Samuel Bing, a longtime dealer in Far Eastern art and artifacts and an influential presence in the growing awareness of Japanese work, opened his new gallery, l'Art Nouveau, to exhibit art and crafts by young artists working in new directions. Bing commissioned the Belgian architect and designer Henri Clemens van de Velde (1863–1957) to design his interiors, and exhibited painting, sculpture, glasswork, jewelry, and posters by an international group of artists and designers.

Graphic design, more ephemeral and timely than most other art forms, began to codify rapidly toward the floral phase of Art Nouveau as Chéret, Grasset, Toulouse-Lautrec, and especially Mucha developed its graphic motifs. From 1895 until 1900, Art Nouveau found its most comprehensive statement in Mucha's work. His dominant theme was a central female figure surrounded by stylized forms derived from plants and flowers, Moravian folk art, Byzantium mosaics, and even magic and the occult. So pervasive was his work that by 1900, *le style Mucha* was often used interchangeably with *l'art nouveau*. This new art was called *Jugendstil* in Germany, *Sezessionstil* in Austria, *Stile Floreale* or *Stile Liberty* (after textiles and furnishings from the London department store) in Italy, and *Modernismo* in Spain.

Mucha's women project an archetypal sense of unreality. Exotic, sensuous, and yet maidenlike, they express no specific age, nationality, or historical period. His stylized hair patterns (Figs. 14-27 and 14-29) became a hallmark of the era in spite of detractors who dismissed this aspect as "noodles and spaghetti." Sarah Bernhardt, who had not been pleased with Grasset's *Joan of Arc* poster or many of the posters for her performances, felt that Mucha's *Gismonda* poster expressed her so well graphically that she signed him to a six-year contract for sets, costumes, jewelry, and nine more posters. The sheer volume of Mucha's output was astounding.

For example, the 134 lithographs for the book *Ilsée, Princesse de Tripoli* (Fig. 14-28) printed in a limited edition of 252 copies, were produced in three months. In addition to graphics, Mucha designed furniture, carpets, stained-glass windows, and manufactured objects. He published pattern books, including *Combinaisons ornementales* in collaboration with Maurice Verneuil (1869–after 1934) and Georges Auriol (1863–1939), that spread Art Nouveau (Figs. 14-30 and 14-31).

In 1904, at the height of his fame, Mucha left Paris for his first American visit. His last major Art Nouveau work was executed in 1909. When Czechoslovakia regained its status as a free nation in 1917, his time and work were centered there, and his last decades were spent primarily producing *Slav Epic,* a series of twenty large murals depicting the history of his native people. When the Germans partitioned Czechoslovakia in 1939, Mucha was one of the first people arrested and interrogated by the Gestapo. When he died a few months later, his beloved homeland was once again under foreign domination, and the world was a vastly different place than it was during the brief energetic years when he carried Art Nouveau to its zenith.

Although Emmanuel Orazi (1860–1934) came to prominence as a poster designer in 1884, when he designed a poster for Sarah Bernhardt, it was not until his static style yielded to the influences of Grasset and Mucha a decade later that he produced his best work. His masterpiece is a 1905 poster for La Maison Moderne (Pl. 27), a gallery competing with Bing's l'Art Nouveau gallery. A sophisticated young lady, drawn in an almost Egyptian profile, is posed before a counter bearing objects from the gallery. La Maison Moderne's logo, centered in the window, is one of many examples of Art Nouveau letterforms applied to trademark design. Other trademarks of Art Nouveau origin, designed for firms such as the American General Electric (Fig. 14-32) and Coca-Cola, have been in continuous use since the 1890s.

Paul Berthon (1872–1909), a student of Grasset, pushed the Art Nouveau style toward softness (Fig. 14-33). He used Grasset's strong contour, stylized Japanese cloud formations, and flowers, but the contour color was muted and blended with the color planes, and the flowers threatened to become repetitive design motifs.

Georges de Feure (1868–1928) had studied with Chéret. His wide-ranging design activities included graphics, theatrical design, porcelains, and—under the influence of Henri van de Velde—furniture and objets d'art. The forms and shapes in de Feure's *Le Journal des Ventes* poster echo this influence (Fig. 14-34).

Art Nouveau found one of its most complete architectural expressions in the work of Hector Guimard (1867–1942), whose iron and glass entrances and pavilions for the Paris Metro achieved visual expression and were constructed with standardized industrial fabrication methods.

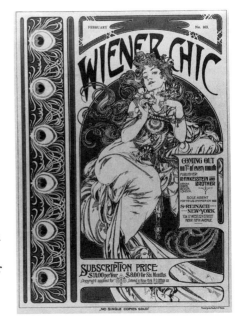

14-29. Alphonse Mucha, cover for *Wiener Chic* ("Vienna Chic"), 1906. This fashion-magazine cover shows Mucha's ornamental patterns and interplay between organic areas for typography and illustration.

14-30. Georges Auriol, cover for *Combinaisons ornementales* ("Ornamental Combinations"), 1900. Auriol's lettering was the prototype for Auriol, one of three widely used Art Nouveau type families he designed for the Peignot foundry in Paris.

14-31. Maurice Verneuil, page from *Combinaisons ornementales,* 1900. With Mucha and Georges Auriol, Verneuil designed Art Nouveau ornaments in a style book for artists and designers.

14-30

14-31

14-32. Trademark for General Electric, c. 1890. This design satisfies the requirements of a successful trademark: It is unique, legible, and unequivocal, which explains how it has survived many decades of changing graphic styles. (A registered trademark of General Electric Company, used by permission.)

14-33. Paul Berthon, poster for *L'Ermitage* magazine, 1900. Even though Berthon used a strong, rigid line, he achieved a soft, mellow quality by specifying inks of limited color or value contrast.

14-34. Georges de Feure, poster for *Le Journal des Ventes,* 1897. De Feure created strong graphic impact by organizing his posters into organic zones of light, dark, and middle tones.

14-35. Eugène Grasset, cover for *Harper's Magazine,* 1892. Grasset's work, combining flowing contours and flat color with an almost medieval flavor, captured the American imagination.

Art Nouveau comes to America

British and French graphic art joined forces to invade America. In 1889, and again in 1891 and 1892, *Harper's* magazines commissioned covers from Eugène Grasset (Fig. 14-35). These first presentations of a new approach to graphic design were literally imported, for Grasset's designs were printed in Paris and shipped by boat to New York to be bound onto the magazines.

British-born Louis Rhead (1857–1926) studied in England and Paris before emigrating to America in 1883. After eight years in New York as an illustrator, he returned to Europe for three years and adopted Grasset's style. Upon his return to America, a prolific flow of posters, magazine covers (Fig. 14-36), and illustrations enabled him to join the self-taught American, William H. Bradley (1868–1962), as the two major American practitioners of Art Nouveau–inspired graphic design and illustration.

The visual poster was adopted in America by the publishing industry, and colorful placards began to appear at the newsstands advertising the new issues of major magazines, including *Harper's, Scribner's,* and *Century.* New books were also advertised with posters. While Rhead embraced Grasset's willowy maidens, contour line, and flat color, he rejected Grasset's pale colors in favor of vibrant combinations. On occasion, Rhead even used such unexpected combinations as a maiden with red contour lines on her bright blue hair, standing before an intense green sky. Rhead's work sometimes mixed a profusion of influences. Decorative patterns left over from Victorian design, forms inspired by the Arts and Crafts Movement, and curving abstract linear patterns are sometimes combined in his designs.

While Rhead adopted the French poster as his model, the uninhibited, energetic, and enormously talented Will Bradley was inspired by English sources. After his father died from wounds received in the Civil War, nine-year-old Bradley and his mother moved from Massachusetts to Ishpeming, Michigan, to live with relatives. His early training in graphic arts began at age eleven, when he became a *printer's*

14-36. Louis Rhead, cover for *Harper's Bazar*, 1894. Dazzling linear patterns animate the background of this cover design. Note the intensity of Rhead's colorful advertisement for Royal Baking Powder on the back cover in contrast to its more typical competitors.

devil for the *Iron Agitator* (later the *Iron Ore*) newspaper. A printer's devil was a young apprentice and errand boy in a printing office, so named because he often became black with ink from cleaning type and presses. When Bradley was seventeen, he used his fifty-dollar savings to go to Chicago and apprentice at Rand-McNally as an engraver. Realizing that engravers did not design or illustrate, and that illustrators and designers did not engrave, he returned to Ishpeming. But Chicago soon beckoned again, and he became a typographic designer at the Knight & Leonard printing company when he was nineteen.

Unable to afford art lessons, Bradley became a voracious student of magazines and library books. As with Frederic Goudy and Bruce Rogers, William Morris and his ideals had enormous impact on Bradley. By 1890, his Arts and Crafts–inspired pen-and-ink illustrations were bringing regular commissions. In early 1894, Brad-

14-37. Will Bradley, covers for *The Inland Printer,* 1894–1895. These cover designs show the range of Bradley's graphic vocabulary: He explored delicate contour line for an overall light effect, complex full-tone drawing, and reduction of the image to black-and-white silhouette masses.

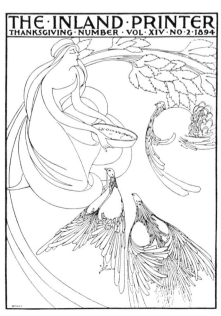

ley became aware of Aubrey Beardsley's work, which led him toward flat shapes and stylized contour. Beginning in 1894, Bradley's work for *The Chap Book* and *The Inland Printer* (Figs. 14-37 through 14-39, and Pl. 28) ignited Art Nouveau in America. His detractors dismissed him as "the American Beardsley," but Bradley used Beardsley's style as a stepping stone to innovative graphic technique and a visual unity of type and image that moved beyond imitation.

Bradley was free-spirited in his approach to typographic design, and flouted all the prevailing rules and conventions. Type became a design element to be huddled in the corner of the space, squeezed into a narrow column, or letterspaced so that lines of many and few letters all became the same length and formed a rectangle. Inspired by the example of the Kelmscott Press, Bradley moved from Chicago to Springfield, Massachusetts, in late 1894 and established the Wayside Press. He

14-39. Will Bradley poster for *The Chap Book*, 1895. Repetition of the figure in a smaller size, overlapping the larger figure, enabled Bradley to create a more complex set of visual relationships.

14-38. Will Bradley, cover for *The Inland Printer*, 1894. A dynamic tension is created between the organic curves and white space of the illustrations and the squared panel of lettering with its dense texture. American Type Founders acquired rights to these letterforms and issued them as the typeface Bradley.

produced books and advertisements and began publication of an art and literary periodical, *Bradley: His Book,* in 1896. Both the magazine and press were critical and financial successes, but the rigors and many roles of the job—editor, designer, illustrator, press manager—threatened Bradley's health. In 1898, he sold Wayside Press to the University Press in Cambridge and accepted a position there.

During a visit to the Boston Public Library in 1895, Bradley had studied its collection of books printed in colonial New England. The vigor of this work, with its Old Style Caslon types, wide letterspacing, sturdy woodcuts, and plain rules, inspired the beginnings of a new direction that became known as the Chap Book Style (Fig. 14-40). Chap books were crudely printed small books formerly sold by traveling peddlers known as chapmen. After the turn of the century, Bradley became a consultant to the American Type Founders, designing typefaces and ornaments. He wrote and designed their series of twelve magazines, *The American Chap-Book.* His demonstration designs, using American Type Founders type and ornaments, were called *The Printer Man's Joy* (Fig. 14-41). His illustration career was swallowed by this passion for type design and layout, and in 1907 thirty-nine-year-old Bradley became art editor of *Collier's* magazine. The last decades of his long career were significant to the evolution of twentieth-century editorial design.

Ethel Reed (b. 1876) became the first woman in America to achieve national prominence for her work as a graphic designer and illustrator (Fig. 14-42). Born and raised in Massachusetts, she became well known as a book illustrator by age eighteen. For four brief years, from 1894 until 1898, she was active as a poster designer for Boston publishers Copeland & Day, and Lamson, Wolffe and Company. Curiously, Reed's career ends abruptly at this point, and her life after age twenty-two is a mystery. Perhaps she either married and abandoned her art or met an untimely death. It is unfortunate that such precocious early work did not see further development.

An art director for Harper and Brothers publications from 1891 until 1901, Edward Penfield (1866–1925) enjoyed a reputation rivaling Bradley's and Rhead's. His monthly series of posters for *Harper's* magazine from 1893 until 1898 portrayed members of the upper class. They were *Harper's* audience, and Penfield frequently depicted them reading or carrying an issue of the magazine. Penfield's first poster for *Harper's* was designed for the January 1894 issue and featured a naturalistic watercolor illustration showing a sophisticated young man purchasing a subscription (Fig. 14-43). During the course of that year, Penfield evolved toward his mature style of contour drawing with flat planes of color. By eliminating the background, he forced the viewer to focus upon the figure and lettering. Penfield drew with a vigorous, fluid line, and his flat color planes were often supplemented

14-40. Will Bradley, cover and pages from a Victor bicycles catalogue, 1898. Geometric zones and letterspaced type combined with curvilinear drawing in early Chap Book graphics printed in a burnt red, olive green, and black.

14-41. Will Bradley, cover design for *The Printer Man's Joy,* 1905. After the turn of the century, Bradley's fascination with colonial printing and woodcuts inspired a shift from Art Nouveau to the bold graphic style typified here.

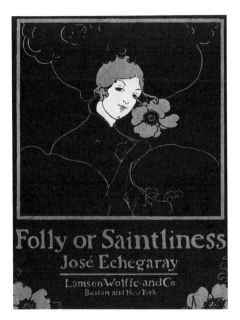

by a masterful stipple technique. In a whimsical 1894 poster for the July issue (Fig. 14-44), a young lady lights a string of fireworks without even looking at them, so preoccupied is she with her reading—the absorbing enjoyment of reading *Harper's* is conveyed. In an 1897 poster (Pl. 29), everyone on a train, including the conductor, is reading *Harper's*. This campaign was wildly successful in promoting *Harper's*, and competitive publications commissioned imitative designs showing the reading public absorbed in *their* magazines. William Carqueville (1871–1946) created similar posters for *Lippincott's* magazine, including a girl dropping her *Lippincott's* after a young boy startles her with a firecracker for the July 1895 issue (Fig. 14-45). After Carqueville left for Paris to continue his study of art, J. J. Gould was hired to continue the campaign (Fig. 14-46).

Several younger artists of the 1890s poster movement were to become major illustrators for magazines and books during the twentieth century. Maxfield Parrish (1870–1966) was rejected as a student by Howard Pyle, who told young Parrish that there was nothing more that Pyle could teach him and that he should develop an independent style. Parrish expressed a romantic and idealized view of the world (Fig. 14-47) in book, magazine, and advertising illustrations during the first three decades of the twentieth century before turning to painting landscapes for reproduction. Joseph C. Leyendecker (1874–1951) became America's most pop-

14-42. Ethel Reed, poster for the book *Folly or Saintliness*, 1895. In an imaginative use of three-color printing, the white face with red lips glows against an otherwise black and orange-brown poster.

14-43. Edward Penfield, poster for *Harper's*, 1894. This image is created by traditional tonal modeling, instead of by the line and color seen in Penfield's work later that same year.

14-44. Edward Penfield, poster for *Harper's*, 1894. Figurative letterforms and the dramatic sense of expectation—the moment before the fireworks begin—create a whimsical concept.

14-46

14-47

14-45. Will Carqueville, poster for *Lippincott's,* 1895. Both the style and concept of Penfield's poster from the preceding Fourth of July are imitated.

14-46. J. J. Gould, poster for *Lippincott's,* 1897. The grainy lithographic crayon quality seen here is the distinguishing feature of Gould's designs.

14-47. Maxfield Parrish, poster for *Scribner's* magazine, 1897. Parrish created an elegant land of fantasy with his idealized drawing, pristine color, and intricate composition.

14-48. Georges Lemmen, cover design for a *Les Vingt* ("The Twenty") exhibition catalogue, 1891. A rising sun, symbolic of the group, rises over a rhythmic sea of swirling lines.

ular illustrator from the World War I era (see Figs. 17-11 and 17-12) until the early 1940s. Leyendecker picked up where Gibson left off in creating beautiful young people for the mass media.

Innovation in Belgium

Art Nouveau sprang to life in Belgium during the middle 1890s. Nestled between France and Germany, this small country had experienced the beginnings of creative ferment during the 1880s when the *Cercle des XX* ("Group of Twenty") formed to enable more progressive art to be exhibited outside the salon establishment. Their daring exhibition program included early exhibits of paintings by Gauguin in 1889 and van Gogh in 1890. The cover design for a *Les Vingt* ("The Twenty") exhibition catalogue by Georges Lemmen (1865–1916) in 1891 demonstrates that Belgian artists were at the vanguard in the momentum toward a new art (Fig. 14-48). By the middle 1890s, Belgian Art Nouveau became a significant force, as architect Baron Victor Horta, designer Henri van de Velde, and artist Jan Toorop (Fig. 14-49; see also Fig. 14-9) were influencing developments throughout Europe.

Van de Velde—an architect, painter, designer, and educator—was a one-man watershed. He synthesized sources including the Japanese print, French Art Nouveau, the English Arts and Crafts Movement, and later the Glasgow School into a unified style. After studying painting in Antwerp and Paris and exploring post-Impressionist styles such as Pointillism, he turned to the study of architecture and joined the *Cercle des XX.* William Morris's example inspired an increasing involvement in design, and van de Velde abandoned his easel and brushes. Interiors, book design, bookbindings, jewelry, and metalwork became major activities. In 1892, van de Velde wrote an important essay, *Déblaiement d'art,* calling for a new art, which would be contemporary in concept and form but possess the vitality and ethical integrity of the great decorative and applied arts of the past. The ornaments and initials designed for a reprint of this essay and for the periodical *Van Nu en Straks* ("Today and Tomorrow") approach pure abstraction (Fig. 14-50), for the basic letter structures are transfigured by dynamic linear rhythms. Van de Velde's work can be seen as a serious effort to innovate new forms for the era. In book design, he broke creative ground, drawing dynamic linear forms that embrace their surrounding space and the intervals between them. His work evolved from forms inspired by plant motifs and symbolic ideas to an abstract style (Fig. 14-51).

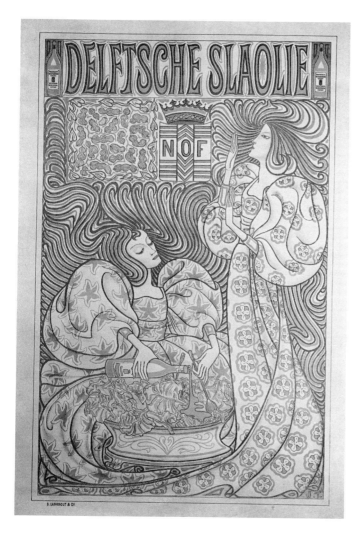

14-51

14-49. Jan Toorop, poster for *Delftsche Slaolie* salad oil, 1894. Printed in yellow and lavender, this poster becomes kinetic through its undulating linear rhythms and close-valued complementary colors.

14-50. Henri van de Velde, initials from *Van Nu en Straks,* c. 1896. Typography was pushed here toward an expression of pure form.

14-51. Henri van de Velde, *Salutations* book cover, 1893. The illustration and lettering are unified by the similarity of forms and line weights.

When this approach was applied to graphic design, van de Velde was, unsurprisingly, a precursor of twentieth-century painting, foretelling the coming of Kandinsky and abstract expression in the twentieth century. His only poster was for a concentrated food product, Tropon, for which he created labeling and advertising in 1899 (Pl. 30). Rather than communicating about the product or depicting people using it, van de Velde engaged the viewer with pure visual form and color. Later, his 1908 book designs for Friedrich Nietzsche's *Also sprach Zarathustra* and *Ecce Homo* were masterworks (Figs. 14-52 through 14-54).

Although van de Velde became an innovator of Art Nouveau, he was far more interested in furthering the Arts and Crafts philosophy than in innovative style as an end in itself. After the turn of the century, his teaching and writing (*The Renaissance in Modern Applied Art,* 1901; *A Layman's Sermons on Applied Art,* 1903) became a vital source for the development of twentieth-century architecture and design theory. An example of his pedagogy is his observation that when a shadow is cast, a complementary form is created on the light-struck side of the shadow's outline, and that this "negative" form is as important as the object casting the shadow. He taught that all branches of art—from painting to graphic design, and from industrial design to sculpture—shared a communal language of form and an equality of importance to the human community. Appropriate materials, functional forms, and a unity of visual organization were demanded. He saw ornament not as decoration but as a means of expression that could achieve the status of art.

Van de Velde brought a moral imperative to his demand for contemporary work to be modern and express the needs of the day. Machine-made objects, he argued,

14-52. Henri van de Velde, title pages for *Also sprach Zarathustra*, 1908. In this monumental Art Nouveau book design, bold graphic shapes fill the pages.

14-53. Henri van de Velde, text pages from *Also sprach Zarathustra*, 1908. Gold ornaments cap each column of type. The chapter-heading design is in the center of the left page, and a chapter section is indicated high on the right page.

14-54. Henri van de Velde, double title page for Friedrich Nietzsche's *Ecce Homo*, 1908. In contrast to the symphonic crescendo of the *Also sprach Zarathustra* title pages, in this design van de Velde's flowing curves weave the quieter harmony of a string quartet.

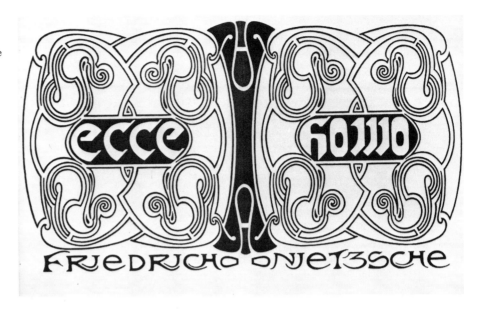

14-55. Privat Livemont, Rajah Coffee poster, 1899. The interplay between the steam from the coffee cup and the product name creates a fascinating interplay of forms.

should be true to their manufacturing process instead of trying, deceitfully, to appear handmade. After the Grand Duke of Saxe Weimar called van de Velde to Weimar as art and design advisor in 1902, he reorganized the Weimar Arts and Crafts Institute and the Weimar Academy of Fine Arts. This was a preliminary step toward Walter Gropius's formation of the Bauhaus in 1919. When World War I broke out, van de Velde returned to his native country. In 1925, the Belgian government, as an expression of their appreciation, named van de Velde, who was then sixty-two, director of the Institut Superieur des Arts Decoratifs in Brussels.

Other 1890s Belgian graphic designers also added original variations to the new art. After six years in Paris, Privat Livemont (1861–1936) returned to his native Belgium. This teacher and painter produced nearly three dozen posters, strongly inspired by Mucha's idealized women, their tendrilous hair, and lavish ornament. His major innovation was a double contour that separates the figure from the background. The dark contour was outlined by a thick, white band, which increased the image's impact when posted on the billboards (Fig. 14-55). Gisbert Combaz (1869–1941) turned from the practice of law to become an artist and art historian specializing in the Far East. He was a leading member of *La Libre Esthetique,* the organization that evolved from the *Cercle des XX* in 1893. His many exhibition posters for this group feature intense color and pushed the Art Nouveau arabesque into an almost mechanical, tense line (Pl. 31).

The German Jugendstil movement

Art Nouveau arrived in Germany, where it was called *Jugendstil* ("young style"). This name was adopted from a new periodical called *Jugend (Youth),* which began publication at Munich in 1896. From Munich, Jugendstil spread to Berlin, Darmstadt, and all over Germany. German Art Nouveau had strong French and British influences, but it still retained strong links to the more traditional academic art that preceded it. The German interest in medieval letterforms—Germany was the only European country that did not replace Gutenberg's textura type with the roman styles of the Renaissance—continued side by side with Art Nouveau motifs (see Fig. 14-59). New printing and manufacturing techniques and the excitement of Jugendstil created tremendous interest in the applied arts, and many German artists embraced graphic and product design.

During the first year *Jugend* was published, the circulation climbed to thirty thousand copies per week. As it walked a fine line between being an arts magazine and a journal of popular entertainment, *Jugend* soon attracted a readership of 200,000 per week. Art Nouveau ornaments and illustrations were on virtually every editorial page. Full double-page illustrations, horizontal illustrations across the top of a page, an abundance of spot illustrations, and decorative Art Nouveau designs brought rich variety to a format that was about half visual material and half text. One unprecedented editorial policy was to allow each week's cover designer the latitude to design a masthead to go with the cover design. Over the course of a year, the *Jugend* logo might appear variously as giant textura letters, tendril-like Art Nouveau lettering, or just the word *Jugend* set in twenty-four-point typography above the image because that week's designer had ignored or forgotten the need to include the logotype in the design. In the cover design for 14 October 1899 by Hans Christiansen (1866–1945), one of the leading artists associated with *Jugend,* the simple, sans serif letterforms are drawn in icy, pale violet with pale pink outlines (Pl. 32). The stylized curves of the letterforms pick up the curves of the flat shapes of the image. In many of his illustrations, Christiansen predates the Fauve movement in his use of flat planes of bright color.

Two of the bright lights in the Jugendstil movement were the young painters Otto Eckmann (1865-1902) and Peter Behrens (1868–1940), who were widely known for their large, multicolor woodblock prints inspired by French Art Nouveau and the Japanese print. Both embraced the applied arts and became frequent contributors of illustrations and decorative designs to *Jugend* and *Pan* magazines. Eckmann's passion for applied art prompted him to auction all his paintings in November of 1894. His letter to the auctioneer bade his paintings a "cordial farewell" and concluded, "may we never meet again." In addition to five covers (Fig. 14-56), illustrations, and numerous decorative nature borders for *Jugend,* Eckmann designed jewelry, objects, furniture, women's fashions, and an important typeface. He became a designer and consultant for the Allgemeine Elektriszitäts Gesellschaft, or AEG, and explored the application of Jugendstil ornament to the graphic and product needs of industry (Fig. 14-57). The Klingspor Foundry was the first German typefoundry to commission new fonts from artists, and in 1900 it released Eckmann's Eckmannschrift (Fig. 14-58; see also Fig. 15-33), which created a sensation and thrust this small, regional foundry into international prominence. Drawn with a brush instead of a pen, Eckmannschrift was a conscious attempt to revitalize typography by combining medieval and roman attributes with the influence of Japanese prints. As the new century opened, Eckmann seemed poised to play a major role in the further evolution of design, but in 1902 this thirty-seven-

14-56. Otto Eckmann, *Jugend* cover, 1896. Jugendstil graphics often blended curvilinear stylization with traditional realism.

14-57

14-58

14-59. Peter Behrens, cover for *Der Bunte Vogel* ("The Colorful Bird") calendar book, 1899. Bold simplicity and typefaces inspired by medieval lettering are typical of Jugendstil.

14-60. Peter Behrens, trademark for Insel-Verlag, 1899. This delightful ship in a circle perched on Art Nouveau waves typifies Jugendstil trademark design.

14-57. Otto Eckmann, cover for an Allgemeine Elektriszitäts Gesellschaft catalogue, 1900. Brush-drawn lettering and ornaments express the kinetic energy of electricity.

14-58. Otto Eckmann, title page for *Eckmann Schriftprobe,* 1901. The blending of contradictory influences—medieval, oriental, and Art Nouveau—produced a wildly popular typeface.

14-61. Peter Behrens, graphic design for *Jugend,* 1904. Evoking peacock feathers and Egyptian lotus designs, a gray and brown structure rises above two columns of textura-inspired type.

year-old designer succumbed to the tuberculosis that had plagued him for years.

In addition to his work for *Jugend,* Peter Behrens experimented with ornaments and vignettes of abstract design throughout two other publications, *Der Bunte Vogel,* (Fig. 14-59) and *Die Insel.* He became artistic advisor to *Die Insel* and its publisher, Insel-Verlag, for which he designed one of the finest Jugendstil trademarks (Fig. 14-60). *Die Insel* was not illustrated, and Behrens gave it a consistent typographic format and program using Old Style typefaces. He also studied design from other cultures and introduced Egyptian motifs into the Jugendstil vocabulary (Fig. 14-61).

The primary German contribution was not Jugendstil, however, but the innovations that developed in reaction to it after the turn of the century, as architects and designers, including Peter Behrens, became influenced by the ideals of the Arts and Crafts Movement, purged of its medieval affections. Designers in Germany, Scotland, and Austria moved rapidly from the floral phase of Art Nouveau toward a more geometric and objective approach to problem solving. This accompanied a shift from swirling organic line and form to a geometric ordering of space. (This birth of the modernist design sensibility is discussed in Chapter 15.)

The English art historian Herbert Read once observed that the life of any art movement is like that of a flower: A budding in the hands of a small number of innovators is followed by full bloom; then the process of decay begins as the influence becomes diffused and distorted in the hands of imitators who understand merely the stylistic manifestations of the movement, rather than the driving passions that forged it. After the turn of the century, this was the fate of Art Nouveau. Before then, Art Nouveau objects and furniture had been primarily one-of-a-kind or limited-edition items. But as the graphic design of posters and periodicals brought Art Nouveau to an ever-widening circle of admirers, far greater quantities were produced. Some manufacturers focused on the bottom line by turning out vast amounts of merchandise and graphics with lower design standards. Lesser talents copied the style, while many of the innovators moved on to other directions. Nevertheless, Art Nouveau lingered, slowly declining, until it vanished in the ashes of World War I. Its legacy is a tracery of the dreams and life-styles of a brief Indian summer in the human saga. Its offspring are twentieth-century designers who adopted, not its style, but its attitudes toward materials, processes, and values.

The Modernist Era:
Graphic design in the first half of the twentieth century

World Events	15 The Genesis of 20th-Century Design	16 The Influence of Modern Art	17 Pictorial Modernism	18 A New Language of Form	19 The Bauhaus & the New Typography
1896 Sousa, *Stars and Stripes Forever*	1895 McNair and Macdonalds, Glasgow fine arts poster				
1897 Thompson discovers the electron	1896 Wright designs *The House Beautiful*	1897 Mallarme, *Un Coup de Des*			
1898 Curie discovers radium	1897 Vienna Secession formed				
1899 Freud, *The Interpretation of Dreams*	1898 *Ver Sacrum* begins publication; Berthold Foundry; Akzidenz Grotesk				
1900 Boxer rebellion	1899 Moser, 5th Vienna Secession poster				
1901 Queen Victoria dies	1900 Behrens, sans serif running text; Klingspor issues Eckmannschrift				
	1901 Klingspor issues Behrensschrift				
1902 Frank Lloyd Wright, the 1st "prairie style" house	1902 Moser, 13th Vienna Secession exhibition poster				
1903 Wright Brothers, 1st airplane flight	1903 Hoffmann & Moser, The Vienna Workshops are established				
1904 Chekhov, *The Cherry Orchard*	1904 Lauweriks teaches geometric grid composition in Germany				
1905 Einstein, Theory of Relativity			1905 Bernhard, Priester matches poster		
1906 San Francisco earthquake	1906 Behrens, Anchor Linoleum pavilion and graphics				
1907 Lumiere Brothers develop their color photographic process	1907 Deutscher Werkbund formed; Behrens joins AEG, designs trademark; Loeffler designs *Fledermaus* poster	1907 Picasso, *Les Demoiselles D'Avignon*			
1908 The Model T Ford is introduced			1908 Hohlwein, PKZ poster		
1909 NAACP formed	1909 Behrens and Bernhard, AEG turbine hall	1909 Marinetti, *Manifesto of Futurism;* Braque, *Pitcher and Violin*			
1910 Stravinsky, *The Firebird*	1910 Behrens, AEG lamp poster	1910 Analytical Cubism		1910 Mondrian learns of Cubism	
1911 Carrier invents the air conditioner			1911 Erdt, Opel poster		
1912 Wilson elected U. S. President		1912 Gris, *Portrait of Picasso*		1912 Wright, Coonley house with geometric stained glass windows	
1913 New York Armory Show		1913 Synthetic Cubism		c. 1913 Malevich, first Suprematist paintings	
1914 World War I begins	1914 Werkbund embraces Muthesius' rationalism	1914 de Chirico, *Departure of the Poet*			
1915 Griffith, *The Birth of a Nation*		1915 Marinetti, "Mountains + Valleys + Streets x Joffre"	1915 Leete, Kitchener "wants you" poster		
1916 Battle of Verdun		1916 Dada founded; Arp explores the role of chance in art		1916 van der Leck, Batavier Line poster	1916 Johnston, Railway Type
1917 Russian Revolution begins		1917 Ball, Dada sound poems; Coburn, *Vortographs*	1917 Klinger, 8th war loan campaign poster; Flagg, "Uncle Sam" poster	1917 De Stijl movement & journal begin	
1918 World War I ends; Czar Nicholas II executed		1918 Apollinaire, *Calligrammes* published; Housmann & Höch, photomontages	1918 Kauffer, *Daily Herald* poster	1918 van Doesburg, *Composition XI*	
1919 U. S. Prohibition begins		1919 Schwitters, Merz exhibition; Heartfield, Grosz & others, Berlin Dada; Leger, *La Fin du Monde . . .*		1919 Lissitzky, *PROUN* paintings and *Beat the Whites with the Red Wedge* poster	1919 Gropius founds Weimar Bauhaus; Feininger informs Bauhaus of de Stijl
1920 U.S. women gain vote					1920 Klee joins Bauhaus
1921 Sacco and Vanzetti convicted					1921 Feininger, *Europäische Graphik* woodcuts
1922 Soviet Union is formed		1922 Dada loses cohesiveness			1922 Kandinsky joins Bauhaus

15 The Genesis of 20th-Century Design

World Events

1923 Hitler, *Mein Kampf*
1924 Mussolini and Fascists consolidate their power in Italy
1925 Fitzgerald, *The Great Gatsby*
1926 NBC, 1st national radio network
1927 Stalin rules Russia; Lindbergh, solo flight across the Atlantic
1928 Warner Brothers, 1st sound motion picture
1929 Stock market crash
1930 Gandhi leads Indian protest against salt tax
1931 Empire State Building
1932 Low point of Depression; Roosevelt elected President
1933 Hitler becomes Chancellor of Germany
1934 Mao Tse-tung leads "Long March"
1935 Rural Electrification Administration
1936 Roosevelt reelected; Spanish Civil War begins
1937 Picasso paints *Guernica*
1938 Munich Pact leads to German occupation of Czechoslovakia
1939 Germany invades Poland, World War II begins; New York World's Fair
1940 Churchill, "blood, toil, tears, and sweat" speech
1941 Japan attacks Pearl Harbor
1942 Bataan "Death March"
1943 Mass production of penicillin
1944 Allied invasion of Normandy (D-Day)
1945 Roosevelt dies; A-bombs dropped; World War II ends
1946 Nuremberg war trials
1947 The Marshall Plan begins
1948 Gandhi is assassinated
1949 Mao Tse-tung's Communist forces capture China
1950 Korean War begins

20 The Modern Movement in America

1924-37 Erte, *Harper's Bazaar* covers
c. 1928 American book designers explore modernist typography; Agha becomes art director of *Vogue*
1933 Beall, *Chicago Tribune* ads
1934 Brodovitch art directs *Harper's Bazaar*
1935 WPA hires artists for design projects
1936 Jacobson, design director for CCA
c. 1937 Beall, REA posters
1930s Bauhaus masters Albers, Bayer, Breuer, Gropius, Mies van der Rohe, Moholy-Nagy immigrate to U.S.
1939 Binder, New York World's Fair poster; Moholy-Nagy, School of Design
1940 Kauffer, Greek resistance poster
1941 Carlu, *America's answer!* Production poster; Binder, Air Corps poster
1942 Sutnar, Sweet's logo
1943 Shahn, *This is Nazi Brutality* poster
1944 Sutnar, *Catalog Design*
1945 CCA "Allied Nations" advertisements
1948 Matter, Knoll chair ads; Bayer begins work on *World Geo-Graphic Atlas*
1950 CCA "Great Ideas" ads begin
1951 Brodovitch, *Portfolio* magazine

16 The Influence of Modern Art

1923 Schwitters, *Merz* magazine
1924 Breton, *Manifesto of Surrealism* Man Ray, *Gun with Alphabet Squares*
1927 Depero, *Dinamo Arani*
1929 Man Ray, *Sleeping Woman*
1933 Nazis raid Heartfield's apartment
1934 Heartfield, "Yuletide" poster

17 Pictorial Modernism

1923 Cooper, London Underground posters; Binder, Vienna music and theater poster
1925 Cassandre, *L'Intransigeant* poster
1926 Schulz-Neudamm, *Metropolis* poster
1927 Cassandre, *Etoile du Nord* poster
1932 Cassandre, *Dubonnet* poster
c. 1936-1943 Hohlwein designs for Nazis
late 1930s Binder, Carlu, Cassandre, & Kauffer to the U. S.
1940s Games, World War II posters

18 A New Language of Form

1923 Mayakovsky & Lissitzky, *For the Voice* published
1924 Lissitzky, *The Isms of Art*; Rodchenko, serial covers, *Mess Mend* books; Rietveld, Schroeder house
1927 Lehning publishes *i10*
1929 Lissitzky, *Russische Ausstellung* poster
1930 van Doesburg, *Manifesto of Art Concret*
1931 van Doesburg dies, *De Stijl* journal ends
1939 Sutnar immigrates to U. S.
1941 Lissitzky dies
1944 Mondrian dies

19 The Bauhaus & the New Typography

1923 Moholy-Nagy replaces Itten at Bauhaus; Bauhaus exhibition, Tschichold attends; Werkman, *1st Next Call*
1925 Bayer, universal alphabet; Tschichold, *elementare typographie*
1926 Gropius, Bauhaus building at Dessau; Bayer, Kandinsky poster
1927 Renner, Futura
1928 Gropius, Moholy-Nagy, & Bayer leave Bauhaus; Tschichold, *Die Neue Typographie*; Zwart, NKF catalogue; Koch, Kabel
1930 Mies van der Rohe moves Bauhaus to Berlin
1931 Gill, *Essay on Typography*
1932 Morison, Times New Roman
1933 Nazis close Bauhaus, arrest Tschichold; Beck, London Underground map
1934 Matter, Swiss travel posters
1935 Matter, *Pontresina* poster
1947 Tschichold joins Penguin books
1950s Sandberg, *experimenta typographica* published

15

The Genesis of Twentieth-Century Design

The turn of a century often seems to cause introspection. As one century closes and a new one begins, writers and artists begin to question conventional wisdom and speculate on new possibilities for changing the circumstances of human culture. For example, the end of the eighteenth century gave birth to a new category of typeface design, which is still called the *modern* style (see Figs. 9-19 through 9-21) two hundred years later. At that same time, the *Neoclassical* revival of Greco-Roman forms in architecture, clothing, painting, and illustration (see Fig. 9-22) replaced Baroque and Rococo design. As the nineteenth century drew to a close and the twentieth century began, designers across the disciplines of architectural, fashion, graphic, and product design searched for new possibilities. Technological and industrial advances fed these concerns. The new design vocabulary of Art Nouveau, discussed in Chapter 14, had challenged the conventions of Victorian design. Curvilinear Art Nouveau proved that inventing new forms, rather than copying forms from nature or historical models, was a viable approach. The potential of abstract and reductive drawing and design was demonstrated by designers in Scotland, Austria, and Germany, who rapidly moved onward from the serpentine beauty of organic drawing as they sought a new aesthetic and design philosophy to address the changing social, economic, and cultural conditions at the turn of a century.

Frank Lloyd Wright and the Glasgow School

During the final years of the nineteenth century, the work of the American architect Frank Lloyd Wright (1867–1959) was becoming known to European artists and designers. Undoubtedly, he was an inspiration for the designers evolving from curvilinear Art Nouveau toward a rectilinear approach to spatial organization. In 1893, Wright began his independent practice. He rejected historicism in favor of a philosophy of "organic architecture," with "the reality of the building" existing not in the design of the façade but in dynamic interior spaces where people lived and worked. Wright defined organic design as having *entity,* "something in which the part is to the whole as the whole is to the part, and which is all devoted to a purpose.... It seeks that completeness in idea in execution which is absolutely *true* to method, *true* to purpose, *true* to character...."

Wright saw *space* as the essence of design, and this emphasis was the wellspring of his profound influence upon all areas of twentieth-century design. He looked to Japanese architecture and design for a model of harmonious proportion and visual poetry; in pre-Columbian architecture and art, he found lively ornament restrained by a mathematical repetition of horizontal and vertical spatial divisions. Wright's repetition of rectangular zones and use of asymmetrical spatial organization were adopted by other designers. In addition to architecture, his design interests included furniture, graphics, fabrics, wallpapers, and stained-glass windows (see Fig. 18-1). At the turn of the century, he was operating at the forefront of the emerging modern movement.

As a young man, Wright operated a basement printing press with a close friend. This experience taught him to incorporate white or blank space as an element in his designs, to establish and work within parameters, and to combine varied materials into a unified whole. During his long career, Wright periodically turned his

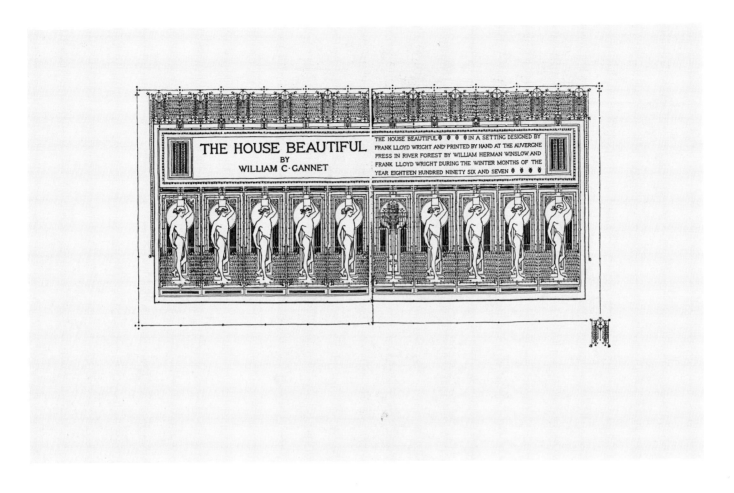

15-1. Frank Lloyd Wright, title page for *The House Beautiful,* 1896–1897. An underlying geometric structure imposed a strong order upon the intricacy of Wright's textural designs.

hand to graphic design. During the winter of 1896–1897, Wright collaborated with William H. Winslow in the production of *The House Beautiful* (Fig. 15-1) by William C. Gannet. Only ninety copies of this extraordinary book were printed, on a handpress using handmade paper at the Auvergne Press. Wright's border designs were executed in a fragile freehand line in a lacy pattern of stylized plant forms.

The Studio and its reproductions of work by Beardsley and Toorop had a strong influence on a group of young Scottish artists who became friends at the Glasgow School of Art in the early 1890s. Headmaster Francis H. Newbery pointed out affinities between the work of two architectural apprentices taking evening classes— Charles Rennie Mackintosh (1868–1928) and J. Herbert McNair (1868–1955)— and the work of two day students—sisters Margaret (1865–1933) and Frances Macdonald (1874–1921). The four students began to collaborate and were soon christened *The Four*. Artistic collaboration and friendship led to matrimony, for in 1899 McNair married Frances Macdonald. The following year, Mackintosh and Margaret Macdonald were wed.

These young collaborators, also known as the Glasgow School, developed a unique style of lyrical originality and symbolic complexity. They innovated a more geometric composition by tempering floral and curvilinear elements with strong rectilinear structure. Their work ranged from melancholy expressions to elegant simplified designs. The Macdonald sisters held strong religious beliefs and embraced symbolist and mystical ideas. The confluence of architectural structure with the sisters' world of fantasy and dreams produced an unprecedented transcendental style that has been variously described as feminine, a fairyland fantasy, and a melancholy disquietude.

Graphic designs by The Four are distinguished by symbolic imagery (Fig. 15-2) and stylized form. Bold, simple lines define flat planes of color. Plate 33, an 1895 poster for the Glasgow Institute of the Fine Arts designed by Margaret and

The Genesis of Twentieth-Century Design

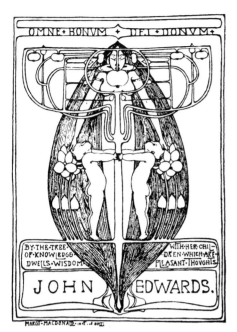

15-2. Margaret Macdonald, bookplate design, 1896. Reproduced in *Ver Sacrum* in 1901 as part of an article on the Glasgow group, this design depicts Wisdom protecting her children within the leaflike shelter of her hair before a symbolic tree of knowledge, whose linear structure is based on Macdonald's metalwork.

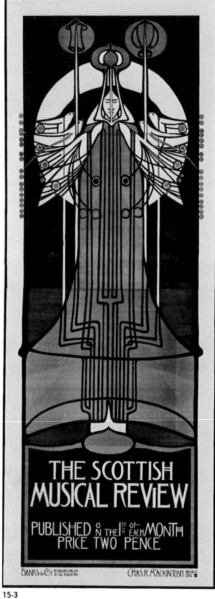

15-3

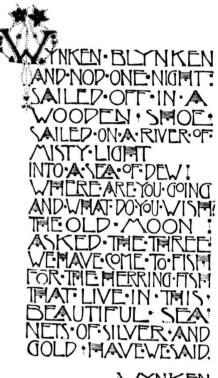

15-4

15-3. Charles Rennie Mackintosh, poster for The Scottish Musical Review, 1896. In this towering image that rises 2.46 meters (over eight feet) above the spectator, complex overlapping planes are unified by areas of flat color. The white ring and birds around the figure create a strong focal point.

15-4. Jessie Marion King, lettering for a nursery rhyme, 1898. The proportions, vertical stress created by the high center stroke of the *E* and *F,* multiple horizontal strokes on the *A* and *H,* and multiple dots reflect King's Glasgow schooling.

Frances Macdonald in collaboration with J. Herbert McNair, demonstrates the rising verticality and integration of flowing curves with rectangular structure that are hallmarks of their mature style. The symbolic figures have been assigned both religious and romantic interpretations. Abstract interpretations of the human figure, such as Mackintosh's Scottish Musical Review poster (Fig. 15-3), had not been seen in Scotland before, and provoked outrage among many observers. But the editor of *The Studio* was so impressed that he visited Glasgow and published two articles in 1897. He reminded *Studio* readers "that the purpose of a poster is to attract notice, and the mildest eccentricity would not be out of place provided it aroused curiosity and so riveted the attention of passers-by. . . . There is so much decorative method in his perversion of humanity that despite all the ridicule and abuse it has excited, it is possible to defend his treatment." German and Austrian artists learned of Glasgow's counter-movement to mainstream Art Nouveau through these articles. The Four were celebrated on the continent, particularly in Vienna, but often ignored in the British Isles. In 1896, the organizers at the annual Arts and Crafts exhibition in London invited them to participate. So dismayed were the hosts, however, that no further invitations were extended.

Mackintosh made notable contributions to the new century's architecture, and major accomplishments were realized in the design of objects, chairs, and interiors as total environments. The Four pioneered interior designs with white walls bathed in light and furnished with a few carefully placed pieces, in contrast to the prevailingly complex interiors of the time. Mackintosh's main design theme is rising vertical lines, often with subtle curves at the ends to temper their junction with the horizontals. Tall slivers of rectangles and the counterpoint of right angles against ovals, circles, and arcs characterize his work. In his furniture, simple structure is accented with delicate decorative ornaments. In the interior designs, every small detail was carefully designed to be visually compatible with the whole. The Four, in their work and their influence on the continent, became important transitions to the aesthetic of the twentieth century.

Among their followers who developed personal styles inspired by the Glasgow School, Jessie Marion King (1876–1949) developed a medieval, fairy style of illustration with stylized lettering (Fig. 15-4), and Annie French (1872–1965) became a prominent London book illustrator. After working in architectural offices and serving as assistant art director for *Black and White* magazine in London, Talwin Morris (1865–1911) was selected in 1893 to become art director of the Glasgow publishing firm of Blackie's after he answered their want ad in the *London Times*. Shortly after moving to Glasgow, Morris established contact with The Four. Even though he was never formally connected to the Glasgow School of Art as a teacher or student, Morris was influenced by their ideas. Blackie's was a volume printer of large editions of popular books for the mass market, including novels, reprints, and encyclopedias, which provided Morris with a forum for applying the geometric spatial division and lyrical organic forms of the Glasgow group to mass communications.

Most of the editions Morris designed were economically printed. He often developed formats for series that could be used over and over again with subtle variations (Figs. 15-5 through 15-7). The sheer volume of his work was a major factor in introducing the English public to Art Nouveau and preparing it to accept the emerging ideas and visual forms of modern architecture and design.

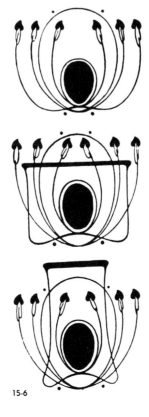

DRAMATIS PERSONÆ

KING OF FRANCE.
DUKE OF FLORENCE.
BERTRAM, Count of Rousillon.
LAFEU, an old Lord at the French court.
PAROLLES, a Follower of Bertram.
First Lord DUMAINE, } Brothers and Captains in the Florentine army.
Second Lord DUMAINE,
RINALDO, a Steward, } Servants to the Count of Rousillon.
LAVACHE, a Clown,
COUNTESS OF ROUSILLON, Mother to Bertram.
HELENA DE NARBON, a Gentlewoman.
WIDOW CAPULET.
DIANA, Daughter to the Widow.
VIOLENTA, } Neighbours to the Widow.
MARIANA,
&c.

15-7

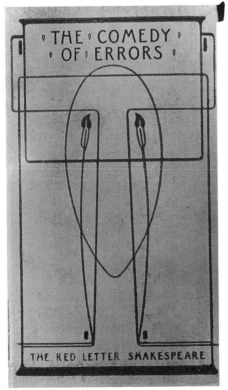

15-5

15-6

15-5. Talwin Morris, binding for *The Comedy of Errors,* c. 1908. Printed in muted green and red on off-white fabric, the standard format for the Red Letter Shakespeare series is typical of the subtle graphic lyricism Morris achieved in economical commercial editions.

15-6. Talwin Morris, page ornaments from the Red Letter Shakespeare series, c. 1908. The name for this small, modestly priced set of Shakespearean plays derives from the two-color printing with the characters' names in red. Between the introduction and the play, each volume had a page with a graceful ornament, printed in black with a red oval, from a series by Morris.

15-7. Talwin Morris, page from *All's Well That Ends Well,* c. 1908. The standard format for the character list in the Red Letter Shakespeare series has this rigorous linear structure printed in red.

The Vienna Secession

In Austria, *Sezessionstil,* or the Vienna Secession, came into being on 3 April 1897, when the younger members of the Künstlerhaus, the Viennese Creative Artists' Association, resigned in stormy protest. Technically, the refusal to allow foreign artists to participate in Künstlerhaus exhibitions was a main issue, but the clash between tradition and new ideas emanating from France, England, and Germany lay at the heart of the conflict, and the young artists wanted to exhibit more frequently. Painter Gustav Klimt (1862–1918) was the guiding spirit who led the revolt; architects Joseph Maria Olbrich (1867–1908) and Josef Hoffmann (1870–1956) and artist-designer Koloman Moser (1868–1918) were key members. Like the Glasgow School from which it drew inspiration, the Vienna Secession became a counter-movement to the floral Art Nouveau that flourished in France and Germany.

Benchmark posters for the Vienna Secession's exhibitions demonstrate the group's rapid evolution from the illustrative allegorical style of Symbolist painting (Fig. 15-8) to a French-inspired floral style (Fig. 15-9) to the mature Vienna Secession style (Pl. 34), which drew inspiration from the Glasgow School. (Compare, for instance, Plate 33 and Figure 15-3 with Plate 34.) Figure 15-8 is the first Vienna Secession exhibition poster. Klimt called upon Greek mythology to show Athena, goddess of the arts, watching Theseus deliver the death blow to the Minotaur. This is an allegory of the struggle between the Secession and the Künstlerhaus. The trees were overprinted later after the Viennese police were outraged by the male nude. This controversy fueled public interest in the artists' revolt.

15-8. Gustav Klimt, poster for the first Vienna Secession exhibition, 1898. The large open space in the center is unprecedented in western graphic design.

15-9. Koloman Moser, Fifth Vienna Secession exhibition poster, 1899. The figure is metallic gold-bronze, and the background is olive green. Yellow-tone paper forms the contour lines for a stunning visual effect.

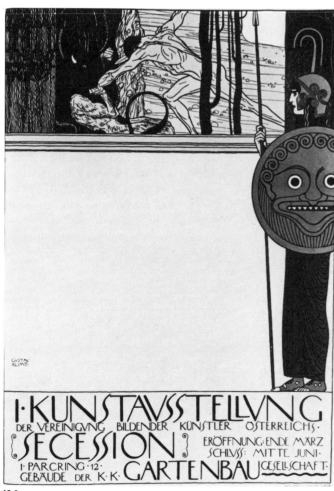

15-8

15-9

I. Jahrg. Heft 1.

Einzelpreis 2 Kronen.

UER·SACRUM

ORGAN·DER
UEREINIGUNG
BILDENDER
KUENSTLER
ÖSTERREICHS·

JANUAR
·1898·

JAEHRLICH·12·HEFTE
IM·ABONNEMENT·6FI=10M·

Alle Rechte vorbehalten.

Verlag Gerlach & Schenk, Wien, VI/1.

15-10. Alfred Roller, cover design for *Ver Sacrum*, initial issue, 1898. Roller used an illustration of a tree whose growth has destroyed its pot, allowing it to take root in firmer soil, to symbolize the Secession.

Figure 15-9, by Moser, demonstrates how quickly the central idealized figures and swooping floral forms of French Art Nouveau were absorbed. A major difference is the Secession artists' love of clean, simple, sans serif lettering, ranging from flat, blocky slabs to fluidly calligraphic forms. For a brief period as the century turned, Vienna became the center for further creative innovation in the final blossoming of Art Nouveau. When Vienna Secession artists rejected the French floral style, they turned toward flat shapes and greater simplicity. Design and craft became increasingly important as this metamorphosis culminated in an emphasis on geometric patterning and modular design construction. The resulting design language used squares, rectangles, and circles in repetition and combination. Decoration and the application of ornament depended on similar elements used in parallel, nonrhythmic sequence. Their geometry was not mechanical and rigid, but subtly organic.

The most beautiful of turn-of-the-century magazines was the Vienna Secession's elegant *Ver Sacrum* (*Sacred Spring*), published from 1898 until 1903. *Ver Sacrum* was more a design laboratory than a magazine. A continuously changing editorial staff, design responsibility handled by a rotating committee of artists, and unpaid contributions of art and design were all focused upon experimentation and graphic excellence. In 1900, there were only three hundred subscribers and a press run of six hundred copies, but work on *Ver Sacrum* enabled the designers to develop innovative graphic design as they explored the merger of text, illustration, and ornament into a lively unity. It had an unusual square format: The 1898–1899 issues were 28 by 28.5 centimeters (11 by 11¼ inches), and the 1900–1903 issues were reduced to 23 by 24.5 centimeters (9 by 9¾ inches). Secession artists loved to produce vigorous linear art, and *Ver Sacrum* covers often combined hand lettering with bold line drawing (Figs. 15-10 through 15-12) printed in color on a colored

15-11. Alfred Roller, cover for *Ver Sacrum*, 1898. A stipple drawing of leaves becomes a frame for the lettering, which sits in a square that gives the impression of a collage element.

15-12. Koloman Moser, cover for *Ver Sacrum*, 1899. A stencil-effect technique for creating images has an affinity, in the reduction of the subject to black-and-white planes, with high-contrast photography.

15-13. Josef Hoffmann, headpiece from the premiere issue of *Ver Sacrum,* 1898. Berries, drawn in the free contour style favored by many Secession artists, flow around a plaque that proclaims "Association of Visual Artists of Austria. Secession."

15-14. Joseph Olbrich, frame for *Ver Sacrum* article title, 1899. The fluid repetition of forms and symmetry of this decorative botanical frame, with its dense black color, bring lively contrast to the typographic page.

background. Decorative ornaments, borders, headpieces (Figs. 15-13 and 15-14), and tailpieces were used generously, but the overall page layouts (Fig. 15-15) were clean and crisp, due to ample margins and careful horizontal and vertical alignment of elements into a unified whole.

Ver Sacrum's unprecedented use of white space in its page layout, sleek-coated stock, and unusual production methods gave an aura of quality. Color plates were tipped in, and fifty-five original etchings and lithographs as well as 216 original woodcuts were bound into the issues during *Ver Sacrum's* six years of publication. Sometimes signatures were printed in color combinations, including muted brown and blue-gray, blue and green, brown with red-orange, and chocolate with gold. When signatures were bound together, four colors, instead of two, appeared on the double spreads. The Vienna Secession artists did not hesitate to experiment: A poem was printed in metallic gold ink on translucent paper; a photograph of an interior was printed in scarlet ink; and for one issue, a linear design by Koloman Moser was embossed on silky smooth, coated white stock in what may have been the first white-on-white embossed graphic design.

Design aesthetics were so important that advertisers were required to commission their advertising designs (Fig. 15-16) from the artists and designers contributing to each issue to ensure a visual design unity. The exceptional linear and geometric design elements gracing *Ver Sacrum's* pages became an important design resource as the Vienna Secession style evolved.

Editorial content included articles about artists and their work, poems contributed by leading writers of the day (Figs. 15-17 and 15-18), and an illustrated monthly calendar (Fig. 15-19). Critical essays were published, including a famous article entitled "Potemkin City" by the polemic Austrian architect Adolf Loos (1870–1933). Because Viennese building façades were cast-concrete fronts mimicking Renaissance and Baroque palaces, Loos accused Vienna of being like the artificial towns of canvas and pasteboard erected in the Ukraine to deceive the Russian Empress Catherine. All areas of design were challenged by Loos, whose other writings roundly condemned both historicism and *Sezessionstil* as he called for a functional simplicity that banished "useless decoration" in any form. Standing alone at the turn of the century, Loos blasted the nineteenth-century love of decoration and abhorrence of empty spaces. To him, "organic" meant not curvilinear but the use of

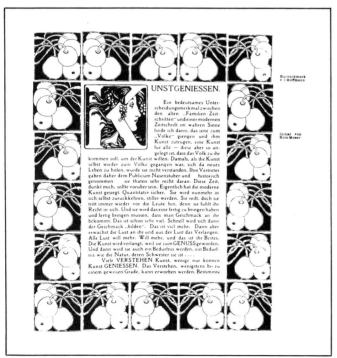

In welken Kronen
wiegt sich der Herbst

Purpurne Blatter
schweben, fallen.

Noch einmal,
mude,
scheint die Sonne.

Am stillen See
sitz ich und starre
in ein gespiegeltes Paradies.

15-17

Prolog.

Seit der alte Papa Wieland
seine liederlichen Musen
abenteuerlich ersuchte,
ihm den Hippogryph zu satteln,
hat schon mancher deutsche Dichter
diesen Tric ihm nachgeäfft.

In das süsse blaue Wunder
unsrer Jungfer Poesie
stippte altklug Mutter Prosa
die didaktisch lange Nase,
und die Töchter des Olympiers
degradirt nun frech zu Jockeys
jeder Schlingel, dem erbärmlich
auf der schlechtgeleimten Leier
nur ein dünnes Därmchen schnurrt.

Ich = bin leider auch nur Mensch.

Dumpf in meine Wiegenlieder
brandete von fern die Ostsee,
und wir Deutschen sind entweder
Dichter oder Philosophen.

Ich bin Dichter. Versefex.

Versefex und degradir drum
jene schlanken Marmorschönen
mit den weltverliebten Herzen
heute selbst zum Stallknechtsdienst.

He. Euterpe. raus den Schinder!
Wiehernd baumt er sich ins Licht.

Sie. Urania' erstmal. bitte.
dort den Strohhalm aus dem Schwanz

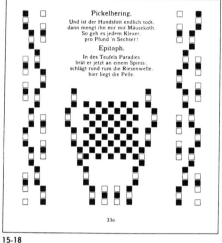

Pickelhering.

Und ist der Hundsfott endlich todt,
dann mengt ihn mir mit Mäusekoth.
So geh es jedem Klexer.
pro Pfund 'n Sechser!

Epitaph.

In des Teufels Paradies
brät er jetzt an einem Spiess:
schlägt rund rum die Riesenwelle.
hier liegt die Pelle.

33o

15-18

15-15. Josef Hoffmann (border) and Koloman Moser (initial), page from *Ver Sacrum,* 1898. Hoffmann's modular berry motif and Moser's figurative initial combine to produce an exquisitely beautiful page.

15-16. Alfred Roller, Koloman Moser, and Frederick Koenig, inside front-cover advertisements for *Ver Sacrum,* 1899. Each ad and the makeup of the whole page are carefully designed to avoid the graphic clutter and clash usually present when small ads are clustered together.

15-17. Adolf Bohm, page from *Ver Sacrum,* 1898. The lyrical contours of trees reflected on a lake provide an appropriate environment for a poem about autumn trees.

15-18. Koloman Moser, pages from *Ver Sacrum,* 1901. As the Prologue and Epitaph demonstrate, Arno Holz's lengthy poem was bracketed with black-and-white patterns of squares, which changed on each page.

human needs as a standard for measuring utilitarian form. His 1906 Villa Karma, built in Switzerland, forecast the simple geometric forms of the 1920s avant-garde.

While the personal monograms by Secession artists convey a communal aesthetic (Fig. 15-20), various members specialized in one or more disciplines: architecture, crafts, graphic design, interior design, painting, printmaking, and sculpture. Moser played a major role in defining the approach to graphic design. His Fromme's calendar poster (Fig. 15-21) moved toward simplified two-dimensional space. Plate 34, Moser's 1902 poster for the thirteenth Vienna Secession exhibition, is a masterpiece of the mature Vienna Secession style. Mathematical patterns of squares and rectangles contrast with the circular forms of the figures and letterforms. This evolution toward elemental geometric form in design was diagrammed by Walter Crane in his book *Line and Form* (Fig. 15-22). Alfred Roller (1864–1935) also made significant innovations in graphic design, with a masterly control of complex line, tone, and form (Fig. 15-23). A set designer and scene painter for theater, Roller's principal work as a graphic designer and illustrator was for *Ver Sacrum* and Secession exhibition posters. Cubism and Art Deco are anticipated in his 1902 poster for the fourteenth Vienna Secession exhibition (Pl. 35), and his poster for the sixteenth Vienna Secession exhibition, later that same year (Fig. 15-24), reduced letterforms to curved-corner rectangles with slashing white curved lines applied to define each character. Roller was willing to sacrifice legibility in order to achieve an unprecedented textural density. Berthold Löffler (1874–1960) also anticipated later developments with his graphic language of thick contours and stylized geometric features. Images in his posters and illustrations became elemental significations rather than depictions (Fig. 15-25).

The Genesis of Twentieth-Century Design

15-19

A D O L F   B Ö H M GUSTAV KLIMT J. M. AUCHENTALLER FERDINAND ANDRI O. SCHIMKOWITZ ERNST STÖHR

JOSEF HOFFMANN LEOPOLD BAUER KOLOMAN MOSER ALFRED ROLLER RUDOLF BACHER EMIL ORLIK

15-20

15-19. Alfred Roller (designer) and Karl Müller (illustrator), *Ver Sacrum* calendar for October 1903. Roller's border has a fairyland exuberance, and the numbers and letterforms are squeezed into rectangles.

15-20. Various designers, personal monograms, 1902. These monograms, designed by members of the Vienna Secession, were included in the catalogue of a 1902 exhibition.

15-21. Koloman Moser, poster advertising Fromme's calendar, 1899. Used by the client with color changes for fifteen years, Moser's design depicts a goddess of personal destiny holding a snake ring and hourglass, symbols for the eternal circle of life and the passing of time.

15-22. Walter Crane, diagram from *Line and Form,* 1900. In retrospect, it almost seems that Crane, in his widely read book, was predicting the evolution of form toward a geometric purity achieved by the Vienna Secession and the post-Cubism avant-garde.

15-21

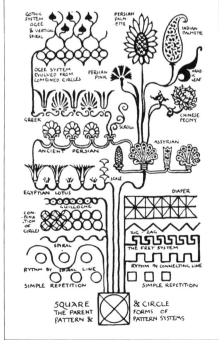

15-22

15-23. Alfred Roller, design for a pocket-watch cover, 1900. Night and day are symbolized by two snails. This drawing almost takes on an oriental yin-yang (positive and negative principles in nature) quality.

15-24. Alfred Roller, poster for the sixteenth Vienna Secession exhibition, 1902. By reducing letterforms to curved-corner rectangles with slashing white curves to define each character, Roller sacrificed legibility in favor of unprecedented textural density.

15-25. Berthold Löffler, poster for a theater and cabaret, c. 1907. Masklike faces glow in intense flat yellow, white, and red against a black background.

15-26. The registered trademark and monogram applied to products of the Vienna Workshops demonstrate the harmony of proportion, lyrical geometry, and clarity of form that characterize its designs.

15-27. Josef Hoffmann, *Wiener Werkstätte* exhibition poster, 1905. A repetitive blue geometric pattern was created by a hand-stencil technique after the lettering and two lower rectangles were printed by lithography. This lettering was combined with other patterns in an advertisement and other posters.

By the turn of the century, both Koloman Moser and Josef Hoffmann had been appointed to the faculty of the Vienna School for Applied Art. Their ideas about clean, geometric design, formed when they stripped the Glasgow influence of its virgins, symbolic roses, and mystical overtones, captured the imagination of their students. With financing from the industrialist Fritz Wärndorfer, Hoffmann and Moser launched the *Wiener Werkstätte* ("Vienna Workshops") in 1903 (Figs. 15-26 and 15-27). An outgrowth of *Sezessionstil,* this spiritual continuum of William Morris's workshops sought a close union of pure and applied arts in the design of lamps, fabrics, and similar objects for everyday use, including books, greeting cards, and other printed matter (Fig. 15-28). Originally formed to produce designs by Moser and Hoffmann, the Vienna Workshops flourished, and many other collaborators participated. Several buildings were executed as total works of art. The

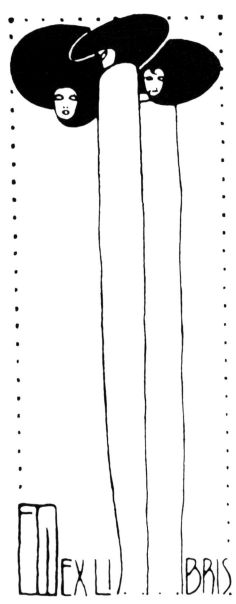

15-28. Josef Hoffmann, bookplate design, 1903. In a large series of figure studies, Hoffmann reduced the image to elongated contours and simple shapes signifying hair or hats.

goal was to offer an alternative to poorly designed, mass-produced articles and trite historicism. Function, honesty to materials, and harmonious proportion were important concerns; decoration was used only when it served these goals and did not violate them. Master carpenters, bookbinders, metalsmiths, and leather workers were employed to work with the designers in the effort to elevate crafts to the standards of fine arts. Moser left the Vienna Workshops in 1907, and his death at age fifty in 1918 cut short the career of a major design innovator.

After 1910, the creative momentum in Vienna declined. But the gulf between nineteenth-century ornament and Art Nouveau on the one hand and the rational functionalism and geometric formalism of the twentieth century on the other had been bridged. The Vienna Workshops survived the economic chaos of World War I and flourished until the Depression Era, when financial difficulties forced their closing in 1932.

Peter Behrens and the new objectivity

During the first decade of the twentieth century, the German artist, architect, and designer Peter Behrens played a major role in charting a course for design in the new century. He sought typographic reform and was an early advocate of sans serif typography. A grid system was used to structure space in his graphic designs. He has been designated "the first industrial designer" in recognition of his designs for such manufactured products as street lamps and teapots. His work for the Allgemeine Elektrizitäts Gesellschaft, or AEG, is considered to be the first comprehensive visual-identification program. In architecture, his early buildings pioneered non-load-bearing glass curtainwalls spanning the spaces between support girders.

Behrens was orphaned at age fourteen. The substantial inheritance from his father's estate provided financial autonomy, which assisted in the evolution of his work. He chose art for his career and studied in Hamburg, then moved to Munich, where a renaissance in German arts and crafts was beginning. His early paintings were of poor people and the industrial landscape, after which he abandoned social realism and embraced the 1890s German *Jugendstil* movement discussed in Chapter 14 (see Figs. 14-59 through 14-61).

In 1900, the Grand Duke of Hessen, who sought to "fuse art and life together," established a new Darmstadt artist's colony, hoping to encourage cultural development and economic growth in light manufacturing, such as furniture and ceramics. The colony's seven artists, including Behrens and Vienna Secession architect Joseph Olbrich, all had experience in the applied arts. Each was granted land to build a home, and Behrens designed his own house and all its furnishings, from furniture to cutlery and china. This experiment in "total design," with unity of diverse parts, later proved invaluable.

German art critics of the period were interested in the relationship of art and design forms to social, technical, and cultural conditions. Behrens was concerned about these issues and believed that after architecture, typography provided "the most characteristic picture of a period, and the strongest testimonial of the spiritual progress" and "development of a people." His typographic experiments were a deliberate attempt to express the spirit of the new era. In 1900, Behrens set his twenty-five-page booklet, *Celebration of Life and Art: A Consideration of the Theater as the Highest Symbol of a Culture,* in sans serif type (Fig. 15-29). German typographic historian Hans Loubier suggested that this booklet may be the first use of sans serif type as running book text. Furthermore, all-capital sans serif type is used in an unprecedented way on the title and dedication pages (Fig. 15-30). The following year, Behrens explored formal geometric design motifs with modular sans serif characters based on a square (Fig. 15-31). The popularity of sans serif types in the twentieth century vindicated Behrens's experiments.

Behrens was not alone in his interest in sans serif typography at the turn of the century. The Berthold Foundry designed a "family" of ten sans serifs, which were variations upon one original font. This Akzidenz Grotesk (called *Standard* in the United States) type family (Fig. 15-32) had a major influence upon twentieth-

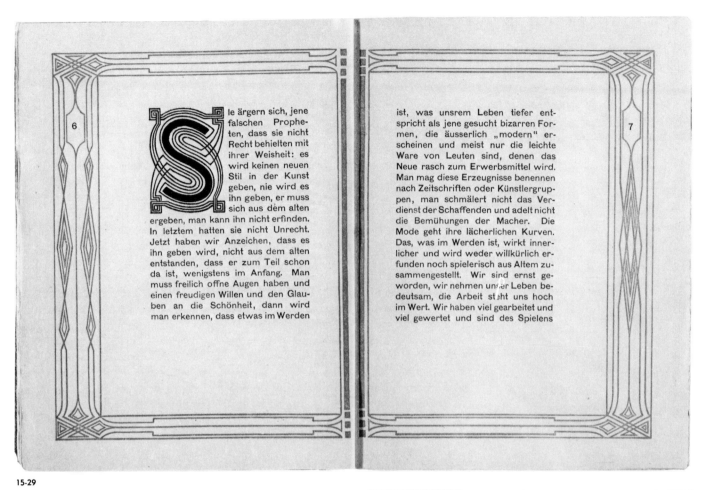

Sie ärgern sich, jene falschen Propheten, dass sie nicht Recht behielten mit ihrer Weisheit: es wird keinen neuen Stil in der Kunst geben, nie wird es ihn geben, er muss sich aus dem alten ergeben, man kann ihn nicht erfinden. In letztem hatten sie nicht Unrecht. Jetzt haben wir Anzeichen, dass es ihn geben wird, nicht aus dem alten entstanden, dass er zum Teil schon da ist, wenigstens im Anfang. Man muss freilich offne Augen haben und einen freudigen Willen und den Glauben an die Schönheit, dann wird man erkennen, dass etwas im Werden

ist, was unsrem Leben tiefer entspricht als jene gesucht bizarren Formen, die äusserlich „modern" erscheinen und meist nur die leichte Ware von Leuten sind, denen das Neue rasch zum Erwerbsmittel wird. Man mag diese Erzeugnisse benennen nach Zeitschriften oder Künstlergruppen, man schmälert nicht das Verdienst der Schaffenden und adelt nicht die Bemühungen der Macher. Die Mode geht ihre lächerlichen Kurven. Das, was im Werden ist, wirkt innerlicher und wird weder willkürlich erfunden noch spielerisch aus Altem zusammengestellt. Wir sind ernst geworden, wir nehmen unser Leben bedeutsam, die Arbeit steht uns hoch im Wert. Wir haben viel gearbeitet und viel gewertet und sind des Spielens

15-29

15-30

15-29. Peter Behrens, text pages for *Celebration of Life and Art: A Consideration of the Theater as the Highest Symbol of a Culture,* 1900. Blue-gray borders and red initials surrounded by rust-colored decoration frame the unprecedented sans serif running text.

15-30. Peter Behrens, title and dedication pages for *Celebration of Life and Art . . . ,* 1900. A sharp angularity characterizes the title page (left), framed by caryatids. On the right, a dedication to the Darmstadt artist's colony is ornamented with controlled curvilinear rhythms.

15-31. Peter Behrens, cover for *Dokumente des Modernen Kunstgewerbes . . .* ("Documents of Modern Applied Arts . . ."), 1901. This decorative geometric design and sans serif lettering based on a square are prophetic of Art Deco design of the 1920s and 1930s.

The Genesis of Twentieth-Century Design

ABCDEFGHIJKLMNOPQRSTUVWXYZ
abcdefghijklmnopqrstuvwxyz

ABCDEFGHIJKLMNOPQRSTUVWXYZ
abcdefghijklmnopqrstuvwxyz

ABCDEFGHIJKLMNOPQRSTUVWXYZ
abcdefghijklmnopqrstuvwxyz

ABCDEFGHIJKLMNOPQRSTUVWX
abcdefghijklmnopqrstuvwxyz

15-32. Berthold Foundry, Akzidenz Grotesk typefaces, 1898–1906. An elegant system of weight contrast is achieved in these pioneering letterforms.

century typography. In addition to the four weights shown in Figure 15-32, Berthold released three expanded and three condensed versions. Akzidenz Grotesk permitted compositors to achieve contrast and emphasis within one family of typefaces. It was a major step in the evolution of the unified and systematized type family. The craftsmen who designed Akzidenz Grotesk achieved a remarkable harmony and clarity, and inspired sans serif typefaces of the post–World War II era.

A sense of urgency existed in the German art and design community. A new century was at hand, and the need to create new forms for a new era weighed heavily upon them. Typographic reform was one of Behrens's major interests. After struggling with a conservative typefounder in an effort to develop a new typeface, Behrens contacted thirty-two-year-old Dr. Karl Klingspor (b. 1868) of the Klingspor Foundry. He agreed to manufacture and release Behrens's first typeface, Behrensschrift (Fig. 15-33), in 1901. Klingspor had just enjoyed unexpected success from the wildly popular Eckmannschrift (Fig. 15-33; see also Fig. 14-58). Behrensschrift was an attempt to reduce any "poetic flourish" that would mark the forms as the work of an individual hand and thereby reduce their universal character. Behrensschrift looks very calligraphic to the late-twentieth-century eye viewing it over sixty years after Paul Renner designed the geometrically constructed Futura (see Figs. 19-37 and 19-38). Relative to ornate Victorian, Art Nouveau, and medieval typefaces dominating new type design at the time, Behrens standardized the strokes used to construct his letterforms. He consciously sought to innovate a new typographic image for the new century and to create a uniquely German type by combining the heavy condensed feeling of black letter, the letter proportions of roman inscriptions, and his standardized letterform construction. Horizontals and verticals are emphasized and diagonals completely eliminated, replaced by curved strokes in letters such as *W* and *V*. Some typographic authorities were outraged by Behrensschrift, but its feather-stroke serifs and clarity, in stunning contrast

15-33. Typefaces released by the Klingspor Type Foundry. Top to bottom: Otto Eckmann's Eckmannschrift, 1900; Peter Behrens's Behrensschrift, an attempt to innovate new typographic forms for the new era, 1901; Behrens-Kursiv, Behrens's italic version of Behrensschrift, 1907; Behrens-Antiqua, his attempt to recapture the clarity and authority of Roman inscriptions, 1908; and Behrens-Medieval, his personal interpretation of Renaissance forms, 1913.

15-34

to the dense black-letter and ornate Art Nouveau typefaces used extensively in Germany at the time, made it a resounding success for both book (Fig. 15-34) and job-printing typography. In the promotional booklet for Behrensschrift, Behrens compared the act of reading text type to "watching a bird's flight or the gallop of a horse. Both seem graceful and pleasing, but the viewer does not observe details of their form or movement. Only the rhythm of the lines is seen by the viewer, and the same is true of a typeface."

In 1903, Behrens moved to Düsseldorf to become director of the Düsseldorf School of Arts and Crafts. Innovative preparatory courses preceded study in specific disciplines, such as architectural, graphic, or interior design. Behrens's purpose was to go back to the fundamental intellectual principles of all form-creating work, allowing the principles of form making to be rooted in the artistically spontaneous, in the inner laws of perception, rather than directly in the mechanical aspects of the work. Students drew and painted natural forms in different media, then made analytical studies to explore linear movement, pattern, and geometric structure. These introductory courses were precursors for the Bauhaus Preliminary Course, where two of Behrens's apprentices, Walter Gropius and Ludwig Mies van der Rohe, served as directors.

A dramatic transformation occurred in Behrens's work in 1904, after the Dutch architect J. L. Mathieu Lauweriks (1864–1932) joined the Düsseldorf faculty. Lauweriks was fascinated by geometric form and had developed an approach to teaching design based on geometric composition. His grids began with a square circumscribed around a circle; numerous permutations then could be made by subdividing and duplicating this basic structure (Fig. 15-35). The geometric patterns

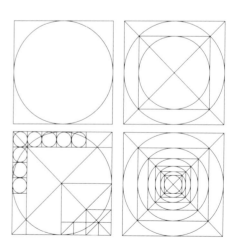

15-34. Peter Behrens, pages from *Manfred* by Georg Fuchs, 1903. Behrensschrift is used systematically with headpieces, tailpieces, and folios.

15-35. These diagrams illustrate Dutch architect J. L. M. Lauweriks's compositional theory elaborating grid systems from a square circumscribed around a circle.

The Genesis of Twentieth-Century Design

15-36. Peter Behrens, Anchor Linoleum exhibition pavilion, 1906. Classical forms and proportions are combined with mathematically derived geometric structure and pattern in a search for a twentieth-century language of form.

thus developed could be used to determine proportions, dimensions, and spatial divisions in the design of everything from chairs to buildings (Fig. 15-36) and graphics (Fig. 15-37). Behrens's application of this theory proved catalytic in pushing twentieth-century architecture and design toward rational geometry as an underlying system for visual organization. His work from this period is part of the tentative beginnings of constructivism in graphic design, where realistic or even stylized depictions are replaced by architectural and geometric structure. Often Behrens used square formats, but more frequently he used rectangles in ratios such as 1 square wide by 1.5 or 2 squares high.

The major event in Behrens's career occurred in 1907, when Emil Rathenau, director of the AEG, appointed Behrens as AEG artistic advisor. Rathenau had purchased European manufacturing rights to Thomas A. Edison's patents in 1883, and the AEG had grown into one of the world's largest manufacturing concerns. Rathenau, a visionary industrialist, sensed the need for a unified visual character to the company's products, environments, and communications. In 1907, the electrical industry was high technology: Electric teakettles were seen as being as advanced as digital electronics are today. As design advisor to the AEG, Behrens began to focus upon the design needs of industry, with design responsibility ranging from large buildings to stationery and electric fans.

The year 1907 also marked the founding in Munich of the Deutscher Werkbund (German Association of Craftsmen), which advocated a "marriage of art with technology." Behrens played a major role in this first organization created to inspire quality design in manufactured goods and architecture. The group's leaders, including Hermann Muthesius, Henry van de Velde, and Behrens, were influenced by William Morris and the English Arts and Crafts Movement, but with significant differences: While Morris was repulsed by the products of the machine age and advocated a return to medieval craftsmanship in romantic protest against the industrial revolution, the Werkbund recognized the value of machines and advocated design as a way to give form and meaning to all machine-made things, including buildings.

With visionary zeal they advanced a philosophy of *Gesamkultur,* which means a new universal culture existing in a totally reformed man-made environment. Design was seen as the engine that could propel society forward to achieve *Gesamkultur.* Soon after it formed, the Werkbund split into two factions. One, headed by

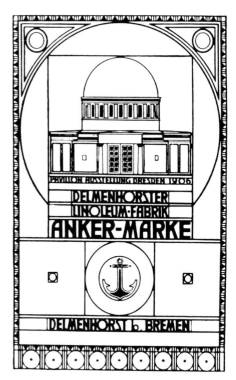

15-37. Peter Behrens, poster for the Anchor Linoleum exhibition pavilion, 1906. Here, Lauweriks's grid theory is applied to graphic design.

15-38. Peter Behrens, AEG trademark, 1907. The new mark was applied to buildings, stationery, products, and graphics in a consistent and redundant manner.

Muthesius, argued for the maximum use of mechanical manufacturing and standardization of design for industrial efficiency. They believed form should be determined solely by function, and wanted to eliminate all ornament. Muthesius saw simplicity and exactness as being both a functional demand of machine manufacture and a symbolic aspect of twentieth-century industrial efficiency and power. A unity of artists and craftsmen with industry, he believed, could elevate the functional and aesthetic qualities of mass production, particularly in low-cost consumer products. The other faction, led by van de Velde, argued for the primacy of individual artistic expression. Behrens attempted to mediate the two extremes, but his work for AEG showed strong tendencies toward standardization. A design philosophy is merely an idle vision until someone creates artifacts that make it a real force in the world, and Werkbund members consciously sought a new design language to realize their goals. Behrens's work for AEG became an early manifestation of Werkbund ideals, and he was sometimes called "Mr. Werkbund."

Behrens's AEG designs represent a synthesis of two seemingly contradictory concepts: Neo-Classicism and *sachlichkeit*. His Neo-Classicism grew from a careful study of art and design from ancient Greece and Rome. Rather than merely copying the stylistic aspects of their work, he found a formal language of harmony and proportion needed to achieve a unity of the parts to the whole. *Sachlichkeit* (loosely translated as common-sense objectivity) was a pragmatic emphasis upon technology, manufacturing processes, and function, in which artistic conceits and questions of style were subordinate to purpose. In concert, these two concepts guided Behrens in his quest for forms to achieve *Gesamkultur*.

An electric lamp poster (Pl. 36) designed by Behrens for AEG in 1907 demonstrates the typographic and spatial parameters of the mature AEG corporate identification program. On 31 January 1908, copyright application was made for his hexagonal AEG trademark (Fig. 15-38). This pictographic honeycomb design containing the firm's initials signifies mathematical order while functioning as a visual metaphor relating the complexity and organization of a twentieth-century corporation to a beehive. Behrens's guide booklet for the AEG pavilion for the 1908 German Shipbuilding Exhibition was an early application of the trademark and corporate typeface (Fig. 15-39). The AEG graphic identity program made consistent use of three linchpin elements that would be present in corporate identity programs as the genre evolved a half-century later: a logo, a typeface, and a consistent layout of elements following standardized formats.

15-39. Peter Behrens, guidebook covers for the AEG pavilion at the German Shipbuilding Exhibition, 1908. A translation drawing reduces the architectural structure to flat planes. The lettering used here became a basis for the AEG visual identification system.

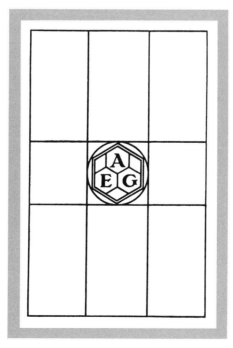

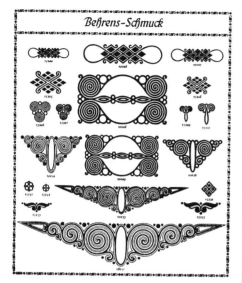

15-40. Peter Behrens, typographic ornaments for Behrens-Kursiv, 1907. Designed for the Klingspor Foundry, these typographic ornaments demonstrate the tempering of Art Nouveau's floral swirls by geometric measurement.

Behrens designed a typeface for AEG's exclusive use to bring unity to its printed materials. At a time when German graphic design was dominated by traditional black letter and decorative Victorian and Art Nouveau styles, Behrens designed a roman-style letterform inspired by classical Roman inscriptions. Initially this was not available in type, so display type on all AEG printed graphics was hand-lettered. In 1908, a typeset variation named Behrens-Antiqua (see Fig. 15-33) was released by Klingspor Foundry, first for the exclusive use of AEG, then later for general use. Behrens had three important goals in designing this new type: It differentiated AEG communications from all other printed matter; its forms were universal rather than individualized by the touch of a specific artist's hand; and it strove for a monumental character that could evoke positive connotations of quality and performance. Behrens-Antiqua possessed the solemn monumental quality of

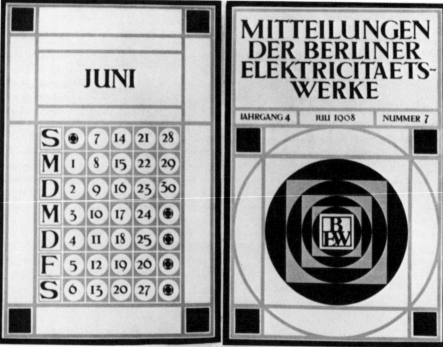

15-41

15-41. Peter Behrens, front and back covers for *Mitteilungen Der Berliner Elektricitaets-Werke (Berlin Electric-Works Magazine),* 1908. Each issue used a different geometric pattern on the front cover, and the graphic theme was echoed by the back-cover calendar design. The front cover is black and lavender; the back black and ochre.

15-42. Peter Behrens, catalogue page for AEG teakettles, 1908. Permutations from the modular system of shapes, handles, materials, and textures are shown. Note the spatial division by rules to create zones of information.

15-42

15-43. Peter Behrens, AEG arc lamp catalogue page, 1907. Shape and proportion are inspired by ancient Greek vases.

LAMPE P.L.Nr. 67216 MIT LATERNE P.L.Nr. 68216

roman letterforms. Ornaments designed for Behrens's Kursiv (Fig. 15-40), Antiqua, and Medieval typefaces were inspired by ancient Greek and Roman ceramic and brass craft objects, whose geometric properties satisfied Behrens's belief that geometry could make ornament universal and impersonal.

The consistent use of graphic devices gave the AEG graphics a unified image (Fig. 15-41). These devices, in addition to modular divisions of space using Lauweriks's grid, included: framing the space by a medium-weight rule; central placement of static elements; exclusive use of Behrens-Antiqua type; use of analogous colors (often two or three sequential colors on the color wheel); and simple objective photographs and drawings with subjects isolated from their environments.

The industrial products designed by Behrens ranged from electric household products, such as teakettles and fans, to street lamps and industrial products, such as electric motors. He brought the formal eye of the painter and the structural approach and professional ethics of the architect to product design. The combination of visual form, working method, and functional concern in his work for AEG products enabled him to produce the body of work that has led some to proclaim Behrens as the "first industrial designer." An innovative use of standardization is

15-44

seen in the design of AEG teakettles with interchangeable parts (Fig. 15-42): three basic kettle forms, two lids, two handles, and two bases. There were three materials—brass, copper-plate, and nickel-plate—and three finishes—smooth, hammered, and rippled. All components were available to assemble three sizes of teakettles, and all of these kettles used the same heating elements and plugs. This system of interchangeable components made it theoretically possible to configure 216 different teakettles, but only about 30 were actually brought to market.

Beginning in early 1907, Behrens designed a large series of AEG arc lamps (Fig. 15-43), which produced intense light by passing an electrical current between two carbon electrodes. These were three hundred times brighter, more energy-efficient, and safer than gas lamps of the time. Since the carbon rods had to be replaced every eight to twenty hours, convenient exterior clips were designed for quick dismantling. Their forms and proportions suggest Lauweriks's grid, while the overall shapes evoke the harmonious design and graceful curves of Greek vases. The arc lamps were widely used in factories, railway stations, and other public buildings.

Behrens sought neutrality and standardization in product designs for machine manufacture. His street lamps and teakettles have simple forms shorn of decoration, with connotations of social class and wealth stripped away. His work pointed toward the new sensibility about design, which matured in the 1920s. This rational approach announced the need for form to emerge from function rather than being an added embellishment.

The AEG corporate design program included applications to architecture ranging from storefronts (Fig. 15-44) to a massive Turbine Hall (Fig. 15-45), which Behrens designed in collaboration with structural engineer Karl Bernhard. This major architectural design by Behrens—with its twenty-two giant exposed exterior steel girders along the sides, glass curtain walls, and form determined by function—became a prototype for future design evolution. During this period, Behrens's apprentices included Walter Gropius, Ludwig Mies van der Rohe, Le Corbusier, and Adolf Meyer. Given these designers' later importance, Behrens's philosophy and the studio shop talk were surely a wellspring for ideas.

At the 1914 Werkbund annual conference (Fig. 15-46), the debate between Muthesius's rationalism and standardization versus van de Velde's expressionism was soundly determined in favor of Muthesius's approach. Up until this 1914 meeting, Behrens played a key role among designers who bolted against Victorian histori-

15-45

cism and Art Nouveau design and advocated a Spartan approach, stripped of decoration. The austere orthodoxy of the International Style, discussed in Chapters 19 and 21, was the evolutionary extension of these beliefs.

Behrens began to accept architectural commissions from other clients in 1911. Graphic and product design occupied less of his time. In 1914 Behrens's contract with AEG was terminated, although he continued to work on AEG projects from time to time. Until his death in 1940, Behrens's design practice centered upon architecture. His work during the opening decades of the century crystallized advanced thinking about design while planting seeds for future developments.

In Germany, as in Scotland and Austria, pioneering designers who were not content with Art Nouveau charted new directions in response to personal and societal needs, and laid the groundwork for the new century. Their works might almost be called *Proto-Modernism,* the initial explorations whose underlying philosophy would reverberate through design activities in the decades ahead.

15-46. Peter Behrens, poster for Deutsche Werkbund exhibition, 1914. The designer is an allegorical torchbearer, in keeping with the Werkbund view that design was an enlightening and humanizing social force. The subtitle reads, "Art in craft, industry and commerce • architecture."

The Influence of Modern Art

16

The first two decades of the twentieth century were a time of incredible ferment and change that radically altered all aspects of the human condition. The social, political, cultural, and economic character of life was caught in fluid upheaval. In Europe, monarchy was replaced by democracy, socialism, and communism. Technology and scientific advances transformed commerce and industry. Transportation was radically altered by the coming of the motorcar (1885) and the airplane (1903). The motion picture (1896) and wireless radio transmission (1895) foretold a new era of human communications. Beginning in 1908 with the Turkish revolution to restore constitutional government and the Bulgarian declaration of independence, colonized and subjugated nations began to awaken and demand independence. The slaughter during the first of two global wars, fought with the destructive weapons of technology, shook the traditions and institutions of Western civilization to their foundations.

Against this turbulence, it is not surprising that visual art experienced a series of creative revolutions that questioned its values, approaches to organizing space, and role in society. The traditional objective view of the world was shattered. Representation of external appearances did not fulfill the needs and vision of the emerging European avant-garde. Elemental ideas about color and form, social protest, and the expression of Freudian theories and deeply personal emotional states occupied many artists. While some of these modern movements—Fauvism, for example—had limited effect upon graphic design, others—Cubism and Futurism, Dada and Surrealism, de Stijl, Suprematism, and Constructivism—directly influenced the graphic language of form and visual communications in this century. The evolution of twentieth-century graphic design closely relates to modern painting, poetry, and architecture. It might almost be said that a fusion of Cubist painting and Futurist poetry spawned twentieth-century graphic design.

Cubism

By introducing a design concept independent of nature, Cubism began a new artistic tradition and way of seeing that ended the four-hundred-year-old Renaissance tradition of pictorial art. The genesis of this movement is the 1907 *Les Demoiselles d'Avignon* (Fig. 16-1) by the Spanish painter Pablo Picasso (1881–1973). Taking cues from the geometric stylizations of African sculpture (Fig. 16-2) and Post-Impressionist Paul Cézanne (1839–1906), who observed that the painter should "treat nature in terms of the cylinder and the sphere and the cone," this painting was a new approach to handling space and expressing human emotions. The figures are abstracted into geometric planes, and classical norms of the human figure are broken. The spatial illusions of perspective give way to an ambiguous shifting of two-dimensional planes. The seated figure is simultaneously seen from a multiplicity of viewpoints.

Over the next few years, Picasso and his close associate Georges Braque (1881–1963) evolved Cubism as the art movement that replaced rendering appearances with the endless possibilities of invented form. Analytical Cubism (Fig. 16-3) is the name given to their work from about 1910–1912. During this period, the artists analyzed the planes of the subject matter, often from different points of view, and

16-1

16-2

used these perceptions to construct a painting composed of rhythmic geometric planes. The real subject became the visual language of form used to create a highly structured work of art. Analytical Cubism's compelling fascination grows from the unresolvable tension of the sensual and intellectual appeal of the pictorial structure in conflict with the challenge of interpreting the subject matter.

Picasso and Braque introduced paper collage elements into their work in 1912. Collage allowed free composition independent of subject matter and declared the reality of the painting as two-dimensional object. The texture of collage elements could signify objects. To denote a chair, for example, Picasso glued oilcloth printed with a chair cane pattern into a painting. Often, letterforms and words from newspapers were incorporated as visual form and for associated meaning.

In 1913, Cubism evolved into what has been called Synthetic Cubism. Drawing upon past observations, the Cubists invented forms that were signs rather than representations of the subject matter. The essence of an object and its basic characteristics, rather than its outward appearance, were depicted. Juan Gris (1887–1927) was a major painter in the development of Synthetic Cubism. His paintings, such as the 1912 *Portrait of Picasso* (Fig. 16-4), combined composition from nature with an independent structural design of the picture space. First, he planned a rigorous architectural structure using golden section proportions and a modular composition grid; then he "laid the subject matter" upon this design scheme. Gris was to have a profound influence upon the development of geometric art and design —his paintings are a kind of halfway house between an art based on perception and an art realized by the relationships between geometric planes.

Among the artists who clustered around Picasso and Braque and joined the Cubist movement, Fernand Léger (1881–1955) also moved Cubism away from the ini-

16-1. Pablo Picasso, *Les Demoiselles d'Avignon,* 1907. The seeds of Cubism are contained in the background spaces that warp and buckle forward toward the picture plane. The personhood of these five figures yields to Picasso's exploration of form and space.

16-2. African mask from the Ivory Coast, undated. Boldly chiseled geometric planes were an exciting revelation for Picasso and his friends. Carved in secrecy and representing awesome spiritual forces, African tribal masks were used in rituals including ancestor worship, puberty, agriculture, and warding off evil spirits.

16-3. Georges Braque, *Pitcher and Violin,* 1909. In this breakthrough image on the road to Analytical Cubism, Braque studied the planes of the motif from different vantage points, fractured them, and pulled them forward toward the canvas surface. The planes shimmer vibrantly in ambiguous positive and negative relationships one to another.

16-5. Fernand Léger, *The City,* 1919. This monumental composition of pure, flat planes signifying the geometry, color, and energy of the modern city led its creator to say, "It was advertising that first drew the consequences" of it.

tial impulses of the founders. From around 1910, Léger took Cézanne's famous dictum about the cylinder, sphere, and cone far more seriously than any other Cubist. Motifs such as nudes in a forest were transformed into fields of colorful stovepipe sections littering the picture plane. Léger might have evolved toward an art of pure color and shape relationships, but his four years of military service among working-class French citizens, and his heightened visual perception that developed during the war, turned him toward a style that was more recognizable, accessible, and populist. He moved closer to his visual experience in paintings like *The City* (Fig. 16-5). Perceptions of the colors, shapes, posters, and architecture of the urban environment—glimpses and fragments of information—are assembled into a composition of brightly colored planes. The letterforms in this painting and in Léger's graphic work for Blaise Cendrar's 1919 book *La Fin du Monde . . . (The End of the World . . .)* pointed the way toward geometric letterforms (Pl. 37). His almost pictographic stylizations of the human figure and objects were a major inspiration for the pictorial modernism that became the major thrust of the revived poster art of the 1920s. Léger's flat planes of color, urban motifs, and the hard-edged precision of his machine forms helped define the modern design sensibility after World War I.

By innovating a new approach to visual composition, Cubism changed the course of painting and graphic design. Its formal language became a catalyst for experiments that pushed art and design toward geometric abstraction and new approaches to pictorial space.

Futurism

Futurism was launched when the Italian poet Filippo Marinetti (1876–1944) published his *Manifesto of Futurism* in the Paris newspaper *La Figaro* on 20 February 1909. Marinetti's stirring words established Futurism as a revolutionary movement for all the arts to test their ideas and forms against the new realities of scientific and industrial society. "We intend to sing the love of danger, the habit of

16-4. Juan Gris, *Portrait of Picasso,* 1912. Cubist planes move forward and backward in shallow space by tonal modulation, while the horizontal, vertical, and diagonal geometry of a grid imposes order.

16-6. Carlo Carrà, *parole in libertà* ("free-word composition"), 1914. The Futurist poets believed that the use of different sizes, weights, and styles of type allowed them to weld painting and poetry because the intrinsic beauty of letterforms, manipulated creatively, transformed the printed page into a work of visual art.

16-7. Filippo Marinetti, *Montagne + Vallate + Strade × Joffre* ("Mountains + Valleys + Streets × Joffre"), 1915. This poem "depicts" Marinetti's journey, which included the war front (lower left), France (upper left), and a visit to Léger (top right).

energy and fearlessness. Courage, audacity, and revolt will be essential elements of our poetry.... We affirm that the world's magnificence has been enriched by a new beauty: the beauty of speed ... a roaring car that seems to ride on grapeshot is more beautiful than the *Victory of Samothrace....* Except in struggle, there is no more beauty. No work without an aggressive character can be a masterpiece." The manifesto voiced enthusiasm for war, the machine age, speed, and modern life. It shocked the public by proclaiming: "We will destroy museums, libraries, and fight against moralism, feminism, and all utilitarian cowardice."

Marinetti and his followers produced an explosive and emotionally charged poetry that defied correct syntax and grammar. In January 1913, Giovanni Papini (1881–1956) began publication of the journal *Lacerba* in Florence, and typographic design was pulled onto the artistic battlefield. The June 1913 issue published Marinetti's article calling for a typographic revolution against the classical tradition. Harmony was rejected as a design quality because it contradicted "the leaps and bursts of style running through the page." On a page, three or four ink colors and twenty typefaces (italics for quick impressions, boldface for violent noises and sounds) could redouble words' expressive power. Free, dynamic, and torpedo-like words could be given the velocity of stars, clouds, airplanes, trains, waves, explosives, molecules, and atoms. A new and painterly typographic design, called *parole in libertá* or *words in freedom,* was born on the page (Figs. 16-6 through 16-10).

Marinetti wrote that a man who has witnessed an explosion does not stop to connect his sentences grammatically, but hurls shrieks and words at his listeners. Marinetti urged poets to liberate themselves from servitude to grammar and open new worlds of expression. Since Gutenberg's invention of movable type, most graphic design had employed a vigorous horizontal and vertical structure, but the

16-6

16-7

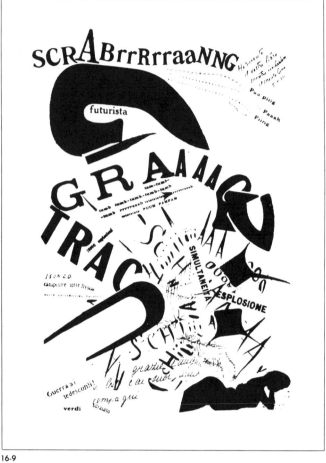

16-9

16-8. Ardengo Soffici, *Bifszf + 18 Simultaneità Chimismi Iirici,* 1915. In this powerful Futurist poem, Soffici contrasts traditional verse with clusters of modulating letterforms used as pure visual form. Diagonal rules link the units and create rhythms from page to page.

16-9. Filippo Marinetti, poem from *Les mots en liberté* ("The words to freedom"), 1919. Noise and speed, two dominant conditions of twentieth-century life, were expressed in Futurist poetry. Here, the confusion, violent noise, and chaos of battle explode above the girl reading her lover's letter from the front. Marinetti's experience in the trenches of war inspired this poem.

16-10. Filippo Marinetti, *chair,* undated. In French, *chair* means *flesh.* In this love poem, mathematical signs mix with words to create lyrical equations, and numbers are used as adjectives expressing intensities.

16-10

Futurist poets cast these constraints to the wind. Freed from tradition, they animated their pages with a dynamic, nonlinear composition achieved by pasting words and letters in place for reproduction from photoengraved printing plates.

The Futurist concept that writing and/or typography could become concrete and expressive visual form has been a sporadic preoccupation of poets dating back at least to the work of the Greek poet Simias of Rhodes (c. 33 B.C.). Called *pattern poetry,* this verse often took the shape of objects or religious symbols. In the nineteenth century, the German poet Arno Holz (1863–1929) reinforced intended auditory effects by such devices as omitting capitalizations and punctuation, varying wordspacing to signify pauses, and using multiple punctuation marks for emphasis. Lewis Carroll's *Alice's Adventures in Wonderland* used descending type sizes and pictorial shape to construct a mouse's tail as part of the mouse's tale (Fig. 16-11).

In 1897, the French Symbolist poet Stéphane Mallarmé (1842–1898) published the poem "Un Coup de Dés" (Fig. 16-12), composed of seven hundred words on twenty pages in a typographic range: capital, lowercase, roman, and italic. Rather

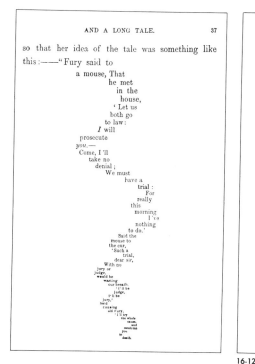

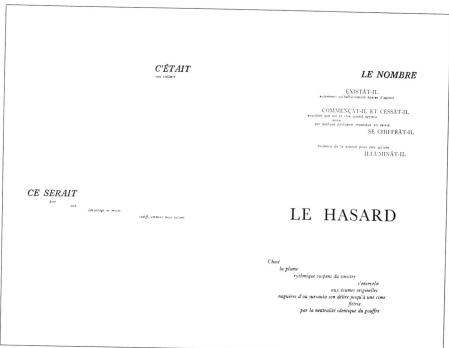

16-12

16-11. Lewis Carroll, typographic image, 1866. Unexpected and totally different from the rest of *Alice's Adventures in Wonderland,* this graphic experiment in figurative typography has received acclaim from both design and literary viewpoints.

16-12. Stéphane Mallarmé, pages from *Un Coup de Dés* ("A Throw of the Dice"), 1897. Mallarmé anticipated the formal and expressive typographic concerns that emerged in the twentieth century when poets and painters became interested in the creative potential of the printed page.

than surrounding a poem with white, empty margins, this "silence" was dispersed through the work as part of its meaning. Instead of stringing words in linear sequence like beads, they were placed in unexpected positions on the page to express sensations and evoke ideas. Moreover, Mallarmé was successful in relating typography to the musical score—the placement and weight of words relate to intonation, importance in oral reading, and rhythm.

Another French poet, Guillaume Apollinaire (1880–1918), was closely associated with the Cubists, particularly Picasso, and was involved in a rivalry with Marinetti. Apollinaire had championed African sculpture, defined the principles of Cubist painting and literature, and once observed that "catalogs, posters, advertisements of all types, believe me, they contain the poetry of our epoch." His unique contribution to graphic design was the 1918 publication of a book entitled *Calligrammes,* poems in which the letterforms are arranged to form a visual design, figure, or pictograph (Figs. 16-13 and 16-14). In these poems he explored the potential fusion of poetry and painting, introducing the concept of simultaneity to the time- and sequence-bound typography of the printed page.

On 11 February 1910, five artists who had joined Marinetti's Futurist movement published the *Manifesto of the Futurist Painters.* Umberto Boccioni (1882–1916), Carlo Carrà (1881–1966), Luigi Russolo (1885–1947), Giacomo Balla (1871–1958), and Gino Severini (1883–1966) declared their intent to: "Destroy the cult of the past. . . . Totally invalidate all kinds of imitation. . . . Elevate all attempts at originality. . . . Regard art critics as useless and dangerous. . . . Sweep the whole field of art clean of all themes and subjects which have been used in the past. . . . Support and glory in our day-to-day world, a world which is going to be continually and splendidly transformed by victorious Science." The Futurist painters were strongly influenced by Cubism, but they also attempted to express motion, energy, and cinematic sequence in their work (Fig. 16-15). They first used the word *simultaneity* in a visual-art context to express concurrent existence or occurrence, such as the presentation of different views in the same work of art.

The *Manifesto of Futurist Architecture* was written by Antonio Sant'Elia (1888–1916). He called for construction based on technology and science, and design for the unique demands of modern life (Fig. 16-16). He declared decoration to be absurd, and used dynamic diagonal and elliptic lines because their emotional power is greater than horizontals and verticals. Tragically, Sant'Elia was killed on the bat-

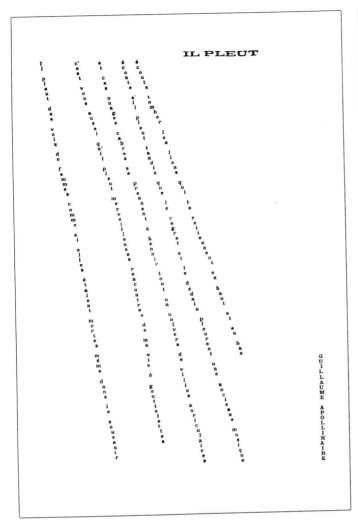

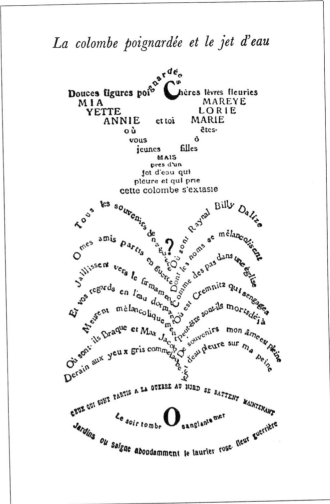

16-14

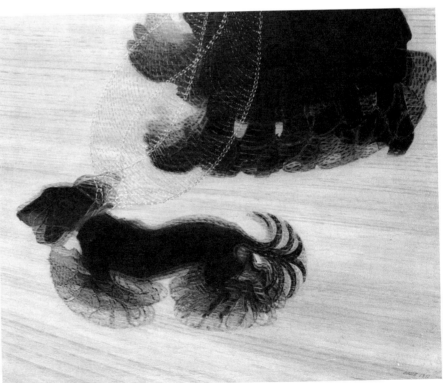

16-13. Guillaume Apollinaire, poem from *Calligrammes,* 1918. Entitled "It's Raining," this poem is composed of letterforms that sprinkle figuratively down the page to relate visual form to poetic content.

16-14. Guillaume Apollinaire, poem from *Calligrammes,* 1918. The typography becomes a bird, a water fountain, and an eye in this expressive design.

16-15. Giacomo Balla, *Dynamism of a Dog on a Leash,* 1912. The Futurist painters sought to introduce dynamic motion, speed, and energy to the static, two-dimensional surface.

16-15

16-16. Antonio Sant'Elia, drawing for the new city of the future, 1914. These drawings were reproduced with Sant'Elia's manifesto in *Lacerba*. After the war, many of his ideas about form developed in architecture, product, and graphic design.

16-17. Fortunato Depero, advertisement for De Marinis & Lorie millinery shop, 1929. The repetition of the legs and transparent layering of black-and-white shapes typify Depero's graphics of the 1920s and 1930s.

tlefield, but his ideas and visionary drawing influenced the course of modern design, particularly Art Deco.

Among the artists who applied Futurist philosophy to graphic and advertising design, Fortunato Depero (1892–1960) produced a dynamic body of work in poster, typographic, and advertising design. This young painter shifted from social realism and symbolism to Futurism in 1913 after seeing a copy of the Futurist paper *Lacerba*. Depero's 1924 poster for the New Futurist Theater Company (Pl. 38) displays his ability to use flat planes of vibrant color, diagonal composition, and angular repetitive forms to produce kinetic motion on the printed page. In 1927 Depero published his *Dinamo Arari,* a compilation of his typographical experiments, advertisements, tapestry designs, and other works. The cover (Pl. 39) proclaimed *Depero Futurista* in a silver and black configuration on heavy blue poster board. Bound by two massive chrome bolts, declaring the book to be a physical object and work of art, this book is a precursor of the artist's book, published by the artist as a creative expression independent of the publishing establishment. From September 1928 until October 1930, Depero worked in New York and designed covers for magazines including *Vanity Fair, Movie Makers,* and *Sparks,* along with advertising designs for the De Marinis & Lorie millinery shop (Fig. 16-17). Although limited to a sophisticated and cosmopolitan audience, the appearance of his Futurist work in American graphic communications proved somewhat influential in America's movement toward modernism. Futurism became a major influence upon other art movements, for its violent, revolutionary techniques were adopted by the Dadaists, Constructivists, and de Stijl. The Futurists initiated the publication of manifestos, typographic experimentation, and publicity stunts (on 8 July 1910, 800,000 copies of Marinetti's leaflet, "Against Past-Loving Venice," were dropped from a clock tower onto Venice crowds), forcing poets and graphic designers to rethink the very nature of the typographic word and its meaning.

Dada

Reacting against a world gone mad, the Dada movement claimed to be antiart and had a strong negative and destructive element. Dada writers and artists were concerned with shock, protest, and nonsense. They bitterly rebelled against the horrors of the world war, the decadence of European society, the shallowness of blind faith in technological progress, and the inadequacy of religion and conventional moral codes in a continent in upheaval. Rejecting all tradition, they sought complete freedom.

The Dada movement developed spontaneously as a literary movement after the poet Hugo Ball (1886–1927) opened the Cabaret Voltaire in Zurich, Switzerland, as a gathering place for independent young poets, painters, and musicians. Dada's guiding spirit was a young Hungarian poet, Tristan Tzara (1896–1963), who edited the periodical *DADA* beginning in July 1917. Tzara joined Ball, Jean Arp (1887–1966, also known as Hans Arp), and Richard Huelsenbeck in exploring sound poetry (Fig. 16-18), nonsense poetry, and chance poetry. He wrote a steady stream of Dada manifestos and contributed to all major Dada publications and events. Chance placement and absurd titles characterized their graphic work (Fig. 16-19). Dadaists did not even agree on the origins of the name Dada, such was the anarchy of this movement. A widely accepted story says that the movement was randomly named by opening a French–German dictionary and quickly pointing to a word, "dada," a child's hobby horse.

The French painter Marcel Duchamp (1887–1968) joined the Dada movement and became its most prominent visual artist. Earlier, he had analyzed his subjects as geometric planes under the influence of Cubism. His painting *Nude Descending a Staircase* (Fig. 16-20) pushed the limits of the static image's ability to record and express motion. To Duchamp, Dada's most articulate spokesman, art and life were processes of random chance and willful choice. Artistic acts became matters of individual decision and selection. This philosophy of absolute freedom allowed Duchamp to create "ready-made" sculpture (Fig. 16-21), such as a bicycle wheel

KARAWANE

jolifanto bambla ô falli bambla

grossiga m'pfa habla horem

égiga goramen

higo bloiko russula huju

hollaka hollala

anlogo bung

blago bung

blago bung

bosso fataka

ü üü ü

schampa wulla wussa ólobo

hej tatta gôrem

eschige zunbada

ɯulubu ssubudu uluɯ ssubudu

tumba ba- umf

kusagauma

ba - umf

(1917)
Hugo Ball

16-18. Hugo Ball, Dada poem, 1917. Sound and sight poems such as this expressed the Dada desire to replace man's logical nonsense with an illogical nonsense.

16-19. This Dada journal cover for "The Bearded Heart," 1922, shows a casual organization of space as found illustrations are randomly dispersed about the page with no particular communicative intent.

16-20. Marcel Duchamp, *Nude Descending a Staircase,* 1912. Duchamp wrote that this painting was "an organization of kinetic elements, an expression of time and space through the abstract presentation of motion."

mounted on a wooden stool, and exhibit "found objects," such as a urinal, as art. The public was outraged when Duchamp painted a mustache on a reproduction of the Mona Lisa. This act was not, however, an attack upon the Mona Lisa. Rather, it was an ingenious assault upon the tyranny of tradition and a public that had lost the humanistic spirit of the Renaissance.

Dada quickly spread from Zurich to other European cities. In spite of the claim that they were not creating art but were mocking and defaming a society that had become insane, several Dadaists produced meaningful visual art that has contributed to graphic design. Dada artists claim to have invented photomontage (Fig. 16-22), the technique of manipulating found photographic images to create jarring juxtapositions and chance associations. Both Raoul Hausmann (1886–1977) and Hannah Höch (1889–1978) were creating outstanding work in the medium as early as 1918.

Kurt Schwitters (1887–1948) of Hanover, Germany, created a nonpolitical off-shoot of Dada that he named *Merz,* coined from the word *kommerz* ("commerce") in one of his collages. Schwitters gave Merz meaning as the title of a one-man art movement. Beginning in 1919, his Merz pictures were collage compositions using printed ephemera, rubbish, and found materials to compose color against color, form against form, and texture against texture (Fig. 16-23). His complex designs combined Dada's element of nonsense and chance with strong design properties. When he tried to join the Dada movement as "an artist who nails his pictures together," he was refused membership for being too bourgeois.

Schwitters wrote and designed poetry that played sense against nonsense (Fig. 16-24). He defined poetry as the interaction of elements: letters, syllables, words, sentences. In the early 1920s, Constructivism became an added influence in

16-21

16-22

16-23

16-21. Marcel Duchamp, *Bicycle Wheel,* 1951
(third version, after the lost original of 1913).
When an object is removed from its usual
context, we suddenly see it with fresh eyes
that respond to its intrinsic visual
properties.

16-22. Hannah Höch, *Da—dandy,* collage
and photomontage, 1919. Images and
materials are recycled, with both accidental
chance juxtapositions and planned decisions
contributing to the creative process.

16-23. Kurt Schwitters, *Merz Picture 19,*
1920. Material gathered from the streets,
alleys, and garbage cans was washed and
cataloged according to size and color for use
as the raw material of art.

16-24. Kurt Schwitters, *W W priimiitittii,*
1920. The Dada poets separated the word
from its language context; these two poems
are intended to be seen as pure visual form
and read as pure sound. Intuitive but highly
structured typographics grew out of the
initial random chance of early Dada poetry.

```
W   W
P B D
Z F M
R F   R F
T Z P F  T Z P F
M W T
R F M R
R K T   P C T
S W   S W
K P T
F   G
K P T
R   Z
K P T
R Z L
T Z P F  T Z P F
H F T L
```

```
priimiitittii.
priimiitittii tisch
tesch
priimiitittii tesch
tusch
priimiitittii tischa
tescho
priimiitittii tescho
tuschi
priimittii
priimiitittii
priimiitittii too
priimiitittii taa
priimiitittii too
priimiitittii taa
priimiitittii tootaa
priimiitittii tootaa
priimiitittii tuutaa
priimiitittii tuutaa
priimiitittii tuutaatoo
priimiitittii tuutaatoo
priimiitittii tootaatuu
priimiitittii tootaatuu
```

16-24

The Influence of Modern Art

16-25. Kurt Schwitters, Théo van Doesburg, and Kate Steinitz, page from *Die Scheuche Marchen* ("The Scarecrow Marches"), 1922. In this modern fairy tale, type and image are wedded literally and figuratively as the *B* overpowers the *X* with verbiage.

Schwitters's work after he made contact with El Lissitzky (1890–1941) and Théo van Doesburg (1883–1931), who invited Schwitters to Holland to promote Dada. Schwitters and van Doesburg collaborated on a book design with typographic forms as the characters (Fig. 16-25). From 1923 until 1932, Schwitters published twenty-four issues of the periodical *Merz,* whose eleventh issue was devoted to advertising typography. During this time Schwitters ran a successful graphic design studio with Pelikan—manufacturer of office equipment and supplies—as a major client, and the city of Hanover employed him as typography consultant for several years. When the German political situation deteriorated in the 1930s, Schwitters spent increasing time in Norway and moved to Oslo in 1937. After Germany invaded Norway in 1940, he fled to the British Isles, where he spent his last years.

In contrast to the artistic and Constructivist interests of Kurt Schwitters, the Berlin Dadaists John Heartfield (1891–1968), Wieland Herzfelde (b. 1896), and George Grosz (1893–1959) held vigorous revolutionary political beliefs and oriented many of their artistic activities toward visual communications to raise public consciousness and promote social change. John Heartfield is an English name adopted by Helmut Herzfelde as a protest against German militarism and the army in which he served from 1914–1916. A founding member of the Berlin Dada group in 1919, Heartfield used the harsh disjunctions of photomontage as a potent propaganda weapon and innovated in the preparation of mechanical art for offset printing. The Weimar Republic and the growing Nazi party were his targets in posters (Figs. 16-26 through 16-28), book and magazine covers (Fig. 16-29), political illustrations, and cartoons. His montages are the most urgent in the history of the technique. Heartfield did not take photographs or retouch images but worked directly with glossy prints acquired from magazines and newspapers. Occasionally, he commissioned a needed image from a photographer. Photography was still considered a poor man's art form, and Heartfield's images met with immediate identi-

WER BÜRGERBLÄTTER LIEST WIRD BLIND UND TAUB.
WEG MIT DEN VERDUMMUNGSBANDAGEN!

16-26

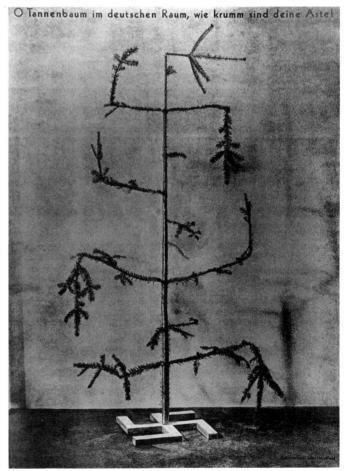

16-27

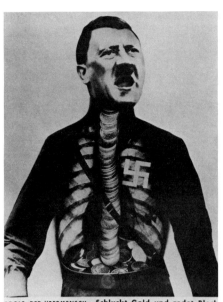

ADOLF, DER ÜBERMENSCH: Schluckt Gold und redet Blech

16-28

16-29

16-30

16-26. John Heartfield, poster attacking the press, 1930. A surreal visual image, a head wrapped in newspaper, appears over a headline declaring that "whoever reads the bourgeois press turns deaf and blind. Away with these bandages which cause stupidity!"

16-27. John Heartfield, yuletide poster, 1934. Under a headline proclaiming "Oh German evergreen, how crooked are your branches," a pathetic Christmas tree symbolizes the pathos of the Third Reich.

16-28. John Heartfield, anti-Nazi propaganda poster, 1935. The headline, "Adolf, the Superman: Swallows gold and talks tin," is visualized by a photomontage x-ray of the Fuehrer showing an esophagus of gold coins.

16-29. John Heartfield, cover for AIZ, 1934. Weapons are turned into a cathedral to symbolize the mentality of national leaders involved in military expansion and an arms race. Note the swastika, dollar mark, and pound sign atop the towers.

16-30. John Heartfield, theater poster, 1955. Heartfield's late work maintains the compositional and montage ideas of his earlier designs, but the biting social comment often yields to a more gentle communication.

fication and comprehension by the working class. After storm troopers occupied his apartment-studio in 1933, Heartfield fled to Prague, where he continued his graphic propaganda and mailed postcard versions of his graphics to Nazi leaders. In 1938, he learned that he was on a secret Nazi list of enemies, and fled to London. He settled in Leipzig, East Germany, in 1950 and designed theater sets and posters (Fig. 16-30). Before his death in 1968, he produced photomontages protesting the Vietnam War and calling for world peace. *Unfortunately Still Timely* is the title given to retrospectives of his graphic art.

Heartfield's younger brother, Wieland Herzfelde, was a poet, critic, and publisher who edited the journal *Neue Jugend,* which was designed by Heartfield (Fig. 16-31). After being jailed in 1914 for distributing communist literature, Wieland started the Malik Verlag publishing house, an important avant-garde publisher of Dada, left-wing political propaganda, and advanced literature. The painter and graphic artist George Grosz was closely associated with the Herzfelde brothers. His biting pen attacked a corrupt society with satire and caricature (Fig. 16-32). He advocated a classless society, and his drawings project an angry intensity of deep political convictions in what he perceived to be a decadent, degenerate milieu.

Having inherited Marinetti's rhetoric and assault upon all artistic and social traditions, Dada was a major liberating movement that continues to inspire innovation and rebellion. Dada was born in protest against war, and its destructive and exhibitionist activities became more absurd and extreme after the war ended. In 1921 and 1922, controversy and disagreement broke out among its members, and the movement split into factions. French writer André Breton (1896–1966), who was associating with the Dadaists, emerged as a new leader who believed that Dada had lost its relevance and that new directions were necessary. Having pushed its negative activities to the limit, lacking a unified leadership, and with its members facing the new ideas that eventually led to Surrealism, Dada floundered and ceased to exist as a cohesive movement by the end of 1922. Dadaists like Schwitters and Heartfield continued to evolve, and produced their finest work after the movement dissolved. Dada's rejection of art and tradition enabled it to enrich the visual vocabulary started by Futurism. Through a synthesis of spontaneous chance actions with planned decisions, Dadaists further rid typographic design of its traditional precepts. Also, Dada continued Cubism's concept of letterforms as concrete visual shapes—not just phonetic symbols (Fig. 16-33).

16-32. George Grosz, cover for *Der Blutige Ernst*, 1919. Responding to postwar decadence, Grosz portrayed this couple against a collage of cabaret advertisements.

16-31. John Heartfield, page from *Neue Jugend*, 1917. In this radical tabloid paper, Heartfield brought the gray newspaper page to life with a visual vitality of Dadaist origin.

16-33. Ilya Zdanevitch, poster for the play *Party of the Bearded Heart*, 1923. A wonderful vitality and legibility result, even though Zdanevitch has combined typographic material from over forty fonts.

Surrealism

With roots in Dada and the Littérature group of young French writers and poets, Surrealism burst onto the Paris scene in 1924, searching for the "more real than real world behind the real"—the world of intuition, dreams, and the unconscious realm explored by Freud. Apollinaire had used the expression "surreal drama" in reviewing a play in 1917. The poet André Breton (1896–1966), founder of Surrealism, imbued the word with all the magic of dreams, the spirit of rebellion, and the mysteries of the subconscious in his 1924 *Manifesto du Surrealisme: "Surrealism,* noun, masc. pure psychic automatism by which it is intended to express, either verbally or in writing, the true function of thought. Thought dictated in the absence of all control exerted by reason, all aesthetic or moral preoccupations."

Tristan Tzara came from Zurich to join Breton, Louis Aragon (1897–1982), and Paul Eluard (1895–1952). He stirred the group on toward scandal and rebellion. These young poets rejected the rationalism and formal conventions dominating postwar creative activities in Paris. They sought ways to make new truths, to re-

16-35

16-34. Giorgio de Chirico, *The Departure of the Poet,* 1914. A member of the short-lived Italian Metaphysical School of Painting, de Chirico created a timeless poetry that stops short of the bizarre or supernatural.

16-35. Max Ernst, collage from *Une Semaine De Bonté,* 1934. Printing techniques obscured the cut edges of Ernst's collages giving them a remarkable unity. His surreal collage concepts have strongly influenced illustration.

veal "the language of the soul." Surrealism ("superreality" in French) was not a style or a matter of aesthetics—rather, it was a way of thinking and knowing, a way of feeling, and a way of life. Where Dada had been negative, destructive, and perpetually exhibitionist, surrealism professed a poetic faith in man and his spirit. Humanity could be liberated from social and moral conventions. Intuition and feeling could be freed. The writers experimented with stream-of-consciousness writing, or automatism, to seek an uninhibited truth.

The impact of the Surrealist poets and writers has been limited to French literary and scholarly circles. It was through the painters that Surrealism affected society and visual communications. While Surrealists often created images so personal that communication became impossible, it also produced images whose feeling, symbols, or fantasy triggered a collective, universal response among large numbers of people. Breton and his friends had speculated about the possibility of surreal painting. They discovered the work of Giorgio de Chirico (1888–1978) and declared him to be the first Surrealist painter. De Chirico painted hauntingly empty vistas of Italian Renaissance palaces and squares that possess an intense melancholy (Fig. 16-34). Vacant buildings, harsh shadows, deep tilted perspective, and enigmatic images combine to communicate feelings far removed from ordinary experience.

Of the large number of artists who joined the Surrealist movement, several significantly influenced visual communications with a major impact on photography and illustration. Max Ernst (1891–1965), a restless German Dadaist who joined Surrealism, used a number of techniques that have been adopted in graphic communications. Fascinated by the wood engravings of nineteenth-century novels and catalogues, Ernst reinvented them by using collage techniques to create strange illustrative images (Fig. 16-35). His *frottage* technique involved using rubbings to

The Influence of Modern Art

16-36

16-37

16-36. René Magritte, *The False Mirror,* 1928. The spectator is unable to reconcile the contradiction of image and space; thus, the poetry of the ambiguous haunts the observer long after seeing the painting.

16-37. René Magritte, *The Blank Signature,* 1965. The Surrealists defied our rational understanding of the world, and their vocabulary of pictorial and symbolic innovations began to seep into the mass media.

16-38. Salvador Dali, *Le Grand Paranoiac,* 1936. The viewer simultaneously sees figures groping in a landscape and a large human head in this oil painting.

compose directly on paper. As he looked at his rubbings, Ernst's imagination invented images in them, much as one sees images in cloud formations. Then he developed the rubbings into drawings of fantastic pictures. *Decalcomania,* Ernst's process of transferring images from printed matter to a drawing or painting, enabled him to incorporate a variety of images into his work in unexpected ways.

This technique has been used extensively in illustration, painting, and printmaking.

The figurative Surrealist painters have been called naturalists of the imaginary. Space, color, perspective, and figures are rendered in careful naturalism, but the image is an unreal dreamscape. The Belgian Surrealist René Magritte (1898–1967) used jolting and ambiguous scale changes, defied the laws of gravity and light, created unexpected juxtapositions, and maintained a poetic dialogue between reality and illusion, truth and fiction (Figs. 16-36 and 16-37). His prolific body of images inspired many visual communications.

The theatrical Spanish painter Salvador Dali (1904–1989) influenced graphic design in two ways. His deep perspectives have inspired attempts to bring depth to the flat, printed page, and his naturalistic approach to simultaneity (Fig. 16-38) has been frequently imitated by designers of posters and editorial images.

Another group of Surrealist painters, the Emblematics, worked with a purely visual vocabulary. Visual automatism (intuitive stream-of-consciousness drawing and calligraphy) was used to create spontaneous expressions of inner life in the work of Joan Miró (1893–1983) and Jean Arp. Miró explored a process of metamorphosis through which he intuitively evolved his motifs into cryptic, organic shapes (Fig. 16-39). As early as 1916, Arp explored chance and unplanned harmonies in works such as *Squares Arranged According to the Laws of Chance*. The organic, elemental forms and open composition of these two artists have been incorporated into design, particularly during the 1950s.

Surrealism's impact on graphic design has been diverse. It provided a poetic example of the liberation of the human spirit. It pioneered new techniques and demonstrated how fantasy and intuition could be expressed in visual terms. Unfortunately, the ideas and images of Surrealism have been exploited and trivialized frequently in the mass media.

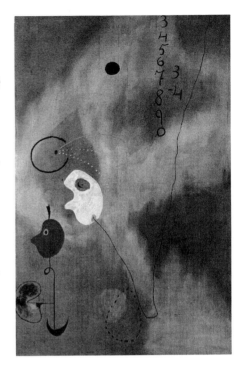

16-39. Joan Miró, *Peinture (Dite L'addition)*, 1925. Because Miró often worked with little conscious direction of his brush, his work became intuitive, spontaneous expressions of the subconscious mind.

Photography and the Modern Movement

Perhaps it was inevitable that the new visual language of the modern movements —with a concern for point, line, plane, shape, and texture, and for the relationships between these visual elements—would begin to influence photography, just as it had affected typography in the Futurist and Dadaist approaches to graphic design. Photography had been invented as a means to document reality with greater accuracy than painting; in the early twentieth century, painting pulled photography into its new realm of abstraction and design.

Francis Bruguiere (1880–1945) began to explore multiple exposures in 1912, pioneering the potential of light recorded on film as a medium for poetic expression. In his photographic abstractions, the play of light and shadow becomes the subject (Fig. 16-40). Another photographer who extended his vision into the realm of pure form was Alvin Langdon Coburn (1882–1966). By 1913, his photographs of rooftops and views from tall buildings focused on the pattern and structure found in the world instead of depicting objects and things (Fig. 16-41). Coburn's jewel-like kaleidoscope patterns, which he called *vortographs* when the series began in 1917, are early nonobjective photographic images. Coburn praised the beautiful design seen through a microscope, explored multiple exposure, and used prisms to split images into fragments.

The technique used in William Henry Fox Talbot's early "photogenic drawings" (see Fig. 11-6) was first revived by the photographer and painter Christian Schad (b. 1894), who began making *schadographs* in 1918. String, bits of fabric, and scrap paper were composed into Cubist-like compositions with other flat materials and small objects on photographic paper in the darkroom. An exposure was then made to record the design.

An American artist from Philadelphia, Man Ray (né Emanuel Rabinovitch, 1890–1976), met Marcel Duchamp and fell under the spell of Dada in 1915. After moving to Paris in 1921, Man Ray joined Breton and others in their evolution from Dada toward Surrealism, with its less haphazard investigation of the role played

The Influence of Modern Art

16-40. Francis Bruguiere, *Light Abstraction,* undated. By cutting and bending paper, Bruguiere composed a photographic composition of forms moving in and out of space.

16-41. Alvin Langdon Coburn, *The Octopus,* 1912. The visual design patterns of shape and tone became Coburn's subject as he viewed the world from unexpected vantage points.

16-40

16-41

by the unconscious and chance in artistic creation. During the 1920s, he worked as a professional photographer while applying Dada and Surrealism to photography, using both darkroom manipulation and bizarre studio setups. He was the first photographer to explore the creative potential of *solarization* (Fig. 16-42), the reversal of the tonal sequence in the denser areas of a photographic negative or print, which adds strong black contours to the edges of major shapes. Solarization is achieved by giving a latent or developing photographic image a second exposure to light. Man Ray's cameraless prints, which he called *rayographs* (Fig. 16-43), were more complex than schadographs. Man Ray frequently made his exposures with moving beams of light, and combined experimental techniques such as solarization with

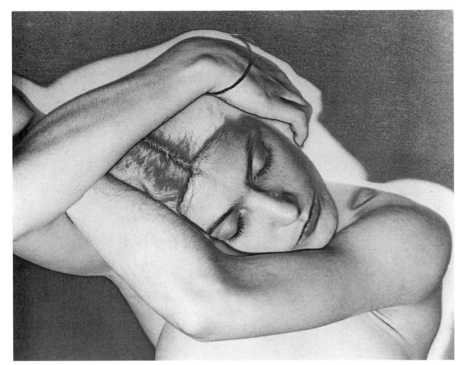

16-42. Man Ray, *Sleeping Woman*, 1929. In this surreal image, the solarization technique is used not just as a visual technique but as a means to plumb the psychic experience.

16-43. Man Ray, *Gun with Alphabet Squares*, 1924. In this "rayograph," multiple exposures and a shifting light source transform the photographic record of the gun and stencil letters into a new order of visual form.

16-44. Man Ray, poster for the London Underground, 1932. Drawing a visual analogy between the London Underground symbol and Saturn, Man Ray propels the trademark into space in an unexpected application of Surrealist dislocation to visual communications.

16-43

-KEEPS LONDON GOING

16-44

the basic technique of placing objects on the photographic paper. He also used distortion, printing through textures, and multiple exposures as he searched for dreamlike images and new interpretations of time and space, applying Surrealism to graphic design (Fig. 16-44) and photography assignments.

The concepts, images, and methods of visual organization from Cubism, Futurism, Dadaism, and Surrealism have provided valuable insights and processes for graphic designers. The innovators of these movements, who dared to walk into a no-man's-land of unexplored artistic possibilities, continue to influence artists, designers, and illustrators to this day.

Pictorial Modernism

17

The European poster during the first half of the twentieth century was a continuation of the 1890s poster, but its course was strongly affected by the modern-art movements and altered by the communication needs of two world wars. Graphic designers involved in the poster, influenced by Cubism and Constructivism yet cognizant of the need to maintain a pictorial reference if their posters were to communicate persuasively with the general public walked a tightrope between the creation of expressive and symbolic images on the one hand and their concern for the total visual organization of the picture plane on the other. This dialogue between communicative imagery and design form generates the excitement and energy of pictorial modernism.

Plakatstil

The reductive, flat-color design school that emerged in Germany early in the twentieth century is called *Plakatstil* ("poster style"). In 1898, fifteen-year-old Lucien Bernhard (1883–1972) attended the Munich Flaspalast Exhibition of Interior Decoration and was overwhelmed by what he saw. Returning home "just drunk with color" from this avant-garde design show, Bernhard began to repaint the proper nineteenth-century decor of the Bernhard home while his father was away on a three-day business trip. Walls, ceilings, and even furniture traded drabness for a wonderland of brilliant color. Upon his return home, the elder Bernhard was not amused. Lucien was called a potential criminal and severely rebuked. He ran away from home that very day and never returned. In Berlin, he was trying unsuccessfully to support himself as a poet when he saw an advertisement for a poster con-

17-1. Lucien Bernhard, poster for Stiller shoes, 1912. Against the brown background, dark letterforms, and black shoe, the inside of the shoe is intense red and the front of the heel is bright orange.

256

test sponsored by Priester matches. The prize was two hundred marks (about fifty dollars at the time), so Bernhard, who had excelled at art in school, decided to enter. His first design showed a round table with a checked tablecloth, an ashtray holding a lighted cigar, and a box of matches. Feeling that the image was too bare, Bernhard painted scantily clad dancing girls in the background. Later that day, he decided that the image was too complex and painted the girls out. When a friend dropped by and asked if it was a poster for a cigar, Bernhard painted out the cigar. Deciding that the tablecloth and ashtray stood out too prominently, Bernhard painted them out as well, leaving a pair of matches on a bare table. Because the entries had to be postmarked by midnight on that date, Bernhard hastily painted the word "Priester" above the matches in blue, wrapped the poster, and sent it off.

Later, Bernhard learned that the jury's immediate reaction to his poster was total rejection. But a late-arriving juror, Ernst Growald of the Hollerbaum and Schmidt lithography firm, rescued it from the trashcan. Stepping back to study the image, Growald proclaimed, "This is my first prize. Here is a genius." Growald convinced the rest of the jury, and Bernhard's first poster was the now-famous Priester matches poster (Pl. 40), which reduced communication to one word and two matches. Color became the visual means that enabled Bernhard to project a powerful message with minimal information.

This self-taught young artist probably did not realize it at the time, but he had moved the visual poster one step further in the process of simplification and reduction of naturalism into a graphic language of shape and sign. Toulouse-Lautrec had started the process, and the Beggarstaffs had continued it, but Bernhard established the approach to the poster of using flat color shapes, the product name, and product image (Fig. 17-1). He would repeat this approach over and over during the next two decades. In addition, he designed over three hundred packages for sixty-six products, using similar elementary graphics.

The outstanding Berlin lithography firm of Hollerbaum and Schmidt recognized that an important style of German poster art was developing in the hands of Bernhard and other young poster artists. It signed Bernhard and five other graphic designers to exclusive contracts. This farsighted business acumen effectively forced anyone wishing to commission posters from these artists to work with the Hollerbaum and Schmidt printing firm. In addition to Bernhard, the group included Hans Rudi Erdt (1883–1918), Julius Gipkens (b. 1883), and Julius Klinger (1876–1950). Comparison of the Stiller shoes poster by Bernhard and the 1911 Opel motorcar

17-2. Julius Gipkens, poster for Heinemann's Wicker Furniture, undated. Gipkens was less reductive than Bernhard and Erdt. The dog and checkered cushion lend an ambience of hearth and home.

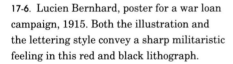

17-4

17-5

17-3. Berthold Type Foundry, Block Type, 1910. Early twentieth-century German sans serif typefaces were based on Bernhard's poster lettering.

17-4. Lucien Bernhard, trademark for Hommel Micrometers, 1912. Every shape and form comprising this figure is derived from Hommel's products.

17-5. Lucien Bernhard, trademark for Manoli cigarettes, 1911. A simple *M* in a circle suggests the minimal forms of forthcoming twentieth-century symbols and trademarks.

17-6. Lucien Bernhard, poster for a war loan campaign, 1915. Both the illustration and the lettering style convey a sharp militaristic feeling in this red and black lithograph.

17-7. Julius Gipkens, poster for an exhibition of captured airplanes, 1917. Stark graphic shapes project boldly against the white field. A symbolic eagle sits triumphantly upon the red, white, and blue indicia of a captured allied aircraft.

17-8. Hans Rudi Erdt, *U-Boats Out!* poster, c. 1916. After 1916, it became evident that submarine warfare was the only possible way that Germany could break the English blockade. Erdt's powerful visual joining of the large *U* with the U-Boat commander peering through a periscope at the sinking vessel served to celebrate Germany's heroes and rally the public behind them.

poster (Pl. 41) by Erdt demonstrates how well Erdt was able to apply the Bernhard formula: flat background color; large, simple image; and product name. Gipkens, like Bernhard, was a self-taught graphic designer who developed a large clientele in Berlin. The fluid, linear drawing of Gipkens's work gave a nervous wiggle to both his lettering and images and became a trademark in his work (Fig. 17-2).

Born and educated in Vienna, Julius Klinger had been associated with the Vienna Secession artists. Sensing a better opportunity for graphic design in Germany, Klinger moved to Berlin, where his style veered from floral Art Nouveau toward decorative shapes of bright, clear color and concise, simple lettering (Pl. 42).

During the early years of Bernhard's poster design career, he developed a sans serif lettering style painted in broad brushstrokes. At first, he did not have any particular concept, but a dense alphabet of unique character gradually developed. This alphabet design impressed a staff member from the Berthold Type Foundry in Berlin, and a typeface design was based on it (Fig. 17-3). When the typeface was released in 1910, Bernhard was quite surprised to see his personal lettering style cast in metal for all the world to use. His sense of simplicity was also applied to trademark design. For Hommel Micrometers in 1912, Bernhard constructed a little mechanical man holding one of the client's sensitive measuring devices (Fig. 17-4). For Manoli cigarettes in 1911, Bernhard reduced the trademark to a simple *M* in a circle printed in a second color (Fig. 17-5).

Bernhard was a pivotal designer. His work might be considered the logical conclusion of the turn-of-the-century poster movement. At the same time, emphasis on reduction, minimalist form, and simplification anticipated the Constructivist movement. As time went on, Bernhard tackled interior design, then studied carpentry to learn furniture design and construction. This led to a study of architecture, and during the 1910s Bernhard was designing furniture, rugs, wallpapers, and lighting fixtures, as well as office buildings, factories, and houses.

A visit to America in 1923 excited Bernhard, and he returned to live in New York. His work was far too modern to gain acceptance in America, and it took him five years to become established as a graphic designer. During that time, he worked as an interior designer. In 1928, Bernhard contracted with the American Type Founders to design new typefaces, resulting in a steady stream of new fonts that captured the sensibilities of the era.

The poster goes to war

The poster reached the zenith of its importance as a medium of communication during World War I (1914–1918). Printing technologies had been perfected, and radio and other electronic means of public communication had not yet come into prominence. In this total global conflict, governments turned to the poster as a major means of propaganda and visual persuasion. Armies had to be recruited, and public morale had to be boosted to maintain popular support for the war effort. In

17-6

this first conflict fought with the armaments of technology—airplanes, zeppelins, heavy artillery, and tanks—fund-raising drives were used to raise vast amounts of money to finance the destruction and prevent governmental bankruptcy. As resources were diverted to the war effort, public support for conservation and home gardening was required to lessen the risk of acute shortages. Finally, the enemy had to be assailed for his barbarism and threat to civilization.

Posters of the Central Powers (led by Germany and Austria-Hungary) and the Allies (led by France and Great Britain, then joined by the United States in 1917) were radically different. In Germany and Austria-Hungary, a design approach that continued the traditions of the Vienna Secession and Bernhard was dominant. Words and images were integrated, and the essence of the communication was conveyed by simplifying images into powerful shapes and patterns. In expressing this design philosophy, Julius Klinger observed that the United States flag was the best poster America had.

Klinger's war posters were reduced to simple pictographic symbols. In his poster for the eighth Bond Drive (Pl. 42), eight arrows piercing a dragon remind the citizens that their contributions have helped wound the enemy. Curiously, Bernhard adopted a medieval approach in several war posters, such as the hand-drawn lithographic poster for the Seventh War Loan (Fig. 17-6). In an almost primeval expression of the ancient Germanic spirit, Bernhard depicts a clenched fist in medieval armor thrusting into the space over the gothic inscription that reads, "This is the way to peace—the enemy wills it so! Thus subscribe to the war loan!"

The simplicity pioneered by Bernhard was used in war posters by Gipkens (Fig. 17-7) and Erdt (Fig. 17-8). A frequent propaganda device was the destruction

17-7

17-8

17-9. Otto Lehmann, poster for a war loan campaign, undated. The cluster of figures and dense lettering create a solid base from which the soldier and flag thrust upward into the white space.

of the enemy's symbol or flag. One of the most effective examples of this approach is Cologne designer Otto Lehmann's (b. 1865) poster depicting industrial workers and farmers holding on their shoulders a soldier taking down a ripped British flag (Fig. 17-9). It proclaims, "Support our men in field gray. Crush England's might. Subscribe to the war loan."

The Allies' approach to graphic propaganda was more illustrative, with literal rather than symbolic imagery used to address propaganda objectives. British posters called upon the need to protect traditional values, the home, and the family. Perhaps the most effective British poster of the war years is the 1915 military recruiting poster by Alfred Leete (1882–1933), showing the popular Lord Horatio Kitchener, British Secretary of War, pointing directly at the viewer (Fig. 17-10). Originally, this image appeared as the 5 September 1914 cover of the *London Opinion* magazine above the headline, "Your country needs you." The Parliamentary Recruiting Committee gained permission to convert it into this powerful frontal eyeball-to-eyeball confrontation that inspired a number of imitations.

Public patriotism ran high when the United States entered the war to "make the world safe for democracy" in "the war to end all wars." Illustrator Charles Dana Gibson offered his services as art director to the division of Pictorial Publicity, a Federal agency that produced over seven hundred posters and other propaganda materials for fifty other governmental agencies. Working without charge, the leading magazine illustrators turned to poster design and grappled with the change in scale from magazine page to poster. Persuasive propaganda replaced narrative interpretations, and suddenly the illustrators had to integrate lettering with the image. James Montgomery Flagg (1877–1960), whose sketchy painting style was widely known, whipped out some forty-six war posters during the year and a half of American involvement in the war, including his American version of the Kitchener poster. Five million copies of Flagg's "Uncle Sam" poster (Pl. 43) were printed, making it one of the most widely reproduced posters in history.

The rising star of illustrator Joseph C. Leyendecker received a boost from his popular posters (Figs. 17-11 and 17-12). Leyendecker's images, painted with slab-like brushstrokes, have a distinctive appearance. His ability to convey the essence of a subject was emerging at this time. This skill held Leyendecker in good stead after the war, for his 322 covers for *The Saturday Evening Post* and countless advertising illustrations, notably for Arrow Shirts and Collars during the 1920s,

17-10

17-11

17-12

17-13. J. Paul Verrees, poster promoting Victory gardens, 1918. Public action—the raising of one's own food—is tied directly to the defeat of the enemy.

17-14. Ludwig Hohlwein, fund-raising poster, 1914. A graphic symbol (the red cross) combines with a pictorial symbol (a wounded soldier) in an appeal with emotional power and visual attention-getting qualities.

17-13

17-14

captured the American experience and attitudes during the decades between the world wars.

Honoring soldiers and creating a cult around national leaders or symbolic figures were two important functions of the poster; ridiculing or disparaging the leaders of the enemy forces was another. In Paul Verrees's unusual attempt at humor (Fig. 17-13), which was seldom seen in propaganda posters, the Kaiser is "canned."

Many posters emphasized the contribution of the public to the war effort by appealing to patriotic emotions. In a poster for the American Red Cross (Pl. 44) by Jesse Wilcox Smith (1863–1935), the viewer is asked if he or she has a service flag, which signifies that the household has supported the Red Cross effort. Smith shared a studio with Elizabeth Shippen Green (1871–1954) and Violet Oakley (1874–1961), both of whom she met while studying with Howard Pyle. The trio became very active as illustrators specializing in magazine and children's book illustrations portraying children, motherhood, and the genre life of the times.

17-10. Alfred Leete, poster for military recruiting, c. 1915. This printed sheet makes eye contact and confronts the spectator.

17-11. Joseph C. Leyendecker, poster for the U.S. Fuel Administration, 1917. A genre scene of a coal company delivery, painted in Leyendecker's choppy brushstrokes, is a reminder to citizens that fuel orders should be placed early.

17-12. Joseph C. Leyendecker, poster celebrating a successful bond drive, 1917. Requested to honor the role of Boy Scouts in the Third Liberty Loan Campaign, Leyendecker combined basic visual symbols —Liberty clad in the flag, holding an imperial shield, and taking a Be Prepared sword from the Scout—that promote patriotism with all levels of society.

The maverick from Munich

A leading Plakatstil designer, Ludwig Hohlwein (1874–1949) of Munich, began his career as a graphic illustrator with work commissioned by *Jugend* magazine as early as 1904. During the first five decades of the century, Hohlwein's graphic art evolved with changing social conditions. The Beggarstaffs were his initial inspiration, and during the years before World War I, Hohlwein took great delight in reducing his images to flat shapes. Unlike the Beggarstaffs and his Berlin rival Bernhard, however, Hohlwein applied a rich range of texture and decorative pattern to his images, as seen in the 1908 poster for Marque PKZ (Pl. 45). Many of these early posters were for clothing manufacturers and retail stores, and it seemed that Hohlwein never repeated himself. In the posters that he designed during World War I, Hohlwein began to combine his simple, powerful shapes with more naturalistic imagery. As evidenced in the 1914 Red Cross fund-raising poster (Fig. 17-14), Hohlwein's work straddles the line between the symbolic posters of other Central Powers graphic designers and the pictorial posters by the Allies. After the war, Hohlwein was much sought after by commercial accounts desiring his style, which was becoming more fluid and painterly, with figures frequently arranged on a flat, white ground and colorful lettering placed around them.

After an unsuccessful 1923 attempt to seize power in the Munich *Putsch,* Adolf Hitler was sent to prison, where he spent his time writing *Mein Kampf,* which set

17-15. Ludwig Hohlwein, poster for the Deutsche Lufthansa, 1936. A mythological winged being symbolizes the airline, German victory in the Berlin Olympics, and the triumph of the Nazi movement.

17-16. Ludwig Hohlwein, concert poster, 1938. A Teutonic she-warrior looms upward because of the low vantage point and a light source striking her from below.

17-15   17-16

forth his political philosophy and plans to take over Germany. He wrote that propaganda "should be popular and should adapt its intellectual level to the receptive ability of the least intellectual" citizens. Hitler was convinced that the more artistically designed posters used in Germany and Austria during World War I were "wrong-headed," while the slogans and popular illustrations from the Allies were more effective.

Hitler had an almost uncanny knack for visual propaganda. When he rose on the German political scene, the swastika was adopted as the symbol for the Nazi party. Uniforms consisting of brown shirts with red armbands bearing a black swastika in a white circle began to appear throughout Germany, as Nazi storm troopers grew in strength and numbers. In retrospect, it seems almost inevitable that the Nazi party would commission a steady stream of posters from Hohlwein, for the evolution of his work coincided closely with Hitler's concept of effective propaganda. As Hitler spoke in his passionate radio addresses to the nation about the "master race" of fair-haired German youth and the triumphant superiority of German athletes, Hohlwein posters carried these images all across the nation (Figs. 17-15 and 17-16). Hitler's ideas gained visual presence, and the repetition of seeing the images over and over again reinforced them. As the Nazi dictatorship consolidated its power and the stormy holocaust of World War II approached, Hohlwein moved toward a bold imperial and militaristic style of tight, heavy forms and strong tonal contrasts (Fig. 17-17).

Post-Cubist pictorial modernism

17-17. Ludwig Hohlwein, recruiting poster, early 1940s. In one of Hohlwein's last posters for the Nazis, a stern and somber soldier appears above the simple question, "And you?"

After World War I, the nations of Europe and North America sought a return to normalcy. The war machinery was turned toward peacetime needs, and a decade of unprecedented prosperity dawned for the victorious Allies. Faith in the machine and technology was at an all-time high, and this ethic gained expression through art and design. Léger's celebration of mechanical, machine-made, and industrial forms became an important design resource, and the Cubist ideas of spatial organization and synthetic imagery inspired an important new direction in pictorial images. Among the graphic designers who incorporated Cubism directly into their work, an American working in London, Edward McKnight Kauffer (1890–1954), and a Russian immigrant to Paris, A. M. Cassandre (né Adolphe Jean-Marie Mouron, 1901–1968), played major roles in defining this new approach.

The term *Art Deco* is used to identify the popular geometric styles of the 1920s and 1930s, and signifies a major aesthetic sensibility in graphics, architecture, and product design during the decades between the two world wars. The influences of Cubism, the Bauhaus, and the Vienna Secession commingled with de Stijl, Suprematism, and a mania for Egyptian, Aztec, and Assyrian motifs. Streamlining, zigzag, moderne, and decorative geometry—these attributes express the simultaneous desires to express the modern era of the machine while still satisfying a passion for decoration. (The term *Art Deco* was coined by British art historian Bevis Hillier in the 1960s, and is derived from the title of the "Exposition Internationale des Arts Décoratifs et Industriels Modernes," a major design exhibition held in Paris in 1925. It was not used for the title of this chapter because graphic designs not encompassed by the term, such as Plakatstil and the wartime propaganda posters, are discussed.)

Kauffer was born in Great Falls, Montana. His formal education was limited to eight years of grammar school because his itinerant fiddler father abandoned the family when Kauffer was three. At age twelve, Kauffer began to work at odd jobs to supplement the family income. At age sixteen, he traveled to San Francisco and worked in a bookstore while taking night-school art classes and painting on weekends. On his way to New York late in 1912, he stopped in Chicago for several months to study at the Art Institute. While there, he saw the famous Armory Show, which traveled to Chicago from New York in 1913. This first American exposure to modern art caused a scandalous uproar. The 16 March 1913 *New York Times* headline proclaimed, "Cubists and Futurists Make Insanity Pay."

Twenty-two-year-old Kauffer responded intuitively to the strength of the work, decided his Chicago teachers were not on top of recent developments in art, and moved to Europe. After living in Munich and Paris, he journeyed to London in 1914 when war broke out. Kauffer's famous 1918 poster for the *Daily Herald* (Pl. 46), although flawed somewhat by the type choice and placement, was a sign that the formal language of Cubism and Futurism could be used with strong communications impact in graphic design. For the next quarter of a century, a steady stream of posters and other graphic design assignments enabled him to apply the invigorating principles of modern art, particularly Cubism, to the problems of visual communications. He designed 141 posters for the London Underground Transport (Figs. 17-18 through 17-20). The writer Aldous Huxley observed that in contrast to the predominant use of money and sex in advertising for everything from scents to sanitary plumbing, Kauffer "prefers the more difficult task of advertising products in terms of forms that are symbolical only to those particular products. . . . He reveals his affinity with all artists who have ever aimed at expressiveness through simplification, distortion, and transposition, and especially the Cubists," to produce "not a copy, but a simplified, formalized and more expressive symbol." When World War II began, Kauffer returned to his native America, where he worked until his death in 1954.

At age fourteen, A. M. Cassandre migrated to Paris from Russia, where he had been born in the Ukraine to a Russian mother and French father. He studied at the Ecole des Beaux Arts and Académie Julian. His graphic design career began when he took a job with Hachard et Compagnie printing firm to earn money for art study and living expenses. From 1923 until 1936, he produced a stunning series of posters that helped revitalize French advertising art. Cassandre's bold, simple designs emphasize two-dimensionality and are composed of broad, simplified planes of color. By reducing his subjects into iconographic symbols, he moved very close to Synthetic Cubism. His love of letterforms is evidenced by an exceptional ability to integrate words and images into a total composition. Cassandre achieved concise statements by combining telegraphic copy, powerful geometric forms, and symbolic imagery created by simplifying natural forms into almost pictographic silhouettes. In his 1925 poster for the Paris newspaper *L'Intransigeant* (Pl. 47), the collage-

17-18. E. McKnight Kauffer, poster for the London Underground, 1922. To make a historical museum interesting, Kauffer selected a dramatic event—the burning of Parliament—and illustrated it with slashing red and orange shapes inspired by Cubism.

TWICKENHAM BY TRAM

THE COLNE RIVER AT UXBRIDGE BY TRAM

17-20

17-19. E. McKnight Kauffer, poster for the London Underground, 1924. Lyrical greens, tans, and grays capture the idyllic quality of the rural location.

17-20. E. McKnight Kauffer, poster for the London Underground, 1924. Kauffer solved the problem of achieving graphic impact with a landscape subject on posters by developing a flat-shape illustration style that distills the essence of the subject into restful blue and green planes.

inspired pictographic image depicts Marianne, the symbolic voice of France, urgently shouting the news that is being received over the telegraph wires. In this masterpiece of composition, Cassandre cropped the client's name as it raced out the upper right-hand corner, leaving the often-used shortened name. Many of Cassandre's finest works were for railways (Fig. 17-21) and steamship lines. In his 1931 poster for the ocean liner *L'Atlantique* (Pl. 48), the ship image is constructed on a rectangle echoing the rectangle of the poster's edges. By exaggerating the scale difference between the ship and tugboat, a monolithic quality is achieved, signifying safety and strength. The severe geometry is softened by the smoke and fading reflection. The iconography of Cassandre's work for Dubonnet (Fig. 17-22) was used by that client for over two decades, in formats ranging from scratch pads to billboards. For the Deberny and Peignot type foundry, Cassandre designed typefaces that were daring innovations in their design qualities (Figs. 17-23 through 17-25). During the late 1930s, Cassandre worked in the United States for clients including *Harper's Bazaar,* Container Corporation of America, and N. W. Ayer. After returning to Paris in 1939, he turned to painting and design for the ballet and theater, which were his major involvements over the next three decades.

In addition to Kauffer and Cassandre, a number of other graphic designers and illustrators incorporated concepts and images from Cubism into their work. Jean Carlu (1900–1989), a promising eighteen-year-old French architectural student, was whipped under the wheels of a Paris trolley car, and his right arm was severed

17-21. A. M. Cassandre, railway poster, 1927. This poster, in addition to being a magnificent abstract design, conveys an intangible aspect of travel—the unknown experience and hope of a destination far in the future—for the "North Star" night train from Paris to Amsterdam.

17-22. A. M. Cassandre, poster for Dubonnet, 1932. Cinematic sequence is used in both word and image: *DUBO* (doubt), as the man eyes the glass uncertainly; *DU BON* (of some good), the beverage is tasted; and *DUBONNET,* the product is identified as the glass is refilled.

17-23. A. M. Cassandre, Bifur typeface, 1929. About half of each letter is omitted. A linear shaded area restores the basic silhouette. Therefore, the eye is able to fill in the missing parts and read the characters.

17-24. A. M. Cassandre, Acier Noir typeface, 1936. In this unique design, each letter is half solid and half outline.

17-25. A. M. Cassandre, Peignot typeface, 1937. In this thick-and-thin sans serif, Cassandre's lowercase actually mixes lowercase with small capitals. Note the design of the ascenders and descenders.

17-22

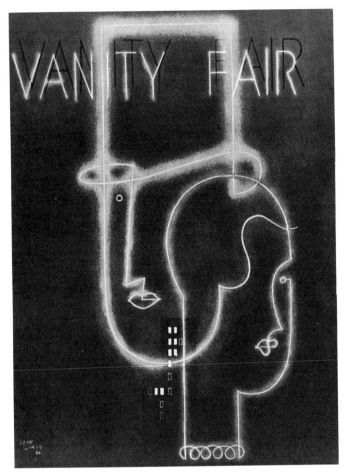

17-27

17-26. Jean Carlu, *Vanity Fair* cover, 1930. This stylized geometric drawing, expressed as the newly invented neon-tube lighting, reflects its Cubist origin. The heads glow vibrantly in red and blue against the dark night sky.

17-27. Paul Colin, poster for the dancer Georges Pomies, 1932. The glowing red and orange figure of Pomies zigs to the right in counterpoint to his brown shadow, which zags to the left against the maroon background. A pulsating musical feeling is generated by the small contour-line white figure with its yellow companions.

from his body. His survival was miraculous, and during long days of recovery he thought intensely about the world and his future. World War I had turned northern France into a vast burial ground. Grids of white crosses stretched for miles where villages and farms had flourished for centuries. France struggled for economic recovery in the face of devastation and hardship. Having to abandon his dream of architecture, young Carlu vowed to become an artist and apply his talents to the needs of his country. With commitment and concentration, he taught himself to draw with his left hand.

Like Cassandre and Kauffer, Carlu understood the modern movements and applied this knowledge to visual communication (Fig. 17-26). Realizing the need for concise statements, he made a dispassionate, objective analysis of the emotional value of visual elements. Then he assembled them with almost scientific exactness. Tenseness and alertness were expressed by angles and lines; feelings of ease, relaxation, and comfort were transmitted by curves. Carlu sought to convey the essence of the message by avoiding the use of "two lines where one would do" or using "two ideas where one will deliver the message more forcefully." To study the effectiveness of communications in the urban environment, he conducted experiments with posters moving past spectators at varying speeds so that message legibility and impact could be assessed and documented.

In 1940, Carlu was in America completing an exhibition entitled "France at War" for the French Information Service display at the New York World's Fair. On 14 June 1940 German troops marched into Paris, and Carlu was stunned to learn that

17-28. Austin Cooper, poster for the Southern Railway, undated. The vocabulary of Cubism operates symbolically for visual communications purposes. Fun and excitement are conveyed by fragments of images and bright color.

his country was capitulating to Hitler. He decided to remain in America for the duration of the war, but this sojourn lasted for thirteen years. Some of his finest work was created during this period, notably the posters designed for the American and Allied war efforts (see Pl. 67). Word and image are interlocked into terse messages of great power in his finest designs.

Paul Colin (1892–1989) started his career as a graphic designer in 1925, when an acquaintance from the trenches of World War I asked the thirty-three-year-old painter if he would like to become the graphics and set designer for the Théâtre des Champs-Elysées in Paris. In program covers and posters, Colin often placed a figure or object centrally before a colored background with type or lettering placed above and/or below this image (Fig. 17-27). These strong, central images are animated by a variety of techniques: creating a double image, often with different

17-29

17-30

drawing techniques and scale changes; using the transparency of overlapping images as a means to make two things into one; or adding color shapes or bands behind or to the side of the central figure to counteract the static placement and create a less stable balance. The simple, sketchy quality of most of Colin's graphic designs enabled him to produce a substantial oeuvre. Estimates about the number of posters he created have ranged from one to two thousand, and some sources credit him with a staggering eight hundred set designs. Whatever the exact numbers, Colin is undoubtedly the most prolific and enduring designer of pictorial modernism. He produced propaganda posters during World War II until the fall of France, and new Colin posters were still being commissioned, printed, and posted throughout Paris during the early 1970s.

A direct application of Cubism to graphic design was made by Austin Cooper (1890–1964) in England. In a series of three collage-inspired posters, he attempted to spark memories of the viewer's earlier continental visits by presenting fragments and glimpses of landmarks (Fig. 17-28). Lively movement is achieved by

17-29. Joseph Binder, poster for the Vienna Music and Theater Festival, 1924. The figures are reduced to flat, geometric shapes, but the proportions and indication of a light and shadow plane retain a sense of naturalism.

17-30. Schulz-Neudamm, poster for the film *Metropolis*, 1926. While the Art Deco idiom often expressed an infatuation with the machine and an unbridled optimism in human progress, in this poster it turns darkly toward a future in which robots replace people.

shifting planes, sharp angles, and the superimposition of lettering and images. In 1924, Cooper made an interesting foray into the use of pure geometric shape and color to solve a communications problem for the London Electric Railway (Pls. 49 and 50). A winter poster proclaimed: "It is warmer down below." Its summer counterpart promised: "It is cooler down below." The geometric forms, rising from the bottom to the top of each poster, change in a rainbow of colors from warm to cool to symbolize the temperature changes as one leaves the cold street in winter—or the hot street in summer—for the greater comfort of the underground railway.

In Vienna, Joseph Binder (1898–1972) studied at the Vienna School of Applied Art, which was under the direction of Alfred Roller, from 1922 until 1926. While still a student, Binder combined various influences, including Koloman Moser and Cubism, into a pictorial graphic design style with strong communicative power. The hallmarks of his work were natural images reduced to basic forms and shapes, like the cube, sphere, and cone, and two flat color shapes used side by side to represent the light and shadow sides of a figure or object. His award-winning poster for the Vienna Music and Theater Festival (Fig. 17-29) is an early manifestation of the uniquely Viennese approach to Art Deco. Binder traveled widely and settled in New York City in 1935. As with so many immigrants to America, his style underwent changes, and he moved toward a highly refined and stylized naturalism in posters and billboards advertising throat lozenges, beer, travel, and public services. In Austria and Germany between the world wars, many other graphic designers constructed pictorial images from geometric planes. Artists such as Schulz-Neudamm, who is widely known for his promotional graphics for Universum-Film Aktiengesellschaft, where he was staff designer for motion picture publicity, created exceptional work in this manner (Fig. 17-30).

In England, Abram Games (b. 1914) was the last major graphic designer of the pictorial modernism philosophy. He began his career on the eve of World War II and became a most important British designer producing educational, instructional, and propaganda graphics during that war. In writing about his philosophy, Games said "the message must be given quickly and vividly so that interest is subconsciously retained. . . . The discipline of reason conditions the expression of design. . . . The designer constructs, winds the spring. The viewer's eye is caught, the spring released." Commonplace images and forms were organized in new ways to make the message more forceful and memorable. Games's poster for the Emergency Blood Transfusion Service (Fig. 17-31) asks the viewer, "If he should fall, is your blood there to save him?" Three ordinary images—a hand, a bottle, and a foot soldier—are combined into a compelling statement that provokes an emotional response from the observer.

European pictorial modernism focused on the total integration of word and image, one of the most enduring currents of twentieth-century graphic design. It began with Bernhard's 1905 Priester matches poster, responded to the communications needs of World War I and the formal innovations of Cubism and other early modern-art movements, and emerged after the war to play a major role in defining the visual sensibilities of the affluent 1920s and economically bleak 1930s. It retained sufficient momentum to provide graphic solutions to communications problems during World War II.

17-31. Abram Games, poster to recruit blood donors, c. 1942. Placing the soldier inside the diagram of the blood transfusion cements the connection between the donor's blood and the soldier's survival.

A New Language of Form

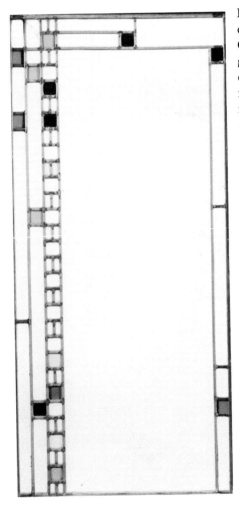

18-1. Frank Lloyd Wright, stained-glass window for the Coonley House, 1912. Before the turn of the century, Wright had begun to organize space into geometric planes. In this window, brilliant square chips of red, orange, and blue create a vibrant counterpoint to the white planes separated by dark strips of lead.

Pictorial modernism was not the only major current of European graphic design during the two decades between the wars. While Kauffer was applying Synthetic Cubism's planes to the poster in England, a formal typographic approach to graphic design emerged in Holland and Russia, where artists saw clearly the implications of Cubism. Visual art could move beyond the threshold of pictorial imagery into the invention of pure form. Ideas about form and composing space from the new painting and sculpture were quickly applied to problems of design. It would be a mistake, however, to say that modern design is a stepchild of the fine arts. As discussed in Chapter 15, the Vienna Secession and Workshops, The Four Macs, Adolf Loos, Peter Behrens, and Frank Lloyd Wright (Fig. 18-1) were all moving a heartbeat ahead of modern painting in their consciousness of plastic volume and geometric form at the turn of the century. A spirit of innovation was present in all the visual arts, ideas were in the air, and by the end of World War I, graphic designers, architects, and product designers were energetically challenging prevailing notions about form and function.

Russian Suprematism and Constructivism

During the second decade of the twentieth century, Russia was torn by the turbulence of World War I and the Russian Revolution. Czar Nicholas II (1868–1918) was overthrown and assassinated, Russia was ravaged by civil war, and the Red Army of the Bolsheviks emerged victorious by 1920. During this period of political trauma, there was a brief flowering of creative art in Russia that had an international influence on twentieth-century graphic design and typography. Beginning with Marinetti's Russian lectures, this decade saw Russian artists absorb the new ideas of Cubism and Futurism with amazing speed and then move on to new innovations.

The Russian avant-garde observed sufficient common traits in Cubism and Futurism to coin the term Cubo-Futurism. Experimentation in typography and design characterized the Futurist artists' books and periodicals, presenting work by the visual and literary art communities. Symbolically, the Russian Futurist books were a reaction against the values of Czarist Russia. The use of coarse paper, handicraft production methods, and handmade additions expressed the poverty of peasant society as well as the meager resources of the artists and writers. The poet Vladimir Mayakovsky's autobiographical play was designed in a dissonant Futurist style by David and Vladimir Burliuk (Fig. 18-2), becoming a model for works by others, including Ilya Zdanevich (Fig. 18-3).

Kasimir Malevich (1878–1935) founded a painting style of basic forms and pure color that he called *Suprematism*. After working in the manner of Futurism and Cubism, Malevich created an elemental geometric abstraction that was new, nonobjective, and pure. Malevich rejected both utilitarian function and pictorial representation, instead seeking the supreme "expression of feeling, seeking no practical values, no ideas, no promised land." Malevich believed the essence of the art experience was the perceptual effect of color. To demonstrate this, perhaps as early as 1913 Malevich made a composition with a black square on a white background (Fig. 18-4), asserting that the feeling this contrast evoked was the essence of art. In

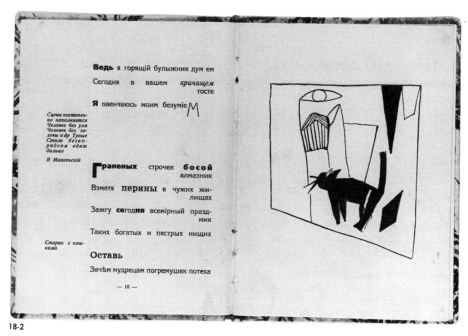

18-2

18-2. David and Vladimir Burliuk, pages
from *Vladimir Mayakovsky—A Tragedy,*
1914. In an effort to relate visual form to
meaning, Russian Futurist graphic design
mixed type weights, sizes, and styles.

18-3. Ilya Zdanevich, pages from *Le-Dantyu
as a Beacon,* 1923. The Burliuk brothers and
the Dadaists inspired Zdanevich's playscript
design, whose lively movements are created
by mixing type sizes and styles, and building
letters with letterpress ornaments.

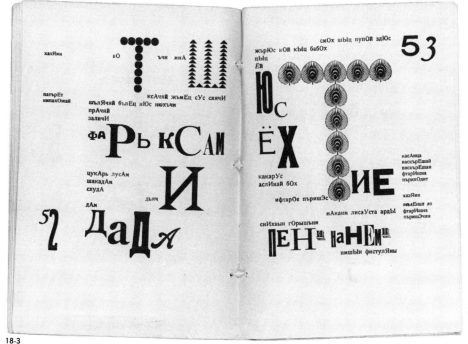

18-3

18-4. Kasimir Malevich, *Black Square,*
c. 1913. A new vision for visual art is as far
removed as possible from the world of
natural forms and appearances.

works such as the 1915 Suprematist Composition (Pl. 51), Malevich saw the work
of art as being a construction of concrete elements of color and shape. The visual
form becomes the content, and expressive qualities develop from the intuitive organization of the forms and colors.

The Russian movement was actually accelerated by the Revolution, for art was
given a social role rarely assigned to it. The "leftist" artists had been opposed to the
old order and its conservative visual art. In 1917, they turned their energies to a
massive propaganda effort in support of the Bolsheviks. But by 1920, a deep ideological split developed concerning the role of the artist in the new communist state.
Some artists, including Malevich and Wassily Kandinsky (1866–1944), argued that
art must remain an essentially spiritual activity apart from the utilitarian needs of
society. They rejected a social or political role, believing the sole aim of art to be
realizing perceptions of the world by inventing forms in space and time. Led by

Vladimir Tatlin (1885–1953) and Alexander Rodchenko (1891–1956), twenty-five artists advanced the opposing viewpoint in 1921, when they renounced "art for art's sake" to devote themselves to industrial design, visual communications, and applied arts serving the new communist society. These Constructivists called on the artist to stop producing useless things and turn to the poster, for "such work now belongs to the duty of the artist as a citizen of the community who is clearing the field of the old rubbish in preparation for the new life." Tatlin turned from sculpture to the design of a stove that would give maximum heat from minimum fuel; Rodchenko forsook painting for graphic design and photojournalism.

An early attempt to formulate Constructivist ideology was the 1922 brochure *Konstruktivizm* by Aleksei Gan (1893–1942). He criticized abstract painters for their inability to break their umbilical cord to traditional art, and boasted that Constructivism had moved from laboratory work to practical application. Gan wrote that tectonics, texture, and construction are the three principles of Constructivism. *Tectonics* represented the unification of communist ideology with visual form; *texture* meant the nature of materials and how they are used in industrial production; and *construction* symbolized the creative process and search for laws of visual organization.

The Constructivist ideal was best realized by the painter, architect, graphic designer, and photographer El (Lazar Markovich) Lissitzky (1890–1941). This indefatigable visionary profoundly influenced the course of graphic design. At age nineteen, after being turned down by the Petrograd Academy of Arts because of ethnic prejudice against Jews, Lissitzky turned to the study of architecture at the Darmstadt, Germany, School of Engineering and Architecture. The mathematical and structural properties of architecture became a basis for his art.

In 1919, Marc Chagall, principal of the art school in Vitebsk located about 250 miles east of Moscow, asked Lissitzky to join the faculty. Malevich was teaching there and became a major influence on Lissitzky, who developed a painting style that he called *PROUNS* (an acronym for "projects for the establishment [affirmation] of a new art"). In contrast to the absolute flatness of Malevich's picture plane, PROUNS (Fig. 18-5) introduced three-dimensional illusions that both receded (negative depth) behind the picture plane (nought depth) and projected forward (positive depth) from the picture plane. Lissitzky called PROUNS "an interchange station between painting and architecture." This indicates his synthesis of architectural concepts with painting; it also shows that PROUNS would point the way to the application of modern painting concepts of form and space to applied design. This is seen in his 1919 poster, *Beat the Whites with the Red Wedge* (Pl. 52). The space is dynamically divided into white and black areas. The emblem of the Bolshevik army, a red wedge, slashes diagonally into the center of a white sphere signifying the "white" forces of Kerenski. The four words of the slogan are placed to reinforce the dynamic movement. Suprematist design elements are transformed into political symbolism that even a semiliterate peasant can understand: Support for the "red" Bolshevik against the "white" forces of Kerenski is symbolized by a red wedge slashing into a white circle.

Lissitzky saw the October 1917 Russian Revolution as a new beginning for mankind. Communism and social engineering would create a new order; technology would provide for society's needs; and the artist/designer (he called himself a constructor) would forge a unity between art and technology by constructing a new world of objects to provide mankind with a richer society and environment. This idealism led him to put increasing emphasis on graphic design, as he moved from private aesthetic experience into the mainstream of community life.

In 1921, Lissitzky traveled to Berlin and made contact with de Stijl, the Bauhaus, Dadaists, and other Constructivists. Postwar Germany had become a meeting ground for Eastern and Western advanced ideas in the early 1920s. Access to excellent German printing facilities enabled Lissitzky's typographic ideas to develop rapidly. His tremendous energy and range of experimentation with photomontage, printmaking, graphic design, and painting enabled him to become the

18-5. El Lissitzky, *PROUN 23,* no. 6, 1919. Lissitzky developed visual ideas about balance, space, and form in his paintings, which became the basis for his graphic design and architecture.

18-6. El Lissitzky, exploratory design for the *Veshch* ("Object") cover, 1921–1922. Perhaps Lissitzky abandoned this concept because he felt that it was not achieving the unity of form that he sought in his graphic designs.

18-7. El Lissitzky, preparatory art for the first cover of *Veshch* ("Object"), 1921–1922. Lissitzky often constructed his designs on a dynamic axis with asymmetrical balance. Weight is often moved high on the page, and letterforms are constructed of geometric elements. Note the different letterform styles drawn for each of the three titles.

18-8. El Lissitzky, title page for *Veshch* ("Object"), 1922. In this page layout, Lissitzky is groping for an organizational system of geometric structure and a way to treat type, geometric elements, and photographic images as elements in an organizational whole. He rapidly realized these goals during the following two years.

18-6

main conduit through which Suprematist and Constructivist ideas flowed into western Europe. Editorial and design assignments for several publications were important vehicles by which his ideas influenced a wider audience.

During the early 1920s, the Soviet government offered official encouragement to the new Russian art, and even sought to publicize it through an international journal (Figs. 18-6 through 18-8). Editor Ilya Ehrenburg was joined by Lissitzky in creating the trilingual journal *Veshch*[Russian]/*Gegenstand*[German]/*Objet*[French]. The title, *Object* in English, was chosen because the editors believed that art meant the creation of new objects, a process that was creating a new collective international style in Europe and Russia in the hands of young creative artists and designers. Realizing that a seven-year period of separation—while Russia was bled by the Revolution and Europe was wasted by war—had seen the evolution of similar movements in art and design, Lissitzky and Ehrenburg saw *Veshch* as a meeting point for the new art and design of different nations. Also, Lissitzky's Berlin period enabled him to spread the message of Russian Constructivism through his frequent Bauhaus visits, important articles, and lectures. Major collaborations included the joint design and editing of a special double issue of *Merz* with Kurt Schwitters in 1924. The editors of *Broom,* a radical American magazine covering advanced literature and art, commissioned title pages and other graphics from Lissitzky. A *Broom* cover layout (Fig. 18-9) shows Lissitzky's practice of making layouts on graph paper, which imposed the modular structure and mathematic order of a grid upon his designs. Advertisements and displays were commissioned by the Pelikan Ink Company (Figs. 18-10 and 18-11). Rebelling against the constraints of metal typesetting, Lissitzky often used drafting instrument construction and paste-up to achieve his designs. In 1925, he correctly predicted that Gutenberg's system belonged to the past, and that photomechanical processes would replace metal type

18-7

18-8

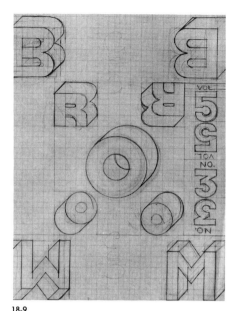

18-9

18-10

18-11

and open new horizons for design as surely as radio had replaced the telegraph.

As a graphic designer, Lissitzky did not decorate the book—he constructed the book by visually programming the total object. In a 1923 book of Vladimir Mayakovsky's poems, *For the Voice*—also translated as *For Reading Out Loud*—(Figs. 18-12 and 18-13, and Pl. 53) Lissitzky designed exclusively with elements from the metal typecase, interpreting the poems in the same way "a violin accompanies a piano." An index of diecut tabs along the right margin is used to make it easy for the reader to find a poem. The title spread for each poem is illustrated with abstract elements signifying the poem's content. The poem "Our March" (Pl. 53) opens with the words, "Beat your drums on the squares of the riots, turned red with the blood of revolution." The title typography is executed in the staccato cadences of a drumbeat, and the red square signifies the town squares of Russia. Visual relationships and contrasts of elements, the relationship of forms to the

18-12

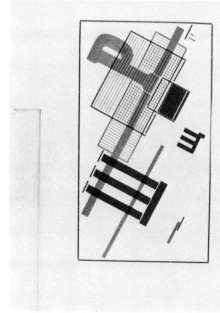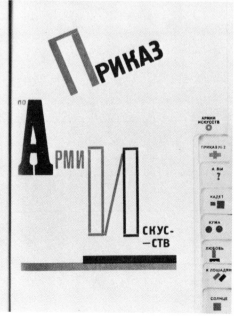

18-13

18-9. El Lissitzky, layout for a *Broom* cover, vol. 5, no. 3, 1922. By making his isometric perspective letterforms upside-down and backwards in the second presentation of the title, Lissitzky brings a subtle vitality to a rigorously symmetrical design.

18-10. El Lissitzky, advertisement for Pelikan carbon paper, 1924. Typewriter type, the manufacturer's signature, and stamped letters expressive of the product's use combine with overlapping planes that relate to the sandwiching of material to produce a business letter with carbons.

18-11. El Lissitzky, poster for Pelikan Ink, 1924. This photogram was produced in the darkroom by composing the objects directly on the photographic paper, then making the exposure by flashing a light held to the left.

18-12. El Lissitzky, cover of *For the Voice* by Mayakovsky, 1923. In contrast to the *Veshch* cover, constructed on a diagonal axis, here a rigid right angle is animated by the counterbalance of the *M* and circles.

18-13. El Lissitzky, pages from *For the Voice* by Mayakovsky, 1923. The poem title, translated as "Order for the Army of the Arts," appears on the right page opposite a dynamic constructivist design.

18-14. El Lissitzky, book cover for *The Isms of Art,* 1924. Complex typographic information is organized into a cohesive whole by the construction of structural relationships.

18-15. El Lissitzky, title page for *The Isms of Art,* 1924. The graphic spirit achieved by medium-weight sans serif type, mathematical division of the space, white areas, and the bold rules established a typographic standard for the modern movement.

18-16. El Lissitzky, text format for *The Isms of Art,* 1924. Rigorous verticals separate the German, French, and English texts, and horizontal bars around the statement of the left page emphasize an important introductory quotation.

18-14

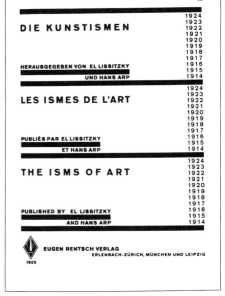

18-15

negative space of the page, and an understanding of such printing possibilities as overlapping color were important in this work.

One of the most influential graphic designs of the 1920s is the book *The Isms of Art 1914–1924* (Fig. 18-14), which Lissitzky edited with the Dadaist Hans Arp. The format that Lissitzky developed for this book is an important step toward the creation of a visual program for organizing information. The three-column horizontal grid structure used for the title page (Fig. 18-15), the three-column vertical grid structure used for the text (Fig. 18-16), and the two-column structure of the contents page became an architectural framework for organizing the illustrated pages of the forty-eight-page pictorial portfolio (Fig. 18-17). Asymmetrical balance, silhouette halftones, and a sensitive feeling for white space are other important design considerations. By using large, bold sans serif numbers to identify the pictures to the captions listed earlier, Lissitzky allows them to become compositional ele-

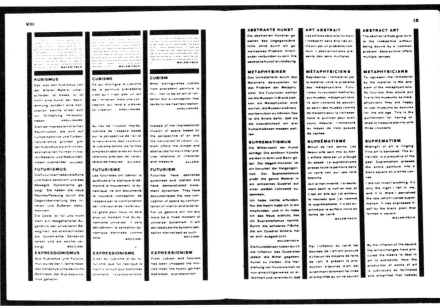

18-16

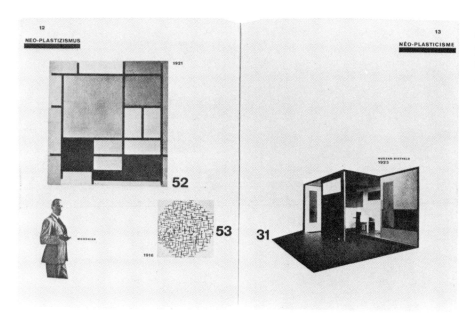

18-17. El Lissitzky, pictorial spread from *The Isms of Art*, 1924. The grid systems of the preceding typographic pages are echoed in the placement of the images, which are one, two, and three columns wide.

ments and expresses an attitude about number and letter as concrete form as well as verbal signal—an attitude adopted by many later twentieth-century graphic designers. Also, the treatment of sans serif typography and bars is an early expression of the modernist style.

Lissitzky explored the potential of montage and photomontage for complex communications messages (Fig. 18-18), and he applied the Constructivist approach to environmental (Fig. 18-19) and exhibition design projects. In 1923, he began an eighteen-year battle with tuberculosis. After returning to Russia in 1925, Lissitzky spent increasing amounts of time with large exhibition projects for the Soviet government (Fig. 18-20) in addition to publications, art direction, and some architectural design projects. In December 1941, six months after Germany invaded Russia, Lissitzky died. Through his social responsibility and commitment to his people, his mastery of technology to serve his goals, and his creative vision, El Lissitzky set a standard of excellence for the designer. Later, typographer Jan

18-18. El Lissitzky, exhibition poster, 1929. In this stark, powerful image, the youth of a collective society are cloned into an anonymous double portrait over the exhibition structure designed by Lissitzky. The image gives equal stature to the female portrait, a significant symbolic communication in a traditionally male-dominated society.

18-19. El Lissitzky, reconstruction of the 1923 PROUN room. The art of constructed relationships was transformed into the prototype of the "total environmental art experience."

18-19

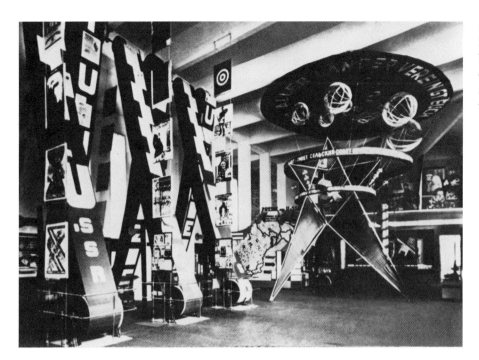

18-20. El Lissitzky, exhibition design for Pressa, 1928. Light, sound, and movement became design elements in Lissitzky's later exhibitions. In this design for the publishing and printing industry, the belts, symbolic of web printing, are in continuous movement.

Tschichold wrote, "Lissitzky was one of the great pioneers. . . . His indirect influence was widespread and enduring. . . . A generation that has never heard of him . . . stands upon his shoulders."

Alexander Rodchenko was an ardent Communist who brought an inventive spirit and willingness to experiment to typography, montage, and photography. His early interest in descriptive geometry led to an analytical precision and definition of form in his paintings. In 1921, Rodchenko abandoned painting and turned to visual communication, because his social views created a sense of responsibility to larger society instead of to personal expression. Collaborating closely with the writer Mayakovsky, Rodchenko produced graphic designs with strong geometric construction, large areas of pure color, and concise, legible lettering. His heavy sans serif hand lettering became the source for the bold sans serif types that are widely used in the Soviet Union.

In 1923, Rodchenko began to design a magazine (Figs. 18-21 through 18-23) for all fields of the creative arts, entitled *Novyi lef* ("Left Front of the Arts"). A design style based on strong, static horizontal and vertical forms placed in machine-rhythm relationships emerged. Overprinting, kiss registration, and photomontage were regularly employed in *Novyi lef*. Rodchenko delighted in contrasting bold, blocky type and hard-edged shapes against the softer forms and edges of photomontages. His interest in photomontage (Fig. 18-24) was a conscious effort to innovate a new illustration technique appropriate to the twentieth century. The beginning of Russian photomontage coincided with the development of montage in film—a new conceptual approach to assembling cinematic information—and shared some of its vocabulary. Some of the common techniques include showing simultaneous action; superimposing images; using extreme close-ups and perspective images, often together; and rhythmic repetition of an image. The concept of serial painting—a series or sequence of independent works unified by common elements or an underlying structure—was applied to graphic design by Rodchenko. In 1924, his series of ten covers for the Jim Dollar *Mess Mend* books (Fig. 18-25) used a standard geometric format printed in black and a second color. The title, number, and photomontage elements change with each edition and express the unique content of each book. The standardized elements bring consistency and economy to the whole series.

Georgy (1900–1933) and Vladimir (1899–1982) Stenberg were talented brothers who collaborated on theatrical designs and film posters (Pl. 54). Mindful of the

18-21. Alexander Rodchenko, cover for *Novyi lef* no. 1, 1923. Five thousand copies of this magazine, *Left Front of the Arts,* were printed. The logo is printed in tight registration, with the top half of the letterforms red and the bottom half black.

18-22. Alexander Rodchenko, cover for *Novyi lef* no. 2, 1923. In one of Rodchenko's early efforts to forge a new illustration technique using photomontage, a red cross-out over-printing the montage negates the old order; young children symbolize the new society.

18-23. Alexander Rodchenko, cover for *Novyi lef* no. 3, 1923. Using a fountain pen as a bomb, a biplane bearing the magazine logo assaults a gorilla representing the old traditional arts of the Czarist regime.

18-24. Alexander Rodchenko, photomontage of Lenin, 1937. Lenin looms above, as a larger-than-life figure, yet his hand makes symbolic contact with the masses. The "podium" is a *Pravda* newspaper proclaiming "Peace! Bread! Land!"

18-26. Salomon Telingater, covers for *Slovo Predstaliaetsia Kirsanovu* ("The Word Belongs to Kirsanov") by K. Kirsanov, 1930. The author's whimsy is reflected in Telingater's rollicking typography that changes tune, tempo, and key as it flows down the page.

18-25. Alexander Rodchenko, paperback book covers, 1924. The series of ten covers for Jim Dollar "Mess Mend" books use a standard geometric format printed in black and a second color. The title, number, and photomontage illustration change, but consistency is achieved through standardization, and the uniqueness of each book is nonetheless expressed.

reproduction difficulties with photographs at the time, they made meticulously realistic drawings for their posters by enlarging film-frame images via projection and grid methods. These three-dimensional illusions were contrasted with flat forms in dynamic, well-designed posters with strong graphic communications qualities.

During the early years after the 1917 Revolution, the Soviet government tolerated the advanced art while more urgent problems commanded its attention. But by 1922 the government, having turned hostile, accused advanced artists of "capitalist cosmopolitanism" and advocated social-realist painting. Although Constructivism lingered as an influence in Soviet graphic and industrial design, painters like Malevich who did not leave the country drifted into poverty and obscurity. Some artists vanished into the Gulag. However, the innovations of this artistic flowering had their further development in the West, and innovative graphic design in the Constructivist tradition continued through the 1920s and beyond. As seen in the work of Salomon Telingater (1903–1969), a dash of Dada vitality was often mixed into Constructivist designs (Fig. 18-26). A witty originality informed Telingater's use of typography and montage elements.

De Stijl (The Style)

The de Stijl movement was launched in the Netherlands in the late summer of 1917. The founder and guiding spirit, Théo van Doesburg (1883–1931), was joined by painters Piet Mondrian (1872–1944), Bart van der Leck (1876–1958), and Vilmos Huszar (1884–1960), the architect Jacobus Johannes Pieter Oud (1890–1963), and others. Working in an abstract geometric style, de Stijl sought universal laws of equilibrium and harmony for art, which could then be a prototype for a new social order.

Mondrian's paintings are the wellspring from which de Stijl's philosophy and visual forms developed. Mondrian had evolved from traditional landscape painting to a symbolic style—influenced by Van Gogh and expressing the forces of nature—when he first saw Cubist paintings by 1911. In early 1912, he moved to Paris and began to introduce the vocabulary of Cubism into his work. Over the next few years, Mondrian purged his art of all representative elements and evolved Cubism toward a pure, geometric abstraction. When war broke out in 1914, Mondrian was in Holland and remained there during the war. The philosopher M. H. J. Schoenmakers decisively influenced his thinking. Schoenmakers defined the horizontal and the vertical as the two fundamental opposites shaping our world, and called red, yellow, and blue the three principal colors. Mondrian began to paint purely abstract paintings composed of horizontal and vertical lines. He felt that the Cubists had not accepted the logical consequences of their discoveries; this was the evolution of abstraction toward its ultimate goal, the expression of pure reality. Mondrian believed true reality in visual art "is attained through dynamic movement in equilibrium . . . established through the balance of unequal but equivalent oppositions. The clarification of equilibrium through plastic art is of great importance for humanity. . . . It is the task of art to express a clear vision of reality."

For a time in the late 1910s, paintings by Mondrian, van der Leck, and van Doesburg were virtually indistinguishable (Fig. 18-27). They had reduced their visual vocabulary to the use of primary colors (red, yellow, and blue) with neutrals (black, gray, and white), straight horizontal and vertical lines, and flat planes limited to rectangles and squares. Plate 55, the 1925 book cover designed by van Doesburg in collaboration with Laszlo Moholy-Nagy (1895–1946) for van Doesburg's book *Grundbegriffe der Neuen Gestaltenden,* shows the application of the de Stijl vocabulary to graphic design. In fact, van der Leck may have been the first to introduce flat, geometric shapes of pure color into his work. In addition, he was creating graphic designs with simple black bars organizing the space and using flat shaped images before the movement formed (Pl. 56 and Fig. 18-28).

With their prescribed visual vocabulary, de Stijl artists sought an expression of the mathematical structure of the universe and the universal harmony of nature. They were deeply concerned with the spiritual and intellectual climate of their

18-27

18-28

18-27. Théo van Doesburg, *Composition XI,* 1918. In the careful balancing of rectangles of primary color on a white field, a purity of form and visual harmony is achieved with an economy of means. The implications for modern design were staggering.

18-28. Bart van der Leck, layout for Batavier Line poster, 1915–1916. In a series of layouts for this poster, van der Leck struggled to bring order to the design by dividing the space into rectangles.

18-29. Piet Mondrian, *Composition in Red, Yellow, and Blue,* 1931. The search for universal harmony became the subject, and the concrete presence of painted form on canvas became the vehicle for expressing a new plastic reality.

18-29

time and wished to express the "general consciousness of their age." The war was sweeping away an old age, and science, technology, and political developments would usher in a new era of objectivity and collectivism. This attitude was widespread during World War I, for many European philosophers, scientists, and artists believed prewar values had lost their relevance. De Stijl sought the universal laws that govern visible reality but are hidden by the outward appearance of things. Scientific theory, mechanical production, and the rhythms of the modern city formed from these universal laws.

In the Dutch language, *schoon* means both pure and beautiful. To de Stijl members, beauty arose from the absolute purity of the work. They sought to purify art by banning naturalistic representation, external values, and expressions of the individual's subjective whims. The content of their work then became universal har-

18-31

18-32

18-30. Vilmos Huszar, cover design for *de Stijl,* 1917. Van Doesburg designed this logo with letters constructed from an open grid of squares and rectangles, and Huszar combined it with his composition and type to create a concise rectangle in the center of the page.

18-31. Vilmos Huszar, title pages for *de Stijl,* 1918. Huszar presented a beautiful study of positive and negative figure–ground spatial relationships and used restrained typography in the issue marking the death of Apollinaire.

18-32. Théo van Doesburg, advertisements and announcements from *de Stijl,* 1921. Five messages are unified by a system of open bars and sans serif typography.

mony, the order that pervades throughout the universe. Mondrian produced a body of paintings of incomparable spiritual and formal quality. His compositions of heroic asymmetrical balance with the tension and balance between elements achieved absolute harmony (Fig. 18-29).

Van Doesburg applied de Stijl principles to architecture, sculpture, and typography. He edited and published the journal *de Stijl* from 1917 until his death in 1931. Primarily funded with his own limited resources, this publication spread the movement's theory and philosophy to a larger audience. *De Stijl* advocated the absorption of pure art by applied art. The spirit of art could then permeate society through architectural, product, and graphic design. Under this system, art would not be subjugated to the level of the everyday object; the everyday object (and, through it, everyday life) would be elevated to the level of art. Mondrian stopped contributing articles to the journal in 1924, after van Doesburg developed his theory of *Elementarism,* which declared the diagonal to be a more dynamic compositional principle than horizontal and vertical construction. *De Stijl* magazine became a natural vehicle to express the movement's principles in graphic designs by Huszar (Figs. 18-30 and 18-31) and van Doesburg (Figs. 18-32 and 18-33), who

18-33. Théo van Doesburg, cover for *de Stijl*, 1922. This format, with type asymmetrically balanced in the four corners of an implied rectangle, was used from 1921 until the last issue, which was published in 1932 after van Doesburg's death. Color was used not as an afterthought or decoration but as an important structural element.

18-34. Théo van Doesburg, *An Alphabet*, 1919. This design uses the square as a rigorous module for the alphabet. A harmony of form is achieved, but the banishing of curved and diagonal lines diminishes character uniqueness and legibility.

18-35. Théo van Doesburg, exhibition poster, 1920. Original lettering was executed in ink for reproduction to promote an international exhibition—*La Section d'Or, Cubists and Neo-Cubists.*

18-36. Théo van Doesburg, Dada poetry from *de Stijl*, 1921. Type size, weight, and style become content to be interpreted when reading the poem aloud.

18-37. El Lissitzky, cover and page from *de Stijl*, 1922. Van Doesburg invited Lissitzky to design and edit a double issue of *de Stijl* that reprinted "A Tale of Two Squares" in a Dutch version.

18-38. Gerrit Rietveld, the Schroeder House, Utrecht, 1924. A new architecture is composed of planes in space.

18-39. Gerrit Rietveld, the Schroeder House dining room, Utrecht, 1924. Dynamic space was created by placing the support post to the left of the corner.

18-36

18-37

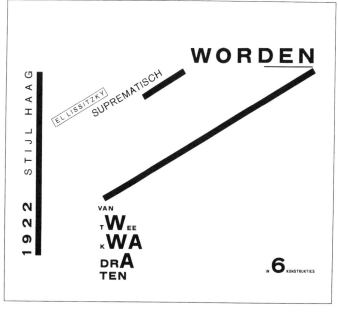

18-38

18-39

18-41

18-40. J. J. P. Oud, facade of the Café de Unie, Rotterdam, 1925. Oud successfully resolved problems of structure, signage, and identification. Architectural and graphic forms of contrasting value and scale are ordered into a harmonious balance.

18-41. Bart van der Leck, page from *Typographie et Composition de Het Vlas,* 1941. Type and image are unified by their form, for both are constructed completely of horizontal, vertical, and diagonal lines separated by spatial intervals.

also imposed horizontal and vertical structure upon the alphabet (Fig. 18-34) and poster designs (Fig. 18-35). Curved lines were eliminated and sans serif typography was favored. Type was often composed in tight rectangular blocks. Asymmetrically balanced layouts were composed on an open implied grid. Red was favored as a second color in printing because, in addition to its graphic power to compete with black, it signified revolution.

Van Doesburg comprehended the liberating potential of Dada and invited Kurt Schwitters to Holland to campaign for it. They collaborated on typographic design projects (see Fig. 16-25), and van Doesburg explored Dada typography and poetry, which he published in *de Stijl* under the pseudonym I. K. Bonset (Fig. 18-36). He saw Dada and de Stijl as opposite but complementary movements: Dada could destroy the old order, then de Stijl could build a new order on the razed site of prewar culture. In 1922, he convened an International Congress of Constructivists and Dadaists in Weimar. One of the Constructivists attending was El Lissitzky, who designed an issue of *de Stijl* (Fig. 18-37).

In architectural experiments, van Doesburg constructed planes in space with dynamic asymmetrical relationships. De Stijl architectural theory was realized in 1924, when Gerrit Rietveld designed the celebrated Schroeder House in Utrecht (Fig. 18-38). This house was so radical that neighbors threw rocks, and the Schroeder children were taunted by their classmates at school. As seen in the dining room (Fig. 18-39), the use of industrial radiators predated the integration of industrial equipment in domestic interiors (the high-tech movement of the late 1970s) by half a century. The following year, Oud designed the Café de Unie (Fig. 18-40) with an asymmetrical facade, projecting de Stijl's vision of order on an environmental scale. Because van Doesburg, with his phenomenal energy and wide-ranging creativity, *was* the de Stijl movement, it is understandable that de Stijl as an organized move-

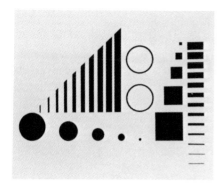

18-42. Henryk Berlewi, *Dynamic Contrasts* Mechano-faktura composition, 1924. The "reading" of this graphic composition is intended to begin with the thin line in the lower-right corner and follow the changing volume of forms, ending with the two outline circles.

18-43. Henryk Berlewi, exhibition poster, 1925. This early application of Mechano-faktura principles to graphic design is for an exhibition held in a Warsaw automobile showroom.

18-43

18-44. Henryk Berlewi, Plutos Chocolates brochure, page 6, 1925. The writer, Aleksander Wat, closely collaborated with the designer to integrate visual form with the copy. Printed in red and black on yellow paper, an implied cross divides the page into quadrants.

ment did not survive his death in 1931 at age forty-seven, even though van der Leck (Fig. 18-41) and others continued to use its visual vocabulary for many years.

The spread of Constructivism

During the war years, the Russian Suprematism and Constructivism and the Dutch de Stijl movements were apparently completely isolated from one another, yet both groups pushed Cubism to a pure geometric art. After the war, their ideas were adopted by artists in other countries, including Czechoslovakia, Hungary, and Poland. The Polish designer Henryk Berlewi (1894–1967) was decisively influenced by Lissitzky's 1920 Warsaw lectures. In 1922–1923, Berlewi worked in Germany and began to evolve his *Mechano-faktura* theory. Believing that modern art was filled with illusionistic pitfalls, he mechanized painting (Fig. 18–42) and graphic design (Fig. 18–43) into a constructed abstraction that abolished any illusion of three dimensions. This was accomplished by mathematical placement of simple geometric forms on a ground. The mechanization of art was seen as an expression of industrial society.

In 1924, Berlewi joined the Futurist poets Aleksander Wat and Stanley Brucz in opening a Warsaw advertising firm, called Roklama Mechano. They introduced modern art forms to Polish society in industrial and commercial advertisements. Their brochure stated that advertising design and costs should be governed by the same principles that govern modern industry and the laws of economy. Advertising

18-45. Ladislav Sutnar, cover design for *Zeneni a vdavani*, 1929. The red triangle creates a strong focal point, unifies the two silhouetted photographs, and becomes the main structural element in a delicately balanced asymmetrical composition.

copy was reorganized for conciseness and impact, and visual layout was adapted to this text (Fig. 18-44). Berlewi hoped that commercial advertising could become a vehicle for abolishing the division between the artist and society.

In Czechoslovakia, Ladislav Sutnar (1897–1976) became the leading supporter and practitioner of functional design. He advocated the Constructivist ideal and the application of design principles to every aspect of contemporary life. In addition to graphics, this prolific Prague designer created toys, furniture, silverware, dishes, and fabrics. The publishing house Druzstevni Prace retained Sutnar as design director. His book jackets and editorial design developed an organizational simplicity and typographic clarity, giving graphic impact to the communication (Fig. 18-45).

In 1919, after completing law studies in Budapest, Hungarian Laszlo Moholy-Nagy turned to nonrepresentational painting influenced by Malevich. In 1921, Moholy-Nagy moved to Berlin, where Lissitzky, Schwitters, and van Doesburg were frequent visitors to his studio. His design for Arthur Lehning's avant-garde publication *i10*—one of the purest examples of de Stijl principles applied to typography—demonstrates the collaboration of Constructivism, de Stijl, and Merz. Moholy-Nagy was assisted by de Stijl member César Domela (b. 1900) in the cover design (Fig. 18-46), and a major piece by Schwitters (Fig. 18-47) was featured in the first issue. The printer was terribly upset by Moholy-Nagy and Domela's com-

ARTHUR MÜLLER LEHNING

i 10

De Internationale Revue **I10** wil een orgaan zijn van alle uitingen van den modernen geest, een dokumentatie van de nieuwe stroomingen in kunst en wetenschap, philosophie en sociologie.
Het wil de gelegenheid geven de vernieuwing op één gebied met die van andere te vergelijken en het streeft naar een zoo groot mogelijken samenhang van al deze onderscheiden gebieden — reeds door het samenbrengen ervan in één orgaan.
Waar dit blad geen enkele bepaalde richting dogmatisch voorstaat, geen orgaan is van een partij of groep, zal de inhoud niet steeds een volkomen homogeen karakter kunnen dragen en veelal meer informatief dan programmatisch zijn.
Een algemeen overzicht te geven van de zich voltrekkende cultureele vernieuwing is zijn doel en het stelt zich, internationaal, open voor alles, waarin deze tot uitdrukking komt.

Die internationale Revue **I10** soll ein Organ aller Aeusserungen des modernen Geistes, der neuen Strömungen der Kunst, Wissenschaft, Philosophie und Soziologie sein. Es soll durch sie ermöglicht werden die Erneuerungen auf einem Gebiete, mit denjenigen auf anderen zu vergleichen, und sie erstrebt schon dadurch einen möglichst engen Zusammenhang der verschiedenen Gebiete, dass sie sie in einem Organ vereinigt.
Da diese Zeitschrift keine Richtung dogmatisch vertritt und sie kein Organ einer Partei oder Gruppe ist, wird ihr Inhalt nicht immer absolut homogen sein und oft mehr einen informativen als programmatischen Charakter haben.
Einen allgemeinen Ueberblick der Erneuerung, die sich in der Kultur volzieht, zu geben: das ist ihr Zweck und, international, öffnet sie sich allem, worin diese zum Ausdruck kommt. **1**

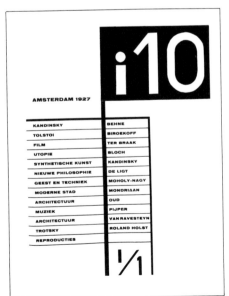

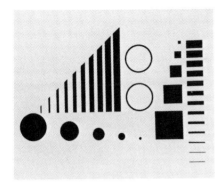

18-42. Henryk Berlewi, *Dynamic Contrasts* Mechano-faktura composition, 1924. The "reading" of this graphic composition is intended to begin with the thin line in the lower-right corner and follow the changing volume of forms, ending with the two outline circles.

18-43. Henryk Berlewi, exhibition poster, 1925. This early application of Mechano-faktura principles to graphic design is for an exhibition held in a Warsaw automobile showroom.

18-43

18-44. Henryk Berlewi, Plutos Chocolates brochure, page 6, 1925. The writer, Aleksander Wat, closely collaborated with the designer to integrate visual form with the copy. Printed in red and black on yellow paper, an implied cross divides the page into quadrants.

ment did not survive his death in 1931 at age forty-seven, even though van der Leck (Fig. 18-41) and others continued to use its visual vocabulary for many years.

The spread of Constructivism

During the war years, the Russian Suprematism and Constructivism and the Dutch de Stijl movements were apparently completely isolated from one another, yet both groups pushed Cubism to a pure geometric art. After the war, their ideas were adopted by artists in other countries, including Czechoslovakia, Hungary, and Poland. The Polish designer Henryk Berlewi (1894–1967) was decisively influenced by Lissitzky's 1920 Warsaw lectures. In 1922–1923, Berlewi worked in Germany and began to evolve his *Mechano-faktura* theory. Believing that modern art was filled with illusionistic pitfalls, he mechanized painting (Fig. 18–42) and graphic design (Fig. 18–43) into a constructed abstraction that abolished any illusion of three dimensions. This was accomplished by mathematical placement of simple geometric forms on a ground. The mechanization of art was seen as an expression of industrial society.

In 1924, Berlewi joined the Futurist poets Aleksander Wat and Stanley Brucz in opening a Warsaw advertising firm, called Roklama Mechano. They introduced modern art forms to Polish society in industrial and commercial advertisements. Their brochure stated that advertising design and costs should be governed by the same principles that govern modern industry and the laws of economy. Advertising

copy was reorganized for conciseness and impact, and visual layout was adapted to this text (Fig. 18-44). Berlewi hoped that commercial advertising could become a vehicle for abolishing the division between the artist and society.

In Czechoslovakia, Ladislav Sutnar (1897–1976) became the leading supporter and practitioner of functional design. He advocated the Constructivist ideal and the application of design principles to every aspect of contemporary life. In addition to graphics, this prolific Prague designer created toys, furniture, silverware, dishes, and fabrics. The publishing house Druzstevni Prace retained Sutnar as design director. His book jackets and editorial design developed an organizational simplicity and typographic clarity, giving graphic impact to the communication (Fig. 18-45).

In 1919, after completing law studies in Budapest, Hungarian Laszlo Moholy-Nagy turned to nonrepresentational painting influenced by Malevich. In 1921, Moholy-Nagy moved to Berlin, where Lissitzky, Schwitters, and van Doesburg were frequent visitors to his studio. His design for Arthur Lehning's avant-garde publication *i10*—one of the purest examples of de Stijl principles applied to typography—demonstrates the collaboration of Constructivism, de Stijl, and Merz. Moholy-Nagy was assisted by de Stijl member César Domela (b. 1900) in the cover design (Fig. 18-46), and a major piece by Schwitters (Fig. 18-47) was featured in the first issue. The printer was terribly upset by Moholy-Nagy and Domela's com-

18-45. Ladislav Sutnar, cover design for *Zeneni a vdavani*, 1929. The red triangle creates a strong focal point, unifies the two silhouetted photographs, and becomes the main structural element in a delicately balanced asymmetrical composition.

INTERNATIONALE REVUE
HOOFDREDACTIE
ARTHUR MÜLLER LEHNING

REDACTEUR
voor ARCHITECTUUR
J. J. P. OUD
voor MUZIEK
WILLEM PIJPER
voor FILM EN FOTO
L. MOHOLY-NAGY

i10
I/1 AMSTERDAM 1927

ARTHUR MÜLLER LEHNING

i 10

De Internationale Revue **I10** wil een orgaan zijn van alle uitingen van den modernen geest, een dokumentatie van de nieuwe stroomingen in kunst en wetenschap, philosophie en sociologie.
Het wil de gelegenheid geven de vernieuwing op één gebied met die van andere te vergelijken en het streeft naar een zoo groot mogelijken samenhang van al deze onderscheiden gebieden — reeds door het samenbrengen ervan in één orgaan.
Waar dit blad geen enkele bepaalde richting dogmatisch voorstaat, geen orgaan is van een partij of groep, zal de inhoud niet steeds een volkomen homogeen karakter kunnen dragen en veelal meer informatief dan programmatisch zijn.
Een algemeen overzicht te geven van de zich voltrekkende cultureele vernieuwing is zijn doel en het stelt zich, internationaal, open voor alles, waarin deze tot uitdrukking komt.

●

Die internationale Revue **I10** soll ein Organ aller Aeusserungen des modernen Geistes, der neuen Strömungen der Kunst, Wissenschaft, Philosophie und Soziologie sein. Es soll durch sie ermöglicht werden die Erneuerungen auf einem Gebiete, mit denjenigen auf anderen zu vergleichen, und sie erstrebt schon dadurch einen möglichst engen Zusammenhang der verschiedenen Gebiete, dass sie sie in einem Organ vereinigt.
Da diese Zeitschrift keine Richtung dogmatisch vertritt und sie kein Organ einer Partei oder Gruppe ist, wird ihr Inhalt nicht immer absolut homogen sein und oft mehr einen informativen als programmatischen Charakter haben.
Einen allgemeinen Ueberblick der Erneuerung, die sich in der Kultur vollzieht, zu geben: das ist ihr Zweck und, international, öffnet sie sich allem, worin diese zum Ausdruck kommt.

1

AMSTERDAM 1927

KANDINSKY	BEHNE
TOLSTOI	BIROEKOFF
FILM	TER BRAAK
UTOPIE	BLOCH
SYNTHETISCHE KUNST	KANDINSKY
NIEUWE PHILOSOPHIE	DE LIGT
GEEST EN TECHNIEK	MOHOLY-NAGY
MODERNE STAD	MONDRIAAN
ARCHITECTUUR	OUD
MUZIEK	PIJPER
ARCHITECTUUR	VAN RAVESTEYN
TROTSKY	ROLAND HOLST
REPRODUCTIES	

I/1

18-46

18-47

18-46. Laszlo Moholy-Nagy, cover design for *i10*, 1927. The designer saw type as form and texture to be composed with a rectangle, lines, and spatial intervals in a balanced asymmetrical composition. Clarity of communication and harmony of form are achieved.

18-47. Kurt Schwitters, *"Sonate in Urlauten,"* 1924 (reproduced in *i10*, 1927). This Dada poem/performance piece was packaged in a constructivist typographic format. Dada destroyed syntax and form; Constructivism pointed the way to a reconstruction of the printed page.

18-48. Laszlo Moholy-Nagy, title page for *i10*, 1927. Among the design ideas that upset the printer are words running vertically, bold sans serif type placed into Old Style text for emphasis, bullets separating paragraphs, and bold bars by the page numbers.

EINLEITUNG:

Fümms bö wö tää zää Uu,

　　　　　pögiff,

　　　　　　　kwii Ee.

Oooooooooooooooooooooooooooooooooo,

　　dll rrrrrr beeeee bö.　　　　　　(A)

　　dll rrrrrr beeeee bö fümms bö,

　　　rrrrrr beeeee bö fümms bö wö,

　　　　beeeee bö fümms bö wö tää,

　　　　　bö fümms bö wö tää zää,

　　　　　fümms bö wö tää zää Uu:

ERSTER TEIL:

Thema 1.

Fümms bö wö tää zää Uu,

　　　　　pögiff,

　　　　　　　kwii Ee.

Thema 2.

Dedesnn nn rrrrrr.

　　　　Ii Ee,

　　　　　mpiff tillff too,

　　　　　　　　tillll,

　　　　　　　Jüü Kaa?

　　　　　　　(gesungen)

Thema 3.

Rinnzekete bee bee nnz krr müü?

　　　　　　　ziiuu ennze, ziiuu rinnzkrrmüü,

　　rakete bee bee.

Thema 4.

Rrummpff tillff toooo?

ÜBERLEITUNG.

Ziiuu ennze ziiuu nnzkrrmüü,

Ziiuu ennze ziiuu rinnzkrrmüü:

　　rakete bee bee? rakete bee zee.

DURCHARBEITUNG.

Fümms bö wö tää zää Uu,

Uu zee tee wee bee fümmmms.

　　Rakete rinnzekete　　　　　(B)

　　rakete rinnzekete

　　rakete rinnzekete

　　rakete rinnzekete

　　rakete rinnzekete

　　rakete rinnzekete

　　Beeeee

　　bö.

fö

　böwö

fümmsbö

　böwörö

fümmsböwö

　böwörötää

fümmsböwötää

　böwörötääzää

1

5

1

2

3

3a

4

3

3a

ü1

ü2

1

395

18-48

plete disregard for the rules of typography, as shown in the opening page of the premiere issue (Fig. 18-48), but eventually he came to understand and appreciate the design. (In 1980, Arthur Lehning stated that although the *i10* cover design has often been attributed to Domela, Lehning's recent retrieval of Moholy-Nagy's cover layouts indicates major responsibility for this design should be credited to him.)

The quest for a pure art of visual relationships that began in Holland and Russia has remained a major influence for the visual disciplines during the twentieth century. One of the dominant directions in graphic design has been geometric construction to organize the printed page. Malevich and Mondrian used pure line, shape, and color to create a universe of harmoniously ordered, pure relationships. This was seen as a visionary prototype for a new world order. Mondrian wrote that art would "disappear in proportion as life gains in equilibrium." The unification of social and human values, technology, and visual form became a goal for those who strived for a new architecture and graphic design.

The Bauhaus and the New Typography

19-1. Lyonel Feininger, "Cathedral," 1919. This woodcut was printed on the title page of the Bauhaus Manifesto.

"It is obvious," wrote Aldous Huxley in 1928, "that the machine is here to stay. Whole armies of William Morrises and Tolstoys could not now expel it. . . . Let us then exploit them to create beauty—a modern beauty, while we are about it." Ideas from all the advanced art and design movements were explored, combined, and applied to problems of functional design and machine production at a German design school, the Bauhaus (1919–1933). Twentieth-century furniture, architecture, product design, and graphics were shaped by the work of its faculty and students, and a modern design aesthetic emerged.

On the eve of world war in 1914, the Belgian Art Nouveau architect Henri van de Velde, who directed the Weimar Arts and Crafts School, resigned his position to return to Belgium. Thirty-one-year-old Walter Gropius (1883–1969) was one of three recommendations he made to the Grand Duke of Saxe-Weimar as a possible replacement. During the war years, the school was closed, and it was not until after the war that Gropius, who had already gained an international reputation for factory designs using glass and steel in new ways, was confirmed as the new director of an institution formed by merging the applied arts-oriented Weimar Arts and Crafts School with a fine arts school, the Weimar Art Academy. Gropius was permitted to name the new school *Das Staatliches Bauhaus,* and it opened on 12 April 1919, when Germany was in a state of terrible ferment. The catastrophic defeat in "the war to end all wars" led to economic, political, and cultural strife. The prewar world of the Kaiser was dead, and a quest to construct a new social order pervaded all aspects of life.

The Bauhaus Manifesto, published in German newspapers, established the philosophy of the new school: "The complete building is the ultimate aim of all the visual arts. Once the noblest function of the fine arts was to embellish buildings; they were indispensable components of great architecture. Today the arts exist in isolation. . . . Architects, painters, and sculptors must learn anew the composite character of the building as an entity. . . . The artist is an exalted craftsman. In rare moments of inspiration, transcending his conscious will, the grace of heaven may cause his work to blossom into art. But proficiency in his craft is essential to every artist. Therein lies the prime source of creative imagination."

Recognizing the common roots of both fine and applied visual arts, Gropius sought a new unity of art and technology as he enlisted a generation of artists in a struggle to solve problems of visual design created by industrialism. It was hoped that the artistically trained designer could "breathe a soul into the dead product of the machine," for Gropius believed that only the most brilliant ideas were good enough to justify multiplication by industry.

The Bauhaus was the logical consequence of a German concern for upgrading design in an industrial society that began in the opening years of the century. As discussed in Chapter 15, the Deutsche Werkbund worked to elevate standards of design and public taste, attracting architects, artists, public and industry officials, educators, and critics to its ranks. The Werkbund attempted to unify artists and craftsmen with industry to elevate the functional and aesthetic qualities of mass production, particularly in low-cost consumer products.

In 1907, Gropius had started his three-year assistantship in Peter Behrens's

19-2. Attributed to Johannes Auerbach, first Bauhaus seal, 1919. The style and imagery of this seal—chosen in a student design competition—express the medieval and craft affinities of the early Bauhaus.

architectural office. Behrens's advocacy of a new objectivity and theories of proportion had an impact on the development of the youthful Gropius's thinking. Henri van de Velde was also an important influence. During the 1890s, van de Velde declared the engineer to be the new architect and called for logical design using new technologies and materials of science: reinforced concrete, steel, aluminum, and linoleum.

The Bauhaus at Weimar

The Bauhaus years in Weimar (1919–1924) were intensely visionary and drew inspiration from expressionism (Figs. 19-1, 19-2, and 19-3). Characterized by a utopian desire to create a new spiritual society, the early Bauhaus sought a new unity of artists and craftsmen to build for the future. Stained glass, wood, and metal workshops were taught by an artist and a craftsman and were organized along medieval *Bauhütte* lines—master, journeyman, apprentice. The Gothic cathedral represented a realization of people's longing for a spiritual beauty that went beyond utility and need, and symbolized the integration of architecture, sculpture, painting, and crafts. Gropius was deeply interested in architecture's symbolic potential and the possibility of a universal design style as an integrated aspect of society.

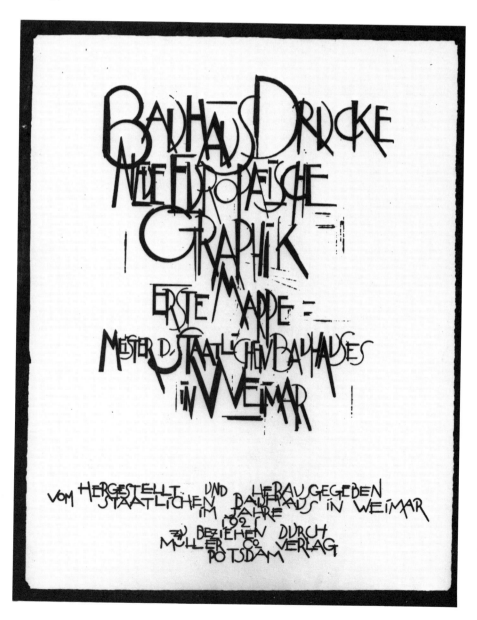

19-3. Lyonel Feininger, woodcut title page for *Europaische Graphik,* 1921. Graphic design during the early Bauhaus years reflected its expressionism and craft orientation.

Advanced ideas about form, color, and space were integrated into the design vocabulary when painters Paul Klee (1879–1940) and Wassily Kandinsky joined the staff in 1920 and 1922, respectively. Klee integrated modern visual art with the work of primitive cultures and children to create drawings and paintings that are charged visual communication. Kandinsky's belief in the autonomy and spiritual values of color and form had led to the courageous emancipation of his painting from the motif and representational elements. At the Bauhaus, no distinction was made between fine and applied art.

The heart of Bauhaus education was the preliminary course, initially established by Johannes Itten (1888–1967). His goals were to release each student's creative abilities, to develop an understanding of the physical nature of materials, and to teach the fundamental principles of design underlying all visual art. Itten put emphasis on visual contrasts and an analysis of Old Master paintings. Itten's methodology of direct experience sought to develop perceptual awareness, intellectual abilities, and emotional experience. In 1923, Itten left the Bauhaus because of disagreement about the conduct of this course. The Bauhaus was evolving from a concern for medievalism, expressionism, and handicraft toward more emphasis on rationalism and designing for the machine. Gropius began to consider Itten's mysticism to be an "otherworldliness," inconsistent with an emerging concern for an objective design language capable of overcoming the dangers of past styles and personal taste.

As early as the spring of 1919, Bauhaus teacher Lyonel Feininger (1871–1956) had become aware of de Stijl and began to make the Bauhaus community cognizant of this movement. The Bauhaus and de Stijl had similar aims, and in late 1920 van Doesburg established contacts with the Bauhaus. In 1921, van Doesburg also moved to Weimar. Until 1923, he lived there and taught courses in de Stijl philosophy that were primarily attended by students from the Bauhaus. He desired a teaching position, but Gropius felt that van Doesburg was too dogmatic in his insistence on strict geometry and an impersonal style. He believed that creating a Bauhaus style or imposing a style upon the students should be vigorously avoided. But even as an outsider, van Doesburg made a strong impact on the Bauhaus by allowing his home to become a meeting place for Bauhaus students and faculty and offering instruction in de Stijl principles. Furniture design and typography were especially influenced by de Stijl, an influence among faculty and students that probably supported Gropius's efforts to lessen Itten's role.

Continuing conflicts between the Bauhaus and the Thuringian government led the authorities to insist that the Bauhaus mount a major exhibition to demonstrate its accomplishments. By this 1923 exhibition, which was attended by fifteen thousand people and brought the Bauhaus international acclaim, romantic medievalism and expressionism were being replaced by an applied design emphasis to the point that Gropius changed the slogan "A Unity of Art and Handicraft" to "Art and Technology, a New Unity." Joost Schmidt's poster for this exhibition echoes Constructivism and machine forms (Pl. 57), reflecting the reorientation occurring at the Bauhaus. A new Bauhaus symbol reflected this shift (Fig. 19-4).

The impact of Laszlo Moholy-Nagy

In this same year, Itten's replacement as head of the preliminary course was the Hungarian Constructivist Laszlo Moholy-Nagy. A restless experimenter, Moholy-Nagy explored painting, photography, film, sculpture, and graphic design. New materials such as Plexiglas, new techniques such as photomontage and the photogram, and visual means including kinetic motion, light, and transparency were encompassed in his wide-ranging investigations. Young and articulate, Moholy-Nagy's presence on the faculty had a marked influence on the evolution of Bauhaus instruction and philosophy, and he became Gropius's "Prime Minister" at the Bauhaus as the director pushed for a new unity of art and technology.

Gropius and Moholy-Nagy collaborated as editors for *Staatliches Bauhaus in Weimar, 1919–1923,* the catalogue for the 1923 exhibition. This record of the first

19-4. Oscar Schlemmer, later Bauhaus seal, 1922. Comparison of the two seals demonstrates how graphic designs can express ideas, for the later seal relates to the geometric style and machine orientation that were emerging.

19-5. Laszlo Moholy-Nagy, title page, Bauhaus exhibition catalogue, 1923. The page structure is based on a rhythmic series of right angles. Stripes are applied to two words to create a second typographic plane.

19-6. Herbert Bayer, cover design, Bauhaus exhibition catalogue, 1923. Geometrically constructed letterforms printed in red and blue on a black background are compressed into a square.

19-7. Laszlo Moholy-Nagy, proposed title page for *Broom,* 1923. This design for the avant-garde magazine shows how thoroughly Moholy-Nagy understood the new visual design vocabulary of Cubism and Lissitzky.

19-8. Laszlo Moholy-Nagy, "typophoto" poster for tires, 1923. The integration of letterforms, photography, and design elements into an immediate and unified communication is realized here.

years was designed by Moholy-Nagy (Fig. 19-5) and the cover (Fig. 19-6) was designed by a student, Herbert Bayer (1900–1985). Moholy-Nagy contributed an important statement about typography, saying that "typography is a tool of communication. It must be communication in its most intense form. The emphasis must be on absolute clarity. . . . Legibility—communication must never be impaired by an *a priori* esthetics. Letters must never be forced into a preconceived framework, for instance a square." In graphic design, he advocated "an uninhibited use of all linear directions (therefore not only horizontal articulation). We use all typefaces, type sizes, geometric forms, colors, etc. We want to create a new language of typography [Fig. 19-7] whose elasticity, variability, and freshness of typographical composition [are] exclusively dictated by the inner law of expression and the optical effect."

In 1922–1923, Moholy-Nagy ordered three paintings from a sign company. These were executed from his graph-paper layouts in colors selected from the firm's porcelain enamel color chart, in keeping with his theory that the essence of art and design was the concept, not the execution, and that the two could be separated. Moholy-Nagy acted on this belief beginning in 1929, when he retained an assistant, Gyorgy Kepes (b. 1906), to complete the execution of Moholy-Nagy's commissions.

Moholy-Nagy's passion for typography and photography inspired a Bauhaus interest in visual communications and led to important experiments in the unification of typography and photography. Moholy-Nagy saw graphic design, particularly the poster, as evolving toward the *typophoto.* He called this objective integration of word and image to communicate a message with immediacy "the new visual literature." The 1923 Pneumatik poster (Fig. 19-8) is an experimental typophoto. In 1923, he wrote that photography's objective presentation of facts could free the

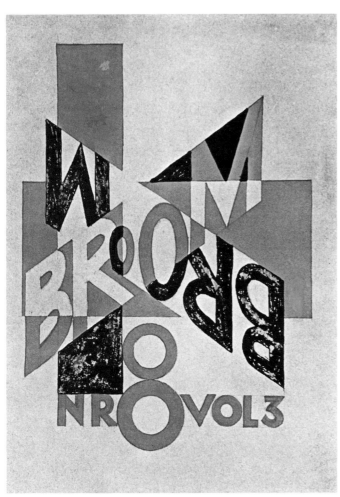

19-7

19-8

19-9

19-10

viewer from depending on another person's interpretation. He saw photography influencing poster design—which needs instantaneous communication—by techniques of enlargement, distortion, dropouts, double exposures, and montage. In typography, he advocated emphatic contrasts and bold use of color. Absolute clarity of communication without preconceived aesthetic notions was stressed.

As a still photographer, Moholy-Nagy used the camera as a tool for design. Conventional compositional ideas yielded to unexpected organization, primarily through the use of light (and sometimes shadows) to design the space. The normal viewpoint was replaced by worm's-eye, bird's-eye, extreme close-up, and angled viewpoints. An application of the new language of vision to forms seen in the world characterizes his regular photographic work. Texture, light and dark interplay, and repetition are qualities of photographs such as *Chairs at Margate* (Fig. 19-9). In his growing enthusiasm over photography, Moholy-Nagy antagonized the Bauhaus painters by proclaiming the ultimate victory of photography over painting.

In 1922, he began to experiment with photograms; the following year he began to make photomontages, which he called *photoplastics*. Moholy-Nagy believed the photogram, because it allowed an artist to capture a patterned interplay of light and dark on a sheet of light-sensitive paper without a camera, represented the essence of photography (Fig. 19-10). The objects he used to create photograms were chosen for their light-modulating properties, and any reference to the objects forming the black, white, and gray patterns or to the external world vanished in an expression of abstract pattern. Moholy-Nagy saw his photoplastics (Fig. 19-11) not as a collage technique but as a forming process to arrive at a new expression that could become both more creative and more functional than straightforward imitative photography. Photoplastics could be humorous, visionary, moving, or insightful, and usually had drawn additions, complex associations, and unexpected juxtapositions.

The Bauhaus at Dessau

Tension between the Bauhaus and the government in Weimar had existed from the beginning, and intensified when a new, more conservative regime came to power and tried to impose unacceptable conditions on the Bauhaus. On 26 December 1924, the director and masters all signed a letter of resignation, effective 1 April 1925, when their contracts expired. Two weeks later, the students signed a letter to the government informing it that they would leave with the masters. Gropius negotiated relocating the Bauhaus with Dr. Fritz Hesse, the mayor of the little provincial town of Dessau. In April of 1925, some of the equipment was moved with

19-9. Laszlo Moholy-Nagy, *Chairs at Margate*, 1935. Juxtaposition of two images is explored by Moholy-Nagy, creating a contrast of pattern and texture and introducing a process of time and change into the two-dimensional image.

19-10. Laszlo Moholy-Nagy, *Photogram*, 1922. Light itself becomes a malleable medium for generating design and form.

19-11. Laszlo Moholy-Nagy, *The World Foundation*, 1927. In this satirical photoplastic, Moholy-Nagy shows "quack-clacking super-geese [pelicans]" observing "the simplicity of the world constructed as a leg show."

19-12. Walter Gropius, the Dessau Bauhaus building, 1925–1926. Considered a landmark in the history of architecture, the Bauhaus building was a series of parts—workshop, classroom, dormitory, and administrative structures—unified into a whole.

faculty and students from Weimar to Dessau, and work began immediately in temporary facilities. A new building complex was designed and occupied in the fall of 1926 (Fig. 19-12), and the curriculum was reorganized.

During the Dessau period (1925–1932), the Bauhaus identity and philosophy came into full fruition. The de Stijl (Fig. 19-13) and Constructivist underpinnings were obvious, but Bauhaus did not merely copy these movements. Rather, clearly understood formal principles evolved, which could be applied intelligently to design problems. The Bauhaus Corporation, a business organization to handle the sale of workshop prototypes to industry, was created. Abundant ideas flowed from the Bauhaus to influence twentieth-century life and design: product design, steel furniture, functional architecture, environmental designs (Fig. 19-14), and typography.

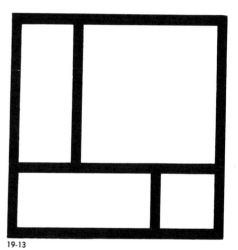

19-13

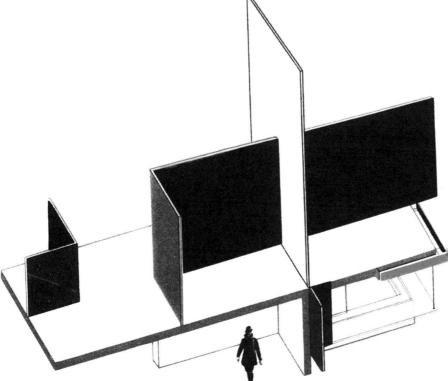

19-14

19-13. Herbert Bayer, symbol for the Kraus stained-glass workshop, 1923. A square is divided by a horizontal line into two rectangles. The top rectangle has the three-to-five ratio of the golden mean. Each rectangle formed is then divided with a vertical to form a square and a smaller rectangle. A harmony of proportion and balance is achieved with minimal means.

19-14. Herbert Bayer, proposed streetcar station and newsstand, 1924. Designed for economical mass production, this structure combines an open waiting area, newsstand, and rooftop advertising panels into a concise modular unit.

19-16

19-15. Herbert Bayer, cover for *Bauhaus* magazine, 1928. A page of typography joins the designer's tools and the basic geometric forms in a photographic still life. This design, which was composed in front of the camera instead of at a drawing board, achieves a rarely seen integration of typography and photography.

19-16. Laszlo Moholy-Nagy, brochure cover for *Fourteen Bauhaus Books,* 1929. Two photoprints of metal type collaged together create an unusual spatial configuration. Blue ink is printed on the upper numeral *14.*

The masters were now called professors, and the medieval-inspired master/journeyman/apprentice system was abandoned. In 1926, the Bauhaus was titled *Hochschule für Gestaltung* ("High school for Form"), and the influential *Bauhaus* magazine (Fig. 19-15) began publication.

This magazine, and the series of Bauhaus books, all but two of which were designed by Moholy-Nagy (Figs. 19-16 through 19-18), became important vehicles for disseminating advanced ideas about art theory and its application to architecture and design. Klee, van Doesburg (see Pl. 55), Mondrian, Gropius, and Moholy-Nagy were editors or authors of volumes in the series.

Five former students were appointed masters, including Josef Albers (1888–1976), who taught a systematic preliminary course investigating the constructive qualities of materials; Marcel Breuer (1902–1981), the head of the furniture workshop, who invented tubular-steel furniture; and Herbert Bayer, who became professor of the newly added typography and graphic design workshop. In Weimar, Gropius had observed Bayer's interest in graphics and encouraged it with periodic assignments (Fig. 19-19), so Bayer's typographic preoccupation preceded the move to Dessau.

In addition to soliciting printing orders from Dessau businesses to help balance the Bauhaus budget, Bayer led the workshop in dramatic innovation in typographic design along functional and Constructivist lines. Sans serif fonts were used almost exclusively, and Bayer designed a universal type that reduced the alphabet to clear, simple, and rationally constructed forms (Fig. 19-20). Arguing that we print and write with two alphabets (capitals and lowercase) that are incompatible in design, and that two totally different signs (capital *A* and small *a*), are used to express the same spoken sound, Bayer omitted capital letters in 1925. He experimented with flush-left, ragged-right typesetting without justification by adding word- or letterspacing. Extreme contrasts of type size and weight were used to establish a hierarchy of emphasis determined by an objective assessment of the relative importance of the words. Bars, rules, points, and squares were used to subdivide the space, unify diverse elements, and call attention to important elements. Elementary forms and the use of black with one bright pure hue were favored. Open composition on an implied grid and a system of sizes for type, rules, and pictorial images brought unity to the designs. Dynamic composition with strong horizontals and verticals characterize Bayer's Bauhaus period.

19-17. Laszlo Moholy-Nagy, dust jacket for *Bauhaus Book 12,* 1925. Printed on architect's translucent tracing paper in red and black ink, this design presented Gropius's modular housing concept in a slashing diagonal. This use of industrial fabrication methods for domestic housing combines economy and social purpose with structural functionalism and aesthetics.

19-18. Laszlo Moholy-Nagy, dust jacket for *Bauhaus Book 14,* 1929. To convey the properties of modern architecture, Moholy-Nagy photographed typography printed on glass with its shadow cast upon a red plane.

19-19. Herbert Bayer, banknote for the State Bank of Thuringia, 1923. Germany's rampant postwar inflation necessitated large-denomination banknotes. Black type overprints a red rectangle, lines, and a textural repetition of the denomination.

19-17

19-18

19-19

19-20. Herbert Bayer, universal alphabet, 1925. This experiment in reducing the alphabet to one set of geometrically constructed characters maximizes the differences between letterforms for greater legibility. The lower forms show different weights. Later, Bayer developed variations, such as the bold, condensed, typewriter, and handwriting styles shown here.

These properties are clearly seen in Bayer's 1926 poster for Kandinsky's sixtieth birthday exhibition (Pl. 58). A communications hierarchy developed from careful analysis of content. Type and image are organized in a functional progression of size and weight from the most important information to supporting details.

The final years of the Bauhaus

In 1928, Walter Gropius resigned his post to resume private architectural practice. At the same time, Bayer and Moholy-Nagy both left for Berlin, where graphic design and typography figured prominently in the activities of each. Former student Joost Schmidt (1893–1948) followed Bayer as master of typography and graphic design (Fig. 19-21). He moved away from strict constructivist ideas and brought in a larger variety of type fonts. Exhibition design (Fig. 19-22) was outstanding under Schmidt, who brought unity to this form through standardized panels and grid-system organization. The directorship of the Bauhaus was assumed by Hannes Meyer (1889–1954), a Swiss architect with strong socialist beliefs, who had been hired to set up the architectural program in 1927. By 1930, conflicts with the municipal authorities forced Meyer's resignation. Ludwig Mies van der Rohe (1886–1969), a prominent Berlin architect whose design dictum "less is more" became a major attitude in twentieth-century architecture, became director.

19-21. Joost Schmidt, *bauhaus* magazine cover, 1929. The format Schmidt designed for the magazine allows effective use of different sizes and shapes of images in the lower two-thirds of the cover.

In 1931, the Nazi party dominated the Dessau City Council and canceled Bauhaus faculty contracts in 1932. Mies van der Rohe tried to run the Bauhaus in an empty telephone factory in Berlin-Steglitz, but Nazi harassment made continuance untenable. The Gestapo demanded the removal of "Cultural Bolsheviks" from the school, with Nazi sympathizers as replacements. The faculty voted to dissolve the Bauhaus, and it closed on 10 August 1933, with a notice to students that faculty would be available for consultation if needed. Thus ended a most important design school of the twentieth century. The growing cloud of Nazi persecution led many Bauhaus faculty members to join the flight of intellectuals and artists to America. In 1937, Gropius and Marcel Breuer were teaching architecture at Harvard University, and Moholy-Nagy established the New Bauhaus (now the Institute of Design) in Chicago. A year later, Herbert Bayer began the American phase of his design career. This Atlantic exodus influenced the course of American design after World War II.

The Bauhaus accomplishments and influences transcend its fourteen-year life, thirty-three faculty members, and about 1,250 students. It created a viable, modern design style that has influenced architecture, product design, and visual communications. A modernist approach to visual education was developed, and the faculty's class-preparation and teaching methods have made a major contribution to visual theory. In dissolving fine and applied art boundaries, the Bauhaus tried to bring art into a close relationship with life by design, which was seen as a vehicle for social change and cultural revitalization.

Years later Herbert Bayer wrote:
for the future
the bauhaus gave us assurance
in facing the perplexities
    of work;
it gave us the know-how to
    work.
a foundation in the crafts,
an invaluable heritage of timeless principles
as applied to the
    creative process.
it expressed again that we are
    not to impose aesthetics
on the things we use, to the
    structures we live in,
but that purpose and form must
    be seen as one.
that direction emerges when one
    considers
    concrete demands,
special conditions, inherent
    character
of a given problem.
but never losing perspective
that one is, after all,
    an artist. . . .

the bauhaus existed for a short
    span of time
but the potentials,
inherent in its principles
have only begun to be realized.
its sources of design remain
    forever full
of changing possibilities. . . .

19-22. Joost Schmidt, exhibition for the Industrial Association of Canned Goods Manufacturers, 1930. Aided by the metal, sculpture, and cabinetmaking workshops, Schmidt led the printing and exhibition design students in creating functional and restrained exhibitions organized on an imaginary grid system.

Jan Tschichold and die neue typographie

Much of the creative innovation in graphic design during the first decades of the century occurred as part of the modern-art movements and at the Bauhaus, but these explorations toward a new approach to graphic design were often only seen and understood by a limited audience outside the mainstream of society. The person who applied these new design approaches to everyday design problems and explained them to a wide audience of printers, typesetters, and designers was Jan Tschichold (1902–1974). The son of a designer and sign painter in Leipzig, Germany, Tschichold developed an early interest in calligraphy, studied at the Leipzig Academy, and joined the design staff of Insel Verlag as a traditional calligrapher (Fig. 19-23). In August 1923, twenty-one-year-old Tschichold attended the first Bauhaus exhibition in Weimar and was deeply impressed. He rapidly assimilated the new design concepts of the Bauhaus and the Russian Constructivists into his work (Fig. 19-24) and became a practitioner of the new typography. For the October 1925 issue of *typographische mitteilungen,* Tschichold designed a twenty-four-page insert entitled "elementare typographie" (Figs. 19-25 through 19-27), which explained and demonstrated asymmetrical typography to printers, typesetters, and designers. It was printed in red and black and featured avant-garde work with Tschichold's lucid commentary. Much German printing at this point *still* used medieval textura and symmetrical layout. Tschichold's insert was a revelation and generated much enthusiasm for the new approach.

His 1928 book, *Die Neue Typographie,* vigorously advocated the new ideas. Disgusted with "degenerate typefaces and arrangements," he sought to sweep the slate clean and find a new asymmetrical typography to express the spirit, life, and visual sensibility of its day. His objective was functional design by the most straightforward means. Tschichold declared the aim of every typographic work to be the delivery of a message in the shortest, most efficient manner. The nature of machine composition and its impact on the design process and product were emphasized.

Tschichold's brochure for the book illustrates this radical new typography (Fig. 19-28), which rejected decoration in favor of rational design planned for communi-

19-23. Jan Tschichold, hand-lettered advertisement for the Leipzig Trade Fair, 1922. Symmetry and historical letterforms characterize Tschichold's youthful work.

cative function. Functionalism, however, is not completely synonymous with the new typography—Tschichold observed that although plain utilitarianism and modern design have much in common, the modern movement sought spiritual content and a beauty more closely bound to the materials used, "but whose horizons lie far beyond." A dynamic force should be present in each design, he argued, for type should be placed in motion rather than at rest. Symmetrical organization was artificial because pure form came before the meaning of the words. Tschichold favored headlines flush to the left margin with uneven line lengths. He believed kinetic

19-24

19-25

19-24. Jan Tschichold, display poster for a publisher, 1924. One of Tschichold's earliest attempts to apply modern design principles, printed in black and gold, proclaims, "Books by Philobiblon are available here in Warsaw."

19-25. Jan Tschichold, cover for "elementare typographie" insert, 1925. A sparse, open functionalism is achieved.

19-26. Jan Tschichold, pages from "elementare typographie," 1925. Bold rules punctuate the space, and Tschichold's essay explains the new approach.

19-26

PROGRAMM DER KONSTRUKTIVISTEN

Die Konstruktivisten stellen sich die Gestaltung des Stoffes zur Aufgabe. Grundlage ihrer Arbeit sind wissenschaftliche Erkenntnisse. Um die Voraussetzung dafür herbeizuführen, dass diese Erkenntnisse in praktischer Arbeit verwertet werden, erstreben die Konstruktivisten die Schaffung des sinnvollen Zusammenhangs (die Synthese) aller Wissens- und Schaffensgebiete.

Alleinige und grundlegende Voraussetzung des Konstruktivismus sind die Erkenntnisse des historischen Materialismus. Das Experiment der Sowjets liess die Konstruktivisten die Notwendigkeit erkennen, dass ihre bisherige, ausserhalb des Lebens stehende, durch wissenschaftliche Versuche ausgefüllte Tätigkeit auf das Gebiet des Wirklichen zu verlegen ist und in der Lösung praktischer Aufgaben ihre Berechtigung erweisen muss.

DIE ARBEITSMITTEL DER KONSTRUKTIVISTEN SIND:

1. Faktur, **2.** Tektonik, **3.** Konstruktion.

Die *Faktur* ist das mit technischer Notwendigkeit ausgewählte und bearbeitete Material.

Die *Tektonik* erwächst aus der, dem Zweck des zu schaffenden Gegenstands entsprechenden, Ausnützung des Materials.

El Lissitzky 1922: Verkleinertes Titelblatt einer amerikanischen Zeitschrift

NEW YORK 1922

KUNST ISMEN 1924
EN 1923
EN 1922
EN 1921
EN 1920
EN 1919
EN 1918
EN 1917
EN 1916
EN 1915
EN 1914
KUNST ISM

HERAUSGEGEBEN VON EL LISSITZKY UND HANS ARP

El Lissitzky 1924: Inserat

DIE KUNST-ISMEN IST EIN BILDERBUCH (21:27 cm), DAS DIE PLASTISCHEN GESTALTUNGEN DES ALLER „ISTISCHEN" KUNSTDEZENNIUMS 1914–24 DARSTELLT. KEIN SCHREIBTISCHPRODUKT EINES KUNSTKRITIKERS. 15 ISMEN, 13 LÄNDER UND 60 KÜNSTLER SIND HIER MIT IHREM CHARAKTERISTISCHEN SCHAFFEN VERTRETEN. EINE REIHE WENIG BEKANNTER WERKE DER BEKANNTEN KÜNSTLER. DIE EINLEITUNG (IN DEUTSCHER, FRANZÖSISCHER UND ENGLISCHER SPRACHE) IST EIN ZWIEGESPRÄCH VON DEN HERREN + UND –.
GEHEFTET FR. 5.80, GEBUNDEN FR. 6.80

Die *Konstruktion* (die Gestaltung) ist eine bis zum Äussersten gehende, formende Tätigkeit: die Organisation des Materials. Nur jeweilige wissenschaftliche Erkenntnisse vermögen der Tektonik oder der Konstruktion Grenzen zu ziehen.

DIE STOFFLICHEN MITTEL SIND:

1. Stoff überhaupt. Die Kenntnis seiner Entstehung und der Veränderungen, die er in der Rohproduktion und in der Verarbeitung erfährt. Seine Eigentümlichkeiten, seine Bedeutung für die Wirtschaft, seine Beziehung zu andern Stoffen. **2.** Die Erscheinungsformen des Stoffes in Raum und Licht: Volumen (die räumliche Ausdehnung), Oberfläche, Farbe. Der Stoff an sich und seine Erscheinungsform können nicht getrennt betrachtet werden, darum stehen die Konstruktivisten im gleichen Verhältnis zu beiden von ihnen.

DIE AUFGABEN DER KONSTRUKTIVISTEN SIND:

1. Herstellung einer Verbindung mit allen Produktionszentren und Haupteinrichtungen des Landes; **2.** Konstruktion von Plänen; **3.** Organisation von Ausstellungen; **4.** Agitation in der Presse:
a) Die Gruppe erklärt rücksichtslosen Krieg gegen alle Kunst.
b) Sie erweist die Unmöglichkeit eines allmählichen Übergangs der vergangenen künstlerischen Kultur in die konstruktiven Formen der neuen Gesellschaft.
c) Sie strebt an, dass die intellektuelle Produktion gleichberechtigt neben der realen Produktion am Aufbau der neuen Kultur teilnimmt. (NACH DEM RUSSISCHEN. Deutsche Bearbeitung von I.T.)

Unser einziger Fehler war, uns mit der sogenannten Kunst überhaupt ernsthaft beschäftigt zu haben. GEORGE GROSZ

197

19-27. Jan Tschichold, pages from "elementare typographie," 1925. Illustrated by Lissitzky's work, Russian Constructivist design is explained.

VORZUGS-ANGEBOT

Im VERLAG DES BILDUNGSVERBANDES der Deutschen Buchdrucker, Berlin SW 61, Dreibundstr. 5, erscheint demnächst:

JAN TSCHICHOLD
Lehrer an der Meisterschule für Deutschlands Buchdrucker in München

DIE NEUE TYPOGRAPHIE

Handbuch für die gesamte Fachwelt und die drucksachenverbrauchenden Kreise

Das Problem der neuen gestaltenden Typographie hat eine lebhafte Diskussion bei allen Beteiligten hervorgerufen. Wir glauben dem Bedürfnis, die aufgeworfenen Fragen ausführlich behandelt zu sehen, zu entsprechen, wenn wir jetzt ein Handbuch der **NEUEN TYPOGRAPHIE** herausbringen.

Es kam dem Verfasser, einem ihrer bekanntesten Vertreter, in diesem Buche zunächst darauf an, den engen Zusammenhang der neuen Typographie mit dem **Gesamtkomplex heutigen Lebens** aufzuzeigen und zu beweisen, daß die neue Typographie ein ebenso notwendiger Ausdruck einer neuen Gesinnung ist wie die neue Baukunst und alles Neue, das mit unserer Zeit anbricht. Diese geschichtliche Notwendigkeit der neuen Typographie belegt weiterhin eine kritische Darstellung der **alten Typographie**. Die Entwicklung der **neuen Malerei**, die für alles Neue unserer Zeit geistig bahnbrechend gewesen ist, wird in einem reich illustrierten Aufsatz des Buches leicht faßlich dargestellt. Ein kurzer Abschnitt „**Zur Geschichte der neuen Typographie**" leitet zum wichtigsten Teile des Buches, den **Grundbegriffen der neuen Typographie** über. Diese werden klar herausgeschält, richtige und falsche Beispiele einander gegenübergestellt. Zwei weitere Artikel behandeln „**Photographie und Typographie**" und „**Neue Typographie und Normung**".

Der Hauptwert des Buches für den Praktiker besteht in dem zweiten Teil „**Typographische Hauptformen**" (siehe das nebenstehende Inhaltsverzeichnis). Es fehlte bisher an einem Werke, das wie dieses Buch die schon bei einfachen Satzaufgaben auftauchenden gestalterischen Fragen in gebührender Ausführlichkeit behandelte. Jeder Teilabschnitt enthält neben **allgemeinen typographischen Regeln** vor allem die Abbildungen aller in Betracht kommenden **Normblätter** des Deutschen Normenausschusses, alle andern (z. B. postalischen) **Vorschriften** und zahlreiche Beispiele, Gegenbeispiele und Schemen.

Für jeden Buchdrucker, insbesondere jeden Akzidenzsetzer, wird „Die neue Typographie" ein **unentbehrliches Handbuch** sein. Von nicht geringerer Bedeutung ist es für Reklamefachleute, Gebrauchsgraphiker, Kaufleute, Photographen, Architekten, Ingenieure und Schriftsteller, also für alle, die mit dem Buchdruck in Berührung kommen.

INHALT DES BUCHES

Werden und Wesen der neuen Typographie
Das neue Weltbild
Die alte Typographie (Rückblick und Kritik)
Die neue Kunst
Zur Geschichte der neuen Typographie
Die Grundbegriffe der neuen Typographie
Photographie und Typographie
Neue Typographie und Normung

Typographische Hauptformen
Das Typosignat
Der Geschäftsbrief
Der Halbbrief
Briefhüllen ohne Fenster
Fensterbriefhüllen
Die Postkarte
Die Postkarte mit Klappe
Die Geschäftskarte
Die Besuchskarte
Werbsachen (Karten, Blätter, Prospekte, Kataloge)
Das Typoplakat
Das Bildplakat
Schildformate, Tafeln und Rahmen
Inserate
Die Zeitschrift
Die Tageszeitung
Die illustrierte Zeitung
Tabellensatz
Das neue Buch

Bibliographie
Verzeichnis der Abbildungen
Register

Typ. Tschichold

Das Buch enthält über **125 Abbildungen,** von denen etwa ein Viertel **zweifarbig** gedruckt ist, und umfaßt gegen **200 Seiten** auf gutem Kunstdruckpapier. Es erscheint im Format DIN A5 (148× 210 mm) und ist biegsam in Ganzleinen gebunden.

Preis bei Vorbestellung bis 1. Juni 1928: **5.00** RM
durch den Buchhandel nur zum Preise von **6.50** RM

Bestellschein umstehend ➡

19-28. Jan Tschichold, brochure for his book, *Die Neue Typographie,* 1928. This brochure, printed in black on yellow, functions as a remarkable didactic example of the principles Tschichold was advocating.

19-29. Jan Tschichold, advertisement, 1932. Asymmetrical balance, a grid system, and a sequential progression of type weight and size determined by the words' importance to the overall communication are aspects of this design.

19-30. Jan Tschichold, exhibition poster, 1937. Black type and a sand-colored circle are used to achieve an economy of means and perfection of balance appropriate to its subject.

19-31. Jan Tschichold, brochure cover for *The Pelican History of Art*, 1947. The classical symmetry of this design has a power and subtlety rivaling Roman inscriptions and the best work of Baskerville and Bodoni.

19-32. Jan Tschichold, paperback book cover, 1950. The Penguin Shakespeare series format illustrates Tschichold's post–World War II philosophy that the graphic designer should draw upon the whole history of design to create solutions expressing content.

asymmetrical design of contrasting elements expressed the new age of the machine. Types should be elementary in form without embellishment; thus, sans serif type, in a range of weights (light, medium, bold, extra bold, italic) and proportions (condensed, normal, expanded), was declared to be *the* modern type. Its wide range of value and texture in the black-and-white scale allowed the expressive, abstract image sought by modern design. Stripped of unessential elements, sans serif type reduces the alphabet to its basic elementary shapes. Designs were constructed on an underlying horizontal and vertical structure. Spatial intervals were seen as important design elements, with white space given a new role as interval and structural element. Rules, bars, and boxes were often used for structure, balance, and emphasis. The precision and objectivity of photography were preferred for illustration. Tschichold showed how the modern art movement could relate to graphic design by synthesizing his practical understanding of typography and its traditions with the new experiments. Tschichold's own prolific design practice set the standard for the new approach in books, job printing, advertisements (Fig. 19-29), and posters (Pl. 59 and Fig. 19-30).

In March 1933, armed Nazis entered Tschichold's flat in Munich and arrested him and his wife. Accused of being a "Cultural Bolshevik" and creating "un-German" typography, he was denied his teaching position in Munich. After six weeks of "protective custody," Tschichold was released and emigrated with his wife and four-year-old son to Basel, Switzerland, where he worked primarily as a book designer. In Switzerland, Tschichold began to turn away from the new typography and to use roman, Egyptian, and script styles in his designs. The new typography had been a reaction against the chaos and anarchy in German (and Swiss) typography around 1923, and he now felt that it reached a point where further development was not possible.

In 1946, he wrote that the new typography's "impatient attitude conforms to the German bent for the absolute, and its military will to regulate and its claim to absolute power reflect those fearful components of the German character [that] set loose Hitler's power and the Second World War." Tschichold began to feel that graphic designers should work in a humanist tradition that spans the ages and

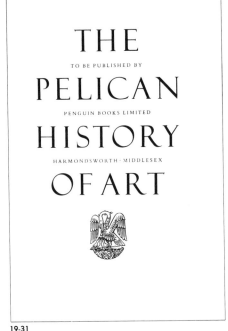

19-31

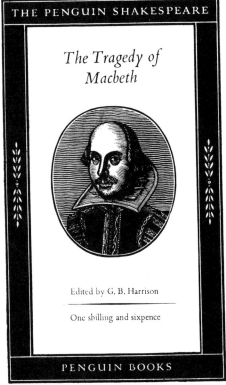

19-32

draws from the knowledge and accomplishments of master typographers of the past. He continued to feel that the new typography was suitable for publicizing industrial products and communication about contemporary painting and architecture, but also believed it was folly to use it for a book of Baroque poetry, for example, and he called reading long pages of sans serif "genuine torture."

During the 1940s, particularly with his 1947–1949 work as typographer for Penguin Books in London (Figs. 19-31 and 19-32), Tschichold led an international revival of traditional typography. While much of his later work used symmetrical organization and classical serif type styles, he advocated freedom of thought and artistic expression. He even endorsed the occasional use of ornamental typography as having "a refreshing effect, like a flower in rocky terrain." He observed that perhaps a person must first lose his freedom (as he did) before one could discover its true value.

Tschichold continued to design and write in Switzerland until his death in 1974. Because he saw the value of the new typography as an attempt at purification, clarity, and simplicity of means, Tschichold was able to bring typographic expression for the twentieth century to fruition. His revival of classical typography restored the humanist tradition of book design, and he made an indelible mark upon graphic design.

Typeface design in the first half of the twentieth century

The passion for the new typography created a spate of sans serif styles during the 1920s. An even earlier twentieth-century English sans serif, Johnston's Railway Type (Fig. 19-33), was commissioned from calligrapher and designer Edward Johnston in 1916 for the exclusive use of the London Underground. Basing his shapes on classical forms from antiquity, Johnston sought the simplest possible design of the basic form of each alphabet character. This typeface is still in use for signage and graphics for the London Underground, and it inspired the Gill Sans series (Fig. 19-34), which was designed by Johnston's friend and former student, Eric Gill (1882–1940) and issued from 1928–1930. This type family, which eventually included fourteen styles, does not have an extremely mechanical appearance because its proportions stem from the roman tradition.

An architectural apprentice drop-out tutored by Johnston at the turn of the century, Eric Gill was a complex and colorful figure who defies categorization in the history of graphic design. His activities encompassed stonemasonry, carving inscriptions for monuments, sculpture, wood engraving, typeface design, lettering, graphic design, and extensive writing. His 1913 conversion to Catholicism intensified his belief that work had spiritual value, and that the artist and craftsman served a human need for beauty and dignity. Around 1925, in spite of his earlier polemics against machine manufacture, he was persuaded by Stanley Morison (1889–1967) of the Monotype Corporation to accept the challenge of type design. His first style, Perpetua, is an antique roman face inspired by the inscription on Trajan's column but subtly redesigned to accommodate the needs of typecasting and printing.

Gill's embrace of historical influences—including the Trajan capitals, medieval manuscripts, the Incunabula, Baskerville, and Caslon—threatened to make him a historicist, but his highly original vision and opinions enabled him to be an innovator who transcended the strong historical influence of much of his work. His work for *The Four Gospels* (Fig. 19-35) demonstrates this synthesis of old and new. The Golden Cockerel type that Gill created for this book is a revitalized roman incorpo-

Gill Sans Light

Gill Sans Light Italic

Gill Sans

Gill Sans Italic

Gill Sans Bold

Gill Sans Bold Italic

Gill Sans Extrabold

Gill Sans Ultrabold

19-34. Eric Gill, the Gill Sans type family, 1928–1930. This family has been widely used in England.

ABCDEFGHIJKLMNOPQRSTUVWXYZ
abcdefghijklmnopqrstuvwxyz
&£1234567890.,;:-!?'‘'""/()

19-33. Edward Johnston, Johnston's Railway Type, 1916. To express the essence of the alphabet, Johnston made the *O* a perfect circle. The capital *M* is a square with the center strokes meeting in the square's exact center. All of the letterforms have a similar elemental design.

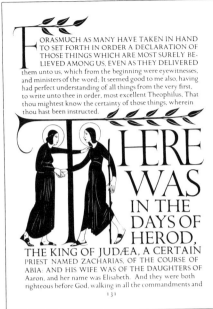

19-35

19-37

19-35. Eric Gill, page from *The Four Gospels*, 1931. Descending type sizes, all capitals on opening lines, unjustified right margins, and initial capitals integrated with illustrations are forged into a unified whole in one of Gill's most original book designs.

19-36. Eric Gill, page from *Essay on Typography,* 1931. In this highly personal and poetic little volume, Gill spoke of industrialism, humanism, letterforms, and legibility, demonstrating his belief in the merit of typographic composition with unjustified lines.

19-37. Paul Renner, folder for Futura, 1927. The early version of Futura released by the Bauer foundry in Germany was more abstract than the version that came to America. The structural relationships in this layout are typical of the new typography.

19-38. Paul Renner, Futura typefaces, 1927–1930. The extensive range of sizes and weights provided the necessary graphic material for printers and designers who adopted the new typography.

rating both Old Style and Transitional qualities. His woodcut illustrations have an archaic, almost medieval quality. However, his total design integration of illustration, capitals, headings, and text into a dynamic whole is strikingly modern.

In his book, *Essay on Typography* (Fig. 19-36), Gill first advanced the concept of unequal line lengths in text type. He argued that the uneven wordspacing of justified lines posed greater legibility and design problems than the use of equal wordspacing and a ragged-right margin. From late 1928 until his death, he worked at Hague and Gill, Printers, using a handpress, hand-set type, handmade paper, and types Gill designed exclusively for the press. This was not, however, a private press in the Arts and Crafts tradition; for Gill said a private press "prints solely what it chooses to print, whereas a public press prints what its customers demand of it."

Inspired by Bayer's universal alphabet (see Fig. 19-20), many geometrically constructed sans serif typefaces were designed during the 1920s. The Futura series (Figs. 19-37 and 19-38) of fifteen alphabets, including four italics and two unusual display styles, was designed by Paul Renner (1878–1956). As a teacher and designer, Renner fought tirelessly for the notion that designers should not just preserve the inheritance that they had been given and pass it on to the next

FUTURA Light
FUTURA Light italic
FUTURA Book
FUTURA Medium
FUTURA Medium Italic
FUTURA Demibold
FUTURA Demibold italic
FUTURA Bold
FUTURA Bold italic
FUTURA Bold condensed
Futura Display
Futura Black
FUTURA INLINE

19-38

abcdefghijklmnopqrstuvwxyz
ABCDEFGHIJKLMNOPQRSTUVWXYZ
abcdefghijklmnopqrstuvwxyz
ABCDEFGHIJKLMNOPQRSTUV WXYZ
abcdefghijklmnopqrstuvwxyz
ABCDEFGHIJKLMNOPQRSTUVWXYZ
abcdefghijklmnopqrstuvwxyz
ABCDEFGHIJKLMNOPQRSTUVWXYZ

19-40

19-39. Rudolf Koch, announcement for Kabel type, c. 1928. Koch's entry into the geometric sans serif style of the 1920s and 1930s is enlivened by unexpected design subtleties. The ornamental design—composed of straight lines—is typical of the period.

19-40. Stanley Morison (typographic advisor), *The Times*, 3 October 1932. Even the masthead, which had been used for 120 years, fell victim to the redesign that introduced Times New Roman.

generation unchanged; each generation must try to solve problems that were inherited and attempt to create a contemporary form true to its own time. Even the mystical medievalist Rudolf Koch (see Fig. 13-25) designed a very popular geometric sans serif typeface, Kabel (Fig. 19-39).

Stanley Morison, typographic advisor to the British Monotype Corporation and the Cambridge University Press, supervised the design of a major twentieth-century newspaper and magazine typeface commissioned by *The Times* of London in 1931. Named Times New Roman (Fig. 19-40), this typeface with short ascenders and descenders and sharp, small serifs was introduced in the 3 October 1932 edition of London's newspaper of record. The typographic appearance of one of the world's preeminent newspapers was radically changed overnight, and the traditionally conservative readers warmly applauded the legibility and clarity of the new typeface. Times New Roman went on to become one of the most widely used typefaces of the twentieth century. Its popularity has been attributed to its remarkable legibility, handsome visual qualities, and the economy achieved by moderately condensed letterforms. By making the stems and curves slightly thicker than in most roman-style letterforms, the designers gave Times New Roman a touch of the robust color that is associated with Caslon type.

The Isotype movement

The important movement toward developing a "world language without words" began in the 1920s, continued into the 1940s, and still has important influences today. The *Isotype* concept involves the use of elementary pictographs to convey information. The originator of this effort was Vienna sociologist Otto Neurath (1882–1945). As a child, Neurath marveled at the way ideas and factual information could be conveyed by visual means. Egyptian wall frescoes in the Vienna Museum and diagrams and illustrations in his father's books fired his imagination. Neurath felt that the social and economic changes following World War I demanded clear communication to assist public understanding of important social issues relating to housing, health, and economics. A system of elementary picto-

GEBURTEN UND STERBEFALLE IN WIEN

19-41

19-42

19-41. Otto Neurath and the Vienna Method, "Births and Deaths in Vienna" chart, c. 1928. Neurath called the Isotype a "language picture," which enabled the reader to make connections. The impact of World War I on mortality and births becomes dramatically evident.

19-42. Gerd Arntz, pictographs for Isotypes, early 1930s. These images show how simplified form and subtle nuances create communicative immediacy.

graphs to present complex data, particularly statistical data, was developed (Fig. 19-41). His charts were completely functional and shorn of decorative qualities. Neurath had ties with the new typography movement, for Tschichold assisted the group briefly in the late 1920s, and Renner's new Futura typeface was adopted for Isotype designs immediately after it became available.

Originally called the *Vienna Method,* the name Isotype (International System of Typographic Picture Education) was selected after Neurath moved to Holland in 1934. A vital group was the Transformation Team, headed by scientist and mathematician Marie Reidemeister (1898–1959). Vast quantities of verbal and numerical data compiled by statisticians and researchers were converted into layout form by the Transformation Team. The layouts were handed over to graphic artists for final execution. One problem was the need to produce large quantities of symbols for charts. Initially, the pictographs were individually drawn or cut from paper. After woodcut artist Gerd Arntz—whose constructivist-inspired prints included archetypal geometric figures—joined the group in 1928, he designed most of the pictographs (Fig. 19-42). Often reduced as small as one-half-centimeter tall, these pictographs were designed to express subtleties such as drunk man, unemployed man, or emigrant man. Arntz cut the pictographs on linoleum blocks, after which they were printed on a letterpress and then pasted into the finished artwork. After 1940, when the Isotype group fled to England, pictographs were duplicated by means of type-high letterpress line blocks. Because of their Germanic background, Neurath and Reidemeister were interned briefly, then were allowed to resume their work in England. In 1942, they were married.

Important among Neurath's many assistants was Rudolph Modley, who came to America during the 1930s and established Pictorial Statistics, Inc., which later became The Pictographic Corporation. This organization became the North American branch of the Isotypes movement.

The Isotype group's contribution to visual communications is the set of conventions they developed to formalize the use of pictorial language. This includes a pictorial syntax (a system of connecting images to create an ordered structure and meaning) and the design of simplified pictographs. The impact of their work upon post–World War II graphic design includes research toward the development of universal visual-language systems and the extensive use of pictographs in signage and information systems.

The prototype for the modern map

The London Underground also sponsored a major graphic design innovation when it made a trial printing of a new subway system map (Fig. 19-43) in 1933. Draftsman Henry C. Beck (b. 1903) submitted an unsolicited design proposal that replaced geographic fidelity with a diagrammatic interpretation. The central portion of the map, showing complex interchanges between routes, was enlarged in proportion to outlying areas. Meandering geographic lines were drawn on a grid of horizontals, verticals, and forty-five-degree diagonals. Bright color coding identified and separated the routes. Although cautious about the value of Beck's proposal, the publicity department printed the trial run and invited public response. When the public found it to be extremely functional, it was developed throughout the system.

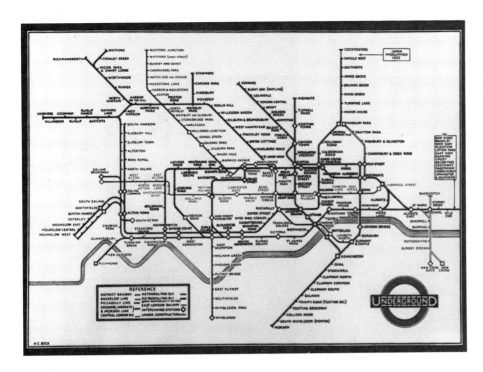

In preparing the camera-ready art for the first trial printing of his map, Beck hand-lettered over 2,400 characters in Johnston's Railway Type! Beck's development and revisions of the London Underground maps over twenty-seven years have made a significant contribution to the visual presentation of diagrams and networks, for his discoveries have inspired many variations around the world.

Independent voices in the Netherlands

In the Netherlands, several designers, influenced by the modern movements and the new typography but very personal and original in their vision, made important contributions. The Dutch designer Piet Zwart (1885–1977) created a synthesis from two apparently contradictory influences: the Dada movement's playful vitality and de Stijl's functionalism and formal clarity. By the time Zwart began graphic design projects at age thirty-six, he had trained as an architect, designed furniture and interiors, and worked in Jan Wils's architectural office. Zwart's interior designs moved toward functionalism and clarity of form after his communication with de Stijl began in 1919; however, he never joined the movement, because although he agreed with its basic philosophy, he found it too dogmatic and restrictive.

By happenstance in the early 1920s, Zwart received his first typographic commissions (Fig. 19-44). As his work evolved, he rejected both traditional symmetrical layout and de Stijl's insistence on strict horizontals and verticals. After making a rough layout, Zwart ordered words, rules, and symbols from a typesetter and playfully manipulated them on the surface to develop the design. The fluid nature of collage technique joined with a conscious concern for functional communication. Zwart designed the space as a "field of tension" brought alive by rhythmic composition, vigorous contrasts of size and weight, and a dynamic interplay between black form and white page (Figs. 19-45 and 19-46). Plate 60, a type specimen brochure page for N. V. Druckerei Trio designed by Zwart in 1930, combines the primary colors of de Stijl with a playful randomness. This page demonstrates the printing firm's large variety of type styles and sizes. Zwart's 1928 catalogue for N. V. Nederlandsche Kabelfabriek (NKF) has a dynamic spatial integration of type and images (Figs. 19-47 and 19-48).

Rejecting the dull grayness of conventional typographic design, Zwart's work became dynamic and arresting. He fractured tradition by taking a new look at the material from which graphic designs are made, just as painters like Picasso and

19-44. Piet Zwart, advertisement for the Laga Company, 1923. In Zwart's first advertising commissions, which came from this flooring manufacturer, the influence of de Stijl principles is evident.

The Bauhaus and the New Typography

Matisse had taken a new look at the material from which paintings are made. Perhaps his "amateur" status—he had no formal training in typography or graphic design—was an asset, for he was uninhibited by rules and methods of traditional professional practice. The need for typography to be in harmony with its era and the available production methods were important concerns for Zwart. Realizing that twentieth-century mass printing made typographic design an important and influential cultural force, he had a strong sense of social responsibility and was concerned for the reader. The function of time as an aspect of the reader's experience was considered as Zwart planned his page designs: He recognized that twentieth-century citizens were bombarded with communications and could not afford the luxury of wading through masses of reading matter. Brief slogans with large letters in bold type and diagonal lines were used to attract the attention of the

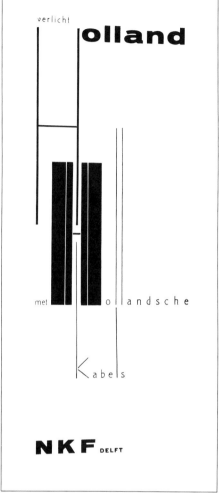

19-46

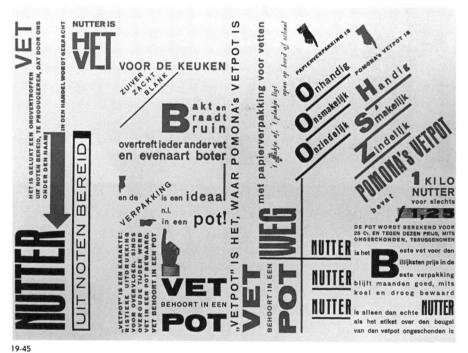

19-45

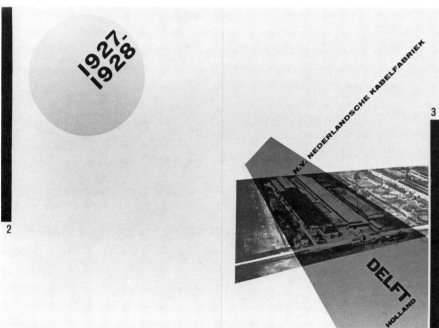

19-47

19-45. Piet Zwart, folder, 1924. Order is achieved in a complex communication by the rhythmic repetition of diagonals, words, letters, rules, and the dingbat hand.

19-46. Piet Zwart, advertisement for the NKF cableworks, 1926. Structured on dynamic verticals, this design is an example of how Zwart, functioning as his own copywriter, would develop simultaneous visual and verbal solutions to the client's communications problem.

19-47. Piet Zwart, pages from the NKF cableworks catalogue, 1928. In a stunning use of asymmetrical balance, the date (printed over a yellow circle) is balanced against a red wedge crossing a blue halftone photograph of the NKF plant. The NKF plant area, overprinted by the red wedge, becomes a purple halftone on a red background.

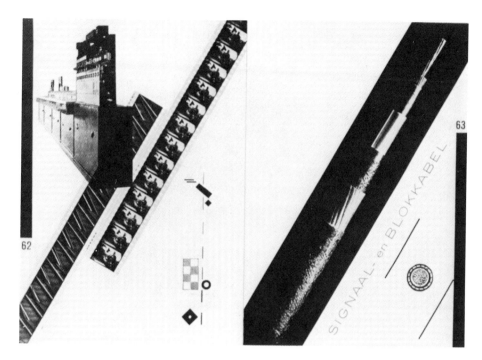

reader, who could quickly grasp the main idea or content and then decide whether to read further. Explanatory matter was organized to make it easy to isolate essential information from secondary material.

Zwart's activities over a long and illustrious career included photography, product and interior design, and teaching. Zwart once called himself a *Typotekt*. This amusing play on words, which expresses the fact that he was an architect who had become a typographic designer, has a deeper meaning, for it also expresses the working process of the new typography. The way that Zwart (as well as Lissitzky, Bayer, and Tschichold) constructed a design from the material of the typecase is analogous to the manner in which an architect's design is constructed from glass, steel, and concrete. His personal logo (Fig. 19-49) is a visual/verbal pun, for the Dutch word *zwart* means *black*.

Another Dutch artist, Hendrik N. Werkman (1882–1945) of Groningen, is noted for his experimentation with type, ink, and ink rollers for purely artistic expression. After his large printing company floundered during the economic dislocations following World War I, Werkman—whose avocation was painting—established a small job-printing firm. Beginning in 1923, he used type, rules, printing ink, brayers, and a small press to produce one-of-a-kind compositions called *druksels* (prints). Also, he began publication of *the next call* (Figs. 19-50 through 19-52), a small magazine of typographic experiments and texts, in 1923. The printing press became a "layout pad," as Werkman composed wood type, wood blocks, and even parts of an old lock directly on the letterpress bed. He loved printing and took joy in beautiful paper, wood textures, and the unique qualities of each nicked and dented piece of wood type. His process of building a design from ready-made components can be compared to the creative process of the Dadaist, particularly in photomontage. Like Lissitzky, he explored type as concrete visual form as well as alphabet communication. A few days before the battle of liberation moved through Groningen in April 1945, Werkman was murdered by the Nazis, and much of his work was destroyed during the battle.

Another important Dutch graphic designer from Groningen province, Paul Schuitema (1897–1973), was educated as a painter during World War I, then turned to graphic design for the Berkel company (Fig. 19-53) in the early 1920s. He made significant use of overprinting and organized his space with rigorous horizontal, vertical, and diagonal movements. Objective photography was integrated with ty-

19-49. Piet Zwart, personal logo, 1927.

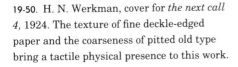

19-50

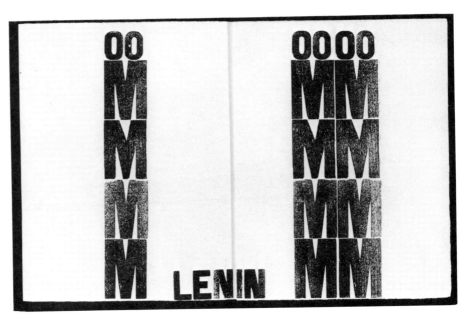

19-51

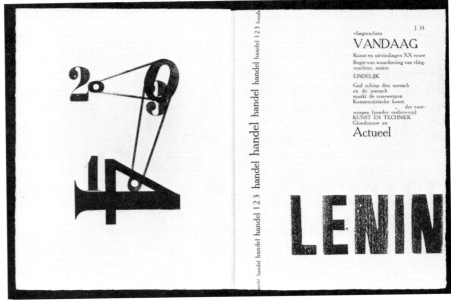

19-52

19-50. H. N. Werkman, cover for *the next call 4,* 1924. The texture of fine deckle-edged paper and the coarseness of pitted old type bring a tactile physical presence to this work.

19-51. H. N. Werkman, pages from *the next call 4,* 1924. In tribute upon the death of Lenin, solemn totems composed of *M*s and *O*s suggest a silent crowd of mourners.

19-52. H. N. Werkman, pages from *the next call 4,* 1924. Composed directly on the press bed, the configuration on the left was achieved by multiple printings with overlapping figures.

pography into a total structure. For thirty years, he taught at the Royal Academy in the Hague.

Willem Sandberg (1897–1984), director and designer at the municipal museums in Amsterdam, emerged as a highly original practitioner of the new typography after World War II. During the war, while hiding and working for the Resistance, he created his *experimenta typographica,* a series of probing typographic experiments in form and space, that was finally published in the middle 1950s (Figs. 19-54 and 19-55) and inspired his later work. Sandberg was an explorer—text settings were often completely unjustified, and sentence fragments were arranged freely on the page with ultrabold or delicate script introduced for accent or emphasis. He rejected symmetry and delighted in bright primary colors and strong contrasts. Crisp sans serif type was combined with large torn-paper collage letterforms with rough edges (Fig. 19-56). Exhibition catalogue text was often printed on coarse, brown wrapping paper, in contrast to coated enamel pages interspersed for halftones.

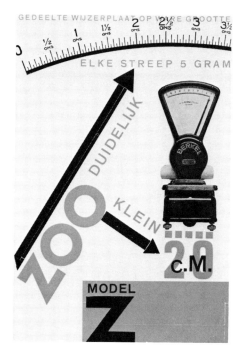

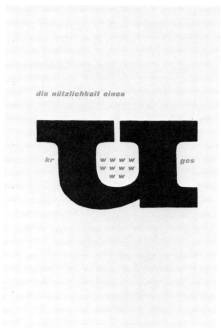

19-54

19-55

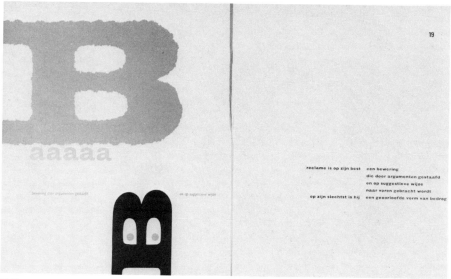

19-56

19-53. Paul Schuitema, brochure cover for the Berkel Model Z scales, before 1929. Arrows moving from the large word *ZOO* ("So") create a double headline: "So clear— every dash 5 grams" and "So small—20 centimeters [wide]." This brochure was printed by letterpress from typographic material assembled on the press bed from Schuitema's layout.

19-54. Willem Sandberg, page from *experimenta typographica,* 1956. In speaking of the utility of jugs, Sandberg transformed the *u* in *Kruges* ("jugs") into a vessel filled with blue letters.

19-55. Willem Sandberg, page from *experimenta typographica,* 1956. Sandberg's sensitive exploration of the negative space between letterforms became enormously influential upon a generation of designers.

19-56. Willem Sandberg, pages from *Keywords,* 1966. Sandberg contrasts scale (large/small), color (red/yellow/blue/black), and edge (torn/sharp). Forms are pushed toward the edges of the spread, and the horizontal movement of lines of type helps establish unity.

In the 1963 cover to *museum journaal voor moderne kunst* (*museum journal of modern art,* Pl. 61), contrasts of scale, color, and edge are used in an asymmetrically balanced layout. The white negative areas around the *m* and *j* are as important as the red letterforms. The torn edges contrast dynamically against the crisp type and razor-edged blue bar, which has an *E* torn from it. Sandberg's work demonstrates that many of the underlying design ideas of the new typography remained vital after World War II.

New approaches to photography

The new typography emphasized objective communication and was concerned with machine production. The camera, a machine for making images, was seen as an appropriate approach to image making. Much of the photography used in conjunction with the new typography was straightforward and neutral. The role of photog-

The Bauhaus and the New Typography

raphy as a graphic communications tool was expanded by Swiss designer/photographer Herbert Matter (1907–1984). While studying painting in Paris under Fernand Léger, Matter became interested in photography and design. In the early 1930s, he worked with Deberny and Peignot typefoundry as a photographer and typographic designer and assisted Cassandre on posters. At age twenty-five, Matter returned to his native Switzerland and began to design posters for the Swiss National Tourist Office. Like Laszlo Moholy-Nagy, Matter thoroughly understood the modern movement's new approaches to visual organization and techniques, such as collage and montage. He applied this knowledge to photography and graphic design. His posters of the 1930s use montage, dynamic scale changes, and an effective integration of typography and illustration. Photographic images become pictorial symbols removed from their normal relationships and composed in a new relationship.

Matter pioneered extreme contrasts of scale and the integration of black-and-white photography, symbols, and color areas (Fig. 19-57). In Matter's 1935 Swiss travel poster, which proclaims that all roads lead to Switzerland, three levels of photographic information combine in a breathtaking expression of space (Fig. 19-58). In the foreground, a cobblestone road photographed from ground level thrusts back into the space. Its motion is stopped by a ridge bearing the famous Swiss roadway that twists and winds over the mountains. Finally, a majestic mountain peak soars up against the blue sky. Plate 62, Matter's 1935 tourist poster for Pon-

19-57. Herbert Matter, travel poster for Switzerland, 1934. The angular shift conveys a sense of movement appropriate to winter sports. A screen tint under the large head introduces a skin tone, while the airbrushed color around the two Swiss crosses is red, and the sky area is pale blue.

19-58. Herbert Matter, poster for the Swiss Tourist Office, 1935. The black-and-white photograph, placed between the flat blue sky and the red typography, has an internal spatial dynamic that captures a feeling of the mountain heights.

19-59. Walter Herdeg, poster for St. Moritz, 1936. Light and shadow create a dynamic, angular composition conveying the thrills of skiing. The trademark sun becomes part of the photograph.

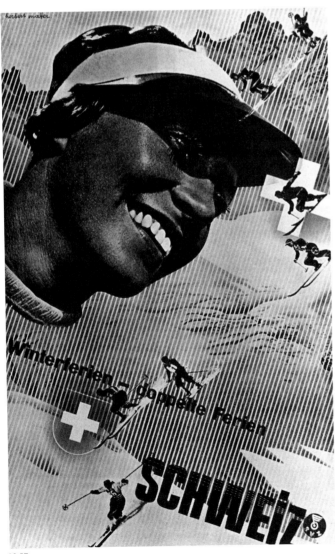

19-57

19-58

tresina, contrasts extreme scale change and uncommon camera angle between the large head and small skier.

Another Swiss graphic designer showing great expertise in the use of photography in graphic design during the 1930s was Walter Herdeg (b. 1908) of Zurich. In publicity materials for Swiss resorts, Herdeg achieved design vitality through the selection and cropping of photographic images. In designs for the St. Moritz ski resort (Fig. 19-59), Herdeg created a graphic unity through the consistent application of a stylized sun symbol and a gestural logotype. During the depths of World War II, Herdeg launched a bimonthly international graphic design magazine entitled *Graphis*. For forty-two years and 246 issues, he published, edited, and designed this publication, which created an unprecedented global dialogue between graphic designers throughout the world.

The new language of form began in Russia and Holland, crystallized at the Bauhaus, and found its most articulate spokesman in Jan Tschichold. The rational and scientific sensibilities of the twentieth century gained a graphic expression. The new typography instead of being a constriction upon creativity, enabled designers of vision to develop visual communications that were functional and expressive. Aspects of the new typography continue to be important influences well into the late twentieth century.

19-59

The Modern Movement
in America

20

The modern movement did not gain an early foothold in the United States. The fabled 1913 Armory Show, which generated a storm of protest when it introduced modern art to America, was not followed by public acceptance of modern art or design. The vitality and inventiveness of advanced European design did not become a significant influence in America until the 1930s. As the billboards in a Walker Evans (1903–1975) photograph demonstrate (Fig. 20-1), graphic design in America during the 1920s and 1930s was dominated by traditional illustration. However, the modern approach slowly gained ground on several fronts: book design, editorial design for fashion and business magazines catering to the affluent, and promotional and corporate graphics.

When Tschichold's "elementare typographie" insert (see Figs. 19-25 through 19-27) was publicized in American advertising and graphic arts publications, it caused considerable excitement and turmoil. Editors and writers savagely attacked it as "typographic fireworks" and a "typographic revolution" of "insane jugglings of type by a band of crazy, foreign type anarchists." But a small number of American typographers and designers recognized the vitality and functionalism of the new ideas. In 1928 and 1929, new typeface designs, including Futura and Kabel (see Figs. 19-38 and 19-39), became available in America, spurring the modern movement forward. A number of book designers, including William Addison Dwiggins (1880–1956), were transitional designers whose work spanned a range from the classical tradition of Goudy and Rogers to the new typography of Tschichold. After

20-1. Walker Evans, untitled, 1936. Evans's Atlanta photograph contrasting decaying homes and Depression Era movie posters demonstrates the gap that often exists between reality and graphic fantasy.

312

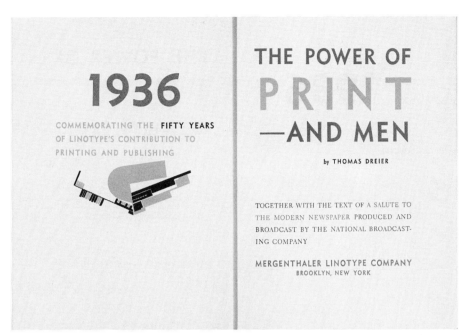

two decades in advertising design, Dwiggins began an involvement in book design for Alfred A. Knopf in 1926. He established Knopf's reputation for excellence in book design, experimenting with uncommon title-page arrangements, two-column book formats, and collagelike stencil ornaments combining the sensibility of the Cubist collage with the grace of traditional ornament (Fig. 20-2). His eighteen typeface designs for Mergenthaler Linotype include Caledonia, a graceful text face; Electra, a modern design with reduced thick and thin contrast; and Metro, Linotype's geometric sans serif created to compete with Futura and Kabel.

Other important book designers of the period include S. A. Jacobs, whose prolific oeuvre includes several books of e. e. cummings's poetry (Fig. 20-3), and Merle Armitage, whose typographic expressions ranged from exquisite Renaissance-inspired designs to books for avant-garde music and dance that helped define the modernist design aesthetic in America (Fig. 20-4).

Lester Beall (1903–1969) was a Kansas City native who moved to Chicago and earned an art history degree in 1926. Beall was primarily self-taught, and his extensive reading and curious intellect formed the basis for his professional development. After gaining experience in the late 1920s and early 1930s as a graphic designer whose work broke with traditional American advertising layout (Fig. 20-5), Beall moved his studio to New York in 1935. In the challenging social and economic environment of the Depression Era, he attempted to develop strong, direct, and exciting visual forms. Beall understood Tschichold's new typography and the Dada movement's random organization, intuitive placement of elements, and role of chance in the creative process. Admiring the strong character and form of nineteenth-century American wood types, Beall delighted in incorporating them into his work of this period. Often, flat planes of color and elementary signs such as arrows were combined with photography, as Beall sought visual contrast and a rich level of information content (Fig. 20-6). Beall's 1937 posters for the Rural Electrification Administration, a Federal agency charged with bringing electricity to the rural areas of America, reduced pro-electricity messages to elemental signs (Pl. 63). One such poster dynamically montaged a photograph of farm children with red and white stripes of the American flag, which echo in the "stripes" of a fence (Pl. 64).

In 1951, Beall moved his studio from New York City to his country home at Dumbarton Farms in Connecticut. In this new environment, and in response to client and social changes, Beall had increasing involvement in the emerging corporate design movement of the 1950s and 1960s (see Chapter 23).

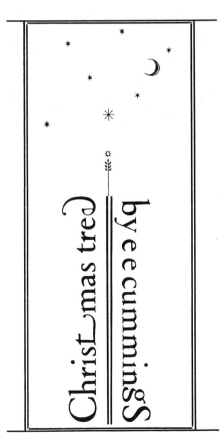

20-3. S. A. Jacobs, title page for *Christmas Tree* by e. e. cummings, 1928. Typography implies an image, which joins with rules and ornaments to suggest a landscape.

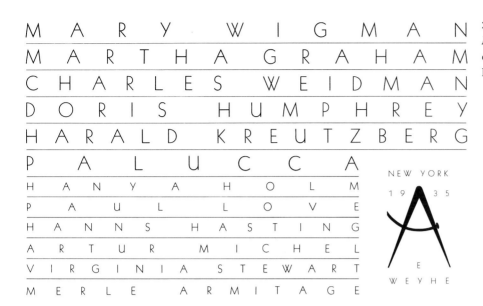

20-4. Merle Armitage, title page for *Modern Dance* by Merle Armitage, 1935. Sans serif capitals are letterspaced and separated by hairline rules.

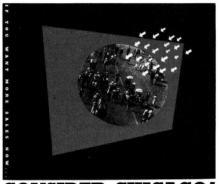

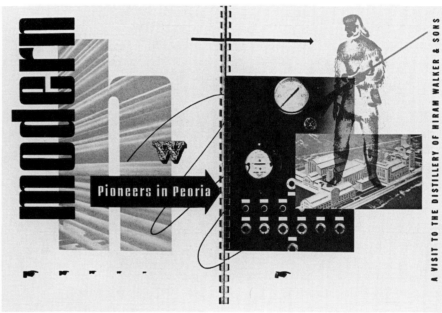

20-6

20-5. Lester Beall, newspaper advertisement for the *Chicago Tribune*, 1933. Red and black shapes, arrows symbolic of a message reaching an audience, and a photograph are combined into a total spatial organization.

20-6. Lester Beall, title pages from a promotional brochure, c. 1935. Victorian wood type contrasts with sans serif type, and photography contrasts with drawing. The strong horizontal movement contrasts with a rhythm of verticals. Images, including a transparent drawing overprinting a photograph, are layered in space.

Immigrants to America

A migratory process began slowly, then reached a crescendo by the late 1930s, as cultural leaders from Europe—including many graphic designers—came to America. The design language they brought with them, and the changes imposed upon their work by their American experience, forms an important phase of the development of American graphic design.

It is a curious coincidence that three individuals who brought European modernism to American graphic design were Russian-born, French-educated immigrants who worked in editorial design for fashion magazines. Erté (né Romain de Tirtoff, b. 1892) was a Russian admiral's son, born in St. Petersburg. After becoming a prominent Paris illustrator and set designer working in the Art Deco manner, he was signed to an exclusive contract from 1924 until 1937 to design covers and fashion illustrations for *Harper's Bazaar* magazine (Fig. 20-7). Erté's covers projected a sophisticated, continental image on the newsstand. Renowned for his fashion designs, set designs, illustrations, and graphics, Erté combined the stylized drawing of pictorial modernism with an exotic decorativeness of Persian complexity to become a major figure in the Art Deco sensibility.

20-7. Erté, *Harper's Bazaar* cover, 1929. Bold blue and white shapes are accented by the stylized fish earring printed in scarlet.

20-8. Martin Munkacsi, editorial photograph from *Harper's Bazaar*, 1934. Rejecting the conventions of the studio, Munkacsi allowed outside locations and the natural movements of his models to suggest innovative possibilities.

The first art director trained in modern design to guide the graphic destiny of a major American periodical was Dr. Mehemed Fehmy Agha (1896–1978). Born in the Ukraine to Turkish parents, Agha studied art in Kiev and received advanced degrees in languages in Paris. After working in Paris as a graphic artist, he moved to Berlin and was there in 1928 when he met Condé Nast, who had come to close down the unprofitable Berlin edition of *Vogue* magazine and was seeking a new art director for the American *Vogue*. Impressed with Agha's graphics, Nast persuaded him to come to New York as *Vogue*'s art director. Energetic and uncompromising, Agha soon took over design responsibilities for *Vanity Fair* (see Fig. 17-26) and *House & Garden* as well. He revitalized Condé Nast's stuffy, dated approach to editorial design by introducing bleed photography, machine-set sans serif type, white space, and asymmetrical layouts.

At the rival *Harper's Bazaar,* which had been purchased by newspaperman William Randolph Hearst in 1913 and revitalized through the use of photography, Carmel Snow became the editor in 1933. She was keenly interested in the visual aspects of the magazine and hired Hungarian Martin Munkacsi (1896–1963) as a staff photographer. Traditional conventions of editorial photography were slapped in the face by Munkacsi's new compositions (Fig. 20-8). Munkacsi was one of a new breed of editorial and advertising photographers who combined the visual dynamic learned from Moholy-Nagy and Man Ray with the fresh approach to photography made possible by the new 35mm Leica "miniature" camera. Invented by an employee of the Leitz Company of Germany in 1913, the introduction of this small portable camera (with a fast *f*/3.4-aperture lens, focal-plane shutter, and a film advance that simultaneously cocked the shutter) had been delayed by World War I. With the addition of faster, higher-resolution films, photography became an extension of the photographer's vision.

Snow invited Alexey Brodovitch (1898–1971) to become art director of *Harper's Bazaar,* where he remained from 1934 until 1958. Brodovitch, a Russian who had fought in the czar's calvary during World War I, immigrated to Paris and established himself as a leading contemporary designer there before heading to the United States in 1930. With a passion for white space and love of razor-sharp type on clear, open pages, he rethought the approach to editorial design (Figs. 20-9 and 20-10). He sought "a musical feeling" in the flow of text and pictures. The rhythmic environment of open space balancing text was energized by the art and photography he commissioned from major European artists, including Henri Cartier-Bresson, A. M. Cassandre, Salvador Dali, and Man Ray. In addition, Brodovitch taught designers how to use photography. His cropping, enlarging, and juxtaposing of images and his exquisite selection from contact sheets were all done with extraordinary intuitive judgment. He saw contrast as a dominant tool in editorial design and paid close attention to the individual page, the spread, and the graphic movement through the editorial pages of each issue.

Joseph Binder, perhaps because of the strong pictorial quality of his designs, received wide acclaim when he migrated to America. He arrived in 1934 for a series of lectures and workshops and, touched by the response to his work, settled in New York the following year. In America, Binder's style became more refined, partly because he had begun to use the airbrush to achieve highly finished forms. His strong Cubist influence yielded to a stylized realism. Binder was an ideal choice to create one of the 1939 New York World's Fair posters (Pl. 65): The trylon and perisphere—emblems of the fair—combine with spotlights, a skyline, and modern transportation images to symbolize America's coming of age on the eve of World War II. World events would soon force the United States to cast aside its provincialism and neutrality, and Binder's World's Fair poster captures America's move into modernism and global power. Traces of Cubism remained in his work, as can be seen in his 1939 poster for iced coffee (Fig. 20-11), in which two-dimensional planes undergird and support the illustrative content. But during his Vienna period (see Fig. 17-29), Binder had constructed images from planes; now the subject matter became dominant, and the design qualities subordinate.

20-9

20-10

20-11

20-9. Alexey Brodovitch (art director) and Man Ray (photographer), pages from *Harper's Bazaar*, 1934. The figure's oblique thrust inspired Brodovitch to construct a dynamic typographic page from several sizes and weights of geometric sans serif types.

20-10. Alexey Brodovitch (art director) and Man Ray (photographer), page from *Harper's Bazaar*, 1934. The forms and texture of the experimental photograph are amplified and complemented by the typographic design.

20-11. Joseph Binder, poster for A & P Coffee, 1939. Flat shapes and airbrushed modulations create strong value contrasts, requiring the viewer to "fill in" the details of Binder's edited naturalism.

The Works Progress Administration poster project

As part of the New Deal of President Franklin Delano Roosevelt, the Federal government created the Works Progress Administration (WPA) in 1935. Direct relief for the unemployed was replaced by work opportunities, and billions of dollars were pumped into the economy as an average of over two million workers were paid from fifteen to ninety dollars per month from 1935 until 1941. Jobs were designed to "help men keep their chins up and their hands in." A poster project was included among the various cultural programs in the WPA Federal Art Projects. From 1935 until 1939, when the Federal Art Projects were abolished, over two million copies of approximately thirty-five thousand designs were produced. Most of the designs were silk-screened, and sculptors and painters joined unemployed illustrators and graphic designers in the studios.

Silk-screen printing's characteristic flat color combined with influences from the Bauhaus, pictorial modernism, and Constructivism to produce a surprisingly modern result (Fig. 20-12) in contrast to the naturalistic illustration dominating much of American mass-media graphics of the era. Government-sponsored cultural events, including theatrical performances and art exhibitions, were frequent subjects for the poster project, as were public-service communications about health, crime prevention, housing, education. Typography was often approached from an aesthetic viewpoint and used as both compositional element and message communicator.

The flight from fascism

The rising tide of Nazism in Europe created the greatest transnational migration of intellectual and creative talent in history. Scientists, authors, architects, artists, and designers left Europe for the haven of North America during the late 1930s, for they realized that freedom of inquiry and expression was in grave danger on the European continent. The artists included Max Ernst, Marcel Duchamp, and Piet Mondrian. When the Nazis closed the Bauhaus in 1933, faculty, students, and alumni dispersed throughout the world and made modern design a truly international movement. Walter Gropius, Ludwig Mies van der Rohe, and Marcel Breuer transplanted the functionalist architectural movement to American shores, and Herbert Bayer and Laszlo Moholy-Nagy brought their innovative approaches to graphic design. Other European graphic designers who came to America and made significant contributions to design include Will Burtin (1908–1972), Jean Carlu, George Giusti (b. 1908), Herbert Matter, and Ladislav Sutnar.

Sponsored by the Association of Arts and Industries, Moholy-Nagy arrived in Chicago in 1937 and established the New Bauhaus. This closed after one year due to inadequate financial support, but Moholy-Nagy managed to open the School of Design in 1939, backed more with imagination and spirit than with economic resources. The primary source of financial support came from Moholy-Nagy and other faculty members, many of whom agreed to teach without pay if necessary. Moholy-Nagy was not the only transplanted European designer who experienced difficulty in bringing his creative work across the Atlantic; both Carlu and Bayer found it difficult to find clients who comprehended their work during their first months in America.

Burtin, recognized as one of Germany's outstanding designers, fled Germany in 1938 after the Nazi regime pressed him to work for it. His work combined a graphic clarity and directness with a lucid presentation of the subject matter. His "Design Decade" cover for the October 1940 cover of *The Architectural Forum* (Pl. 66) demonstrates his ability to bring together structural form and symbolic information into a cohesive whole: The dates, printed on acetate, combine with the architect's tools to symbolize design during the preceding decade; shadows become integral forms in the design. Burtin had a keen understanding of science and began to design for Upjohn pharmaceuticals, interpreting such complex subjects as bacteriology (Fig. 20-13). This involvement was suspended in 1943, when he worked for the government designing training manuals, followed by three years as art director

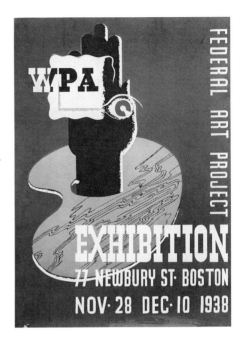

20-12. Works Progress Administration poster, 1938. Often designed by artists who would rather be painting than producing graphics, the WPA posters combined elements of pictorial modernism with other graphic forms, such as the slab-serif lettering shown here.

20-13. Will Burtin, cover for the first issue of *Scope,* 1941. To signify the new "miracle drugs" under development, a color illustration is superimposed over a black-and-white photograph of a hand holding a test tube.

The Modern Movement in America

20-14. Egbert Jacobson, logo for Container Corporation of America, 1936. This logical symbol, combining the major product and suggesting the national scope of the firm, was innovative for its time.

20-15. A. M. Cassandre, advertisement for Container Corporation of America, 1938. A strong statement, "Research, experience, and talent focused on advanced paperboard packaging," is given a near-hypnotic graphic impact.

of *Fortune* magazine. In 1948, he became a design consultant for Upjohn and other companies, making a major contribution to the visual interpretation of graphic information (see Fig. 20-42).

A patron of design

A major figure in the development of American modern design beginning in the 1930s was a Chicago industrialist, Walter P. Paepcke (1896–1960), who founded the Container Corporation of America in 1926. At a time when most products were shipped in wooden containers, Paepcke pioneered the manufacture of paperboard and corrugated-fiber containers. Acquisitions and expansion enabled Container Corporation to become a national company and the nation's largest producer of packaging materials. Paepcke was unique among the captains of industry of his generation, for he recognized that design could serve both a pragmatic business function and become a major cultural thrust by the corporation. In 1936, Paepcke hired Egbert Jacobson (1890–1966) to become the first director of Container Corporation's new department of design. As with Peter Behrens's design program for AEG early in the century, Container Corporation's new visual signature (and its implementation) was based on two ingredients: the vision of the designer and a supportive client. Jacobson had an extensive background as a color expert, and this knowledge was put to use as mill and factory interiors were transformed from drab industrial grays and browns to bright colors. A new trademark was designed (Fig. 20-14), and graphic materials such as stationery and invoices were redesigned with a consistent format using Futura type and a standard color combination of black and shipping-carton tan.

Paepcke was an advocate and patron of design. He had maintained a long-standing interest in the Bauhaus, which may have been a response to the school's experiments with paper materials and structures. Moved by Moholy-Nagy's com-

20-15

20-16

20-17

financial support to the Institute of Design. By the time of Moholy-Nagy's tragic early death from leukemia on 24 November 1946, the Institute was on a firm educational and organizational footing.

Container's advertising agency was N. W. Ayer, where art director Charles Coiner (1898–1989) made a major contribution. Beginning in May 1937, A. M. Cassandre was commissioned to design a series of advertisements for Container that turned the conventions of American advertising upside-down. The traditional headline and body copy were replaced by a dominant visual that extended a simple statement about Container Corporation (Fig. 20-15). In contrast to the long-winded copywriting of the 1930s, many of these advertisements only had a dozen words. These efficient communications separated Container Corporation from the general din of advertising.

Cassandre was also commissioned to design covers for *Harper's Bazaar* by Alexey Brodovitch (Fig. 20-16). When Cassandre decided to return to Paris in 1939, Container Corporation continued his general approach by commissioning advertisements from other artists and designers of international stature, including Herbert Bayer (who was retained as a consulting designer by Jacobson then served as chairman of Container's department of design from 1956 to 1965), Fernand Léger, Man Ray, Herbert Matter, and Jean Carlu.

The war years

While World War I was primarily fought in trenches far removed from urban populations, World War II was fought with lightning invasions by mechanized divisions and aerial bombardments of industry and cities. While the war's trauma disrupted the ability of many governments to produce graphic propaganda, a diverse group of painters, illustrators, and designers received commissions from the U.S. Office of War Information. America's wartime graphics spanned the range of possibilities from brilliantly conceived posters to training materials and amateurish cartoons.

In 1941, as America's entry into the global conflict became increasingly inevitable, the Federal government began to develop propaganda posters to promote production. Charles Coiner became art consultant to the Office of Emergency Management as America's colossal defense buildup began. He commissioned Jean Carlu to create one of the finest designs of his career, the famous "America's answer! Production" poster (Pl. 67). Visual and verbal elements are inseparably interlocked into an intense symbol of productivity and work. Over 100,000 of these posters were produced for distribution throughout the country, and Carlu was recognized with a top award by the New York Art Director's Club Exhibition.

Intense feelings about Hitler, Pearl Harbor, and the war seemed to pull powerful communications from the graphic designers, illustrators, and fine artists commissioned to create posters for the Office of War Information. Illustrator John Atherton (1900–1952), whose credits included numerous *Saturday Evening Post* covers, penetrated to the heart of the problem of careless talk, gossip, and discussion of troop movements as a source of enemy information (Fig. 20-17). Joseph Binder's 1941 poster proposal for the U.S. Army Air Corps is potent in its simplicity and beauty of design (Fig. 20-18). E. McKnight Kauffer, commissioned to design a series of stunningly simple posters to boost the morale of the occupied Allies, produced a 1940 poster for Greece (Pl. 68) bearing the Greek headline that translates to "We Fight for the Liberty of All." Kauffer combined a classical Greek head with an American flag to make a powerful graphic symbol—two dissimilar graphic elements signifying the unity of two nations. The angry social realist Ben Shahn (1898–1969), whose powerful style of awkward shapes had addressed social and economic injustice during the depression, reached a larger audience in posters conveying Nazi brutality (Pl. 69). His 1943 poster for the U.S. Office of War Information achieves communicative power from intense graphic forms: the prisonlike closing of the space with a wall; the hood masking the victim's identity; the simple,

20-16. A. M. Cassandre, cover for *Harper's Bazaar*, 1939. A pink perfume bottle forms the nose, lipstick creates a mouth, and a puff of powder colors a cheek in an almost textbook demonstration of simultaneity.

20-17. John Atherton, poster for the U.S. Office of War Information, 1943. The placement of the two-part headline implies a rectangle within the space. This symmetry is animated by the off-center placement of the white cross.

The Modern Movement in America

20-18

20-19

straightforward headline; and the factual urgency of the telegraphic message.

The posters Herbert Bayer produced during and after the war were surprisingly illustrative compared to his ardent insistence on Constructivism during his Dessau Bauhaus period. Sensitive to his new audience and oriented toward communications problem solving, Bayer moved into an almost pictographic illustration style that was combined with the hierarchy of information and the strong underlying composition he pioneered at Dessau. In his poster promoting egg production, the large white egg centered against the black sky becomes a strong focal point (Fig. 20-19). The headline to the left balances the flaming town to the right, and the diagonal subheading echoes the diagonal shadow cast by the egg.

When one compares Bayer's 1949 poster for polio research (Fig. 20-20) with his 1926 poster for the Kandinsky Jubilee Exhibition (see Pl. 58), these two graphic designs are clearly worlds apart. The Kandinsky poster was designed by a twenty-six-year-old typography teacher at a young school optimistically hoping to build a new social order by design; the polio research poster is the work of a forty-eight-year-old designer living in a foreign land after having seen the death of twenty-six million people in Europe during World War II. The Dessau Bauhaus had been closed for political reasons; now it sat in mute testament to the hopes and dreams of a generation, locked behind the "iron curtain" that divided Europe after the war. The photography and typography of Bayer's Bauhaus period yielded to hand-painted illustration and hand-lettering, but the commitment to functional communication, the integration of letterforms and imagery, and the asymmetrical balance remained constant.

During World War II, Container Corporation innovated new uses for paperboard packaging, which freed metals and other strategic materials for the war effort. A "Paperboard Goes to War" advertising campaign (Figs. 20-21 and 20-22) continued the design experimentation of the earlier institutional ads. Before the war, there was still a degree of public concern about the strength of paperboard—this campaign prepared the way for its extensive use after the war. Each advertisement showed a specific use of a Container Corporation product in the war effort. Herbert Bayer, Jean Carlu, and Herbert Matter joined Jacobson in creating powerful telegraphic statements that went directly to the essence of the communications problem, using strong visuals and two or three lines of typography whose angled thrust picked up diagonal compositional lines from the illustration or montage. The next series of Container Corporation advertisements commemorated the twenty-eight allied nations who were fighting together during World War II, with the ad for each country illustrated by an artist from that nation (Fig. 20-23).

20-18. Joseph Binder, poster for the U.S. Army Air Corps, 1941. A symbolic suggestion of great depth is achieved by the scale change between the close-up aircraft wing and the formation of aircraft.

20-19. Herbert Bayer, poster to encourage egg production, c. 1943. The primary colors of de Stijl are used in altered form: The headline is blue, the flames are red, and the area to the left of the egg is a muted yellow.

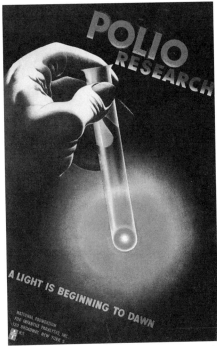

20-20

20-22

20-23

20-21. Herbert Matter, advertisement for Container Corporation of America, 1942. A dramatic thunderstorm reinforces the copy concept that paperboard packaging protects goods from weather and spoilage. The lightning becomes a strong focal point, connecting the two areas of typography.

20-22. Herbert Matter, advertisement for Container Corporation of America, 1943. In this "Paperboard Goes to War" advertisement, a unified complex of images telegraphs global scope, paperboard boxes, and food for our troops.

20-23. Willem de Kooning, "The Netherlands" advertisement for Container Corporation of America, 1945. Once selected to visualize their native lands or states, the fine artists participating in these campaigns were given the freedom of their artistic convictions.

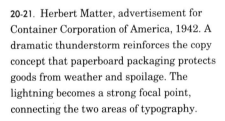

20-20. Herbert Bayer, poster supporting polio research, 1949. The diagonal shaft of the test tube leads the eye from the red and blue headline to the flowing yellow light that is beginning to dawn, linking the elements in the same manner as the thick black bars of Bayer's Bauhaus work.

After the war

Seeking another institutional advertising campaign using fine art, Container Corporation decided to honor the states by commissioning paintings by a native artist from each of the then forty-eight states. A simple copy line appeared under each full-color painting, followed by the Container Corporation logotype. Both the nations and states series served to advance a Bauhaus ideal: the union of art with life. Artists were commissioned to express visually their homelands or states, and these works of art were reproduced as part of the pragmatic need of Container Corporation to speak to its diverse audiences.

After completion of the series of advertisements commemorating the states, Container developed what is perhaps the most brilliant institutional campaign in the history of advertising. Paepcke and his wife Elizabeth were attending the Great Books discussion group conducted in Chicago by Robert M. Hutchins and Mortimer Adler. These two scholars were also editing the Great Books of the Western World series, which included two volumes discussing the ideas contained in the series. Paepcke approached Adler with the possibility of an institutional ad campaign presenting the great ideas of Western culture. Each would have an artist's graphic interpretation of a great idea specified by Adler and his colleagues. Walter and Elizabeth Paepcke joined Egbert Jacobson and Herbert Bayer as a jury to select the visual artists who would be asked to bring graphic actualization to these abstract concepts. Beginning in February 1950, this unprecedented institutional campaign transcended the bounds of advertising, as ideas about liberty, justice, and human rights (Figs. 20-24 and 20-25) were conveyed to an audience of business leaders, investors, prospective employees, and molders of public opinion. Over three decades, 157 visual artists created artwork for almost two hundred "Great Ideas" advertisements. The campaign separated Container Corporation from its army of competitors, and made Container appear somehow different to its diverse markets, for a company whose management spent a portion of its advertising budget conveying great ideas by outstanding artists and designers must likewise possess positive social and cultural qualities. This campaign continued for over three decades.

Alexey Brodovitch grew in skill and assurance as an editorial designer through the 1940s and 1950s. He had a remarkable gift for identifying and assisting new talent. Photographers Richard Avedon (b. 1923) and Irving Penn (b. 1917) both received early commissions and advice from Brodovitch. Art Kane (b. 1925) was

20-25

20-24. Herbert Bayer, "Great Ideas" advertisement for Container Corporation of America, 1954. Protection from injustice and oppression is clearly expressed by the blue and white hands warding off black arrows penetrating into the yellow page.

20-25. Herbert Bayer, "Great Ideas" advertisement for Container Corporation of America, 1960. Theodore Roosevelt's admonition that the "love of soft living and the get-rich-quick theory of life" were threats to America find expression in a collage of images of affluence and decadence.

another Brodovitch protégé. Kane worked as a photo retoucher and art director of *Seventeen* magazine before turning to photography. He is a master of symbolism, multiple exposure, and the reduction of photography to essential images needed to convey the essence of content with compelling conviction.

During the early 1950s, Brodovitch designed the short-lived visual arts magazine *Portfolio* (Figs. 20-26 through 20-28). At the height of his graphic powers, Brodovitch gave this publication an elegance and visual flow that has seldom been matched. The pacing, cropping of images, and use of color and texture were extraordinary. Large images, dynamic space, and inserts on colored or textured papers changed the tactile and perceptual experience of reading a magazine.

In addition to his free-lance design commissions for Container Corporation of America, Herbert Matter received design and photographic assignments from many clients, including *Vogue, Fortune,* and *Harper's Bazaar.* In 1946, he began a twenty-year period as graphic design and photography consultant to the Knoll Associates furniture design and manufacturing firm, and produced some of his finest work for this design-oriented client. His 1948 advertisements for molded-plastic chairs by Eero Saarinen are remarkable in their dynamic compositions (Fig. 20-29). Biomorphic shapes, while quite fashionable during the late 1940s and early 1950s in painting, furniture, and other design forms, became trapped in this time frame and are now associated with the sensibilities of the period. It is a tribute to Matter's strong sense of design fundamentals that the advertising series he created for Saarinen furniture has maintained a design vitality long after the forms of the era have become dated.

During the 1950s, Matter, after a quarter of a century integrating graphic and photographic elements, turned toward more purely photographic solutions. His ability to convey concepts with images is shown in the 1956 folder (also used as

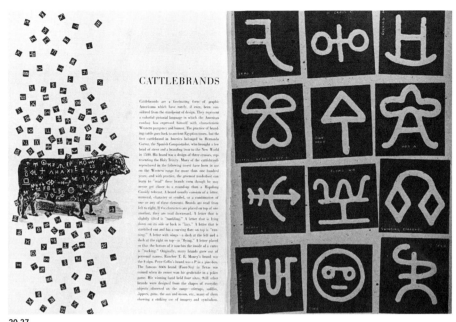

20-27

20-26. Alexey Brodovitch, cover for *Portfolio,* 1951. Screen tints produce the illusion that translucent rectangles of pink and blue-gray have been placed on the stencil logo slashing down the black cover.

20-27. Alexey Brodovitch, pages from *Portfolio,* 1951. Brodovitch's mastery of contrast is seen in the scale change between the small, scattered cattle brands around the well-stamped bull and the large cattle brands of the portfolio's first page. Also, rough-textured paper contrasts with slick, coated white stock.

advertisements on two consecutive right-hand pages of magazines) unveiling a new line of molded-plastic pedestal furniture (Fig. 20-30). A strange object wrapped in paper appears on the cover of the brochure, printed in full color on translucent paper. Underneath, the reader finds a Saarinen pedestal chair bearing a fashionable model. The surprise value of this sequence is that this new furniture has just one pedestal leg—the viewer, first seeing the cover, does not recognize the shape of the traditional four-legged chair.

With his powerful shapes and well-defined subjects, Joseph Binder remained a force on the American design scene until the 1960s. His ubiquitous military recruiting posters (Fig. 20-31), which were among the last manifestations of pictorial modernism, were ingrained into the American consciousness during the 1950s. The geometric and symbolic shapes of pictorial modernism were converted into monolithic masses that became symbols of military might and the technological accomplishments of a new era of sophisticated weaponry.

Born to Italian and Swiss parents, George Giusti worked in both Italy and Switzerland before coming to New York City in 1938 and opening a design office. Gius-

20-28. Alexey Brodovitch, foldout photographic essay from *Portfolio,* 1951. Stretching about 138 centimeters (4½ feet), this layout of images from the Mummer's Parade is punctuated with vertical columns of film strips. Graphic design only rarely becomes this sequential and kinetic.

20-29. Herbert Matter, advertisement for Knoll Associates, 1948. Photographs of organic chair components combine with flat, yellow "shadows" in an advertisement with the energy of a Calder mobile.

20-30. Herbert Matter, brochure covers introducing a Knoll chair, 1956. On the translucent cover, the warm browns of the kraft paper are keyed to the orange logo. On the inner cover, the crisp black and white of the girl's clothing and the white chair are accented with a red logo, cushion, and lipstick.

20-31

20-32

20-31. Joseph Binder, recruiting poster for the U.S. Navy, c. 1954. Traces of Cassandre's steamship posters remain, but the strength expressed is more powerful and forbidding.

20-32. George Giusti, cover for *Holiday,* 1960. Part Cubism and part expressionism, this simplified and colorful design depicts the legend of Romulus, the founder of Rome, and his twin Remus, who were raised by a wolf.

20-33. Ladislav Sutnar, Sweet's Catalog Service symbol, 1942. Disarmingly simple and possessing a beautifully harmonious figure–ground relationship, this symbol established the typographic character for Sweet's printed material.

20-34. Ladislav Sutnar, cover for *Catalog Design,* 1944. This book presented Sutnar's emerging philosophy of structuring information in a logical and consistent manner. The geometrically constructed letterforms are alternated in blue and orange, and the grid pattern is printed in black.

ti's great gift as a graphic designer is an ability to reduce forms and images to a simplified, minimal essence. His images become iconographic and symbolic. Giusti used freehand drawing and included evidence of process in his work—an image painted in transparent dyes will have areas of flooded and blotted color, and his three-dimensional illustrations often include the bolts or other fasteners used to assemble the elements. For all of their simplicity, Giusti's images retain a human warmth. Beginning in the 1940s and continuing well into the 1960s, Giusti received frequent commissions for his bold iconographic images for advertising campaigns and for cover designs of *Holiday* and *Fortune* magazines (Fig. 20-32).

Informational and scientific graphics

Ladislav Sutnar came to New York as design director of the Czechoslovakian Pavilion at the New York World's Fair in 1939, the year Hitler had summoned Czechoslovakia's leaders to Berlin and informed them that Prague would be destroyed from the air unless additional Czech territory was surrendered to him. In New York, Sutnar became a vital force in the evolution of modern design in the United States. A close association with Sweet's Catalog Service (Fig. 20-33) enabled Sutnar to place an indelible mark upon the design of industrial product information.

Since 1906, Sweet's had provided a compendium of architectural and industrial product information. Working closely with Sweet's research director, Knut Lönberg-Holm, Sutnar defined informational design as a synthesis of *function, flow,* and *form. Function* he defined as utilitarian need with a definite purpose: to make information easy to find, read, comprehend, and recall. *Flow* was his term for the logical sequence of information. Sutnar felt the basic unit to be not the page but the "visual unit," which is the double-page spread. He rejected traditional margins as rigid containers creating barriers to visual flow and employed bleeds extensively. He used shape, line, and color as functional elements to direct the eye as it moved through the design seeking information.

As Sutnar approached problems of *form,* static and uniform arrangements of catalogue information gave way to dynamic information patterns and clear, rational organization. Symmetrical typography was discarded because it lacked a relationship to the functional flow of information. Visual articulation of type— underlining, size and weight contrasts, spacing, color, and reversing—was used to aid searching, scanning, and reading. A simple visualization language with emphasis upon graphic charts, diagrams, and pictures was used to clarify complex information and save the reader's time. The upper-right corner, which Sutnar considered the visual entry point for each layout, was used for identifying information. Optical unity was achieved by a systematic use of signs, shapes, and color. As design of *Sweet's Catalog* became more functional, the writing style became more compact and factual, using brief, concise statements. In two landmark books, *Catalog Design* (Fig. 20-34) and *Catalog Design Progress* (Figs. 20-35 through 20-38), Sutnar documented and explained his design approach to a generation of designers and their clients.

A major graphic design accomplishment of the late 1940s and 1950s and an important milestone in the visual presentation of data was the publication of the *World Geo-Graphic Atlas* (Figs. 20-39 and 20-40) by Container Corporation in 1953. In an introduction, Paepcke spoke of a need for "a better understanding of other peoples and nations." Herbert Bayer was the designer and editor of this volume, and labored for five years on the project. Once again, Paepcke behaved in a manner unlike the conventional businessman: A corporation published, for the information of its clients and suppliers, plus distribution to libraries and museums, a 368-page book filled with 120 full-page maps of the world, supported by 1,200 diagrams, graphs, charts, symbols, and other graphic communications about the planet—hardly a typical business decision! Bayer assembled information from multiple scientific disciplines, including geography, astronomy, climatology, economics, and sociology, and presented it through symbols, charts, and diagrams. He was ahead of his time in his effort to inventory earth resources and study the

20-35

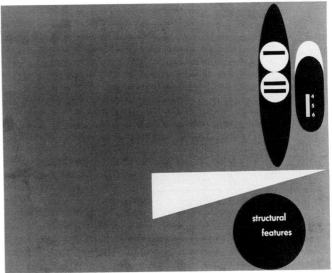

20-36

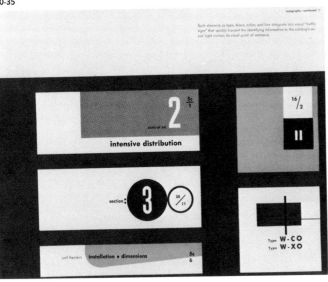

20-37

20-38

planet as a series of interlocking geophysical and life systems. Even more propheti-cally, the final section of the *World Geo-Graphic Atlas* discusses the conservation of resources, addressing population growth and resource depletion. Bayer called for careful management and development of earth resources, international coopera-tion, and increased agricultural productivity.

Will Burtin made a significant contribution to the visualization of scientific pro-cesses. He believed that visual communications should be based on four principal realities: man, as measure and measurer; light, color, and texture; space, time, and motion; and science. Man, according to Burtin, is the most important consideration of a designer, for as a measure, the "dimensions of his hands, his eyes, his entire body" become the standard against which any design is assessed. As measurer, Burtin believed a person's "emotional, physical, and intellectual response" and un-derstanding of the information communicated should be the yardstick used to mea-sure or evaluate a design. Burtin saw science and the scientific method as having great value when applied to all areas of people's social and psychological lives, including art. Science allows people "to see the workings of nature, makes trans-parent the solid, and gives substance to the invisible." In the midst of all this, Burtin saw the designer as a "communicator, link, interpreter, and inspirer," able to make comprehensible the knowledge of science.

Through graphic and exhibition design, Burtin made scientific knowledge visible.

20-35. Ladislav Sutnar, title page for *Catalog Design Progress,* 1950. Bars and rectangles containing type become compositional elements to be balanced in dynamic equilibrium.

20-36. Ladislav Sutnar, section divider page from *Catalog Design Progress,* 1950. The coding on the ovals, following a system used throughout the book, indicates that this is "part one, section two, topics four, five, and six: structural features." The triangle points the reader forward.

20-37. Ladislav Sutnar, page from *Catalog Design Progress*, 1950. These designs demonstrate how systems of identifying information can use line, shape, color, and type to create "visual traffic signs" in the upper-right corner (each visual unit's point of entrance) to assist the user in the search for information.

20-38. Ladislav Sutnar, page from *Catalog Design Progress*, 1950. The construction of page layouts for an electron tubes catalog is shown. A consistent horizontal band and three-column grid were the unifying graphic themes of this particular catalog.

20-39. Herbert Bayer, page from the *World Geo-Graphic Atlas*, 1953. Bayer used color coding, symbols, cross-sections, and illustrations to provide a visual inventory of earth resources.

20-40. Herbert Bayer, page from the *World Geo-Graphic Atlas*, 1953. Bayer used R. Buckminster Fuller's Dymaxion Projection, a map that shows the globe in two dimensions without distortion, as a base for pictographs representing population and rectangles of black dots symbolizing energy consumption. Immediate comparisons can be made between population and energy use.

20-41. Will Burtin, exhibition of the Uranium-235 atom. Time-lapse photography created a two-dimensional expression of Burtin's three-dimensional model.

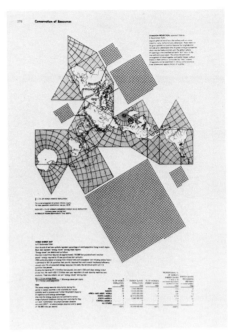

20-39   20-40

His model of a Uranium-235 atom (Fig. 20-41) contained ninety-two miniature electric lights on fine steel rods that rotated around the nucleus, representing electrons. This model, enclosed in a translucent blue sphere, articulated the physical and kinetic qualities of the atom. Burtin's most ambitious presentation of scientific process was his 1958 Upjohn Cell Exhibit (Fig. 20-42). This model of half a human red blood cell, 7.3 meters (24 feet) in diameter, was enlarged about a million times. Viewers physically entered and walked inside to view the minute structures that make up the fundamental biological unit of human life. Developed from fuzzy microphotographs and numerous consultations with scientists, Burtin's graphic articulation of cell structures and processes had great educational value.

Many of the design nomads who brought European design concepts to the United States arrived virtually penniless and with minimal possessions. But they were armed with talent, ideas, and a strong belief in design as a valuable human activity that could contribute to the improvement of human communication and the human condition. The American experience was greatly enriched by their presence.

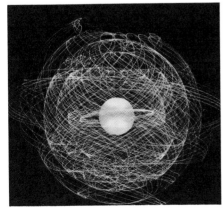

20-41

20-42. Will Burtin, Upjohn Cell Exhibit, 1958. The plastic model was imbued with life through the use of moving, pulsating lights glowing through the structure.

20-42

The Information Age:
Graphic design in the global village

World Events	21 The International Typographic Style	22 The New York School	23 Corporate Identity and Visual Systems	24 The Conceptual Image	25 A Global Dialog
	1930s Bill, Stankowski, and others, constructivist graphic design	1939 Thompson, his 1st *Westvaco Inspirations*			
1940 Churchill, "blood, toil, tears, and sweat" speech		1940 *Print* magazine, 1st issue; Steinweiss joins Columbia Records	1940 Golden becomes art director of CBS		
1941 Japan attacks Pearl Harbor		1940s Rand, *Directions* covers			
1942 Bataan "Death March"	1942 Bill, *Moderne Schweizer Architektur*				
1943 Mass production of penicillin					
1944 Allied Invasion of Normandy (D-Day)	1944 Herdeg, *Graphis* 1st issue	1945 Lustig, New Directions book covers			
1945 Roosevelt dies; A-bombs dropped; World War II ends	1945 Bill, *USA Baut* poster				
1946 Nuremberg war trials		1946 Rand, *Thoughts on Design*	1946 Dorfsman joins CBS		
1947 The Marshall Plan begins	1947 Ruder & Hofmann join Basel School of Design; Martin joins Cincinnati Museum		1947 Pintori joins Olivetti		
1948 Gandhi assassinated	1948 Huber, *Gran premio dell' Autodrome* poster				
1949 Mao Tse-tung's Communist forces capture China	1949 Vivarelli, *For the Elderly* poster	1949 Doyle Dane Bernbach founded			
1950 Korean War begins	1950 Odermatt opens studio; Zapf designs Palatino; Ulm School of Design planned	1950s Brodovitch's editorial design classes inspire a generation			
1951 UNIVAC I, 1st mass-produced computer			1951 Golden, CBS symbol; Fogleman joins CIBA		
1952 Eisenhower elected President; Korean War ends	1952 de Harak opens New York studio				
1953 Hillary & Norgay climb Mt. Everest	1953 Stankowski, Standard Elektrik Lorenz AG logo	1953 Wolf art directs *Esquire*	1953 Fogleman defines "corporate identity"	1953 Trepkowski, "Nie!" poster	
1954 Senate censures McCarthy; Supreme Court bans segregation	1954 Frutiger, Univers designed		1954 Matter, New York, New Haven, and Hartford Railroad program	1954 Testa, Pirelli graphics; Push Pin Studio forms	
1955 Sabin, oral polio vaccine	1955 Casey joins MIT	1955 Bass, *Man with the Golden Arm* graphics			
1956 Soviets crush Hungarian Revolution			1956 Rand, IBM logo; Pintori, Olivetti Electrosumma 22 poster	1956 Trepkowski dies; Tomaszewski leads Polish movement, evolves toward a colorful collage approach	
1957 USSR launches 1st earth satellite, Sputnik I	1957 Miedinger, Haas Grotesque (later named Helvetica by Stempel foundry)	1957 Brownjohn, Chermayeff, & Geismar formed	1957 Eckerstrom, new CCA logo		
1958 Supreme Court orders school desegregation	1958 Froshaug designs Ulm *Journal*	1958 Storch redesigns *McCall's*			
1959 Castro ousts Batista from Cuba	1959 *Neue Grafik*, 1st issue; Hofmann, *Giselle* poster	1959 Brodovitch retires, Wolf art directs *Bazaar*; *Communication Arts*, 1st issue	1959 Runyan, Litton annual report; Golden dies	1959 *Twen* magazine launched	
1960 Kennedy elected President	1960 Müller-Brockmann, *der Film* poster	1960 Bass, *Exodus* graphics	1960 Beall, International Paper logo; Chermayeff & Geismar, Chase Manhattan identity		
1961 Bay of Pigs fails; Peace Corps established		1961 Thompson, final *Westvaco Inspirations*			
1962 Cuban missile crisis; Carson, *Silent Spring* spurs environmental movement		1962 Lubalin designs *Eros*	1962 Aicher & staff, Lufthansa identity system	1962 Berg joins CBS Records	1962 Fletcher, Forbes, & Gill founded; Venturi, Grand's Restaurant supergraphics
1963 Kennedy assassinated; Johnson becomes President	1960s de Harak, McGraw-Hill covers				1963 Tanaka design studio opens
1964 Tonkin Gulf Resolution escalates Vietnam War; Johnson wins election		1960s Lois, *Esquire* "statement" covers	1964 Chermayeff & Geismar, Mobil identity program	1964 Massin designs *The Bald Soprano*; Gloser, *The Sound of Harlem* album cover	1964 Kamekura, Tokyo Olympics posters; Tissi, E. Lutz advertisements

25 A Global Dialog

1966 Solomon, Sea Ranch environmental graphics

1968 Weingart joins Basel School of Design faculty

1970 Friedman teaches "New Wave" typography in U. S.

1972 Weingart, 1st American lecture series

1974 Sato, *New Music Media* poster

1975 Igarashi, isometric alphabets; Fukuda, impossible optical illusions; Kunz, *Typographic Interpretations*

1970s *Postmodernism* designates design breaking with modernism

1979 Greiman, China Club graphics; Vanderbyl, California Public Radio poster; Scher, CBS Records jazz posters; Greiman & Odgers, Cal Arts graphics

1981 Memphis exhibition in Milan

1983 Longhauser, *Groves* poster; Igarashi, calendar poster; Fili & Scher, Retro designs

1984 Duffy Design Group formed; 1st Macintosh computer; Brody, constructive & deconstructive type in *The Face*

1985 300 dpi laser printer

1987 Stone, Stone type family

24 The Conceptual Image

1966 Kieser, *Alabama Blues* poster; Wilson & Moscoso, psychedelic posters

1967 Glaser, *Dylan* poster

1968 Grapus founded; Serrano, *Day of the Heroic Guerrilla* poster

1970 Zaid, Hiller's *Art Deco* cover; Max, Love graphics

1970s Richards, Pirtle, and others: Texas becomes a major design center

1975 Cieslewicz, *Amnesty International* poster

1976 Rambow, 1st S. Fischer-Verlag poster; Davis, *For Colored Girls . . .* poster

1977 McMullan, *Anna Christie* poster

1980 Janiszewski, Solidarity logo; Rambo, *Die Hamletmachine* poster

1981 Grapus, *No Neutrons Mr. Reagan* poster

1988 Rambow, *Southafricans Roulette* poster

23 Corporate Identity and Visual Systems

1965 Bass, Continental Airlines logo; Eckerstrom, Fogleman, & Vignelli form Unimark

1968 Wyman, Mexico City Olympics; Bass, AT&T "Bell" logo

1972 Massey, Labor Department identity; Aicher & staff, Munich Olympics

1974 Cook & Shanosky, transportation symbol system

1977 U. S. National Parks Unigrid system

1984 Los Angeles Olympics; Bass, AT&T "globe" logo

1986 Rand, NeXT logo

22 The New York School

1968-71 Lubalin, *Avant Garde* magazine

1970 International Typeface Corporation formed; Lubalin & Carnase, Avant Garde typeface

21 The International Typographic Style

1965 Hofmann, *Graphic Design Manual*

1967 Ruder, *Typography: A Manual of Design*

1968 Ulm School of Design closes; Stankowski, Berlin design program; Zapf, *Manuale Typographicum*

1970s The International Typographic Style becomes dominant throughout the world

1980 Müller-Brockmann, *concert poster series* poster

World Events

1965 Watts riots, Medicare established

1966 Chinese Cultural Revolution

1967 Six Day Arab-Israeli War

1968 Martin Luther King & Robert F. Kennedy assassinated; Nixon elected

1969 U. S. lunar landing

1970 Massive protest against the Vietnam War; Kent State students shot

1971 Cigarette advertising banned from television

1972 Watergate break-in; Steinem founds *Ms.*

1973 Vice President Agnew resigns

1974 Nixon resigns presidency; Ford becomes president

1975 World population exceeds 4 billion people

1976 U. S. Bicentennial; Carter elected president

1977 Carter pardons draft evaders

1978 Nicaraguan Revolution begins

1979 Khomeini replaces Shah in Iran; Thatcher is British Prime Minister

1980 Reagan elected President; Afghan rebels fight Soviets

1981 Columbia makes 1st space shuttle mission

1982 AT&T monopoly disbanded; Falkland Islands War

1983 Strategic Defense Initiative, called "Star Wars, " is launched

1984 Reagan reelected

1985 Gorbachev heads USSR

1986 Space shuttle *Challenger* explodes

1987 Stock market crashes

1988 Bush elected president

1989 Berlin Wall comes down

1990 Iraq invades Kuwait

1991 Kuwaiti War; Soviet coup fails

21

The International Typographic Style

21-1. Ernst Keller, exhibition poster, 1931. Dynamic diagonals and a constructed geometric image effectively express modern architecture.

During the 1950s, a design style emerged from Switzerland and Germany that has been called *Swiss design* or, more appropriately, the *International Typographic Style*. The objective clarity of this design movement won converts throughout the world. It remained a major force for over two decades, and its influence continues into the 1990s. Detractors of the International Typographic Style complain that it is based on formula and results in a sameness of solution; advocates argue that the style's purity of means and legibility of communication enable the designer to achieve a timeless perfection of form, and they point to the inventive range of solutions by leading practitioners as evidence that neither formula nor sameness is indigenous to the style, except in the hands of lesser talents.

The visual characteristics of this international style include: a visual unity of design achieved by asymmetrical organization of the design elements on a mathematically constructed grid; objective photography and copy that present visual and verbal information in a clear and factual manner, free from the exaggerated claims of much propaganda and commercial advertising; and the use of sans serif typography set in a flush-left and ragged-right margin configuration. The initiators of this style believe that sans serif typography expresses the spirit of a progressive age, and that mathematical grids are the most legible and harmonious means for structuring information.

More important than the visual appearance of this work is the attitude that its early pioneers developed toward their profession. These trailblazers defined design as a socially useful and important activity, rejecting personal expression and eccentric solutions in favor of a more universal and scientific approach to design problem solving. In this paradigm, the designer defines his or her role not as an artist but as an objective conduit for spreading important information between components of society. Achieving clarity and order is the ideal.

Pioneers of the movement

More than any other individual, the quality and discipline found in the Swiss design movement can be traced to Ernst Keller (1891–1968). In 1918, Keller joined the Zurich *Kunstgewerbeschule* ("School of Applied Art") to teach the advertising layout course and develop a professional course in design and typography. In teaching and in his own lettering, trademark, and poster design projects, Keller established a standard of excellence over the course of four decades. Rather than espousing a specific style, Keller advocated that the solution to the design problem should emerge from its content. Fittingly, the range of his work encompasses diverse solutions. His 1931 poster for an exhibition of Walter Gropius's contemporary architecture has a geometric pictographic hand holding a trowel (Fig. 21-1). Quite different is the 1948 exhibition poster (Fig. 21-2), with almost medieval overtones and rigorous symmetrical balance. A gentle and unassuming man, Keller initiated a climate of excellence in Swiss graphic design.

The roots of the International Typographic Style grew from de Stijl, the Bauhaus, and the new typography of the 1920s and 1930s. Two principal links between the earlier Constructivist graphic design and the new movement that formed after World War II are two Swiss designers who studied at the Bauhaus, Théo Ballmer

(1902–1965) and Max Bill (b. 1908). Ballmer, who studied briefly at the Dessau Bauhaus under Klee, Gropius, and Meyer during the late 1920s, made an original application of de Stijl principles to graphic design, using an arithmetic grid of horizontal and vertical alignments. In 1928, Ballmer's poster designs achieved a high degree of formal harmony as he used an ordered grid to construct visual forms. In the *buro* poster (Fig. 21-3), both the black word and its red "reflection" are carefully developed on the underlying grid. The other lettering on this poster shows an understanding of van Doesburg's experiments with geometric letterforms. However, Ballmer's lettering is more refined and graceful. While the grid used to build the forms in the *buro* poster is invisible, in Ballmer's 1928 *norm* poster (Pl. 70) the grid becomes visible. Rather than employing the asymmetrical horizontals and verticals of Mondrian's paintings, Ballmer used absolute mathematical construction.

Max Bill's work encompassed painting, architecture, engineering, sculpture, and product and graphic design. He attended the Bauhaus from 1927 until 1929 and studied with Gropius, Meyer, Moholy-Nagy, Albers, and Kandinsky, after which he moved to Zurich. It was in 1931, when he embraced the concepts of Art Concret, that Bill began to find his way clearly.

Eleven months before his death, in April 1930, Théo van Doesburg formulated a *Manifesto of Art Concret,* which called for a universal art of absolute clarity in which the visually controlled arithmetical construction of the painting would be completely created from pure, visual elements—planes and colors. Because these pure elements have no meaning other than themselves, the result is a painting that has no meaning except itself. Of course, graphic design is the antithesis of this concept in one sense, since a graphic design without symbolic or semantical meaning ceases to be a graphic communication and becomes fine art. However, Art Concret can nonetheless be applied to the structural aspect of graphic design.

As the 1930s gave way to the war years and Switzerland sat in splendid neutrality in the midst of a ravaged Europe, Bill constructed layouts of geometric elements organized with absolute order (Figs. 21-4 through 21-6). Mathematical proportion, geometric spatial division, and the use of Akzidenz Grotesk type (particularly the medium weight) are aspects of his work of this period. He explored the use of the ragged-right margin and indicated paragraphs by an interval of space instead of a paragraph indent in some of his 1940s book designs. In his 1945 American architecture exhibition poster (Pl. 71), Bill carefully balanced diamond-shaped photographs on a grid, almost creating the effect of an arrow exploding—some of the

21-2. Ernst Keller, exhibition poster, 1948. The medieval town crest and rough-hewn letterforms with calligraphic slashed serifs project a traditional, old-world feeling appropriate to the subject.

21-3. Théo Ballmer, poster for *buro*, 1928. Traces of the grid of squares used to construct this poster remain as the thin white lines between the letterforms.

21-4. Max Bill, poster for a Christmas exhibition and sale, 1940. Dynamic positive and negative shapes and visual harmony are created by the repetition of star shapes and careful alignment of points and edges.

21-3

21-4

21-5. Max Bill, typographic book cover, 1942. Mathematical precision is achieved by the alignment of typography down the center of the page, creating harmony and order in an asymmetrical layout. Akzidenz Grotesk type reflects the functional geometry of the architecture in the book.

diamonds that would make up a big wedge shape composed of photographs have been pulled out into the white ground to equalize the figure and ground. The evolution of Bill's art and design was based on the development of cohesive principles of visual organization. Important concerns include: linear division of space into harmonious parts; modular grids; arithmetic and geometric progressions, permutations, and sequences; and the equalization of contrasting and complementary relationships into an ordered whole. In 1949, he concluded "that it is possible to develop an art largely on the basis of mathematical thinking."

In 1950, Bill became involved in the planning of the curriculum and buildings for the *Hochschule für Gestaltung* ("Institute of Design") in Ulm, Germany. This school, which operated until 1968, attempted to establish a center of research and training to address the design problems of the era with educational goals similar to those of the Bauhaus. Among the cofounders, Otl Aicher (b. 1922) played a major role in developing the graphic design program (see Figs. 23-32 through 23-35). Bill left the Ulm directorship in 1956, and the school evolved along scientific and methodological approaches to design problem solving. English typographer Anthony Froshaug (1920–1984) joined the Ulm faculty as professor of graphic design from 1957 until 1961 and set up the typography workshop. Froshaug's design of the Ulm journal's first five issues (Fig. 21-7) represents a paradigm of the emerging style.

The Ulm School of Design included a study of semiotics, the general philosophical theory of signs and symbols, in its curriculum. Semiotics has three branches: semantics, the study of the meaning of signs and symbols; syntactics, the study of how signs and symbols are connected and ordered into a structural whole; and pragmatics, the study of the relation of signs and symbols to their users. Also, principles of Greek rhetoric were reexamined for application to design.

In counterpoint to Max Bill's evolution toward a strong purist approach to graphic design from the 1930s to the 1950s, there was also a strong tendency toward complexity in this period. During the same era, Max Huber (b. 1919) brought

21-6. Max Bill, exhibition poster, 1951. Bill used two sizes of type to form a cross, then repeated this configuration in smaller type, establishing a hierarchy of information. Depth is implied by the descending sizes of typography.

21-7

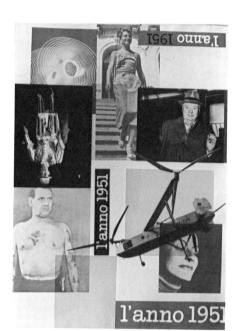

21-9

21-10

21-8. Max Huber, yearbook cover, 1951. An informal balance of halftones printed in red, black, and blue combines with yellow rectangles to turn the space into an energy-charged field.

21-9. Anton Stankowski, trademark for Standard Elektrik Lorenz AG, 1953. A dynamic equilibrium is achieved by this asymmetrical construction within an implied square, signifying telecommunications transmitting and receiving.

21-10. Anton Stankowski, calendar cover for Standard Elektrik Lorenz AG, 1957. This geometric configuration symbolizes transmission and radiation to signify the outward communication made possible by the client's radio and telephone products.

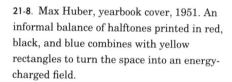

21-7. Anthony Froshaug, cover for the *Journal of the Hochschule für Gestaltung* in Ulm, Germany, 1958. The four-column grid system, use of only two type sizes, and graphic resonance of this format were widely influential.

an extraordinary vitality and complexity to his work. After studying the formal ideas of the Bauhaus and experimenting with photomontage as a student at the Zurich School of Arts and Crafts, Huber moved south to Milan, Italy, and began his career. Returning to his native Switzerland during the darkest period of the war, Huber collaborated with Max Bill on exhibition design projects. After his return to Italy in 1946, Huber produced dazzling graphics. Bright, pure hues were combined with photographs in intense, complex visual organizations (Fig. 21-8). Huber took advantage of the transparency of printing inks by layering shapes, typography, and images to create a complex stratum of graphic information. In his 1948 poster for Monza motorcars (Pl. 72), Huber visualized speed and movement with typography racing back in perspective and arrows arcing forward to give depth to the printed page. Sometimes Huber's designs are pushed to the edge of chaos, but he always tried to use balance and alignment to maintain order in the midst of complexity.

Functional graphics for science

German-born Anton Stankowski (b. 1906) worked as a graphic designer in Zurich from 1929 until 1937, where he enjoyed close contacts with many of the leading artists and designers of Switzerland, including Max Bill, Herbert Matter, and Richard P. Lohse. During his Zurich period, Stankowski was particularly innovative in photography, photomontage, and darkroom manipulation of images. Visual pattern and form were explored in his close-up photographs of common objects, whose texture and detail were transformed into abstract images.

In 1937, Stankowski moved to Stuttgart, Germany, where he painted and designed for over five decades. A dialogue is evident between Stankowski's painting and his design: Ideas about color and form from his paintings often find their way into his graphic designs; conversely, his wide range of form experimentation in searching for design solutions often provides shapes and compositional ideas for his fine art.

World War II and military service, including a period as a prisoner of war after his capture by the Russians, interrupted Stankowski's career. After the war, his work started to crystallize into what was to become his major contribution to graphic design: the creation of visual forms to communicate invisible processes and

21-11. Anton Stankowski, image from a calendar for Viessmann. Cool-blue curved elements change to a bright orange after passing through the red bar in the center of the page, symbolizing the transfer of heat and energy in furnace boilers manufactured by Viessmann.

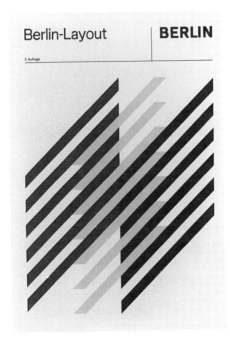

21-12. Anton Stankowski, cover for *Berlin Layout*, 1971. The red, yellow, and blue design on this cover is an image originally developed in Stankowski's painting.

physical forces (Figs. 21-9 through 21-11). The abilities Stankowski brought to this search were a strong mastery of Constructivist design, an intellectual acumen for science and engineering, and a burning curiosity. Research and an intellectual comprehension of the subject preceded his designs, for only after such research can a designer invent forms that become symbols of unseen scientific and engineering concepts. Stankowski tackled the unseen, ranging from electromagnetic energy to the internal workings of a computer, and transformed the underlying concept for these forces into visual designs.

In 1968, the Senate of the city of Berlin charged Stankowski and his studio with developing a comprehensive design program for that city. Consistent design standards for architectural signage, street signs, and publications were developed. Instead of designing a trademark or unique typographic logo for use as the unifying visual element, Stankowski developed a *tectonic element* that is consistently used on all material. This is a long horizontal line with a short vertical line rising from it, becoming a symbol for the then-divided city of Berlin (the vertical line represents the Berlin Wall, which, until 1989, separated the Russian-occupied portion of the city from the rest of Berlin. The word "Berlin," set in medium Akzidenz Grotesk, is always placed in the right side of the tectonic element (Fig. 21-12).

New Swiss sans serif typefaces

The emerging International Typographic Style gained its alphabetical expression in several new sans serif typestyles that were designed in the 1950s. The geometric sans serif styles, mathematically constructed with drafting instruments during the 1920s and 1930s, were rejected in favor of new designs inspired by the nineteenth-century Akzidenz Grotesk fonts. In 1954, a young Swiss designer working in Paris, Adrian Frutiger (b. 1928), created a visually programmed family of twenty-one sans serif fonts named Univers (Fig. 21-13). The palette of typographic variations —limited to regular, italic, and bold in traditional typography—was expanded sevenfold. Conventional nomenclature was replaced by numbers: The normal or regular weight is called Univers 55, and the family ranges from Univers 39 (light/extra condensed) to Univers 83 (expanded/extrabold). Because all twenty-one fonts have the same x-height and ascender and descender lengths, they form a uniform whole that can be used together with complete harmony (Fig. 21-14). The size and weight of the capitals are closer to the size and weight of the lowercase characters; therefore, the color of a Univers text setting is more uniform than that of most earlier typestyles. Frutiger labored for three years on Univers. To produce the Univers family, the Deberny-Peigot foundry in Paris invested over 200,000 hours of machine engraving, retouching, and final hand punching to create the thirty-five thousand matrices needed to produce all twenty-one fonts in the full range of sizes.

In the middle 1950s, Edouard Hoffman of the HAAS type foundry in Switzerland decided that the Akzidenz Grotesk fonts should be refined and upgraded. Hoffman collaborated with Max Miedinger, who executed the designs, and their new sans serif with an even larger x-height than Univers's was released as the New Haas Grotesque. When this design was produced in Germany by D. Stempel AG in 1961, the Germans shocked Hoffman by naming the face Helvetica (Fig. 21-15), which is the traditional Latin name for Switzerland that appears on its postage stamps. Helvetica's well-defined forms and excellent rhythm of positive and negative shapes made it the most specified typeface internationally during the 1960s and 1970s. But because Helvetica's various weights, italics, and widths were developed by different designers in several countries, the original Helvetica family lacked the cohesiveness of Univers. As digital typesetting became prevalent in the 1980s, versions of the Helvetica family with more systemic compatibility were developed.

A master of classical typography

While German and Swiss designers were forging the International Typographic Style, a major German typeface designer evolved from the traditions of calligraphy and Renaissance typography. A tremendous admiration for Rudolf Koch and Ed-

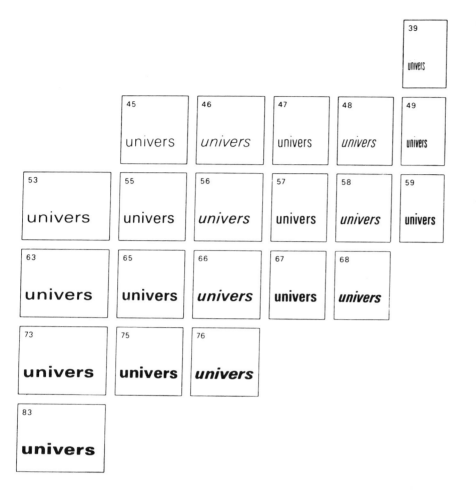

21-13. Adrian Frutiger, schematic diagram of the twenty-one Univers styles, 1954. Starting with Univers 55, which has the proper black-and-white relationships for book setting, Frutiger expanded the forms (fonts to the left of Univers 55), condensed the forms (fonts to the right of Univers 55), and made the stroke weights lighter (fonts above Univers 55) and darker or bolder (fonts below Univers 55).

21-14. Bruno Pfäffli of Atelier Frutiger, composition with the letter *u*, c. 1960. The variety of contrasts that Adrian Frutiger achieved with his program of twenty-one variations of Univers, all of which can be used together to achieve dynamic contrasts of weight, tone, width, and direction, is shown in this composition.

Helvetica
Helvetica Italic
Helvetica Medium
Helvetica Bold
Helvetica Bold Condensed

21-15. Edouard Hoffman and Max Miedinger, Helvetica typeface, 1961. The basic version of Helvetica released by the Stempel foundry in 1961 is shown, along with some of the variations developed later.

Palatino
Palatino Italic
Palatino Semibold
Palatino Bold

Melior
Melior Italic
Melior Semibold
Melior Bold Condensed

Optima
Optima Italic
Optima Semi Bold

21-16. Hermann Zapf, typefaces: Palatino, 1950; Melior, 1952; and Optima, 1958. These alphabets have a harmony and elegance seldom achieved in typeface design.

ward Johnston proved to be the catalyst that launched the career of Hermann Zapf (b. 1918). A native of Nuremberg, Germany, Zapf entered the graphic arts as an apprentice photo retoucher at age sixteen. A year later, he started his study of calligraphy after acquiring a copy of Koch's *Das Schreiben als Kunstfertigkeit*, a manual on calligraphy. Four years of disciplined self-education followed, and at age twenty-one Zapf's first typographic involvement began when he entered Koch's printing firm. Later that year, Zapf became a free-lance book and typographic designer, and at age twenty-two the first of his more than fifty typefaces was designed and cut for the Stempel foundry. Zapf developed an extraordinary sensitivity to letterforms in his activities as a calligrapher, typeface designer, typographer, and graphic designer, all of which contributed to his view of typeface design as "one of the most visible visual expressions of an age."

Zapf's triumvirate of typefaces designed during the late 1940s and the 1950s are widely regarded as major type designs (Fig. 21-16): Palatino (released in 1950) is a roman style with broad letters, strong serifs, and elegant proportions somewhat reminiscent of Venetian faces; Melior (1952) is a modern style that departs from earlier models through its vertical stress and squared forms; Optima (1958) is a thick-and-thin sans serif with tapered strokes. While Zapf's typeface designs are based on a deep understanding of the past, they are original inventions designed with a full understanding of twentieth-century technologies. To the complex and technically demanding craft of typeface design, Zapf brings the spiritual awareness

Słowo jest potęgą. Utrwalone w piśmie, zdobywa nie dającą się obliczyć ani przewidzieć władzę nad myślą i wyobraźnią ludzi, panuje nad czasem i przestrzenią. Tylko myśl pochwycona w sieć liter żyje, działa, tworzy. Wszystko inne roznosi wiatr. Każdy postęp w rozwoju umysłu ludzkiego, wszystkie jego zdobycze narodziły się kiedyś wśród tych wątłych badylków, wschodzących na karcie papieru.   Jan Parandowski

j O u N t
i I e H i m s
P E A d F h M s z
J f A b B h l r y
C D c G
n K k g L S
Q o p q
U V v x
w R W
X Y Z

Das Wort ist eine Macht. Dauerhaft gemacht durch die Schrift, gewinnt es eine unberechenbare und ungeahnte Gewalt über Gedanken und Einbildungskraft der Menschen; es beherrscht die Zeit und den Raum. Nur der ins Netz der Buchstaben eingefangene Gedanke lebt, wirkt, schafft. Alles andere wird vom Winde verweht. Jeder Fortschritt in der Entwicklung des menschlichen Verstandes, alle seine Errungenschaften waren irgendwann inmitten dieser kleinen und feinen Stengel, die auf dem Blatt Papier keimen, geboren.

21-17. Hermann Zapf, page from *Manuale Typographicum,* 1968. Parandowski's quotation about the power of the printed word to "govern time and space" inspired this graphic field of tension radiating from the central cluster.

21-18. Hermann Zapf, page from *Manuale Typographicum,* 1968. Using his Michelangelo typeface, Zapf organized this page with classical symmetry and exquisite intervals between letters. The subtle shadow relief of the ruled lines suggests an inscription-like quality.

of a poet who is capable of inventing new forms to express the current century and preserve it for posterity.

In the area of book design, Zapf's two editions of *Manuale Typographicum,* published in 1954 and 1968, are outstanding contributions to the art of the book (Figs. 21-17 and 21-18). Encompassing eighteen languages and more than a hundred typefaces, these two volumes consist of quotations about the art of typography, with a full-page typographic expression for each quotation selected. Zapf, like Eric Gill, combines a great love and understanding of the classical traditions of typography with a twentieth-century attitude toward space and scale.

Design in Basel and Zurich

The further development of the International Typographic Style occurred in two cities, Basel and Zurich, located 70 kilometers (about 50 miles) apart in northern Switzerland. Fifteen-year-old Emil Ruder (1914–1970) began a four-year composi-

21-19

STADT THEATER BASEL

21-20

21-21

tor's apprenticeship in 1929, and attended the Zurich School of Arts and Crafts when he was in his late twenties. In 1947, Ruder joined the faculty of the Basel School of Design (*Allegemeine Gewerbeschule*) as a typography teacher, and continued in this position for the rest of his life. Ruder called upon his students to strike a correct balance between form and function and taught that type loses its purpose when it loses its communicative meaning. Legibility and readability therefore became dominant concerns. His classroom projects developed sensitivity to negative or unprinted spaces, including the spaces between and inside letterforms. Ruder advocated systematic overall design and the use of a complex grid structure to bring all elements—typography, photography, illustration, diagrams, and charts—into harmony with each other while allowing for design variety. Problems of unifying type and image were addressed.

More than any other designer, Ruder realized the implications of Univers and the creative potential unleashed by the unity of proportion that allowed the intermixing of all twenty-one members of this type family. Ruder and his students exhaustively explored the contrasts, textures, and scale possibilities of the new face in both commissioned and experimental work (Fig. 21-19). His methodology of typographic design and education was presented in his 1967 book, *Typography: A Manual of Design*, which had a worldwide influence.

In 1947, Armin Hofmann (b. 1920) began teaching graphic design at the Basel School of Design, after completing his education in Zurich and working as a staff designer for several studios. At the same time, Hofmann opened a design studio in collaboration with his wife, Dorothe. Hofmann applied a deep sense of aesthetic values and understanding of form to both teaching and designing. As time passed, Hofmann evolved a design philosophy based on the elemental graphic-form language of point, line, and plane, replacing traditional pictorial ideas with a modernist aesthetic. In his work and in his teaching, Hofmann seeks a dynamic harmony where all the parts of a design are unified. He sees the relationship of contrasting elements as the means to breathe life into visual design. These contrasts include light to dark, curved lines to straight lines, form to counterform, and dynamic to

21-19. Emil Ruder, book jacket for an anthology of Dada poetry, reproduced in *Typography: A Manual of Design,* 1967. The contrast created by combining different fonts becomes a graphic metaphor for the chance randomness of the Dadaists. The consistent x-height of the Univers family unifies these diverse letters.

21-20. Armin Hofmann, logotype for the Basel Civic Theater, 1954. This hand-lettered logotype anticipates the tight spacing and capital ligatures of phototypography. The control of spatial intervals between letterforms is magnificent.

21-21. Armin Hofmann, poster for the Basel theater production *Giselle,* 1959. An organic, kinetic, and soft photographic image contrasts intensely with geometric, static, and hard-edged typographic shapes.

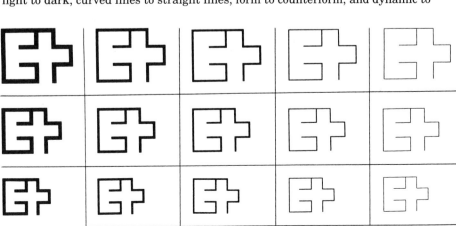

21-22. Armin Hofmann, trademark for the Swiss National Exhibition, Expo 1964. A memorable form is created by linking an *E* for Exhibition and the Swiss cross. The open bottom of the cross allows the white space of the page to flow into the symbol.

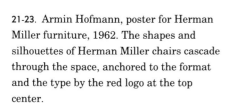

21-24

21-25

21-23. Armin Hofmann, poster for Herman Miller furniture, 1962. The shapes and silhouettes of Herman Miller chairs cascade through the space, anchored to the format and the type by the red logo at the top center.

21-24. Armin Hofmann, poster for a lace exhibition, 1969. Hofmann is a master at reducing a design to its essentials. The black surrounding the photograph and typography turns this poster into a strong focal point on the street.

21-25. Armin Hofmann, exterior sculpture for the Disentis, Switzerland, high school, 1975. The altered direction of the boards of the molds used to cast the concrete relief produces a vigorous textural contrast.

static, with resolution achieved when the creator brings the total into an absolute harmony. As with music, painting, or dance, design moves to a higher place of expression when this resolution is accomplished.

Hofmann works in diverse areas, including posters, advertising, and logo design (Figs. 21-20 through 21-24). His environmental graphics, which take the form of letterforms or abstract shapes based on letterforms, are often incised into molded concrete (Fig. 21-25). In 1965, Hofmann published *Graphic Design Manual,* a book that presented his application of elemental design principles to graphic design.

Zurich designers, including Carlo L. Vivarelli (b. 1919), were also forging the new movement in the late 1940s (Fig. 21-26). Swiss design began to coalesce into a unified international movement when the journal *New Graphic Design* began publication in 1959 (Figs. 21-27 through 21-29). The editors were Vivarelli and three other Zurich designers who played a major role in the evolution of the International Typographic Style: Richard P. Lohse (b. 1902), Josef Müller-Brockmann (b. 1914), and Hans Neuburg (b. 1904). This trilingual periodical began to present the philosophy and accomplishments of the Swiss movement to an international audience. Its format and typography were a living expression of the order and refinement achieved by Swiss designers.

Emerging as a leading theorist and practitioner of the movement, Josef Müller-Brockmann sought an absolute and universal graphic expression through an objective and impersonal presentation communicating to the audience without the interference of the designer's subjective feelings or propagandistic techniques of persuasion. A measure of his success can be gauged by observing the visual power and impact of his work. Posters created by Müller-Brockmann in the 1950s are as fresh and contemporary as the latest fashion and communicate their message with a remarkable intensity and clarity (Fig. 21-30). His photographic posters treat the image as a symbol (Figs. 21-31 and 21-32). In his celebrated concert posters, the language of Constructivism creates a visual equivalency to the structural harmony of the music to be performed (Fig. 21-33).

The *der Film* exhibition poster (Fig. 21-34) is one of Müller-Brockmann's masterpieces. It demonstrates the universal design harmony achieved by mathematical spatial division. The poster is in the three-to-five ratio of the golden mean, considered since Greek times to be the most beautifully proportioned rectangle. This rectangle is divided into fifteen squares, or modules—three across the horizontal dimension and five down the vertical dimension. The top nine modules form a

21-26. Carlo L. Vivarelli, *For the Elderly* poster, 1949. The contrasting juxtaposition of an organic, human, and textured photograph with sharp geometric typography intensifies the meaning of both. The angle of illumination on the face contributes a dramatic impact in this poster, conceived to create an awareness of the elderly and their problems.

21-27. Carlo L. Vivarelli, cover for *New Graphic Design* 2, 1959. The mathematical structure of the organizational grid signifies the scientific and functional design philosophy of the Swiss movement.

21-28. Hans Neuburg, pages from *New Graphic Design* 7, 1960. The layout of this article about an exhibition design by Max Bill reveals asymmetrical balance and use of white space.

21-26

21-27

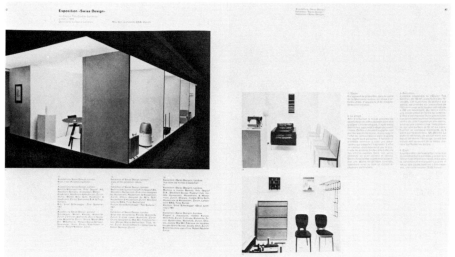

21-28

21-30

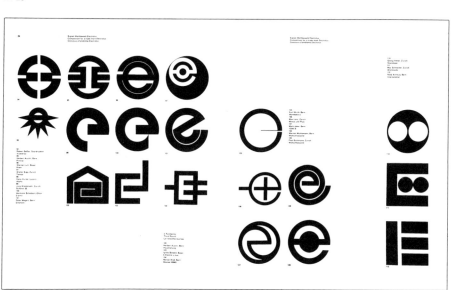

21-29

21-29. Hans Neuburg, pages from *New Graphic Design* 13, 1962. Entries in a trademark-design competition are organized on a grid of squares with space intervals that create an overall movement from upper left to lower right.

21-30. Josef Müller-Brockmann, *American books today* exhibition poster, 1953. In this early poster, the white curvilinear shapes forming the book counter the vertical red and blue stripes.

The International Typographic Style

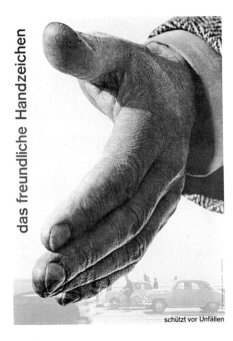

21-31. Josef Müller-Brockmann, Swiss Auto Club poster, 1954. *The friendly hand sign* (shown in a huge black-and-white photograph) *protects from accidents* (symbolized by the traffic scene overprinted in red). This is a superb example of Müller-Brockmann's use of photography as objective information.

21-32. Josef Müller-Brockmann, public awareness poster, 1960. To heighten public awareness of noise pollution, the red type shouts "less noise," and the photograph graphically depicts the discomfort of noise pollution.

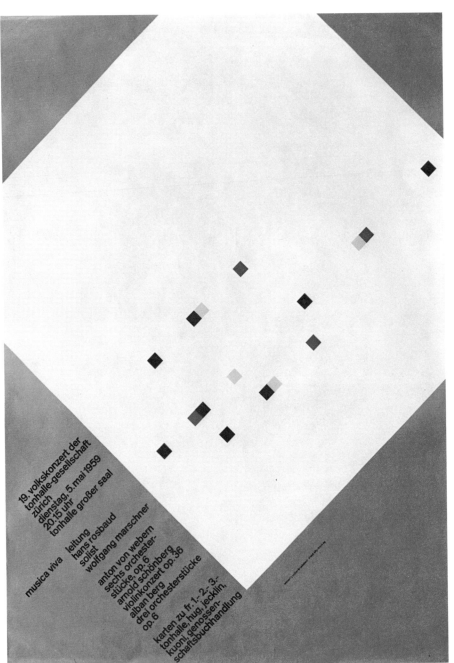

21-33

square, the title fills three units, and three are below the title. *Film* occupies two units, and the secondary typographic information aligns with the front edge of the F in *Film*. This design organization grew out of functional communication needs: The title projects clearly at great distances against the field of black, and the overlapping of *Film* in front of *der* is a typographic equivalent to the cinematic techniques of overlapping images and dissolving from one image to another. For all its elemental simplicity, this poster successfully combines effective communication of information, expression of the content, and visual harmony.

In a 1980 exhibition poster, Müller-Brockmann revealed the nature of the grid structures underlying his work (Fig. 21-35). The importance of color in his work can be seen in Plate 73, a poster for an exhibition of lamps. The modulated and glowing multicolor disks symbolize the radiant energy of lighting fixtures. Through his writing, teaching, and work, Müller-Brockmann is the Swiss designer whose impact was most influential as this national movement grew beyond Swiss borders.

In a country with such outstanding design schools as Switzerland, Siegfried Odermatt (b. 1926) is a rarity: the self-educated graphic designer. Originally he planned to become a photographer, but after working in photographic studios for several years, Odermatt turned to design and typography. After a period of employment in several advertising agencies, Odermatt opened his own studio in 1950.

Working for corporate clients in the areas of trademark development, informational graphics, advertising, and packaging, Odermatt played a major role in defining the International Typographic Style as applied to the communications of business and industry. He combined clean, efficient presentation of information with a dynamic visual quality, using straightforward photography with drama and impact. Ordinary images are turned into convincing and engaging photographs through the careful use of cropping and lighting, with attention to shape and texture as qualities that cause an image to reach out from the page (Figs. 21-36 through 21-38). Odermatt expresses originality through the idea, not through vi-

21-33. Josef Müller-Brockmann, *musica viva* concert poster, 1972. The red, yellow, and blue squares march in musical rhythm on the tilted white diamond. Typography and shapes align in harmonious juxtaposition.

21-34. Josef Müller-Brockmann, *Of the Film,* exhibition poster, 1960. The elementary simplicity of this poster's graphic power is remarkable. Against a black field, the word *Film* is white, the word *der* is gray, and the other typography is red.

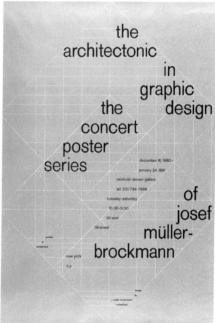

21-35. Josef Müller-Brockmann, exhibition poster, 1980. The grid, always underlying Müller-Brockmann's designs, becomes visible as a major element in this poster.

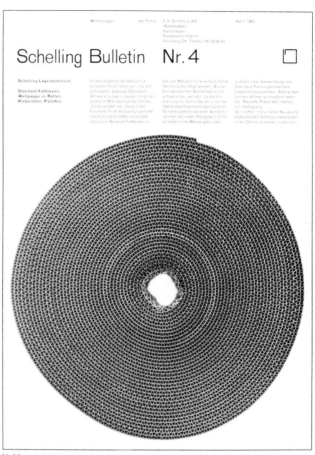

21-37

a

Nervös, überarbeitet, reizbar? Gönnen Sie sich mehr Ruhe und
– Nervocalmin, das bewährte Nervenstärkungsmittel bei
Schlaflosigkeit, Angstgefühl und nervösen Zuständen.
Nervocalmin ist selbst bei längerem Gebrauch vollkommen
unschädlich und führt nicht zur Gewöhnung; auch der empfind-
liche Magen verträgt es gut.

apotheke sammet
beim Hauptbahnhof
Zürich
Bahnhofstrasse 106
Telefon 051 25 51 33

21-36. Siegfried Odermatt, Apotheke
Sammet advertisement, 1957. Odermatt's
advertisements for this pharmacy's
private-label medicines used large, arresting
close-up photography. The trademark
clones the initials of the client's name.

21-37. Siegfried Odermatt, cover for
Schelling Bulletin, No. 4, 1963. This folder
for a paperboard and packaging
manufacturer shows Odermatt's unexpected
photographic view of an ordinary object.

21-38. Siegfried Odermatt, inside pages for
Schelling Bulletin, No. 4, 1963. A four-
column grid unifies typography with product
photography.

sual style—graphic design is always seen as an instrument of communication, and
the visual tools used are typography, photography, and constructive drawing.

Much of Odermatt's work is purely typographic, and he is willing to take great
liberties with the traditions of typography. It is his belief that a one-color typographic design can achieve the visual impact and power of full-color graphics
through the strength of the concept and the manipulation of visual form, space,
shape, and tone. By his fresh and original manipulations of the graphic elements,
Odermatt has made a mockery of those designers who say that there are only so
many ways to divide and organize the space of the printed page. Unlike many
Swiss designers, Odermatt employs an element of the playful and the uninhibited
in his work. A young designer who joined his studio in the early 1960s, Rosmarie
Tissi (b. 1937) (Fig. 21-39), also has a strong playful element in her work. In 1968,
she became an equal partner with Odermatt in the studio Odermatt & Tissi. This
studio loosened the boundaries of the International Typographic Style and introduced elements of chance, the development of surprising and inventive forms, and
intuitive visual organization into the vocabulary of graphic design. This phase of
the studio's development marked the beginning of a break with the traditions of
Swiss design and will be discussed in Chapter 25.

During the post–World War II era, there was a growing spirit of internationalism. Increased trade enabled multinational corporations to operate in over a
hundred different countries. The speed and pace of communications were turning
the world into a "global village." There was a need for communicative clarity, multilingual formats to transcend language barriers, and elementary pictographs and
glyphs to enable people from around the world to comprehend signs and information. The new graphic design developed in Switzerland helped fulfill these needs,
and the fundamental concepts and approach developed in Switzerland began to
spread throughout the world.

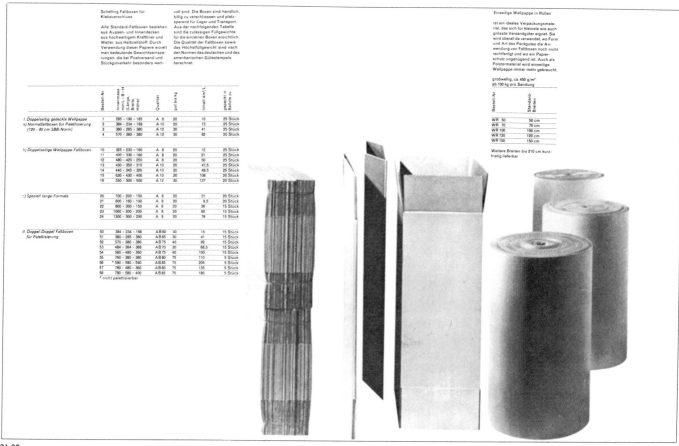

21-38

The International Typographic Style in America

The Swiss movement had a major impact upon postwar American design. A ripple of influence in the 1950s turned into a tidal wave during the 1960s and 1970s. One designer who softened the beaches for this invasion of modern typography into America was Noel Martin (b. 1922). He was one of the first American designers beginning his career after the war who explored the potential of European modernist typographic design in the postwar era. After a fine-arts education and completion of his World War II military service, Martin became the first staff graphic designer at the Cincinnati Museum of Art in 1947. The museum had a small metal typesetting and printing shop in the basement, and this became his laboratory to learn graphic design. Lacking teachers or precedents, he turned to the museum's library, where periodicals and books enabled him to learn about modern European typographic design. As his work evolved (Figs. 21-40 and 21-41), Martin became a catalyst for the use of typography by American designers whose sensibilities lay not with traditional narrative illustration but with the language of form, shape, and color developed by European modern art and design. His critical eye for proportion and balance resulted in disarmingly simple arrangements of elements in space. Martin organized important graphic design exhibitions, including the first American exhibition of modern Swiss graphic design in 1958. Martin never became a disciple of the Swiss movement, and applying the principles of order and clarity from European modernism is only part of his oeuvre: His wonderful typographic production includes historical paraphrases of Bodoni and Caslon, expressionistic experiments, and lively designs using Victorian typefaces.

Another self-taught graphic designer who embraced the potential of European modernism, Rudolph de Harak (b. 1924), began his career in Los Angeles in 1946. Four years later, de Harak moved to New York, and in 1952 he formed his own design studio. During the 1950s, de Harak took great delight in bringing structural

21-39. Rosmarie Tissi, Univac advertisement, 1965. A dynamic, powerful image is created by the careful cropping and placement of two telephone receivers.

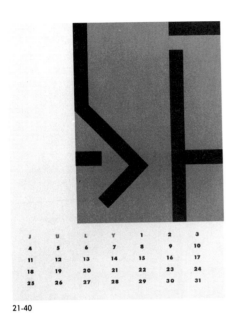

21-40

21-41

21-40. Noel Martin, page from a calendar for J. W. Ford Typographers, 1954. A composition using thirty-six-point metal rules was made up and printed over a blue rectangle by letterpress. The word *July* is printed in red to separate it from the black numbers on the same grid.

21-41. Noel Martin, page from *The War We Are In,* foreign affairs booklet, 1960. Diagonal structure and bold red rules against a black background bring urgency to a list of major conflicts after World War II. The red daggers signify Sino-Soviet involvement.

order to his work. His ability to compose with simple graphic elements is demonstrated in a 1956 *Esquire* magazine illustration (Fig. 21-42), where photographs and simple geometric shapes combine to express the content of an article on psychological testing.

De Harak's evolution has been a continuing quest for communicative clarity and visual order, which are the qualities he regards as vital to effective graphic design. He recognized these qualities in Swiss design during the late 1950s and began to apply aspects of the movement to his work. Grid structures and asymmetrical balance were used. Responding to the legibility and formal perfection of Akzidenz Grotesk before it was available in the United States, de Harak obtained specimen sheets from European foundries so that he could assemble headlines for his designs. These combine purity of form with elemental images expressive of the content. A series of album covers for Westminster Records (Fig. 21-43) evoked a conceptual, mental image of the music's structure.

During the early 1960s, de Harak initiated a series of over 350 book jackets for McGraw-Hill Publishers that were designed using a common typographic system and grid (Fig. 21-44). The subject of each book was articulated by visual configurations that ranged from elemental pictographs to abstract geometric structures. In his 1964 cover for *Personality and Psychotherapy* (Pl. 75), vertical lines of orange, green, and purple form an elusive dualistic head to communicate the intangible and complex aspects of personality. Because this large series of paperback books covered academic subject areas including psychology, sociology, management, and mathematics, de Harak's approach appropriately expressed a high intellectual con-

21-42. Rudolph de Harak, illustration for *Esquire,* 1956. A hand reaching into the page to take the exclamation mark combines with a dynamic complex of pictures and triangles to suggest several aspects of an article on psychological testing.

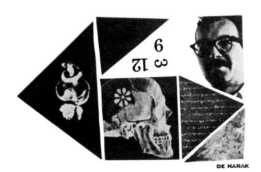

21-42

21-43. Rudolph de Harak, album cover for Bach Concertos, 1961. The mathematical perfection of Bach's music is evoked by a complex optical illusion with four quadrants.

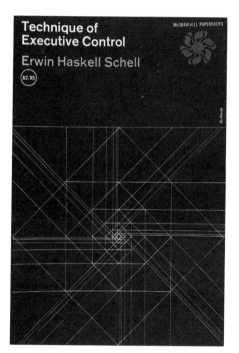

21-44. Rudolph de Harak, cover for *Technique of Executive Control,* 1964. The geometric structure, with its concentration of lines in the center, symbolizes centralization of management authority.

21-45. Jacqueline S. Casey, announcement for the Ocean Engineering program, 1967. A classic typographic grid sits above an x-ray of a chambered nautilus shell superimposed upon a wavelike repetition of fluid shapes.

tent. This series altered the course of book-jacket design in the United States.

The International Typographic Style was rapidly embraced in corporate and institutional graphics during the 1960s and remained a prominent aspect of American design for over two decades. A noteworthy example of this is the graphic design group at the Massachusetts Institute of Technology, where a sustained level of quality and imagination has been maintained. In the early 1950s, MIT established a graphic design program enabling all members of the university community to benefit from free, professional design assistance on their publications and publicity material. This was a very early recognition of the cultural and communicative value of design by an American university, and MIT developed a design approach based on a commitment to the grid and sans serif typography. The MIT staff has been innovative in the use of designed letterforms and manipulated words as vehicles to express content. This approach evolved in the work of Jacqueline S. Casey (b. 1927), director of the Design Services Office; Ralph Coburn (b. 1923); and Dietmar Winkler (b. 1938), a German-trained designer who worked with Casey and Coburn from 1966 until 1971.

21-45

The International Typographic Style

21-46

21-47

21-48

21-46. Ralph Coburn, poster for the MIT jazz band, 1972. A staccato repetition of the letterforms of the word *jazz* establishes musical sequences and animates the space.

21-47. Dietmar Winkler, poster for a computer programming course, 1969. The word *Cobol* is constructed of elemental forms and repeated in red, white, and blue segments against a black background.

21-48. Jacqueline C. Casey, poster for an MIT open house, 1974. Stencil letterforms announce the open house, and the open *O* does double duty as a concrete symbol of the opening of the campus to visitors.

21-49. Arnold Saks, *Inflatable Sculpture* poster for the Jewish Museum, 1968. This sequence of bars that bend and expand as they move up the poster becomes a symbol for the action of energy upon pliable materials, graphically articulating the essence of inflatable sculpture.

The Design Services Office produces publications and posters (Figs. 21-45 and 21-46) announcing concerts, speakers, seminars, exhibitions, and courses on the university campus. These frequently use solid-colored backgrounds. The use of graphic form to express technical and scientific information is demonstrated by Dietmar Winkler's 1969 poster for a computer-programming course (Fig. 21-47). While photography is sometimes employed, most of the solutions are typographic. In a sense, letterforms become illustrations, for the design and arrangement of the letters in key words frequently become the dominant image (Fig. 21-48).

Part of the rapid spread of the International Typographic Style resulted from the ability of elemental forms to express complex ideas with clarity and directness, as seen in the Inflatable Sculpture exhibition poster (Fig. 21-49) by Arnold Saks (b. 1931). The design movement that began in Switzerland and Germany, then outgrew its native boundaries to become truly international, was particularly useful when a diverse body of informational materials, ranging from signage to publicity, needed to be unified into a coherent body. The resulting growing awareness of design as a logical tool for large organizations after World War II caused a growth in corporate design and visual identification systems. During the middle 1960s, the development of corporate design and the International Typographic Style were linked into one movement. This will be discussed in Chapter 23.

21-49

The New York School

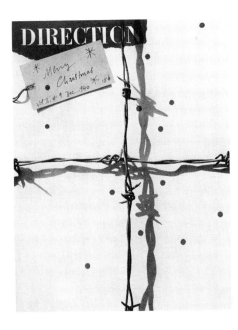

22-1. Paul Rand, cover for *Direction* magazine, 1940. This design shows the important role of contrast in Rand's work. A Christmas package wrapped with barbed wire instead of ribbon was a grim reminder as the world hurled deeper into global war. The handwritten Christmas tag on a crisp rectangle contrasts sharply with the mechanical stencil lettering of the logo on a torn-edged collage element.

As we have seen, the first wave of modern design in America was imported by talented emigrants from Europe seeking to escape the political climate of totalitarianism. These individuals brought Americans a firsthand introduction to the European avant-garde. The 1940s saw further steps toward an original American approach to modernist design. While borrowing freely from the language of form developed by European designers, Americans developed attitudes and invented forms that added to the tradition of graphic design. European design was theoretical and highly structured; American design was pragmatic, intuitive, and more informal in its approach to organizing space. Just as Paris had been the most democratic city in the world with great receptivity to new ideas and images during the late nineteenth and early twentieth centuries, New York City assumed that role during the middle twentieth century. It may have been that these cultural incubators nurtured creativity because the prevailing climate enabled individuals to realize their potential. Or, the existing climate may have been a magnet that attracted individuals of great talent and potential. In either case, New York became the cultural center of the world in the middle of the twentieth century, and graphic design innovation ranked high among its accomplishments.

Despite the European underpinnings, unique aspects of American culture and society dictated an original approach to modern design. The United States is an egalitarian society with capitalistic attitudes and values, limited artistic traditions, and a diverse ethnic heritage. Emphasis was placed upon the expression of ideas and an open, direct presentation of information. In this highly competitive society, novelty of technique and originality of concept were much prized, and designers sought simultaneously to solve communications problems and satisfy a need for personal expression. This phase of American graphic design began with strong European roots during the 1940s, gained international prominence for its original viewpoints in the 1950s, and continues today.

Pioneers of the New York School

Perhaps more than any other American designer, Paul Rand (b. 1914) initiated this American approach to modern design. When he was twenty-three years old, Rand began the first phase of his design career as a promotional and editorial designer for *Apparel Arts, Esquire, Ken, Coronet,* and *Glass Packer.* His magazine covers broke with the traditions of American publication design. A strong knowledge of the modern movement, particularly the works of Klee, Kandinsky, and the Cubists, led Rand to an understanding that freely invented shapes could have a self-contained life, both symbolic and expressive, as a visual-communications tool. His ability to manipulate visual form (shape, color, space, line, value) and skillful analysis of communications content, reducing it to a symbolic essence without being sterile or dull, allowed Rand to become widely influential while still in his twenties. The playful, visually dynamic, and unexpected often find their way into his work. He seized upon collage and montage as a means to bring concepts, images, textures, and even objects into a cohesive whole (Figs. 22-1 and 22-2).

From 1941 until 1954, Paul Rand worked at the Weintraub advertising agency, applying his design approach to advertisements. His collaborations with Bill Bern-

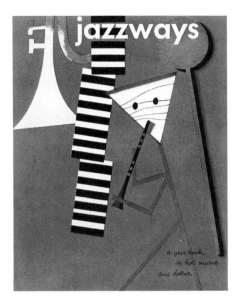

22-3

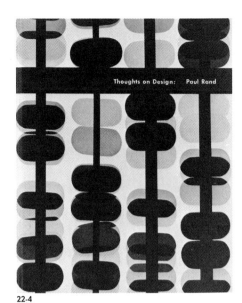

22-4

22-2. Paul Rand, *Jazzways* yearbook cover, 1946. Collage technique, elemental symbolic forms, and dynamic composition were graphic qualities of Rand's work in the late 1930s and 1940s.

22-3. Paul Rand, Ohrbach's advertisement, 1946. A combination of elements—the logotype, photograph, decorative drawing, and type—are playfully combined into a unity. The image visually reinforces the headline.

22-4. Paul Rand, cover for *Thoughts on Design,* 1946. A photogram, created by making several exposures of an abacus placed on photographic paper in the darkroom, becomes a metaphor of the design process—moving elements around to compose space—and provides a visual record of this process.

bach became a prototype for the art/copy team working closely together to create a synergistic visual-verbal integration. Campaigns they created for clients including Ohrbach's department store featured entertaining puns and wordplay supported by Rand's whimsical integration of photography, drawing, and logo (Fig. 22-3). After leaving the agency, Rand became an independent designer with increasing emphasis upon trademark and corporate design. *Thoughts on Design,* his 1946 book illustrated with over eighty examples of his work, inspired a generation of designers (Fig. 22-4).

Paul Rand understands the value of ordinary, universally understood signs and symbols as tools for translating ideas into visual communications (Figs. 22-5 and 22-6). To engage the audience successfully and communicate memorably, he knows that the designer's alteration, juxtaposition, or interpretation is necessary to make the ordinary into something extraordinary. Sensual visual contrasts mark his work. Playing red against green, organic shape against geometric type, photographic tone against flat color, cut or torn edges against sharp forms, and the textural pattern of type against white margins are some of the contrasts in which he delights. In addition, he has been willing to take risks by exploring uproven ideas. In his 1968 cover design for the American Institute of Graphic Arts (Pl. 75), a red "A. Eye. G. A." plays hide-and-seek against the green background as a pictographic clown face plays hide-and-seek with an organic abstraction. Design becomes play, and the Futurist concept of simultaneity is evoked.

For all his visual inventiveness, Rand defines design as the integration of form and function for effective communication. The cultural role of the designer is defined as upgrading rather than as serving the least common denominator of public taste. During the early period of Rand's career, he made forays into the vocabulary of modern art but never parted from an immediate accessibility of image. This was a major hallmark of his contribution—perhaps there is a limit to how far a designer can follow the modern painter into the uncharted realm of pure form and subjective expression without losing the vital foothold on public communication.

During a design career in a life cut tragically short by illness, Alvin Lustig (1915–1955) incorporated his subjective vision and private symbols into graphic design. Born in Colorado, Lustig bounced between the east and west coasts and between architecture, graphic design, and interior design. At age twenty-one, he operated a graphic design and printing business from the rear of a Los Angeles drugstore. On projects for the Ward Ritchie Press, Lustig created abstract geometric designs using type rules and ornaments.

Sensing that Lustig's work was created by an "artist who might possess a touch of genius," publisher James Laughton of New Directions in New York began to

22-5

22-6

commission book and jacket designs from him (Figs. 22-7 through 22-10). As New Directions published books of outstanding literary quality, Lustig's design approach—searching for symbols to capture the essence of the contents and treating form and content as one—found a receptive response from its literary audience. A comparable expression was achieved by his designs for classical music recordings (Fig. 22-11). Lustig believed in the importance of painting to design and design education, and considered the artist's pure research into private symbols to be the wellspring for the public symbols created by the designer. By 1950, he was becoming increasingly involved in design education, but his eyesight had begun to fail, and he was totally blind by the autumn of 1954. In the face of this overwhelming tragedy for an artist, Lustig continued to teach and design until his death over a year later. One is compelled to wonder what the impact of this perceptive man upon design and visual education might have been had he lived a normal lifespan.

In 1940, twenty-four-year-old Alex Steinweiss (b. 1916) was named art director of Columbia Records. The modern design sensibilities of the 1940s were applied to record-album design as Steinweiss searched for visual forms and shapes to express music (Fig. 22-12). Steinweiss had an informal approach to space—elements were placed casually on the field with an informal balance that sometimes bordered on a random scattering of forms. Steinweiss initiated a commitment to quality and appropriate expression of musical content that continues over five decades later within the musical recording industry.

Bradbury Thompson (b. 1911) emerged as one of the most influential graphic designers in postwar America. After graduation from Washburn College in his hometown of Topeka, Kansas, in 1934, Thompson worked for printing firms there for several years before moving to New York. His designs for *Westvaco Inspirations* from 1939 until 1961 had tremendous impact. His thorough knowledge of printing and typesetting, combined with an adventurous spirit of experimentation, allowed him to expand the range of design possibilities. *Westvaco Inspirations,* a four-color publication demonstrating printing papers, used letterpress plates of art and illustration borrowed from advertising agencies and museums. With a limited budget for new plates or artwork, Thompson used the typecase and printshop as his "canvas, easel, and second studio." He discovered and explored the potential of eighteenth- and nineteenth-century engravings as design resources (Fig. 22-13). Large, bold, organic and geometric shapes were used to bring graphic and symbolic power to the page. Letterforms and patterns, such as the details from halftone reproductions in Figure 22-14, were often greatly enlarged and used as design elements or

22-5. Paul Rand, poster for the film *No Way Out,* 1950. Rand's design language—integrating photography, typography, and graphic shapes, and surrounding active form with white space—is in marked contrast to the conventional film posters shown in this photograph.

22-6. Paul Rand, monograph cover, 1953. An exuberance of shape and whimsical images have been recurring themes in Rand's advertisements and children's books.

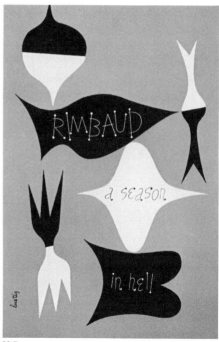

22-7

22-8

22-9

22-10

22-7. Alvin Lustig, cover for Arthur Rimbaud's *A Season in Hell,* 1945. Sharp black-and-white biomorphic figures on a deep-red field suggest the French poet's spiritual descent into hell, and his failures in love and art.

22-8. Alvin Lustig, cover for Tennessee Williams's *27 Wagons Full of Cotton,* 1949. A delicate magnolia flower brutally nailed to rough siding—these contradictory photographic symbols represent the underlying violence and hatred behind the civilized façade in human affairs. Lustig understood the frail human spirit and brutal environmental forces articulated in Williams's plays.

22-9. Alvin Lustig, cover for Federico Garcia Lorca's *3 Tragedies,* 1949. In this stunning montage of five photographic images, the author's name and title become objects photographed in the world.

22-10. Alvin Lustig, cover for Tennessee Williams's *Camino Real,* 1952. The typographic, posterlike title contrasts crisply with the graffiti-marred wall upon which it is posted.

22-11. Alvin Lustig, album cover for Vivaldi, 1951. Moving like music notes along the median line, the abstracted letters forming the Italian composer's name echo the background triangular shapes in a composition of warm colors.

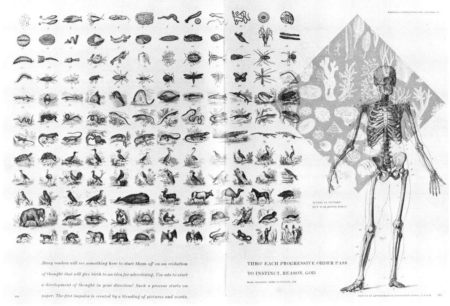

22-12. Alex Steinweiss, album cover for Beethoven's *Symphony No. 5,* 1949. This collage of elements, a *5* constructed of geometric shapes, casual script writing, positive and negative images of the composer, a pink bar, and a white circle on a blue background, are typical of Steinweiss's vocabulary.

22-13. Bradbury Thompson, pages from *Westvaco Inspirations,* 151, 1945. The vast storehouse of printed images now in the public domain was deftly probed and became part of the modern design vocabulary.

22-14. Bradbury Thompson, pages from *Westvaco Inspirations,* 186, 1951. This spirited collage opens an issue, "Enlarging upon Printing," which explores such possibilities as enlarging halftone dots.

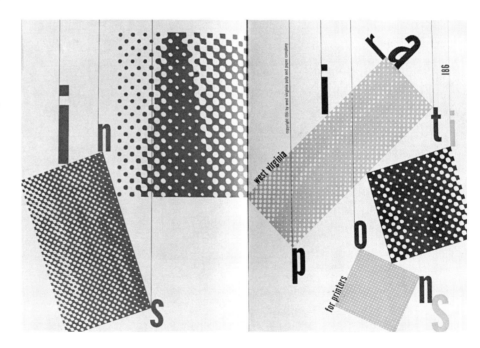

to create visual patterns and movements. Four-color process plates would be taken apart and used to create designs (Fig. 22-15) and often overprinted to create new colors. Typography gained expression through scale and color (Fig. 22-16). In sum, Thompson achieved a rare mastery of complex organization, form, and visual flow. In one of his most famous designs, for the 1958 *Westvaco Inspirations,* 210 (Pl. 76), letterforms from the word *Westvaco* are used to construct a winking, speaking typographic mask, echoing the stylized geometry of the African masks in Somoroff's photograph. The photograph, loaned for use as a printing specimen, was the catalyst for Thompson's typographic invention.

During the 1960s and 1970s, Thompson turned increasingly to a classical approach to book and editorial format design. Readability, formal harmony, and a sensitive use of Old Style typefaces have marked his work for periodicals such as *Smithsonian* and *ARTnews,* postage stamps, and a steady flow of books, including the monumental *Washburn College Bible.*

22-15. Bradbury Thompson, pages from
Westvaco Inspirations, 210, 1958. Starting
with a multiple-exposure photograph of a
saxophone player, Thompson reversed it
from a black circle on the left and
overprinted it in primary colors on the right.

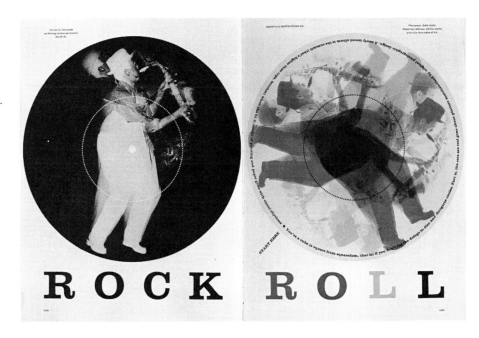

22-16. Bradbury Thompson, pages from
Westvaco Inspirations, 216, 1961. The final
issue used complex typography to interpret
the American Civil War. In this spread, a
painting reproduced on the preceding pages
is printed in yellow and black, blue and red,
red, and red and yellow as it moves across
the page behind the letterforms.

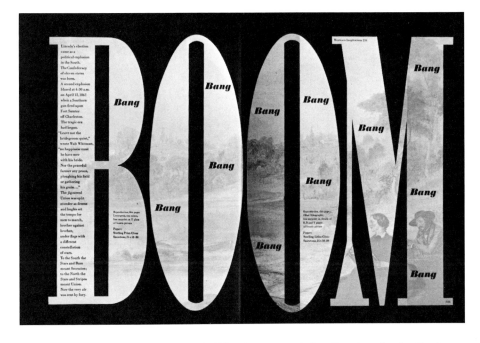

The sensibilities of the New York School were carried to Los Angeles by Saul
Bass (b. 1921). This native New Yorker was educated and worked in his home city
until 1950, when he moved to California. Two years later, he opened his own studio. Paul Rand's use of shape and asymmetrical balance during the 1940s was an
important inspiration for Bass. But while Rand's carefully orchestrated compositions used complex contrasts of shape, color, and texture, Bass frequently reduced
the graphic design to a single dominant image, usually centered in the space.

Bass has a remarkable ability to identify the nucleus of a design problem. This is
then expressed with images that become glyphs, or elemental pictorial signs, that
exert great graphic power (Fig. 22-17). Although Bass stripped visual complexity
from American graphic design and reduced the communication to a simple pictographic image, his work is not simply the elemental graphics of Constructivism—
chunky forms are cut from paper with scissors or drawn with a brush, and freely
drawn, decorative letterforms are as likely to be used in his work as typography or
handwriting. There is a robust energy about his forms, and an almost casual qual-

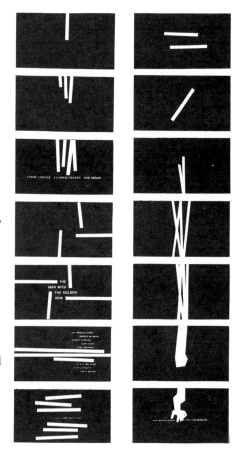

22-17. Saul Bass, billboard for Pabco Paints, early 1950s. The process of painting is reduced to a multicolored stripe. The happy people who look ahead by using quality paint are articulated by three simple marks signifying satisfied customers.

22-18. Saul Bass, symbol for *The Man with the Golden Arm*, 1955. This consistent and memorable visual identifier was flexible enough for uses ranging from minute newspaper advertisements to large-scale posters.

ity about their execution. While images are simplified to a minimal statement, they lack the exactitude of measurement or construction that could make them rigid.

The motion picture had long used traditional portraits of actors and actresses in promoting films when producer/director Otto Preminger commissioned Bass to create unified graphic materials for his films, including logos, theater posters, advertising, and animated film titles. The first comprehensive design program unifying both print and media graphics for a film was the 1955 design program for Preminger's *The Man with the Golden Arm*. As the symbol for this film about drug addiction, Bass developed a thick pictographic arm that thrusts downward into a rectangle composed of slablike bars, then bracketed the arm with the name of the film (Fig. 22-18). The titles for this motion picture broke new ground as well (Fig. 22-19): Accompanied by staccato jazz, a single white bar thrusts down onto the screen, followed by three more; when all four reach the center of the screen, typography appears, listing the featured performers. All of these elements except one bar, retained for continuity, fade. Then, four bars sweep in from the top, bottom, and sides to frame the film-title typography, which suddenly appears. This kinetic sequence of animated bars and typography continues in perfect synchronization to the throbbing wail of jazz music through the credits. Finally, the bars thrust into the space and transform into the pictographic arm of the logo. From this beginning, Bass became the acknowledged master of the film title. He pioneered an organic process of forms that appear, disintegrate, reform, and transform in time and space. This combination, recombination, and synthesis of form was carried over into the area of printed graphics.

A typical Bass motion picture design program can be seen in the 1960 graphics for *Exodus*. Bass created a powerful pictograph of arms reaching upward and struggling for a rifle, conveying the violence and strife connected with the birth of the nation of Israel. This mark was used in a comprehensive publicity program, including newspaper, magazine, and trade advertisements (Fig. 22-20), posters and film titles, and even stationery, shipping labels, and other routine printed matter. Each individual item was approached as a unique communications problem. Diversity was achieved while the strong graphic qualities of the mark ensured continuity. In the poster for *Exodus* (Pl. 77), the trauma of Israel's birth is expressed by two levels of reality: the two-dimensional logo, and the photographically frozen moment when this image is engulfed in flames. The simplicity and directness of Bass's work enables the viewer to interpret the content immediately (Fig. 22-21).

In addition to his film graphics, which represent a major contribution to the evolution of graphic design, Bass has created numerous corporate identity programs. He also has directed a number of films, ranging from the outstanding short film *Why Man Creates,* which uses a kaleidoscope of film techniques probing the

22-19. Saul Bass, film titles for *The Man with the Golden Arm,* 1955. Abstract graphic elements create a spare, gaunt intensity reflecting the character of the film. Graphic design for film was revolutionized.

8TH SAN FRANCISCO INTERNATIONAL FILM FESTIVAL·OCTOBER 14TH TO 27TH 1964 CORONET THEATRE

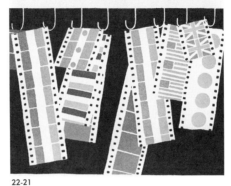

22-20

22-21

22-20. Saul Bass, trade advertisement for *Exodus,* 1960. To communicate that *Exodus* was all wrapped up or "in the can," a film can was wrapped in a Hebrew newspaper, tied, and labeled with a tag bearing the logo.

22-21. Saul Bass, *8th San Francisco International Film Festival* poster, 1964. The white space separating the two black squares also becomes the film-editing bar, holding colorful shots of the flags from participating countries.

nature of human creativity and expression, to a feature-length motion picture.

George Tscherny (b. 1924) is a native of Budapest, Hungary, who immigrated to the United States as a child and received his visual education there. Tscherny served as head of the graphic design department for the New York design firm George Nelson & Associates before opening his own design office in 1956. Tscherny has functioned as an independent designer, which is somewhat unique in a profession where partnerships, large staffs, and staff positions are the norm. The particular gift that this intuitive and sensitive man brings to the design process is an ability to seize the essence of the subject and express it in stunningly simple terms. The results are elegant and to the point; other designers have found his designs so disarmingly simple and appropriate that "Why didn't I think of this?" is a common reaction. Tscherny's vocabulary of techniques for solving design problems includes the purely typographic, photography, simple calligraphic brush drawing, and the bold, simple shapes that he delights in cutting from colored papers. Regardless of technique, Tscherny's process of reducing complex content to an elemental graphic symbol expressing the underlying order or basic form of the subject is constant (Figs. 22-22 and 22-23).

22-22. George Tscherny, dance program cover, 1958. At first glance, this appears as a beautiful color study in positive and negative space. Then the viewer realizes that with two pieces of cut paper, Tscherny has captured the renowned modern dancer, Martha Graham, in one of her classic poses.

22-23. George Tscherny, exhibition catalogue covers, 1961. José de Rivera is a Constructivist sculptor whose parabolic curves twist and bend in space. Tscherny expressed this quality by photographing type that he had bent and twisted.

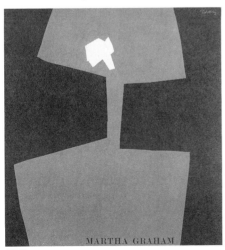

MARTHA GRAHAM

22-22

22-23

22-24. Ivan Chermayeff, album cover for Beethoven's *Eroica*, 1957. Through trial-and-error collage, Chermayeff presented each letter as a visual element with uncommon and unexpected relationships to the other letters.

Among youthful designers entering the profession, important work was done by the firm of Brownjohn, Chermayeff, and Geismar, founded in 1957 in New York City. Calling their firm a "design office" instead of an "art studio," reflected their attitudes toward design and the design process. Robert Brownjohn (1925–1970) had studied painting and design under Moholy-Nagy and architecture under the distinguished architect-teacher Serge Chermayeff; Ivan Chermayeff (b. 1932), son of Serge Chermayeff, had worked as an assistant to Alvin Lustig and as a record album designer; and his close friend from graduate school, Tom Geismar (b. 1931), had served two years with the United States Army as an exhibition designer and then free-lanced. Their initial contribution to American graphic design sprang from a strong aesthetic background and an understanding of the major ideas of European modern art, which had been reinforced by their contacts with the elder Chermayeff, Moholy-Nagy, and Lustig. A communicative immediacy, a strong sense of form, and a vitality and freshness characterized their work in the early months of the partnership. In typographic collages for a variety of projects, including the record-album cover for Beethoven's *Eroica* (Fig. 22-24), texture, color, and typeforms were used in unexpected combinations. Images and symbols were combined with a surreal sense of dislocation to convey the essence of the subject in book jackets (Figs. 22-25 and 22-26). Typographic solutions, such as the record-album cover for Manchito and his orchestra (Fig. 22-27), used color repetition and unusual letterforms to express the subject matter. A particularly fine sense of both typographic and art history, developed in the principals' wide-ranging educational backgrounds, enabled these young designers to chart a course based on problem solving. Solutions grew out of the needs of the client and the limitations of the problem in hand.

An organizational and project-management expertise for handling large, multicomponent projects became evident in 1958, when Brownjohn, Chermayeff, and Geismar were commissioned to design a major exhibition for the United States Pavilion at the Brussels World's Fair (Fig. 22-28). Here they presented the scale and character of the American urban environment, not by duplicating a typical street scene but through an environmental-scale, three-dimensional, typographic assemblage expressing the vitality and spirit of the city.

In 1960, Brownjohn left the partnership and moved to England, where he made significant contributions to British graphic design, especially in the area of film titles. Particularly inventive was the title design for the motion picture *Goldfinger*.

22-25. Tom Geismar, cover for *Common Sense and Nuclear Warfare*, c. 1958. Photomontage powerfully conveys a person's vulnerability to nuclear war. The atomic blast becomes a visual metaphor for the human brain, graphically echoing the title.

22-26. Ivan Chermayeff, cover for Henry Miller's, *The Wisdom of the Heart*, 1959. The author's verbal metaphor becomes a powerful visual metaphor through the unexpected juxtaposition of a graphic sign and a photographic image.

22-25

22-26

22-27. Robert Brownjohn, album cover for Machito and his orchestra, 1959. A visual pattern of abstract shapes is formed by repeating the bottom portions of letterforms that have been broken into fragments by a stencil-lettering effect.

22-28. Brownjohn, Chermayeff, and Geismar, United States Pavilion for the Brussels World's Fair, 1958. Fragments of signage become planes in space communicating a sense of place: the American urban landscape.

Brownjohn's typographic designs for the credits were 35mm color slides projected upon a moving human body filmed in real time. This integration of two-dimensional graphics with figurative cinematography launched a number of other experimental titling efforts. Meanwhile, the firm, renamed Chermayeff & Geismar Associates after Brownjohn's departure, played a major role in the development of postwar corporate identity, discussed in the next chapter.

An editorial design revolution

During the 1940s, only a moderate number of American magazines were designed well. These included *Fortune,* a business magazine whose art directors included Will Burtin and Leo Lionni (b. 1910); *Vogue,* where Alexander Liberman replaced Dr. Agha as art director in 1943; and *Harper's Bazaar,* where Alexey Brodovitch continued as art director until his retirement in 1958. One of Dr. Agha's assistants at *Vogue* during the 1930s, Cipe Pineles (b. 1910), made a major contribution to editorial design during the 1940s and 1950s, first as art director at *Glamour,* then at *Seventeen, Charm,* and *Mademoiselle.* Pineles often commissioned illustrations from fine artists, resulting in editorial pages that broke with conventional imagery. Her publication designs were characterized by a lyrical appreciation of color, pattern, and form (Fig. 22-29). Pineles became the first woman admitted to membership in the New York Art Director's Club, breaking the bastion of the male dominated professional design societies.

Over the course of the 1950s, a revolution in editorial design occurred, spurred in part by the design classes Brodovitch taught first at his home and then at the New School for Social Research in New York. The seeds for an expansive, design-oriented period of editorial graphics were sown in these classes. One of his students, Otto Storch (b. 1913), wrote later that "Brodovitch would dump photostats, type proofs, colored pieces of paper, and someone's shoe lace, if it became untied, on a long table together with rubber cement. He would fold his arms and with a sad expression challenge us to do something brilliant." Brodovitch's students learned to examine each problem thoroughly, develop a solution from the resulting understanding, and then search for a brilliant visual presentation. Brodovitch's impact

22-29. Cipe Pineles, cover for *Seventeen,* 1949. Stripe patterns and a mirror-image reflection achieve a graphic vitality.

upon a generation of editorial designers and photographers who came into their own during the 1950s was phenomenal, and editorial design experienced one of its greatest eras.

Storch, working as an art director at Dell publishing, was unhappy with the level of subject matter in his assignments. He was keenly interested in Brodovitch's design of *Harper's Bazaar* and joined the art directors, photographers, fashion and general illustrators, and packaging, set, and typographic designers who gathered to learn from the master. After class one evening in 1946, Brodovitch reviewed Storch's portfolio and advised him to quit his job because he showed potential but his position did not. A seven-year period of free-lancing followed, after which Storch joined the McCall's Corporation as assistant art director for *Better Living* magazine. In 1953, Storch was named art director of *McCall's*. When this major women's publication developed circulation problems in the late 1950s, a new editor named Herbert Mayes was brought in to revitalize the magazine. Mayes gave Storch a free hand to upgrade the graphics in 1958, and an astounding visual approach developed. Typography was unified with photography by designing the type to lock tightly into the photographic image (Fig. 22-30). Headlines often became parts of illustrations. For example, an article title, "Why Mommy Can't Read," was written on a pair of glasses, which were then photographed. Type warped and bent (Fig. 22-31), or became the illustration, as in a tight rectangle of over sixty capital Baskerville *Z*'s linked with the title "Bored of Education," for an article discussing how some children found school so dull that it put them to sleep.

Scale was explored in the large-format publication. Small objects became large graphics. Various subjects, including a beautiful ear of fresh summer corn in the food section of the magazine (Fig. 22-32) and a close-up of a woman's lips as she put on lipstick, were presented as full, double-page layouts. Storch and the photographers who worked with him went to great pains to produce photographic essays that were unexpected and poetic. Foods and fashions were often shot on location instead of in the studio. Full-bleed, double-page photographs were designed with preplanned areas for the type. For an article on breakfasts around the world, Storch photographed the foods on the wing of a transatlantic airplane (Fig. 22-33).

Storch ranks among the major innovators of the period. His philosophy that idea, copy, art, and typography should be inseparable in editorial design (Fig. 22-34) influenced both editorial and advertising graphics. In 1967, he became very involved with photography. Success had made the management at *McCall's* more conservative, and opposition to Storch's creative layout was building. After nearly

22-30. Otto Storch (art director) and Paul Dome (photographer), pages from *McCall's*, 1961. These introductory pages to a feature on frozen foods unify typography and photography into a cohesive structure.

fifteen years as art director of *McCall's,* he resigned to concentrate on editorial and advertising photography.

After gaining experience in studios and an advertising agency, Vienna-born Henry Wolf (b. 1925) became art director of *Esquire* in 1953. Wolf also studied under Brodovitch, and he redesigned *Esquire's* format with greater emphasis on the use of white space and large photographs. When Brodovitch retired in 1958, Wolf replaced him as art director of *Harper's Bazaar.* Wolf sought to make the magazines he designed visually beautiful. He experimented with typography, making it very large to fill the page on one spread and then using petite headlines on other pages. Wolf's vision of the magazine cover was an exquisitely simple image conveying a visual idea (Fig. 22-35). The sophistication and inventiveness of photography commissioned by *Harper's Bazaar* during his tenure were extraordinary (Figs. 22-36 and 22-37).

22-31. Otto Storch (art director) and Dan Wynn (photographer), pages from *McCall's,* 1961. Typography bends with the elasticity of a soft mattress under the weight of the sleeping woman.

22-32. Otto Storch (art director and photographer), pages from *McCall's,* 1965. The soft beauty of an ear of corn fills the pages. The title for this feature is a photograph of a handmade sign from a roadside market.

22-33

22-35

22-34

22-33. Otto Storch (art director and photographer), pages from *McCall's,* 1965. For an article on breakfasts around the world, Storch photographed food on the wing of an international jet liner.

22-34. Otto Storch (art director) and Allen Arbus (photographer), pages from *McCall's,* 1959. Typography sprinkles from the hand and foot of moving models. A dynamic color effect is achieved because one model wears a red dress against a black background, while the other wears a black-and-white outfit against a red background.

22-35. Henry Wolf, cover for *Esquire,* 1958. "The Americanization of Paris" is signified by a packet of "instant red wine," satirizing the creeping spread of American technology, customs, and conveniences. The editor received letters asking where instant wine could be purchased.

22-36. Henry Wolf, cover for *Harper's Bazaar,* 1959. This refracted image is typical of the imaginative visual solutions Wolf brought to ordinary design problems. As a subtle touch, the logo is refracted as well.

22-37. Henry Wolf, cover for *Harper's Bazaar,* 1959. The colors of the peacock feather are echoed by the eye makeup in this arresting juxtaposition.

22-38. Henry Wolf, cover for *Show,* 1963. On this Valentine's Day cover, an x-ray machine locates the model's graphic red heart.

In 1961, Wolf left *Bazaar* to design the new *Show* magazine (Fig. 22-38), a short-lived periodical that explored new design territory as a result of Wolf's imaginative and elegant art direction. He then turned his attention toward advertising (Fig. 22-39) and photography. Among the other editorial art directors of this wonderful era of magazine design, Allen Hurlburt (1911–1983) art directed *Look* magazine from 1953 until 1968, and brought relevance, intelligence, and a keen sense of scale to this publication. Some of the photographic essays used in *Look* during the 1960s raised editorial design and photography to a high aesthetic level.

In the late 1960s, broad factors at work in America ended the era of large pages, lavish photography, and design dominating content. A two-decade period of ever-growing affluence was yielding to inflation and economic problems. Television was robbing magazines of their traditional role of providing popular fiction entertainment and eroding their advertising revenue. At the same time, public concerns about the Vietnam War, environmental problems, the rights of minorities and women, and a host of other issues produced a need for a different kind of publica-

22-36

22-37

22-38

tion. The public demanded a higher information content, and skyrocketing postal rates, paper shortages, and escalating paper and printing costs shrunk the large-format periodicals. *McCall's* and *Esquire,* for example, went from 25.5 by 33.4 centimeters, (10⅛ by 13⅛ inches) to what became the fairly standard format size of 21 by 27.5 centimeters (8½ by 11 inches). Others, including *Life, Look,* and the *Saturday Evening Post,* ceased publication.

22-39. Henry Wolf, advertisement for Olivetti, 1960s. In a surreal art gallery, Olivetti's product design is honored for its artistic quality.

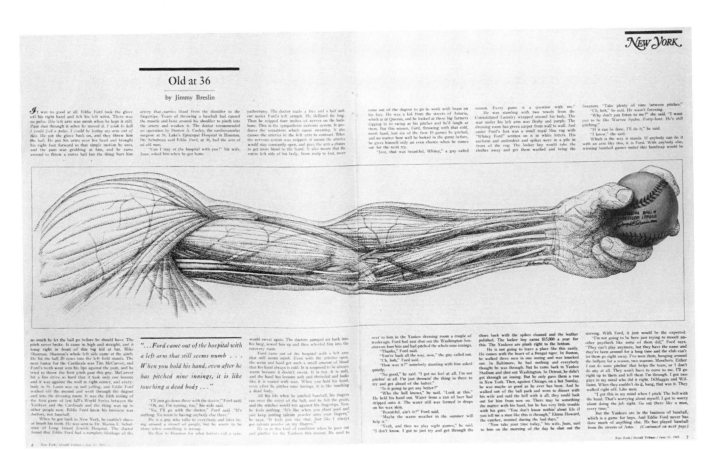

22-40

Editorial design after the decline

Soothsayers predicted the death of the magazine as a communications form during the 1960s. However, a new, smaller-format breed of periodicals addressing the specific interests of specialized audiences emerged and thrived. Advertisers who wished to reach the specific audiences of these more specialized magazines bought advertising space. This new editorial climate, with more emphasis on content, longer text, and less opportunity for lavish visual treatment, necessitated a new approach to editorial design. Layout became more controlled, and the use of a consistent typographic format and grid—undoubtedly under the influence of the International Typographic Style—became the norm.

The harbinger for the future evolution of the magazine as a graphic communications form can be found in the work of Peter Palazzo, design editor of the *New York Herald Tribune* from 1962 until 1965. Palazzo received considerable acclaim for his overall typographic design of this newspaper, the editorial design approach of the *Book Week Supplement* and *New York* magazine, and the conceptual power of many of the images he commissioned. In the weekly *New York* magazine section, Palazzo established a three-column grid and a consistent size and style for article titles, which were always bracketed by a thick ruled line above and a thin rule below (Fig. 22-40). Palazzo made a little white space go a long way: a band of space across the top of an editorial spread here, a vacant left-hand column with the title at the top there, and an illustration containing open spaces on another page. The total effect was somewhere between the newspaper (with its dominant masses of text) and the magazine design of the period (with engaging visuals and ample white space). His cover designs used simple, direct symbolic images making editorial comment on important issues (Fig. 22-41). After the *New York Herald Tribune* ceased publication in April 1967, the *New York* supplement continued as a well-known city magazine.

The design approach developed in New York spread to other major communications centers, such as Chicago and Los Angeles when designers including Saul

22-41. Peter Palazzo (art director), cover for *New York*, 1965. For a special issue discussing women's problems and desires for greater freedom and equality, Palazzo applied eye shadow and mascara to the Statue of Liberty.

22-40. Peter Palazzo (art director), editorial design for *New York,* 1965. Palazzo combined a transparent anatomical drawing of an arm with a photograph of a baseball to express the arm problems of a leading major league pitcher.

22-42. Dugald Stermer (art director) and Carl Fischer (photographer), cover for *Ramparts,* 1967. With the black-and-white intensity and lost-and-found forms of a Rembrandt etching, this universal indictment of man's inhumanity to man gains a sudden immediacy through the presence of American soldiers at the crucifixion scene.

22-43. Dugald Stermer (art director), cover for *Ramparts,* 1967. Because the editors' names are clearly visible on the burning draft cards, this graphic depiction of civil disobedience takes on the quality of a self-documented crime.

Bass, whose education and formative work were in New York, relocated throughout the country. During the late 1960s, American graphic design slowly started to become a national profession. New typesetting and printing technology permitted excellent work to be produced in smaller cities. Two national design magazines—*Print,* published in New York from 1940, and *Communication Arts,* launched in the San Francisco area in 1959—communicated to an increasingly national design community.

A new breed of editorial art directors, who were as much editors as designers, emerged in other cities, including Atlanta and San Francisco. They helped shape the editorial viewpoints and philosophies of their publications. One prototype for this new editorial designer is Dugald Stermer (b. 1936), who left a studio job in Texas in 1965 to return to his native California and become art director of *Ramparts* magazine. Public opposition to the Vietnam War and concern for a host of other social and environmental issues were exploding, and *Ramparts* became the journal of record for the movement. Stermer developed a format using Times Roman typography with capital initials, two columns of text on the page, and centered titles and headings. The dignity and readability of classical, traditional typography thus packaged the most radical periodical of the era. It was in the use of images, which were often full-page illustrations or photographs on covers and at the beginnings of articles, that Stermer made a major contribution to graphic design. He did not commission images to illustrate the articles or topics—he used images as a separate communication to provide "information, direction, and purpose" distinct from the printed word (Fig. 22-42).

Stermer and editors Warren Hinkle, Robert Scheer, and Sol Stern came perilously close to being indicted for conspiracy as a result of the December 1967 cover design (Fig. 22-43). At a time when many young Americans were burning their Selective Service registration cards as a matter of conscience, this cover depicted

22-42

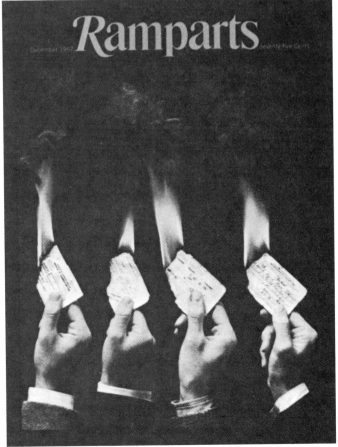

22-43

22-44

22-45

four hands holding burning facsimile draft cards of Stermer and the three editors. In a country that constitutionally guarantees freedom of speech, this may be the only case on record in which the state attempted to convict an art director and subpoenaed him to testify before a grand jury as a result of art directing. Convincing arguments by attorney Edward Bennet Williams persuaded the grand jury not to indict the four.

In contrast to the consistent format adopted by Stermer, the design of *Ms.* magazine by Bea Feitler (1938–1982) depended heavily upon a diversity of typographic style and scale to bring vitality and expression to this journal of the women's movement for equal rights and opportunities. Social conventions and standard design thinking were challenged by the *Ms.* 1972 Christmas cover (Fig. 22-44). The traditional holiday greeting, normally expressing "good will to men," is directed toward "people." The notion that magazine covers must be pictorial to attract attention is overcome by the use of close-value color. Feitler has an original approach to typography and design, depending not on consistency of style but on a finely tuned ability to make appropriate choices uninhibited by current fashion or standard typographic practice. In a single issue of *Ms.* magazine, her graphic range included fifteenth-century French Renaissance Garamond with ornamental initials, simple geometric sans serif types, and novelty and illustrated letterforms. All were carefully used to express the content of an article (Fig. 22-45). After her tenure at *Ms.,* Feitler became active as a free-lance designer of periodicals and books. She sometimes negotiated to receive book royalties in an industry where designers, unlike authors, normally work for fixed fees.

A number of currents—the conceptual approach to cover design, the role of art director expanding into editorial matters as defined by Stermer, and the growing interest in nostalgia, ephemera, and popular culture partly inspired by 1960s Pop Art—dovetailed in the work of Mike Salisbury (b. 1941), who in 1967 became the art director of *West,* the Sunday supplement of the *Los Angeles Times.* For a period of five years, until the newspaper terminated this outstanding periodical due to inadequate advertising revenue to meet production costs, Salisbury made *West* a vital expression of California culture (Fig. 22-46). The visual delights of popular artifacts, ranging from orange-crate labels to blue jeans advertising (Fig. 22-47) to customized cars, were featured in editorial spreads researched by Salisbury and designed with a combination of randomness and order in original layouts that intensified the pages of *West.*

22-44. Bea Feitler, cover for *Ms.* magazine, 1972. The lime-green typography against a fluorescent pink background projected joyously from newsstands.

22-45. Bea Feitler, pages from *Ms.* magazine, 1972. Typography and decoration are a direct expression of the content.

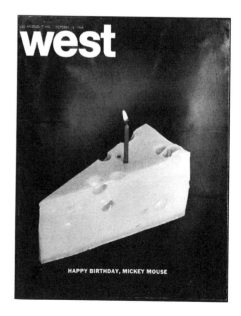

22-46. Mike Salisbury (art director) and Rod Dyer (photographer), cover for *West,* 1968. Salisbury's first conceptual cover for *West* simply presented a slice of birthday cheese for a renowned mouse.

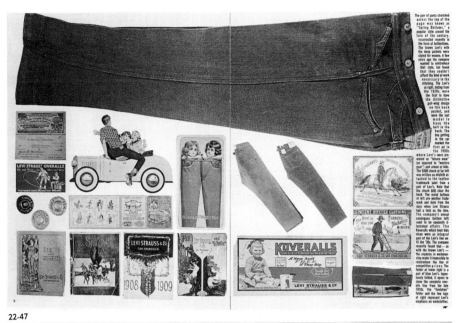

22-47

22-48

22-47. Mike Salisbury, pages from *West*, late 1960s. Here the art director became a visual historian, researching and selecting old Levi's advertisements and products for a pictorial essay.

22-48. Mike Salisbury, pages from *Rolling Stone*, 1974. Diverse typefaces are contained in shapes, plaques, and boxes. Full two-page photographs produce a lively graphic pacing.

In 1974, Salisbury redesigned the entire format of *Rolling Stone*, a rock and roll newspaper that was repositioned as a tabloid magazine. The element of surprise became Salisbury's primary design tool to give *Rolling Stone* a visual energy. Typography was used differently for each article in an issue, and the range of illustrations and photographic approaches knew no bounds. In addition to redefining *Rolling Stone*'s format, Salisbury established an uninhibited, freewheeling design approach that influenced the layout of many popular, specialized, and regional periodicals for a decade (Fig. 22-48). Salisbury also worked as a consultant designer or art director for *Oui, City,* and *New West* (Fig. 22-49). By the early 1980s, over half a billion copies of magazines had been distributed with covers or concepts created by him.

22-49. Mike Salisbury, cover for *New West*, 1979. A typographic cover about serious water-supply issues gains visual impact through the *trompe l'oeil* realism of water spilled onto the type.

The new advertising

The 1940s were a lackluster decade for advertising. A pile-driver repetition of hyperbolic slogans, movie-star testimonials, and exaggerated claims were mainstays of the decade, punctuated by occasional design excellence. On 1 June 1949, a new advertising agency, Doyle Dane Bernbach, opened its doors at 350 Madison Avenue

We regret to inform you your school stuff is ready at Ohrbach's

22-51

22-50. Bob Gage (art director), Bill Bernbach, and Judy Protas (writers), Ohrbach's advertisement, 1958. A "catty lady" discovers why a friend dresses so well on an ordinary income: She gets high fashion at low prices from Ohrbach's.

22-51. Charlie Piccirillo (art director) and Judy Protas (writer), back-to-school advertisement for Ohrbach's, 1962. Conventional seasonal clichés yield to a direct presentation of the joys and sorrows of everyday life. White space effectively focuses the reader's attention toward the headline and image on crowded newspaper pages.

in New York City with a staff of thirteen and less than half a million dollars in client accounts. Copywriter Bill Bernbach (1911–1982) was the partner with responsibility for the creative area, and his initial staff consisted of art director Bob Gage and copywriter Phyllis Robinson. Doyle Dane Bernbach "took the exclamation mark out of advertising" as they talked intelligently to consumers. Their first client was a budget department store badly in need of a fresh image (Figs. 22-50 and 22-51). For each campaign, they developed a strategy surrounding any important advantage, useful difference, or superior feature of the product. In order to break through the indifference of consumers bombarded by perpetual commercial messages, Bernbach sought an imaginative package for this information, and it is here that he made his major contribution, for words and images were combined in a new way. Traditionally, a copywriter's headline and body copy were sent to the art director, who then made a layout. In the Bernbach approach, a synergistic relationship between visual and verbal components was established. Paul Rand had developed a bellwether approach to advertising in the 1940s, integrating words and phrases in a freer organization with visual metaphors and puns seldom seen in advertising. Now, Bernbach and his colleagues smashed through the boundaries separating verbal and visual communications and evolved the visual/verbal syntax: word and image fused into a conceptual expression of an idea so that they become completely interdependent (Figs. 22-52 and 22-53).

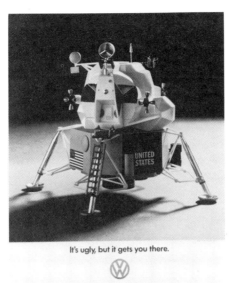

It's ugly, but it gets you there.

22-52

22-53

22-52. Helmut Krone (art director) and Julian Koenig (writer), Volkswagen advertisement, 1960. An economical car is made lovable, as conventional exaggerated claims and superlatives are replaced with straightforward facts, marketing "strange little cars with their beetle shapes" to a public used to luxury and high horsepower as status symbols.

22-53. Jim Brown (art director) and Larry Levenson (writer), Volkswagen advertisement, 1969. Appearing in newspapers all across America immediately after the lunar landing, this advertisement gained phenomenal impact from its continuity with the earlier ads. The visual link between a car and the space vehicle reinforces the concept of a homely but well-engineered, reliable vehicle.

This new advertising saw a new working relationship, as writers and art directors worked as "creative teams." In addition to Bob Gage, Bill Taubin, Helmut Krone (b. 1925), Len Sirowitz (b. 1932), and Bert Steinhauser rank among the art directors who produced outstanding creative work in collaboration with Doyle Dane Bernbach copywriters. Because concept becomes dominant, the design of many Doyle Dane Bernbach advertisements is reduced to the basic elements necessary to convey the message: a large arresting visual image, a concise headline of bold weight, and body copy that stakes its claim with factual and often entertaining writing instead of puffery and meaningless superlatives. Often the visual organization is symmetrical, for design arrangement is not allowed to distract from the straightforward presentation of an idea. Advertising stereotypes were replaced by real people from America's pluralistic society (Fig. 22-54). The potency of this approach was demonstrated when a public-service ad influenced congressional action (Fig. 22-55) and Steinhauser, the art director, received a letter from President Lyndon B. Johnson after the bill was passed.

22-54

22-55

22-54. Bill Taupin (art director) and Judy Protas (writer), subway poster, c. 1965. The stereotypes of mass communication were replaced by real people, breaking down the taboos against ethnic models during the 1960s.

22-55. Bert Steinhauser (art director) and Chuck Kollewe (writer), political action advertisement, 1967. Readers are startled by the image and challenged to participate in the political process by writing to congresspeople who voted for and against the rat-extermination bill.

Doyle Dane Bernbach became a training ground for what became called "the new advertising." Many writers and art directors who developed there participated in spin-off agencies as the boutique agency, a small shop with emphasis on creativity rather than on full marketing services, challenged the dominance of the monolithic multimillion-dollar agencies during the flowering of advertising creativity in the 1960s. The notion of the advertising superstar was fed by a proliferation of awards, competitions, professional periodicals, and annuals.

The first regular television broadcasting had started in 1941, and immediately after World War II it began its spectacular growth as an advertising medium. By the early 1960s, it became the second largest medium (after newspapers) in terms of total advertising revenue and the largest medium in major national advertising budgets. Print art directors began to turn toward the design of television commercials. At its best, this ubiquitous communication form began to expand public understanding of cinematic form, as techniques from experimental film were incorporated; at its worst, television's commercials became a bane upon the public consciousness.

Since the "new advertising" developed at the same time as the "new journalism," a spate of comparisons was inevitable. The new journalism of writers like Tom Wolfe (b. 1931) replaced journalism's traditional objectivity with subjective responses as a component part of reportage. The journalist experienced a story as a participant rather than as a dispassionate observer. By contrast, although the new advertising continued advertising's orientation toward persuasive selling techniques and subjective emotional appeals, the techniques used became more honest, literate, and tasteful. In the 1970s, advertising became increasingly involved in "positioning" products and services against their competitors, and the general level of print advertising creativity declined.

American typographic expressionism

A playful graphic design trend that began in the 1950s and continued into the 1960s among New York graphic designers was an interest in figurative typography. This took many forms—letterforms became objects, objects became letterforms. Gene Federico (b. 1919) was one of the first graphic designers who delighted in using letterforms as images (Fig. 22-56). Another approach to figurative typography used the visual properties of the words themselves, or their organization in the space, to express an idea. Don Egensteiner's "Tonnage" advertisement (Fig. 22-57) is an example of the visual organization of type taking on connotative meaning. Typography was sometimes scratched, torn, bent, and vibrated to express a concept or introduce the unexpected into the printed page.

22-56. Gene Federico (art director), advertisement for *Woman's Day,* 1953. In this double-page advertisement from the *New Yorker* magazine, the perfectly round Futura *O* provides bicycle wheels—an early example of figurative typography.

22-57. Don Egensteiner (art director), advertisement for Young and Rubicam Advertising, 1960. The heavy, one-word headline crashes into the body copy to accomplish a major communications objective: to gain attention.

Another typographic trend that began slowly in the 1950s was a reexamination of the nineteenth-century decorative and novelty typography that had been rejected for many decades under the influence of the modern movement. This revival of interest was inspired by Robert M. Jones, art director of RCA Victor Records, who established the private Glad Hand Press in 1953. Jones had a fondness for colonial and nineteenth-century printing, and exercised this interest in hundreds of pieces of graphic ephemera produced at the press. In addition, he often set typography for his record-album designs using wood type. Jones's interest inspired a revival of discarded typographic forms and a lessening of prejudice toward the decorative and outmoded.

Phototypography, the setting of type by exposing negatives of alphabet characters to photographic paper, was attempted as early as 1893 with limited results. During the 1920s, inventors in England and America moved closer to success. The year 1925 saw the quiet dawning of a new era of typography with the public announcement of the Thothmic photographic composing machine, invented by E. K. Hunter and J. R. C. August of London. A keyboard produced a punched tape to control a long, opaque master film with transparent letterforms. As a given letter moved in position in front of a lens, it was exposed to photographic paper by a beam of light. The Thothmic was the harbinger for a graphic revolution a half-century later.

Commercially viable photographic display typesetting in the United States began when the Photolettering firm was established in New York in 1936. It was headed by Edward Rondthaler (b. 1905), who had been instrumental in perfecting the

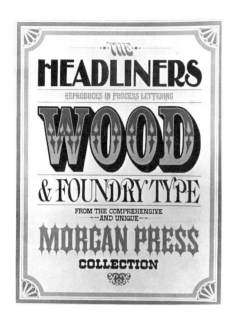

22-58. John Alcorn, cover for a phototype specimen booklet, 1964. The symmetrical mixture of decorative fonts approximates the nineteenth-century wood-type poster, but the spacing and use of color are innovative.

22-59. Herb Lubalin, typogram from a Stettler typeface announcement poster, 1965. Marriage, "the most licentious of human institutions," becomes an illustration through the joined *R*s.

22-60. Herb Lubalin (designer) and Tom Carnase (letterer), proposed publication logo, 1967. In this masterpiece of figurative typography, the ampersand enfolds and protects the "child" in a visual metaphor for motherly love.

Rutherford Photolettering Machine, which sets type by exposing film negatives of type characters onto photopaper. Although phototypography had the potential to replace the rigid quality of metal type with a dynamic new flexibility, for over two decades it was used only as an alternative method to set type, with some production advantages and disadvantages. A major advantage of phototype was a radical reduction in the cost of introducing new typestyles. The large-scale expansion of phototype during the 1960s was accompanied by new designs and reissues of old designs. A specimen book (Fig. 22-58) designed by John Alcorn (b. 1935) introduced Morgan Press nineteenth-century typefaces as phototype from Headliners Process Lettering. This was one of many phototype collections making Victorian faces widely available. Graphic designers rethought the value of supposedly outmoded forms and incorporated them in their work.

A typographic genius was needed to define the aesthetic potential of phototypography by understanding its new flexibility and exploring the possibilities it opened for graphic expression. Herb Lubalin (1918–1981), a generalist *ne plus ultra* whose achievements include advertising and editorial design, symbol and typeface design, posters and packaging, has been hailed as the typographic genius of his time. Major thrusts of American graphic design—including the visual/verbal concept orientation of Doyle Dane Bernbach and the trends toward figurative and more structured typography—unified in Lubalin's work. Space and surface became his primary visual considerations. He abandoned traditional typographic rules and practice and looked at alphabet characters as both visual form and message communication.

Discontented with the rigid limitations of metal type in the 1950s, Lubalin would cut apart his type proofs with a razor blade and reassemble them. Type was compressed until letters joined into ligatures, and enlarged to unexpected sizes; letterforms were joined, overlapped, and enlarged; capital *O*s became receptacles for images. The traditional separation between word and image collapsed for Lubalin: Words and letters could become images; images could become a word or a letter. Photographs of objects, including a rock and a bakery roll, replaced words in headlines. This typographic play engages the reader and requires participation. Lubalin practiced design not as an art form or craft created in a vacuum but as a means to give visual form to a concept or a message. In his most innovative work, concept and visual form are yoked into a oneness that has been called a *typogram*, meaning a brief, visual, typographic poem. Making type talk, Lubalin's wit and strong message orientation enabled him to transform words into ideographic typograms about the subject (Figs. 22-59 through 22-62).

When the decade of the 1960s opened, most display typography was the hand-set, cold metal type of Gutenberg's day. But this five-hundred-year-old craft was being rendered obsolete by phototype. By the end of the decade, metal type was virtually a thing of the past. More than any other graphic designer, Lubalin explored the creative potential of phototypography and how the fixed relationships of letterforms marching upon square blocks of metal could be exploded by phototype's dynamic and elastic qualities. In phototype systems, letterspacing can be compressed to extinction, and forms can overlap. A greater range of type sizes is available, and type can be set to any size required by the layout or enlarged to huge sizes without losing sharpness. Special lenses can be used to expand, condense, italicize, backslant, or outline letterforms. Lubalin incorporated these possibilities into his work—not just as technical or design ends in themselves, but as potent means to intensify the printed image and express content.

During the metal-type era, hundreds of thousands of dollars had to be invested in the deployment of a single new typestyle: Punches and matrices had to be manufactured for every size of handset and hot-metal keyboard type; then each typesetting firm had to purchase a large stock of metal type in each size and variation of roman, bold, italic, and so on to meet client requests. Phototypography reduced this process to the relatively inexpensive creation of simple film fonts, and a proliferation of typeface designs to rival the Victorian era began. Visual Graphics Corpora-

22-61. Herb Lubalin, proposed New York City logo, 1966. The isometric perspective implied by the forty-five-degree angles creates a dynamic tension between two- and three-dimensionality.

22-62. Herb Lubalin, Ice Capades logo, 1967. An ice skate and nineteenth-century engraving are evoked by this figurative and illustrative logo.

22-63. Herb Lubalin, page from *Eros*, 1962. Lubalin's design approach included overlapping or touching letterforms, compressing the space between the words, and squeezing words and images into a rectangle.

22-64. Herb Lubalin, pages from *Eros*, 1962. The pictorial essay closes with a photograph of the young president and his wife opposite a quotation from Stephen Crane, which became a chilling forewarning of Kennedy's assassination the following year.

tion, manufacturer of the Phototypositor display typesetting machine, which put excellent photodisplay type in design studios and printing firms all across America, sponsored a National Typeface Design Competition in 1965. Lubalin's posters demonstrating the dozen winning designs spurred the awareness of phototypography and its design potential. Plate 78 illustrates the poster announcing the Davida Bold typeface, with the four stanzas of the Peter Piper tongue twister sharing a common capital *P*. When his detractors wondered whether his typography suffered from a decline in legibility due to tight spacing and overlapping forms, Lubalin responded that "sometimes you have to compromise legibility to achieve impact." Lubalin was a very complete designer, whose attentiveness to detail and typographic experimentation raised other designers' typographic sensitivities, inspiring them to try new things.

Lubalin also made significant contributions in editorial design during the 1960s. A host of editorial redesigns, including two for the ill-fated *Saturday Evening Post,* accompanied his collaboration with publisher Ralph Ginzburg on a series of magazines. A hardbound quarterly journal called *Eros,* launched in 1962 with a massive, direct-mail campaign, was billed as the magazine of love. Its ninety-six-page, advertising-free format allowed Lubalin to explore scale, white space, and visual flow. In a photographic essay about President John F. Kennedy (Figs. 22-63 and 22-64), scale changes ranging from a double-page bleed photograph to pages jammed with eight or nine photographs established a lively pace. After pondering over photographic contact sheets, Lubalin designed layouts of remarkable vitality (Figs. 22-65 and 22-66). Believing that typeface selection should express content and be governed by the visual configuration of the words, Lubalin used a variety of display types in *Eros,* including giant condensed sans serifs, novelty faces, and delicate Old Style romans. Although the visual and written content of *Eros* was tame in comparison to the explicit material permitted a decade later, Ginzburg was tried and convicted of sending obscene material through the mails. After exhausting all appeals, he was imprisoned for eight months in 1972.

In 1967, Ginzburg launched *Fact* magazine featuring explosive editorial exposés of hallowed institutions and sacred cows. Lubalin's graphic treatment on a frugal production budget harbingered the restrained economics of inflationary 1970s publishing. Lacking funds to hire ten different illustrators or photographers for each issue, Lubalin commissioned one guest illustrator per issue to do all the work for a unified fee. Design economy was achieved by the standardized format using Times Roman Bold titles and Times New Roman subtitles (Fig. 22-67).

Ginzburg and Lubalin closed out the decade with the square-format *Avant*

22-63

22-64

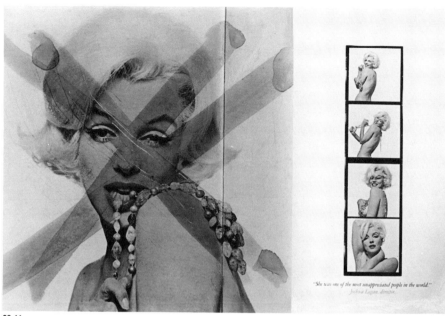

22-66

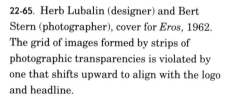

22-67

22-65. Herb Lubalin (designer) and Bert Stern (photographer), cover for *Eros,* 1962. The grid of images formed by strips of photographic transparencies is violated by one that shifts upward to align with the logo and headline.

22-66. Herb Lubalin (designer) and Bert Stern (photographer), pages from *Eros,* 1962. An expansive vitality is created by enlarging a transparency that had been crossed out with a marker by its subject, Marilyn Monroe. A totem of images from the same shooting session balances it on the opposite page.

22-67. Herb Lubalin (designer) and Etienne Delessert (illustrator), pages from *Fact,* 1967. The "illustration" for this article is symbolic restatement of the headline.

Garde, a lavishly visual periodical that published visual essays, fiction, and reportage. Born amidst the social upheavals of civil rights, women's liberation, sexual freedom, and antiwar protest, this magazine became one of Lubalin's most innovative achievements. His layouts have a strong underlying geometric structure, but this is not the classical geometry of the Basel and Zurich designers; it is the exuberant and optimistic order of the expansive American character, unencumbered by a sense of tradition or any thought of limitations that cannot be overcome (Fig. 22-68). The logotype for *Avant Garde,* composed of tightly integrated capital ligatures, was developed into a family of typefaces bearing the same name (Fig. 22-69).

By 1970, typeface design began to occupy more of Lubalin's time (Fig. 22-70). Lubalin saw the designer's task as projecting a message from a surface using three interdependent means of expression: photography, illustration, and letterforms. As time passed, his love for letterforms and the satisfaction he drew from working with them grew. Although photography and, more recently, illustration have been

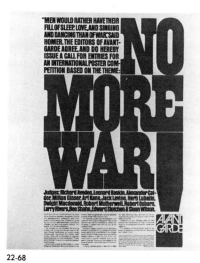

22-68

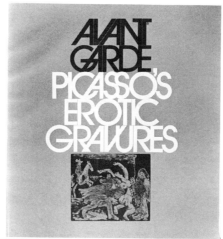

22-69

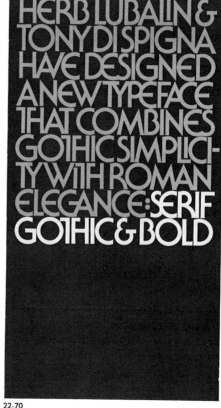

22-70

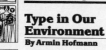

22-71

22-68. Herb Lubalin, advertisement for *Avant Garde*'s antiwar poster competition, 1967. Unity and impact, rarely achieved in purely typographic design, result from complex information being compressed into a rectangle, thereby surrounding the bright blue headline with the typographic power of brass knuckles.

22-69. Herb Lubalin (designer) and Pablo Picasso (lithographer), title page for *Avant Garde,* 1969. The *Avant Garde* logo becomes a typeface filled with extraordinary ligatures in this heading for a special issue devoted to Picasso's erotic lithographs.

22-70. Herb Lubalin and Tony DiSpigna, Serif Gothic and Bold typestyle, 1972. Despite the name, a hint of serifs appears on this somewhat rotund, geometrically constructed style. Alternate characters and capital ligatures allow spatial maneuvering and compression.

22-71. Herb Lubalin, cover for *U&lc,* 1974. Fifty-nine typographic units, seven illustrations, and sixteen rules—a total of eighty-two separate elements—are integrated into an information-filled page.

The New York School

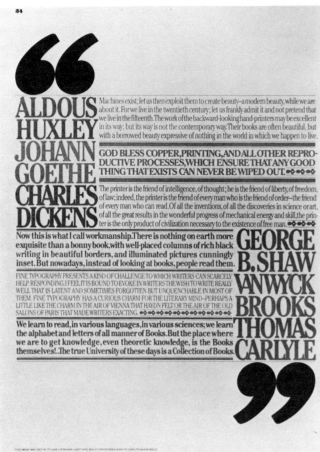

22-72

22-73

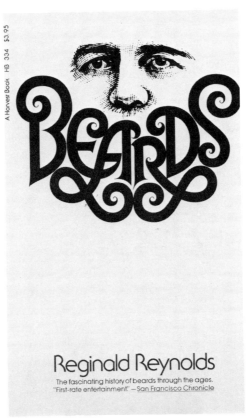

Family Circle

22-74. Herb Lubalin (art director) and Alan Peckolick (designer), *Family Circle* magazine logo, 1967. Visual alignment and overlapping create a strong unified logo from two words.

22-75. Harris Lewine (art director), Alan Peckolick (designer), and Tom Carnase (letterer), book jacket for *Beards,* 1975. Figurative typography and the Futurist concept of simultaneity are unified as the title becomes a beard.

22-75

22-72. Herb Lubalin, type specimen page from *U&lc,* 1978. A tight square of typography is bracketed by huge quotation marks in the generous margins.

22-73. Herb Lubalin, type specimen page from *U&lc,* 1978. An informal layout gains cohesiveness from the large words pinwheeling around an implied central axis.

recognized as art forms, this status still eludes typography. Perhaps the pervasive presence of alphabetic communication in industrialized cultures leads people to take type's potent aesthetic qualities for granted, and the imposition of a technical process between the mind and eye of the artist and the final work runs counter to the traditional notion of art as precious artifact.

As the design of new typefaces increased, design piracy became a vital issue. Original typeface designs requiring hundreds of hours of work could now be photo-copied by unscrupulous operators who produced instant film fonts but did not com-pensate the designers. To enable designers to be adequately compensated for their designs while licensing and producing master fonts available to all manufacturers, Lubalin joined with phototypography pioneer Edward Rondthaler and typographer Aaron Burns in establishing the International Typeface Corporation in 1970. Thirty-four fully developed type families and about sixty additional display faces were developed and licensed during ITC's first decade. As with the Helvetica fonts, emphasis was placed on a large x-height and short ascenders and descenders. With Lubalin as design director, ITC began a journal, *U&lc,* to publicize and demon-strate its typefaces. As Lubalin said, after over three decades of designing for clients, he was now his own client. The complex, dynamic style of this tabloid-size publication and the popularity of ITC typefaces had a major impact on typographic design of the 1970s (Figs. 22-71 through 22-73).

From the time that Lubalin left his position as vice president and creative direc-tor of the Sudler and Hennessey advertising agency in 1964, he formed partner-ships and associations with a number of associates, including graphic designers Ernie Smith and Alan Peckolick (b. 1940) and lettering artists Tony DiSpigna (b. 1943) and Tom Carnase. These artists have demonstrated stylistic affinities with Lubalin while achieving unique creative solutions to a diverse range of problems (Figs. 22-74 and 22-75).

George Lois

Among the young art directors and copywriters who passed through Doyle Dane Bernbach during the late 1950s, George Lois (b. 1931) became the *enfant terrible* of American mass communications. Lois's energetic efforts to sell his work, including such legendary tactics as climbing out on the three-story ledge of the A. Goodman & Company president's office demanding that his poster be accepted (Fig. 22-76), combined with a tendency to push concepts to the very limit of propriety, earned him this reputation. Lois adopted the Bernbach philosophy that fully integrated visual/verbal concepts were vital to successful message conveyance. Lois wrote that an art director must treat words "with the same reverence that he accords graph-ics, because the verbal and visual elements of modern communication are as indi-visible as words and music in a song." His designs are deceptively simple and single-mindedly direct (Figs. 22-77 through 22-79). Backgrounds are usually stripped away to enable the content-bearing verbal and pictorial images to interact unhampered, a technique he learned at Bernbach, his third agency. At age twenty-eight, he left Bernbach to cofound Papert, Koenig and Lois, which grew to $40 million per year in billing in seven short years. On three subsequent occasions, Lois left an agency partnership to form yet another advertising agency.

In 1962, *Esquire* was in serious trouble. If any two consecutive issues had lost money on newsstand sales, it would have folded. After being *the* man's magazine in America, *Esquire* was losing the younger audience to *Playboy,* founded by former *Esquire* staff member Hugh Hefner in 1960. *Esquire* editor Harold Hayes asked Lois to develop effective cover designs for the literate but nearly bankrupt maga-zine. Lois felt that design—a harmony of elements—had no place on a magazine cover. Instead, he opted for the cover as a statement that captured the reader with a spirited comment on a major article. An ability to stay closely in touch with one's times is a vital requirement for someone in visual communications, and many of Lois's most innovative concepts grew from his ability to understand and respond to the people and events of his era. Over the next decade, Lois designed over ninety-

22-76. George Lois, subway advertisement poster for Goodman's Matzos, 1960. The large-scale cracker anticipates the 1960s Pop-Art fascination with large-scale everyday objects.

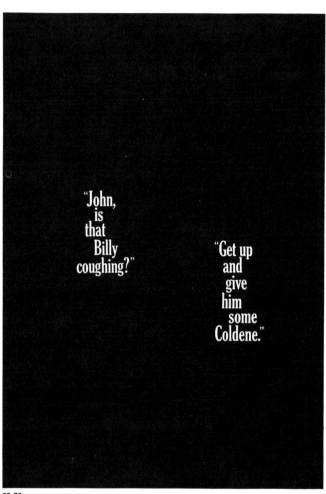

22-78

22-77. George Lois, advertisement for Allerest, 1961. Phonetic spelling and typeface selection permit type to "talk" in the voice of an allergy sufferer.

22-78. George Lois, advertisement for Coldene, 1961. In contrast to the coarse hard-sell advertising of most over-the-counter pharmaceutical products, a simple black page with twelve words becomes a midnight exchange between concerned parents.

two *Esquire* covers, mostly in collaboration with photographer Carl Fischer (b. 1924). These covers helped capture the audience, and by 1967 *Esquire* turned a $3 million profit.

Lois felt that Fischer was one of the few photographers who understood ideas. Their collaborative efforts created covers that challenged, shocked, and often provoked the audience. Unexpected combinations of images and photographic montage techniques served to intensify an event or make a satirical statement. The 24 November 1963 murder of presidential assassin Lee Harvey Oswald, witnessed by millions on television, was visualized by showing a young boy watching the event on television while eating a hamburger with a cola. The terror of the Vietnam War was presented by a solid-black cover with large, white Bodoni letters proclaiming, "Oh my God—we hit a little girl," a quotation from an article telling the "true story of M Company from Fort Dix to Vietnam."

Lois's skills in persuading people to participate in photographs resulted in powerful images. In 1968, Lois persuaded boxer Muhammad Ali, who had been stripped of his world heavyweight championship title because as a conscientious objector he refused military service, to pose for the April 1968 *Esquire* cover as Saint Sebastian, the legendary Christian martyr condemned by Roman Emperor Diocletian and shot by archers (Pl. 79). As Richard Nixon mounted his second pres-

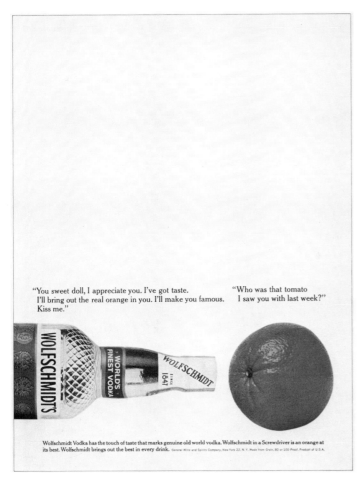

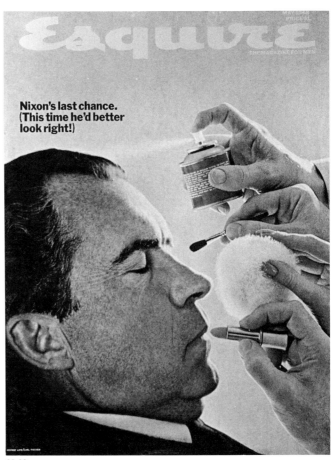

"You sweet doll, I appreciate you. I've got taste. I'll bring out the real orange in you. I'll make you famous. Kiss me."

"Who was that tomato I saw you with last week?"

Wolfschmidt Vodka has the touch of taste that marks genuine old world vodka. Wolfschmidt in a Screwdriver is an orange at its best. Wolfschmidt brings out the best in every drink. General Wine and Spirits Company, New York 22, N. Y. Made from Grain, 80 or 100 Proof. Product of U.S.A.

Nixon's last chance. (This time he'd better look right!)

22-80

22-79. George Lois, advertisement for Wolfschmidt's, 1962. Blatant symbolism and outrageous humor combine in an inventive technique. The piece also establishes continuity, for the preceding week's advertisement had featured the loquacious bottle talking to a tomato.

22-80. George Lois (designer) and Carl Fischer (photographer), *Esquire* cover, May 1968. This composite photograph of presidential candidate Richard M. Nixon being made up for a television appearance is typical of Lois's audacity.

idential campaign in 1968, Lois combined a stock photograph of the candidate with Fischer's photograph of four hands applying makeup (Fig. 22-80). This concept grew out of Lois's recollection of the 1960 presidential campaign, when Nixon lost the race to John F. Kennedy partly because Nixon's "five o'clock shadow made him look evil." After the cover ran, Lois received a call from one of Nixon's staffers, who berated Lois because the lipstick was "an attack on Nixon's masculinity." Lieutenant William Calley, placed on trial for his alleged role in the killing of over one hundred children, women, and old men in the Vietnam village of My Lai, was photographed posing with a group of oriental children for the November 1970 cover.

Born of an excitement for European modernism and fueled by economic and technological expansion, the New York School was a dominant force in graphic design from the 1940s until the 1970s, and many of its practitioners, young turks who revolutionized American mass communications in the 1940s or 1950s, continue to design in the 1990s, as their design practices reach the half-century mark.

Corporate Identity and Visual Systems

olivetti
82 Diaspron

23-1. Giovanni Pintori, poster for the Olivetti 82 Diaspron, c. 1958. A schematic diagram demonstrating the mechanical action of the typewriter key combines with a photograph of the machine to communicate two levels of information about the product.

The technological advances during World War II were staggering. After the war, productive capacity turned toward consumer goods, and many people believed that the outlook for the capitalist economic structure could be unending economic expansion and prosperity. With this bright view of the future in mind, "Good design is good business" became a rallying cry in the graphic design community during the 1950s. Prosperity and technological development appeared to be closely linked to the increasingly important corporations, and the more perceptive of these were becoming aware of the need to develop a corporate image and identity among diverse audiences. Design was seen as a major way to shape a reputation for quality and reliability.

The use of visual marks for identification has been in existence for centuries, of course. In medieval times, proprietary marks were compulsory as a means of enabling the guilds to control trade. By the 1700s, virtually every trader and dealer had a trademark or stamp. The arrival of the industrial revolution, with its mass manufacturing and marketing, caused visual identification and trademarks to gain in value and importance. But the visual identification systems that began during the 1950s went far beyond trademarks or symbols. The national and multinational scope of many corporations had made it difficult for them to maintain a cohesive image, but by unifying all communications from a given organization into a consistent design system, a cohesive image could be projected to accomplish identifiable goals.

Pintori at Olivetti

The first phase in the development of postwar visual identification resulted from pioneering efforts by strong individual designers who put their personal imprint upon a client's designed image. This was the case with Peter Behrens at AEG (see Chapter 15) and with the Olivetti Corporation, an Italian typewriter and business machines company that has had a dual commitment to humanist ideals and technological progress since its 1908 founding by Camillo Olivetti. Adriano Olivetti (1901-1970), son of the founder, became president in 1938. He had a keen sense about the contribution that graphic, product, and architectural design could make to an organization. In 1936, Olivetti hired twenty-four-year-old Giovanni Pintori (b. 1912) to join the publicity department. For a thirty-one-year period, Pintori put his personal stamp upon Olivetti's graphic images. The logotype that Pintori designed for the firm in 1947 consisted of the name in lowercase sans serif letters, slightly letterspaced. Identity was achieved not through a systematic design program but through the general visual appearance of promotional graphics.

Pintori's ability to generate graphic metaphors for technological processes is shown in a 1956 poster for the Olivetti Elettrosumma 22 (Pl. 80). An informal structure of brightly colored cubes with numerals suggests the adding and mathematical building process that takes place when using this calculating machine. There is a casual and almost relaxed quality to Pintori's organization of space. And yet even extremely complex designs have a feeling of simplicity because of his ability to combine small elements into unified structures through a repetition of size and visual rhythms. This complexity of form was well suited to Olivetti's publicity needs during the 1940s and 1950s, for the firm sought a high-technology image to promote advanced industrial design and engineering. Pintori was particularly adept at using simplified graphic shapes to visualize the mechanisms and processes (Fig. 23-1). His abstract configurations suggested the function or purpose of the product being advertised. Olivetti's corporate policy has focused upon design excellence and cultural programming, and the firm has received international recognition for its commitment to design excellence.

Design at CBS

The Columbia Broadcasting System of New York City moved to the forefront of corporate identity design as a result of two vital assets: CBS President Frank Stanton, who understood art and design and their potential in corporate affairs, and William Golden (1911–1959). As CBS art director for almost two decades, Golden brought uncompromising visual standards and keen insight into the communications process. The effectiveness of the CBS corporate identity did not depend on a regimented design program or application of a specific style to all of the corporation's communications. Rather, the quality and intelligence of each successive design solution enabled CBS to establish an ongoing and successful corporate identity.

Golden designed one of the most successful trademarks of the twentieth century for CBS (Fig. 23-2). When the pictographic CBS eye first appeared as an on-air logo on 16 November 1951, it was superimposed over a cloud-filled sky and projected an almost surreal sense of an eye in the sky. After one year, Golden suggested to Frank Stanton that they might abandon the eye and seek another logo. Stanton reminded Golden of the old adage, "Just when you're beginning to get bored with what you have done is probably the time it is beginning to be noticed by your audience." The eye remained. In applying this trademark to the corporation's multitude of printed material, from shipping labels to press releases, care and concern were used in even the most modest graphic designs. Dogmatic consistency in using the CBS trademark was not considered necessary. It was used in print with a variety of different company signatures, and Golden and his staff avoided forcing it where it did not belong. Even in printed advertising, it continues to be omitted whenever it conflicts with the rest of the design. The effectiveness of the CBS sym-

23-2. William Golden, CBS Television trademark, 1951. Two circles and two arcs construct a pictographic eye. Translucent and hovering in the sky, it symbolizes the awesome power of images projected through the air into every home.

Corporate Identity and Visual Systems

23-3. William Golden, program kit cover for Du Pont Show of the Month, 1957. Classified advertising typography is layered over the actor's face. Tight cropping and the leftward glance convey a mystery program.

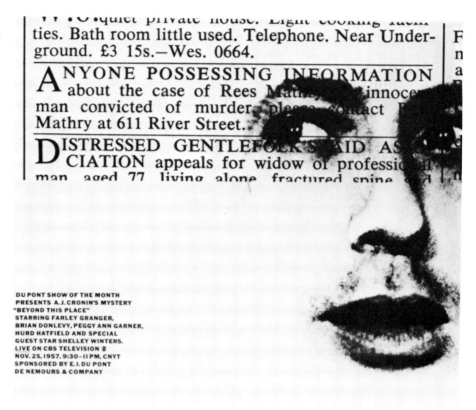

23-4. William Golden (designer) and Ben Shahn (illustrator), trade advertisement for CBS Television, 1957. Textured shopping carts and text type unify into a horizontal band. This tonal complexity contrasts with a bold headline in the white space above and the staccato repetition of the black wheels and logotype across the bottom.

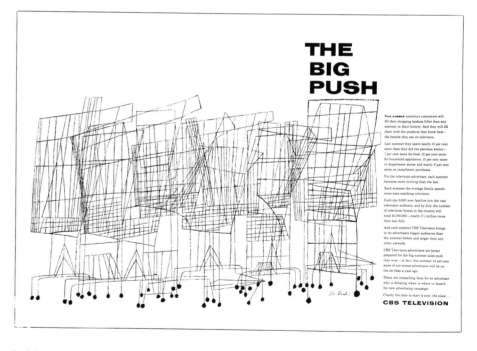

bol demonstrated to the larger management community that a contemporary graphic mark could compete successfully with traditional illustrative or alphabetic trademarks.

A corporate philosophy and approach to advertising emerged in the late 1940s and early 1950s. Advertisements for CBS Television (Figs. 23-3 and 23-4) by Golden and for CBS Radio by Lou Dorfsman (b. 1918), a young art director who joined CBS in 1946, combined simplicity of idea with a straightforward and provocative visual presentation (Figs. 23-5 through 23-8). Typography and image were arranged in well-ordered relationships using white space as a design element.

23-5

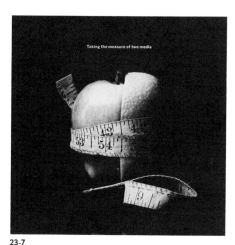

23-7

23-8

23-6

23-5. Lou Dorfsman (designer) and Andy Warhol (illustrator), program advertisement for CBS Radio, 1951. This early advertisement has the open, direct presentation typical of Dorfsman's work.

23-6. Lou Dorfsman (designer) and Edward Sorel (illustrator), advertisement for a CBS special program, 1964. To overcome the graphic jungle of the American newspaper, Dorfsman's program ads were simple and direct, but executed with distinction.

23-7. Lou Dorfsman, sales presentation cover, undated. An old adage, "It's like comparing apples and oranges"—becomes a photographic metaphor of the cost-effectiveness of two communications media.

23-8. Lou Dorfsman, advertisement for a program series, 1968. Image combination carried tremendous shock value and gained viewers for important news programs.

In a 1959 lecture at a design conference, Golden called upon designers to have a sense of responsibility and a rational understanding of the function of their work. He declared the word *design* to be a verb, "in the sense that we design something to be communicated to someone," and added that the designer's primary function is ensuring that the message is accurately and adequately communicated. Painters including Feliks Topolski, René Bouche, and Ben Shahn were commissioned to create illustrations for CBS advertisements. The climate of creative freedom encouraged them to accept these commissions and resulted in a high artistic level relative to newspaper and trade publication advertisements of the period. A classic example of this approach is the 1957 "The Big Push" (Fig. 23-4), which appeared in business and advertising trade publications during a booming economy. The text reveals that Americans will purchase more than in any other summer in history, and recommends television advertising during this big summer sales push. The provocative headline, amplified by Shahn's drawing, lends dignity and taste to the commercial message.

Stanton's recognition of the importance of design resulted in designers being given executive and administrative authority. In 1951, Golden was named creative director in charge of advertising and sales promotion for the CBS Television Network, and in 1954, Dorfsman was named director of advertising and promotion for the CBS Radio Network. Because the advertising was created by internal graphic designers instead of by advertising agencies, a unified approach between advertising and other graphics was maintained.

After Golden's sudden death at age forty-eight, Dorfsman became the creative director of CBS Television. As art director of the CBS Radio Network during the 1950s, he had forged a design approach that combined a pragmatic sense of effective communication with intuitive and imaginative problem solving. Dorfsman advocated no single philosophic use of certain typefaces, spatial layouts, or the same illustrative and photographic approaches; rather, his overall quality of problem solving and standards of visual organization during four decades with CBS enabled him to project an exemplary image for the corporation. Dorfsman was named director of design for the entire CBS Corporation in 1964, and vice president in 1968, in

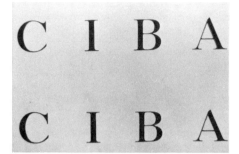

23-9. CIBA design staff, corporate identity program, 1953–1960. A graphic consistency in trademark use resulted because each new application was kept consistent with all previous ones.

keeping with Stanton's philosophy that design is a vital area that should be managed by professionals.

Eero Saarinen (1910–1961) designed a new CBS headquarters building in 1966, and Dorfsman designed all aspects of the typographic information, right down to the numerals on the wall clocks, numbers on elevator buttons, exit signs, and elevator-inspection certificates. These last two items required Fire Department and City Building Inspection approval before they could replace their mandatory but graphically inferior predecessors. Dorfsman has also applied his graphic design sense to film, computer animation in the production of promotional spots, informational materials, and network title sequences. The CBS approach to corporate image and design is not dependent on a system or style, but on the management policy toward design and the creative abilities of its design personnel. The strength of this approach is a varying and dynamic corporate design that can shift with company needs and evolving sensibilities; the potential danger is that, if management or design authority move into less insightful hands, there is no fallback position.

The CIBA corporate design program

An early effort toward a comprehensive international corporate design program was launched by CIBA—the Society for Chemical Industry in Basel—which had grown from a small manufacturer of brilliant chemical dyes into a global chemicals, plastics, and pharmaceuticals firm in the early 1950s. In mid-1951, James K. Fogleman (b. 1919) was hired as design director of an American subsidiary, CIBA Pharmaceutical Products Incorporated of Summit, New Jersey, and he began to evolve a design program. The lengthy corporate name was reduced to CIBA, consistently printed in an outline Egyptian type style. A range of three typefaces was used for product identification; Fogleman believed that this variety of style and weight was necessary for design flexibility. In 1953, he persuaded CIBA in Summit to adopt a standardized, square format for promotional material. In addition to the recognition value of the infrequently used shape, economics was a key factor in its adoption—artwork could be used throughout a series, and gang runs of promotional materials for several products significantly reduced production costs.

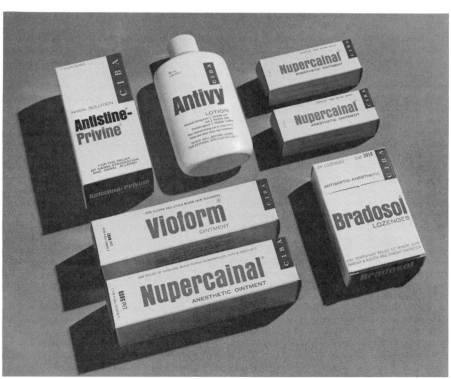

23-10

In a talk before a 1953 international conference of CIBA employees, Fogleman spoke of the "need for integrated design, or a controlled visual expression of corporate personality, which plays a large role in achieving *corporate identity*." Speaking before the management committee in Basel, he called for "a sense of unity, clarity or singleness of viewpoint," and argued that "policies are necessary which will, after a period, tie together into a unified or corporate expression of the company's character and personality." CIBA's Basel headquarters became concerned about the need for a uniform corporate identity, and a logo designed by Fritz Beuhler of Basel was selected for international use. The initials *C I B A* were letterspaced to about the width of the capital height in transitional-style letterforms.

The importance of the CIBA program was not in the logo but in the almost programmatic consistency with which it was applied to packaging, stationery, signage, promotional graphics, and vehicles (Figs. 23-9 and 23-10). Fogleman popularized the corporate-image concept through frequent lectures and writing. He urged his audiences to see each communication, including advertising, as having two functions: the immediate communicative need (to promote a particular product or identify a plant, for example), and the development of a firm's reputation and image, which may be the more important function in the long run.

The New Haven Railroad design program
A short-lived but highly visible effort at corporate identity occurred in 1954, when Patrick McGinnis, president of the New York, New Haven, and Hartford Railroad, launched a corporate design program. The New Haven Railroad was in the midst of a technological updating with new engines, cars, and signal systems. McGinnis felt that a contemporary logo and design program, replacing the old logotype and olive-green/Tuscan-red color scheme, would enable the firm to project a modern and progressive image to industry and passengers. Herbert Matter was commissioned to design the new trademark. He developed a geometric capital *N* above an *H* and a red, black, and white color scheme (Fig. 23-11). The traditional industrial feeling of slab-serif type, long associated with the railroad industry, was updated to project a curiously modern feeling due to the mathematical harmony of parts.

Marcel Breuer was commissioned to design the interiors and exteriors of the new trains. Using Matter's color scheme and logo, Breuer designed a passenger train that looked like a Russian Constructivist painting roaring along the New Haven's 1,700 miles of track. The dingy gray and earth tones previously used for freight cars were replaced by solid red or black. Plans called for implementation of a comprehensive corporate identity program encompassing everything from stations to matchbooks, but the commuter railroad developed financial woes and suffered from a consumer uprising in protest of late trains, poor scheduling, and rising fares. On 20 January 1956, McGinnis resigned as president and the corporate identity program came to a screeching halt. The new management continued to apply the logo and color scheme whenever possible. Printed pieces designed by Matter offered a degree of guidance, and the strength of the logo and color scheme provided some semblance of continuity.

Corporate identification comes of age
While World War II left most industrial countries devastated, the manufacturing capacity of the United States escaped undamaged. An era of unprecedented industrial expansion took place, with large corporations playing an important role in developing and marketing products and services. During the 1950s and 1960s, many American designers—including Paul Rand, Lester Beall, Saul Bass, and design firms such as Lippencott & Marguiles and Chermayeff & Geismar—embraced corporate visual identification as a major design activity.

After playing a pivotal role in the evolution of American editorial and advertising design during the 1940s and early 1950s, Paul Rand became more involved in trademark design and visual identification systems in the 1950s. Rand realized that to be functional over a long period of time, a trademark should be reduced to

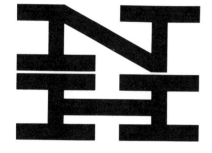

23-11. Herbert Matter, New York, New Haven, and Hartford Railroad trademark, 1954. The mathematical harmony of parts demonstrates how alphabetic forms can be unified into a unique gestalt.

23-10. CIBA design staff, CIBA pharmaceutical packaging system, 1956–1960. Typeface selection, symbol placement, spatial division, and color were used consistently, creating a unified corporate image.

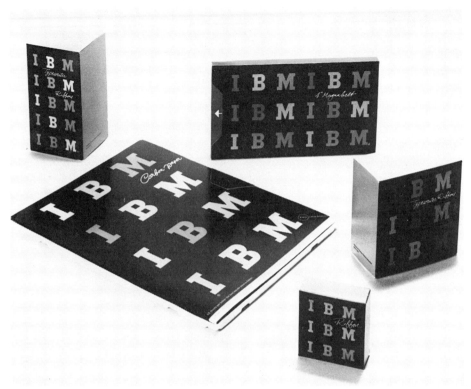

IBM IBM
IBM IBM
IBM IBM

23-12. Paul Rand, IBM trademark, 1956. Here is the original design, along with outline versions and the eight- and thirteen-stripe versions currently being used.

23-13. Paul Rand, IBM package designs, late 1950s. A strong corporate identification was produced by a repeat pattern of blue, green, and magenta capital letters on the black package fronts; white handwritten product names, and blue package tops and sides.

elementary shapes that are universal, visually unique, and stylistically timeless.

Rand's trademark for International Business Machines (Fig. 23-12) was developed from an infrequently used typeface called City Medium, designed by Georg Trump in 1930. This is a geometrically constructed slab-serif typeface designed along similar lines as the geometric sans serif styles. Redesigned into the IBM corporate logo, a powerful and unique alphabet image emerged, for the slab serifs and square negative spaces in the *B* lent a unity and uniqueness. In the 1970s, Rand updated the logo by striping it to unify the three forms and evoke scan lines on video terminals. Package designs by Rand show the application of the logo in the 1950s (Fig. 23-13) and after its redesign in the 1970s (Fig. 23-14).

Eliot Noyes, IBM's consulting design director during the late 1950s, wrote that the IBM design program sought "to express the extremely advanced and up-to-date nature of its products. To this end we are not looking for a theme but for a consistency of design quality which will in effect become a kind of theme, but a very flexible one." The IBM design program was flexible enough to avoid stifling the creativity of designers working within the guidelines of the program. The model developed by IBM, with design consultants such as Rand and internal staff design departments whose managers have authority for maintaining the corporate visual identity, has produced an evolving design program while maintaining a continuing level of quality.

23-14. Paul Rand, IBM package design, 1975. After two decades, the original packaging design program was replaced by an updated design using the eight-stripe logo.

After a 1959 study of the "public faces" of the Westinghouse Corporation, a decision was made to redesign its "Circle-W" trademark. Rand was commissioned to symbolically incorporate the nature of the company's business in a new mark that would be simple, memorable, and distinct (Fig. 23-15). General graphic forms, rather than specific signs or symbols, suggest Westinghouse products by evoking wires and plugs, electronic diagrams and circuitry, and molecular structures. Rand also developed a typeface for Westinghouse and applied these new elements to packaging, signage, and advertising.

Rand's 1965 redesign of the trademark for the American Broadcasting Company (Fig. 23-16) reduced the information to its simple essence while achieving a memo-

23-15. Paul Rand, Westinghouse trademark, 1960. This design, evocative of electronic diagrams and circuitry, is depicted as it might be constructed in an animated film sequence.

23-16. Paul Rand, American Broadcasting Company trademark, 1965. The continuing legacy of the Bauhaus and Herbert Bayer's universal alphabet informs this trademark, in which each letterform is reduced to its most elemental configuration.

23-17. Paul Rand, NeXT trademark, 1986. The four-letter name is separated into two lines to, in Rand's words, "startle the viewer" and give a common word an uncommon image. The black box at a twenty-eight-degree angle signifies the Next computer, which is a black box.

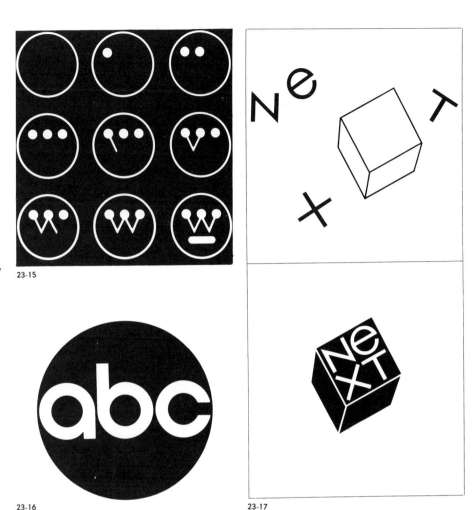

23-15

23-16

23-17

rable and unique image. The NeXT computer logo (Fig. 23-17) was designed in 1986, after IBM agreed to "loan" its long-time design consultant to a competitive computer company.

The annual report to stockholders, a legal publication required by Federal law, evolved from a dry financial report into a major communications instrument during the postwar period. Landmarks in this evolution include the IBM annual reports designed by Rand during the late 1950s. The 1958 IBM annual report (Fig. 23-18) established a standard and style for corporate literature, using graphic design to express advanced technology and organizational efficiency. Los Angeles designer Robert Miles Runyan also played a major role in redefining this genre, notably in his 1959 Litton Industries annual report (Fig. 23-19), which created an elegant editorial environment for the client's message through the use of large symbolic photographs.

Lester Beall helped launch the modern movement in American design during the late 1920s and early 1930s (see Figs. 20-5 and 20-6, and Pls. 63 and 64). During the last two decades of his career, Beall did pioneering corporate identity programs for many corporations, including Martin Marietta, Connecticut General Life Insurance, and International Paper Company. Beall contributed to the development of the corporate identity manual, a firm's book of guidelines and standards for implementing its program. Beall's manuals specifically prescribed the permissible uses and forbidden abuses of the trademark. If a plant manager in a small town retained a sign painter to paint the trademark and name on a sign, for example, the corporate design manual specified the exact proportions and placement. In discussing his mark for International Paper Company, one of the largest paper manufacturers in the world, Beall wrote, "Our assignment was to provide management with a strong mark that could be readily adapted to an immense variety of applica-

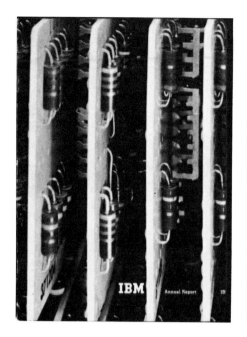

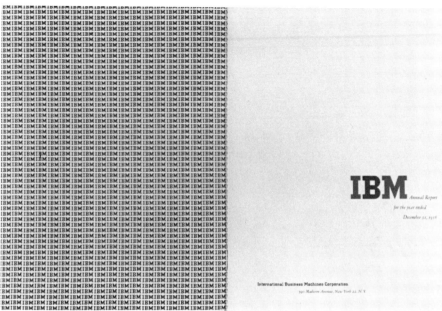

23-18. Paul Rand, IBM annual report, 1958. Influential design qualities here include close-up photography of electronic components that almost become abstract patterns, simple dramatic photographs of products and people, and a typographic system combining clarity with restrained elegance.

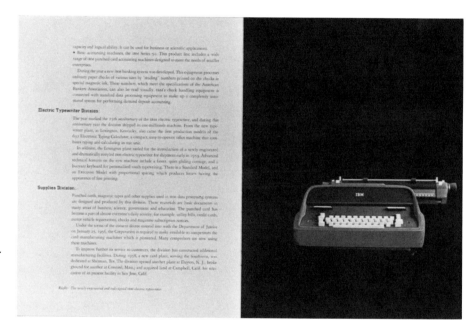

23-19. Robert Miles Runyan (designer) and Ovid Neal (photographer), Litton Industries annual report cover and interior pages, 1959. An editorial ambience is produced by full-color, bleed, still-life photographs showing Litton products with artifacts signifying areas of corporate activity.

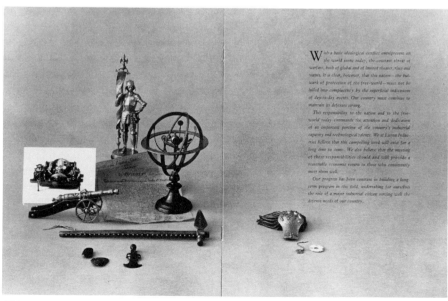

23-19

23-20. Lester Beall, International Paper Company trademark, 1960. Initials, tree, and upward arrow combine in a mark whose fundamental simplicity—an isometric triangle in a circle—assures a timeless harmony.

23-21. Lester Beall, International Paper Company trademark, 1960. For a forest-products company, stenciling the mark on a tree is one of numerous applications that must be considered.

23-22. Lester Beall, International Paper Company packaging, 1960. Used in repeated patterns, the mark becomes a decorative element.

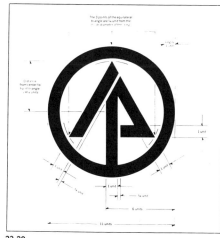

23-20

23-21

tions. This ranged from its bold use on the barks of trees to its intricate involvement in repeat patterns, carton designs, labels, trucks [Figs. 23-20 through 23-24]. In addition to its functional strength, the new mark is a powerful force in stimulating and integrating divisional and corporate identity with positive psychological effects on human relations." The International Paper Company trademark was controversial in the design community when it first appeared: The letters *I* and *P* are distorted to make a tree symbol, and critics questioned whether letterforms should be altered to this extreme. The continuing viability of this mark since its inception indicates that Beall's critics were overly cautious.

Chermayeff & Geismar Associates moved to the forefront of the corporate identification movement in 1960 with a comprehensive visual image program for The Chase Manhattan Bank of New York. Chase Manhattan's new logo was composed of four geometric wedges rotating around a central square to form an external octagon (Fig. 23-25). It was an abstract form unto itself, free from alphabetic, pictographic, or figurative connotations. Although it does have general overtones of security or protection because the four elements confine the square, this trademark demonstrated that a completely abstract form could successfully function as a visual identifier for a large organization. A distinctive sans serif typeface was designed for use with the logo. The selection of an expanded letter grew out of Chermayeff & Geismar's study of the client's design and communications needs. Urban signage, for instance, is often seen by pedestrians at extreme angles, but an

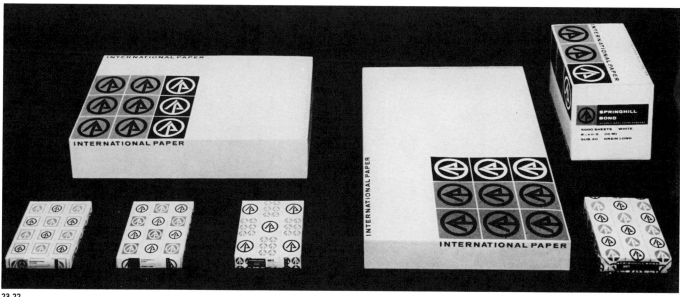

23-22

Corporate Identity and Visual Systems

23-23

23-24

23-23. Lester Beall, International Paper Company truck, 1960. Transportation applications extend the identity program throughout the society.

23-24. Lester Beall, International Paper Company sign, 1960. Workmen fabricate a large scale illuminated sign.

23-25. Chermayeff & Geismar Associates, The Chase Manhattan Bank corporate identity program, 1960. Consistent use of the trademark, color, and new typeface began to build recognition value through the process of visual redundancy.

23-26. Chermayeff & Geismar Associates, typeface and signage for The Chase Manhattan Bank, 1960. Architectural signage requires attention to the texture and surface of building materials, integration of signage and architectural form, and the effects of distance and viewing angle upon legibility.

extended letterform retains its character recognition even when viewed under these conditions (Fig. 23-26). The uncommon presence of the expanded sans serif form in the Chase Manhattan corporate design system launched a fashion for this kind of letterform during the first half of the 1960s. Consistency and uniformity in the application of both logo and letterform enabled redundancy, in a sense, to become a third identifying element.

The Chase Manhattan Bank corporate identification system became a prototype for the genre. It led many corporate managers to seriously evaluate their corporate image and the need for an effective and unique visual identifier. The rapid recognition value gained by the Chase Manhattan mark indicated that a successful logo could, in effect, become an additional character in the inventory of symbolic forms that every person carries mentally. Tom Geismar observed that a symbol must be memorable and have "some barb to it that will make it stick in your mind." At the

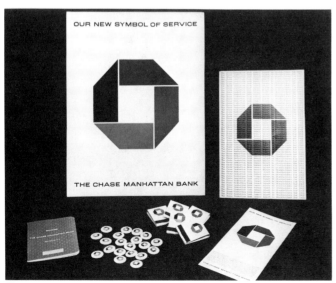

23-25

23-26

23-28

23-27. Chermayeff & Geismar Associates, Mobil Oil trademark, 1964. The old pictorial trademark, a red flying horse, was replaced by a simple and direct presentation of a memorable word.

23-28. Chermayeff & Geismar Associates, Mobil service station exhibition, c. 1968. A predominance of cylinder forms and a thematic repetition of circular bands brings design order to a type of retail outlet long noted for visual pollution and clutter.

same time, it must be "attractive, pleasant, and appropriate. The challenge is to combine all those things into something simple."

One of Chermayeff & Geismar's most far-reaching corporate design programs was for Mobil Oil, a multinational corporation operating in over a hundred countries. The trademark (Fig. 23-27), executed in an elemental geometric sans serif typeface, is the ultimate in simplicity. The word *Mobil* is executed in five vertical strokes, the angle of the *M,* and two circles. The name became the trademark, with the round, red *O* separating this word from the visual presentation of other words. This emphasis on the circle is projected as a visual theme throughout the identification program and in the design of Mobil gas stations (Fig. 23-28).

Chermayeff & Geismar have produced over one hundred corporate design programs, including the trademarks illustrated in Figure 23-29. In addition to corporate identification, Chermayeff & Geismar have developed innovative exhibition techniques, one of which they call the "supermarket principle." A large variety of objects are clustered in a manner that will communicate an insight. At the 1976 Nation of Nations exhibition in Washington, D.C., installed for the United States Bicentennial, for example, an exhibition of diverse spinning wheels brought to America from European countries communicated the cultural variety and diversity of the people who ventured across an ocean seeking a better life. By stacking illu-

23-29. Chermayeff & Geismar Associates, trademarks for (left to right, top row to bottom) The American Film Institute, 1964; Time Warner, 1990; the American Revolution Bicentennial, 1971; Screen Gems, 1966; Burlington Industries, 1965; the National Broadcasting Company, 1986; Rockefeller Center, 1985; and the National Aquarium in Baltimore, 1979.

Corporate Identity and Visual Systems

AT&T

AT&T

CELANESE

CONTINENTAL AIRLINES

GIRL SCOUTS

MINOLTA

UNITED

United Way

WARNER COMMUNICATIONS

YWCA

23-30

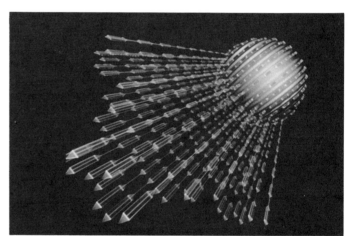

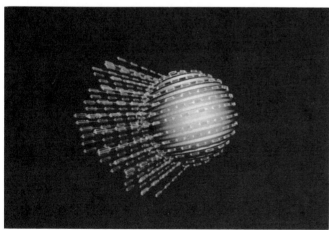

23-31. Saul Bass & Associates, AT&T computer-graphics animation identification tag, 1984. A spinning globe gathers electronic bits of information, then transforms into the AT&T trademark.

minated logos and signs identifying several American corporations in many foreign countries and languages, the concept of global trade was projected. Chermayeff & Geismar continue to accept a steady stream of smaller projects, such as posters, requiring immediate, innovative solutions. The evolution of an "office style" is rejected in favor of allowing the solution to evolve from the problem.

Saul Bass's mastery of elemental form (see Figs. 22-17 through 22-21) was applied to visual identification problems as his firm—Saul Bass & Associates, later

23-30. Saul Bass & Associates, trademarks for (left to right, top row to bottom) AT&T (Bell), 1969; AT&T (Globe), 1984; Celanese, 1965; Continental Airlines, 1965; Girl Scouts, 1978; Minolta, 1980; United Airlines, 1974; United Way, 1972; Warner Communications, 1974; and YWCA, 1988.

renamed Saul Bass/Herb Yeager & Associates—produced iconic and often widely imitated trademarks. Bass believes that a trademark must be readily understood yet possess elements of metaphor and ambiguity that will attract the viewer again and again. Many Bass trademarks have become important cultural icons (Fig. 23-30). Within two years after Bass redesigned the Bell Telephone System bell trademark, its recognition rose from 71 to over 90 percent of the public. After the AT&T long-distance telephone network was split from the local Bell system telephone companies in 1984, Bass designed a new mark that repositioned the firm from "the national telephone system" to "a global communications company" with information bits circling the globe. This concept was expressed in computer-graphics animation as the identification tag for AT&T television commercials (Fig. 23-31).

Programmed visual identification systems
The impetus of the International Typographic Style and the visual identity movement joined together during the 1960s with the development of highly systematic design programs planned to combine complex and diverse parts into a unified whole. The 1962 Lufthansa German Airlines identification system, conceived and produced at the Ulm Institute of Design, is a prototype. The principles of the International Typographic Style were extended into a design program addressing all visual communication needs of a large corporation. This program was designed by Otl Aicher in collaboration with Tomas Gonda (1926–1988), Fritz Querengässer, and Nick Roericht. The working premise was that an extensive organization could achieve a uniform, and thus significant, corporate image by systematic arrangement and use of constant elements. A flying crane image in use since the 1930s was retained but enclosed in a circle and used in a manner subordinate to the name *Lufthansa* in a consistent letterspacing arrangement (Fig. 23-32). The air-freight service combined the crane icon with an isometric package and bold lines to create an arrow configuration (Fig. 23-33). Standardization reduced paper formats to an economical number. Grid systems (Fig. 23-34) and detailed typographic specifications were worked out to take into account every visual communications need, from foodservice packaging to timetables and aircraft identification. A blue and yellow color scheme was applied throughout. Uniforms, packaging, the character of photographs to be used in ads and posters, and aircraft interiors and exteriors were all addressed by this massive system (Fig. 23-35). The Lufthansa corporate identity program became an international prototype for the closed identity system with every detail and specification addressed for absolute uniformity.

23-32. Otl Aicher in collaboration with Tomas Gonda, Fritz Querengässer, and Nick Roericht, pages from the Lufthansa corporate identity manual, 1962. Every typographic detail was systematically determined.

23-33. Otl Aicher in collaboration with Tomas Gonda, Fritz Querengässer, and Nick Roericht, page from the Lufthansa corporate identity manual, 1962. The supercargo double trademark gains unity through consistent line weight.

23-32

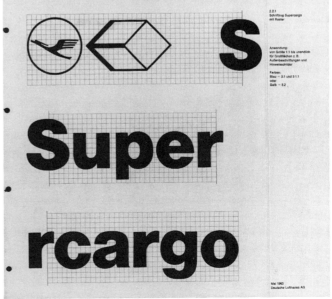

23-33

Corporate Identity and Visual Systems

23-34. Otl Aicher in collaboration with Tomas Gonda, Fritz Querengässer, and Nick Roericht, page from the Lufthansa corporate identity manual, 1962. Every publications possibility was anticipated by a series of carefully constructed grid formats.

23-35. Otl Aicher in collaboration with Tomas Gonda, Fritz Querengässer, and Nick Roericht, aircraft identification from the Lufthansa corporate identity manual, 1962. Color and insignia become standardized.

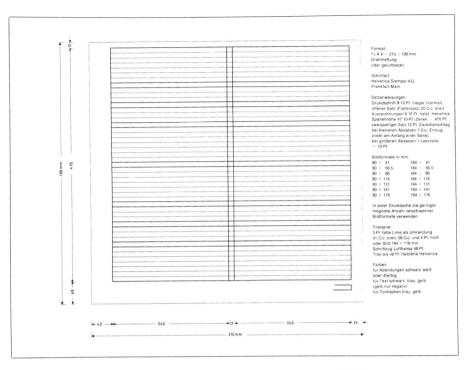

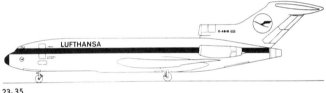

23-35

23-36. Ralph Eckerstrom, trademark for Container Corporation of America, 1957. A flat image becomes an isometric optical illusion, signifying packaging while provoking visual interest.

Container Corporation became an early advocate of systematic corporate identity in the 1960s. A new corporate logo (Fig. 23-36) had been developed by the design staff under design director Ralph Eckerstrom. The corporate initials were packaged in a rectangle with two corners shaved at a forty-five-degree angle to imply an isometric box. Eckerstrom stated the requirements of a corporate identification program: "As a function of management, design must be an integrated part of overall company operation and directly related to the company's business and sales activities. It must have continuity as a creative force. It must reflect total corporate character. Unless it meets these requirements, the company image it seeks to create will never coalesce into a unified whole, but will remain a mosaic of unrelated fragments."

John Massey (b. 1931), who joined Container Corporation in 1957, became the director of design in 1964. Under his direction, corporate design and the International Typographic Style merged. Visual identification and systems design in general—and design in Chicago in particular—were broadly influenced. Massey adopted Helvetica as the corporate typeface, and developed standardized grids for all signage and publications. A strong advocate of design consistency and unity, Massey used thematic and visual continuity in such diverse communications materials as the annual report to stockholders and trade advertising as early as 1961. The Great Ideas of Western Man advertising campaign, which had undergone pendulum swings of typographic style during the 1950s, entered a two-decade period of typographic continuity.

In 1966, Container Corporation established the Center for Advanced Research in Design, an independent design studio that worked on advanced and experimental projects and received commissions from other organizations. For example, the center developed a comprehensive visual identification system for Atlantic Richfield, a major oil company whose name changed to Arco.

Active as a painter and printmaker, Massey explores "geometric patterns and

23-37. John Massey, and other Container Corporation of America staff designers, including Jeff Barnes, Bill Bonnell, and Joe Hutchcroft, publication covers and calendars, 1966–1978. Graphics from two decades show consistency and excellence in the corporate design program.

volumes as they relate to the order of the universe." This sense of order, and the bringing of a wholeness to a sphere of activity, strongly informed Massey's work as a corporate design manager, as evidenced in Container Corporation publications (Fig. 23-37). Container Corporation was purchased by Mobil Oil in 1976, then sold to the Jefferson Smurfit company in 1986. Decentralized and lacking an autonomous identity, Container Corporation's era as a design patron drifted to a close.

Unimark, an international design firm that grew to 402 employees in forty-eight design offices around the world, was founded in Chicago in 1965 by a group of partners including Ralph Eckerstrom, James Fogleman, and Massimo Vignelli (b. 1931). Unimark rejected individualistic design and believed that design could be a system, a basic structure set up so that other people could implement it effectively. The basic tool for this effort was the grid, standardizing all graphic communications for dozens of large Unimark clients, including Alcoa, Ford Motor Company, JCPenney, Memorex, Panasonic, Steelcase, and Xerox. Helvetica was the preferred typeface for all Unimark visual identity systems, because it was believed to be the most legible. Objectivity was Unimark's goal as it spread a generic conformity across the face of multinational corporate communications. The design programs it created were rational and so rigorously systematized that they became virtually foolproof as long as the standards were maintained.

The graphic excellence of Unimark design programs can be seen in the Knoll program (Fig. 23-38), directed by Massimo Vignelli, who was Unimark's Director of Design and headed the New York office. This program set the standard for furniture-industry graphics for years to come. But Unimark's far-flung design empire—with offices in major North American cities, England, Australia, Italy, and South Africa—was vulnerable to the effects of recession in the early 1970s, and a retrenchment process began.

Corporate Identity and Visual Systems

23-38. Massimo Vignelli and the Unimark New York office staff, Knoll Graphics, 1966–1970s. Knoll is renowned for its furniture designs, so the graphic program projected an appropriate image of a design-oriented company.

23-39. Vignelli Associates, cover designs for *Skyline* magazine, 1979. Dividing space into bands of information and using large-scale type—here as a metaphor for the New York skyline—are important aspects of the Vignelli vocabulary.

23-39

The Unimark philosophy continued as its founders and the legion of designers they trained continued to implement its ideals. When the New York office closed, Vignelli Associates was founded by Massimo and Lella Vignelli in 1971. Their typographic range expanded beyond Helvetica to include such classical faces as Bodoni, Century, Garamond, and Times Roman, but the rational order of grid systems and emphasis upon lucid and objective communication remained a constant (Fig. 23-39) as Vignelli continued to put his imprint upon the evolution of information design.

23-40. John Massey, trademark for the U.S. Department of Labor, 1974. By striping the *L* forms, Massey expressed the American flag's stars and stripes.

The Federal Design Improvement Program

In May 1974, the United States Government initiated the Federal Design Improvement Program in response to a growing awareness of design as an effective tool for achieving objectives. This was coordinated by the Architectural and Environmental Arts Program (later renamed the Design Arts Program) of the National Endowment for the Arts. All aspects of federal design, including architecture, interior space planning, landscaping, and graphic design, were upgraded under the program. The Graphics Improvement Program, under the direction of Jerome Perlmutter, set forth to improve the quality of visual communications and the ability of governmental agencies to communicate effectively to citizens. The prototype federal graphic standards system was designed by John Massey for the Department of Labor. Problems identified by this case study included outmoded, unresponsive, and impersonal images, a lack of uniform and effective communications policies, and insufficient image continuity. Massey's goals for the new design program were "uniformity of identification; a standard of quality; a more systematic and economic template for publication design; a closer relationship between graphic design (as a means) and program development (as an end) so that the proposed graphics system will become an effective tool in assisting the department to achieve program objectives."

A graphic standards manual established a cohesive system for visual identification and publication formats. Standards for format sizes, typography, grid systems, paper specifications, and colors realized tremendous economies in material and time. These standards, however, were carefully structured so that the creativity and responsiveness to each communications project would not be seriously hampered. With the mechanics of the printing and format predetermined, Department of Labor staff designers were able to devote their time to the creative aspects of the problem at hand.

The Department of Labor communications mark (Fig. 23-40) is composed of two interlocking letter *L*s, forming a diamond configuration around a star. A set of publication format sizes provided economy of production and minimized paper waste, while a series of grid systems and uniform typographic specifications for these publication formats ensured consistency (Fig. 23-41). Routine printed materials, including stationery, envelopes, and forms, were given standardized formats.

23-41. John Massey, typographic cover format from the U.S. Department of Labor graphic standards manual, 1974. Standard formats bring economy and efficiency to the design process.

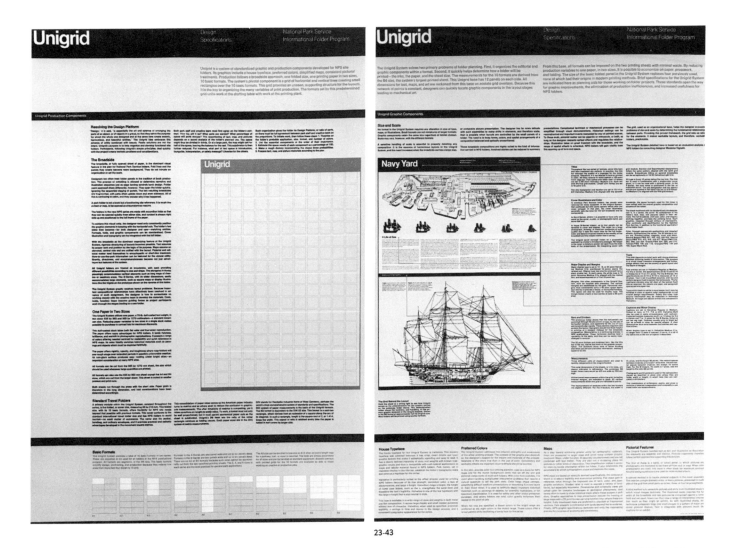

23-43

23-42. Massimo Vignelli (consulting designer), Vincent Gleason (art director), and Dennis McLaughlin (graphic designer), Unigrid system for the National Park Service, 1977. Design specifications for the Unigrid system and standard formats are presented on a large broadside.

23-43. Massimo Vignelli (consulting designer), Vincent Gleason (art director), and Dennis McLaughlin (graphic designer), Unigrid system for the National Park Service, 1977. The reverse side of the material shown in Figure 23-42 demonstrates and specifies all graphic components on a sample broadside.

Over forty different federal departments and agencies initiated visual identification programs, and many of the leading designers in America were called upon to develop them. One of the most successful is the *Unigrid* system, developed in 1977 for the United States National Park Service by Vignelli Associates in collaboration with the Park Service Division of Publications headed by Vincent Gleason.

The Unigrid (Figs. 23-42 and 23-43) unified the hundreds of informational folders used at about 350 national park locations. It is based on exquisitely simple basic elements: ten format sizes, all derived from the Unigrid; broadside or full-sheet presentation of the folders, instead of layouts structured on folded panels; black title bands with park names serving as logotypes; horizontal organization of illustrations, maps, and text; standardized typographic specifications; and a master grid coordinating design in the studio with production at the printing plant. A single white dull-coated paper in a standard size is used, allowing economical carload purchases. Typography is restricted to Helvetica and Times Roman in a limited number of sizes and weights.

The standardized format of the Unigrid enables the Park Service publications staff to focus upon achieving excellence in the development and presentation of pictorial and typographic information (Fig. 23-44). The program proved so successful that a format was also developed for the Park Service's series of 150 handbooks. The Unigrid's continued vitality and effectiveness prove the value of design systems for large organizations.

To attract outstanding architects and designers to governmental service, traditional civil service procedures were supplemented by portfolio reviews conducted by professionals. Designers were recruited by a publicity campaign with the theme,

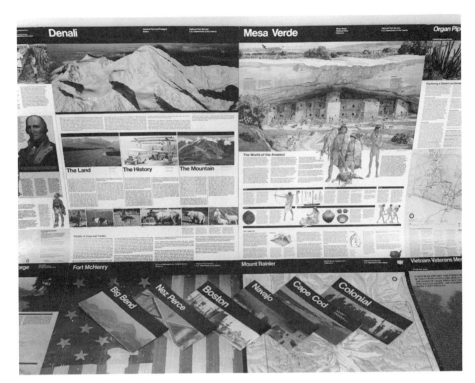

23-44. National Park Service publications staff, including Vincent Gleason (chief), and designers Melissa Cronyn, Nicholas Kirilloff, Dennis McLaughlin, Linda Meyers, Phillip Musselwhite, and Mitchell Zetlin, publications created with the Unigrid, 1977–1990.

23-44. National Park Service publications staff, including Vincent Gleason (chief), and designers Melissa Cronyn, Nicholas Kirilloff, Dennis McLaughlin, Linda Meyers, Phillip Musselwhite, and Mitchell Zetlin, publications created with the Unigrid, 1977–1990.

"Excellence attracts excellence." But by 1980, momentum for federal design excellence became a casualty of the Reagan administration's tax cuts and huge Federal deficits. Many established design programs for such agencies as NASA and the Park Service were maintained, while others sank back toward mediocrity.

Transportation signage symbols

Major international events, large airports, and other transportation facilities handling international travelers have commissioned graphic designers to create pictographs as part of overall signage programs to communicate important information and directions quickly and simply. The development of these sign-and-symbol systems involved considerable time and expense, and near-duplication of effort often occurred. In 1974, the United States Department of Transportation commissioned the American Institute of Graphic Arts (AIGA), the nation's oldest professional graphic design organization, to create a master set of thirty-four passenger- and pedestrian-oriented symbols for use in transportation-related facilities. A consistent and interrelated group of symbols bridging language barriers and simplifying basic messages at domestic and international transportation facilities was the goal.

The first step was the compilation and inventory of symbol systems developed for individual transportation facilities and international events (Fig. 23-45). A committee of five prominent graphic designers, headed by Thomas H. Geismar, acted as evaluators and advisors on the project. The Department of Transportation provided the AIGA with a list of message areas. Examples, manuals, and research from around the world were gathered and compiled. Prior solutions to the thirty-four subject areas were evaluated by each member of the advisory committee, after which the committee attempted to determine the best approach to each symbol. Some existing symbols were determined to be adequate for inclusion in a system; in other subject categories, a totally new glyph was needed. The final set of symbols (Fig. 23-46) was designed and drawn by the outstanding design partnership of Roger Cook (b. 1930) and Don Shanosky (b. 1937), of Cook and Shanosky Associates in Princeton, New Jersey. Clarity of image was their overriding goal—the resulting symbol system combined overall harmony with a visual consistency of line, shape, weight, and form. This effort represented an important first step toward the goal of unified and effective graphic communications transcending cul-

First Aid

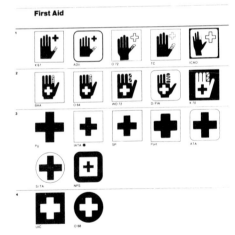

23-45. Various artists/designers, nineteen First Aid symbols from various systems throughout the world. Semantic, syntactic, and pragmatic values of existing programs were evaluated by the committee. Then a summary recommendation by the advisory committee was used by Cook and Shanosky for guidance in developing the symbol system.

23-46. Roger Cook and Don Shanosky, signage symbol system for the U.S. Department of Transportation, 1974. The thirty-four symbols were introduced to a wide audience by this black, red, and tan poster.

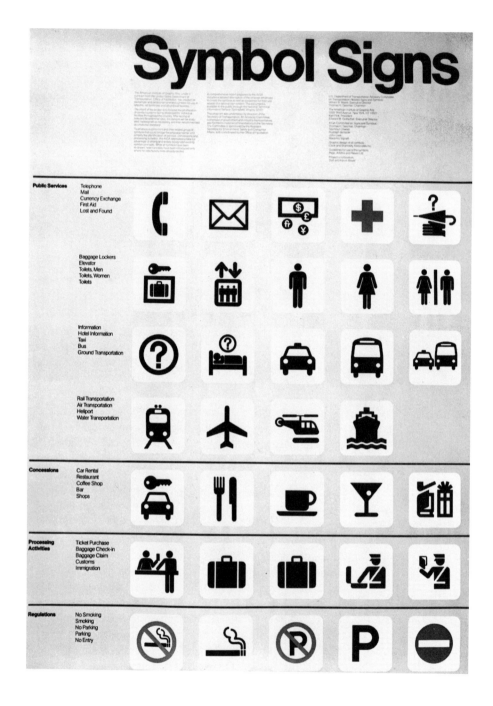

tural and language barriers in a shrinking world. A 288-page book published by the Department of Transportation provides invaluable information about the design process and evaluation used to arrive at the system.

Design systems for the Olympic Games

By the late 1960s, the concept of comprehensive design systems had become a reality. Planners realized that comprehensive planning for large organizations or events was not only functional and desirable but actually necessary, if large numbers of people were to be accommodated. This was particularly true in international events, including World's Fairs and Olympic Games, where an international and multilingual audience had to be directed and informed. Among many outstanding design efforts, the design programs for the 1968 Mexico City Nineteenth Olympiad, the 1972 Munich Twentieth Olympiad, and the 1984 Los Angeles Twenty-third Olympiad were milestones in the evolution of graphic systems.

A theme—"The young of the world united in friendship through understanding"—was adopted by the organizing committee of the Nineteenth Olympiad, chaired by Mexican architect Pedro Ramirez Vazquez. Realizing that an effective information system encompassing environmental directions, visual identification, and publicity was needed, Vazquez assembled an international design team, with American Lance Wyman (b. 1937) as director of graphic design and British industrial designer Peter Murdoch (b. 1940) as director of special products.

Because the Nineteenth Olympiad took place in and around Mexico City itself, rather than in a special location built for the purpose, the design system had to be deployed throughout one of the world's largest cities. Traffic control, urban logistics, and a multilingual audience compounded the scope of the challenge. During Wyman's initial analysis of the problem, he determined that the solution should reflect the cultural heritage of Mexico instead of the design tastes of New York or Basel. An exhaustive study of ancient Aztec artifacts and Mexican folk art led him to incorporate two design ideas: the use of repeated multiple lines to form patterns, and the Mexican love of bright, pure hues. Throughout the country, arts and crafts, adobe homes, paper flowers, the marketplace, and clothing sang with joyous, pure color, and this exuberant color spirit figured importantly in Wyman's planning.

A logotype for the Olympiad was the first graphic item developed (Fig. 23-47), and it formed a basis for the further evolution of the design program. The five rings of the Olympiad symbol were overlapped and merged with the numeral *68*. This emblematic symbol was then combined with the word *Mexico*. The repeated-stripe pattern observed in traditional Mexican art was used to form the letters. Following development of the logotype, Wyman extended it into a display typeface (Fig. 23-48), which could be applied to a range of graphics, from tickets to billboards and from uniform patches to giant color-coded balloons hovering over the arenas. The

23-47. Lance Wyman, logo for the Nineteenth Olympiad, 1966. This sequence shows the development of the logo, and how it was extended into a dynamic animated film.

23-48. Lance Wyman, alphabet for the Nineteenth Olympiad, 1967. Composed of five bands or ribbons, the alphabet echoes design motifs from early Mexican folk arts.

Corporate Identity and Visual Systems

23-49. Lance Wyman, Eduardo Terrazas, and Manuel Villazon, sports symbols for the Nineteenth Olympiad, 1967. Pictographs of the sports equipment permitted immediate identification by an international audience.

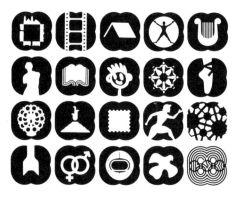

23-50. Lance Wyman and Eduardo Terrazas, cultural symbols for the Nineteenth Olympiad, 1967. The cultural events expressed as pictographs are a Youth Reception, Film Festival, Youth Camp, World Art Exhibition, Music and Performing Arts Festival, Sculptors' Conference, Poets' Reunion, Children's Art Festival, Folklore Festival, Ballet, Folk Arts Festival, Olympic Flame, Stamp Exhibit, Olympiad History Exhibition, Nuclear Energy Exhibition, Space Research Exhibition, Human Genetics and Biology, Olympiad Facilities Exhibition, Advertising in Service of Peace, and Films of Olympiad Games.

23-51. Lance Wyman, Mexican Olympiad postage stamps, 1967–1968. A series of stamps depicts silhouette figures engaged in different sports and printed over brilliant color backgrounds. The images were designed to flow from stamp to stamp in a continuous design.

system encompassed pictographic symbols for athletic (Fig. 23-49) and cultural (Fig. 23-50) events, formats for the Department of Publications, site identification, directional signs for implementation by the Department of Urban Design throughout the city, informational posters, maps, postage stamps (Fig. 23-51), film titles, and television spots. Tickets designed by Lance Wyman and Beatrice Cole were coded in a universal visual language of colors and symbols (Pl. 81). The top portion identified the sport (by pictograph) and location, and the bottom portion identified the date and time, color-coded to the day of the week and coordinated with the program of events. The middle portion was coded to the color of the seating area and used pictographs to identify the gate, ramp, row, and seat.

For the exterior environmental signage system, Wyman and Murdoch collaborated on the development of a complete system of modular functional components with interchangeable parts (Fig. 23-52). These combined directional and identificative signage (Fig. 23-53) with mailboxes, telephones, water fountains, and so on. Color was used in both decorative and pragmatic ways: Information kiosks were vibrant with colorful pictographs (Fig. 23-54); the rainbow of colors used to identify major routes on the official map was painted on the curbs of the corresponding streets; a person wishing to travel from the hotel on Avenue Universidad to the track-and-field races at the stadium on the Avenue de Los Insurgents Sur (identified by a pictograph of a foot) followed the purple line along Avenue Universidad until it crossed the red line at the intersection with the Avenue de Los Insurgents Sur, after which the person could follow the red line along the curve until arriving at the stadium, where a large footrace pictograph announced the sporting event held in that location. This design system was so effective that the New York Times proclaimed, "You can be illiterate in all languages [and still navigate the surroundings successfully,] so long as you are not color-blind."

In antiquity, the Olympiad concept embraced the physical and intellectual unity of the whole person. In an effort to restore this concept, nineteen cultural events were added to the 1968 program, requiring a set of pictographic representations. To immediately separate cultural from athletic events, the cultural symbols were placed in the silhouetted shape formed by the 68 of the logo. Wyman's goal was to create a design system that was completely unified, easily understood by people of all language backgrounds, and flexible enough to meet a vast range of applications. Measured in terms of graphic originality, innovative functional application, and its value to thousands of visitors to the Nineteenth Olympiad, the graphic design system developed by Wyman and his associates in Mexico was one of the most success-

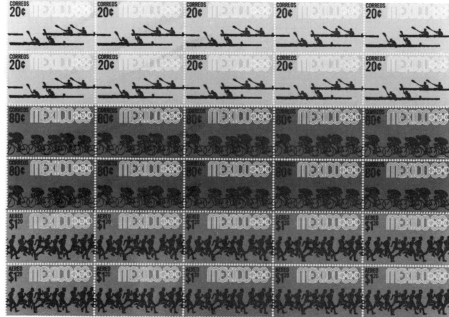

23-51

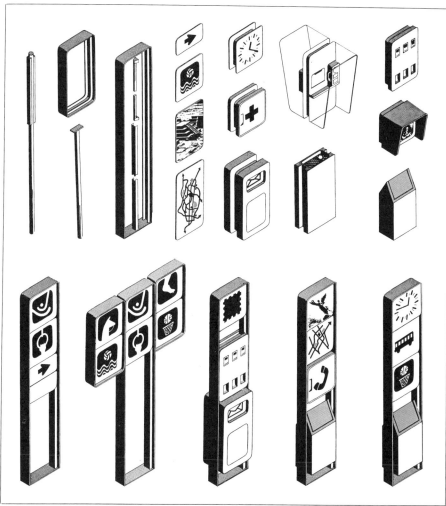

23-52

23-52. Peter Murdoch, preliminary studies for the Nineteenth Olympiad signage and facilities, 1968. Modular components were assembled into units throughout the city.

23-53. Peter Murdoch (structures) and Lance Wyman (graphics), Nineteenth Olympiad signage system, 1968. The flexible system enabled appropriate information to be disseminated throughout the city.

ful in the evolution of visual identification. After completing the two-year Olympiad project, Wyman returned to New York City and reestablished his design firm, where the expertise gained on the Mexican project has been applied to comprehensive design programs for shopping plazas and zoos.

For the 1972 Twentieth Olympiad in Munich, Germany, Otl Aicher directed a design team in the development and implementation of a more formal and systematized design program. An identification manual (Fig. 23-55) established standards for use of the symbol, a radiant sunburst/spiral configuration centered beneath the Olympiad rings and bracketed by two vertical lines. Univers was selected as the typeface, and a system of publication grids was established. The color palette consisted of a partial spectrum composed of two blues, two greens, yellow, orange, and

23-54. Peter Murdoch (structures) and Lance Wyman (graphics), Nineteenth Olympiad information kiosk, 1968. Thirty brightly colored information kiosks were placed in strategic locations.

23-55. Otl Aicher and his staff, Twentieth Olympiad graphics standards manual pages, c. 1970. Every detail of the graphics program was determined.

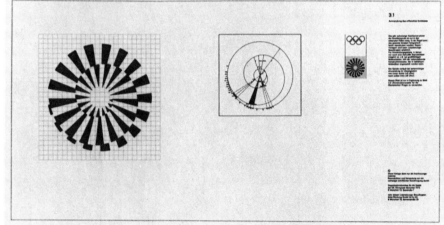

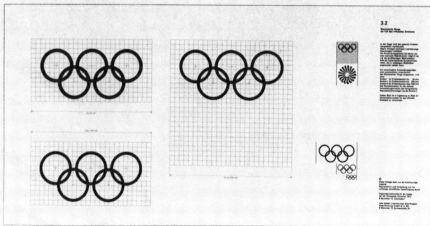

three neutral tones (black, white, and a middle-valued gray); red was excluded. Excluding one segment of the spectrum in this way created a unique color feeling generated by the harmony of analogous colors, and projected a festive air.

An extensive series of pictographs was drawn on a modular square grid divided by horizontal, vertical, and diagonal lines (Fig. 23-56). A pictograph was designed for each Olympiad sport (Fig. 23-57), emphasizing the motion of the athletes and the diagrammatic indications of their equipment—immediate identification was achieved in spite of language barriers. These pictographs were widely used in printed graphics (Fig. 23-58) and identification signs. The cool geometry of the pictographs counterpointed another level of imagery: high-contrast, posterized photographs of athletes that were used on publications (Fig. 23-59) and a series of

23-56

23-57

23-56. Otl Aicher, grid for the Twentieth Olympiad pictographs, c. 1972. The complexity of the grid allowed an infinite range of solutions.

23-57. Otl Aicher and his staff, sports pictographs for the Twentieth Olympiad, c. 1970.

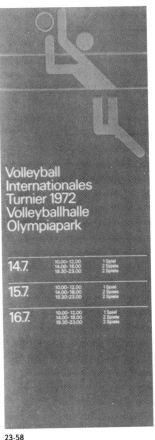

Volleyball
Internationales
Turnier 1972
Volleyballhalle
Olympiapark

14.7.	10.00–12.00 14.00–18.00 19.30–23.00	1 Spiel 2 Spiele 2 Spiele
15.7.	10.00–12.00 14.00–18.00 19.30–23.00	1 Spiel 2 Spiele 2 Spiele
16.7.	10.00–12.00 14.00–18.00 19.30–23.00	1 Spiel 2 Spiele 2 Spiele

Bogenschießen
Internationales
Testturnier 1972
Bogenschießanlage
Hirschanger
Englischer Garten

| 22.5. | 10.00–13.00
14.00–17.00 | 90m Männer
70m Frauen
70m Männer
60m Frauen |
| 23.5. | 10.00–13.00
14.00–17.00 | 50m Männer
50m Frauen
30m Männer
30m Frauen |

23-58

Bulletin 6

| Septembre 1971
Rapport officiel du
Comité organisateur
concernant
la préparation
des Jeux
de la XXe Olympiade
Munich
1972 | September 1971
Official report
by the
Organizing Committee
on the preparations
for the Games
of the XXth Olympiad
Munich
1972 | September 1971
Offizieller Bericht des
Organisations-
komitees über die
Vorbereitungen
für die Spiele
der XX. Olympiade
München
1972 |

23-59

twenty-two commemorative posters depicting major Olympiad sports, using the modified-spectrum palette of four cool and two warm colors. Each poster had a wide expanse of one dominant color as a ground for a posterized photograph of athletic competition. The poster for track events (Pl. 82), for example, defines the track and runners in the lighter green and two shades of blue against a dark-green field. Other posters in the series had orange, yellow, blue or gray as their primary background color.

The 1984 Los Angeles Twenty-third Olympiad saw a sprawling urban city transformed into a joyous environment of color and shape, unifying twenty-eight athletic sites, forty-two cultural locations, and three Olympic Villages for housing athletes into an exuberant celebration of the event. Hundreds of designers and architects working for over sixty design firms were involved in this vast project. Continuing the practice of combining a symbol specifically designed for this edition of the Olympics with the traditional linked rings, the Los Angeles Olympic Organizing Committee selected a dynamic "star-in-motion" configuration (Fig. 23-60) in a 1980 competition by leading Los Angeles design firms.

Lacking the huge government subsidies of many earlier Olympic games, the Organizing Committee decided to use twenty-six existing athletic facilities, adding only one new swimming pool and a cycling track. The design problem was well defined: How to temporarily transform these far-flung facilities to create a unified celebratory feeling, express the international character of the games, and invent a designed environment that will work effectively both on-site and for the global television audience? For help in answering these questions, the Organizing Committee called upon two design firms to spearhead the effort. An architectural firm, The Jerde Partnership, directed by Jon Jerde and David Meckel, joined with an environmental and graphic design firm, Sussman/Prejza & Co., headed by Deborah Sussman and Paul Prejza, to collaborate on planning the visual vocabulary—architecture, color, graphics, and signage—for this massive event. Due to the limited

23-58. Otl Aicher and his staff, informational graphics for the Twentieth Olympiad, 1972. The pictographs function as signifiers and illustrations.

23-59. Otl Aicher and his staff, cover for the Twentieth Olympiad *Bulletin,* 1971. The format grid becomes a part of the illustration.

23-60. Jim Berté (designer) and Robert Miles Runyan (art director), symbol for the games of the Twenty-third Olympiad, 1980. The "star-in-motion" is generated by three weights of horizontal lines.

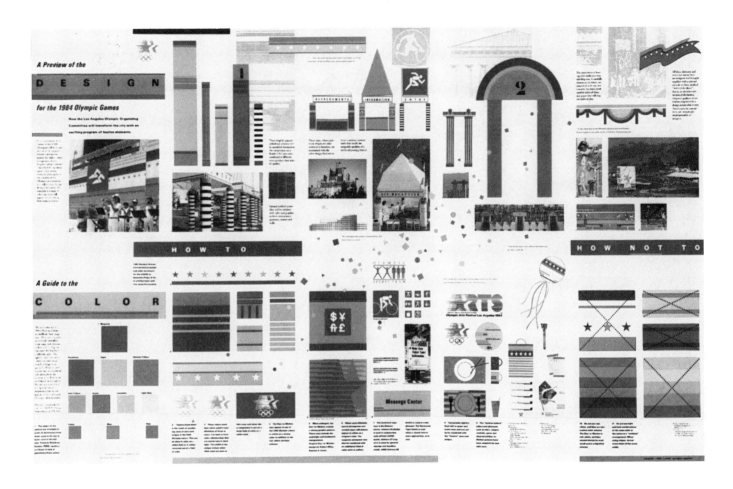

23-61. Debra Valencia (designer) and Deborah Sussman (art director), design guide for the Twenty-third Olympiad, 1983. The design parameters allow diversity within a fixed range of possibilities.

amount of time from the start of the design process to the start of the Olympic games, existing technologies, prefabricated parts, and rented items were used extensively. The brief time-frame of the Olympics combined with Los Angeles's mild, dry climate to permit the use of fragile and ephemeral materials.

A parts kit was assembled to provide a uniform idiom for designing components and environments. Forms were simple and basic: Sonotube columns, normally used as molds for casting concrete columns, but used here as columns themselves, were decorated with colorful painted stripes; the sonotubes were lined up to make colonnades, combined with rented tents to make colorful pavilions, or topped with flat graphic pediments echoing the forms of earlier Olympics. A poster-size design guide (Fig. 23-61) was produced to provide all participants with consistent parameters for using the parts kit. Gateways and monumental towers were built from aqua and magenta scaffolding and punctuated with ornaments and banners.

Sussman selected a bright, vibrant palette, with hot magenta as the basic color. Its primary supporting palette consisted of vivid aqua, chrome yellow, and vermilion. A secondary palette included yellow, green, lavender, and light blue, with violet, blue, and pink accents. Graphic forms were derived from the stars and stripes of the American flag combined with the stripes of the star-in-motion logo. These elements were freely pulled apart, recreated in the dazzling color palette, and combined in a layering of stripes—light against dark, thick against thin, and warm against cool. Plate 83, a periodical cover designed by Deborah Sussman, demonstrates the color palette and use of stripe and star imagery.

These graphic patterns were used extensively on entryways and sports arenas, providing a dynamic backdrop for events telecast around the globe to over two billion viewers. Each sports arena was transformed with its own color combinations and graphic motifs (Fig. 23-62), developed from the design guidelines. Entryways to the sporting events became festive colonnades (Fig. 23-63). Imaginative

Corporate Identity and Visual Systems

22-62

22-63

23-64

23-62. The Jerde Partnership and Sussman/Prejza & Co., Twenty-third Olympiad stadium graphics, 1984. Magenta and chrome yellow contrast with blue and green accents.

23-63. The Jerde Partnership, Sussman/Prejza & Co., and Daniel Benjamin, entrance to the Twenty-third Olympiad swimming competition, 1984. The swimming pictograph is white against a magenta field. The sonotubes have black and white stripes with orange capitals and bases. All information booths have yellow "wizard's hat" tents for easy identification.

23-64. The Jerde Partnership and Sussman/Prejza & Co., Twenty-third Olympiad village entry, 1984. Scaffolding, fabric, sonotubes, and spheres create a festive entryway.

23-65. Sussman/Prejza & Co., identification signage for the Twenty-third Olympiad, 1984. Magenta squares with directional arrows, aqua stars, and vermillion bars glow against a chrome-yellow background.

23-65

possibilities for combining the temporary forms were explored in designing environments, such as the Olympic Village entries (Fig. 23-64). The informational signage system (Fig. 23-65) was consistent yet flexible. Economical materials, such as hollow-core doors, styrene panels, and the ever-present sonotubes were painted in the bright colors, and then Univers typography, bright bars of color, and large star-and-confetti patterns were applied. Staff uniforms, street banners, and food packaging extended the graphic theme to all aspects of the event. Scores of designers and design firms produced Olympic graphics and environments conforming to the design guide developed by the principal design firms; it is not possible to list all of them here. The 1984 Los Angeles Olympics thus occurred within an environment of joyous graphics, which brought a festive vitality to the event. In a sense, graphics helped restore the Olympics as an international celebration after political boycotts (1980, 1984) and terrorist activities (1972) had tainted the Olympics.

Complex international events, large governmental entities, and multinational corporations have required graphic designers to develop complex design systems to manage information flow and visual identity. While accomplishing these pragmatic goals, design systems can also create a spirit or resonance, helping to express and define the very nature of the large organization or event.

The Conceptual Image

24

24-1. Armando Testa, poster for Pirelli, 1954. The strength of a bull elephant is bestowed upon the tire by the Surrealist technique of image combination.

Sensing that traditional narrative illustration did not address the needs of the times, post–World War I pictorial modernism reinvented the communicative image to express the age of the machine and the advanced visual ideas of the period. In a similar quest for new imagery, the decades after World War II saw the development of the conceptual image in graphic design. Images conveyed not merely narrative information but ideas and concepts. Mental content joined perceived content as motif. The illustrator interpreting a writer's text yielded to the graphic imagist making a statement. Instead of scooping a rectangle out of illusionistic space on a printed page, this new breed of image makers was often concerned with the total design of the space and the integration of word and image. In the exploding information culture of the second half of the twentieth century, the entire history of visual arts was available as a library of potential forms and images to the graphic artist. In particular, inspiration was gained from the advances of twentieth-century art movements: the spatial configurations of Cubism; the juxtapositions, dislocations, and scale changes of Surrealism; the pure color loosened from natural reference by Expressionism and Fauvism; and the retreading of mass-media images by Pop Art. Graphic artists had greater opportunity for self-expression, created more personal images, and pioneered individual styles and techniques. The traditional boundaries between the fine arts and public visual communications became blurred.

The creation of conceptual images became a significant design approach in Poland, the United States, Germany, and even Cuba. It also cropped up around the world in the work of individuals whose search for relevant and effective images in the post–World War II era led them toward the conceptual image. In the most original work of the Italian graphic designer Armando Testa (b. 1917), for example, metaphysical combinations are used to convey elemental truths about the subject. Testa was an abstract painter until after the war, when he established a graphic design studio in his native Turin. His 1950s publicity campaigns for Pirelli tires had an international impact upon graphic design thinking (Fig. 24-1). Testa called upon the vocabulary of Surrealism by combining the image of a tire with immediately recognizable symbols. In his posters and advertisements, the image is the primary means of communication, and he reduces the verbal content to a few words or just the product name. Testa effectively used more subtle contradictions, such as images made of artificial materials (Fig. 24-2), as a means of injecting unexpected elements into graphic design.

The Polish poster
The violence of World War II swept over Europe on 1 September 1939 with Hitler's lightning invasion of Poland from the north, south, and west without a declaration of war. Seventeen days later, Soviet troops invaded Poland from the east, and a six-year period of devastation followed. Poland emerged from the war with enormous population losses, devastated industry, a wrecked agriculture, and the capital city of Warsaw almost completely eradicated. Printing and graphic design, like so many aspects of Polish society and culture, had ceased to exist. It is a monumental tribute to the resilience of the human spirit that an internationally renowned Polish school of poster art emerged from this devastation.

410

24-2. Armando Testa, rubber and plastics exhibition poster, 1972. A hand holding a plastic ball is a direct and appropriate image for this trade exhibition. When one realizes that the hand itself is made of synthetic materials, the impact is intensified.

In the communist society established in Poland after the war, the clients were state-controlled institutions and industry. Graphic designers joined filmmakers, writers, and fine artists in the Polish Union of Artists, which established standards and set fees. Entry into the union came after completion of the educational program at either the Warsaw or the Krakow Academies of Art. Entry standards for these schools are rigorous, and the number of graduates produced is carefully controlled to equal the need for design.

The earliest Polish poster artist to emerge after the war was Tadeusz Trepkowski (1914–1956). During the first decade after the devastation, Trepkowski expressed the tragic memories and aspirations for the future that were deeply fixed in the national psyche. Trepkowski's approach involved reducing the imagery and words until the content was distilled into its simplest statement. In his famous 1953 antiwar poster (Pl. 84), Trepkowski reduced his passionate statement to just one word: "No!" A few simple shapes symbolizing a devastated city, superimposed over a silhouette of a falling bomb, say the rest.

Henryk Tomaszewski (b. 1914) became the spiritual head of Polish graphic design after Trepkowski's early death and became an important impetus for the movement from his position as professor at the Warsaw Academy of Fine Arts. The poster became a source of great national pride in Poland, and its role in the cultural life of the nation is unique. Electronic broadcasting lacked the frequency and diversity of Western media, and the din of economic competition was less pronounced in a communist country. Therefore, posters for cultural events, the circus, movies, and politics become important communications. In 1964, the Warsaw International Poster Biennial began, and Muzeum Plakatu—a museum devoted exclusively to the art of the poster—was established in Wilanow near Warsaw. During the 1950s, the Polish poster began to receive international attention. Tomaszewski led in developing an aesthetically pleasing style escaping from the somber world of tragedy and remembrance into a bright, decorative world of color and shape (Fig. 24-3). In an almost casual collage approach, designs were created from torn and cut pieces of colored paper, then printed by the silkscreen process. Typical of this style is the film poster for *Rzeczpospolita Babska* (Fig. 24-4) by Jerzy Flisak (b. 1930). The symbolic female figure has a pink, doll-like head with round, rouged cheeks and a heart-shaped mouth. The circus poster has flourished as a lighthearted expression of the magic and charm of this traditional entertainment since

24-3. Henryk Tomaszewski, poster for the play *Marie and Napoleon,* 1964. Tomaszewski led Polish graphic design toward a colorful and artistic expression.

24-4. Jerzy Flisak, cinema poster for *Rzeczpospolita Babska,* undated. Bright red, pink, orange, yellow, and green project the festive quality of the 1950s Polish poster.

24-3

24-4

24-5

24-6

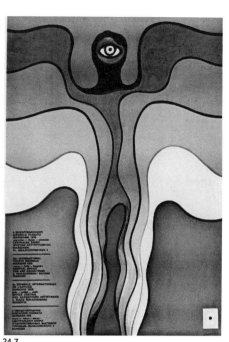

24-7

1962, when concern about mediocre circus publicity inspired a juried program to select a dozen circus posters per year for publication by the Graphic Arts Publishers in Warsaw. The word *cyrk* ("circus") is the only type or lettering on each poster (Fig. 24-5). Strips of typographic information giving full particulars for the specific engagement appear under the poster image on kiosks and walls.

The next major tendency in Polish posters started to evolve during the 1960s and reached a crescendo during the 1970s. This was a tendency toward the metaphysical and Surrealism, as a darker, more somber side of the national character was addressed. It has been speculated that this represented either a subtle reaction to the social constraints of the dictatorial regime or a despair and yearning for the autonomy that has so often been denied the Polish nation during its history. One of the first graphic designers to incorporate this new metaphysical sensitivity into his work was Franciszek Starowiejski (b. 1930). In his 1962 poster for the Warsaw Drama Theater, a serpent hovers in space coiling around two circles that become shaking hands (Fig. 24-6). This enigmatic image was a harbinger of things to come in Starowiejski's work, which sometimes tends toward the slime-and-gore school of graphics, and in the work of a number of other Polish graphic designers. Jan Lenica (b. 1928) pushed the collage style toward a less innocuous and more menacing and surreal communication in posters and experimental animated films. Then during the middle 1960s, he began using flowing, stylized contour lines that weave through the space and divide it into colored zones, which form an image (Fig. 24-7).

Lenica and Starowiejski were joined in their break with the mainstream of Polish poster design by several others of the emerging generation who realized that the Polish poster was in danger of fossilizing into an academic national style. This potential pitfall has been avoided, as designers including Waldemar Swierzy (b. 1931) have arrived at unique personal visions. Approaching graphic design with a painterly viewpoint, Swierzy draws upon both twentieth-century fine art and folk art for inspiration. This prolific artist, who has created over a thousand posters with virtuoso skill, uses a wide variety of media. He often incorporates acrylics, crayon, pencil, and watercolor into a design. In his famous poster for the American rock musician Jimi Hendrix (Fig. 24-8), Swierzy animated the large portrait with swirling energetic gestures that give the impression that the artist defaced an immaculately rendered portrait by drawing graffiti-like gestures into the wet paint with the brush handle. The spontaneous quality of much of his work is deceptive, for Swierzy generally devotes three weeks to each poster and sometimes executes a poster five or more times before being satisfied with the results.

24-8. Waldemar Swierzy, Jimi Hendrix poster, 1974. The electric vitality of the gestures on the cobalt-blue portrait suggests the vigorous energy of hard-rock music.

24-9. Roman Cieslewicz, Amnesty International poster, 1975. A monumental statement about anonymous victims of political persecution emerges from the massive, totemlike image.

24-10. Roman Cieslewicz, Krackow Temporary Theater poster, 1974. In this surreal image, the tradition of hunting for an image in the clouds proves fruitless.

24-5. Roman Cieslewicz, circus poster, 1962. Bright collage elements superimpose the word *Cyrk* and a clown upon a high-contrast photograph of an elephant.

24-6. Franciszek Starowiejski, Warsaw Drama Theater poster, 1962. The cube drawn in perspective centered below the snake is crucial, for it transforms the flat page into deep space, forcing the strange complex above it to float.

24-7. Jan Lenica, Warsaw Poster Biennale poster, 1976. Meandering arabesques isolate a series of bands, ranging from yellow to dark green, while metamorphosing into a winged being.

An exiled Polish poster artist, Roman Cieslewicz (b. 1930), has been living in Paris since the 1960s. Closely associated with the Polish avant-garde theater, Cieslewicz has taken the poster, a public art form, and transformed it into a metaphysical medium to express profound ideas that would be difficult to articulate verbally (Figs. 24-9 and 24-10). Cieslewicz's techniques include enlarging collage, montage, and halftone images to a scale that turns the dots into texture, setting up an interplay between two levels of information: the image and the dots that create it.

In 1980, shortages of food, electricity, and housing led to strikes and the formation of the illegal Solidarity labor union, whose logo (Fig. 24-11), designed by Jerzy Janiszewski, became an international symbol of struggle against oppression. As a result of government censorship during Poland's social unrest, the country's posters addressed issues ranging beyond Poland's boundaries, rather than internal political struggles such as the banning of Solidarity. An external subject is seen in a poster by Marian Nowinski (b. 1944), an eloquent symbol about censorship (Fig. 24-12). Nowinski laments censorship and suppression, not only of Chilean poet Pablo Neruda, but of the entire Chilean people, expressing solidarity with the Chilean struggle for democracy and independence by transcending the immediate to create a powerful statement about censorship and the suppression of ideas everywhere.

The legalization of Solidarity and its overwhelming victory in May 1989 elections ended one-party communist rule, marking the beginning of a new era in Polish history. For half a century, the Polish poster developed as a result of a conscious decision by the government to sanction and support poster art as a major form of expression and communication. The posters have been creative statements trafficking in ideas rather than in commodities. Despite the governmental changes, a tra-

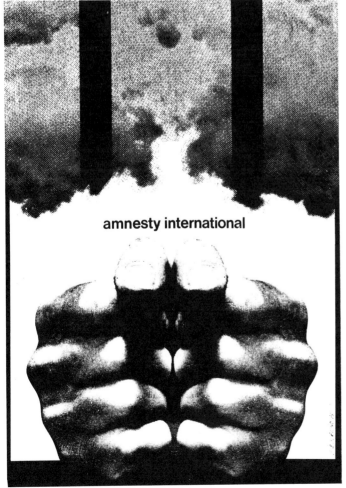

24-9

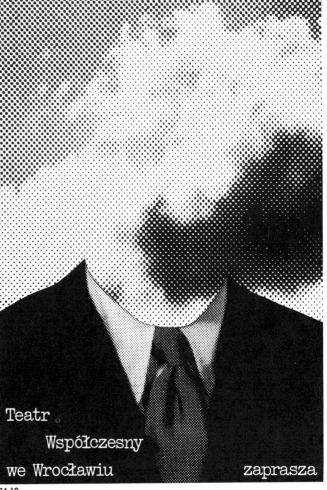

24-10

24-11. Jerzy Janiszewski, Solidarity logo, c. 1980. Crude letterforms evoke street graffiti, and the crowded letters become a metaphor for people standing solidly together in the street.

24-12. Marian Nowinski, political poster, 1979. A book bearing the name of Chilean poet Pablo Neruda, whose works were banned and burned by the Pinochet regime, is nailed down and defaced by large metal spikes.

dition of excellence, bolstered by strong design education, may ensure a continuing poster art form in Poland; inventiveness is already being demonstrated by younger graphic designers entering the profession. (And *profession* is the right word in Poland, where graphic art is accorded the status of more traditional disciplines, such as architecture and medicine.)

American conceptual images

During the 1950s, the Golden Age of American Illustration was drawing to a close. For over fifty years, narrative illustration had ruled American graphic design, but improvements in paper, printing, and photography caused the illustrator's edge over the photographer to decline rapidly. Traditionally, illustrators had exaggerated value contrasts, intensified color, and made imagery appear crisper than life to create more convincing images than photography. But now, improvements in photographic materials and processes enabled photography to expand its range of lighting conditions and image fidelity. The death of illustration was somberly predicted as photography made rapid inroads into illustration's traditional market. But as photography stole illustration's traditional function—the creation of narrative and descriptive images—a new approach to illustration emerged.

A primary wellspring of this more conceptual approach to illustration began with a group of young New York graphic artists. Art students Seymour Chwast (b. 1931), Milton Glaser (b. 1929), Reynolds Ruffins (b. 1930), and Edward Sorel (b. 1929) banded together and shared a loft studio. Upon graduation from Cooper Union in 1951, Glaser received a Fulbright Scholarship to study etching under Giorgio Morandi in Italy, and the other three friends found employment in New York advertising and publishing. Free-lance assignments were solicited through a joint publication called *The Push Pin Almanac.* Published bimonthly, it featured interesting editorial material from old almanacs illustrated by the group. When Glaser returned from Europe in August 1954, the Push Pin Studio was formed. After a time, Ruffins left the studio and became a prominent decorative and children's-book illustrator. In 1958, Sorel started free-lancing (see Fig. 23-6) and emerged as a major political satirist of his generation. Meanwhile, Chwast and Glaser maintained a collaborative studio for over two decades. *The Push Pin Almanac* became the *Push Pin Graphic,* and this experimental magazine provided a forum for developing new ideas.

Push Pin's philosophy, techniques, and personal visions had a major impact. Graphic design has often been fragmented into component parts of image making and layout or design. Like turn-of-the-century graphic designers Mucha and Bradley, Glaser and Chwast united these components into a total communication conveying the individual vision of the creator. As with turn-of-the-century poster designers, Push Pin artists were interested in the total conception and design of the printed page. Using art and graphic history from Renaissance paintings to comic books as a data bank of form, images, and visual ideas, the Push Pin artists freely paraphrased and incorporated a multiplicity of inspirations into their work, often reinventing these eclectic sources into new and unexpected forms.

Milton Glaser's singular genius is hard to categorize, for over the course of several decades he "reinvented himself as a creative force" by exploring new graphic techniques and new motifs. During the 1960s, Glaser created images of flat shapes formed by thin, black ink contour lines with color added by adhesive color films (Fig. 24-13). This almost schematic drawing style echoed the simple iconography of comic books, the flowing curvilinear drawing of Persian and Art Nouveau arabesques, the flat color of the Japanese print and Matisse cutouts, and the dynamic of contemporary Pop Art. As with other graphic designers whose work captured and expressed the sensibilities of their times, Glaser was widely imitated. Only his ability to maintain a steady stream of innovative conceptual solutions, along with his restless exploration of different techniques, prevented him from being consumed by his followers.

While the forms created by this technique are formed by the edge, another ap-

24-13. Milton Glaser, record album cover for *The Sound of Harlem,* 1964. In this early example of Glaser's contour-line-and-flat-color period, the figures are weightless shapes flowing in musical rhythm.

24-14. Milton Glaser, poster for *The Shadowlight Theatre,* 1964. A dictionary of strange characters unleashed from Glaser's ink bottle are halftones reversed from the background.

24-15. Milton Glaser, *One Print, One Painting* exhibition poster, 1968. The dense purple-black field is created by overprinting the deep blue of the numerals and the red of the typography, with the thin white line of the isometric box glowing vividly.

proach developed by Glaser evolved from the mass. Inspired in the late 1950s by oriental calligraphic brush drawing and Picasso aquatints, Glaser began making gestural silhouette wash drawings that tease the viewer by only suggesting the subject, requiring the viewer to "fill in" the details from his or her own imagination. An example of this is the 1964 *Shadowlight Theatre* poster for a performance of a contemporary interpretation of the Balinese shadow play (Fig. 24-14). The figures are printed against a rich black field in a *split fountain*—the ink reservoir on the printing press is filled with several ink colors, which are blended by the ink rollers. The baroque figures take on an eerie glow as their color flickers from yellow-green to red to brown.

For Glaser, geometric forms, words, and numbers are not merely abstract signs but tangible entities with an object-life that allows them to be interpreted as motifs, just as figures and inanimate objects are interpreted by an artist. His approach to sign and symbol is seen in the 1968 *One Print One Painting* exhibition poster (Fig. 24-15), in which an isometric cube comes alive with the magical ability to warp and bend the large numerals. In the rejected poster design for the Museum of Modern Art's Dada and Surrealism exhibition, the words themselves take on a metaphysical afterlife as objects (Fig. 24-16). "Dada" is impaled through the tabletop to hover over its wayward offspring, "Surrealism." Like the art movements it represents, this design defies rational interpretation.

Glaser's concert posters and record-album designs achieve a singular ability to combine his personal vision with the essence of the content. When Gertrude Stein complained to young Pablo Picasso that the portrait he painted of her during the winter of 1905–1906 did not look like her, he reportedly advised her that, in time, it would; to this day, the public image of Gertrude Stein is contained in Picasso's portrait. The same is true of Glaser's 1967 image of the folk-rock singer Bob Dylan (Pl. 85). The popular singer is presented as a black silhouette with brightly colored hair patterns inspired by Islamic design. Nearly six million copies of the poster were produced for inclusion in a best-selling record album. As did Flagg's Uncle Sam poster (see Pl. 43), it became a graphic icon in the collective American experience. A photographer told Glaser about being on assignment on the Amazon River and seeing the poster in a hut at a remote Indian village.

In contrast to the simplicity of the Dylan poster, Glaser's interpretation of Johann Sebastian Bach is extremely complex (Fig. 24-17). Glaser's personal associations—"particularly in terms of the music's structure and geometry—were details from an Islamic rug, a series of geometric references including grids, overlapping discs, and a variety of perspective lines. Reference to certain natural forms—leaves, trees, and landscapes—point to pastoral aspects in Bach's work." In addi-

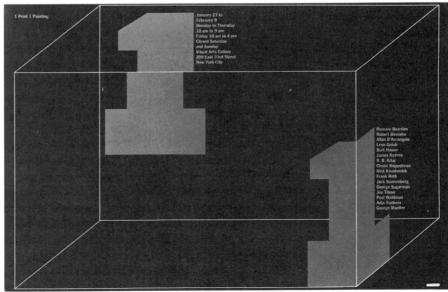

24-17

24-18

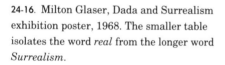

24-16. Milton Glaser, Dada and Surrealism exhibition poster, 1968. The smaller table isolates the word *real* from the longer word *Surrealism.*

24-17. Milton Glaser, Johann Sebastian Bach poster. Although separated by a black gulf, the landscape and portrait are unified graphically by the diagonal lines. In addition, the shape of Bach's head and neck repeats the silhouette of the tree.

24-18. Milton Glaser, Poppy Records poster, 1968. Symbolizing a new, independent recording company seeking to break through the monolithic conventions of the recording industry, Glaser's brilliant orange and red poppy blooms from a granite cube.

tion, Glaser often called upon Surrealism's vocabulary as a vehicle to express complex concepts (Fig. 24-18).

Chwast's vision is very personal, yet communicates on a universal level. He frequently uses the technique of line drawings overlaid with adhesive color films, and experiments with a large variety of media and substrata. Echoes of children's art, primitive art, folk art, expressionist woodcuts, and comic books appear in his imaginative reinventions of the world. Chwast's color is frontal and intense. In contrast to Glaser's spatial depth, an absolute flatness is usually maintained. Chwast's innocent vision, love of Victorian and figurative letterforms, and ability to integrate figurative and alphabetic information has enabled him to produce unexpected design solutions.

Chwast's album cover for *The Three Penny Opera* (Pl. 86) demonstrates the ability to synthesize diverse resources—the German expressionist woodcut, Surreal spatial dislocations, and dynamic color found in primitive art—into an appropriate expression of the subject. In his 1965 moving announcement for Elektra Productions (Fig. 24-19), each letter in the word lumbers across the space endowed with its own form of transportation. The nineteenth-century woodtype poster, with its multiplicity of type styles, has been revived by Chwast and invigorated with bright color and illustrations to allow its graphic complexity to speak to the citizens of yet another century (Fig. 24-20). From antiwar protest (Fig. 24-21) to food packaging (Fig. 24-22) and magazine covers, Chwast has reformulated earlier styles to express new concepts in new contexts. With an outrageously uninhibited layout style, Chwast continued the *Push Pin Graphic* after his partnership with Glaser was dissolved in the mid-1970s.

Both Chwast and Glaser developed a number of novelty display typefaces. Often, these began as lettering for assignments, then were developed into full alphabets. Figure 24-23 shows the logo Chwast developed for Artone ink, based on a lowercase ink-drop *a;* the gradated version of Blimp based on old woodtypes; a geometric face inspired by the logo Glaser designed for a film studio; a typeface based on lettering first developed for a *Mademoiselle* poster; and the Buffalo typeface, originally devised for a French product named "Buffalo Gum," which was never produced.

The term "Push Pin Style" became widely used for the studio's work and influence, which spread around the world. The studio hired other designers and illustrators in addition to Glaser and Chwast, and a number of these younger

24-19

24-20. Seymour Chwast, graphic statement about war, 1967. Red, orange, lavender, and blue letterforms pull Victorian typography into a twentieth-century context. The copy line uses the propaganda technique of the positive endorsement that evokes a negative response in the viewer.

individuals, who worked for the studio and then moved on to free-lance or to other positions, extended the boundaries of the Push Pin Style. This so-called style is less a set of visual conventions, or a unity of visual techniques or images, than it is an attitude about visual communications, an openness to try new forms and techniques, and an ability to integrate word and image into a conceptual and decorative whole.

An enormously influential young graphic designer in the late 1960s and early 1970s, Barry Zaid (b. 1939) joined Push Pin for a few years during this period. A Canadian who majored first in architecture and then in English during college before becoming a self-taught graphic designer and illustrator, Zaid worked in Toronto and then London before joining Push Pin Studio. As a graphic archeologist basing his work upon a thorough study of the graphic vernacular of bygone eras, Zaid became an important force upon the revivalism and historicism that were prevalent in graphic design during this period. He made a number of forays into Victorian graphics (Fig. 24-24) and was particularly prominent in the revival of

24-21. Seymour Chwast, poster protesting the bombing of Hanoi, 1968. A mundane advertising slogan gains a new life when combined with a blue woodcut with offset-printed green and red areas.

24-22. Seymour Chwast, package for Love Drops candies, 1974. A lighthearted line of Pushpinoff candies showed just how decorative and appealing packages could be.

24-20

24-21

24-22

24-24

24-23. Seymour Chwast, display typeface designs. Chwast playfully echoes Victorian, Art Nouveau, Op Art, and Art Deco forms.

24-24. Barry Zaid, 7-Up billboard, 1969. To create a nostalgic reminder of summer leisure, Zaid began with a Victorian chromolithograph, then painted a bottle in the little girl's hand and added a sign and the lettering.

1920s Art Deco decorative geometric forms (Figs. 24-25 and 24-26), including the cover to the 1970 book *Art Deco* by English art historian Bevis Hillier. Zaid's historicism did not merely mimic the nostalgic forms of his motifs, for his spatial organization, scale, and color were of his own time.

Among other illustrators who passed through Push Pin Studio, James McMullan (b. 1934) revived watercolor, a medium that had declined from a position second only to oil paint for fine art and illustration, and restored it as a means of graphic expression. McMullan achieved prominence during the 1960s for energetic ink-line and watercolor illustrations that often combined multiple images with significant changes in spatial depth and image size and scale. Moving into the 1970s, McMullan's watercolor technique became increasingly masterly, and he developed a photodocumentative approach of sharply increased detail and realism. At the same time, however, a concern for total design asserted itself, and McMullan began to make fluid lettering an important part of his images. In his 1977 poster for Eugene O'Neill's play *Anna Christie* (Fig. 24-27), the intimate spatial level of the figure sitting in an interior is superimposed over an ocean scene. The dual image combines to communicate the locale of the play while creating an engaging spatial interplay.

Another Push Pin alumnus who moved into a total design approach is Paul Davis (b. 1938), who first appeared in the *Push Pin Graphic* with a series of primitive figures painted on rough, wood panels with superimposed targets. From this beginning, Davis moved toward a painting style of minute detail that drew upon primitive Colonial American art as a resource. Davis evolved into a master of meticulous naturalism in which the solid shapes of his forms projected a convincing weight and volume. Like McMullan, Davis often became involved in a painterly integration of image and words. In his 1976 poster for the play *For Colored Girls . . .* (Pl. 87) the title is written in a graffiti rainbow behind the sensitive portrait. The theater and its address are executed in the mosaic tiles of New York subway signs.

The Push Pin school of graphic illustration and design presented an alternative to the narrative illustration of the past, the mathematical and objective typographic and photographic orientation of the International Typographic Style, and the formal concerns of the New York School. Warm, friendly, and accessible, Push Pin designs project vitality with unashamed allusions to other art and lush color. Although not formally associated with the Push Pin Studio, graphic designer Richard Hess (b. 1934) turned to illustration and developed a rendering style somewhat allied to that of Paul Davis. Hess has more of a tendency toward Surrealism than Davis, and often drew inspiration from the spatial manipulations of René Magritte. An understanding of the folklore and imagery of nineteenth-century America enabled Hess to produce a number of images that thoroughly captured the essence of this earlier period (Fig. 24-28).

The Push Pin group did not maintain a monopoly on the conceptual image in America, for a number of independent voices forged individual approaches to com-

24-25

24-26

munications problem solving while combining the traditional conceptualization and layout role of the graphic designer with the image-making role of the illustrator. One such person, Arnold Varga (b. 1926), practically reinvented the retail newspaper advertisement. Varga entered the field in 1946. Beginning in the middle 1950s, his newspaper advertisements for two Pittsburgh department stores—Joseph P. Horne & Co. and Cox's—indicated that this usually pedestrian form of visual design could be turned into memorable image-building communications. Many of his ads used carefully integrated white space and headlines with large, simple illustrations to break through the monotonous gray of the newspaper page. Varga is particularly noted for the lighthearted, entertaining copy in his advertisements. A multiple-image picture and caption approach such as the gourmet shop advertisement for Joseph P. Horne (Fig. 24-29), achieved notable public response—people actually offered to buy this advertisement to hang on their walls!

The conceptual image is not the exclusive province of the illustrator/designer, for art directors called upon the entire range of image-making possibilities in their search for means to convey concepts and ideas. This is particularly true in the work of graphic designers in the musical recording industry. Art and music share a common idiom of expression and experience. We use the same words—including *rhythm, texture, tone, color,* and *resonance*—as we struggle to convey the spiritual dimension of both visual and auditory perception. The design staff of CBS Records operated at the forefront of the graphic interpretation of music. The conceptual image emerged as a significant direction in album design during the early 1960s

24-25. Barry Zaid, book jacket for Bevis Hillier's *Art Deco*, 1970. In this orange, green, and black cover, 1920s decorative geometry is reinvented in the context of the sensibilities of a half century later.

24-26. Barry Zaid, cover for the Australian *Vogue* magazine, 1971. The rotund geometric forms of Leger and pictorial modernism are evoked here.

24-27. James McMullan, *Anna Christie* poster, 1977. McMullan often calls attention to the physical properties of the medium. For example, the red background behind the figure changes into painterly strokes that become lettering.

24-28. Henrietta Condak (art director) and Richard Hess (illustrator), record album cover for Charles Ives's *The 100th Anniversary,* 1974. The complex format used on Victorian-era circus posters enables Hess to depict many images from the composer's time.

24-29. Arnold Varga, newspaper advertisement for Joseph P. Horne, c. 1966. The joys of food and cooking are conveyed. (Reproduced from a proof not showing the Horne logo at the bottom of the page.)

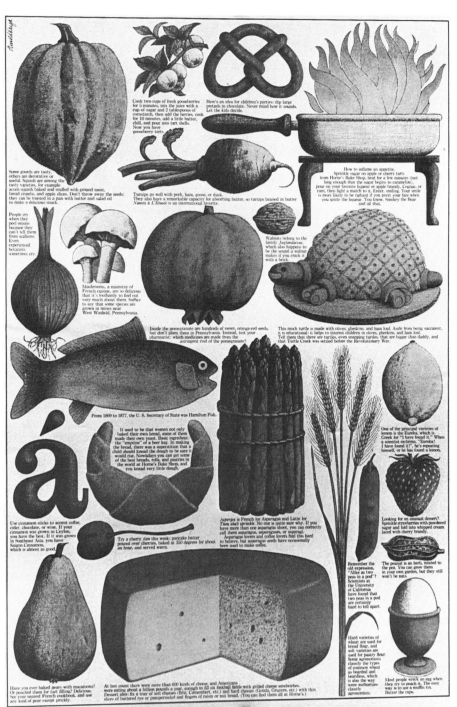

24-29

after Bob Cato became head of the creative services department and hired John Berg (b. 1932), who served as art director at CBS's Columbia Records until 1984. Photographs of musicians performing and portraits of composers yielded to more conceptual images, as in Berg's 1963 *William Tell Overture* album (Fig. 24-30). For two decades, Berg and his staff wrested the maximum potential from 144 square inches of design area. The art director became a conceptualizer and collaborator, working with illustrators and photographers to realize imaginative expressions for the spectrum of musical experience. The fantastic, the real, and the surreal joined the classical and outrageous in Columbia Records' graphic repertoire (Fig. 24-31).

Consistent corporate identification is irrelevant in the music industry, for specific recording artists or musical selections rather than the reputation and longevity of manufacturer are the audience's overriding concerns. Sometimes a sense of corporate identity was created for a series of albums by a given composer or group. For example, Berg designed a large series of album covers for the musical group Chicago (Fig. 24-32), each featuring a logotype in lettering reminiscent of bold nineteenth-century Victorian scripts. This logo has appeared as a hand-painted sign on wood, a chocolate bar, tactile leathercraft, a wall sign being painted by sign painters, and even as the shape of a high-rise building in a bird's-eye-view illustration. Some of the most memorable graphic images from the 1960s, 1970s, and 1980s were birthed as covers of Columbia Records albums. The rapid replacement of the long-playing record by the compact disc in the early 1990s altered music graphics from a format approaching that of the small poster to smaller formats more resembling the book jacket.

Illustrative, conceptual images and the influence of Push Pin Studios often mingled with wild West, Mexican, and Native American images and colors in the regional school of graphic design that emerged in Texas during the 1970s and became a major force in the 1980s. A high level of aesthetic awareness, an open friendliness, and a strong sense of humor characterize graphic design from the Lone Star state. Intuitive approaches to problem solving combine with a pragmatic emphasis upon content. Texas designers acknowledge the importance of Stan Richards, head of The Richards Group in Dallas, as a catalytic figure in the emergence of Texas as a major design center. The work of Woody Pirtle (b. 1943), one of many major Texas designers who worked for Richards during their formative years, epitomizes the originality of Texas conceptual images. His logo for Mr. and Mrs. Aubrey Hair (Fig. 24-33) evidences an unexpected wit, while his Knoll "hot seat" poster (Fig. 24-34) ironically combines the clean Helvetica and generous white space of modernism with a regional iconography. In 1988, Pirtle moved on to join the Manhattan office of the British design studio Pentagram (see Figs. 25-2 through 25-6).

During the 1970s, the Texas design boom accompanied a bustling economy, for this oil-producing state prospered as petroleum prices skyrocketed. Texas design even managed to survive a severely depressed economy after oil prices collapsed in the 1980s during a period of international overproduction. But Texas was not the only new center for design—the 1980s saw graphic design in the United States become a truly national profession. Outstanding practitioners emerged all around the country, often far from the traditional centers. *Print* magazine, the graphic

24-30. John Berg, record album cover for the *William Tell Overture*, 1963. As happened in "the new advertising," complex visual organization has been replaced by the simple presentation of a concept.

24-31. John Berg (art director) and Virginia Team (designer), record album cover for the Byrds' *Byrdmaniax*, 1971. An enigmatic image transcends normal portraiture, as masklike faces emerge from the surface.

24-32. John Berg (art director) and Nick Fasciano (illustrator), record album cover for Chicago, 1974. Images of nineteenth-century Chicago, from the stockyards to the great fire, are executed in hand-tooled leatherwork.

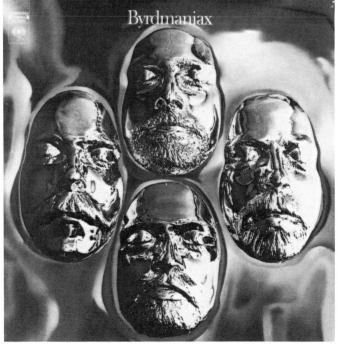

24-31

24-32

24-33. Woody Pirtle, logo for Mr. and Mrs. Aubrey Hair, 1975. In this graphic pun, the comb relates to the client's name, which is spelled by the comb's teeth.

24-34. Woody Pirtle, poster for Knoll furniture, 1982. A "hot" pepper becomes a red and green chair, signifying the availability of Knoll's "hot" furniture in Texas.

design periodical founded in 1940, instituted a regional design annual in 1981 to reflect the emerging national scope of the discipline.

The poster mania

In contrast to postwar Polish posters, which were patronized by governmental agencies as a national cultural form, the poster craze that erupted in the United States during the 1960s was a grass-roots affair fostered by a climate of social activism. The civil rights movement, the vast public protest against the Vietnam War, the early stirrings of the women's liberation movement, and a search for alternative life-styles figured into the social upheavals of the decade. The posters of the period were hung on apartment walls more frequently than they were posted in the streets. These posters made statements about social viewpoints instead of advertising commercial messages. The first wave of poster culture emerged from the late-1960s hippie subculture centered in the Haight-Ashbury section of San Francisco. Because the media and general public related these posters to antiestablishment values, rock music, and psychedelic drugs, they were called *psychedelic posters*.

The graphics movement that expressed this cultural climate drew from a number of resources: the flowing, sinuous curves of Art Nouveau, the intense optical color vibration associated with the brief Op Art movement popularized by a Museum of Modern Art exhibition, and the recycling of images from popular culture or by manipulation (such as reducing continuous-tone images to high-contrast black and white) that was prevalent in Pop Art.

Many of the initial artists in this movement were largely self-taught, and their primary clients were rock-and-roll concert and dance promoters. These dances were intense perceptual experiences of loud music and light shows that dissolved the environment with throbbing fields of projected color and bursting strobes. This experience was paralleled graphically in posters using swirling forms and lettering warped and bent to the edge of illegibility, frequently printed in close-valued complementary colors. Figure 24-35, designed by Robert Wesley "Wes" Wilson (b. 1937), evidences the Art Nouveau influence of swirling lines and letterforms, which are variants of Alfred Roller's Art Nouveau alphabets (see Fig. 15-24). Wilson was the innovator of this style and created many of the stronger images. According to newspaper reports, respectable and intelligent businessmen were unable to decipher the lettering on these posters, yet they communicated well enough to fill auditoriums with a younger generation. Other prominent members of this brief movement included Kelly/Mouse Studios and Victor Moscoso (b. 1936), the only major artist of the style with formal art training (Fig. 24-36).

Some aspects of the psychedelic poster movement were used in the wildly popular poster art of New York designer Peter Max (b. 1937). In his series of posters during the late 1960s, the Art Nouveau qualities of psychedelic poster art were combined with more accessible images and less strident colors. His most famous image, the 1970 *Love* graphic (Fig. 24-37), combined the fluid organic line of Art Nouveau with the hard, black contour of the comic book and Pop Art. In his finest work, Max experimented with images and printing techniques. The 1970 *Toulouse-Lautrec* poster (Fig. 24-38), adapted from a book jacket designed by Max for a biography of the tragic post-Impressionist, used turn-of-the-century lettering superimposed over the hat. A photograph of a bacchanal scene is printed in the letterforms using two split-fountain impressions. Cool colors are printed as a halftone; the reverse of this image is then printed in warm colors for a strange graphic effect created on the printing press.

During the early 1970s, the poster mania reached its peak. As with the rats in Albert Camus's allegorical novel, *The Plague*, it was almost as though people suddenly realized one day that the posters were gone. American poster art of inventive quality retreated to the university campus, which is one of the few surviving pedestrian environments in America. Since universities present a large number of events, the campus is an ideal poster-communications environment. A number of

24-35

24-36

24-37

prominent poster designers emerged from university design faculties. For example, Lanny Sommese (b. 1944) became a prolific poster designer (Fig. 24-39) at Penn State University during the 1970s. Drawn images were executed in a free, casual manner more reminiscent of European printmaking and graphic illustration than of American sources. Often, these images were drawn small and then greatly enlarged, which radically changed the image and the line quality. During his graduate study, Sommese photographed hundreds of wood engravings from nineteenth-century science magazines, which he later used in surreal collages.

David Lance Goines (b. 1945) proves that even in the late-twentieth-century era of overspecialization, it is possible for the individual artist or craftsman to define a personal direction and operate as an independent creative force with total control over his or her work. The eldest of eight children, this Oregon native had an early interest in calligraphy that blossomed into serious study at the University of California at Berkeley. Goines was expelled from the university at age nineteen for his participation in the free speech movement. He learned graphic arts as an apprentice pressman at the radical Berkeley Free Press, where he wrote, printed, and bound a book on calligraphy. When the Berkeley Free Press failed in 1971, Goines acquired it, renamed it the Saint Hieronymous Press, and continued to print and publish books while developing his poster style. Offset lithography and graphic design are unified in Goines's work, becoming a medium for personal expression and public communications. He designs, illustrates, and hand-letters posters, makes the negatives and plates, and then operates the press to print the edition. This thoughtful and scholarly designer has evolved a highly personal style that integrates diverse sources of inspiration. Symmetrical composition, simplified line drawing, quiet planes of flat color, and subtle stripes rimming the contours of his forms are characteristics of his poster style (Fig. 24-40).

During the 1980s, a conservative decade characterized by economic disparity between rich and poor, environmental indifference, and limited social activism, many American posters were produced as decorative objects. Limited-edition images of photographs or paintings became posters rather than reproductions because the artist's name and often a title—frequently letterspaced in elegant, all-capital type—were added. These were sold in specialty shops and department stores. Typical subjects included flowers, high-performance sports cars, and fruit presented against simple backgrounds with exquisite composition and lighting.

24-35. Wes Wilson, Buffalo Springfield/Steve Miller Blues Band concert poster, 1967. Printed in intensely vibrating and contrasting colors, the message was deciphered, rather than read, by its viewers.

24-36. Victor Moscoso, Big Brother and the Holding Company concert poster, 1966. This long-haired hippie, with his pinwheel eyes, top hat, and giant cigarette, becomes an iconic cult figure of the era.

24-37. Peter Max, "Love" poster, 1970. Max's split-fountain printing resulted in the word and linear drawing appearing as purple dissolving to blue, while the background fades from green to yellow to orange to pink.

Undergrad Student HUB GALLERY/MAY 4–JUNE 10
Art Exhibition ZOLLER GALLERY/AUG. 12–SEPT. 9

24-39

24-38. Peter Max, *Toulouse-Lautrec* book jacket and poster, 1970. Red, yellow, and purple lettering contains a period image signifying the post-Impressionist painter's bohemian life-style.

24-39. Lanny Sommese, art exhibition poster, 1979. Easels and eyes create a compelling image in the white silhouette of a head cut from an engraved interior.

24-40. David Lance Goines, classical film screening poster, 1973. A directness of image and composition gains graphic distinction from a poetic sense of color and sensitive drawing.

24-40

European visual poets

Poetry was once defined as bringing together unlike things to create a new experience or evoke an unexpected emotional response. In Europe, beginning in the 1960s and continuing into the 1990s, there emerged a poetic approach to graphic design based on imagery and its manipulation through collage, montage, and both photographic and photomechanical techniques. These graphic poets stretched time and typography, merged and floated objects, and fractured and fragmented images in a sometimes disturbing but always engaging manner. The conservative, traditional, and expected were rejected by these graphic designers, who defined the design process not as form arrangements or construction but as the invention of unexpected images to convey ideas or feelings. A receptive audience and client list developed for book and album covers, magazine designs, and posters for concerts, television, and radio.

A master of this movement is Gunther Kieser (b. 1930), who began his free-lance career in 1952. This brilliant imagist has consistently demonstrated an ability to invent unexpected visual content to solve communications problems. Kieser brings together images or ideas to create a new vitality, new arrangement, or synthesis of disparate objects (Fig. 24-41). His poetic visual statements always have a rational basis that links expressive forms to communicative content; it is this ability that separates him from design practitioners who use fantasy or Surrealism as ends rather than means.

An expansive quality is often present in Kieser's designs. Sometimes this is achieved by scale (Fig. 24-42); in other designs, by color or value contrast. In the late 1970s and early 1980s, Kieser began to construct fictitious objects that are convincingly real. Viewers stop in their tracks to study the huge posters bearing color photographs of Kieser's private visions to determine if they are having delusions. In a poster for the 1978 Frankfurt Jazz Festival (Fig. 24-43), Kieser and photographer Hartmann almost convince us that a moss-covered tree stump can grow in the shape of a trumpet. It sprouts a new branch with the same inevitability as the annual return of the jazz festival.

Launched in Munich in 1959, the German periodical *Twen,* whose name—derived by chopping the last two letters from the English word *twenty*—signified the age group of sophisticated postadolescents to whom the magazine was addressed, featured excellent photography used in dynamic layouts by art director Willy Fleckhouse. With a genius for cropping images and using typography and white

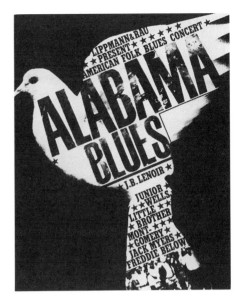

24-41. Gunther Kieser, Alabama Blues concert poster, 1966. In this stark black-and-white poster, a dove with typography inspired by nineteenth-century woodtype becomes a potent symbol of the longing for freedom and justice contained in the folk blues music.

24-42. Gunther Kieser (designer) and Hartmann (photographer), Berlin Jazz Days poster, 1975. A portrait 119.5 centimeters (about four feet) tall rips through the graphics of a bygone era, conveying the historical roots of jazz. A powerful *trompe l'oeil* effect of a poster peeling from the wall to reveal a presence beneath is created.

24-43. Gunther Kieser (designer) and Hartmann (photographer), Frankfurt Jazz Festival poster, 1978. Kieser almost convinces us that a moss-covered tree stump can grow in the shape of a trumpet.

24-42

24-43

24-45

24-44. Willy Fleckhouse (art director), cover for *Twen,* 1970. Graphic communications often become political symbols in the struggle between alternative value systems and generations.

24-45. Willy Fleckhouse (art director), pages from *Twen,* 1970. Sensitive cropping, a full-page photographic symbol, and white space create a dynamic and expansive layout.

space in unexpected ways, Fleckhouse made the bold, uninhibited pages of *Twen* a milestone in editorial design. While the Brodovitch tradition of editorial design was undoubtedly a resource for Fleckhouse, the dynamic of scale, space, and poetic images in *Twen* created a provocative and original statement (Figs. 24-44 and 24-45).

One of the most innovative image makers in late twentieth-century design is Gunter Rambow (b. 1938) of Frankfurt, Germany, who often collaborated with Gerhard Lienemeyer (b. 1936) and Michael van de Sand (b. 1945). In Rambow's graphic designs, the medium of photography is manipulated, massaged, montaged, and airbrushed to convert the ordinary into the extraordinary. Everyday images are combined or dislocated, then printed as straightforward, documentary black-and-white images in an original metaphysical statement of poetry and profundity. In a series of posters commissioned by the Frankfurt book publisher S. Fischer-Verlag for annual distribution beginning in 1976 (Fig. 24-46), the book has been used as a symbolic object, altered and transformed to make a statement about itself as a communications form. The book as a means of communicating with vast numbers of people was symbolized by a huge book emerging from a crowd scene, and the book as a door or window opening upon a world of new knowledge was symbolized by turning the cover of the book into a door one year and a window the next (Fig. 24-47). These metaphysical and symbolic advertisements carried no verbal information except the logo and name of the client, giving the audience of editors and publishers memorable and thought-provoking visual phenomena rather than a sales message.

Rambow often imbues straightforward photographs with a sense of magic or mystery (Fig. 24-48), and uses collage or montage as a means for creating a new graphic reality. Often images are altered or combined and then rephotographed. In the 1980 poster for the play *Die Hamletmaschine* (Fig. 24-49), a photograph of a wall was placed under a photograph of a man standing in front of this wall, then the top photograph was torn away. The final rephotographed image presents the viewer with a perplexing impossibility. This image seems to be capable of self-destruction—a figure appears to possess the existential ability to negate itself. The iconic power of Rambow's images can be seen in the 1988 *Südafrikanisches Roulette (Southafricans Roulette)* theatre poster (Pl. 88), designed by Rambow and photographed by Rambow and van de Sand. A bandaged hand with a bloodstain shaped like the continent of Africa conveys the pathos of suffering and revolution.

Other German practitioners of the imagist approach to graphic design include Hans Hillman (b. 1925), whose illustrations frequently combine two images in the

24-46. Gunter Rambow (designer), Gunter Rambow and Michael van de Sand (photographers), S. Fischer-Verlag poster, 1976. The portability of the book is conveyed in memorable fashion.

24-47. Gunter Rambow (designer), Gunter Rambow and Michael van de Sand (photographers), S. Fischer-Verlag poster, 1980. The book and the concept of reading as a "window on the world" gain intensity from the sunlight streaming from this volume.

24-48. Gunter Rambow (designer and photographer), Gunter Rambow and Gerhard Lienemeyer (typographers), poster for the play *Antigone,* 1978. Pathos and isolation are conveyed by the burning chair photographed from a low vantage point at dusk.

manner of Salvador Dali's simultaneous image technique, and Holger Matthies (b. 1940), whose bold images are overlapped and manipulated.

France has been a source of innovative and poetic graphic designers. During the 1960s, literary and graphic design communities throughout the world were astounded and delighted by the experimental typography of French designer Robert Massin (b. 1925), who designed editions of poetry and plays for the Paris publisher Editions Gallimard. As a young man, Massin apprenticed in sculpture, engraving, and letter-cutting under his father. Rather than seeking formal design training, he learned graphic design under typographic designer Pierre Faucheux. In its dynamic configurations and use of letterforms as concrete visual form, Massin's work has affinities with Futurist and Dada typography. But his intensification of both narrative literary content and visual form into a cohesive unity expressing the author's meaning is uniquely original. His designs for Eugene Ionesco's plays combine the pictorial conventions of the comic book with the sequencing and visual flow of the cinema. The drama is enacted through Henry Cohen's high-contrast photographs (Fig. 24-50)—each character is assigned a typeface for his or her speaking voice (Fig. 24-51), and is identified not by name but by a small photographic portrait. By printing typography via letterpress onto sheets of rubber and then manipulating and photographing it, Massin created unprecedented figurative typography (Fig. 24-52), while a large argument in the play provided him with an opportunity for an explosive typographic event (Fig. 24-53). Visual vitality, tension, and confusion appropriate to the play are graphically conveyed. In his design for Ionesco's *Delire a Deux* (Fig. 24-54), words become the expressionistic image. Massin's manipulations of typography anticipated the elastic spatial possibilities inherent in bit-mapped computer graphics of the 1980s. His many years of research into letterforms and their history led to the important 1970 book, *Letter and Image,* which explores the pictorial and graphic properties of alphabet design through the ages.

24-49. Gunter Rambow, poster for the play *Die Hamletmaschine,* 1980. A chilling sense of anonymity is produced by this self-inflicted act of vandalism.

24-50–24-53. Robert Massin (designer) and Henry Cohen (photographer), cover and double-page spreads from Eugene Ionesco's *La Cantatrice Chauve* ("The Bald Soprano"), 1964. The pictorial directness of the comic book is combined with the expressive letterforms of Futurist poetry.

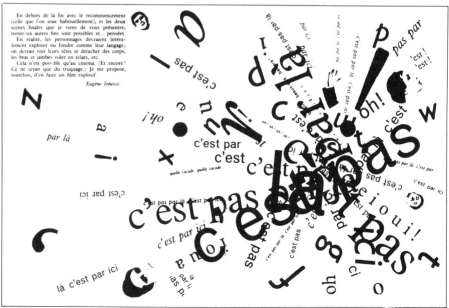

24-54. Robert Massin, pages from Eugene Ionesco's *Delire a Deux*, 1966. The words leap and run and overlap and smear into ink blots in a calligraphic homage to the nonrepresentational, surreal ideas of Ionesco, who is master of the Theater of the Absurd.

During the May 1968 student revolts in Paris, the streets were filled with posters and placards, mostly handmade by amateurs. Three young graphic designers, Pierre Bernard (b. 1942), François Miehe (b. 1942), and Gerard Paris-Clavel (b. 1943), were deeply involved in the radical politics of the day. Publicity and design, they believed, were directed toward creating artificial demands in order to maximize profits, so they joined forces to turn their graphic design toward political, social, and cultural rather than commercial ends. Seeking to address real human needs, they formed the Grapus studio in 1970 to realize this mission. Bernard and Paris-Clavel had both spent a year in Poland studying under Henryk Tomaszewski, who stressed an attitude of being both artist and citizen. His teaching advocated an intellectual rigor and clear personal conviction about the world. Grapus was a collective; intensive dialogue took place about the meaning and means of every project. In these days, French left-wing radicals were called *crapules staliniennes* ("Stalinist scum"). This phrase was melded with the word *graphic* to produce the

24-55. Grapus, political poster, 1981. During the international controversy about nuclear missiles in Europe, Grapus's "No Neutrons Mr. Reagan" was picked up by mass media throughout the world and became a typographic icon for a political position.

24-56. Grapus, theater poster, 1982. The play title, *Gevrey-Chambertin,* is the name of a popular brand of champagne. The cola bottle with a pacifier therefore becomes a particularly potent symbol.

group's name. The starting point of Grapus's problem solving was a thorough analysis and lengthy discussion about content and message. The most significant aspects of the problem and the kernel of the message were determined; then a graphic expression of the essence of the content was sought.

Major political issues were often crystallized and given a public icon by Grapus posters (Fig. 24-55). The icon was then extended through buttons, bumper stickers, small tabloid handouts, and dimensional street displays. Grapus favored universal icons with readily understood meanings: hands, wings, sun, moon, fireworks, blood, and flags. Images were cultural icons to be blended, combined, blurred, defaced, and reinvented. Typographic refinement and technical polish yielded to handwritten headlines and scrawled graffiti, creating a raw vitality and energy. Often a palette of primary colors was used for its intense graphic power. The commonplace became new and unexpected (Fig. 24-56).

Grapus has been motivated by dual goals of achieving social or political change while striving to realize creative artistic impulses. A 1982 poster (Pl. 89) for an exhibition of Grapus graphics has a central figure holding a dimensional arrow pointing toward the exposition. Bounding into the space on a jack-in-the-box spring, it layers an arresting group of cultural icons: the ubiquitous yellow smile face, Mickey Mouse's ears, and Hitler's hair and moustache. Its eyes are the communist and French tricolor indicia, and a small television antenna sprouts from the top of its head. Grapus spawned many imitators, and the shocking verve of its statement was copied by fashionable advertising.

The Third World poster

From the end of World War II until the dismantling of the Iron Curtain in 1989, the industrialized nations formed two groups: the capitalist democracies of western Europe, North America, and Japan, and the communist block led by the Soviet Union. The emerging nations of Latin America, Asia, and Africa have been called the Third World. In social and political struggles, ideas are weapons, and the poster is a major vehicle for spreading them. The medium is a good one, for access to newspapers, radio, and television is often limited in these countries, where the poster is used with the intensity and frequency of World War I European posters, with rich color bringing vitality and beauty to drab, overpopulated urban slums.

In this context, posters become vehicles to challenge authority, express dissent, or demonstrate solidarity with the oppressed. These oppositional posters are political messages operating outside the traditional censorship of government, business, and newspapers. Some of them are spontaneous expressions, crude folk art created by unskilled hands, while others are created by accomplished artists. In both cases, the artists/advocates who create this work have an agenda and seek to alter viewers' perspectives.

Third World posters address two constituencies: In their native lands, they speak about political and social issues, motivating people toward the designer's side in a political or social struggle; a secondary audience exists in the industrial democracies, where distributors such as Liberation Graphics in Alexandria, Virginia, make posters available to Westerners who feel strongly about international issues. They purchase and display posters to show personal support and solidarity with, for example, the struggle against apartheid in South Africa.

Cuba became a major center for poster design after the revolutionary force led by Fidel Castro defeated the regime of President Fulgenico Batista on New Year's Day of 1959. Over the next two years, a Marxist course was charted, leading to a complete breakdown in diplomatic ties with the United States and a close association with the Soviet block. The creative arts had been virtually ignored under Batista, but three meetings in June 1961 enabled artists and writers to meet with governmental leaders to forge a mutual understanding. At the final meeting on June 30, Castro delivered his lengthy address, "Words to the Intellectuals," defining his policy toward the creative arts. Castro assured artists and writers "that freedom of form must be respected," but freedom of content was seen as a more subtle and

24-57. Raul Martinez, poster celebrating the Cuban people, c. 1970. Leaders and workers are cheerfully depicted in a comic book drawing style and bright, intense color.

24-58. Artist unknown, poster for COR, the Commission for Revolutionary Action, 1967. Clouds parting to reveal a glimpse of the orange sun symbolize the ill-fated 26 July 1953 assault on the Santiago army barracks, which launched the Cuban revolution.

24-57

24-58

complex matter. He advised that artists and intellectuals "can find within the Revolution a place to work and create, a place where their creative spirit, even though they are not revolutionary writers and artists, has the opportunity and freedom to be expressed. This means: within the Revolution, everything; against the Revolution, nothing." The creative community was told that each person could "express freely the ideas he wants to express," but that "we will always evaluate his creation from the Revolutionary point of view." Castro defined "the good, the useful, and the beautiful" as whatever is "noble, useful, and beautiful" for "the great majority of the people—that is, the oppressed and exploited classes." Popular art forms—cinema and theater, posters and leaflets, songs and poetry—and propaganda media were encouraged. Traditional painting and sculpture were seen as relatively inefficient in reaching large audiences with the Revolutionary message.

Under these terms, artists and writers admitted to the union receive salaries, work space, and materials. Graphic designers produce their work for a variety of government agencies with specific missions. Leading Cuban graphic designers include Raul Martinez, a painter who creates illustrative designs (Fig. 24-57), and Felix Beltran (b. 1938), who was educated in New York. Beltran served as art director for the Commission for Revolutionary Action, which creates internal ideological propaganda and maintains public consciousness of the Revolution by promoting commemorative days (Fig. 24-58) and past leaders.

Bureaus and institutes have responsibility for motion pictures, musical and theatrical events, publishing, and exhibition programs, and use graphics to promote these cultural events. Emphasis is upon outreach—unlike many countries where cultural programs are only available to the urban population, a serious attempt is made to reach the rural areas. Film posters are lively and happy affairs printed in an uninhibited palette of bright silk-screened colors.

Posters and leaflets for export throughout the Third World are produced by OSPAAAL (Organization of Solidarity with Asia, Africa, and Latin America) to support revolutionary activity and build public consciousness for ideological viewpoints. OSPAAAL posters are printed via offset and use elemental symbolic images readily comprehended by people of diverse nationalities, languages, and cultural backgrounds. The Castro government sees itself as being involved in an ideological

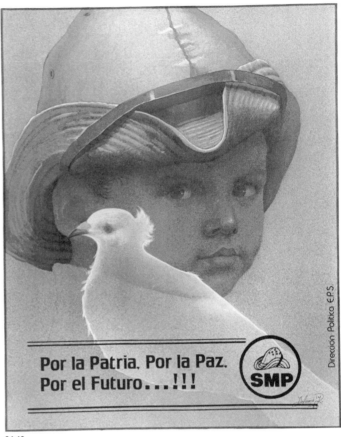

24-60

24-59. Elena Serrano, "Day of the Heroic Guerrilla" poster, 1968. An iconographic image of Che Guevara transforms into a map of South America in a radiating image signifying revolutionary victory.

24-60. Jose Salome Garcia Riveria, "For Country, For Peace, for The Future!" poster for the political office of the Sandinista Popular Militia, 1985. Cool-green tones are accented with glowing yellow and white highlights. The hat symbolizes the Sandinista movement.

war against "Yankee Imperialism" for the hearts and minds of people in the emerging Third World countries. The eye of the beholder is tantalized while revolutionary consciousness is formed through repeated exposure. The international distribution of OSPAAAL graphics is evidenced by the presence of Arabic, English, French, and Spanish typography on each poster.

Lacking artistic traditions, Cuban graphic designers have assimilated a variety of resources. Graphic styles from America—Pop Art, the psychedelic poster, and Push Pin Studio—and the Polish poster are important inspirations. The "heroic worker" school of romanticized realism of the Soviet Union and China is avoided. The icon, ideograph, and telegraphic message are far more effective in developing nations. Myth and reality have been unified in a powerful graphic symbol based on the image of Ernesto ("Che") Guevara. A leader of the Cuban revolution, Guevara left Cuba in the mid-1960s to lead guerillas in the South American country of Bolivia. On 9 October 1967, he was gunned down in the jungle village of Higuera. Graphic designers have converted Che's image, one of the most reproduced images of the late twentieth century, into a symbolic icon (Fig. 24-59) representing struggle against oppression throughout the Third World. The look of high-contrast photography conveys the fallen guerilla wearing a beard and a beret with a star; his head tilts slightly upward. This "trademark" becomes everyman, with a potency transcending Che and South America. A specific person, Ernesto Guevara, was converted into the mythic hero or savior who sacrificed his life so others might live.

The most recent flowering of a national poster movement occurred in Nicaragua after the Sandinistas ousted the Somoza dictatorship in 1979. Art schools had only been accessible to the elite, and the Nicaraguan people had no vehicles for artistic expression. After coming to power, the Sandinista government established a na-

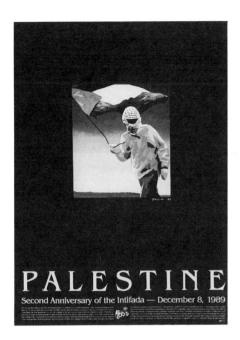

24-61. Salim Yaqub, poster commemorating the second anniversary of the Intifada, 1989. An illustration of a youthful protester is surrounded by an ominous black field.

tional art school. Nicaraguan artists have a vibrant sense of color, scale, and composition. Many exquisite posters are imbued with warmth and tenderness, and have achieved international acclaim. Self-taught Nicaraguan artist Jose Salome Garcia Riveria has created a series of posters delicately rendered in luminous, subtle color. Elemental images of peace and the future, such as a beautiful young child and dove (Fig. 24-60), are easily understood by everyone.

International solidarity posters address political struggle in one country or region but are created by graphic artists living elsewhere. These artists and their sponsors show support for a cause in an effort to increase public consciousness and concern. The posters speaking out against apartheid in South Africa, for example, are not created there, for it is illegal to produce antigovernment graphics, and the black majority does not have access to art training or printing facilities. But graphic artists in other countries, including Cuba, the United States, and Europe (see Pl. 88), produce posters that speak against apartheid. By default, a South African graphic heritage is being formed by artists outside the nation's boundaries.

Graphic images have also become an important weapon in the conflict between Israel and the Palestinians. The *Intifada,* or uprising, of Palestinians in the Israeli-occupied West Bank and Gaza territories began in December 1987. This conflict between rock-throwing Palestinian teenagers and children and the Israeli army has become an international subject for protest graphics. The 1989 poster (Fig. 24-61) by San Francisco artist Salim Yaqub (b. 1963), commemorating the second anniversary of the Intifada, has been circulated around the globe.

The importance of conceptual images in the second half of the twentieth century developed in response to many factors. Ideas and forms from modern art have filtered into popular culture. By usurping graphic art's documentary function, photography and video have repositioned graphic illustration into a more expressive and symbolic role. The complexity of the political, social, and cultural ideas and emotions graphic artists need to communicate can frequently be presented more effectively by iconic and symbolic, rather than narrative, images.

25   A Global Dialogue

25-1. Alan Fletcher, Colin Forbes, and Bob Gill, cover for *Graphis*, 1965. Asked to design a cover for this magazine carrying an article about their work, the designers mailed this parcel containing material for the article from London to Zurich with a request that it be returned unopened. Upon its return, a color photograph was made documenting its journey through the postal system. Thus, the package that carried the work to the publication also became the package that carried *Graphis* to its readers.

In 1966, the German graphic designer Olaf Leu wrote that German design no longer had any national attributes. Observing that while some might favor this development, Leu also acknowledged that others regret it. At that time, the purist geometry of the International Typographic Style and the uninhibited freedom of American design coexisted as important influences upon German design, as well as on design activity around the globe. A period of international dialogue had begun. Just as events in Southeast Asia or the Middle East directly affect Europe, the Americas, and Japan, conceptual innovation and visual invention spread like wildfire. An international culture embracing the fine arts, performing arts, and design spans national boundaries, extending from traditional centers to every corner of the globe. This has been spurred by graphic arts technology, which makes professional typography and printing possible in regional centers and developing countries, and by the rapid growth of graphic design education.

During the 1980s, the rapid development of electronic and computer technology began to change the processes and appearance of design. Overnight express mail, fax machines, global televisual communications such as the continuous Cable News Network, and direct-dial international long-distance telephone service all served to further shrink the human community into Marshall McLuhan's "global village." The advanced technology of the late twentieth century creates a cultural milieu of simultaneity—ancient and modern cultures, Eastern and Western thought, handicraft and industrial production—until past, present, and future blur into a continuum of information and visual form. This complex world of cultural and visual diversity combines with electronic and computer technology to create an explosive and pluralistic era for graphic design.

Postwar English graphic design illustrates the new internationalism. Both the purist modernism from Switzerland and the graphic expressionism from New York were assimilated. The potential pitfall of becoming a colony to these pervasive international influences was successfully avoided by outstanding English designers who made significant contributions to the international dialogue. Herbert Spencer (b. 1924) became an important voice in renewing British graphic design after the trauma of World War II through his writing, teaching, and graphic design practice. Spencer's thorough understanding of modern art and design was translated into a rare typographic sensitivity and structural vitality. As editor and designer of the journal *Typographica* and author of an influential 1969 book which informed the postwar generation about the accomplishments of earlier twentieth-century designers, *Pioneers of Modern Typography,* Spencer helped spur the worldwide dialogue.

The locus of postwar British design has been a design partnership that began in 1962 when Alan Fletcher (b. 1931), Colin Forbes (b. 1928), and Bob Gill formed the studio Fletcher, Forbes, and Gill. In 1965, after Gill left the partnership and architect Theo Crosby (b. 1925) joined the firm, the name was changed to Crosby, Fletcher, Forbes. Exhibition design, historic conservation, and industrial design were added to the firm's activities. As additional partners were added, the name of the studio was changed to Pentagram, but continued growth made even this five-pronged name obsolete, for Pentagram had sixteen partners and 130 employees in its London, New York, and San Francisco offices by 1990.

25-2. Alan Fletcher, bus poster for Pirelli slippers, 1965. The bus passengers supply the heads and shoulders for the photographic bodies wearing Pirelli slippers, giving the client twice as many square feet of advertising space as he purchased.

Intelligence and appropriate design solutions growing out of the needs of the problem are the hallmarks of Pentagram design (Fig. 25-1). An ability to evaluate the problem thoroughly and invent a dynamic visual solution became evident in the mid-1960s in such design solutions as Fletcher's 1965 bus poster for Pirelli slippers (Fig. 25-2), which used the bus passengers as part of the design. Thorough evaluation of the communications problem and the specific nature of the environmental conditions under which the design was to appear combined with wit and a willingness to try the unexpected (Figs. 25-3 and 25-4). This, perhaps, summarizes the essence of the Pentagram approach to graphic design.

We, the undersigned, deplore and oppose the Government's intention to introduce admission charges to national museums and galleries

Write in protest to your MP and send for the petition forms to Campaign Against Museum Admission Charges 221 Camden High Street London NW1 7BU

25-3. Colin Forbes, poster protesting museum admission charges, 1970. A slight change in the wording of a petition being circulated to protest admission fees to public museums, plus two dozen famous signatures, turns an ordinary document into a memorable poster.

25-4. Alan Fletcher, stationery for a film company, 1968. A "corporate identity program" for a firm whose main product is the creativity of the three partners uses an unconventional photograph of the group. The white shirts become the sheet of paper. By dividing the image, Fletcher designed business cards for the three partners using the same full-color separations.

25-5. Colin Forbes, symbol for the Zinc Development Association Die Casting Conference, 1966. Pentagram solutions seem to appear magically from the requirements of the problem. An opportunity to render the year of a conference in the male and female components of a die-casting mold occurs only once each decade.

25-6. Alan Fletcher and Georg Staehelin, logo for an exclusive boutique, 1968. By assembling ornamented initials from five different Renaissance designs, an unexpected graphic expression of the name is conveyed.

25-6

In the best English tradition, Pentagram's English partners combines a sense of the contemporary (Fig. 25-5) with a strong historical understanding (Fig. 25-6). The firm's design solutions range from clean geometric forms in corporate identity systems to a warm historicism in packaging design and graphics for smaller clients. Even the vernacular of Pop Art is called upon when appropriate. Conceptual, visual, and often expressive of British wit, the attitudes that this studio brought to graphic design enabled Britain to establish an international presence in graphic design just as it did at the turn of the century and in the years after World War I.

Postwar graphic design in Japan

Japan, an island nation off the east coast of Asia, has over 120 million people and a population density of about 729 persons per square mile. Eighty percent of the island consists of rugged, uninhabitable mountains, and both food and fuel have to be imported. Japan retained an isolated and feudal society until the middle of the nineteenth century. Its rapid industrial development throughout the course of the twentieth century, particularly during the decades since World War II, is a major testament to the will and energy of the Japanese people. During the postwar period, technological leadership and an awareness of western social patterns and life-styles raised philosophic issues for Japanese graphic designers, as they sought to maintain national traditions while incorporating international influences. The tree-planting poster (Fig. 25-7) by Ryuichi Yamashiro (b. 1920) demonstrates just how successfully this could be accomplished, as Eastern calligraphy and spatial concerns unite with a Western communications concept.

Modernist design was not widely adopted in Japan before the 1950s; the 1931 effort to incorporate Bauhaus concepts into the curriculum at the Shin School of Design and Architecture in Tokyo had a short life. One of the students during that period, Yusaku Kamekura (b. 1915), apprenticed to an architect and then worked as art director for several Japanese cultural magazines from 1937 until 1948. During the postwar recovery period, Kamekura emerged as such an influential design leader that he earned the name "Boss" in Japanese design circles. Under his leadership, Japanese graphic designers dispelled the widely held belief that visual communications must be hand-drawn, and the notion of applied arts' inferiority to fine art faded as Japanese designers established their professional status.

European Constructivism is a major resource for the Japanese design movement. However, the systematic organization and strong theoretical foundation of Constructivism is tempered by a traditional Japanese inclination toward intuitive problem-solving activity and a heritage of simplified emblematic form. But instead of the relational asymmetrical balance of European Constructivism, Japanese designers are more prone to central placement and the organization of space around

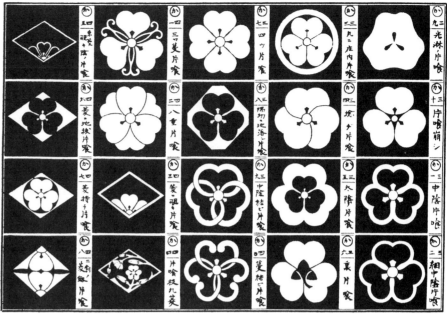

25-8

25-7. Ryuichi Yamashiro, poster for a tree-planting campaign, 1961. The Japanese characters for tree, grove, and forest are repeated to form a forest.

25-8. Japanese traditional crests and modern graphic design share direct frontal presentation of simplified images, symmetrical composition, and a refined use of line and space.

25-9. Yusaku Kamekura, booklet cover, 1954. Torn-paper Japanese characters bearing Bodoni letterforms, spelling out the same word as the Japanese forms, typify Kamekura's synthesis of Oriental and Occidental forms.

25-10. Yusaku Kamekura, magazine cover, 1957. Resonant wedges of black, red, and purple create kinetic rhythms. The kiss registration evidences the disciplined skill of Japanese printers.

a median axis, reflecting the compositional traditions of many Japanese arts and crafts. An important design inspiration for the Japanese graphic designer is the traditional family symbol or crest, the *mon* (Fig. 25-8), which has been in use for a thousand years. These simplified designs of flowers, birds, animals, plants, and household objects contained in a circle were applied to belongings and clothing.

Kamekura charted the course of this new Japanese movement through the vitality and strength of his creative work, his leadership in founding the Japan Advertising Art Club to bring professionalism and focus to the new discipline, and the establishment of the Japan Design Center in 1960. Kamekura became managing director of this organization, which brought Japan's leading graphic designers together with industry.

Technical discipline, a thorough understanding of printing techniques, and careful construction of the visual elements characterize Kamekura's work (Figs. 25-9 and 25-10). When global attention focused on Japan for the 1964 Olympics, the logo and posters created by Kamekura for these events received international acclaim and established Japan as a center of creative design activity (Figs. 25-11 and

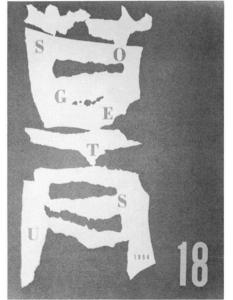

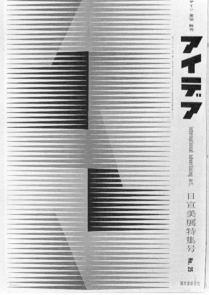

25-9

25-10

25-11. Yusaku Kamekura, Tokyo Olympics logo and poster, 1964. Three simple symbols —the red sun of the Japanese flag, the Olympic rings, and the words, *Tokyo 1964*— combine into an immediate and compelling message.

25-12). Kamekura's works are strikingly modern yet often evoke the poetic traditions of Japanese art (Fig. 25-13), and the emblematic simplicity of his Constructivist geometry (Figs. 25-14 and 25-15) is created by an extraordinary complexity, yet all parts are unified into an expressive whole.

An imaginative approach to photographic design was developed by Masuda Tadashi (b. 1922). While still a student, he was drafted under the Student Mobilization Law and spent three years in the Japanese Navy during World War II. Afterwards, he joined the prominent Dentsu Advertising Agency. A growing involvement in photographic illustration to solve graphic design problems, combined with his interest in collaborative and team design, culminated in the establishment of the Masuda Tadashi Design Institute in 1958. Many art directors and graphic designers view photographers and illustrators as subcontractors—button and pencil pushers—on call to give form to the designer's concepts. Tadashi's collaborative approach, however, with the group working as a team, allowed unexpected solutions and new ways of seeing things (Fig. 25-16) to emerge. Type placement on, above, or below the photograph is usually done with great sensitivity. A favored layout approach is to design a structure of fine, ruled lines as a vessel to contain the typographic information. Color is used very effectively: Bright colored backgrounds are sometimes contrasted against objects of contrasting hue, and a uniform color cast is often used to unify an image. Focal points, such as the rich blue paper wrapping the printing plates in a 1964 *Brain* cover (Fig. 25-17), are examples of this use of one intense color in an otherwise muted photograph.

As Japanese design evolved, the Constructivist impulse was extended by original thinkers who bestowed expression and individual vision upon the vocabulary of geometric form. Kazumasa Nagai (b. 1929), a sculpture major at the Tokyo University of Fine Arts and Music, turned to graphic design after graduating in 1951. His oeuvre might be considered as an ongoing research into linear form and the properties of line as a graphic medium for spatial modulation. His fine arts explorations through drawings and prints investigating the nature of line are the wellspring for his posters, abstract trademarks, and advertisements. Nagai's linear patterns are sometimes combined with photographs and create deep spatial vistas (Fig. 25-18), and the technical perfection of his designs and their printed production is formidable. His 1984 poster for a Paris exhibition of works by twelve Japanese graphic designers, "Tradition et Nouvelles Techniques" (Pl. 90), creates a universe of geometric forms evoking planets and energy forces moving in space.

25-12. Yusaku Kamekura (designer) and Osamu Hayasaki (photographer), Tokyo Olympics poster, 1964. A meticulously planned and lighted photograph becomes an emblematic expression of the footrace.

25-13. Yusaku Kamekura (designer) and Saburo Kitai (photographer), poster for a ski resort, 1968. The bird's-eye view and indeterminate space express the "small man/ vast world" concept of traditional Oriental painting.

25-12

25-13

25-14. Yusaku Kamekura, poster for the Osaka World Exposition, 1970. Japanese designers' imaginations are constantly tested by the need to invent new sun images as part of the heritage of "the land of the rising sun."

25-15. Yusaku Kamekura, poster for a stereo manufacturer, 1980. Technical perfection in stereo sound is signified by bright yellow, pink, and blue traceries darting around a black linear triangle on a deep blue field.

25-16. Masuda Tadashi (designer) and Imamura Masaaki (photographer), advertisement for Atorie Sha, 1960. Imaginative photography transforms matches signifying many ideas into a wonderful graphic blossom.

25-17. Masuda Tadashi (designer) and Doki Mitsuo (photographer), cover for *Brain* magazine, 1964. To illustrate an article on typography, metal printing plates are wrapped in typographic printed proofs, which are torn to reveal the contents.

While Nagai bases his designs on line, Ikko Tanaka (b. 1930) uses plane and shape as the nucleus for his graphic language. After graduating from Kyoto Municipal College of Fine Arts in 1950, Tanaka worked as a textile designer before shifting to graphic design. Over the course of the 1950s, Tanaka assimilated the modern design language developed at the Bauhaus, eventually opening Tanaka

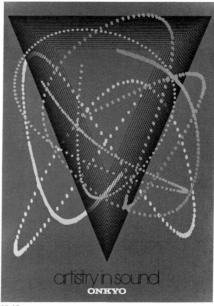

25-14

25-15

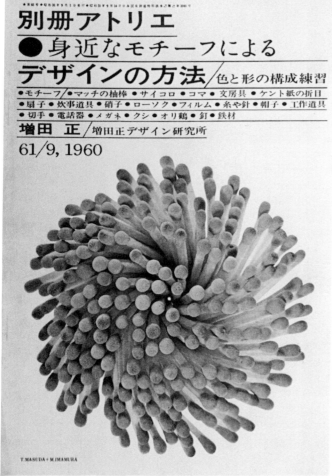

25-16

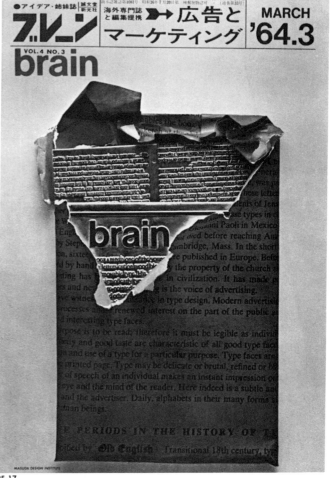

25-17

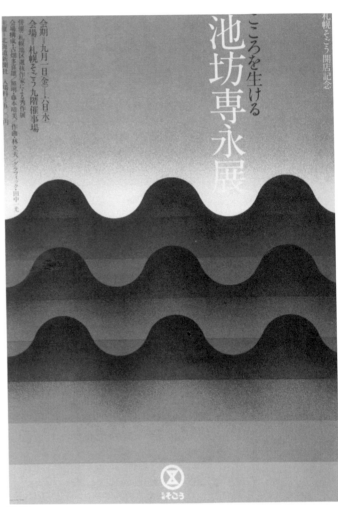

25-18

25-19

Design Studio in 1963. Tanaka is a pluralistic designer who has explored many directions. Two underlying visual concepts in much of his work are grid structure and vibrant planes of color, exploring warm/cool contrast, close-valued color, and analogous color ranges. Traditional Japanese motifs, including landscape (Fig. 25-19), Kanze Noh Theater, calligraphy, masks, and woodblock prints, are reinvented in the form language of modern design. In some of his most original works, color planes are arranged on a grid to signify stylized and expressive portraits, as seen in his 1981 poster for "Nihon Buyo" at the Asian Performing Arts Institute (Pl. 91). Tanaka has created a remarkable range of emotions and personalities through this approach.

Takenobu Igarashi (b. 1944) is a paradigm of the blending of Eastern and Western ideas. After graduating from Tama University in 1968, Igarashi earned a graduate degree from the University of California, Los Angeles. Upon returning to Japan, he discovered that design firms and corporations were not receptive to a designer who had spent time abroad, so he opened his own design office in 1970. Much of Igarashi Studio's work is in trademark, corporate identity, environmental, and product design. By 1976, Igarashi's experiments with alphabets drawn on isometric grids were attracting clients and international recognition (Fig. 25-20). The isometric alphabets have evolved into three-dimensional alphabetic sculptures that Igarashi calls *Architectural Alphabets*. These have been applied to signage as part of visual identity programs (Figs. 25-21). Igarashi achieves unexpected variety in his isometric alphabets. The exploding letters of the Expo '85 poster (Fig. 25-22) become a metaphor for the materials and processes of the built environment. In 1983, Igarashi began a ten-year project of designing the Igarashi Poster Calendar,

25-20. Takenobu Igarashi, shopping bag for Citizen's Watch Company, 1976. The flying blocks signify the passing of time.

25-18. Kazumasa Nagai, corporate-image advertisement for Toshiba Corporation, 1982. A surreal landscape of linear patterns expresses the title, "Toshiba's electronics technology . . . for man and his future."

25-19. Ikko Tanaka, poster for Senei Ikenobo's flower arrangement, 1974. The mountains and waves of traditional woodblock prints are evoked by a rhythmic sequence of blue and blue-green bands under a graduated tan sky.

25-21. Takenobu Igarashi, trademark for Parco Part 3 department store, 1981. Letters assembled of geometric segments lend themselves to flat relief and three-dimensional interpretation in environmental signage.

25-22. Takenobu Igarashi, poster for Expo'85, 1982. A blue background is animated by warm planes of color. The subject of the international science and technology exposition, dwellings and surroundings, is evoked by the structurelike forms.

starting with five years for the Museum of Modern Art in New York and then continuing with five more for the Alphabet Gallery in Tokyo. As shown in the 1990 calendar (Pl. 92), each month has a different design theme and each number is a unique drawing. After ten years, Igarashi will have designed 6,226 numbers.

Igarashi notes that 95 percent of his design is based on a grid system. His work is formed from an elemental form language: the dot, the smallest component of design; lines, which define positions and create boundaries between planes; grids, whose x and y axes bring mathematical order to his work; surfaces, which can be visual and tactile; flat or dimensional planes; and the creative language of circle, triangle, and square. Igarashi's best works achieve boundlessness (Fig. 25-23), an expansive power created by color, texture, and ambiguity.

The design vocabulary of Tadanori Yokoo (b. 1936) replaces the order and logic of Constructivism with the restless vitality of Dada and a fascination with mass media, popular art, and comic books. During the mid-1960s, Yokoo used the comic book technique of black line drawing as a vessel to contain flat areas of photomechanical color. Photographic elements were often collaged into the designs, and traditional Japanese images were translated into the Pop Art idiom (Fig. 25-24). During the late 1960s and into the 1970s, Yokoo's design vocabulary and range of art and printing techniques became increasingly uninhibited. Nudes painted with fluorescent paint then appear photographed under ultraviolet light, a samurai warrior in front of a rear-projected image of the Arch of Triumph in Paris raises his foot to reveal a portrait painted on his sole, and collaged butterflies flutter daintily above the lava flow from an erupting volcano. The *Sixth International Biennial Exhibition of Prints in Tokyo* poster (Fig. 25-25) combines a variety of techniques: a halftone group portrait in pink; a sky with an airbrushed brown band across the top and a red one at the horizon; calligraphic writing on vertical bands, as found in earlier oriental art; and a monumental, montaged figure towering over the lighthouse on the bank across the water. During the 1970s and 1980s, Yokoo's work often moved toward unexpected and even mystical images (Fig. 25-26). An artist

25-24

25-25

25-23. Takenobu Igarashi, poster for the Kanagawa Art Festival, 1984. A universe composed of dots evokes boundless time and space.

25-24. Tadanori Yokoo, poster for Koshimaki Osen, 1966. East and West meet in a virtual catalogue of images and techniques.

25-25. Tadanori Yokoo, poster for a printmaking exhibition, 1968. As Yokoo began to open his densely packed spaces and expand his range of printing techniques, he moved from Pop Art to personal statement.

often speaks for a generation; in Yokoo's case, he expresses the passions and curiosity of a Japanese generation that grew up with American mass popular culture and electronic media—television, movies, radio, and records. Accordingly, shifting values and a rejection of tradition find symbolic expression in Yokoo's uninhibited graphics, and he gained a reputation not unlike the "cult figure" status attained by rock musicians such as the Beatles. Perhaps more than any other visual artist of his generation, Yokoo translates this phenomenon into his work.

Designs by Shigeo Fukuda (b. 1932) are disarmingly simple, as readable and immediate as a one-panel cartoon, and yet they engage the viewer with their unexpected violations of the spatial logic and universal order. After completing his education at the Tokyo University of Fine Arts, Fukuda soon became known for his unconventional view of the world, a concept at the heart of his work. The disarming

25-26. Tadanori Yokoo, exhibition poster, 1973. The reds, blues, and golds of a Persian carpet frame an enigmatic black rectangle, where two plates of food hover inexplicably.

25-27. Shigeo Fukuda, "Victory 1945" poster, 1975. The simple act of turning the shell back toward the gun signifies the folly of war.

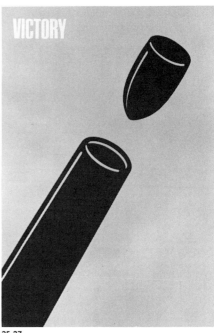

25-26

25-27

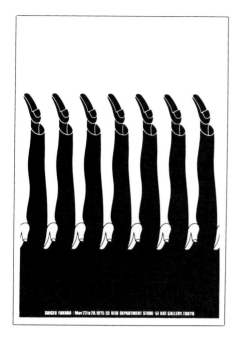

25-28. Shigeo Fukuda, exhibition poster for Keio department store, 1975. "Impossible" optical illusions frequent Fukuda's work.

25-29. Shigeo Fukuda, teacups, 1975. Fukuda's visual puns and illusions are expressed three-dimensionally in toys, products, and sculpture.

directness of his work is seen in "Victory 1945," awarded first prize in an international competition for a poster commemorating the thirtieth anniversary of the end of World War II (Fig. 25-27). In other works, he expresses a nonverbal concept or presents an inexplicable visual phenomenon (Fig. 25-28). His images are a construct of memory and association rather than a direct impression of the senses.

Playfulness and humor are abundant in Fukuda's work. The enigma and contradictions of Dada and Surrealism are reinvented—not with high-minded seriousness, but with a joyful affection for everyday life (Fig. 25-29). Given his humor and simplified drawing, one might ask what separates Fukuda's work from ordinary comics. Intentional ambiguity and purposefulness pervade his work, giving it a life beyond the ephemeral or disposable. With the simplest of means, a complex idea is projected with disarming clarity and unexpected imagery.

The Japanese understand nonverbal communication, in part because Zen Buddhism teaches the use of all five senses in receiving communication, and even states that "silence is communication." In this tradition, Koichi Sato (b. 1944) brings delicate color motifs and metaphysical forms to his quietly poetic designs. Sato graduated from Tokyo University of Art and Music in 1968 and opened his own studio two years later. His painting of a white tray—which he tilted so the blue-colored water filling it graduated toward one end of the tray—became an important inspiration for his evolution. His first use of gradation in his graphic design is in a 1974 concert poster (Fig. 25-30).

Sato thinks in opposites: traditional/futuristic; organic/mechanic; East/West; light/dark. He writes haiku poetry, and his graphic designs share the multiple levels of meaning and expression of deep emotion found in this traditional form. Auras and glowing luminosity are found in his work (Fig. 25-31), and many of his works from the 1980s are glowing fields of color, integrated with Japanese calligraphy. In Sato's 1984 concert poster, "Eclipse Music '84" for Map Company, Ltd. (Pl. 93), the red background turns the yellow and blue calligraphy into a kinetic expression of the surging energy of the music.

The postwar miracle of Japan, as it rose from the ashes of defeat to become a leader in technology and manufacturing, is paralleled by its emergence as a major center for graphic creativity. Contemporary Japanese graphic design has a strong emphasis upon the aesthetic dimension, not at the expense of communicating the client's message, but as a means to reinforce and extend it.

25-31

25-30. Koichi Sato, New Music Media poster for the May Corporation, 1974. A black fish, glowing pale-green water, and a black box with outside shading emit a quiet poetry.

25-31. Koichi Sato, image poster for the Yuny supermarket, 1985. A metaphysical event in a subtle palette of blues creates a poetic image for the client.

Supermannerism and supergraphics

Like so many art history labels, *Supermannerism* was first used as a disparaging term. Mannerism is the term generally used to label the stylish art of the 1500s, which broke with the natural and harmonious beauty of the High Renaissance. This word, describing a departure from the norm that takes liberties with the classical vocabulary of form, was elevated to Supermannerism by the advocates of the purist modern movement to describe work by young architects whose expanded design vocabulary embraced the Pop Art notion of changing scale and context and introduced zigzag diagonals into the cool formal vocabulary of the right angle. Supermannerism rejected the machine aesthetic and simple geometric forms of the International Style.

In the 1960s, the application of graphic designs to architecture in large-scale environmental graphics extended the formal concepts of Art Concret and the International Typographic Style. *Supergraphics* became the popular name for bold geometric shapes of bright color, giant Helvetica letterforms, and huge pictographs warping walls, bending corners, and flowing from the floor to the wall and across the ceiling. Supergraphics can expand or contract space as its scale changes relative to the architecture. Psychological as well as decorative values were addressed as designers created forms to enliven dismal institutional architecture, reverse or shorten the perspective of endless hallways, and bring vitality and color to the built environment.

The most controversial and original Supermannerist architect is Philadelphia-born Robert Venturi (b. 1925), who looked at the vulgar and disdained urban land-

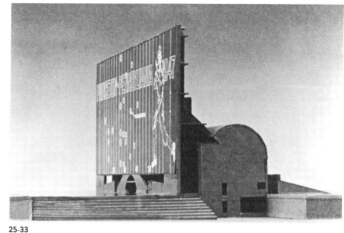

25-33

25-32. Robert Venturi, interior of Grand's Restaurant, 1962. Giant stencil letterforms, repeated in mirror image on the opposite wall, alter the scale and space of the environment. *(Photograph by Lawrence S. Williams.)*

25-33. Robert Venturi, competition model for the Football Hall of Fame, 1967. A vast, kinetic electronic graphics display dominates the building, as information replaces structure as the dominant "subject" of architecture. *(Photograph by George Pohl.)*

scape of billboards, electric signs, and pedestrian buildings and found a vitality and functional purpose there. He urged designers to learn from the hyperbolic glitter of Las Vegas. Venturi saw the building not as sculptured form but as a component of the larger urban traffic/communication/interior/exterior environmental system. Uncommon uses and juxtaposition of materials, graphic elements from the commercial roadside strip, billboards, and environmental-scale lettering were freely added to his architectural vocabulary. Perhaps the large graphic wall decorations of his 1962 diner-inspired Grand's Restaurant (Fig. 25-32) in West Philadelphia (now destroyed) were the impetus for the Supergraphics concept. Venturi sees graphic communications and new technologies as important tools for architecture—his proposal for the Football Hall of Fame (Fig. 25-33) used a giant illuminated sign that would have been visible for miles on the approaching interstate highway.

Supermannerist architect Charles W. Moore (b. 1925) designed a large condominium project at Gualala, California, in the mid-1960s. He called upon graphic designer Barbara Stauffacher Solomon (b. 1932) to bring the walls and ceilings of this large architectural project to life through the application of color and shape (Fig. 25-34). Solomon, a San Francisco native and painter who had studied graphic

25-34. Barbara Stauffacher Solomon, supergraphics for Sea Ranch, 1966. Vibrant primary colors, Helvetica letterforms, arcs, and slashing diagonals form a strong counterpoint to the architectural structure and the brilliant California sunshine streaming through the windows.

design at the Basel School of Design during the late 1950s, used a vocabulary of pure hue and elementary shape in compositions that transformed the totality of the space. In 1970, the American Institute of Architects presented its medal to Solomon for "bold, fresh, and exciting designs clearly illustrating the importance of rational but vigorous graphics in bringing order to the urban scene."

Both the name Supergraphics and the idea caught the public's fancy, and by 1970 Supergraphics was being incorporated into corporate identification systems, decorating shops and boutiques, and brightening factory and school environments, creating an impetus toward greater graphic-design involvement in environmental graphics.

Post-Modern Design

In the 1970s, the term *Post-Modernism* came into use to label the work of architects and designers who were breaking with the International Style that had been prevalent in architecture and design since the Bauhaus. A general feeling developed that the modern era was drawing to a close in art, design, politics, and literature. The social, economic, and environmental awareness of the period caused many to feel that the modern aesthetic was no longer relevant to what was rapidly becoming a post-industrial society of shrinking resources. New technologies and social concerns pushed designers toward unprecedented forms to express the needs and feelings of the era.

Post-Modernism sent shock waves through the design establishment as it challenged the order and clarity of design, particularly corporate design. (Some observers reject the term Post-Modern, arguing that it is merely a continuation of the modern movement. *Late Modernism* and *Mannerism* are proffered as alternative terms for late twentieth-century design.) Design forms have political and social meaning, expressing the attitudes and values of their time; Post-Modernism gained a strong foothold among the generation of American designers who emerged in the 1970s. Perhaps the International Typographic Style had been so thoroughly refined, explored, and accepted that a backlash was inevitable. The 1970s were called the "me generation" because the social protest of the late 1960s gave way to more self-absorbed, personal involvements. The intuitive and playful aspects of Post-Modernism reflect the personal involvement. Post-Modern designers place a form in space because it "feels" right, rather than to fulfill a rational communicative need. As radically different as a psychedelic poster and a corporate design manual might be, both are *corporate* design, for or relating to a unified body of people with common values. Much Post-Modernist design, on the other hand becomes subjec-

25-35. Rosmarie Tissi, advertisement for E. Lutz & Company, 1964. The space comes to life through subtle shifts and angles that throw the page into a state of suspended animation.

25-36. Siegfried Odermatt, advertisement for Union, 1968. Overlapping and cropping the logo, printed in black and blue-gray, bring the vitality and impact of pure form to the newspaper page.

25-37. Siegfried Odermatt, advertisement for Union, 1969. The white logo on a red background is folded and bent into a pure expression of dynamic form.

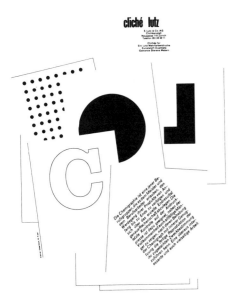

25-35

25-36

25-37

tive and even eccentric; the designer becomes an artist performing before an audience as surely as a musician in the park, and the audience either responds or passes on.

The umbrella term *Post-Modernism* does not tell the whole story, because while architecture may fit rather neatly into simple stylistic boxes (Victorian, Art Nouveau, Modern, and Post-Modern), graphic design is far too pluralistic and diverse to fit such a simplistic system of styles. Just three examples of graphic design expressions having no parallel in architecture are the Push Pin Style, the psychedelic poster, and the typographic designs of Herb Lubalin. Graphic design, rapidly changing and ephemeral, was never dominated by the International Style the way architecture was. Post-Modern graphic design can be loosely categorized into several major directions: the early extensions of the International Typographic Style by Swiss designers who broke with the dicta of the movement; *New Wave Typography,* which began in Basel, Switzerland, through the teaching and research of Wolfgang Weingart (b. 1941); the exuberant mannerism of the early 1980s, with significant contributions from the Memphis group in Milan, Italy, and from San Francisco designers; *Retro,* the eclectic revivals and eccentric reinventions of earlier models, particularly European vernacular and modern design from the decades between the world wars; and the electronic revolution spawned by the Macintosh computer in the late 1980s, which drew upon all of the earlier thrusts.

Post-Modern graphic design first emerged in the work of individuals trained in the International Style of Typography who enlarged its formal vocabulary in the 1960s. The main thrust of the International Typographic Style was toward neutral and objective typography; the playful, unexpected, or disorganized were rarely allowed to encroach upon its cool clarity and scientific objectivity. One of the earliest indications that a younger generation of graphic designers was starting to break with the International Typographic Style is the 1964 advertisement (Fig. 25-35) for the printer E. Lutz & Company by Rosmarie Tissi. Different kinds of copy, printed by the client—headlines, text, halftones, and solids—are illustrated by elemental symbols. Instead of these images being lined in boxes ordered on a grid, as one might expect from a Swiss designer, the five images appear as if they have been intuitively and randomly placed in a pile. The ruled lines forming the edges of the squares upon which these images rest have lost-and-found edges that force the viewer to fill in the missing lines.

In 1966, Siegfried Odermatt designed a trademark for the Union Safe Company that is the antithesis of Swiss design, for the letterforms in the word "Union" are jammed together to form a compact unit suggesting the sturdy strength of the product, sacrificing legibility in the process. In full-page newspaper advertisements for Union (Figs. 25-36 and 25-37), placed during prestigious banking conferences, Odermatt treated this logo as pure form to be manipulated visually, creating a plastic dynamic on the newspaper page. Odermatt and Tissi have always used strong graphic impact, a playful sense of form, and unexpected manipulation of space in the context of finding a logical and effective solution to a design problem.

When Odermatt and Tissi have turned to typeface design, their originality of form has produced unexpected letterforms, as can be seen in Tissi's 1980 advertisement for Englersatz AG (Fig. 25-38), which features her typefaces. A 1981 presentation folder designed by Tissi for the printing firm Anton Schöb (Pl. 94) achieves a typographic vitality by overlapping and combining letterforms. Placing text typography on geometric shapes whose configuration is generated by the line lengths of the text is a technique the pair frequently used during the 1980s.

Another Swiss designer with a strong interest in complexity of form is Steff Geissbuhler (b. 1942), who joined the Geigy pharmaceutical company in the mid-1960s. In a capabilities brochure for the publicity department (Fig. 25-39), Geissbuhler's swirling typographic configuration becomes a circular tunnel moving back into space. Geissbuhler moved to Philadelphia and established an independent design practice before joining Chermayeff & Geismar Associates as a partner. Geissbuhler's complexity of form is never used as an end in itself; the dynamic of

25-38. Rosmarie Tissi, advertisement for Englersatz AG, printers, 1980. The whimsical geometric shapes of Tissi's typefaces engage the viewer with their texture and dimension.

25-39. Steff Geissbuhler, brochure cover for Geigy, 1965. Legibility is sacrificed in favor of dynamic visual organization.

25-40. Steff Geissbuhler, poster for Blazer financial services, 1974. A kinetic repetition of forms moving across the space suggests travel in one of five posters used as decorative and functional wall displays.

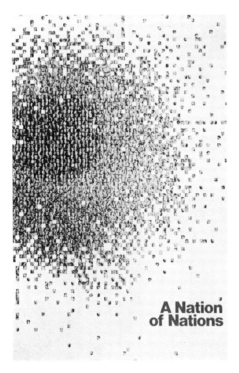

25-41. Steff Geissbuhler, poster for the Nation of Nations Exhibition, 1976. To symbolize America as a nation of immigrants, hundreds of portrait photographs of immigrants are assembled into a complex configuration that seems to expand and contract in space.

multiple components forming a whole grows from the fundamental content of the design problem at hand (Figs. 25-40 and 25-41).

Odermatt, Tissi, Geissbuhler, and others working in the 1960s did not rebel against the International Style; rather, they expanded its parameters. This was followed by a revolt, which began in the 1970s as practitioners and teachers schooled in the International Style sought to reinvent typographic design. These new directions were quickly labeled *New Wave Typography*.

New Wave Typography

Just as Herbert Bayer, Jan Tschichold, and others innovated a new approach to typographic design in the 1920s, a new approach in opposition to the cool formalism of the modernist tradition emerged first in Switzerland, then spread around the world. In 1964, young Wolfgang Weingart, who had already completed a three-year apprenticeship in typography and studied art (Fig. 25-42), arrived in Basel from southeastern Germany to study with Emil Ruder. Weingart joined Armin Hofmann on the faculty of the Basel School in 1968. Originally, Weingart had worked under the influence of Ruder and Hofmann; when he began to teach, however, he determined that he must teach type differently from his mentors. Weingart began to question the typography of absolute order and cleanness. He wondered if perhaps the International Style had become so refined and prevalent throughout the world that it had reached an anemic phase. Rejecting the right angle as an exclusive organizing principle, Weingart achieved a joyous and intuitive design with a richness of visual effects. Ideology and rules collapsed in the face of his boundless energy. Drawing upon broad technical knowledge and a willingness to explore the untried, he heated up the intensity of the page.

From 1968 until 1974, Weingart worked with lead type and letterpress systems (Figs. 25-43 through 25-45). In his teaching and personal projects, he consciously sought to breathe a new spirit into the typography of order and neatness by questioning the premises, rules, and surface appearances that were hardening the innovations of the Swiss masters into an academic style in the hands of their followers. Time-honored traditions of typography and visual language systems were rethought: Why must paragraphs be indicated by indents? What other ways could be invented to divide text visually? Why not change weights in midword? To emphasize an important word in a headline, Weingart often reversed it from a chunky, black rectangle. Wide letterspacing, discarded in the fetish for tight type in the revolution from metal to photographic typographic systems in the 1960s, was explored. Responding to a request to identify the kind of typographic design he created, Weingart's list included sunshine type, bunny type, ant type, five-minute type, typewriter type, and for-the-people type. This sense of humor and expressive use of language metaphor to define his work finds close parallels in his typographic invention.

But by the mid-1970s, Weingart set off in a new direction when he turned his attention toward offset printing and film systems. The printer's camera was used to alter images and the unique properties of the film image were explored. Weingart began to move away from purely typographic design and embraced collage as a medium for visual communication (Fig. 25-46). A new technique—the sandwiching or layering of images and type that have been photographed as film positives—enabled him to overlap complex visual information (Fig. 25-47), juxtapose textures with images (Fig. 25-48), and unify typography with pictorial images in unprecedented ways. He took particular delight in the graphic qualities of enlarged halftone dots (Fig. 25-49) and the moiré patterns that are produced when these dot patterns are overlapped and then shifted against each other. His design process involves multiple film positives and masks that are stacked, arranged, then exposed with careful registration to produce one negative, which goes to the printer. In color work such as the 1982/83 Kunstkredit exhibition poster (Pl. 95), the process is extended into an interaction of layers of modulated color warping and bending the space.

25-42. Wolfgang Weingart, part of a German typesetter's examination, 1963. The strong influence of Swiss typography is evident.

25-43. Wolfgang Weingart, experimental text setting, 1969. Traditional wordspacing and letterspacing concepts dating to the medieval manuscript were called into question.

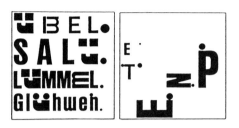

25-44. Wolfgang Weingart, typographic experiments, 1971. A form-and-space exploration relates bullets to letterforms. Four German words explore inverted lowercase m forms to make a B and e, while colons and apostrophes combine to form accented u letterforms.

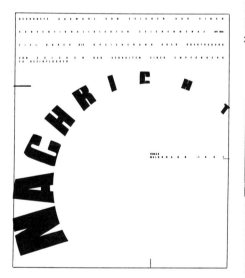

25-45. Wolfgang Weingart, cover for a typographic journal, 1971. The baseline and capline become arcs slicing away parts of the letters in the word Nachricht (Information).

25-46. Wolfgang Weingart, announcement from Typografische Monatsblätter magazine, 1974. This early layered collage, with overlapping images and complex drop-outs, uses numbers and arrows, rather than left-to-right and top-to-bottom sequencing, to direct the reader through the page.

Hausanschlußkästen aus Isolierstoff	BEG	Berliner Elektrizitäts-Gesellschaft	
Hausanschlußsicherungen		1000 Berlin	
Berührungsschutz für den Netzanschluß		Postfach 437	
Steuerleitungsklemmen		Fernruf	59 67 21
Endverschlußrichter			

BEG

25-42

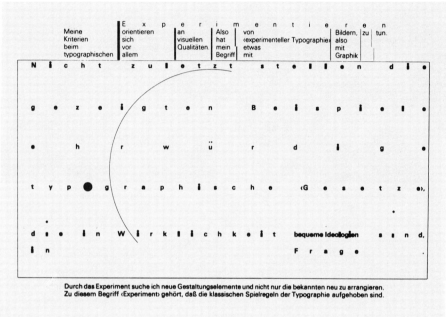

25-43

25-46

Weingart advocates the "Gutenberg approach" to graphic communications: the designer, like the early typographic printers, should strive to maintain an involvement in all aspects of the process (including concept, typesetting, prepress production, and printing) to ensure the realization of his or her vision. By the time homogenized versions of Weingart's innovations were assimilated into the main-

25-47

25-48

25-49

stream of graphic design, he had moved on to new explorations, including, since 1984, computer investigations.

In October 1972, Weingart traveled to America and delivered presentations at eight prominent design schools. His new design sensibility fell on fertile soil. Young designers who spent time at Basel—including Dan Friedman (b. 1945), April Greiman (b. 1948), and Willi Kunz (b. 1943)—came to America to teach and practice. A new typographic vocabulary began to filter into an American design profession restless with the redundancy of sans serif and grid-based corporate systems. Weingart and others who pioneered the typographic new wave strongly reject the notion of style and see their work as an attempt to expand the parameters of typographic communication; yet their work was so widely imitated, especially in design education, that it gave rise to a prevailing typographic style of the late 1970s and 1980s. Specific design ideas explored by Weingart and his students in the late 1960s and early 1970s and adopted a decade later include: letterspaced sans serif type; bold stair-step rules; ruled lines punctuating and energizing the space; diagonal type; mixing italic type and/or weight changes within words; and type reversed from a series of bars.

Dan Friedman, who studied at the Ulm Institute of Design in 1967–1968 and at the Basel School of Design from 1968–1970, rethought the nature of typographic forms and how they could operate in space (Fig. 25-50). After returning to America, he taught courses at Yale University and Philadelphia College of Art in 1970–1971. At a time when letterpress typography was collapsing but the new photographic and computer-generated processes were still evolving, Friedman addressed the problem of teaching the basics of a new typography through syntactic and semantic investigations (Fig. 25-51). After exploring principles of rhythm, harmony, and proportion, students were given a neutral message in 30-point Univers 55 and 65. A sequence of design operations ranging from simple to complex was made with the message, generating the effects of message variation through changes in the following: position; weight and scale; slant (roman to italic); line-, word-, and letterspacing; clustering; symbolic gesture; and pictorial confrontation. Another concern was an evaluation of legibility and readability, for Friedman believed "that legibility (a quality of efficient, clear, and simple reading) is often in conflict with readability (a quality which promotes interest, pleasure, and challenge in reading)." Friedman challenged the students to make their work both functional and aesthetically unconventional. Exploration of the various elemental spacings gives

25-47. Wolfgang Weingart, exhibition poster, 1977. A kaleidoscope of shifting images and forms calls experience of the museum and its art into play.

25-48. Wolfgang Weingart, cover for the Japanese design magazine *Idea,* 1979. Although he had never visited Japan, Weingart combined imagery evocative of his impressions of that land: snowcapped Mount Fujiyama, rolling fog, industry, a rising sun, earthquakes, and fragile blossoms (which are a halftone made by placing flowers directly in an engraver's camera).

25-49. Wolfgang Weingart, exhibition poster, 1982. Moiré patterns are created by layered film positives.

25-50

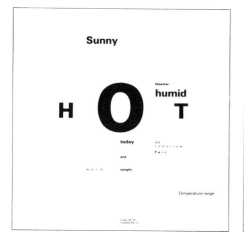

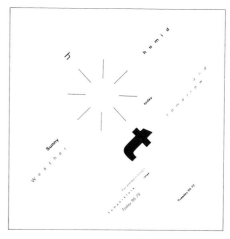

25-51. Dan Friedman (instructor) and Rosalie Hanson (student), typographic permutations, 1970. Working with a daily weather report, Friedman's students were challenged to explore contrasts: functional/unconventional; legibility/readability; simple/complex; orderly/disorderly; legible/unpredictable; static/dynamic; banal/original.

25-50. Dan Friedman, cover for *Typografische Monatsblätter* magazine, 1971. Letterforms become kinetic objects moving in time and space in a metaphorical landscape.

some of these works a quality of being *deconstructed*—that is, the syntactic structure has been pulled apart. But even in the most random solutions, an underlying structure is evident. The 1973 publication of this work in the journal *Visible Language* had a widespread influence upon typographic education in America and in other countries.

Friedman's graphic designs, furniture, and sculptural works are paradigms of the emerging Post-Modern currents. His formal background at Ulm and typographic experimentation at Basel were synthesized as he played formal structure against spontaneous and expressive forms (Figs. 25-52 and 25-53). Texture, surface, and spatial layering are explored in his work; the organic and the geometric are contrasted. Friedman believes that forms can be amusing to look at, and provocative, and he freely injects these properties into his work.

On the west coast, April Greiman established a studio in Los Angeles after studying with Weingart and Hofmann in Basel during the early 1970s. Weingart observed that "April Greiman took the ideas developed at Basel in a new direction, particularly in her use of color and photography. All things are possible in America!" While Greiman draws from the design vocabulary developed at Basel, using forms such as the step-rule at the bottom of the Luxe logotype (Fig. 25-54) which was inspired by the step-pattern of the stairways in ruins at an archaeological site that Weingart visited on his travels, she evolved a new attitude toward space (Figs. 25-55 through 25-57). Typographic design has usually been the most two dimensional of all the visual disciplines; Greiman achieves a sense of depth in her typographic pages. Overlapping forms, diagonal lines that imply perspective or reverse perspective, gestured strokes that move back in space, overlap, or move behind geometric elements, and floating forms that cast shadows are the means used to make forms move forward and backward from the surface of the printed page.

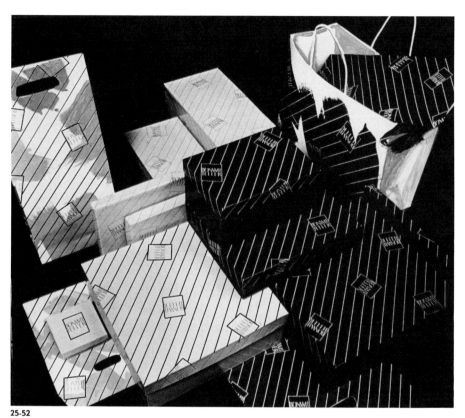

25-52

25-53

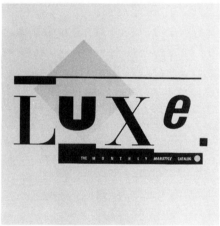

25-54

25-52. Dan Friedman (in association with Anspach Grossman Portugal, Inc.), Bonwit Teller gift-packaging proposal, 1977. Spontaneous handmade forms are layered with mechanical linear patterns and typography.

25-53. Dan Friedman, order form for Chicken Little's, 1978. Rational clarity is juxtaposed with a loose, decorative spontaneity.

25-54. April Greiman, masthead for *Luxe,* 1978. The step-rule, mixture of letterspaced and italic type, and isolation of each letter as an independent form reflect Greiman's Basel heritage.

Greiman's typographic space operates with the same governing principle defined by El Lissitzky in his PROUN paintings but never applied to his typographic designs.

Strong tactile qualities are found in Greiman's work, as textures including enlarged four-color process screens and repetitive dot patterns or ruled lines contrast with broad, flat shapes of color or tone. The intuitive dispersal of numerous elements could collapse into chaos, but a "point–counterpoint" organizational system

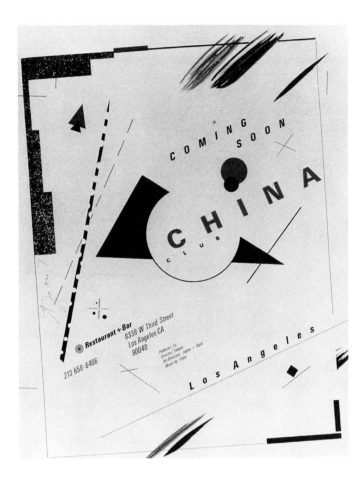

25-56

25-55. April Greiman, advertisement for China Club, 1980. Overlapping forms and movements in and out of space dissolve the flat typographic page.

25-56. April Greiman, invitation for China Club, 1980. The space is energized by gestural and geometric forms moving in counterpoint to the typographic structure.

25-57. April Greiman and Jayme Odgers, poster for California Institute of the Arts, 1979. The printed surface is redefined as a continuum of time and space.

maintains order by pulling the eye into the page through dominant elements that quickly give way to others as the viewer moves through the page's richness of form.

In collaboration with the photographer Jayme Odgers (b. 1939), Greiman moved graphic design and photographic illustration into a new realm of dynamic space. Graphic elements become part of the "real space" of photographs. Wide angle photographs by Odgers with extreme depth of field have objects thrusting into the picture space from the peripheral edges.

Swiss-born Willi Kunz played a role in introducing the new typography developed at Basel into the United States. After apprenticing as a typesetter, Kunz completed his post graduate studies at the Zurich School of Arts and Crafts. Kunz moved to New York City in 1970 and worked there as a graphic designer until 1973, when he accepted a one-year appointment to teach typography at the Basel School of Design as Weingart's sabbatical-leave replacement. Inspired by the research of Weingart and his students, and with the type shop at his disposal, Kunz

25-57

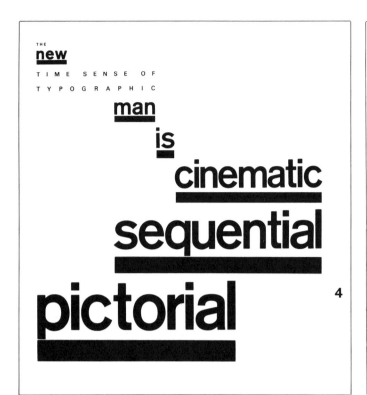

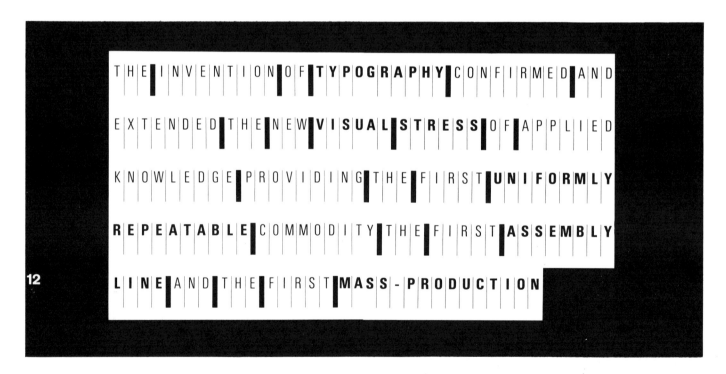

25-58. Willi Kunz, pages from *12 T y p o graphical Interpretations,* 1975. McLuhan noted that Kunz understood "the resonant interval in structuring designs."

began a series of typographic interpretations of writings by Canadian philosopher Marshall McLuhan. These were hand printed and published under the title *12 T y p o graphical Interpretations* (Fig. 25-58). McLuhan's thoughts on communications and printing were visualized and intensified by contrasting type weights, sometimes within the same word; geometric stair-step forms; unorthodox letter-, word-, and linespacing; lines and bars used as visual punctuation and spatial elements; and textural areas introduced into the spatial field.

After Kunz returned to New York and established his design office, his 1978 exhibition poster for photographer Fredrich Cantor (Fig. 25-59) was hailed as a

25-59. Willi Kunz, photography exhibition poster, 1978. A dynamic equilibrium between diverse parts is achieved.

25-60. Willi Kunz, lecture and exhibition announcement for the Columbia University School of Architecture, Planning, and Preservation, 1984. Form is shaped by a search for communicative clarity.

25-61. Kenneth Hiebert, poster for an exhibition and symposium, 1979. A formal, underlying grid structure is implied, but a playful intuitive process of form exploration led Hiebert to unexpected relationships.

25-59

25-60

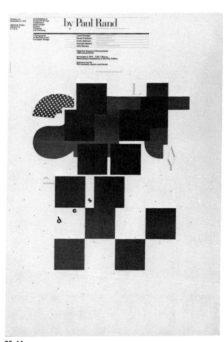

25-61

"quintessential example of Post-Modern design." The contrasting sizes of the photographs, the mixed weight of the typography, the diagonal letterspaced type, and the stepped pattern of dots covering part of the space all heralded the typographic new wave.

Kunz does not construct his work on a predetermined grid; rather, he starts the visual composition and permits structure and alignments to grow from the design process. He builds his typographic constellations with concern for the essential message, with the structure unfolding in response to the information to be conveyed. He has been called an "information architect" who uses visual hierarchy and syntax to bring order and clarity to messages, as seen in a lecture series and exhibition schedule announcement (Fig. 25-60). Kunz's working method is not unlike the process used by Piet Zwart (see Figs. 19-45 through 19-49): He believes design must be resolved working with the actual typographic materials, and generally does not spend a large amount of time working on preliminary sketches. After the basic ideas are formed, he has actual type material set, then develops the final solution from a careful probing of the organizational possibilities of the project.

As the New Wave Typographic spread, many designers working in the International Typographic Style began to test their precepts against the exploratory design attitudes that were emerging. Dada photomontage techniques were used; grids were established, then violated; functional elements of the 1920s new typography were used as decorative elements; and designers began to define the overall space as a field of tension, much as Zwart had done half a century earlier. Moreover, intuition and play reentered the design process. This can be seen in the work of the prominent designer and educator Kenneth Hiebert (b. 1930), who retained the harmonious balance achieved through experience with grid systems but, in designs such as his 1979 art/design/play poster for a Paul Rand exhibition (Fig. 25-61), introduced texture, a small dot pattern, a wider typeface range, and shifted forms on the grid.

The Memphis style and the San Francisco school

A new sensibility in Post-Modern design was catapulted into international prominence as the 1970s closed and the 1980s began. This style was pluralistic, eclectic, and deeply enamored with texture, pattern, surface, color, and a playful geometry. It almost seemed that the rational ethic of the modern design movement was being flaunted and mocked by designers willing to introduce whimsy and exaggerated form and proportions into their work. Innovation occurred in many cities and countries around the globe, with important contributions from diverse groups, including architects and product designers in Milan, Italy, and graphic designers in San Francisco, California.

An important inspiration for all areas of design emerged in 1981, when global attention was concentrated upon an exhibition of the Italian design group Memphis, led by eminent Italian architectural and product designer Ettore Sottsass (b. 1917). The group chose the name *Memphis* to reflect their interest in the inspiration of both contemporary popular culture and the artifacts and ornaments of ancient cultures. Function became secondary to the iconic image of surface pattern and texture, color, and fantastic forms in their lamps, sofas, and cabinets. The Memphis sensibility (see Fig. 25-64) embraces exaggerated geometric forms in bright (even garish) colors, bold geometric and organic patterns, often printed on plastic laminates, and allusions to earlier cultures, such as marble and granite used in columnlike table and chair legs evocative of Greco-Roman architecture. In Memphis designs, form no longer follows function—it becomes the *reason* for the design to exist. The Memphis graphic design section was headed by Christoph Radl (Fig. 25-62). The experimental attitude, fascination with tactile and decorative color pattern, and exuberant geometry had a direct influence upon Post-Modern design throughout the world. The Memphis style, exploding upon the scene just as the prosperous 1980s began, helped set the stage for an extravagant decorativeness in design.

25-62. Christoph Radl and Valentina Grego, Memphis logo designs, early 1980s. The Memphis vocabulary of form and pattern is given typographic expression in this series of logo designs.

25-63. William Longhauser, poster for Michael Graves's exhibition, 1983. The letterforms retain their legibility while being transformed into decorative geometric forms evoking a Post-Modern architectural landscape.

The vocabulary of form used by Post-Modernist architect Michael Graves (b. 1934) became another source of design inspiration. Graves became known in the 1960s for private houses designed in a minimalist style of orthodox Modernism influenced by Le Corbusier. In the late 1970s, he rebelled against the modernist tradition and sought a richer architectural vocabulary. Classical colonnades and loggias were revived with formal elements inspired by Cubist paintings. Graves's geometry is not the cool purism of Mies van der Rohe; it is an energetic, high-spirited geometry of decorative surfaces and tactile repetitive patterns. His vocabulary of forms is expressed in a 1983 poster designed by the outstanding Philadelphia graphic designer William Longhauser (b. 1947) for an exhibition of Graves's works (Fig. 25-63). In this poster, which became an influential Post-Modern design in itself, an overall background pattern of repetitive dots is produced by the letters *M I C H A E L* letterspaced on a grid.

The design community and art schools in San Francisco were strongly influenced by the International Style. This direction was punctuated by the flowering of the psychedelic poster in the late 1960s (see Figs. 24-35 and 24-36), proving to Bay Area graphic designers that tremendous potential for innovative form and color existed. In the early 1980s, San Francisco Post-Modern design emerged quickly, earning the city a reputation as a major center for creative design. Many San Francisco designers stubbornly resisted the pressure to grow into large studios to capitalize upon their growing reputations, preferring to maintain single-designer offices. Three of these designers, Michael Vanderbyl (b. 1947), Michael Manwaring (b. 1942), and Michael Cronin (b. 1951), figured prominently in the evolution of the medium. An ongoing dialogue between these and other San Francisco designers enabled them to learn from each other as they forged the Bay Area Post-Modern style. Their shared vocabulary of graphic possibilities conveyed a cheerful optimism, a warm sense of humor, and an unbridled attitude about form and space. Freely drawn gestures, a sunny palette of pastel hues, and intuitive composition are often found in their work.

Vanderbyl's 1979 poster for California Public Radio (Pl. 96) is an important early harbinger of the emerging style. The bright palette, the repetition of ruled lines,

25-64. Michael Vanderbyl, promotional mailer for Simpson Paper Company, 1985. Diagonal placement of Memphis designs and the green word *Innovation* with its textured pattern and mixed fonts echo the uninhibited vigor of the Italian design studio.

25-65. Michael Vanderbyl, Post-Modern architecture poster, 1984. An "innovative" Post-Modern building sticks out its tongue at an "obsolete" modern building, the stereotypical and oft-criticized "boring glass box."

and the overall pattern of radio waves on the gray background foretell the new movement. Vanderbyl's forms are carefully selected for their symbolic meaning: The blue rectangle over the eyes and red triangles over the ear and flaring away from the mouth signify the auditory, non-visual medium of radio. Vanderbyl paid homage to the exuberant furniture and textile designs of Memphis in a promotional mailer for Simpson Paper Company (Fig. 25-64), and turned his wit on Post-Modern architecture in a poster series that used graphic images to make editorial comments about aspects of the movement (Fig. 25-65). In graphics for products ranging from woolen knit caps (Fig. 25-66) to office furniture (Fig. 25-67), Vanderbyl combines a casual Post-Modern vitality with a typographic clarity echoing his background in the ordered typography of the International Style.

In Bay Area Post-Modern design, design elements are given symbolic roles and become part of the content. A lyrical resonance permeates the color, form, and texture in Michael Manwaring's graphic and environmental designs. In his series

25-65

25-66

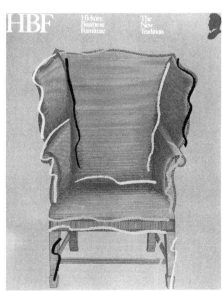

25-67

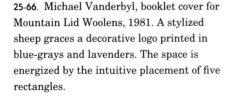

25-68. Michael Manwaring, display poster for Santa Cruz, 1984. A diagonal, torn-edged, chrome-yellow shape with purple rubber stamps is bracketed by a blue-striped area containing a magenta logo and a full-color photograph.

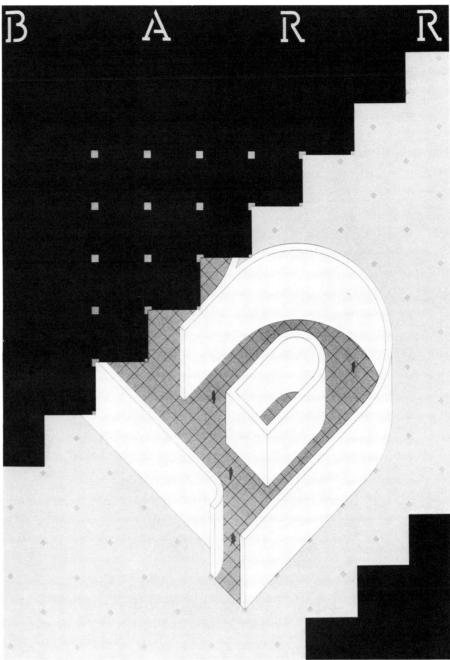

25-69. Michael Manwaring, brochure cover for Barr Exhibits, 1984. Post-Modern designers delighted in pastel shades: pink dots pepper the gray background and turquoise diagonal shape. The viewer participates in the design by deciphering the half-hidden, tan-and-white *B*.

25-66. Michael Vanderbyl, booklet cover for Mountain Lid Woolens, 1981. A stylized sheep graces a decorative logo printed in blue-grays and lavenders. The space is energized by the intuitive placement of five rectangles.

25-67. Michael Vanderbyl, cover for an HBF business furniture catalogue, 1985. The basic structure of a gray chair on a lighter gray page is restated in bold gestural strokes in vermillion, purple, turquoise, and peach.

of posters for Santa Cruz clothing (Fig. 25-68), graphic forms and color serve the function of a traditional headline, making a statement about the quality and desirability of the products. The exaggerated claims of mass communication have robbed words of their potency; graphic designers can communicate a mood, an attitude, or a resonance through the language of design. In his brochure cover for Barr Exhibits (Fig. 25-69), the juxtaposition of a dimensional exhibition in the shape of the letter *B* against a grid pattern of small squares signifying floor plans and structural elements conveys the essence of the client's activity. In the hands of San Francisco designers, cliche-dominated design areas such as wine labels—where elegant scripts, letterspaced Old Style type, and line drawings of vineyards had been prevalent—were reinvented (Fig. 25-70).

Although the San Francisco designers share a formal vocabulary of gesture, shape, palette, and intuitive spatial arrangement, personal attitudes are evident in their work. Michael Cronin often builds his compositions with shapes, which become symbolic vessels or containers for color. His 1983 Beethoven Festival Poster (Pl. 97), designed with Shannon Terry, relates a silhouette profile of Beethoven to the flame signifying his passion through the form correspondence of flame and hair. A repetition of diagonal and curved forms brings order and harmony to the composition. Three treatments of display typography are unified by their structural relationship to the edges of the rectangle and the green architectural elements.

The ornamental and mannerist Post-Modern design spawned by diverse international sources, including Memphis, Michael Graves, and San Francisco designers, became a dominant design direction during the 1980s. During a decade whose economic expansion and materialism were fueled by abundant energy supplies and heavily leveraged debt, architects around the world decorated facades with arches, pediments, and colonnades, then embellished them with marble, chrome, and pastel colors. Graphic designers used lush palettes and ornamented their work with gestures, textures, and decorative geometric elements. Surface and style became ends in themselves.

Retro and vernacular design

During the 1980s, graphic designers gained a growing understanding and appreciation of their history. Books, design magazines, and exhibitions all contributed to this awareness. A movement based on historical revival first emerged in New York and spread rapidly throughout the world. Called *Retro* by some designers, it was based on an uninhibited eclectic interest in modernist European design from the first half of the century, a flagrant disregard for the "rules" of proper typography, and a fascination with kinky and mannered typefaces designed and widely used during the 1920s and 1930s, then banished after World War II. This prefix charges the words *retroactive* and *retrograde* with implications of "backward-looking" and "contrary to the usual." Retro may be considered an aspect of Post-Modernism due to its interest in historical revivals, yet it paraphrases modern design from the decades between the wars rather than Greco-Roman and Renaissance motifs. The term *vernacular design* referring to the commonplace artistic and technical expression broadly characteristic of a locale or historical period, is closely related to Retro design. Vernacular design is the paraphrasing of earlier, more commonplace

25-70. Michael Manwaring, wine label for Hanna Wine, 1986. The die-cut shape is aesthetic and pragmatic: It differentiates from competitive products and becomes an identifying form not unlike a trademark.

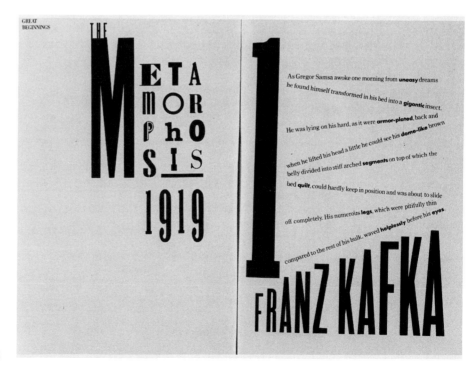

25-71. Paula Scher, *Great Beginnings* spread for the Koppel and Scher promotional booklet, 1984. Typographic ideas paraphrasing Russian Constructivism, Futurism, and Dada are freely combined and reinvented.

graphic forms, such as baseball cards, matchbook covers, and unskilled commercial illustrations and printing from earlier decades.

The New York approach to Retro began with a small number of designers, including Paula Scher (b. 1948), Louise Fili (b. 1951), and Carin Goldberg (b. 1953). They rediscovered earlier twentieth-century graphics, ranging from the turn-of-the-century Vienna Secession to modernist but decorative European typefaces that were popular during the two decades between the World Wars. Their approach to space, color, and texture is often personal and original. Unorthodox attitudes about the rules and regulations of "proper" design and typography permit them to take risks and experiment by exuberantly mixing fonts, using extreme letterspacing, and printing type in subtle color-on-color combinations. They are, however, typographic precisionists seeking a sublime level of visual organization. In many Retro designs, typography does not play second fiddle to illustration and photography, but moves to center stage to become figurative, animated, and expressive. The self-consciously eclectic aspects of Retro continue a trait of New York design: Scher credits Seymour Chwast of Push Pin Studios and his use of Victorian, Art Nouveau, and Art Deco forms as an important inspiration; Fili worked with the late Herb Lubalin, who often called upon the extravagance of Victorian and Art Nouveau typographic themes. Retro moved New York's tradition of historicism forward into the 1920s and 1930s.

Paula Scher, outspoken and with an ironic sense of humor, worked as a graphic designer for CBS Records during the 1970s, where healthy budgets enabled her to function as an art director who developed concepts, commissioned outstanding illustrations and photography, and designed typography to complement the image. The music industry's interest in novel and original graphics provided opportunities to experiment with offbeat solutions, but the high-flying recording industry crashed in 1978, as inflation, skyrocketing production costs, and slumping sales took a powerful toll. By 1979, the adversity of tight budgets on many projects forced Scher to develop typographic solutions, as she drew upon her imagination, art and design history sources, and her fascination with little-used typefaces in the backs of type-specimen books. Art Deco, Russian Constructivism, and outmoded, little-used typefaces were incorporated into her work.

Plate 98 shows the inspiration of Russian Constructivism upon Scher's typographic promotional posters for CBS Records in 1979. She did not copy the earlier Constructivist style, but used its vocabulary of forms and form relationships, reinventing and combining them in unexpected ways. Space and color are totally different from those of her sources. The floating weightlessness of Russian Constructivism is replaced by a dense packing of forms in space with the weight and vigor of old wood-type posters. After Scher formed the Koppel and Scher studio in partnership with Terry Koppel in 1984, their *Great Beginnings* booklet (Fig. 25-71) announced their new partnership with period typographic interpretations of the first paragraphs of great novels. Retro went national in 1985 when Scher designed the first of two folios for a paper manufacturer, presenting twenty-two complete fonts of "An eclectic collection of eccentric and decorative type," including such anomalies as the 1911 decorative script *Phyllis,* the playful 1925 *Greco Rosart* (renamed *Greco Deco* by Scher), and a quirky thick-and-thin sans serif *Trio.* Designers suddenly had access to complete fonts of eccentric 1920s and 1930s typefaces whose availability had vanished with hand-set metal type. The close paraphrasing of resources has been a controversial aspect of some Retro designs (Fig. 25-72), for some skeptics question how closely a designer might legitimately quote an earlier source.

Retro design thrived in book jacket design. The work of Louise Fili is highly personal and intuitive. As a student, an opportunity to work in the college type shop inspired a deep love for typography. After working for Herb Lubalin, Fili was art director of Pantheon Books from 1978 to 1989 before opening her own studio. Her earlier work evidenced Lubalin's influence, then grew in power and originality

25-72. Paula Scher, Swatch Watch poster, 1985. A famous Herbert Matter poster from the 1930s (see Fig. 19-57) is unabashedly paraphrased for Swatch, the Swiss watch manufacturer.

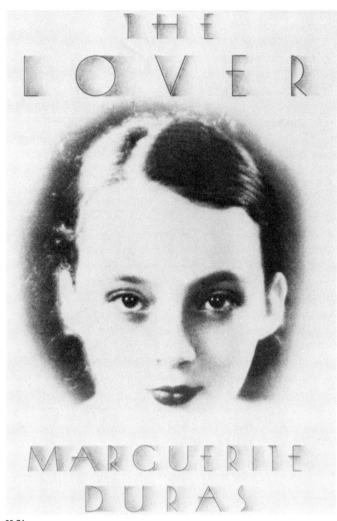

25-74

25-73. Louise Fili, book cover for *When Things of the Spirit Come First,* 1983. Lettering with eccentric shape and proportion is drawn with modulated tones.

25-74. Louise Fili, book cover for *The Lover,* 1985. A delicately vignetted photograph is used with lettering that seems to cast soft shadows.

from this initial starting point. Fili routinely vacationed in Europe each summer after the annual crunch of producing cover designs for Pantheon's huge fall list, and her travels inspired the development of an original approach to American book jacket design. The dimensional letterforms on the signs of little Italian seashore resorts built between the World Wars fascinated her, and she began photographing them. In the flea markets and used-book stalls of French and Italian cities, she began collecting European graphics from the 1920s, 1930s, and 1940s. These vernacular graphics incorporated textured backgrounds, silhouetted photographs, and modernistic sans serif typefaces that were sometimes decorated or given exaggerated proportions. After World War II, design sensibilities shifted and these typestyles and techniques fell into disuse, and when typography converted from metal type to photographic and digital methods in the 1960s and 1970s, these old faces were seen as outmoded and were not converted to the new processes. Fili responded to them with fresh eyes and began to introduce them into her work. Her eclecticism can be called reinvention, because she does not copy her sources, but uses them as background influences. Fili's work is elegant and refined, possessing great subtlety and even softness. Seeking the proper graphic resonance for each book, she searches for the appropriate typeface, color scheme, and imagery by producing volumes of tissue layouts. Although the death of hand-set metal typography has meant the loss of many old faces that are simply unavailable, Fili has refused to let this limit her possibilities. She has worked around this problem when wanting to use a now-forgotten face—such as Iris, a condensed sans serif with thin horizontal strokes, or Electra Seminegra, a bold geometric sans serif face with inverted triangles for the crossbar of the capital *A*—by restoring letterforms from old printed specimens and commissioning hand-lettering of the missing letters or even of the entire title and message. In Fili's book covers, color and imagery also seem to resonate with the essence and spirit of the literature, almost as though she has developed a sixth sense for interpreting the author's work (Figs. 25-73 and 25-74).

Carin Goldberg studied design and painting then worked as an assistant to Lou Dorfsman at CBS in the 1970s, where she developed a fine-tuned reverence for type. Every type proof entering the offices was hand-altered and improved. She worked at CBS Records under Paula Scher, where the emphasis was upon innovation, so Scher's influence upon Goldberg was not directly stylistic. Rather, Scher's curiosity, reverence for design history, and attitude toward her work became vital influences. When Goldberg opened her own design office, she began to focus upon book jackets because her primary interest was in single-surface, posterlike areas. Goldberg describes her work as being 90 percent intuitive and acknowledges the influence of early modernist posters upon her work, especially the work of Cassandre. Goldberg's early experience as a painter informs her attitude toward space, as does an architectural orientation that comes from shared classes with architects in school and space adjacent to her husband's architectural office. Her ability to "paint with her t-square"—functioning as a typographic precisionist with a painterly orientation—explains the personal attitude that underlies her work, transcending her myriad eclectic sources (Figs. 25-75 and 25-76).

Lorraine Louie (b. 1955), who grew up, studied design, and worked in San Francisco before migrating to New York, is one of numerous younger designers who embraced the general resonance of the Retro approach. Shape, spatial composition, and color are primary vehicles in her work. She designed several series of book jackets with a unifying graphic distinctiveness, while maintaining individuality for each book through imaginative color combinations and imagery. Her format for the Vintage Contemporaries series (Fig. 25-77) uses a consistent set of typographic sizes, styles, and placement. Letterspacing, drop shadows, dot patterns, and the arrangement of geometric shapes create a consistency over many volumes. Geometric zones contain author's name, book title, and illustration. Another series for *The*

25-75

25-76

25-75. Carin Goldberg (designer) and Frank Metz (art director), book cover for *The Sonnets of Orpheus*, 1987. Design motifs of the Vienna Workshops and sans serif lettering banded by black rectangles and decorative patterns are revived for a book jacket.

25-76. Carin Goldberg (designer) and Gene Greif (illustrator), book cover for *Where Water Comes Together with Other Water*, 1987. Wavy ornaments signifying water were added to the Eagle typeface by Goldberg.

25-78

25-77. Lorraine Louie (designer), Judith Loeser (art director), and Marc Tauss (photographer), book cover for *Bright Lights, Big City*, 1984. The saga of a young man who sets out to conquer the Big Apple during the affluent 1980s is illustrated.

25-78. Lorraine Louie (designer) and Susan Mitchell (art director), cover for *The Quarterly*, 1987. Over this series, Louie invented a vast vocabulary of colorful shapes, organized with an unerring sense of balance.

Quarterly literary anthology (Fig. 25-78) has a large *Q* as a sign for the publication. Each issue is energized by colorful geometric shapes balanced within the space.

Daniel Pelavin (b. 1948) dates his affinities for 1930s and 1940s work to pre–World War II architecture and furniture at Michigan State University, where he earned his undergraduate degree. The school's Union Building had a large "late moderne" lounge. Several years of industrial arts and drafting classes in high school, and apprenticeships after college in the Detroit design studio system, developed Pelavin's formidable lettering and rendering skills. His imagery, paraphrasing the work of Gustav Klimt and the Vienna Workshops, combines their diverse decorative patterns into a lively whole (Fig. 25-79). When Pelavin interprets the streamlined forms of Art Deco graphics and architecture from the 1930s and 1940s, he combines a reductive stylization with precise mechanistic forms (Fig. 25-80). Pelavin has designed an extensive library of pictographs, created in related sets of images, used extensively by clients from all around America.

Perhaps the Retro idiom emerged because many designers born in the 1940s and 1950s carried memorable impressions of artifacts experienced as children, which then became part of their vocabulary of provocative forms. When Scher and Fili created their first designs in what later became known as Retro idioms, many veteran designers, raised on formal purity and typographic refinement, were appalled to see the return of these exiled letterforms and eccentric spatial organizations. But Retro, like New Wave Typography in the late 1970s and early 1980s, refused

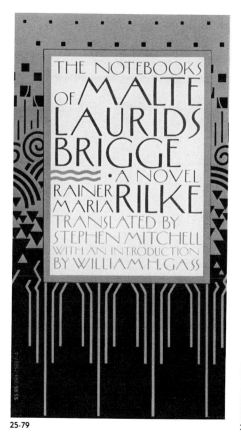

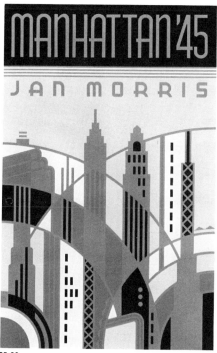

25-79   25-80

25-79. Daniel Pelavin (designer) and Judith Loeser (art director), book cover for *The Notebooks of Malte Laurids Brigge,* 1985. The lettering is inspired by a Gustav Klimt poster (see Fig. 15-8).

25-80. Daniel Pelavin (designer) and Victoria Wong (art director), book cover for *Manhattan '45,* 1985. A palette of metallic gold, dark pink, warm gray and black evokes a feeling of the era.

to go away, as more and more designers and clients responded to its energy and fresh approach. It crept into the design vocabulary as designers courageously (or timidly) dared to use such eccentric typefaces as Empire, Bernhard Fashion, and Huxley. Many art directors consider Retro as part of their repertoire, to be called upon as needed to express the proper resonance for a given assignment. Precise spacing, scale relationships, and color combinations give the best Retro designs their stunning vitality.

Other original voices explored reinvention of historical models quite differently from New York Retro designers. At the Duffy Design Group in Minneapolis, Minnesota, Joe Duffy (b. 1949) and Charles S. Anderson (b. 1958)—who left the Duffy firm and formed his own design office in 1989—designed nostalgic revivals of vernacular and modernistic graphic arts from the first half of the century. Anderson recalls growing up in the small town of Boone, Iowa, and being impressed by old graphics from the 1940s that had never been thrown away. The walls of an old print shop in town were covered with graphics from an earlier decade, and a retired artist who had created ubiquitous clip art as a newspaper illustrator made indelible impressions. Inspiration for Minnesota-based Retro ranged from delight in the humble, coarsely printed spot drawings found on old matchbook covers and newspaper ads (Fig. 25-81), to the warmth of traditional typefaces and nineteenth-century woodcuts applied by Duffy and Anderson to grocery-store packaging (Fig. 25-82), to decorative emblematic labels (Fig. 25-83) and trademarks recalling postage stamps, official seals, and pictorial trademarks of an earlier time. The power of graphic design was demonstrated by the Classico spaghetti sauce labels, when sales of this product, packaged in old-style mason jars with ornately illustrated and designed labels, soared to $90 million within two years in spite of a limited advertising budget.

Anderson's graphics for French Paper Company, an innovator in recycled printing papers, reflect combined decorative elegance and graphic whimsy (Fig. 25-84). Historical graphic resources as diverse as Aztec ornament and Ouija boards were

25-81. Charles S. Anderson, Marine Midland Auto Financing Division trademark, 1985. This nostalgic automobile and line technique evoke newspaper spot illustrations of the 1930s and 1940s.

25-83

25-82. Charles S. Anderson (designer and illustrator) and Lynn Schulte (illustrator), label designs for Classico pasta sauce, 1985. Duffy Design Group countered the garish color and strident typography of many mass-marketed grocery packages with subtle color and elegant typography.

25-83. Joe Duffy and Charles S. Anderson, identity program for various lines of Chaps/Ralph Lauren clothing, 1987. The Chaps brand name inspired a saluting scout printed in earth tones and red accents.

plumbed for their form and color. Anderson's work reflects a genuine enchantment with textural properties, as enlarged details from cheap printing, such as comic books, and overall patterns of spot illustrations find their way into his designs.

The pluralism of late-twentieth-century design enables San Francisco designer Michael Mabry (b. 1955) to freely synthesize sources as diverse as Cubism and vernacular pictorial trademarks. In the late 1980s, Mabry began to synthesize his knowledgeable modernist sensibility with a fascination for vernacular graphics, resulting in publicity and packaging spanning the gulf between two currents from the first half of the century (Fig. 25-85).

Meanwhile, in London, one of the original visions of the 1980s emerged as Neville Brody designed graphics and album covers for rock music and art directed English magazines, including *The Face* and *Arena*. Although Brody has been influenced by the geometric forms of the Russian Constructivist artists, especially Rodchenko, and by Dada's experimental attitudes and rejection of the canons of the ruling establishment, it would misrepresent his philosophy and values to label him a Retro designer reinventing past styles. As an art student in the late 1970s, Brody wondered if "within mass communications, the human had been lost completely." Confronting the decision between pursuing fine art or graphic design, Brody thought, "Why can't you take a painterly approach within the printed medium? I wanted to make people more aware rather than less aware, and with the design that I had started to do, I followed the idea of design to reveal, not to conceal." Brody's work evolved from an effort to discover an intuitive yet logical approach to design, expressing a personal vision that could have meaning to his audience.

Brody has stated that he did not learn the rules of correct typography, leaving him free to invent working methods and spatial configurations. His typographic configurations become icons, projecting an absolute emblematic authority evoking heraldry and military emblems (Fig. 25-86). He designed a series of geometric sans serif typefaces for *The Face,* bringing a unique graphic image to the magazine. Headlines took on the power of objects, each carefully crafted to express content

25-84. Joe Duffy and Charles S. Anderson, booklet cover for French Paper Company, 1985. Muted colors and an overall pattern of spot illustrations lend a mellow resonance.

25-85. Michael Mabry, packaging for Zele citrus-flavored beverage, 1985. The vocabulary of Cubism, Constructivism, and Cassandre are evoked in the shapes and visual syntax of this label.

25-86. Neville Brody, record album cover design for Parliament, 1985. Hand-lettered words are executed with a mechanistic and mathematical perfection in this album cover executed in black, red, and yellow-orange against a textured gray-green field.

25-84

25-85

25-86

25-87. Neville Brody, editorial page from *The Face* No. 53, September, 1984. Circular, horizontal, vertical, and diagonal elements are carefully constructed into an expressive graphic statement. The roman *e* reverses from the slanted rectangle.

(Fig. 25-87). Brody viewed the magazine as a dimensional object existing in time and space and having a continuity from issue to issue. This continuity was explored when graphic elements such as the contents page logo were deconstructed into abstract glyphs over several months (Fig. 25-88). Brody's ability to load a layout with levels of meaning is seen in the opening spread of an interview with Andy Warhol (Fig. 25-89): The repeated photograph echoes Warhol's use of repeated images; the large *W* is actually the *M* from a feature on the popular singer Madonna from the month before, turned upside-down and bringing a small portion of a photograph and part of a headline with it, paraphrasing Warhol's use of existing graphic material. The oval within a circle and the cross above it reference the sexuality of Warhol's life and work.

Seldom have a designer's hard-won accomplishments been plundered and plagiarized as Brody's distinctive work was in the late 1980s. As clones of his typefaces and emblematic logo designs appeared all around the world, Brody designed a new quarterly magazine, *Arena,* using the clean, informational attributes of Helvetica type in dynamic ways. Large scale, strong value contrasts, and clear, simple layouts characterize this publication.

25-88. Neville Brody, contents page logos from *The Face* Nos. 49, 52, and 55, 1984. Over eight or nine issues, the word *contents* was deconstructed from a readable word into abstract marks as Brody investigated an organic process of change and the role of visual coding in the editorial environment.

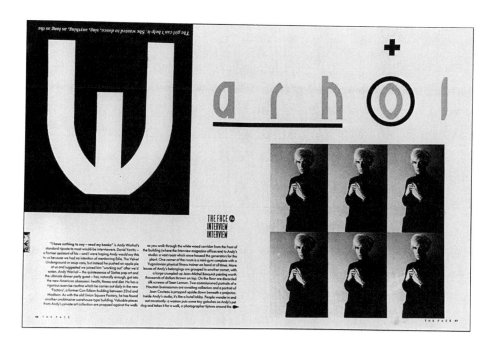

25-89. Neville Brody, editorial pages for *The Face* No. 59, March 1985. Type and image become objects composed against each other to achieve a dynamic whole.

The computer-graphics revolution

By providing designers with new processes and capabilities, new technology often enables designers to create unprecedented images and forms. Apple Computer's 1984 introduction of the first-generation Macintosh computer, based on technology pioneered in the Lisa computer, foretold a graphic revolution soon to occur. It displayed *bit-mapped* graphics; that is, its screen presented information as dots called *pixels,* with 72 dots per inch (dpi) on the screen. Its "intuitive interface" with the user was achieved via a desktop "mouse" device, whose movement controlled a pointer on the screen. By placing the pointer on an icon (Fig. 25-90) and pressing a button on the mouse, a user controlled the computer intuitively, permitting him or her to focus upon writing, drawing, or design instead of machine operation. The first printers for the Macintosh computer output typography and images at 72 dpi; the output was called bit-mapped fonts, early examples of which (Fig. 25-91) were designed by Susan Kare (b. 1954) of the Apple Computer design department. Letterform design was dictated by the matrix of dots in these early efforts.

While many designers rejected and decried this new technology as "primitive" during its infancy, others embraced it as an innovative new tool capable of expand-

25-90. Susan Kare (graphic designer) and Bill Adkins (computer programmer), icons for the 128K Macintosh computer, 1984. Pictographs are the language permitting a new interface between man and machine.

25-91. Susan Kare, screen fonts for the Macintosh computer, 1984. The low-resolution dot pattern dictates the letterform design and jagged edges.

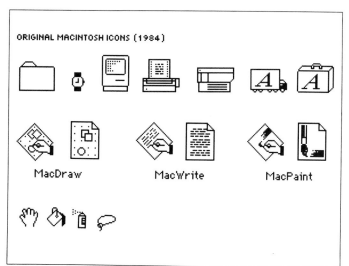

ORIGINAL MACINTOSH ICONS (1984)

MacDraw   MacWrite   MacPaint

FONTS FOR ORIGINAL MACINTOSH (1984)

CHICAGO 12
ABCDEFGHIJKLMNOPQRSTUVWXYZ
abcdefghijklmnopqrstuvwxyz 1234567890

NEW YORK 12
ABCDEFGHIJKLMNOPQRSTUVWXYZ
abcdefghijklmnopqrstuvwxyz 1234567890

GENEVA 12
ABCDEFGHIJKLMNOPQRSTUVWXYZ
abcdefghijklmnopqrstuvwxyz 1234567890

25-90

25-91

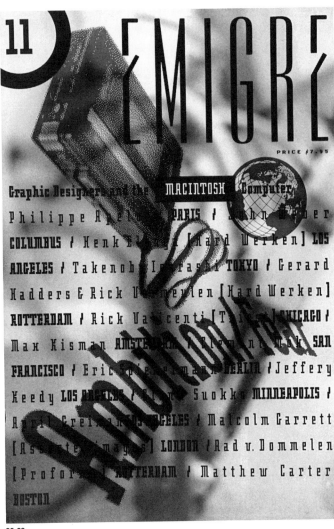

25-93

25-92. April Greiman, poster for the Los Angeles Institute of Contemporary Art, 1986. Computer output, printed as layers of lavender, blue-gray, red-orange, and tan, overlap and combine into an even fuller palette of color.

25-93. Rudy VanderLans, cover for *Emigre* 11 magazine, 1989. Typography is bit-mapped, bent, stretched, and layered with digitized imagery.

ing the language of design and the very nature of the design process. Los Angeles designer April Greiman explored the visual properties of bit-mapped fonts, the layering and overlapping of computer-screen information, and the tactile patterns and shapes made possible by this new technology. In her first graphic design using Macintosh output (Fig. 25-92), bit-mapped type and computer-generated textures were photostatted to large size and pasted up with conventional typesetting. As computers and their software became more powerful, a new spatial elasticity became possible in typography and imagery. Rudy VanderLans (b. 1955), a newspaper designer in San Francisco, began to edit, design, and publish a magazine, *Emigre*. Its experimental approach helped define and demonstrate the capabilities of the new technology, both in its editorial design (Fig. 25-93) and in the work and interviews of designers from around the world that were included in its pages.

In 1985, Apple Computer introduced the Laserwriter, a dot-matrix printer whose 300-dpi output enables its typographic output to more closely duplicate typesetting. A page-description programming language called PostScript, developed by Adobe Systems, Inc., enables printers to output text, images, graphic elements, and their placement on the page. PostScript fonts are not simply made up of dots; rather, they are stored as electronic instructions and data. Characters are generated by electronically drawing outlines, which are then filled in as solid forms. Letterforms are drawn with Bezier curves—mathematically generated lines producing nonuniform curvatures (in contrast to curves with uniform curvature, called arcs), defined by four control points. Bezier curves' ability to create complex shapes with smooth

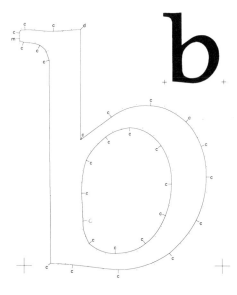

25-94. Sumner Stone, digitized data for Stone Medium *b*, 1985. The outline Bezier curves and filled laser-printed output are shown.

endpoints makes them particularly useful for creating letterforms (Fig. 25-94) and computer graphics.

Pages designed on the computer screen can be output at 72 dpi on a low-resolution printer, 300 dpi on a laser printer, or 1,270 or 2,540 dpi on a high-resolution output device, such as a Linotron imagesetter. This new technology has revolutionized graphic design. Page-layout programs made possible by PostScript permit the actual design of full pages on the screen. The term *desktop publishing* became popular to describe the electronic layout and design of pages, positioning type and image on the screen before printing them as a single unit.

A virtual explosion in typeface development resulted. The digital type foundry became a new reality, thanks to font-design software that permitted greater efficiency and flexibility. VanderLans's partner, Zuzana Licko (b. 1951) of Emigre Fonts, typifies the new typeface designer. Her first fonts were designed for low-resolution technology, then were converted to companion high-resolution versions as the technology progressed (Fig. 25-95). The first type family developed for the new PostScript page-description language was Stone (Fig. 25-96), designed by Sumner Stone (b. 1945). Trained as a calligrapher and mathematician, Stone was type director of Adobe Systems before opening his own type foundry in 1990. The Stone family has three versions—serif, sans serif, and informal—which share basic letterform proportions and structure. There are eighteen fonts, as the serif, sans serif, and informal versions each have three roman and three italic weights.

When typeface designers developed a typeface for a Linotype or Monotype machine, they could take the specific nature of the typesetting equipment into account. Today, however, the designer of a PostScript typeface develops fonts to be used on many output devices, including low-resolution display screens; dot-matrix, thermal, and very-high-resolution printers, and developing output systems that do

25-95. Zuzana Licko, digital typefaces, late 1980s. Oakland, Emperor, and Emigre were originally designed as bit-mapped fonts for 72-dpi resolution. Modula and Matrix are higher-resolution versions of the latter two fonts.

We Read Best What We Read Most (Oakland 8)

We Read Best What We Read Most (Emperor 14)

We Read Best What We Read Most (Modula)

We Read Best What We Read Most (Emigre 14)

We Read Best What We Read Most (Matrix)

25-96. Sumner Stone, the Stone type family, 1987. This typographic arrangement by Min Wang shows the harmony of the serif, sans serif, and informal versions.

not yet exist. Moreover the environment in which type is used has expanded dramatically, with people in many disciplines, not just designers and typesetters, making typographic decisions and creating typeset documents. A comparison can be made to George Eastman's invention of the Kodak camera (see Fig. 11-12): Just as photography was wrested from the exclusive use of specialists and made available to the general public in the 1880s, typography left the exclusive domain of professionals and became accessible to a large universe of people in the 1980s.

Rapid advances in computer-graphics technology enabled designers to achieve unprecedented results. By the early 1990s, accelerating progress in computers, software, and output devices enabled graphic designers to achieve results virtually identical to those of conventional working methods, and also explore unprecedented possibilities. The promise of seamless on-screen color graphics had arrived, and many prominent designers, including Lance Hidy (b. 1946) and April Greiman, energized their work through advanced computer graphics. Hidy achieved prominence in the early 1980s as a poster designer employing flat-shape color silhouettes with affinities to turn-of-the-century designers, including the Beggarstaffs and Edward Penfield. As he embraced the new technology, his working method changed, for instead of exploring color through many hand-painted sketches, he was able to change and evaluate many color palettes quickly on the screen. In his 1990 poster for the Sioux City Public Library (Pl. 99), Hidy digitized 35mm color photographs of a person reading a book, a tree, a bird, and a sky. The computer enabled him to size, crop, position, and colorize each image to assemble the final design—all on his screen. In printing proofs, Hidy and master screen printer Rob Day (b. 1954) explored bit-mapped images of the digitized sky pattern in versions ranging from 36 to 126 pixels per inch (Fig. 25-97). The 36- and 54-dpi patterns seemed too coarse, and the high-resolution patterns caused a moiré effect with the mesh of the printing screen, so the 72-dpi pattern was used instead. Computer graphics enabled Hidy to explore options and supplement flat planes of color with textural areas.

Other 1980s developments included the introduction of powerful electronic image processors, including Scitex systems, which electronically scan images and permit extensive editing, and Quantel Video and Graphic Paintboxes. These systems permit precise color control and allow images to be overlapped, combined, and altered. Photography is losing its status as a documentation of reality, because these new processes allow seamless and undetectable image manipulation. In a 1985 photomontage for Mead Paper Company, designer Woody Pirtle created a surreal book whose pages open to allow objects and figures to float out into an expansive sky (Pl. 100). To create a 1987 poster for a health-care symposium, "Shaping the Future of Health Care" (Pl. 101) April Greiman "built" the poster by combining images digitized into the machine—photographs of a flag and an eagle, an x-ray, and a drawing of the medical profession's traditional caduceus symbol—with color shapes and gradations and a video clip of hands shot live into the Paintbox. A wide variety of effects, including mosaicking, fading, outlining, overlapping, and increasing or decreasing levels of transparency, enables complex iconography to evolve as an integrated and organic whole.

The impact of technology upon graphic design is becoming even more pronounced. The merger of video and print technology is leading to unprecedented graphic possibilities. Optical disks, video capture-and-edit capabilities, and interactive print-and-time-based media are expanding graphic design activity, promising to bring continued opportunities to explore the uncharted potential of new tools.

  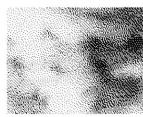

25-97. Lance Hidy, digitized sky patterns for the Sioux City Public Library poster, 1990. Shifts in resolution alter the image significantly.

Epilogue

At the time of this writing, human affairs are undergoing a new revolution comparable to the industrial revolution that launched the machine age. Electronic circuitry, microprocessors, and computer-generated imagery threaten to radically alter our culture's images, communications processes, and the very nature of work itself. Graphic design, like many other spheres of activity, is undergoing profound changes. The graphic design community is responding to this new age of electronic circuitry by an involvement in media graphics, systems design, and computer graphics. As has happened so often in the past, the tools are changing with the relentless advance of technology, but the essence of graphic design remains unchanged. That essence is to give order to information, form to ideas, and expression and feeling to artifacts that document human experience.

The need for clear and imaginative visual communications to relate people to their cultural, economic, and social lives has never been greater. As shapers of messages and images, graphic designers have an obligation to contribute meaningfully to a public understanding of environmental and social issues. Graphic designers have a responsibility to adapt new technology and to express the zeitgeist of their times by inventing new forms and new ways of expressing ideas. The poster and the book, vital communications tools of the industrial revolution, will continue in the new age of electronic technology as art forms, and graphic designers will help to define and extend each new generation of electronic media.

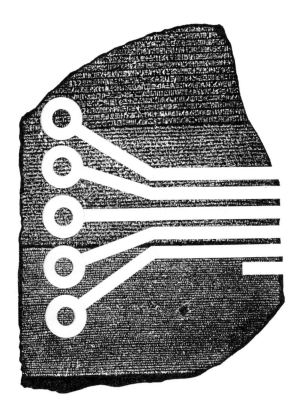

Selected Bibliography

The complete bibliography for this book contains over five thousand entries including books, journal articles, tapes and notes from interviews, lectures, presentations, and actual artifacts such as books, posters, and other graphic designs. Of necessity, this bibliography is limited to books selected for further reading on specific topics. Books covering more than one section or chapter are listed at the first area of coverage. Lists of general surveys and periodicals appear at the end of the bibliography.

Part I. The Prologue to Graphic Design:
The visual message from prehistory through the medieval era

1. The Invention of Writing
Collon, Dominique. *First Impressions*. London: British Museum, 1987.
Gelb, I. J. *A Study of Writing*. Rev. Ed. Chicago: University of Chicago, 1952.
Giedon, S. *The Eternal Present: The Beginning of Art*. New York: Pantheon, 1962.
Grazisosi, Paolo. *Paleolithic Art*. New York: McGraw-Hill, 1960.
Huyghe, Rene. *Larousse Encyclopedia of Prehistoric and Ancient Art*. New York: Prometheus Press, 1962.
Jackson, Donald. *The Story of Writing*. New York, 1981.
Leakey, Richard E., and Lewin, Roger. *Origins*. New York: Dutton, 1977.
Parrot, Andre. *The Arts of Assyria*. New York: Golden Press, 1961.
Porada, Edith. *Ancient Art in Seals*. Princeton, NJ: Princeton, 1980.
Strommenger, Eva. *5000 Years of Mesopotamian Art*. New York: Abrams, n.d.
Teissier, Beatrice. *Ancient Near Eastern Cylinder Seals*. Los Angeles, CA: University of California Press, 1984.

2. **Graphic Communications in Ancient Egypt**
Allen, Thomas George. *The Book of the Dead or Going Forth by Day*. Chicago: University of Chicago Press, 1974.
Breasted, James. *Development of Religion and Thought in Ancient Egypt*. Gloucester, MA: Scribner's, 1959.
Budge, Sir E. A. Wallis, Kt. *The Dweller on the Nile*. New York: Benjamin Blom, 1972.
———. *The Book of the Dead*. London, 1909.
———. *The Rosetta Stone in the British Museum*. New York: AMS Press, 1976.
Grayson, A. Kirk and Redford, Donald B. *Papyrus and Tablet*. Englewood Cliffs: Prentice-Hall, 1973.
Michalowski, Kazimierz. *Art of Ancient Egypt*. New York: Abrams, 1978.
Petrie, Sir W. M. Flinders. *Buttons and Design Scarabs*. Great Britian: Biddles Limited, 1974.
Rossiter, Evelyn. *The Book of the Dead*. Fribourg-Geneve: Productions Liber SA, 1979.
The Trustees of the British Museum. *Introductory Guide to the Egyptian Collection*. Oxford: The University Press, 1971.

3. The Asian Contribution

Carter, Thomas F., revised by Goodrich, L. Carrington. *The Invention of Printing in China and Its Spread Westward.* New York: Ronald Press, 1955.

Chang, Leon Long-Yien. *Four Thousand Years of Chinese Calligraphy.* Chicago: University of Chicago, 1990.

DeVinne, Theodore L. *The Invention of Printing.* New York: Francis Hart & Co., 1876.

Kapleau, Philip. *The Three Pillars of Zen.* New York: Beacon, 1967.

Tsien, Tsuen-Hsuin. *Written on Bamboo and Silk.* Chicago: University of Chicago Press, 1962.

Twitchett, Denis. *Printing and Publishing in Medieval China.* New York: Beil, 1983.

Williams, C. A. S. *Outlines of Chinese Symbolism and Art Motives.* New York: Dover, 1976.

4. The Alphabet

Anderson, Donald M. *The Art of Written Forms.* New York: Holt, Reinhart and Winston, 1969.

Bickerman, E. J. *Chronology of the Ancient World.* Ithaca: Cornell, 1968.

Diringer, David. *The Alphabet: A Key to the History of Mankind.* 3rd Ed. New York: Funk and Wagnalls, 1968.

————. *The Book Before Printing: Ancient, Medieval, and Oriental.* New York: Dover, 1982.

————. *Writing.* New York: Praeger, 1962.

Doblerhoffer, Ernest. *Voices in Stone.* New York: Viking, 1961.

Fairbank, Alfred. *A Book of Scripts.* London: Faber, 1977.

Hutchinson, James. *Letters.* New York: Van Nostrand Reinhold, 1983.

Kraus, Theodor. *Pompeii and Herculaneum: The Living Cities of the Dead.* New York: Abrams, 1975.

Logan, Robert K. *The Alphabet Effect: The Impact of the Phonetic Alphabet on the Development of Western Civilization.* New York: Morrow, 1986.

Nesbitt, Alexander. *The History and Technique of Lettering.* New York: Dover, 1950.

Roberts, Colin H., and Skeat, T. C. *The Birth of the Codex.* London: Oxford University Press, 1983.

Sutton, James, and Bartram, Alan. *An Atlas of Typeforms.* New York: Hastings House, 1968.

Trudgill, Ane. *Traditional Penmanship.* Lakewood: Watson-Guptill, 1989.

Turner, E.G. *Greek Manuscripts of the Ancient World.* London: Institute of Classical Studies, 1986.

Ullman, B. L. *Ancient Writing and Its Influence.* New York: Longmans, Green, 1932.

5. The Medieval Manuscript

Alexander, J. J. G. *Italian Renaissance Illuminations.* London: Chatto & Windus, 1977.

————. *The Decorated Letter.* New York: Braziller, 1978.

Backhouse, Janet. *The Illuminated Manuscript.* Oxford: Phaidon Press, 1979.

Banks, Doris H. *Medieval Manuscript Bookmaking.* Metuchen, NJ: Scarecrow Press, 1989.

Brown, Peter. *The Book of Kells.* London: Thames and Hudson, 1980.

D'Ancona, P., and Aeschlimann, E. *The Art of Illumination.* London: Phaidon Press, 1969.

Fairbank, Alfred. *The Story of Handwriting.* New York: Watson-Guptill, 1970.

Fremantle, Anne. *Age of Faith.* New York: Time-Life, 1965.

Hassall, A. G. and W. O. *The Douce Apocalypse.* New York: Thomas Yoseloff, 1961.

Henderson, George. *From Durrow to Kells: The Insular Gospel-books 650-800.* London: Thames and Hudson, 1987.

Ker, N. R. *Medieval Scribes, Manuscripts, and Libraries.* London: Scholar Press, 1978.

Morison, Stanley. *Selected Essays on the History of Letterforms in Manuscript and Print*. Cambridge: University of Cambridge Press, 1983.

Mutherich, Florentine, and Gaehde, Joachim E. *Carolingian Painting*. New York: Braziller, 1976.

Nordenfalk, Carl. *Celtic and Anglo-Saxon Painting*. New York: Braziller, 1977.

Pognon, Edmond. *Les Tres Riches Heures du Due de Berry: 15th Century Manuscript*. Fribourg: Productions Liber SA, 1979.

Weitzmann, Kurt. *Late Antique and Early Christian Book Illumination*. New York: Braziller, 1977.

Welch, Stuart Cary. *Persian Painting: Five Royal Safavid Manuscripts of the Sixteenth Century*. New York: Braziller, 1976.

Williams, John. *Early Spanish Manuscript Illumination*. New York: Braziller, 1977.

Part II. A Graphic Renaissance:
The origins of European typography and design for printing

6. Printing Comes to Europe

Amman, Jost, and Sachs, Hans. *The Book of Trades*. Reprint. New York: Dover, 1973.

Beaty, Nancy Lee. *The Craft of Dying: A Study in the Literary Tradition of the* Ars Moriendi *in England*. New Haven: Yale, 1970.

Blades, William. *The Life and Typography of William Caxton*. London, 1861.

Breitkopf, Johnnaes G. I. *Versuch den Ursprung der Spielkarten, Die Einführung des Leinenpapieres, und den Anfang der Holzschneidekunst in Europa*. Leipsic, 1784.

Carter, John, and Muir, Percy H. *Printing and the Mind of Man*. London: Cassell, 1967.

Chatto, William Andrew. *A Treatise on Wood Engraving*. London: Chatto and Windus, Piccadilly, 1861.

Colin, Clair. *A Chronology of Printing*. Cassell, 1969.

Dowding, Geoffrey. *An Introduction to the History of Printing Types*. Clerkenwell: Wace and Company, n.d.

Eisenstein, Elizabeth L. *The Printing Revolution in Early Modern Europe*. Cambridge: University of Cambridge Press, 1983.

Gress, Edmund. *The Art and Practice of Typography*. New York: Oswald, 1917.

Haebler, Konrad. *Incunabula: Original Leaves Traced by Konrad Haelber*. Munich: Werss and Company, 1927.

Hansard, Thomas. *Typographia: An Historical Sketch of the Origin and Progress of the Art of Printing*. London: Baldwin, Cradock & Joy, 1825.

Hellinga, Lotte. *Caxton in Focus: The Beginning of Printing in England*. London: British Library, 1982.

Lavarie, Norma. *The Art and History of Books*. New York: Heineman, 1968.

Lehmann-Haupt, Hellmut. *Gutenberg and the Master of the Playing Cards*. New Haven: Yale, 1966.

Lockombe, Philip. *The History and Art of Printing*. 1771.

McLuhan, Marshall. *The Gutenberg Galaxy: The Making of Typographic Man*. Toronto: University of Toronto, 1962.

McMurtrie, Douglas C. *The Book: The Story of Printing and Bookmaking*. New York: Oxford, 1943.

Morison, Stanley. *German Incunabula in the British Museum*. New York: Hacker Art Books, 1975.

———, and Day, Kenneth. *The Typographic Book*. London: Ernest Benn, and Chicago: University of Chicago, 1963.

Norton, F. J. *Printing in Spain 1501–1520*. Cambridge: University of Cambridge Press, 1966.

7. The German Illustrated Book

Anzewlewsky, Fedja. *Dürer: His Art and Life.* New York: Alpine, 1980.

Bliss, Douglas Percy. *A History of Wood-Engraving.* London: J. M. Dent and Sons, 1928.

Dodgson, Cambell. *Catalog of Early German and Flemish Woodcuts, Vols. I and II.* London: British Museum, 1903.

Dürer, Albrecht. trans. Nichol, R. T. *Of the Just Shaping of Letters.* New York: Dover, 1965.

————. *Underweysung der Messung mit dem Zirckel und Richtscheyt.* Nuremberg, 1525.

Gilver, William. *Masterworks in Wood: The Woodcut Print.* Portland: Portland Art Museum, 1976.

Hind, Arthur M. *An Introduction to a History of Woodcut.* Boston and New York: Houghton Mifflin, 1935.

Hoetink, Hans. *Dürer's Universe.* Woodbury, NY: Barron's, 1971.

Hollstein, F. W. H. *German Engravings Etchings and Woodcuts CA. 1400–1700.* Amsterdam: Menno Hertzberger, 1962.

Johnson, A. P. *Selected Essays on Books and Printing.* New York: Van Gendt, 1970.

Kurth, Dr. Willi. *The Complete Woodcuts of Albrecht Dürer.* New York: Crown, 1946.

Muther, Richard. *German Book Illustration of The Gothic Period and The Early Renaissance (1460–1530).* Metuchen, N.J.: Scarecrow Press, 1972.

Panofsky, Erwin. *The Life and Art of Albrecht Dürer.* Princeton: Princeton University Press, 1955.

Rossiter, Henry Preston. *Albrecht Dürer: Master Printmaker.* Boston: Museum of Fine Arts, 1971.

Strauss, Walter L. *The German Single-Leaf Woodcut, 1550–1600.* New York: Abrams, 1975.

Talbot, Charles W., ed. *Dürer in America: His Graphic Work.* New York: Macmillan, 1971.

Wilson, Adrian. *The Making of the Nuremberg Chronicle.* Amsterdam: Nico Israel, 1976.

8. Renaissance Graphic Design

Armstrong, Elizabeth. *Robert Estienne the Royal Printer: An Historical Study of the Elder Stephanus.* Cambridge: Cambridge University Press, 1954.

Benson, John Howard. *The First Writing Book.* New Haven: Yale, 1955.

Bernard, Auguste. trans. Ives, George B. *Geofroy Tory.* New York: Houghton Mifflin, 1909.

DeVinne, Theodore L. *A Treatise on Title-pages.* 1901. Reprint. New York: Haskell House, 1972.

Johnson, A. P. *Selected Essays on Books and Printing.* New York: Van Gendt, 1970.

Johnson, Fridolf. *A Treasury of Bookplates from the Renaissance to the Present.* New York: Dover, 1977.

le Be, Pierre. *Modeles de lettres de Pierre le Be.* Paris, 1601.

Lowry, Martin. *The World of Aldus Manutius.* Ithica: Cornell, 1979.

McCrillis, John O. C. *Printer's Abecedarium.* Boston: Godine, 1974.

McKitterick, David, ed. *Stanley Morison and D. B. Updike: Selected Correspondence.* London: Scholar Press, 1972.

Meynell, Sir Francis, and Simon, Herbert, eds. *Fleuron Anthology.* Boston: Godine, 1979.

Morison, Stanley. *First Principles of Typography.* Cambridge: Cambridge University Press, 1936.

Mortimer, Ruth. *French 16th Century Books (Vols. I and II).* Cambridge: The Belknap Press of Harvard University Press, 1964.

Schreiber, Fred. *The Estiennes: An Annotated Catalog.* New York: E. K. Schreiber, 1982.

Tannenbaum, Samuel A. *The Handwriting of the Renaissance*. New York: Ungar, 1930.

Williamson, Hugh. *Methods of Book Design*. New Haven: Yale, 1983.

9. An Epoch of Typographic Genius

Ball, Johnson. *William Caslon: Master of Letters*. Kineton: The Roundwood Press, 1973.

Bartram, Alan. *The English Lettering Tradition from 1700 to the Present Day*. London: Lund Humphries, 1986.

Berry, W. Turner, and Johnston, A. F. *Catalog of Specimens of Printing Types by English and Scottish Printers and Founders 1665–1830*. New York: Garland, 1983.

Bodoni, Signora, and Orsi, Luigi, eds. *Manuale Tipografico*. Parma, 1818.

Bultin, Martin. *William Blake 1757–1827*. London: Tate Gallery, 1990.

Carter, Harry, trans. *Fournier on Typefounding*. New York: Lenox Hill, 1972.

Didot, A. Ambroise Firmin. *Essai sur la typographie*. Paris, 1851.

Fournier, Pierre Simon. *Manuel Typographique, Vol. I & II*. Paris, 1764 & 1768.

Franklin V, Benjamin. *Boston Printers, Publishers, and Booksellers: 1640–1800*. Boston, G. K. Hall, 1980.

Holloway, Owen E. *French Rococo Book Illustration*. New York: Transatlantic Arts, 1969.

Hutt, Allen. *Fournier, the Compleat Typographer*. London: Frederick Muller, Ltd., 1972.

Lowance, Mason I., Jr., and Bumgardner, Georgia B., eds. *Massachusetts Broadsides of the American Revolution*. Amherst: University of Massachusetts, 1976.

Osborne, Carole Maroot. *Pierre Didot the Elder and French Book Illustration*. New York: Garland, 1985.

Pardoe, F. E. *John Baskerville of Birmingham: Letter-Founder and Printer*. London: Frederick Muller, 1975.

Pignatti, Terisio. *The Age of Rococo*. New York: Paul Hamlyn, 1966.

Plomer, Henry R. *English Printer's Ornaments*. New York: Burt Franklin, 1924.

Sewter, A. C. *Baroque and Rococo*. New York: Harcourt Brace Jovanovich, 1972.

Twyman, Michael. *Printing 1770–1970*. London: Eyre & Spottiswoode, 1970.

Part III. The Industrial Revolution:
The impact of industrial technology upon visual communications

10. Typography for an Industrial Age

Bidwell, John, ed. *Specimens of Type . . . American Type Founders Co.* New York: Garland, 1981.

Bruce, David, Jr. and Eckman, James, eds. *History of Typefounding in the United States*. New York: The Typophiles, 1981.

Day, Kenneth, ed. *Book Typography 1815–1965 in Europe and the United States of America*. Chicago: University of Chicago, 1965.

Gowan, Al. *T. J. Lyons: A Biography and Critical Essay*. Boston: Society of Printers, 1987.

Gray, Nicolete. *Nineteenth Century Ornamented Typefaces*. Berkeley and Los Angeles: University of California, 1976.

Huss, Richard E. *The Development of Printer's Mechanical Typesetting Methods 1822–1925*. Charlottesville: University of Virginia, 1973.

Kelly, Rob Roy. *American Wood Type: 1828–1900: Notes of the Evolution of Decorative and Large Types*. New York: De Capo, 1969.

Lewis, John. *Typography/Basic Principles*. New York: Reinhold, 1966.

Mosley, James. *British Type Specimens before 1831: A Hand List*. Oxford: Bodleian Library, 1984.

Reed, Talbot Baines. *A History of the Old English Letter Foundries.* Revised and enlarged by A. F. Johnson. London: 1952.

Silver, Rollo G. *Typefounding in America: 1787–1825.* Charlottesville: University of Virginia, 1965.

Southward, John. *Practical Printing: A Handbook for the Art of Typography.* London: Printer's Register Office, 1882. Reprint, New York: Garland, 1980.

Tracy, Walter. *Letters of Credit: A View of Type Design.* London: Gordon Fraiser, 1986.

11. Photography, the New Communications Tool

Arnold, H. J. P. *William Henry Fox Talbot: Pioneer of Photography and Man of Sciences.* London: Hutchinson Benham, 1977.

Buckland, Gail. *Fox Talbot and the Invention of Photography.* Boston: Godine, 1980.

Jammes, Andre. *William H. F. Talbot, Inventor of the Positive-Negative Process.* New York: Macmillan, 1973.

Lassam, Robert. *Fox Talbot: Photographer.* Wiltshire, England: Compton, 1979.

Newhall, Beaumont. *The History of Photography.* New York: Museum of Modern Art, 1964.

Pollack, Peter. *The Picture History of Photography.* New York: Abrams, 1969.

Rosenblum, Naomi, ed. *A World History of Photography.* New York: Abbeville, 1981.

Snyder, Joel. *American Frontiers: Timothy O'Sullivan.* New York: Aperture, 1981.

Talbot, William Henry Fox. *The Pencil of Nature.* London: Longman, Brown, Green and Longmans, 1844–46.

Weinbergen, Norman S. *The Art of the Photogram: Photography without a Camera.* New York: Taplinger, 1981.

12. Popular Graphics of the Victorian Era

Abbott, Charles D. *Howard Pyle, A Chronicle.* New York: Harper's, 1925.

Alistair, Allen, and Hoverstadt, Joan. *The History of Printed Scraps.* London: New Cavendish Books, 1983.

Annenberg, Maurice. *A Typographic Journey through The Inland Printer.* Baltimore: Maran Press, 1977.

Black, Mary. *American Advertising Posters of the Nineteenth Century.* New York: Dover, 1976.

Crane, Walter. *Walter Crane as a Book Illustrator.* London: Academy Editions, 1975.

Dobson, Austin. *Thomas Bewick and His Pupils.* London: Chatto and Windus, Piccadilly, 1884.

Durant, Stuart. *Victorian Ornamental Design.* London: Academy Editions, and New York: St. Martin's Press, 1972.

Freeman, Larry. *Louis Prang: Color Lithographer.* Watkins Glen, NY: Century House, 1971.

Hillier, Bevis. *100 Years of Posters.* New York: Harper and Row, 1972.

Jarvis, Simon. *High Victorian Design.* Woodbridge, Suffolk: Boydell, 1983.

Jones, Owen. *The Grammar of Ornament.* Reprint, New York: Portland House, 1986.

Konody, Paul George. *The Art of Walter Crane.* London: G. Bell, 1902.

Lehmann-Haupt, Hellmut. *The Book in America.* New York: Bowker, 1951.

McClinton, Katharine Morrison. *The Chromolithographs of Louis Prang.* New York: Clarkson N. Potter, 1973.

McLean, Ruari. *Victorian Book Design and Colour Printing.* 2nd Ed. Berkeley: University of California Press, 1972.

Marzio, Peter C. *The Democratic Art.* Boston: Godine, 1979.

Mott, Frank Luther. *A History of American Magazines.* Cambridge: Belknap Press of Harvard University, 1957.

Muir, Percy. *Victorian Illustrated Books.* New York: Praeger, 1971.

Pitz, Henry C. *Howard Pyle: Writer, Illustrator, Founder of the Brandywine Press*. New York: C. N. Potter, 1975.

Shove, Raymond H. *Cheap Book Production in the United States, 1870 to 1891*. Urbana: University of Illinois Library, 1937.

Spencer, Isabel. *Walter Crane*. London: Studio Vista, 1975.

Stern, Madeleine B. *Publishers for Mass Entertainment in Nineteenth Century America*. Boston: G. K. Hall, 1980.

Wornum, Ralph N. *Analysis of Ornament*. London: Chapman and Hall, 1879.

13. The Arts and Crafts Movement

Anscombe, Isabelle, and Gere, Charlotte. *Arts and Crafts in Britain and America*. London: Academy Editions, 1978.

Arts and Crafts Exhibition Society. *Arts and Crafts Essays*. London: Longmans Green and Company, 1893.

Ashbee, Charles R. *An Endeavor towards the Teaching of John Ruskin and William Morris*. London: Edward Arnold, 1901.

————.*Craftsmanship in Competitive Industry*. Camden: Essex House, 1908.

————, ed. *The Manual of the Guild and School of Handicraft*. London: Cassell, 1892. Reprint, New York: Garland, 1977.

Bell, Malcolm. *Edward Burne-Jones*. London: Bell, 1892.

Bell, Quintin. *Ruskin*. New York: Braziller, 1963.

Black, Mary. *American Advertising Posters of the Nineteenth Century*. New York: Dover, 1976.

Bruckner, D. J. R. *Frederic Goudy*. New York: Abrams, 1990.

Carter, Sebastian. *Twentieth Century Type Designers*. London: Trefoil, 1987.

Cave, Roderick. *The Private Press*. New York: Watson-Guptill, 1971.

Cobden-Sanderson, Thomas James. *Ecce Mundus* and *The Arts and Crafts Movement*. Hammersmith: Hammersmith Pub. Society, 1902–1905. Reprint, New York and London: Garland, 1977.

Colebrook, Frank. *William Morris: Master Printer*. Council Bluffs, Iowa: Yellow Barn Press, 1989.

Crane, Walter. *Of the Decorative Illustration of Books Old and New*. London: Bell, 1896.

————.*William Morris to Whistler*. London: Bell, 1911.

Crawford, Alan. *C. R. Ashbee. Architect, Designer, and Romantic Socialist*. New Haven: Yale, 1985.

Fairclough, Oliver. *Textiles by William Morris and Morris and Co: 1861–1940*. New York: Thames and Hudson, 1981.

Ferebee, Ann. *A History of Design from the Victorian Era to the Present*. New York: Van Nostrand Reinhold, 1970.

Franklin, Colin. *The Ashendene Press*. Dallas: Birdwell, 1986.

Gibbs-Smith, C. H. *The Great Exhibition of 1851*. London: Her Majesty's Stationery Office, 1951.

Gillow, Norah. *William Morris: Designs and Patterns*. London: Bracken, 1988.

Goudy, Frederic W. *Typologia*. Berkeley: University of California, 1940.

————. *The Alphabet and Elements of Lettering*. Berkeley: University of California, 1952.

————. *Goudy's Type Designs*. 2nd Ed. New Rochelle, NY: Myriade Press, 1978.

Keynes, Geoffrey. *William Pickering: Publisher*. Revised Edition. London: Galahad Press, 1969.

Konody, Paul George. *The Art of Walter Crane*. London: Bell, 1902.

Ludwig, Coy L. *The Arts and Crafts Movement in New York State, 1890s–1920s*. Hamilton, NY: Gallery Association of New York State, 1983.

Mackail, J. W. *The Life of William Morris*. New York: Oxford, 1950.

McLean, Ruari. *Modern Book Design from William Morris to the Present Day*. London: Faber & Faber, 1958.

Morris, William. Gaunt, William, ed. *Selected Writings*. London: Falcon Press, 1948.
———. Peterson, William S., ed. *The Ideal Book: Essays and Lectures on the Art of the Book*. Berkeley: University of California, 1983.
———. *William Morris by Himself: Designs and Writings*. Boston: New York Graphic Society, 1988.
Naylor, Gillian. *The Arts and Crafts Movement*. Cambridge: MIT Press, 1971.
Parry, Linda. *William Morris Textiles*. London: Weidenfeld and Nicol, 1983.
Ransom, Will. *Private Presses and Their Books*. New York: Bowker, 1929.
Rogers, Bruce. *Paragraphs on Printing*. New York: William E. Rudge's Sons, 1943.
Rosenberg, John D. *The Darkening Glass: A Portrait of Ruskin's Genius*. New York: Columbia, 1961.
Sparling, H. Halliday. *The Kelmscott Press and William Morris, Master Craftsman*. London: Macmillan, 1924.
Smart, William. *John Ruskin: His Life and Work*. New York: Heywood, 1973.
Stansky, Peter. *Redesigning the World; William Morris, the 1880s, and the Arts and Crafts*. Princeton: Princeton University Press, 1985.
Thompson, Susan Otis. *American Book Design and William Morris*. New York: R. R. Bowker, 1977.
Triggs, Oscar Lovell. *Chapters in the History of the Arts and Crafts Movement*. Chicago, 1902. Reprint, New York: Arno Press, 1979.
Vallance, Aymer. *William Morris: His Art, His Writings, and His Public Life*. London: George Bell and Sons, 1897.
Volpe, Todd, and Cathers, Beth. *Treasures of the American Arts and Crafts Movement*. New York: Abrams, 1988.

14. Art Nouveau

Arwas, Victor. *Belle Epoque Posters and Graphics*. New York: Rizzoli, 1978.
———. *Berthon and Grasset*. New York: Rizzoli, 1978.
Aslin, Elizabeth. *The Aesthetic Movement: Prelude to Art Nouveau*. London: Elek Books, 1969.
Bavilli, Renato. *Art Nouveau*. London: Cassell, 1987.
Beardsley, Aubrey. *The Early Work of Aubrey Beardsley*. London: Lane, 1899.
———. *The Later Work of Aubrey Beardsley*. London: Lane, 1901.
Beeh, Wolfgang. *Jugendstil: Kunst um 1900*. Darmstadt: Roether, 1982.
Bradley, William H. *Will Bradley: His Chap Book*. New York: The Typofiles, 1955.
Brinckmann, Justus. *Jugendstil*. Dortmund, Germany: Havenberg, 1983.
Broido, Lucy. *The Posters of Jules Cheret*. New York: Dover, 1980.
Bargiel, Rejane. *Steinlen affichiste: catalog raisonne*. Lausanne, France: Editions du Grand-Pont, 1986.
Castleman, Riva, and Wittrock, Wolfgang. *Henri de Toulouse-Lautrec*. New York: The Museum of Modern Art, 1985.
Cate, Phillip Dennis, and Hitchings, Sinclair Hamilton. *The Color Revolution*. Santa Barbara, CA, and Salt Lake City, UT: Peregine Smith, 1978.
Cate, Phillip Dennis, Finby, Nancy, and Kiehl, David W. *American Posters of the 1890s*. New York: Abrams, 1987.
Chibbett, David. *The History of Japanese Printing and Book Illustration*. Tokyo: Kodansha, 1977.
Cirker, Hayward and Blanche. *The Golden Age of the Poster*. New York: Dover, 1971.
Constantine, Mildred, and Fern, Alan M. *Word and Image*. New York: Museum of Modern Art, 1968.
Delevoy, Robert L., Culot, Maurice, and Brunhammer, Yvonne. *Guimard, Horta, Van de Velde*. Paris: Musee des Arts Decoratifs, 1971.
Fields, Armond. *George Auriol*. Layton, UT: Peregrine Smith, 1985.
Eschmann, Karl. *Jugendstil*. Kastellann, Germany: Aloys Henn Verlag, 1976.
Gerhardus, Maly and Dietfried. *Symbolism and Art Nouveau*. Oxford: Phaidon Press, 1979.
Gibson, David. *Designed to Persuade: The Graphic Art of Edward Penfield*. Yonkers, NY: Hudson River Museum, 1984.

Gillon, Edmund V., Jr. *Art Nouveau: An Anthology of Design and Illustration from the Studio.* New York: Dover, 1969.

Hermand, Jost. *Jugendstil: Kunst um 1900.* Stuttgart: Metzlersche, 1965.

Hiesinger, Kathryn B., ed. *Art Nouveau in Munich: Masters of the Jugendstil.* Munich: Prestel-Verlag, 1988.

Hofstatter, Hans H. *Art Nouveau: Prints, Illustrations, and Posters.* New York: Greenwich House, 1968.

Horning, Clarence P. *Will Bradley: His Graphic Art.* New York: Dover, 1974.

Houfe, Simon, ed. *The Birth of* The Studio: *1893–1895.* Woodbridge, Suffolk: Baron, n.d.

Hutchison, Harold F. *The Poster.* New York: Viking, 1968.

Julien, Edouard. *The Posters of Toulouse-Lautrec.* Monte Carlo: Andre Sauret, 1966.

Keay, Carolyn. *American Posters of the Turn of the Century.* London: Academy Editions, 1975.

Kempton, Richard. *Art Nouveau: An Annotated Bibliography.* Los Angeles: Hennessey & Ingalls, 1977.

Levy, Merwyn. *Liberty Style: The Classic Years 1889–1910.* New York, 1986.

Madsen, Stephan T. *Sources of Art Nouveau.* New York: Da Capo, 1975.

Margolin, Victor. *American Poster Renaissance.* New York: Watson-Guptill, 1975.

Mucha, Juri. *Alphonse Mucha.* New York: St. Martin's Press, 1971.

Nyns, Marcel. *Georges Lemmen.* Antwerp: de Sikkel, 1954.

Osthaus, Karl Ernst. *Van de Velde.* Hagen: Folkwang, 1920.

Plasschaert, A. *Jan Toorop.* Amsterdam: Vorst & Tas, 1929.

Read, Brian. *Aubrey Beardsley.* New York: Bonanza, 1968.

Richards, Maurice. *Posters at the Turn of the Century.* New York: Walker, 1968.

Ricketts, Charles. *A Defence of the Revival of Printing.* London: Ballentine Press, 1909.

Sainton, Roger. *Art Nouveau Posters and Graphics.* New York: Rizzoli, 1977.

Selz, Peter, and Constantine, Mildred, eds. *Art Nouveau.* New York: Museum of Modern Art, 1959.

Sharp, Dennis. *Henri Van de Velde, Theatres 1904-1914.* London: The Architectural Association, 1974.

Solo, Dan X. *Art Nouveau Display Alphabets.* New York: Dover, 1976.

Sterner, Gabriele. *Jugendstil Art Deco Malerei and Grafik.* Munich: Wilhelm Heyne Verlag, 1981.

Sunshine, Linda. *The Posters of Alphonse Mucha.* New York: Harmony Books, 1975.

Taylor, John Russell. *The Art Nouveau Book in Britain.* Edinburgh: Paul Harris Publishing, 1979.

Terrence, Kathy. *An Art Nouveau Album.* New York: Dutton, 1981.

Velde, Henri Van de. *Deblaiement d'Art.* Brussels: Monnom, 1894.

————. *Die Renaissance im Modernen Kunstgewerbe.* Berlin: Cassirer, 1903.

Verneuil, M. M. P., Auriol, G., and Mucha, A. *Combinaisons Ornementales.* Paris: Librairie Centrale des Beaux Arts, 1901.

Weisser, Michael. *Im Stil der "Jugend."* Frankfurt: Fricke, 1979.

Part IV. The Modernist Era:
Graphic design in the first half of the twentieth century

15. The Genesis of Twentieth-Century Design

Ades, Dawn, *et al. The 20th Century Poster: Art of the Avant Garde.* New York: Abbeville, 1984.

Adlmann, Jan Ernst. *Vienna Moderne: 1898–1918.* Houston: University of Houston, 1979.

Banham, Reyner. *Theory and Design in the First Machine Age.* New York: Praeger, 1967.

Baroni, Daniele, and D'Auria, Antonio. *Kolo Moser: Graphic Artist and Designer.* New York: Rizzoli, 1986.

Behrens, Peter. *Feste des Lebens und der Kunst, eine Betrachtung des Theaters als Höchsten Kultursymbols.* Leipzig: Eugen Diederichs, 1900.

Billcliffe, Roger. *Charles Rennie Mackintosh: The Complete Furniture, Furniture Drawings, and Interior Designs.* London: J. Murry, 1986.

Bliss, Douglas Percy. *Charles Rennie Mackintosh and Glasgow School of Art.* Glasgow: Glasgow School of Art, 1979.

Bruckhardt, Lucius. *The Werkbund: History and Ideology, 1907–1933.* New York: Barron's, 1977.

Buddensieg, Tilmann. *Industrialkultur: Peter Behrens and the AEG.* Cambridge, MA: MIT Press, 1984.

Campbell, Joan. *The German Werkbund: The Politics of Reform in the Applied Arts.* Princeton: Princeton University Press, 1978.

Clair, Jean, *et al. Vienne 1880-1938: L'Apocalypse Joyeuse.* Paris: Editions du Centre Pompidou, 1986.

Crane, Walter. *The Bases of Design.* London: G. Bell & Sons, 1898.

———. *Line and Form.* London: G. Bell & Sons, Ltd., 1900.

Eisler, Max. *Gustav Klimt.* Vienna: Rikola, 1921.

Fenz, Werner. *Koloman Moser.* Salzburg and Vienna: Residenz Verlag, 1984.

Fleischmann, Benno. *Gustav Klimt.* Vienna: Deuticke, 1946.

Garvey, Eleanor M., Smith, Anne B., and Wick, Peter A. *The Turn of a Century 1885–1910: Art Nouveau—Jugendstil Books.* Cambridge, MA: Harvard, 1970.

Hanks, David A. *The Decorative Designs of Frank Lloyd Wright.* New York: Dutton, 1979.

Haslam, Malcolm. *In the Nouveau Style.* Boston: Little, Brown, 1989.

Hoeber, Fritz. *Peter Behrens.* Munich: Georg Muller and Eugen Rentsch, 1913.

Hoepfner, Wolfram. *Das Haus Wiegand von Peter Behrens in Berlin-Dahlem.* Mainz: von Zabern, 1979.

Hoffman, Werner, trans. by Goodwin, Inge. *Gustav Klimt.* Greenwich, CT: New York Graphic Society, 1974.

Howarth, Thomas. *Charles Rennie Mackintosh and the Modern Movement.* London: Routledge and Kegan Paul, 1952.

Kadatz, Hans-Joachim. *Peter Behrens.* Leipzig: VEB E. A. Seemann Verlag, 1977.

Kallir, Jane. *Viennese Design and the Wiener Werkstätte.* New York: Braziller, 1986.

Koschatzky, Walter, and Kossatz, Horst-Herbert. *Ornamental Posters of the Vienna Secession.* London: Academy Editions, 1974.

Lane, Terence. *Vienna 1913.* Melbourne: National Gallery of Victoria, 1984.

Latham, Ian. *Josef Maria Olbrich.* London: Academy Editions, 1980.

Loos, Adolf. *Spoken into the Void: Collected Essays 1897–1900.* Cambridge, MA: MIT, 1982.

Loubier, Hans. *Die Neue Deutsche Buchkunst.* Stuttgart: Felix Krais Verlag, 1921.

MacLeod, Robert. *Charles Rennie Mackintosh: Architect and Artist.* New York: Dutton, 1983.

MacMillan, Andy, and Futagawa, Yukio. *Charles Rennie Mackintosh: The Glasgow School of Art.* Tokyo: A. D. A. Edita, 1979.

Meehan, Patrick J., ed. *Truth Against the World: Frank Lloyd Wright Speaks for an Organic Architecture.* New York: Wiley, 1987.

Messina, Maria Grazia. *Hoffmann: i "mobili semplici" Vienna 1900/1910.* Florence: Galleria dell'Emporio, 1977.

Meyer, Christian. *Josef Hoffmann: Architect and Designer 1870–1956.* Vienna: Galerie Metropol, 1981.

Nebehay, Michael Christian. *Ver Sacrum: 1898–1903.* New York: Rizzoli, 1977.

Noever, Peter, and Oberhuber, Oswald. *Josef Hoffmann: Ornament Zwischen Hoffnung und Verbrechen.* Vienna: Beim Herausgeber, 1987.

Peter Behrens and Nurnberg. Munich: Prestel, 1980.

Pevsner, Nikolaus. *Charles R. Mackintosh.* Milan: Il Balcone, 1950.

———. *The Sources of Modern Architecture and Design.* London: Thames and Hudson, 1968.

Powell, Nicolas. *The Sacred Spring: The Arts in Vienna 1898–1918*. Greenwich, CT: New York Graphic Society, 1974.

Sarmany-Parsons, Ilona. *Gustav Klimt*. New York: Crown, 1987.

Schuster, Peter-Klaus, ed. *Peter Behrens und Nurnberg*. Munich: Prestel-Verlag Munchen, 1980.

Schweiger, Werner J., et al. *Koloman Moser: 1868–1918*. Vienna: Hochschule für Angewandte Kunst in Wien, 1979.

———. *Wiener Werkstaette: Design in Vienna 1903–1932*. New York: Abbeville, 1984.

Tummers, Nic H. M. *J. L. Lauweriks, zijn werk en zigninvloed op architectuuren vormgevingrond 1910: DeHagenerlmpls*. Hilversum, The Netherlands: Uitgeverij F. van Saane, 1968.

Varnedoe, Kirk. *Vienna 1900: Art, Architecture, and Design*. New York: Museum of Modern Art, 1986.

Vergo, Peter. *Art in Vienna 1898–1918*. London: Phaidon, 1975.

———. *Vienna 1900: Vienna, Scotland, and the European Avant-Garde*. Edinburgh: Her Majesty's Stationery Office, 1975.

Vienna Secession. *Katalog der Kunst Ausstellung der Vereinigung Bildenden Künstler Österreichs*. Vienna: No. 1–14, 1898–1902.

Weber, Wilhelm. *Peter Behrens*. Berlin: Pfalzgalerie Kaiserslautern, 1966.

Werde, Stuart. *The Modern Poster*. New York: Museum of Modern Art, 1988.

Windsor, Alan. *Peter Behrens: Architect and Designer*. New York: Whitney, 1981.

16. The Influence of Modern Art

Ades, Dawn. *Photomontage*. London: Thames and Hudson, 1976.

Apollinaire, Guillaume. *The Cubist Painters, Aesthetic Meditations, 1913*. New York: Wittenborn, 1962.

———. *Calligrammes*. Paris: Editions Gallimard, 1925.

Apollonio, Umbro, ed. *Futurist Manifestos*. New York: Viking Press, 1973.

Baldacci, Paolo, and Daverio, Philippe. *Futurism 1911–1918*. Milan: Galleria Daverio, 1988.

Baxandall, Lee. *Radical Perspectives in the Arts*. Middlesex: Penguin Books, 1972.

Benson, Timothy O. *Raoul Hausmann and Berlin Dada*. Ann Arbor, MI: UMI Research Press, 1987.

Cassou, Jean, and Leymarie, Jean. *Fernand Leger Drawings and Gouaches*. Greenwich, CT: New York Graphic Society, 1973.

Cendrars, Blaise. *La Fin Du Monde. . .* Reprint: Paris: Pierre Seghers, 1949.

Cohen, Arthur A. *The Avant Garde in Print*. Vols. I–V. New York: Ex Libris, 1983.

Crane, Arnold W. *Man Ray Photo Graphics*. Milwaukee: Milwaukee Art Center, 1973.

Damase, Jacques. *Revolution Typographique*. Geneve: Galerie Motte, 1966.

De Rache, Andre, ed. *Joan Miro*. Brussels: Gemeentelijke Casino, 1971.

Elderfield, John. *Kurt Schwitters*. London: Thames and Hudson, 1985.

Enyert, James. *Bruguiere: His Photographs and His Life*. New York: Knopf, 1977.

Ernst, Max. *Une Semaine De Bonte*. New York: Dover, 1976.

Foster, Steven B., ed. *Dada/Dimensions*. Ann Arbor, MI: UMI Research Press, c. 1985.

Fraser, James, and Heller, Steven. *The Malik Verlag 1916–1947, Berlin, Prague, New York*. New York: Goethe House, and Madison, NJ: Fairleigh Dickinson University, 1985.

Freeman, Judi. *The Dada and Surrealist Word-Image*. Cambridge, MA: MIT, 1989.

Fry, Edward F. *Cubism*. London: Thames and Hudson, 1966; and New York: Oxford, 1978.

Greenberg, Allen Carl. *Artists and Revolution: Dada and the Bauhaus. 1917–1925*. Ann Arbor, MI: UMI Research Press, 1979.

Habasque, Guy. *Cubism*. Paris: Skira, 1959.

Haenlein, Carl-Albrecht. *Dada Photomontagen*. Hannover: Kestner-Gesellschaft Hannover, 1979.

Hausmann, Raoul, and Schwitters, Kurk. *PIN*. London: Gaberbocchus Press, 1962.

Heartfield, John. *Photomontages of the Nazi Period*. New York: Universe, 1977.

Hubert, Renee Riese. *Surrealism and the Book*. Berkeley: California, 1988.

Huelsenbeck, Richard. *Memoirs of a Dada Drummer*. New York: Viking, 1969.

Hulten, Pontus, ed. *Futurism and Futurisms*. New York: Abbeville, 1986.

Kahn, Douglas. *John Heartfield: Art and Mass Media*. New York: Tanam, 1985.

Kozloff, Max. *Cubism/Futurism*. New York: Charter House, 1973.

Lippard, Lucy R. ed. *Dadas on Art*. Englewood Cliffs: Prentice-Hall, 1971.

Lista, Giovanni. *Futurismo e Fotografia*. Milano: Multhipla Edizioni, 1979.

Little, Roger. *Guillaume Apollinaire*. London: Athlone Press, 1976.

Marinetti, Filippo T. Edited by R. W. Flint. *Marinetti Selected Writings*. New York: Farrar, Straus, and Giroux, 1971.

Martin, Marianne W. *Futurist Art and Theory 1909–1915*. Oxford: Clarendon Press, 1968.

Michaud, Guy. *Mallarme*. New York: New York University Press, 1965.

Nadeau, Maurice. *The History of Surrealism*. Cambridge, MA: Harvard, 1989.

Newell, Kenneth B. *Pattern Poetry: A Historical Critique from the Alexandrian Greeks to Dylan Thomas*. Boston: Marlborough House, 1976.

Passamani, Bruno. *Fortunato Depero*. Luglio: Bassano Del Grappa, 1970.

Read, Herbert. *A Concise History of Modern Painting*. New York: Praeger, 1959.

Richardson, Tony, and Stangos, Nikos, eds. *Concepts of Modern Art*. New York: Harper and Row, 1974.

Rosenbaum, Robert. *Cubism and Twentieth-Century Art*. New York: Abrams, 1966.

Rye, Jane. *Futurism*. London: Studio Vista, 1972.

Samaltanos, Katia. *Apollinaire: Catalyst for Primitivism, Picabia, and Duchamp*. Ann Arbor, MI: UMI Research Press, 1984.

Schmalenbach, Werner. *Fernand Leger*. New York: Abrams, 1976.

Schwartz, Arturo. *Man Ray: Rigour of Imagination*. New York: Rizzoli, 1972.

Scudiero, Maurizio. *Futurismi Postali*. Rovereto: Longo Editore, 1986.

————, and Leiber, David. *Depero Futurista & New York:* Rovereto: Longo Editore, 1986.

Siepmann, Eckhard. *Montage: John Heartfield*. Berlin: Elefanten Press Galerie, 1977.

Steegmuller, Francis. *Apollinaire, Poet among the Painters*. Freeport: Books for Libraries Press, 1971.

Steinitz, Kate Trauman. *Kurt Schwitters, A Portrait from Life*. Berkeley and Los Angeles: University of California Press, 1968.

Sylvester, David. *Magritte*. New York: Praeger, 1969.

Tisdall, Caroline, and Bozzolla, Angelo. *Futurism*. New York and Toronto: Oxford, 1978.

17. Pictorial Modernism

Binder, Carla (compiler). *Joseph Binder*. Vienna: Anton Schroll & Co., 1976.

Brown, Robert K., and Reinhold, Susan. *The Poster Art of A. M. Cassandre*. New York: Dutton, 1979.

Cooper, Austin. *Making A Poster*. London: The Studio, Ltd., 1938.

Darracott, Joseph. *The First World War in Posters*. New York: Dover, 1974.

Delhaye, Jean. *Art Deco Posters and Graphics*. New York: Rizzoli, 1978.

Encyclopedia des arts decoratifs et industriels modernes au XXeme siecle. Vol. I–VII. Paris: Impr. nationale, 1925.

Green, Oliver. *Art for the London Underground*. New York: Rizzoli, 1990.

Gluck, Felix. *World Graphic Design: Fifty Years of Advertising Art*. New York: Watson-Guptill, 1969.

Haworth-Booth, Mark. *E. McKnight Kauffer: A Designer and His Public*. Madison, CT: Fraser, 1979.

Hillier, Bevis. *Art Deco of the 20s and 30s*. London: Studio Vista, and New York: Dutton, 1968.

————. *The World of Art Deco*. New York: Dutton, 1971.

Hitler, Adolf. *Mein Kampf (My Battle)*, trans. E. T. S. Dugdale. Boston: Houghton Mifflin, 1933.

Hohlwein, Ludwig. *Hohlwein Posters*. New York: Dover, 1976.

Kauffer, E. McKnight. *The Art of the Poster*. London: Cecil Palmer, 1924.

Menten, Theodore. *Advertising Art in the Art Deco Style*. New York: Dover, 1975.

Metzl, Ervine. *The Poster: Its History and Its Art*. New York: Watson-Guptill, 1963.

Mouron, Henri. *A. M. Cassandre*. New York: Rizzoli, 1985.

Rawls, Walston. *Wake Up America! World War I and the American Poster*. New York: Abbeville, 1988.

Schau, Michael. *J. C. Leyendecker*. New York: Watson-Guptill, 1974.

Thomson, Oliver. *Mass Persuasion in History*. Edinburgh: Paul Harris, 1977.

Tolmer, A. *Mies en Page. The Theory and Practice of Layout*. London: The Studio, 1930.

18. A New Language of Form

Anikst, Mikhail. *Soviet Commercial Design of the Twenties*. New York: Abbeville Press, 1987.

————, and Chernevich, Elena. *Russian Graphic Design 1880–1917*. New York: Abbeville, 1990.

Baburina, Nina. *The Soviet Political Poster 1917–1980*. New York: Viking, 1988.

Baljeu, Joost. *Theo van Doesburg*. New York: Macmillan, 1974.

Bann, Stephen, ed. *The Tradition of Constructivism*. New York: Viking, 1974.

Barooshian, Vahan D. *Russian Cubo-Futurism: 1910–1930*. The Hague: Mouton, 1974.

Barron, Stephanie, and Tuchman, Maurice, eds. *The Avant-Garde in Russia, 1910–1930: New Perspectives*. Cambridge, MA: MIT Press, 1980.

Beeren, Wim, et. al. *Kazimir Malevich 1878–1935*. Amsterdam: Stedelijk Museum, 1988.

Blake, Patricia, ed. *Vladimir Mayakovsky: The Bedbug and Selected Poetry*. Princeton: Princeton University Press, 1975.

Bojko, Szymon. *New Graphic Design in Revolutionary Russia*. London: Lund Humphries, 1972.

Bowlt, John E., ed. and trans. *Russian Art of the Avant-garde: Theory and Criticism 1902–1934*. New York: Viking, 1976.

Charters, Ann and Samuel. *I Love: the Story of Vladimir Mayakovsky and Lili Brik*. New York: Farrar, Straus & Giroux, 1979.

Chernevich, Elena. *Russian Graphic Design, 1880–1917*. New York: Abbeville, 1990.

Cohen, Arthur A. ed. *ExLibris 6: Constructivism & Futurism: Russian and Other*. New York: ExLibris, 1977.

Compton, Susan P. *The World Backwards: Russian Futurist Books 1912–16*. London: British Museum Publications, 1978.

Constantine, Mildred, and Fern, Alan. *Revolutionary Soviet Film Posters*. Baltimore: Johns Hopkins, 1974.

Contensou, Bernadette, and Lemoine, Serge. *Domela: 65 ans D'Abstraction*. Paris: MAM Musee d'Art Moderne, 1987.

Doig, Allan. *Theo van Doesburg: Painting into Architecture, Theory into Practice*. Cambridge: Cambridge University Press, 1986.

Elliott, David. *Rodchenko and the Arts of Revolutionary Russia*. New York: Pantheon, 1979.

Foresta, Merry, Naumann, Francis, and Foster, Stephen C, et. al. *Perpetual Motif: The Art of Man Ray*. New York: 1988.

Friedman, Mildred, ed. *De Stijl: 1917–1931. Visions of Utopia*. New York: Abbeville Press, 1982.

Franciscono, Marcel. *The Modern Dutch Poster: The First Fifty Years 1890–1940.* Cambridge, MA: MIT Press, 1987.

Grey, Camilla. *The Great Experiment: Russian Art 1863–1922.* New York: Abrams, 1962.

Jaffe, Hans. *De Stijl.* New York: Abrams, 1971.

———. *Mondrian und De Stijl.* Obenmarspforten: Galerie Gmurzynska, 1979.

Karginov, German. *Rodchenko.* London: Thames and Hudson, 1979.

Khan-Magomedov, S. O. *Rodchenko: The Complete Work.* Cambridge, MA: MIT Press, 1987.

King, David, and Porter, Cathy. *Images of Revolution: Graphic Art from 1905 Russia.* New York: Pantheon, 1983.

Lissitzky-Kuppers, Sophie, ed. *Lissitzky: Life Letters Texts.* London: Thames and Hudson, 1967.

Lodder, Christina. *Russian Constructivism.* New Haven: Yale, 1983.

Markov, Vladimir. *Russian Futurism: A History.* London: MacGibbon & Kee, 1969.

Martinet, Jan. *H. N. Werkman 'druksel' prints and general printed matter.* Amsterdam: Stedelijk Museum, 1977.

———. *The Next Call.* Utrecht: uitgeverij Reflex, 1978.

Milena, Richard and Kalinovska. *Art into Life: Russian Constructivism 1914–1932.* New York: Rizzoli, 1990.

Milner, John. *Vladimir Tatlin and the Russian Avant-Garde.* New Haven: Yale, 1983.

Mondrian, Piet. *Plastic Art and Pure Plastic Art.* New York: Wittenborn, 1951.

Neumann, Eckhard. *Functional Graphic Design in the 20's.* New York: Reinhold, 1967.

Nisbet, Peter. *El Lissitzky: 1890–1941.* Cambridge, MA: Harvard University Art Museums, 1987.

Overy, Paul. *De Stijl.* London: Studio Vista, 1969.

Rubinger, Krystyna; Bojko, Szymon; and Bowlt, John E., et. al. *Women Artists of the Russian Avantgarde, 1910–1930.* Köln: Galerie Gmurzynska, 1980.

Rickey, George. *Constructivism: Origins and Evolution.* New York: Braziller, 1967.

Seuphor, Michel. *Piet Mondrian.* New York: Abrams, n.d.

Spencer, Herbert. *Pioneers of Modern Typography.* London: Lund Humphries, 1969.

———, ed. *The Liberated Page.* San Francisco: Bedford Press, 1987.

Stapanian, Juliette R. *Mayakovsky's Cubo-Futurist Vision.* Houston: Rice, 1986.

Van Straaten, Evert. *Theo Van Doesburg: Schilder en Architect.* 'S-Gravenhage, The Netherlands: SDU Uitgeverij, 1988.

White, Stephen. *The Bolshevik Poster.* New Haven, CT: Yale, 1988.

Woroszylski, Wiktor. *The Life of Mayakovsky.* New York: Orion Press, 1970.

19. The Bauhaus and the New Typography

Albers, Josef. *Search Versus Research.* Hartford, CT: Trinity College Press, 1969.

———. *Interaction of Color.* New Haven, CT: Yale, 1975.

Bauhaus Journal. Munchen: Kraus Reprint, 1977.

Barker, Nicolas. *Stanley Morison.* Cambridge, MA: Harvard, 1972.

Bayer, Herbert; Gropius, Walter; and Gropius, Ise, eds. *Bauhaus 1919–1928.* New York: Museum of Modern Art, 1938.

———. *Herbert Bayer: Painter Designer Architect.* New York: Reinhold, 1967 and London: Studio Vista, 1967.

Blaser, Werner. *Mies van der Rohe: less is more.* Zurich: Wasser Verlag, 1986.

Brady, Elizabeth. *Eric Gill: Twentieth Century Book Designer.* Metuchen: The Scarecrow Press, 1974.

Brewer, Roy. *Eric Gill: The Man Who Loved Letters.* London: Frederick Muller Ltd., 1973.

Broos, Kees. *Piet Zwart.* The Hague: Gemeentemuseum, 1973.

Chanzit, Gwen F. *The Herbert Bayer Collection and Archive at the Denver Art Museum.* Denver: Denver Art Museum, 1988.

Dearstyne, Howard. *Inside the Bauhaus*. New York: Rizzoli, 1986.

Franciscono, Marcel. *Walter Gropius and the Creation of the Bauhaus at Weimar: The Ideals and Artistic Theories of its Founding Years*. Champaign/Urbana, Il: Illinois, 1971.

Geelhaar, Christian. *Paul Klee and the Bauhaus*. Greenwich, CT: New York Graphic Society, 1973.

Gill, Eric. *An Essay on Typography*. London: Sheed and Ward, 1931.

Gropius, Walter, et. al. *Offset Buch und Werbekunst, Heft 7*. Leipzig: Der Offset-Verlag GMBH, 1926.

Gropius, Walter, ed. *The Theatre of the Bauhaus*. Middletown, CT: Wesleyan University, 1961.

Gropius, Walter. *The New Architecture and the Bauhaus*. Cambridge, MA: MIT Press, 1965.

Gropius, Walter, and Moholy-Nagy, Laszlo, ed. *Staatliches Bauhaus Weimar, 1919–1923*. Munchen: Kraus Reprint, 1980.

Hahn, Peter. *Bauhaus Berlin*. Weingarten: Kunstverlag Weingarten GmbH, 1985.

Haus, Andreas. *Moholy-Nagy: Photographs and Photograms*. New York: Pantheon Books, 1980.

Hight, Eleanor M. *Moholy-Nagy: Photography and Film in Weimar Germany*. Wellesley: Wellesley College Museum, 1985.

Itten, Johannes. *Design and Form: The Basic Course at the Bauhaus and Later*. New York: Reinhold, 1963.

Kagan, Andrew. *Paul Klee: Art & Music*. Ithaca, NY: Cornell, 1983.

Kandinsky, Wassily. *Concerning the Spiritual in Art*. New York: Wittenborn, 1947.

———. *Point and Line to Plane*. New York: Dover, 1979.

———. *Complete Writings on Art*. New York: Hall, 1982.

Klee, Paul. *Pedagogical Sketchbook*. New York: Praeger, 1953.

Kostelanetz, Richard. *Moholy-Nagy*. London: Allen Lane, 1974.

Kroll, Friedhelm. *Bauhaus 1919–1933*. Dusseldorf: Verlagsgruppe Bertelsmann GmbH, 1974.

Marzona, E. and Fricke, R., ed. *Bauhaus Photography*. Cambridge, MA: MIT Press, 1969.

McLean, Ruari. *Jan Tschichold: Typographer*. London: Lund Humphries, 1975.

Moholy-Nagy, Laszlo. *The New Vision and Abstract of an Artist*. New York: Wittenborn, 1947.

———. *Vision in Motion*. Chicago: Paul Theobald, 1947.

Moholy-Nagy, Sibyl. *Experiment in Totality*. Cambridge, MA: MIT Press, 1969.

Moran, James. *Stanley Morison: His Typographic Achievement*. London: Lund Humphries, and New York: Hastings House, 1971.

Muller, Fridolin, ed. *Piet Zwart*. Teufen, Switzerland: Niggli, 1966.

Naylor, Gilliam. *The Bauhaus Reassessed: Sources and Design Theory*. London: Herbert, 1985.

Neumann, Eckhard. *Bauhaus and Bauhaus People*. New York: Van Nostrand Reinhold, 1970.

Passuth, Krisztina, and Senter, Terence A. *L. Moholy-Nagy*. London: Arts Council of Great Britian, 1980.

Plant, Margaret. *Paul Klee: Figures and Faces*. London: Thames and Hudson, 1978.

Poling, Clark V. *Kandinsky's Teaching at the Bauhaus: Color Theory and Analytical Drawing*. New York: Rizzoli, 1986.

Roh, Franz, and Tschichold, Jan, eds. *foto-auge*. Stuttgart: Akademischer Verlag Dr. Fritz Wedekind, 1929.

Schlemmer, Oskar. *Man: Teaching Notes from the Bauhaus*. Cambridge, MA: MIT Press, 1971.

Schmidt, Joost, Entwurf. *Offset Buch und Werbekunst, 1926*. Dessau, Germany: Dünnhaupt, 1926.

Skelton, Christopher. *Eric Gill: The Engravings*. Boston: David Godine, 1990.

Speaight, Robert. *The Life of Eric Gill*. London: Methuen, 1966.

Thorp, Joseph. *Eric Gill*. London: Jonathan Cape, 1929.

Tower, Beeke Sell. *Klee and Kandinsky at the Bauhaus*. Ann Arbor, MI: UMI Research Press, 1981.

Tschichold, Jan. *Die neue typographie*. Berlin: Verlag Des Bildungsverbandes, 1928.

———. *Asymmetric Typography*. English edition. New York: Reinhold, 1967.

———. *Designing Books*. New York: Wittenborn, Schultz, Inc., 1951.

Whitford, Frank. *Bauhaus*. London: Thames and Hudson, 1984.

Wingler, Hans Maria. *The Bauhaus: Weimar Dessau Berlin Chicago*. Cambridge, MA: MIT Press, 1969.

20. The Modern Movement in America

Chanzit, Gwen Finkel. *Herbert Bayer and Modernist Design in America*. Ann Arbor, MI: UMI Research Press, 1987.

———. *The Herbert Bayer Collection and Archive at the Denver Art Museum*. Seattle: University of Washington, 1988.

DeNoon, Christopher. *Posters of the WPA*. Los Angeles: Wheatley, 1987.

Duncan, Alastair. *American Art Deco*. New York: 1986.

Ehrlich, Frederic. *The New Typography and Modern Layouts*. New York: Stokes, 1934.

Goudy, Frederic. *Why Go Modern*. New York: Diamant Typographic Service, 1944.

Grundberg, Andy. *Brodovitch*. New York: Abrams, 1989.

Hurlburt, Allen. *Publication Design*. New York: Van Nostrand Reinhold, 1976.

Jacobson, Egbert, ed. *Seven Designers Look at Trademark Design*. Chicago: Theobold, 1952.

Johnson, J. Stewart. *The Modern American Poster*. New York: Museum of Modern Art, 1983.

Judd, Denis. *Posters of World War II*. New York: St. Martin's Press, 1973.

Kepes, Gyorgy. *Language of Vision*. Chicago: Paul Theobald, 1945.

———. *The New Landscape*. Chicago: Paul Theobald, 1956.

Lönberg-Holm, K., and Sutnar, Ladislav. *Catalog Design*. New York: Sweet's Catalog Service, 1944.

———. *Catalog Design Progress: Advancing Standards in Visual Communications*. New York: Sweet's Catalog Service, 1950.

Massey, John, ed. *Great Ideas*. Chicago: Container Corporation of America, 1976.

McMurtrie, Douglas C. *Modern Typography and Layout*. Chicago: Eyncourt Press, 1929.

Remington, Roger, and Hodik, Barbara J. *Nine Pioneers of American Graphic Design*. Cambridge, MA: MIT Press, 1989.

Rhodes, Anthony. Victor Margolin, ed. *Propaganda: The Art of Persuasion, World War II*. New York: Chelsea House, 1976.

Sutnar, Ladislav. *Package Design: The Force of Visual Selling*. New York: Arts, 1953.

Tibbel, John. *The American Magazine: A Compact History*. New York: Hawthorne Books, 1969.

Weber, Eva. *Art Deco in America*. New York: Exeter Books, 1985.

Zeman, Zbynek. *Selling the War: Art and Propaganda in World War II*. London: Orbis, 1978.

Part V. The Information Age:
Graphic design in the global village

21. The International Typographic Style

Aicher, Otl. *Typographie*. Berlin: Ernst and Sohn, 1988.

Bill, Max. *Modern Swiss Architecture 1925–1945*. Basel: Verlag Karl Werner, 1945.

Diethelm, Walter. *Visual Transformations*. Zurich: ABC Verlag, 1982.

Frutiger, Adrian. *Type Sign Symbol*. Zurich: ABC Verlag, 1981.

———. *Signs and Symbols: Their Design and Meaning*. New York: Van Nostrand Reinhold, 1989.

Gasser, Manuel. *Exempla graphica*. Zurich: Hug and Sohne, 1967.

Gerstner, Karl, and Kutler, Marcus. *Die Neue Grafik/The New Graphic Art*. New York: Hastings House, 1959.

Gerstner, Karl. *Designing Programmes*. Teufen AR, Switzerland: Arthur Niggli, 1968.

———, trans. by Stephenson, Dennis Q. *Compendium for Literates: A System for Writing*. Cambridge, MA: MIT, 1968.

Grieshaber, Judith M. and Kröplien. *Die Philosophie der Neuen Grafik*. Stuttgart: Edition Cantz, 1990.

Henrion, F. H. K. *Top Graphic Design*. Zurich: ABC Verlag, 1983.

Hofmann, Armin. *Graphic Design Manual*. New York: Van Nostrand Reinhold, 1965.

Hüttinger, Eduard. *Max Bill*. Zurich: ABC Editions, 1978.

Lindinger, Herbert, ed. *Ulm Design: The Morality of Objects*. Cambridge: MIT Press, 1990.

Maier, Manfred. *Basic Principles of Design*. New York: Van Nostrand Reinhold, 1980.

Müller-Brockmann, Josef. *The Graphic Artist and His Design Problems*. Teufen AR, Switzerland: Verlag Arthur Niggli, 1968.

———. *Grid Systems*. Niederteufen: Verlag Arthur Niggli, 1981.

Papanek, Victor. *Design for the Real World*. New York: Pantheon, 1970.

Rotzler, Willy, and Garamond, Jacque N. *Art and Graphics*. Zurich: ABC Verlag, 1983.

Rotzler, Willy. *Constructive Concepts*. New York: Rizzoli, 1989.

Ruder, Emil. *Typography: A Manual of Design*. New York: Hastings House, 1981.

Ruegg, Ruedi. *Basic Typography: Design with Letters*. New York: Van Nostrand Reinhold, 1989.

Schmidt, Helmut. *Typography Today*. Tokyo: Seibundo Shinkosha, 1980.

Stankowski, Anton. *Bildpläne*. Stuttgart: Edition Cantz, 1979.

———. *Visual Presentation of Invisible Processes*. Teufen AR: Verlag Arthur Niggli AG, 1966.

Wichmann, Hans, ed. *Armin Hofmann: His Work, Quest and Philosophy*. Springer, Verlag, 1990.

Zapf, Hermann. *Hermann Zapf: ein Arbeitsbericht*. Hamburg, Germany: Maxmillian-Gesellsch, 1984.

———. *Manuale Typographicum*. Cambridge, MA: MIT Press, 1954.

———. *Manuale Typographicum*. Frankfurt: Z-Press, 1968.

———. *Typographic Variations: On Themes in Contemporary Book Design*. Myriade Press, 1978.

22. The New York School

Burns, Aaron. *Typography*. New York: Reinhold, 1961.

Carter, Rob. *American Typography Today*. New York: Van Nostrand Reinhold, 1989.

Dobrow, Larry. *When Advertising Tried Harder*. New York: Friendly Press, 1984.

Hurlburt, Allen. *Layout: The Design of the Printed Page*. New York: Watson-Guptill, 1977.

Kamakura, Yusaku, ed. *Paul Rand: His Work from 1946–1958*. New York: Knopf, 1959.

Lee, Marshall, ed. *Books for Our Time*. New York: Oxford, 1951.

Lois, George, and Pitts, Bill. *The Art of Advertising: George Lois on Mass Communications*. New York: Abrams, 1977.

McLuhan, Marshall. *The Mechanical Bride*. New York: Vangard, 1951.

———.*Culture is our Business*. New York: McGraw-Hill, 1970.

———. *From Cliche to Archetype*. New York: Viking Press, 1970.

————. and Fiore, Quentin. *The Medium is the Massage*. New York: Bantan, 1967.

————. *Understanding Media: The Extensions of Man*. New York: McGraw-Hill, 1964.

————. *Verbo-Voco-Visual Explorations*. New York: Something Else Press, 1967.

Rand, Paul. *Thoughts on Design*. New York: Van Nostrand Reinhold, 1970.

————. *Paul Rand: A Designer's Art*. New Haven: Yale, 1985.

Rondthaler, Edward. *Life with Letters—As They Turned Photogenic*. New York: Hastings House, 1981.

Snyder, Gertrude, and Peckolick, Alan. *Herb Lubalin: Art Director, Graphic Designer, and Typographer*. New York: American Showcase, 1985.

Thompson, Bradbury. *The Art of Graphic Design*. New Haven: Yale, 1988.

Woods, Gerald, Thompson, Philip, and Williams, John. *Art without Boundaries*. London: Thames and Hudson, 1972.

23. Corporate Identity and Visual Systems

Bass, Saul, et. al. *Saul Bass and Associates*. Tokyo: Seibundo Shinkosha, 1978.

Consuegra, David, ed. *ABC of World Trademarks*. Bogota, Columbia: Primera editions, 1988.

Golden, Cipe Pineles; Weihs, Kurt; and Strunsky, Robert, eds. *The Visual Craft of William Golden*. New York: Braziller, 1962.

Helms, Janet Conradi. *A Historical Survey of Unimark International and Its Effect on Graphic Design in the United States*. Ames, IA: Iowa State University, 1988.

Herdeg, Walter. *Film & TV Graphics*. Zurich: The Graphis Press, 1967.

————. *Film & TV Graphics 2*. Zurich: The Graphis Press, 1976.

Hess, Dick, and Muller, Marion. *Dorfsman and CBS*. New York: American Showcase, 1987.

Igarashi, Takenobu, ed. *World Trademarks and Logotypes II*. Tokyo: Graphic-sha, 1987.

Iinkai, Kokomasu. *Corporate Design Systems: Identity through Design*. New York: PBC International, 1985.

Napoles, Veronica. *Corporate Identity Design*. New York: Van Nostrand Reinhold, 1988.

Rosen, Ben. *The Corporate Search for Visual Identification*. New York: Van Nostrand Reinhold, 1970.

Rotzler, Willy. *Constructive Concepts*. New York: Rizzoli, 1977.

Schmittel, Wolfgang. *Corporate Design International*. Zurich: ABC Editions, 1984.

Shapira, Nathan H., et. al. *Design Process: Olivetti, 1908–1978*. Milan, Italy: Olivetti, 1979.

Vignelli, Massimo and Lella. *Design: Vignelli*. New York: Rizzoli, 1981.

24. The Conceptual Image

Alcorn, John, et. al. *The Push Pin Style*. Palo Alto, CA: Communication Arts, 1970.

Chwast, Seymour. *The Left-Handed Designer*. New York: Abrams, 1985.

Czestochowski, Joseph S. *Contemporary Polish Posters*. New York: Dover, 1979.

Davis, Paul. *Faces*. New York: Friendly Press, 1985.

————. *Paul Davis Posters and Paintings*. New York: Dutton, 1977.

Glaser, Milton. *Milton Glaser: Graphic Design*. Woodstock, NY: Overlook Press, 1972.

————. *The Milton Glaser Poster Book*. New York: Harmony Books, 1977.

Heller, Steven. *Innovators of American Illustration*. New York: Van Nostrand Reinhold, 1986.

Hornig, Norbert. *Leipziger Plakatkunst*. Leipzig: VEB E. A. Seeman, 1985.

Kowalski, Tadeusz. *The Polish Film Poster*. Warsaw: Filmowa Agencja Wydawnicza, 1957.

McMullan, James. *Revealing Illustrations*. New York: Watson-Guptill, 1981.

Rambow, Gunther. *Plakate von Gunther Rambow im Museum Wiesbaden*. Wiesbaden, Germany: Museum Wiesbaden, 1988.

Stermer, Dugald. *The Art of Revolution, Castro's Cuba: 1959–1970*. New York: McGraw-Hill, 1970.

Wesselius, Jacqueline. *Grapus 85*. Utrecht, The Netherlands: Reflex Verlag, 1985.

25. A Global Dialog

Adobe Systems Incorporated. *Adobe Type 1 Font Format*. Mountain View, CA: Adobe Systems, 1990.

Aldersey-Williams, Hugh. *New American Design*. New York: Rizzoli, 1988.

Branzi, Andrea. *The Hot House: Italian New Wave Design*. Cambridge, MA: MIT Press, 1984.

Brody, Neville. *The Graphic Language of Neville Brody*. New York: Rizzoli, 1988.

Elam, Kim. *Expressive Typography*. New York: Van Nostrand Reinhold, 1990.

Fukuda, Shigeo. *Visual Illusion*. Tokyo: Rikuyosha, 1982.

———. *Posters of Shigeo Fukuda*. Tokyo: Mitsumura Tosho Shuppan, 1982.

Gaetan-Picon, Genevieve, et. al. *L'Affiche Japonaise*. Paris: Musee de l'Affiche, 1979.

Gorb, Peter, ed. *Living by Design: Pentagram*. London: Lund Humphries, 1978.

Greiman, April. *Hybrid Imagery: The Fusion of Technology and Graphic Design*. New York: Watson-Guptill, 1990.

Herring, Jerry, et. al. *Design in Texas*. Houston: Graphic Design Press, 1986.

Horn, Richard. *Memphis*. Philadelphia: Running Press, 1985.

Igarashi, Takenobu. *Space Graphics*. Tokyo: Shoten Kenchiku-sha, 1983.

———.*Seven Graphic Designers*. Tokyo: Graphic-sha Publishing Company, 1985.

———. *Igarashi Alphabets*. Zurich: ABC Editions, 1987.

Kamekura, Yusaku, et. al. *The Works of Yusaku Kamekura*. Tokyo: Rikuyo-sha, 1983.

Levin, Kim. *Beyond Modernism*. New York: Harper and Row, 1988.

Nagai, Kazumasa. *The Works of Kazumasa Nagai*. Tokyo: Kodansha, 1985.

Pierce, Donald L., Jr. *100 Texas Posters*. Houston: Graphic Design Press, 1985.

Radice, Barbara. *Memphis: Research, Experiences, Results, Failures, and Successes of the New Design*. New York: Rizzoli, 1984.

Sottsass, Ettore, et. al. *Sottsass Associati*. New York: Rizzoli, 1988.

Sparke, Penny. *Modern Japanese Design*. New York: Dutton, 1987.

———. *Italian Design: 1870 to the Present*. London: Thames and Hudson, 1988.

Stone, Sumner. *On Stone: The Art and Use of Typography on the Personal Computer*. San Francisco: Bedford Arts, 1991.

Tadashi, Masuda. *Works of the Masuda Tadashi Design Institute*. Tokyo: Seibundo shinkosha, 1966.

Tanaka, Ikko. *Posters of Ikko Tanaka*. Tokyo: 1981.

———. *The Work of Ikko Tanaka*. Tokyo: 1975.

Tanikawa, Koichi. *100 Posters of Tadanori Yokoo*. Tokyo: Kodansha, 1978.

Thackara, John, ed. *Design After Modernism*. London: Thames and Hudson, 1988.

White, Jan V. *Graphic Design for the Electronic Age*. New York: Watson-Guptill, 1988.

Wozencroft, John. *The Graphic Language of Neville Brody*. New York: Rizzoli, 1988.

Yokoo, Tadanori. *Tadanori Yokoo*. Woodbury, NY: Barron's, 1977.

———. *The Complete Tadanori Yokoo*. Tokyo: Kodansha, 1971.

General surveys

Barnicoat, John. *A Concise History of the Poster*. London: Thames and Hudson, 1972.

Berry, W. Turner, Johnson, A. F., and Jaspert, W. P. *The Encyclopaedia of Type Faces*. London: Blandford, 1958.

Booth-Clibborn, Edward, and Baroni, Daniele. *The Language of Graphics*. New York: Abrams, 1980.

Gallo, Max. *The Poster in History*. New York: American Heritage, 1974.

Garner, Anne, ed. *The 1325 Greatest Moments in the History of Graphic Design (so far)*. Montana State University, 1987.

Gottshall, Edward M. *Typographic Communications Today*. Cambridge, MA: MIT Press, 1989.

Gress, Edmund G. *The Art and Practice of Typography*. New York: Oswald, 1917.

Heller, Steven and Chwast, Seymour. *Graphic Style from Victorian to Post-modern*. New York: Abrams, 1988.

Hellier, Bevis. *Posters*. New York: Stein and Day, 1969.

Lewis, John. *Anatomy of Printing*. London: Faber and Faber, 1970.

Malhotra, Ruth, et. al. *Das frühe Plakat in Europa und den USA*. Vol. I–III. Berlin: Gebr. Mann Verlag, 1973.

Moran, James, ed. *Printing in the 20th Century*. New York: Hastings House, 1974.

Müller-Brockmann, Josef. *A History of Visual Communications*. New York: Hastings House, 1967.

———, and Müller-Brockmann, Shizuka. *History of the Poster*. Zurich: ABC Editions, 1971.

Pitz, Henry C. *Two Hundred Years of American Illustration*. New York: Random House, 1977.

Sparke, Penny. *Design Source Book*. Secaucus, NJ: Chartwell, 1986.

Wrede, Stuart. *The Modern Poster*. New York: Museum of Modern Art, 1988.

Updike, Daniel Berkeley. *Printing Types: Their History, Forms, and Use*. Cambridge: Harvard University Press, 1937.

Major periodicals

Ars Typographica. Vol. 1–3. Douglas C. McMurtrie, editor. New York: Douglas C. McMurtrie, 1918–1934.

Bauhaus Journal. No. 1–15. Dessau, Germany: 1926–1931.

The Century Guild Hobby Horse. Arthur H. Mackmurdo, ed. London: 1884–1888.

Communication Arts. Vol. 1 No. 1, 1959—Vol. 33 No. 3, 1991.

De Stijl. Vol. I–VII. Theo van Doesburg, ed. 1917–1931. Reprint, Amsterdam: Athenaeum, 1968.

The Dolphin. Vols. I–IV. New York: Limited Editions Club, 1933–1941.

The Fleuron: A Journal of Typography. No. 1–7. Stanley Morison, ed. London: The University Press (Cambridge), 1923–1930. Reprint. Westport, CT: Greenwood, 1970.

Graphis. Vol. 1 No. 1, 1944—Vol. 47 No. 2, 1991.

Journal of the Ulm School of Design. No. 1–21. Ulm, Germany: 1958–1968.

Jugend. Munich: 1896-1910.

Neue Grafik. (New Graphic Design). Richard P. Louse, Josef Müller-Brockmann, Hans Neuberg, and Carlo L. Vivarelli, eds. No. 1–16. Zurich: 1959–1963.

Novum Grebrauchgraphik (formerly *Grebrauchgraphik*). Vol. 1 No. 1, 1925; Vol. 62 No. 5, 1991.

Print. Vol. 1 No.1, 1940—Vol. 45 No. 4, 1991.

The Studio. London: 1893–1900.

Van Nu en Straks. Brussels and Antwerp: 1892–1901.

Ver Sacrum, Organ der Vereinigung Bildender Küenstler österreichs. Vol. 1–6. Vienna: 1898–1903.

Visible Language. (formerly *The Journal of Typographic Research*.) Vol. 1 No. 1, 1967—Vol. 23 No. 4, 1989.

Picture Credits

Designers and designers' estates, clients, and private collections are primary sources for illustrative material and reproduction permissions. Designers and clients providing reproduction permissions are identified in the picture captions. The following archives, museums, corporations, and libraries also provided images for reproduction.

AEG Firmen-archiv, Frankfurt/M., Germany: Figs. 15-38, 15-41, 15-42, 15-43, 15-45 • Agora Excavations, American School of Classical Studies, Athens: Figs. 4-7, 4-8 • Albright-Knox Art Gallery, Buffalo, NY: Fig. 16-15. Alma H. Law Archive, Scarsdale, NY: Figs. 18-22, 18-23 • Arnold H. Crane Collection, Chicago: Fig. 16-43 • Art Institute of Chicago: Fig. 16-4 • Athenaeum-Polak & Van Gennep, Amsterdam: Figs. 18-30, 18-31, 18-32, 18-33, 18-36, 18-37 • Asia Society, New York, from the collection of Dr. Paul Singer: photograph, Fig. 3-5 • Bauhaus Archiv, Berlin: Figs. 19-21, 19-22 • Bavarian National Museum, Munich: Fig. 11-4 • Biblioteca Nacional, Madrid: Figs. 5-11, 5-12, 5-13 • Bibliothèque Nationale, Paris: Figs. 5-2, 6-15, 9-1, 9-2, 12-14 • Bill Graham, San Francisco, CA: Fig. 24-35, poster #61, copyright 1967 • Birmingham Public Library, Birmingham, England; Reference Library, Local Studies Department: Fig. 9-12 • Bodleian Library, University of Oxford: Figs. 5-14, 5-15 • British Library, London: Pl. 10, Figs. 3-13, 5-6, 18-2, 18-3 • British Museum, London: Fig. 1-4; Pls. 2, 3; Figs. 2-2, 2-14, 2-15, 2-16; Department of Egyptian Antiquities, Figs. 4-2, 5-10 • Commune di Como, Como, Italy: Fig. 16-16 • Cooper Union, Herb Lubalin Study Center, New York, NY: Figs. 22-59, 22-60, 22-61, 22-62, 22-63, 22-64, 22-65, 22-66, 22-67, 22-68, 22-69, 22-70, 22-71, 22-72, 22-73, 22-74 • D. Stempel AG, Frankfurt/M., Germany: Fig. 13-26 • Dutch Architectural Institute, Amsterdam/Rotterdam, The Netherlands: Fig. 18-40 • Editions Gallimard, Paris: Figs. 16-15, 16-16, 24-49–24-53 • Egyptian Antiquities Museum, Cairo: Fig. 2-1 • Ex Libris, New York, NY: Figs. 18-25, 18-26 • Family Dog: Fig. 24-36, copyright 1966, Victor Moscoso, artist • Fine Arts Museum, Nice, France: Fig. 14-3 • French Tourist Office: Pl. 1; Fig. 1-1 • George Eastman House, Rochester, NY: Figs. 11-1, 11-10, 11-16, 11-17, 11-18, 11-19, 11-20, 11-22, copyright Arch. Phot, Paris/SPADEM/VAGA, New York, 1891: Figs. 11-24, 11-25, 16-40, 16-41, 16-42, 19-9, 19-10, 19-11 • Gernsheim Collection, The Harry Ransom Humanities Research Center, The University of Texas at Austin: Figs. 11-2, 11-3 • Herakleion Museum, Crete: Pl. 5 • Her Majesty's Stationery Office, Norwich, UK: Pl. 47 • Hessische Landes-und Hochschulbibliothek, Darmstadt: Fig. 5-16 • Hirmer Fotoarchiv, Munich: Fig. 2-8 • The Hirshhorn Museum, Washington, DC: Fig. 18-1 • Houghton Library, Harvard University, Cambridge, MA: Figs. 8-33, 13-24, 13-25, 14-5, 14-6, 14-7, 14-51, 14-52, 14-53, 14-54, 14-59, 15-16, 15-18, 15-19, 19-39 • Iraq Museum, Baghdad: Fig. 1-9 • Jules Cheret Museum, Nice: Fig. 14-3 • Kunsthistorisches Museum, Vienna: Pl. 7 • Library of Congress, Washington, DC: Figs. 3-16, 7-19, 8-2, 8-10, 8-34, 9-10, 9-25, 12-21, 12-26, 13-1, 15-1, 20-1; The Poster Collection: Pls. 33, 44, 64, 65, 67, 68, 69, 71; Figs. 12-4, 12-10, 12-11, 12-15, 12-23, 14-35, 14-36, 14-42, 14-43, 14-44, 14-45, 14-46, 14-49, 17-6, 17-13, 17-14, 17-15, 17-16, 17-17, 17-19, 17-31, 19-1, 20-12, 20-19, 20-20, 20-31, 21-6; The Rosenwald Collection: Pls. 9, 12, 13, 14, 19; Figs. 6-7, 6-8, 6-12, 6-14, 7-4, 7-5, 7-7, 7-8, 7-9, 7-10, 7-20, 7-24, 7-28, 8-7, 8-8, 8-9, 8-11, 8-12, 8-14, 8-15, 8-16, 8-24, 8-

Index

Colophon

Printing and Binding: Arcata/Halliday, United States of America

Color Separation: Excel Graphics Arts Limited, Hong Kong

Typography: Dix Type, Inc., Syracuse, NY
Text: 9/12 New Century Schoolbook
Captions: 8/10 New Century Schoolbook
Chapter titles: 24/24 New Century Schoolbook Bold

Design: Monika Keano and Philip B. Meggs